Tru64™ UNIX File System
Administration Handbook

Steven M. Hancock

**Digital
Press**

Boston • Oxford • Auckland • Johannesburg • Melbourne • New Delhi

Library of Congress Cataloging-in-Publication Data
Hancock, Steven.
    Tru64 Unix file system administration handbook/Steven M. Hancock
        p. cm.
    Includes bibliographical references and index.
    ISBN 1-55558-227-3 (alk. paper)
        1. UNIX (Computer file). 2. Operating systems (Computers). 3. File organization (Computer science) I. Title.

QA76.76.O63 H34465 2000
005.75'85—dc21   00-040492

British Library Cataloguing-in-Publication Data
A catalogue record for this book is available from the British Library.

The publisher offers special discounts on bulk orders of this book.
For information, please contact:

Manager of Special Sales
Butterworth–Heinemann
225 Wildwood Avenue
Woburn, MA 01801-2041
Tel: 781-904-2500
Fax: 781-904-2620

For information on all Digital Press publications available, contact our World Wide Web home page at: http://www.bh.com/digitalpress

10 9 8 7 6 5 4 3 2
Printed in the United States of America

Dedication

To JoEllen

Contents

List of Figures

Chapter 7

List of Tables

Appendix C

Preface

As of this writing, roughly 70 percent of the top 100 most visited sites on the Internet are Tru64™ UNIX systems. Top national laboratories from the U.S. Departments of Defense and Energy, NASA, and the Environmental Protection Agency depend on Compaq's high-performance UNIX™ product. In addition, some of the top companies from the fields of banking, telecommunications, retail, pharmaceuticals, and manufacturing rely on Tru64 UNIX for the security of their data and performance of their file systems. From the author's direct experience, it is known that many of the system administrators for these systems have benefited from knowledge included in this book. They were able to get better performance or recover lost data that wouldn't have been possible without some of this "inside" information. Much of this information is not publicly available for a variety of reasons. Mainly, the information is either part of internal technical documents provided to customers on an "as-needed" basis, is documented only in source code, or is included in manuals or reference pages that are not organized in a file system–centric fashion. The *Tru64 UNIX File System Administration Handbook* is an attempt to correct that lack of information availability.

In addition, much of the material presented here has been used successfully by the author to teach internal seminars to software support specialists in the Customer Support Center (CSC). When CSC management made the bold decision to train specialists from other declining specialty areas into the rapidly growing UNIX business, this material became the basis for a series of highly successful seminars. The seminar materials were used for what became known as UNIX University. This program continues today. Anyone with a solid background in any modern operating system such as OpenVMS™, Windows NT®, or another flavor of UNIX can quickly ramp up in Tru64 UNIX specifics and be successful in a short period. So, much of this material has been "road tested" in teaching a high percentage of those specialists currently supporting the product.

Intended Audience

This book is written primarily for systems administrators, systems engineers, software engineers, software support specialists, and others who must optimize the performance of and perform advanced troubleshooting on the Tru64 UNIX file systems.

It is assumed that the reader is familiar with basic UNIX system administration. Also, this book was designed as a companion to Matthew Cheek's book *Digital UNIX™ Systems Administration Guide*, so that material will be referred to occasionally. Other references and recommended reading can be found in the bibliography at the end of this text.

A Note on Versions

This book is based on Tru64 UNIX version 5.0a, which was internally code-named "zinc" within Compaq. During most of this writing, zinc was not a released product; therefore, some test cases have been tested on field test software or verified on a 5.0 system only. Every effort has been made to ensure that the functionality was not changed by the time 5.0a shipped to customers. Many of the major functionality changes were included in 5.0, which was a shipping product for approximately six months. The 5.0 code stream is also known internally as the "steel" stream. We may use that terminology in this text as well. Most of the material is also applicable to prior versions from the "platinum" release stream (e.g., 4.0, 4.0a, 4.0b, 4.0c, 4.0d, 4.0e, 4.0f, and 4.0g), as well as from the "gold" releases (e.g., 3.2c, 3.2d, 3.2e, 3.2f, and 3.2g). Any behavior that may have been release-based, or changed in a particular release stream, will be so noted.

On the Tru64 UNIX Name

It should be noted that some nontechnical aspects changed while this work was in progress. Compaq and Digital™ companies merged, so many of the references to Digital are simply mentioned out of habit or legal naming requirements. Also, Compaq's UNIX product has undergone a change of names over time. Most people know that the 64-bit UNIX product was built on a Mach kernel developed at Carnegie Mellon University. The Open Software Foundation (now part of the Open Group), or OSF™, took this kernel, added a UNIX interface, and rebadged it with the name OSF/1™. When Digital added some system management and other tools to this framework, it became the original DEC OSF/1™ product. The name later changed to Digital UNIX around the time that the 3.2c version was released. Recently, the name changed again, following the merger of Digital Equipment Corporation™ (DEC) with Compaq Computer Corporation, to Tru64 UNIX because clearly Digital UNIX reflected neither the product's new ownership nor its 64-bit nature. The new name reflects these issues quite well.

Conventions Used in this Book

In this book, we use some different font and style conventions to refer to different aspects of the operating system. The typeface we use throughout much of this work is Adobe Garamond 11.5 point.

Any new terminology we introduce is presented in **bolded** font the first time we mention it to emphasize the importance of the new term.

For output from commands typed on a system and actual output, we use Courier font in 8.5 point size.

Example:

```
# cd /dev

# ls -l disk/dsk46a
brw-------  1 root    system  19,593 Mar 15 11:04 disk/dsk46a
```

or

```
# file rdisk/dsk46a
rdisk/dsk46a:  character special (19/594) SCSI #2 RZ28D disk
#1 (SCSI ID #6) (SCSI LUN #0)
```

When we refer to actual UNIX commands, we always try to include the UNIX convention of citing the reference page number on which you can find the command in parentheses immediately following the command name. We also use *italics* to make the command name stand out.

Example:

". . . initialized when the disk is formatted, and may be changed later with the *disklabel(8)* command."

The Organization of this Book

This book is organized into nine chapters and three main topic categories. Each chapter covers a different aspect of the file systems on Tru64 UNIX systems. The first three chapters discuss background topics for storage, Logical Storage Manager (LSM™), and UNIX file systems architecture. The next three chapters include coverage of the three most popular file system types: UFS, AdvFS™, and NFS™. Finally, we look at example case studies for configuring and tuning "typical" systems and troubleshooting and recovering from some common problems.

- Chapter 1 introduces file systems administration terminology. In addition, our discussion of some seemingly simplistic UNIX file systems helps to fill in the gaps in the knowledge of many users who may think they already know this topic.

- Chapter 2 discusses storage concepts and administration, including disk concepts, storage and RAID technologies, and Tru64 UNIX device and I/O subsystem management.

- Chapter 3 discusses the logical storage manager (LSM). It includes details of the LSM architecture, creating logical volumes correctly, and methods for using LSM in the most efficient manner.

- Chapter 4 introduces Tru64 UNIX file system architecture, including the virtual file system, caches, and internal structures for gathering information and tuning.

- Chapter 5 covers the UNIX file system. It details the UFS on-disk structure and covers tools and techniques for creating, tuning, troubleshooting, and correcting problems.

- Chapter 6 explains the basics of the Advanced File System (AdvFS). This discussion is comprehensive, begins with basic AdvFS administration, and concludes with the advanced utilities. This chapter and Chapter 7 should be considered the real "meat" of this text because the information is truly invaluable for anyone interested in learning as much as possible about this exciting product.

- Chapter 7 discusses advanced topics in the AdvFS on Tru64 UNIX. In this chapter, we introduce concepts like the regular and metadata file tags, the on-disk structure, and troubleshooting problems. We conclude with topics such as configuring and tuning your AdvFS for performance.

- Chapter 8 covers configuring and tuning some typical environments. This chapter covers some typical types of systems that have been designed and tuned to handle specific applications. As before, we build on and refer to the earlier material in developing this chapter.

1

Introduction

One hundred percent of the shots you don't take, don't go in.
—*Wayne Gretzky*

The file system is a critically important part of any computing environment. This statement is particularly true for large, complex environments such as electronic commerce, Internet sites, electronic mail systems, high-speed computing systems, and On Line Transaction Processing systems (OLTP). For any such system, data—more than any other single factor—drive its sizing and configuration. The purpose of this book is to assist readers to make their Tru64 system perform at its best.

In this chapter, we cover some introductory topics in file systems. In the first two sections, we discuss the "what" and the "why" for this book to give readers an understanding of why such a book is absolutely essential in today's complex environments. Then, we acknowledge that we use a lot of jargon on this journey toward optimal file systems performance, so we attempt to remove as much of the ambiguity in terminology as possible. Finally, we enter some introductory topics in file system administration from the user's perspective. We conclude with a discussion of the often misunderstood topic of discretionary access controls and access control lists.

1.1 What is File Systems Administration?

In Tru64 UNIX, as in any UNIX environment, the file system has a consistent "look and feel" and is the highest layer in the storage management hierarchy of the system. These days, this user interface of most UNIX environments is defined by the POSIX 1003.2 standard. Tru64 UNIX is no exception to this rule. By design, the file system users don't have any understanding of the implementation details but see only files with certain attributes containing their data. A UNIX system user simply manipulates files using a set of commands such as *cat(1)* or *grep(1)*. This notion is powerful because the system users can create an environment in which they can do useful work, but the underlying structure details are hidden.

The system administrator or engineer must ensure that the file system's underlying structure remains a hidden detail. When the user begins to notice a performance issue that hampers work progress, then it is time to consider making some changes. Fortunately, lots of tools are at your disposal to accomplish this task. So, what exactly is this task?

File system administration is a term that is usually attached to someone's job description but can have many different meanings depending on whom you talk to. For our purposes, we define this term as an activity that consists of two equally important tasks: (1) design and (2) management. At many smaller sites, a single system administrator accomplishes both tasks. Larger sites tend to divide the tasks of design and management into multiple people or even multiple departments within an organization. The engineering group is usually responsible for design, whereas the operations group takes care of the day-to-day management.

1.1.1   Design

The design task is concerned with either how to put a new system together to perform its appointed job (or jobs) or planning for future upgrades as system workload changes. An example of a design task would be to start by analyzing the expected workload of the system. This task is usually accomplished by running a benchmark with some sample data on a test environment. The task is to decide, based on the benchmark results, whether to design the system such that the input/output (I/O) load can be spread across multiple controllers or to increase memory so that a cache size can be increased, for example.

1.1.2   Management

Management, on the other hand, involves monitoring performance, tuning, troubleshooting, and recovering from failures. These tasks are the day-to-day activity of the average systems administrator. An example of a management task is that in talking to users, they are complaining about performance during a specific period of the day. You realize that, based on performance monitoring, a user cron job runs at that time every day. That user says that performance of his compute-intensive job has been running slow recently, too. You realize that the advanced file system (AdvFS) those users are sharing is badly fragmented, so you implement an online defragmenter, which restores performance of the file system.

You also decide to proactively implement a defragment process that runs each night on that file system.

As you can see from the examples, the design and management tasks that constitute file system administration are related but not the same. Therefore, both systems administrators and engineers involved in either of these tasks can benefit from an in-depth understanding of the file system.

1.2 Why a Book Dedicated to File Systems Administration?

There are three primary reasons why this book is a necessity for any Tru64 UNIX administrator. First, storage growth in recent years has outpaced our ability to manage it effectively. We will attempt to provide better strategies than those traditionally employed to deal with this issue. Second, a large site will most likely not get optimal performance from its Tru64 UNIX systems with configurations and parameter settings straight "out-of-the-box." Therefore, we provide hints for how to optimize the performance and reliability of your storage subsystems. Although this book is particularly geared toward those large-site administrators, customers with systems that are not large, but are still critical, can benefit from some, if not all, of the information we provide here. The third reason a text dedicated to file systems administration is needed is to help readers develop good file system management skills.

1.2.1 Managing Growth

Strong evidence suggests that storage is growing at a tremendous rate. Tru64 UNIX customers commonly have 30 gigabyte file systems and larger. For purposes of this book, we consider a single file system with more than 30 gigabytes as a large file system. The author has seen file systems greater than 200 gigabytes in use at several sites. This kind of large file system simply cannot be left alone without regular monitoring and maintenance.

Explosive storage system growth has forced customers to rethink traditional storage management strategies. Traditional file systems strategies simply don't scale up, and increasing storage capacities has led to problems that didn't exist when a large file system was around 1 gigabyte. For example, the *fsck(8)* tool, which checks and corrects problems in UFS following a system crash, takes exponentially longer to complete as a file system's size grows. As a result, the AdvFS has become very popular for customers with larger storage requirements. As a log-based file system, AdvFS needs only to back out uncommitted transactions in the log if a system crash occurs, resulting in significant recovery time savings for a large file system.

Another example of a strategy that needs to be rethought is backup and recovery. In a 24-hour work environment, a file system cannot be taken offline to produce a consistent backup. Traditionally, UNIX file systems were backed up in an unmounted state, possibly even in single-user mode. Of course, this method doesn't work for a 24-hour, e-business system. AdvFS assists us in another way by providing the clone file systems feature. Clone file systems can be created and backed up while the file system is still in use. We will discuss the significant features of AdvFS in Chapter 6.

1.2.2   Optimization

Tru64 UNIX (formerly Digital UNIX) is a powerful, yet complex product. Compaq engineers developing this high-performance, 64-bit operating system have done a superb job of delivering a system that scales from the workstation all the way up to the largest enterprise customers with reasonable performance. This wide range of supported platforms and sized systems from a single operating system virtually guarantees that the defaults will not be tuned properly for your specific situation. Therefore, it is important to understand how the system can be tuned to optimize performance.

Any compute-intensive task clearly requires a lot of data with which to operate. Alpha™ processor–based systems, on which Tru64 UNIX runs, are the highest performing 64-bit processors on the market. Therefore, data throughput is important to realize the full capabilities of the Alpha processor. The purpose of this book is to give readers all the tools necessary to design a new Tru64 UNIX file system or to tune an existing file system to perform at its best.

1.2.3   Developing Good Practice

Developing good file systems administration practices early in one's career is important in order to preserve one's career later on. In other words, file systems administration is serious business. We have seen too many Tru64 UNIX system administrators who lost critical data or credibility because they failed to follow good practice. For example, the most common mistake administrators make is failing to test their backups or

blocks on disk. In order to make this function happen the way that it's supposed to, several components and activities take place "under the hood." In this section, we explore the organization of the entire I/O subsystem, which exists as a set of drivers and other routines in the UNIX kernel. Figure 1–1 illustrates that the I/O subsystem is the part of the kernel that sits between the user processes and the disk controller hardware.

FIGURE 1–1
Tru64 UNIX
Input/Output
Subsystem

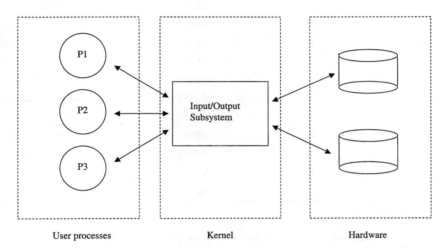

| User processes | Kernel | Hardware |

The input/output subsystem includes not only all of the supported file system types (see section 1.3.2, File System Type) but also the virtual file system, LSM, buffer cache, Prestoserve™, and disk device driver. Each of these components are discussed in greater detail in different sections of this book. The interaction among the components is shown in Figure 1–2. As you can see from this diagram, an application can access blocks on a disk in a lot of different ways. Each of these methods is strictly defined by a set of interfaces into the kernel. Users don't necessarily ever see those interfaces because they simply execute commands from a shell prompt; however, the programmer uses the interfaces by calling system calls or library functions from within an executing program. Thus, the system calls define the user-level interface. Other interfaces, such as between AdvFS and the buffer cache, are actually internal kernel routines that are not available to the user-level programmer.

As a means of illustration, we consider some examples of different applications that are representative of how the interfaces work. Table 1–1 summarizes the different examples of applications named "A" through "L" in Figure 1–2 and how each application interacts with the different I/O subsystem components.

TABLE 1–1   Tru64 UNIX I/O Subsystem Component Interaction

APPLICATION	FILE SYSTEM	DESCRIPTION
A	UFS	VFS/UFS/UBC/LSM
B	UFS	VFS/UFS/UBC
C	UFS	VFS/UFS/UBC/Presto
D	UFS	VFS/UFS/UBC/Presto/LSM
E	UFS	VFS/AdvFS/UBC/Presto/LSM
F	AdvFS	VFS/AdvFS/UBC/Presto
G	AdvFS	VFS/AdvFS/UBC/LSM
H	AdvFS	VFS/AdvFS/UBC
I	AdvFS	VFS/AdvFS/DirectIO
J	AdvFS	VFS/AdvFS/DirectIO/LSM
K	Raw	Raw/LSM
L	Raw	Raw

FIGURE 1–2
Tru64 UNIX I/O
Subsystem
Component
Interaction

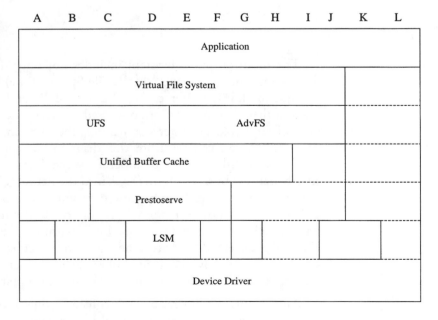

Example:

Applications A and B are standard user files on a UFS. In the former case, the file system utilizes an LSM logical volume, and in the latter case, it simply uses a regular disk drive. Applications D and C are the same as A and B, but with a Prestoserve accelerator being used.

Example:

A commercial database product such as Oracle™ can completely bypass the file system and access the disk directly, as shown in the figure as application "J." It can also use an LSM logical volume to access the disks as in application "I" in the figure. This type of access is common in large database applications. Because they are sophisticated applications, databases are able to manage the storage more efficiently without the overhead of a file system. In doing so, they expect to gain some performance advantage.

1.5 UNIX File Types

Most UNIX users are not aware that the file system actually supports many different types of files because in the course of doing their work they usually encounter only regular and directory files. Tru64 UNIX supports all standard UNIX file types, including regular, directory, symbolic links, block and character device special, named pipes, and sockets. Each of these types is discussed in the following sections.

The *ls(1)* or *file(1)* commands can be employed by any user on a system to examine the file type. Table 1–2 lists each file type and information given by these two utilities:

TABLE 1–2 Supported File Types in Tru64 UNIX

FILE TYPE	LS(1)	FILE(1)
Regular	-	depends[2]
Directory	d	directory
Symbolic Link	l	symbolic link to <file/dir>
Character Special	c	character special (maj/min)
Block Special	b	block special (maj/min)
Named Pipes	p	fifo
Local Socket	s	socket

1.5.1   Regular Files

A regular file can contain any kind of data, such as an executable program, a text file, or source code. The UNIX operating system imposes no structure on the regular file—it is simply a sequentially ordered data structure. In other operating systems, such as OpenVMS or MVS™, the file system interprets and structures data on disk differently depending on its declared usage. In UNIX, this function is left up to the application.

Example:

```
# ls -l smauth.log
-rw-r--r--   1 root    system   9482 Feb 27 17:17 smauth.log

# file smauth.log
smauth.log:   ascii text
```

1.5.2   Directories

A directory is a type of file that lists a table of names and inodes for files contained within that directory. Because the name of a file is not found in the inode of the file, that association is made by the contents of the directory files of the system. Directories are created using the *mkdir(1)* command and removed using the *rmdir(1)* command or, in some cases, by using a recursive *rm(1)*.

Example:

```
# mkdir test

# ls -ld test
drwxr-xr-x   2 root    system   8192 Aug 28 22:23 test

# rmdir test
```

1.5.3   Symbolic Links

A symbolic link is a pointer to another file or directory. Symbolic links differ from hard links in that they have their own inode number associated with them. Hard links are simply another reference (or directory entry) to the same inode on the same file system. Symbolic links can span file systems. Notice that the size of a symbolic link is equal to the number of characters in the link itself. The reason for this is, not surprisingly, that the data stored in a symbolic link are the string of the path to which the link points.

Example:

```
# ls -ld /usr/tmp
lrwxrwxrwx   1 root    system   10 Jun 29 18:15 /usr/tmp ->
../var/tmp
```

when *mkfifo(1)* is issued with no flags in the first case. We create a second named pipe below with a different mode than the default by utilizing the '-m' flag.

```
# mkfifo FIFO
# mkfifo -m 755 FIFO.2
# ls -l FIFO*
prw-r--r--   1 root    system    0 Mar 16 21:38 FIFO
prwxr-xr-x   1 root    system    0 Mar 16 21:39 FIFO.2
```

Regardless of how they are created, named pipes can be removed just like regular files by using the *rm(1)* command.

1.5.6 Local Sockets

Local sockets are seen with an 's' is the file type field using 'ls -l.' They are created by programs using the *socket(2)* system call in the domain of "AF_UNIX." They are also used by some facilities in Tru64 UNIX as another means of interprocess communication.

Example:

Below we have an example of a file that already exists in the /dev directory on most Tru64 UNIX systems that use the syslog facility. Any other process that wants to send a message to the syslog daemon can do so by opening this domain socket and writing to it.

```
# cd /dev
# ls -l log
srw-rw-rw-   1 root    system    0 Feb 26 16:25 log
# file log
log: socket
```

Example:

The *logger(1)* command is provided for any user to log a message into the system logs on a Tru64 UNIX system. This example illustrates that although the user "hancock" does not have privileges to write directly to the messages file, the syslog daemon does this on the user's behalf. The *logger(1)* command communicates with the syslog daemon using the "log" socket.

```
jackson> whoami
hancock

jackson> logger "test"

jackson> grep test /var/adm/messages
grep: can't open /var/adm/messages
```

```
jackson> ls -l /var/adm/messages
-rw-r----- 1 root adm 4487984 Mar 16 22:22 /var/adm/messages

jackson> su
Password:

# grep test /var/adm/messages
Mar 16 22:18:56 jackson hancock: test
```

1.6   Some Useful UNIX Commands

You can use several common user-level or administrator's tools to gather information about your files and file systems. The system administrator often needs to determine which users or applications are filling up one or more of the file systems. Techniques and tools are available to assist in the search for the "culprit." Although our list is not exhaustive, we discuss some of them in this section.

1.6.1   Where Have My Blocks Gone?

In this section, we explore the system administrator task of trying to find out where the file or files are that can be removed from the system to free up space. This need is often the result of a file system becoming full, or you need the information because you are simply performing routine file system maintenance. We examine some of the commands that can be used to perform this task and give helpful examples.

The first of these useful commands is called disk free, or *df(1)*. This command is one of the most useful that a system administrator can use to find out usage for all of the mounted file systems in the environment. Using *df(1)* with no options displays the usage statistics for all of the mounted file systems. The default for Tru64 UNIX is to show the output in disk blocks (512 bytes per block).

Example:

```
# df /test
Filesystem       512-blocks Used  Available Capacity Mounted on
/dev/vol/vol01 1070346    22690 94062     3%      /test
```

Also, to make Tru64 UNIX show this information in kilobytes, use the -k switch.

```
# df -k /test
Filesystem       1024-blocksUsed  Available Capacity Mounted on
/dev/vol/vol01 535173     11345 47031     3%      /test
```

In addition to block and kilobyte usage data, the *df(1)* command allows you to look at inode information. This information is mostly useful for UFS because it could be an indication that the file system needs to have its inodes increased. Unfortunately, the only way you can do that is by backing up your data and remaking the file system with an increased inode count. We detail how you can do that in our *newfs(8)* discussion in Chapter 5. System users may experience a symptom of this problem when they try to use a utility to write to a file system that is out of inodes. The error message is the same as for a full file system: "file system full." A programmer would see an ENOSPC errno return from a program that issues a *write(2)*. The following example is the output of "df –i."

Example:

```
# df -i /test
Filesystem      512-blocks  Used  Available Capacity Iused Ifree  %Iused Mounted on
/dev/vol/vol01  1070346     22690 940620       3%     118927 13423  90%    /test
```

In addition to *df(1)*, the *find(1)* command is also useful for finding out file system usage. The difference, however, is that *find(1)* can be used to discover where the usage on the file system actually resides. One of the best ways to use *find(1)* is if a file system is found to be full using *df(1)*, but you are not sure where the blocks are going. If you assume that the usage goes to one or a small number of large files, then *find(1)* can be used to identify those files. Here's an example showing *find(1)* syntax for finding files larger that 5 MB on a file system called /test.

Example:

In this example, we illustrate a typical system administrator's task: find out where the big files are on a file system. Here, we're looking for any file over 5 MB in size on the file system /test and printing out the results in two different ways. The first result is just a list of files, whereas the second is a long listing output similar to what *ls(1)* provides.

```
# find /usr -size +5000k -xdev -print
/usr/bin/X11/dtadvfs
/usr/bin/X11/real-netscape
/usr/bin/ladebug
/usr/ccs/lib/cmplrs/cc/gemc_cc
/usr/lib/classes.zip
/usr/lib/xemacs-21.1.7/bin/xemacs-21.1.7
/usr/lib/DIA/FMG_CTR__DEF_RUL_LIB.KNL
/usr/opt/TruCluster/clu_genvmunix
/usr/share/sysman/kits/jre.exe

# find /usr -size +5000k -xdev -ls
 9329 10488 -r-x------ 1 root  bin  10731552 Dec 15 15:28 /usr/bin/X11/dtadvfs
```

```
 10905 18040 -rwxr-xr-x 1 bin   bin   18472960 Jan 12 03:07 /usr/bin/X11/real-
netscape
 16531 6568 -r-xr-xr-x 1 root   system   6725632 Nov 2 09:35 /usr/bin/ladebug
 5325 5752 -r-xr-xr-x 1 bin   bin   5890048 Jan 11 22:18 /usr/ccs/lib/cmplrs/cc/
gemc_cc
 16736 8576 -rw-r--r-- 1 bin   bin   8780861 Jun 11 1999 /usr/lib/classes.zip
 17997 6144 -rwxr-xr-x 1 bin   bin   6283984 Dec 3 02:43 /usr/lib/xemacs-21.1.7/
bin/xemacs-21.1.7
 22723 12344 -rw-r--r-- 1 root   system   12639144 Jan 13 1999 /usr/lib/DIA/
FMG_CTR__DEF_RUL_LIB.KNL
 25670 22648 -rwxr-xr-x 1 root   system   23186528 Jan 13 00:36 /usr/opt/TruClus-
ter/clu_genvmunix
 3530 5344 -r--r--r-- 1 bin   bin   5465521 Jan 12 03:12 /usr/share/sysman/kits/
jre.exe
```

The *du(1)* command allows for finding the disk usage for a given directory. The *du(1)* command, as opposed to *find(1)*, is more useful if the usage is not a small number of large files but rather a large number of smaller files. In that case, *find(1)* gives lots of output that would have to be sifted through by hand. Good system administrators wouldn't waste time doing that but could use the *du(1)* command to narrow down the usage by subdirectory starting from the mount point. By default, *du(1)* prints the usage for a directory in blocks and crosses file system boundaries, but by using a few simple switches, more tailored results can be obtained. The following example illustrates this point.

Example:

This simple usage example illustrates how you can use *du(1)* in three different ways to find out the block usage beneath a directory called /usr. The default output from *du(1)* gives the result in 512-byte blocks and crosses file system boundaries.

```
# df
Filesystem          512-blocks      Used  Available  Capacity    Mounted on
root_domain#root        262144    182088      68816       73%    /
proc                         0         0          0      100%    /proc
usr_domain#usr         1433600   1145838     227360       84%    /usr
usr_domain#var         1433600     28000     227360       11%    /var
jack2:/usr/staff/k2    8129148   2716750    4599482       38%    /usr/staff/k2
/dev/vol/volbig       32579526         2   29321570        0%    /big

# du -s /usr
3861690 /usr
```

Because /usr could have all kinds of stuff mounted below it, we'd like to avoid crossing file system boundaries. Therefore, we use the '-x' flag.

```
# df
Filesystem          512-blocks      Used   Available   Capacity   Mounted on
root_domain#root        262144    182088       68816       73%    /
/proc                        0         0           0      100%    /proc
usr_domain#usr         1433600   1145838      227360       84%    /usr
usr_domain#var         1433600     28000      227360       11%    /var
jack2:/usr/staff/k2    8129148   2716750     4599482       38%    /usr/staff/k2
/dev/vol/volbig       32579526         2    29321570        0%    /big

# du -sx /usr
1144942 /usr
```

Also, because people tend to think in kilobytes more than in blocks, we get the usage in kilobytes by using the '-k' switch.

```
# du -sxk /usr
572471 /usr
```

Example:

This more complex example shows the use of *du(1)* to figure out which files to clean up in the /usr/var file system.

```
# df /usr/var
Filesystem       512-blocks   Used     Available   Capacity   Mounted on
var_domain#var   970368       499790   343488      60%        /usr/var

# cd /usr/var

# du -sxk *
4286 X11
0   X11R6
216499 adm
98  ase
0   checklist.setup
153 dt
8   esnmp
8   join
3480 kdbx
8   log
19  lsm
8   named
8   news
11055 nsr
11780 opt
8   preserve
18  presto
8   quota.group
16  quota.user
20  run
8   rwho
18  shlib
784 spool
8   subsys
```

```
447   tcb
32   tmp
307   yp

# du -sxk nsr/*
2766 nsr/cores
6275 nsr/index
611  nsr/logs
1337 nsr/mm
41   nsr/res
17   nsr/tmp
# du -sxk nsr/cores/*

9   nsr/cores/ansrd
9   nsr/cores/nsrd
9   nsr/cores/nsrexecd
9   nsr/cores/nsrindexd
9   nsr/cores/nsrmmd
2713 nsr/cores/nsrmmdbd

# du -sxk adm/*
0   adm/MM0msgs
1   adm/X0msgs
177  adm/acct
6410 adm/backuplog
10016 adm/binary.errlog
50112 adm/crash
64   adm/cron
48   adm/defragcron.log
8   adm/dev
32   adm/dms
112  adm/etc
0   adm/fee
8   adm/home
61   adm/lastlog
338  adm/lmf
47263 adm/log
8   adm/mdec
4488 adm/messages
2080 adm/messages.old.gz
8   adm/mountdtab
8   adm/opt
7   adm/pacct
86891 adm/patch
8   adm/proc
64   adm/ris
72   adm/sbin
302   adm/sendmail
8   adm/shlib
1234 adm/smlogs
8   adm/subsys
8   adm/sys
8   adm/syslog
442   adm/syslog.dated
9   adm/update
840   adm/usr
```

not be manipulated by other users. The sticky bit on a regular file implies that on an executable file, the text portion of the program is retained in memory after the program has stopped running. It will continue to reserve space in the swap file.

Example:

This example shows what the long list output from *ls(1)* shows for a regular file and a directory file when the sticky bit is cleared and when it is set.

```
# chmod 1755 redhat.ps

# ls -l redhat.ps
-rwxr-xr-t   1 hancock    wku1    7250 Apr 13 18:15 redhat.ps

# chmod 1644 redhat.ps

# ls -l redhat.ps
-rw-r--r-T   1 hancock    wku1    7250 Apr 13 18:15 redhat.ps

# mkdir temp

# ls -ld temp
drwxr-xr-x   2 root       wku1    8192 Aug 29 09:26 temp

# chmod 1755 temp

# ls -ld temp
drwxr-xr-t   2 root       wku1    8192 Aug 29 09:26 temp
```

1.6.2.2 UNIX File Times

Three times are associated with each file in a UNIX file system. These times are known as the mtime, ctime, and atime, as described in the following paragraphs.

The default time shown using the '-l' switch to the *ls(1)* command is to show the time of last modification (the mtime). Thus, any time the data blocks for the file are modified in any way, such as when appending the file, this time is updated. The following example illustrates how appending a file updates the mtime.

Example:

This example shows how an append process on a regular file updates its mtime.

```
# ls -l pak.txt
-rw-r--r--   1 hancock wku1    1099 May 18 17:26 pak.txt

# echo "This is a test" >> pak.txt

# ls -l pak.txt
-rwxr-xr-x   1 hancock wku1    1114 Aug 29 09:10 pak.txt
```

The ctime is often erroneously referred to as the file's creation time, when in fact it is the last time the inode for the file was modified. The ctime is set to its initial value at the time a file is created, but it can also be changed whenever the mode for the file is changed, for example. Some other examples of regular UNIX commands that update a file's inode information would be *chgrp(1)* or *chown(1)*. These commands update the group ownership and user ownership of a file, respectively.

Example:

Here, we show that the ctime for the file named pak.txt is updated simply by changing permissions on the file.

```
# ls -lc pak.txt
-rw-r--r--   1 hancock wkul    1099 May 26 12:49 pak.txt
# chmod 755 pak.txt
# ls -lc pak.txt
-rwxr-xr-x  1 hancock wkul    1099 Aug 29 09:08 pak.txt
```

Last, the atime is the time that the file was last accessed. In this context, "accessed" means that the data blocks have been read, not referring to reading the inode information. For example, performing an "ls –l <file>" would be an access to the directory containing the file to find out the inode information but not the file itself.

Example:

This example illustrates how reading the data blocks using the *cat(1)* command updates the atime for the file.

```
# ls -lu pak.txt
-rw-r--r--   1 hancock wkul    1099 Aug 28 13:53 pak.txt
# cat pak.txt > /dev/null
# ls -lu pak.txt
-rw-r--r--   1 hancock wkul    1099 Aug 29 09:06 pak.txt
```

1.6.2.3 Sparse Files

A sparse file is simply a regular file that has less file system space allocated to it than the size indicated by its stat structure. This is accomplished by using the *lseek(2)* system call to skip past the end of allocated space and then the *write(2)* system call to write something. If the intervening space is more than the file system block size, then no space is allocated.

You can use *ls(1)* with the '-s' switch to determine whether a file is sparse. This gives the actual usage in kilobytes in the first column. A typical example of a sparse file is a crash dump,[3] which is shown as follows:

Example:

```
# ls -ls vmcore.2
19928 -rw-r-----   1 root    system   100644864 Aug 22 19:34
vmcore.2
```

One way to create a sparse file without writing a program is by using the *dd(1)* command with the oseek keyword as shown in the following example.

Example:

Here is a demonstration of how you could use *dd(1)* to create a sparse file, if you were so inclined.

```
# dd if=/dev/zero of=sparse.out oseek=10000 count=1
1+0 records in
1+0 records out

# ls -ls
total 16
16 -rw-r--r--   1 root    system   5120512 Feb 28 19:47
sparse.out
```

1.7   Access Control Lists (ACLs)

Tru64 UNIX supports the notion of access control lists (ACLs). An ACL is an object that is associated with a file and that contains entries specifying the access that individual users or groups of users have to the file. ACLs provide a straightforward way of granting or denying access for a specified user or group of users. Using only the standard UNIX permission bit mechanism, without ACLs, granting access to the granularity of a single user who is not the owner of the file can be cumbersome.

ACLs represent what is also known as extended file attributes associated with Tru64 UNIX files. Only those Tru64 UNIX file system types that support property lists support ACLs. At present, those file systems are the NFS, UFS, and AdvFS. See the *proplist(4)* reference page for more information about property lists.

Although ACLs are often associated with elevated security, your system does not have to be running enhanced (or C2) level security in order to use ACLs. This common misconception often prevents customers from employing this useful feature.

ACLs are a POSIX (defined by standard P1003.6) extension to the traditional UNIX permissions, thus they may not be fully supported by all utilities. The archive utilities [*pax(1)*, *tar(1)*, *cpio(1)*, *dump(8)*, *restore(8)*, *vdump(8)*, and *vrestore(8)*] support files with extended file attributes; however, third-party archive utilities, such as *gzip(8)* or *gtar(1)*, may not support extended file attributes and, consequently, if they are used on those kind of files, the attributes could be lost.

1.7.1   Discretionary Access Algorithm

We've already discussed the standard UNIX permissions in a previous section. Now, we look at the algorithm for how this mechanism would work when ACLs are employed.

A process may request to read a file, write to a file, or execute/search a file. To determine this access, the Tru64 UNIX algorithm is applied to the ACL of the file. In general terms, the access check is performed on the ACL entries in the following order:

1.   the file owner

2.   a named user

3.   a user belonging to the owning group, together with any named groups

4.   a user belonging in any named groups

5.   others

When a match on one of these users is made, the ACL is no longer searched, and the granted or denied permissions take effect. For example, if a user is specified as a named user, and all permissions in the entry are set to deny access to that user, then the user is denied access. The groups the user may belong to are not checked to see if the user may have access through the groups' permissions. The somewhat simplified algorithm is as follows:

1.   If the user requesting access is the file owner, and the requested mode is granted by the ACL entry, then access is granted: else access is denied.

2.   If the user is a named user in the ACL, and the requested mode is granted by the ACL entry, then access is granted: else access is denied.

3.   If the user is in the owning group of the file, or is a member of any named groups, and the requested access mode is granted by the ACL entry of the owning group or the ACL entry of any of these named groups, then access is granted: else access is denied.

4. If the user is a member of any of the named groups, and the requested access mode is granted by the ACL entry of any of these named groups, then access is granted: else access is denied.

5. If the requested access mode is granted by the "other" entry, then access is granted: else access is denied.

1.7.2   Examining a File's ACL

The *dxsetacl(1)* or *getacl(8)* commands can be used to examine a file or directory's ACLs. If no ACLs are set, then these utilities simply show the standard UNIX permissions for the file or directory.

ACL entries have three fields, each separated by colons, as follows:

1. Entry type, such as user, group, or other

2. A group, user ID, or name. If empty, refers to the owning user.

3. The permission bit settings

The following example illustrates examining ACL setting for a newly created file and directory.

Example:

Here, we show how you can use the *getacl(8)* command to examine a newly created file called testfile.dat and a newly created directory called testdir. You can see that the initial ACLs are the same as the normal UNIX permissions.

```
# touch testfile.dat
# ls -l testfile.dat
-rw-r--r--   1 root   system   0 Feb 28 20:26 testfile.dat
# getacl testfile.dat
#
# file: testfile.dat
# owner: root
# group: system
#
user::rw-
group::r--
other::r-
# mkdir testdir
# ls -ld testdir
drwxr-xr-x   2 root   system   8192 Feb 28 21:59 testdir
# getacl testdir
#
```

```
# file: testdir
# owner: root
# group: system
#
user::rwx
group::r-x
other::r-x
```

Now that we've shown you how to examine a file's ACL with the *getacl(8)* command, we show you how to set the ACL in the following section.

1.7.3   Setting an ACL on a File or Directory

If a system administrator wishes to allow one user special access to a specific file or directory, then the ACL can be the only method for accomplishing this task. It is usually for cases in which standard UNIX permissions will not take care of the kind of policy you wish to implement. We can imagine scenarios where this is the case, but ultimately it is up to you as the system administrator to decide when this access is appropriate. The following example shows how to set an ACL for an individual user on a file.

Example:

Our example here shows how to set a user permission on a file called testfile.dat for the user named martin. Because martin is a trustworthy user, we give him full access to our important file.

```
# getacl testfile.dat
#
# file: testfile.dat
# owner: root
# group: system
#
user::rw-
group::r--
other::r--

# setacl -u user:martin:rwx testfile.dat
# getacl testfile.dat
#
# file: testfile.dat
# owner: root
# group: system
#
user::rw-
user:martin:rwx
group::r--
other::r--
```

Sometimes it is necessary to allow a group of users special access to a file or directory. The following example is a continuation of the previous example and shows how to additionally set an ACL for a group user on a file.

Example:

Here, we show you how to use the *setacl(8)* utility to set appropriate group permissions on a file called testfile.dat. You can see that the group field has been set to allow read access for the crash group.

```
# setacl -u group:crash:r-- testfile.dat
# getacl testfile.dat
#
# file: testfile.dat
# owner: root
# group: system
#
user::rw-
user:martin:rwx
group::r--
group:crash:r--
other::r--
```

The following example shows how it is possible to explicitly deny access to a file to a single user or group of users. In this case, the user hancock and group wkul are denied access to this file.

Example:

```
# setacl -u user:hancock:--- testfile.dat
# getacl testfile.dat
# file: testfile.dat
# owner: root
# group: system
#
user::rw-
user:martin:rwx
user:hancock:---
group::r--
group:crash:r--
other::r--

# setacl -u group:wkul:--- testfile.dat
#
# getacl testfile.dat
#
# file: testfile.dat
# owner: root
# group: system
#
user::rw-
user:martin:rwx
user:hancock:---
```

```
group::r--
group:crash:r--
group:wkul:---
other::r-
```

1.8   Backups

We bring up the topic of backups here to stress their importance. As for the mechanics of how to do a backup—with the exception of *btcreate(8)*, which we cover here—we discuss those topics in chapters 3, 5, and 6. You have many options. Regardless of what option you choose, it is vitally important that you develop and follow a sound and tested backup strategy as part of the proper management of any Tru64 UNIX system.

The following are your backup choices:

■ *System disk backup.* You should always keep at least one full backup of your system disk at all times. You should also remake these backups any time you make any changes to the system such as installing patches, upgrading, or any major system configuration changes. An acceptable system disk backup can be made using *btcreate(8),* which we discuss a bit later.

■ *Full backup.* This is a complete data backup on a regular basis, usually nightly. The frequency with which you back up your system depends on how volatile the data are.

■ *Incremental backup.* Incremental backups are used when regular full backups cannot be used because the data are updated too frequently or there is too much data to practically perform regular full backups. Usually, incremental backups are used in conjunction with full backups.

1.8.1   Btcreate

The *btcreate(8)* utility is a handy way to make a bootable tape containing a full system backup from which you can later restore in case of a disaster. This backup is particularly useful if you do not have ready access to a bootable medium such as the operating system CD or a Remote Installation Services (RIS) server. On the other hand, there used to be a short list of supported hardware for bootable tape, so we suggest you should make sure the hardware you have works with the tool before continuing. Compaq support is your best resource for this kind of information.

If *btcreate(8)* is a viable option for you based on the hardware you have, then we recommend using it for your system disk backup as part of your overall backup strategy. *Btcreate(8)* simply utilizes *vdump(8)* to perform the backup itself, so the data can be restored using standard tools as well. The following example illustrates how that can be done.

Example:

This rather lengthy example shows how the *btcreate(8)* utility can be used to create a bootable backup tape of the critical file systems on your Tru64 UNIX system.

```
# /usr/sys/bin/btcreate
      BOOTABLE TAPE CREATION
The btcreate utility creates a bootable standalone system (SAS)
kernel on tape. The SAS kernel has a built-in memory file
system (mfs), which contains the commands, files, and directories
needed to restore the system image.
The btcreate utility prompts you for information. Default answers,
if applicable, are enclosed in square brackets ([]). To select
a default answer, press the Return Key at the prompt. Type q at
any prompt to exit the utility; any information you supplied up to
that point is ignored.
The btcreate utility prompts you for the following:
  - name of the a kernel configuration file
  - disk partition to contain the SAS kernel
  - tape device to use for backup operations
  - list of file systems to back up
  - list of files and directories to back up
Do you want to continue (y/n) [y]:
      SELECTING A KERNEL CONFIGURATION FILE
The kernel configuration file, located in the /usr/sys/conf directory,
defines the run-time behavior of the kernel. The btcreate utility
uses this file to build the SAS kernel. You must specify which kernel
configuration file to use.

Enter the name of the kernel configuration file [JACKSON]:

  SELECTING MFS FILE SYSTEM OPTION

You can build the miniroot file system on a memory file system (mfs)
to save space on disk. An mfs file system is a UFS in virtual memory.

Answer yes if you want to create the miniroot file system in memory.
Answer no if you want to create the miniroot file system on disk.

Do you want to use an MFS file system? (y/n) [y]:

  SELECTING LOCATION FOR TEMPORARY FILES

The btcreate utility requires 70,120 (512 blocks) of disk in the
/usr file system for the temporary files that are created during
the process of bootable tape creation.
If you have space constraints in the /usr file system, then you
can use disk space in file systems other than the one /usr/sys is
located on.
When this flag is used, all necessary temporary space needed by
btcreate will be used in the specified directory.
```

Answer yes if you want btcreate to use the space available in /usr/sys.
Answer no if you want btcreate to use some other area for temp files.

Do you want temporary files to be created in /usr/sys ? (y/n) [y]:

SELECTING A TAPE DEVICE

The SAS kernel and file systems are backed up to a no-rewind tape
device. You must specify which tape device is to contain the kernel
and file systems.

Enter the name of the tape device [nrmt0h]:

Verifying tape... Done.

SELECTING FILE SYSTEMS

You must specify which file systems you want to include on the tape
device. Each entry consists of the device name, mount point, and
file system type separated by a space or tab as follows.

   device_name   mount_point   fs_type

To help with your selections, information about your local file
systems follows.

```
root_domain#root    /                advfs
usr_domain#usr      /usr             advfs
var_domain#var      /usr/var         advfs
var_domain#tmp      /tmp             advfs
var_domain#local    /usr/local2      advfs
/dev/vol/volbig     /usr/staff/k2    ufs
```

Press the Return Key after each entry or at the prompt to end input.

Enter your selection: root_domain#root / advfs

root_domain#root / advfs selected for back up.

Enter your selection: usr_domain#usr /usr advfs

usr_domain#usr /usr advfs selected for back up.

Enter your selection: var_domain#var /usr/var advfs

var_domain#var /usr/var advfs selected for back up.

Enter your selection: var_domain#local /usr/local2 advfs

var_domain#local /usr/local2 advfs selected for back up.

Enter your selection:

Have you completed your selections (y/n) [y]:

CUSTOMIZING THE MINIROOT FILE SYSTEM
You have the option of adding files and directories to the miniroot
file system. Each entry consists of two fields separated by a space
or tab as follows.

    file   destination

The first field specifies the absolute pathname of the file or directory
on the currently running system. The second column specifies the
absolute pathname on the miniroot file system.

Press the Return Key after each entry or at the prompt to end input.

Enter your selection:

You did not select a file or directory to back up.
Is this correct (y/n) [y]:

No files will be added to the miniroot file system.

   VERIFYING USER INPUT

This section summarizes your selections. You have the option
of accepting or modifying any selection. If you want to exit
the utility discarding all information gathered, type a q at
the prompt.

```
Kernel Configuration File specified  : /usr/sys/conf/JACKSON
Disk Partition                       : mfs
Tape Drive                           : nrmt0h
File systems included                : yes
Miniroot customizations              : no
```

The following file systems were specified for backup:

```
Device_Name    Mount_Point  File_Type Size
root_domain#root /   advfs  184750
usr_domain#usr /usr     advfs  1645790
var_domain#var /usr/var  advfs  663852
var_domain#local /usr/local2 advfs  166386
```

Are the answers correct? (y/n) [y]:

   Proceeding to create Bootable tape...

Creating a new kernel...

```
Moving the new kernel to /usr/sys/bin/vmunix.
Creating device files on mfs...
procprod: using MfsBase 0x140010000
procprod: pid 2765, MfsBase 140010000, 30720 sectors, output ==> "/var/tmp/pro"
procprod: wrote 15728640 bytes
Getting copy of kernel...
Merging file system into kernel...
Merging sboot into kernel...
pmerge sboot into kernel...
performing dd...
1+0 records in
1+0 records out
performing cat...
deleting /usr/sys/bin/vmunix.boot.2740...
Moving /usr/sys/bin/vmunix.tmp.2740 to /usr/sys/bin/vmunix.boot.2740...
Making tape bootable kernel...
Writing vmunix...
39561+0 records in
39561+0 records out
Dumping the file system root_domain#root of type advfs
path  : /
dev/fset : root_domain#root
type  : advfs
advfs id : 0x3516a170.000d0029.1
vdump: Date of last level 0 dump: the start of the epoch
vdump: Dumping directories
vdump: Dumping 94184427 bytes, 237 directories, 3166 files
vdump: Dumping regular files
```

```
vdump: Status at Fri Mar 10 08:02:06 2000
vdump: Dumped 91374170 of 94184427 bytes; 97.0% completed
vdump: Dumped 208 of 237 directories; 87.8% completed
vdump: Dumped 3155 of 3166 files; 99.7% completed

vdump: Status at Fri Mar 10 08:02:10 2000
vdump: Dumped 94184419 of 94184427 bytes; 100.0% completed
vdump: Dumped 238 of 237 directories; 100.4% completed
vdump: Dumped 3165 of 3166 files; 100.0% completed
vdump: Dump completed at Fri Mar 10 08:02:10 2000
Dump finished.

Dumping the file system usr_domain#usr of type advfs

path   : /usr
dev/fset : usr_domain#usr
type   : advfs
advfs id : 0x3516a183.0000fd0b.1
vdump: Date of last level 0 dump: the start of the epoch
vdump: Dumping directories
vdump: Dumping 884270127 bytes, 1177 directories, 26375 files
vdump: Dumping regular files

vdump: Status at Fri Mar 10 08:08:12 2000
vdump: Dumped 106445265 of 884270127 bytes; 12.0% completed
vdump: Dumped 20 of 1177 directories; 1.7% completed
vdump: Dumped 2441 of 26375 files; 9.3% completed

vdump: Status at Fri Mar 10 08:13:18 2000
vdump: Dumped 206390280 of 884270127 bytes; 23.3% completed
vdump: Dumped 284 of 1177 directories; 24.1% completed
vdump: Dumped 6844 of 26375 files; 25.9% completed

vdump: Status at Fri Mar 10 08:18:18 2000
vdump: Dumped 303021229 of 884270127 bytes; 34.3% completed
vdump: Dumped 491 of 1177 directories; 41.7% completed
vdump: Dumped 9038 of 26375 files; 34.3% completed

vdump: Status at Fri Mar 10 08:23:23 2000
vdump: Dumped 406135193 of 884270127 bytes; 45.9% completed
vdump: Dumped 600 of 1177 directories; 51.0% completed
vdump: Dumped 10565 of 26375 files; 40.1% completed

vdump: Status at Fri Mar 10 08:28:23 2000
vdump: Dumped 505718728 of 884270127 bytes; 57.2% completed
vdump: Dumped 769 of 1177 directories; 65.3% completed
vdump: Dumped 17865 of 26375 files; 67.7% completed

vdump: Status at Fri Mar 10 08:33:23 2000
vdump: Dumped 605172019 of 884270127 bytes; 68.4% completed
vdump: Dumped 945 of 1177 directories; 80.3% completed
vdump: Dumped 20273 of 26375 files; 76.9% completed

vdump: Status at Fri Mar 10 08:38:23 2000
vdump: Dumped 725887870 of 884270127 bytes; 82.1% completed
vdump: Dumped 1047 of 1177 directories; 89.0% completed
vdump: Dumped 24979 of 26375 files; 94.7% completed

vdump: Status at Fri Mar 10 08:45:54 2000
vdump: Dumped 826176376 of 884270127 bytes; 93.4% completed
vdump: Dumped 1132 of 1177 directories; 96.2% completed
```

```
vdump: Dumped 25482 of 26375 files; 96.6% completed

vdump: Status at Fri Mar 10 08:50:57 2000
vdump: Dumped 877212299 of 884270127 bytes; 99.2% completed
vdump: Dumped 1151 of 1177 directories; 97.8% completed
vdump: Dumped 26298 of 26375 files; 99.7% completed

vdump: Status at Fri Mar 10 08:51:36 2000
vdump: Dumped 884270127 of 884270127 bytes; 100.0% completed
vdump: Dumped 1177 of 1177 directories; 100.0% completed
vdump: Dumped 26375 of 26375 files; 100.0% completed

vdump: Dump completed at Fri Mar 10 08:51:36 2000
Dump finished.
Dumping the file system var_domain#var of type advfs
path   : /usr/var
dev/fset : var_domain#var
type   : advfs
advfs id : 0x3516a1d5.0005140d.1
vdump: Date of last level 0 dump: the start of the epoch
vdump: Dumping directories
vdump: Dumping 339092442 bytes, 399 directories, 1695 files
vdump: Dumping regular files

vdump: Status at Fri Mar 10 08:57:30 2000
vdump: Dumped 76082020 of 339092442 bytes; 22.4% completed
vdump: Dumped 7 of 399 directories; 1.8% completed
vdump: Dumped 107 of 1695 files; 6.3% completed

vdump: Status at Fri Mar 10 09:02:42 2000
vdump: Dumped 234109745 of 339092442 bytes; 69.0% completed
vdump: Dumped 39 of 399 directories; 9.8% completed
vdump: Dumped 379 of 1695 files; 22.4% completed

vdump: Status at Fri Mar 10 09:07:54 2000
vdump: Dumped 331937021 of 339092442 bytes; 97.9% completed
vdump: Dumped 344 of 399 directories; 86.2% completed
vdump: Dumped 1397 of 1695 files; 82.4% completed

vdump: Status at Fri Mar 10 09:08:08 2000
vdump: Dumped 339092539 of 339092442 bytes; 100.0% completed
vdump: Dumped 399 of 399 directories; 100.0% completed
vdump: Dumped 1695 of 1695 files; 100.0% completed
vdump: Dump completed at Fri Mar 10 09:08:08 2000
Dump finished.
Dumping the file system var_domain#local of type advfs
path   : /usr/local2
dev/fset : var_domain#local
type   : advfs
advfs id : 0x3516a1d5.0005140d.3
vdump: Date of last level 0 dump: the start of the epoch
vdump: Dumping directories
vdump: Dumping 84237409 bytes, 84 directories, 784 files
vdump: Dumping regular files

vdump: Status at Fri Mar 10 09:12:55 2000
vdump: Dumped 84237409 of 84237409 bytes; 100.0% completed
vdump: Dumped 84 of 84 directories; 100.0% completed
vdump: Dumped 784 of 784 files; 100.0% completed
```

```
vdump: Dump completed at Fri Mar 10 09:12:55 2000
Dump finished.
Rewinding the tape.
btcreate.log file has been created on /var/adm directory.
  End of system image creation on tape.
```

Now, we can easily use this tape to recover selected files if we remember that the first part of the tape needs to be skipped because it is the bootable portion and is not a *vdump(8)* archive. A complete restore of an entire file system is possible, although we don't show it here.

```
# cd /tmp

# mt rewind

# mt -f /dev/nrmt0h fsf 1

# vrestore -i
vrestore: Date of the vdump save-set: Fri Mar 10 07:56:58 2000
(/) ls

.:
#.mrg...login                    #.mrg..DXsession
.Xauthority                      .advfs_hostlist
.asWedit-prefs                   .cshrc
.dt/                             .dtprofile
.elm/                            .login
.lsof_sunny                      .netscape/
.new...cshrc                     .new...login
.new...profile                   .new..DXsession
.profile                         .proto...cshrc
.proto...login                   .proto...profile
.proto..DXsession                .proto..DXsession.FailMRG
.proto..DXsession.PreMRG         .rhosts
.sh_history                      .sysman/
.tags                            .xsession-errors
Dxsession                        DXsession.PreMRG
Dxterm                           GENERIC
Mail/                            News/
O3D.out                          PCITMP1
PCITMP2:                         PCITMP3
backup/                          bin
cdrom/                           check_cd
core                             core.aseagent
crash/                           dev/
etc/                             genvmunix
guru/                            home/
j/                               junk/
kits/                            lib
master                           mbox
mdec/                            mnt/
mnt2/                            nsmail/
nsr                              opt/
osf_boot                         patches/
proc/                            quota.group
```

```
quota.user              real.profile
rz1.label               sbin/
shlib/                  subsys/
sys/                    tcb/
test/                   tmp/
usr/                    var
vmunix                  vmunix.pre_isp
webmnt/
```

1.9   Adding New File Systems to Your Environment

One of the most important tasks you will need to accomplish as a systems administrator is setting up new file systems. The process is straightforward at the simplest level, but it can be complex when you begin to look at all of the different options. If you are new to the process, it can appear to be a daunting task. We suggest you start out simply and become more sophisticated as you learn about the different options available to you.

Although we cover only a few file system types in any detail in this text, Tru64 UNIX supports many of them. Our discussion in Chapter 4 details how the actual mounting is accomplished by the operating system through the virtual file system (VFS); however, right now we would like to introduce to you the procedure by which you can add new file systems to your environment. The following lists the steps to perform to add a new file system to a Tru64 UNIX system.

1. Identify a block special device or logical volume to hold the file system.[4]

2. Identify on which directory you would like the new file system to be mounted. Create the directory if it doesn't already exist.

3. Create the file system.

4. Mount the file system.

5. Set up to mount the file system at boot time.

Steps 1 and 3 above are covered in chapters 5 and 6 for the UFS (and MFS) and AdvFS types, respectively. Step 2 is up to you, and we cannot make that decision for you. Most UNIX systems have a directory already on them called /mnt, which can be used by the system administrator for temporary mounts. Tru64 UNIX is no exception. We suggest that you use this directory for becoming familiar with mounting and unmounting file systems. You will often find that you need to mount a file system in a temporary location before allowing users to have access to it. This is the main purpose of the /mnt directory.

In the following sections, we discuss the latter two steps in the process.

1.9.1   Mounting File Systems

The concept of mounting a file system is an old one in operating systems. The operation's primary purpose is to make the file system available to the system users. With few exceptions, the file systems can either be mounted from the command line by the system administrator or can be mounted at boot time.[5] In this section, we are mostly concerned with the former function, which is one of the system administrator's most important roles.

The *mount(8)* command is used in Tru64 UNIX for mounting file systems on a mount point directory. This command has many options, and we can't possibly hope to cover all of them in any detail. Some of the options that are specific to a file system type may be discussed further in the chapter that deals with it. For example, the AdvFS-specific mount options are covered in Chapter 6.

The syntax for the *mount(8)* command is given as follows:

Syntax:

```
mount [-d] [-r | -u | -w] [-o argument,...] [-t [no]type]
file-system directory

mount [-el] [-t [no]type]

mount -a [-fv] [-t [no]type]

mount [-d] [-r | -u | -w] [-o argument,...] [-t [no]type]
file-system | directory
```

Table 1–3 lists the valid flags for the *mount(8)* command. Some flags are valid only for certain file system types. We have given those flags for UFS, AdvFS, and NFS in the columns marked with U, A, or N, respectively.

TABLE 1–3   Flags for the *mount(8)* Command

FLAG	DESCRIPTION	U	A	N
file system	Specifies the block special device for UFS, a domain#fileset for AdvFS, or a nodename:/directory for NFS.	X	X	X
directory	Specifies a mount point directory on the system on which the file system will be mounted.	X	X	X
-a	Attempts to mount all of the file systems listed in the /etc/fstab file.	X	X	X

TABLE 1–3   Flags for the *mount(8)* Command (Continued)

FLAG	DESCRIPTION	U	A	N
-d	Mounts the file system even if it has not passed consistency checking. This flag should be used with caution.	X	X	
-e	Lists all file system mount points.	X	X	X
-f	Performs a "fake" mount without actually mounting anything. This function is used to verify options.	X	X	X
-l	Shows the mount table and lists all of the mount options used for the mount.	X	X	X
-o argument	Allows you to specify a list of comma-separated arguments to pass to the *mount(8)* for the particular file system type.	X	X	X
-r	Mounts the file system with read-only access. This function is equivalent to the "–o ro" flag.	X	X	X
-t [no]type	Allows you to specify the type of file system on which you are trying to mount.	X	X	X
-u	Performs a remount of the specified file system in order to update in-memory structures.	X	X	X
-v	Verbose mode.	X	X	X
-w	Mounts the file system with read-write access. This function is equivalent to the "-o rw" flag.	X	X	X

TABLE 1–4   *Mount(8)* Optional Arguments

FLAG	DESCRIPTION	U	A	N
dual	See Chapter 6.		X	
atimes	Flushes to disk file access time changes for reads of regular files. This is the default behavior when neither atimes nor noatimes is specified.	X	X	
noatimes	Marks file access time changes made for reads of regular files in memory, but does not flush them to disk until other file modifications occur. This is not standard behavior.	X	X	
rw	Use of this flag allows read-write access to the specific file system.	X	X	X
rdonly or ro	Use of this flag allows read-only access to the specified file system.	X	X	X
rq	This flag is the same as rw, except it is used with file systems for which quotas have been enabled.	X	X	
sw	Allows block special device to be used for swap space.	X		
dirty	Allows a file system to be mounted even if it was not cleanly unmounted.	X	X	
dev	Allows access to block and character special devices. This is the default if neither dev nor nodev is specified.	X	X	X

TABLE 1–4   *Mount(8)* Optional Arguments (Continued)

FLAG	DESCRIPTION	U	A	N
nodev	Disallows access from the file system to either block or character special devices from that mounted file system. This security is useful for NFS mounts where you don't have control over the root on the server system.	X	X	X
suid	Allows SUID execution from this file system. This is the default if neither suid nor nosuid are specified.	X	X	X
nosuid	Prohibits SUID execution of programs from that mounted file system. This security is useful for NFS mounts where you don't have control over the root on the server system.	X	X	X
sync	Causes all writes to be written immediately to disk as well as to the buffer cache before returning a success.	X	X	X
nosync	Specifies that writes may indicate success before data are written to disk.	X	X	X
smsync2	Enables the alternate smooth sync policy, in which dirty data do not get written to disk until they are dirty and aged sufficiently. See Chapter 4 for our discussion of this feature.	X	X	
exec	Allows binary execution of programs on this file system. This is the default if neither exec nor noexec are specified.	X	X	X
noexec	Prohibits execution of programs that reside on that file system. This security is useful for NFS mounts where you don't have control over the root on the server system.	X	X	X
grpid	Newly created files inherit the parent directory's group ID. This is the default and matches BSD's semantics.	X	X	X
nogrpid	The SVID III semantics are applied.	X	X	X
delayed	Metadata updates are delayed rather than flushed synchronously, and the metadata are flushed by the sync daemon.	X		
nodelayed	Metadata updates are flushed to disk synchronously.	X		
bg	Attempts to retry the mount in the background, if the first mount attempt fails. Use this flag if the NFS server may not be up when this node will be mounting file systems. If the server is not available at client boot time, the client will not hang on boot.			X
fg	Retries in the foreground.			X
retry=n	Sets the number of mount failure retries to *n*.			X
rsize=n	Sets the read buffer size to *n* bytes.			X
wsize=n	Sets the write buffer size to *n* bytes.			X

TABLE 1–4   *Mount(8)* Optional Arguments (Continued)

Flag	Description	U	A	N
timeo=n	Sets the initial NFS timeout period for UDP mounts to *n* tenths of a second. NFS continually adjusts the timing as a function of network response time.			
maxtimo=n	Sets the maximum value, in seconds, that is allowed between request transmissions. [UDP mounts only]			X
retrans=n	Sets the number of NFS retransmissions to *n*.			X
intr	Allows hard-mounted file system operations to be interrupted.			X
nintr	Prevents hard-mounted file system operations from being interrupted, unless the thread is terminated (e.g., by a SIGKILL or an AST).			X
soft	Returns an error if the server does not respond.			X
hard	Retries the request until the server responds.			X
nfsv2	Normally, the *mount(8)* command tries to use version 2 of the NFS protocol exclusively.			X
nfsv3	The *mount(8)* tries to use version 3 of the NFS protocol. If the server does not support it, then version 2 is used. This is the default.			X
proto=type	Specifies the network transport to be used. Both udp or tcp are supported.			X
port=n	Sets the server IP port number to a specified value of *n*. The default is to query the portmap daemon on the server for the port number (normally port 2049).			X
proplist	Allows the use of extended attributes (property list), including ACLs, on this file system. The NFS server exporting this file system must be running the proplistd daemon. See our discussion of property lists and ACLs earlier in this chapter.			X
vers=n	Specifies the version of the NFS protocol. You can specify either version 2 or version This is the same as nfsv2 and nfsv3 options respectively.			X
acdirmin=n	Holds cached directory attributes for at least *n* seconds.			X
acdirmax=n	Holds cached directory attributes for no more than *n* seconds. The maximum value you can specify is 3600.			X
acregmin=n	Holds cached file attributes for at least *n* seconds.			X
acregmax=n	Holds cached file attributes for no more than *n* seconds. The maximum value you can specify is 3600.			X
actimeo=n	Sets all four attributes' cache timeout values to *n*.			X
noac	Does not set attribute caching. This argument is equivalent to actimeo=0.			X
nocto	Does not get a fresh attribute when opening a file.			X

1.9.2 Mounting File Systems at Boot Time

File systems that are specified in the /etc/fstab file are mounted at boot time. The fstab file is scanned by the *bcheckrc(8)* script that is executed when the system boots up. At that time, any UFSs have *fsck(8)* run on them in the order specified by the fsck field. Any file systems that are clean are mounted; if not, the *fsck(8)* is performed in preen mode to clean up any inconsistencies. See Chapter 5 and Appendix C for more details on what *fsck(8)* does. Any AdvFS file systems listed in the fstab file are activated at this time.

Six fields in the /etc/fstab file are each separated by white space. The structure of the entries in the file are as follows:

```
file_system mount_point fstype options backup fsck
```

Each of these fields has the following meaning:

file_system: The name of the file system. For UFS, it is the block special device, for AdvFS it is the domain#fset, and for NFS it is the node:/directory to be mounted.

mount_point: The directory on which the file system will be mounted.

fstype: The file system type to which this entry refers.

options: Any options to be passed to *mount(8)*.

backup: A nonzero value specifies whether the file system will be backed up. A zero or empty field indicates that the file system is to be ignored by *dump(8)*.

fsck: The pass order for the file systems.

For UFS, this is the pass number for *fsck(8)*. It is a numeric value that indicates the order in which the file systems should have *fsck(8)* run on them at boot time. The root file system must be 1, and all others should be 2 or greater. If a zero is present, or the entry is empty, then *fsck(8)* is not performed on the file system.

For AdvFS, this is the pass number for the *quotacheck(8)* to perform consistency checks needed for the the file system. The root file system must be 1, and all others should be 2 or greater. If a zero is present, or the entry is empty, then *quotacheck(8)* is not performed on the file system.

TABLE 1–5 *Mount(8)* Options Specified Only in /etc/fstab

OPTION	DESCRIPTION	U	A	N
dirty	Specifies that the file system can be mounted even if it was not cleanly unmounted.	X		
userquota [=filename]	User quotas will be enforced on this file system. Perform a *quotacheck(8)* at boot time for consistency checking.	X	X	
groupquota [=filename]	Group quotas will be enforced on this file system. Perform a *quotacheck(8)* at boot time for consistency checking.	X	X	
xx	Ignore this entry in the /etc/fstab file.	X	X	X

You can use a handy shortcut for mounting or unmounting file systems, if the file system is already listed in the /etc/fstab file. That is, you can simply use *mount(8)* or *umount(8)* with either the mount point directory or the file system alone and leave off the rest of the fields. The *mount(8)* command consults the /etc/fstab file for the rest of the information.

Example:

Here is an example of using the shorthand method for mounting a file system called /big listed in the fstab file.

```
# grep big /etc/fstab
/dev/vol/volbig /big ufs rw 0 3

# mount /big

# df /big
Filesystem      512-blocks Used Available Capacity Mounted on
/dev/vol/volbig 32579526      2   29321570       0%       /big
```

Alternatively, you could use the file system name as well.

```
# umount /big

# mount /dev/vol/volbig

# df /big
Filesystem      512-blocks Used Available Capacity Mounted on
/dev/vol/volbig 32579526      2   29321570       0%       /big
```

1.9.3   Unmounting File Systems

The command for unmounting mounted file systems in Tru64 UNIX is the *umount(8)* command. The command simply makes a file system unavailable for access by the system users.

The following is the supported syntax for the *umount(8)* command.

Syntax:

```
umount -a | -A -b [-fv] [-t type] [-h host]
umount [-fv] file-system... | directory...
```

TABLE 1–6   Flags for the *umount(8)* Command

FLAG	DESCRIPTION
file-system	The name of the file system that you would like to unmount.
directory	The name of the mount point directory that you would like to unmount.
-A	Attempts to unmount all the file systems that are currently mounted.
-a	Attempts to unmount all the file systems that are listed in the /etc/fstab file.
-b	Broadcasts a message to all server machines in the subnetwork to remove the client host's name from their NFS mountdtab files.
-f	Performs a fast NFS unmount operation that causes remote file systems to be unmounted without notifying the server.
-h host	Unmounts all file systems listed in the /etc/fstab file that are remotely mounted from host.
-a -t type	Unmounts all file systems listed in the /etc/fstab file that are of the specified type.
-v	Verbose mode.

Table 1–6 lists the valid flags for the *umount(8)* command.

Example:

Below, we give a simple example of the use of the *umount(8)* command to unmount a file system mounted on the mount point directory /big.

```
# df /big
Filesystem      512-blocks  Used  Available Capacity  Mounted on
/dev/vol/volbig 32579526       2   29321570       0%        /big

# umount -v /big
/dev/vol/volbig: Unmounted from /big
```

Example:

The *umount(8)* command does not work if files are open on the mount point. In this example, we demonstrate how the *fuser(8)* command shows which users are using the file system, so they can be removed (killed).

```
# cd /big

# pwd
/big

# umount /big
/big: Device busy

# fuser -cuv /big
fuser: 2 reference(s) on directory /big

PID     UID   USERNAME   COMMAND   REFERENCE
21761   0     root       fuser     cdir
14175   0     root       sh        cdir
```

1.10   Summary

In this chapter, we have introduced the topic of file systems administration in the Tru64 UNIX environment. The I/O subsystem in the Tru64 UNIX environment was discussed, which should put the following chapters in this text in perspective for you. Our goal for the rest of the book is to discuss the layers of the I/O subsystem and finally to wrap it all up in chapters 8 and 9 with examples and case studies for setting up and troubleshooting real Tru64 UNIX systems. We also discussed access control lists, which are useful for setting and managing accesses to files on the file system. They provide a flexible and POSIX standard addition to the standard UNIX permissions. Then, we covered backup strategies. We cannot stress enough the importance of a sound backup strategy. Finally, we discussed mounting and unmounting file systems both at boot time and at the command line.

Now that we have completed our discussion of the introductory material in file systems, we move on to storage management.

Notes

1.   The author has developed specialized tools for recovering some files, but if customers did not follow good backup practices, then this help was not covered by their standard support contract.

2.   The *file(1)* command attempts to interpret the data in a regular file based on information in /etc/magic.

3.   Beginning in Tru64 UNIX version V4.0D, crash dumps are compressed internally, so they are no longer written by *savecore(8)* as sparse files.

4.   In the case of NFS, you would be identifying a remote node and directory to be mounted.

5.   We'll ignore for the moment that the automounter and TruCluster software can also mount file systems.

2

Storage and Device Management

> Do not go where the path may lead, go instead
> where there is no path and leave a trail.
> — *Ralph Waldo Emerson*

As we discussed in Chapter 1, the I/O subsystem consists of many layers. The lowest layer in the architecture is the device driver that interacts with the storage hardware. Therefore, a discussion of the Tru64 UNIX I/O subsystem would not be complete without a discussion of the organization of storage and the way in which devices are managed. Because one of our ultimate objectives is to optimize the performance of the file systems and because the file systems are the upper layers in the I/O subsystem hierarchy, it stands to reason that file system performance depends on performance at the lower layers. File system performance is bounded at the top end by the performance of all the layers between the file system and the devices. Also, given this dependency, we would conclude that device management problems would cause file system problems and would ultimately be seen by the end-user applications. Experience shows us that this situation is exactly what occurs with real systems like those we examine in our coverage of case studies later.

This chapter does not attempt to make you an expert in Tru64 UNIX disk devices or drivers; however, it does provide enough background information to give readers a better understanding of how the higher layers in the I/O subsystem interact with the device management layer. In this chapter, we begin with basic storage terminology. This background is necessary when we get to following sections in this chapter and the later chapter on the UNIX file system.

2.1 Storage Systems Concepts

To better understand how UNIX file systems are implemented, you should know some of the terminology of storage. In this section, we examine generic concepts of storage and disk drive parlance, so these ideas will make sense in the context of the internal workings of the storage management subsystem.

2.1.1   Disk Drive Terminology

Disk drive technology has been around in the computer business for a long time. In the "old" days, names like Winchester drive and DASD were common to refer to disk drive technology. These days we simply refer to them as disks, disk drives, or disk devices. These are drives based on a single, individual spindle that constitute a storage subsystem. Sometimes a redundant array of independent disks (RAID) device, which can comprise many individual disks, is referred to as a single disk because it presents itself to UNIX that way. For our purposes in this section, we refer to concepts related to a single disk device, and later sections cover the RAID device concepts and terminology.

A **disk drive** is a mechanical device. It consists of moving parts such as servos and drive motors that can wear out after a certain period. Despite this long-term wear, these devices have become very reliable over time, with very high mean time between failure (MBTF) associated with them. An MBTF of greater than 500,000 hours is very common these days, which means that unless a manufacturing defect is present, the drives will likely outlive the useful life of the computer system to which they are attached. Historically, understanding the mechanics of the disks was important because they were used in calculations for optimal UNIX file system structure and so forth. We see later that these calculations still exist, but they are far less relevant than they used to be with the advent of hardware and software RAID products that mask this underlying detail. Understanding that these devices still do fail is also important. A single block or an entire drive can go bad, but in either case the failures can be hidden from the operating system's point of view using RAID techniques.

A **spindle** is a single, rotating axle to which the platters that contain the data on the disk are attached. A single circumference of a disk platter under a single head located a fixed distance from the disk spindle is known as a **track**. This is the amount of data that can be read by a single drive head in one rotation of the platter. A disk **sector** is a fixed-size piece of a track located on a disk. A disk **block** is a fixed-size, contiguous area on a disk. It is the minimum amount of information transferred between the operating system and a disk, thus it is the minimally addressable entity on a disk device. For all Compaq-supported disk drives, the disk sector and block are the same and are equal to 512 bytes of data.

A **head** is a physical device that reads the data on a single side of a platter. All heads for a single drive are connected to a device known as an **actuator arm** that moves all the heads together. Because all the heads must move simultaneously and can read data in parallel, a logical construct known as a **cylinder** was developed to describe all the tracks located on all the platter sides located the same fixed distance from the disk spindle. Because a **seek** is the most time-consuming event needed to read and write data to or from a disk drive, it is important to reduce the number of them. One way this task is accomplished is to place related data in the same or adjacent cylinders, thus the concept of a cylinder group was developed. A **cylinder group** simply refers to a contiguous set of cylinders used to store file system data, which we cover in greater detail in our UFS discussion in Chapter 5.

2.1.2 Controller Technology

A **controller** is another one of those terms that can have many meanings depending on the context in which it is used. In the context of this chapter, we simply use the term as another name for an adapter. Thus, a small computer system interface (SCSI, pronounced "scuzzy") controller is simply a device that converts signals from the computer system's main I/O bus to the SCSI standard protocol. A RAID controller is a device that connects to a standard bus interface like SCSI and translates the I/Os to a set of devices connected in a fashion on the back end of the device. Thus, a RAID controller is much more sophisticated and complex than a simple SCSI adapter. A RAID controller has a central processing unit (CPU) and memory associated with it and runs a specialized program, called the **firmware**, that determines how the device can be configured and how it will react to various events.

Disk drives used to have a large array of controller technology, which has evolved over time. Many of the older controllers were proprietary in nature. Compaq (on the Digital side) delivered many legacy controllers, such as DSSI™, and Sun Microsystems' high-end legacy controller was known as the Intelligent Peripherals Interconnect (IPI™). In addition, IDE, Enhanced IDE, and ATAPI are the most popular controllers in PC systems.

Today, most storage attached to UNIX systems is connected using the SCSI bus standard. Later, we cover SCSI in greater depth because the standard has evolved over time. There is no such thing as a single SCSI adapter; there are many to support the different speeds and signal types that the standards allow. Even with these changes, the SCSI standard has simplified disk interconnects considerably from the old days of proprietary disk protocols.

2.1.3   SCSI Bus Concepts

SCSI is not just one standard, but actually is a suite of standards. In this section, we explain the different SCSI terminology and develop concepts needed later to discuss interaction between SCSI devices and the host.

2.1.3.1   Terminology

Many terms have been developed to discuss the SCSI protocol. We are going to give you a brief overview of some of them that are relevant to our discussion in this section.

In fact, the term **protocol** is usually discussed with respect to networking because it refers to a "conversation" in much the same way as the English language is one protocol used as communication between human beings. More technically, a protocol is a mechanism for exchange of information between two entities. In the case of a computer network, the two entities are host computers or specialized networking equipment. In a disk specification, such as SCSI, the entities could be hosts, disks, tape drives, or many other supported devices. The SCSI specification defines things such as the supported commands a host can use when communicating with a device, signaling levels, and supported cable lengths and interfaces.

Devices are interconnected to each other on a SCSI **bus**, with termination at either end. On the bus are two types of devices. The first type is called an **initiator**, which can begin a SCSI conversation on a bus. The second type is a **target**, which is the recipient of the SCSI conversation. Some devices, such as a host adapter, can be either an initiator or a target, depending on the situation. Other devices, such as a disk, can only be a target. Each device on the bus has a unique target number associated with it. In SCSI parlance, this is known as the SCSI ID for the device. The SCSI ID has significance only for the bus its device is connected to and refers to one of the signal lines for the bus. Each SCSI ID has eight logical unit numbers (LUNs), numbered from 0 to 7, which can be assigned to up to eight different devices at a particular target address. A **nexus** is defined as a device path that includes its bus, target, and LUN numbers.

2.1.3.2   Timing

As the standards have evolved, so have the timing parameters of the bus. The original SCSI standard was single-ended and narrow (eight data lines) with a 5 MB/second data transfer rate. Later, the SCSI 2 standard evolved, and the differential bus was introduced. This advance allowed the bus speed to be doubled to 10 MB/second, and cable lenths were greatly increased. Another feature introduced in SCSI 2 was the wide bus. The wide bus supported 16 data lines, so data transfer speed doubled again to 20 MB/second using a fast, wide differential SCSI bus. Even faster speeds are defined in the SCSI 3 specifications, up to a fast 160 MB/second.

2.1.3.3 SCSI Types and Specifications

SCSI (or what is now commonly referred to as SCSI 1) was the original SCSI specification proposed by the American National Standards Institute (ANSI). Work on the specification was first begun in 1982 and was originally designed to support workstations (ANSI X3.131-1986). It supported a single-ended, narrow bus structure with maximum support for only eight devices. The maximum speed that could be achieved was only 5 MB/second and only supported a maximum bus length of six meters. In addition, the roughly 200-page document defined only six devices. Although this standard was useful and became used in many small computer systems, it had significant weaknesses, particularly for larger systems. Technology and system sizes began to change significantly, thus the need for improvements became evident. Hence, the committee began working in 1992 on the second revision of the standard.

The SCSI 2 specification (ANSI X3.131-1994) was the result of the second committee's work and is still in widespread use today. This standard was a great improvement because it defined much faster device speeds, four new devices, fast and wide concepts, differential device specifications, and new cabling standards. In addition, it allowed for multiple initiators on a single bus at one time, thus paving the way for clustering technologies like Compaq's TruCluster product. The new standard allows for up to 16 devices per SCSI 2 bus and for up to 8 LUNs per device. The SCSI 2 specification was vastly better than SCSI 1 and brought SCSI into the mainstream of computing both for low-end and high-end systems.

As of this writing, the SCSI 3 specification is emerging as the new SCSI standard. SCSI 3 is different from its predecessors in that it is really an architecture for adding new interfaces and devices into the standard. It has been intelligently crafted with the thought that any useful standard must continue to evolve and never remain static. To date, many devices have implemented various pieces of the specification to one degree or another. For example, the popular Ultra and Ultra Wide SCSI (also known as Fast 20 and Fast 20 Wide) devices are an implementation of part of the SCSI 3 standard. These two devices fall under the SCSI parallel interface (SPI), which is a synchronous extension of the SCSI standard with a negotiated period of between 50 and 96 nanoseconds. As a result, the Ultra standard is roughly twice the speed of regular Fast SCSI, allowing for a 20 MB/second transfer rate for narrow devices and 40 MB/second for wide. The SCSI 3 standard increases the number of supported LUNs per device from 8 to 64.

2.1.4   Caching Techniques

Most SCSI devices in use today are intelligent and contain some kind of cache onboard, which allows them to better handle bursts in the data being transferred to or from the device. Any device with a cache usually includes a management mechanism known as its **cache policy**, and some devices even support more than one. There are two main cache policies for SCSI devices: the write-back cache and the write-through cache. Each cache policy has its benefits for a particular situation. The write-back cache is preferable for write operations because the device can signal that the write operation is complete as soon as the data are written to the cache, rather than waiting for the data to be written to persistent storage. The write-through cache, on the other hand, reduces response to reads because they are satisfied from the cache, rather than from the disk. Naturally, for any device with a cache, some sort of battery backup should be provided so that data corruption can be avoided should a power disruption occur.

As previously mentioned, RAID controllers can be complex. In order for an I/O that comes from the operating system to be written to a physical disk in a RAID set, the controller has to perform calculations and manipulations to provide the needed redundancy. Because this work the controller must do could introduce some delay for each I/O, a cache is usually included with the controller to handle periodic I/O bursts. Also, when a cache is utilized, the controller fools the host computer into thinking that the I/O is complete when it is written to the memory but not when written to the disk. Thus, the operating system continues to operate under the assumption that the data are safely on disk, when in fact they are not. Therefore, controller cache should not be used without the additional feature of a battery backup so that if power to the controller is lost, the cache will be flushed and the data will not be in an inconsistent state. This kind of inconsistent state is also known as data **corruption**. The system must be designed to ensure that data corruption never occurs.

Modern RAID controllers usually support caches that utilize one or both of two methods. The following two sections explain these caching methodologies and reasons why you might use one over the other. Compaq StorageWorks™ HSZ™ controllers support both types.

2.1.4.1 Write-Through Caching

Write-through caching means that when the block is written to the controller, it is also written to the disk at the same time. Thus, the writes are mostly synchronous, but reads can be gotten directly from the cache, thus bypassing the need to read the disk block back into the cache. So, this method maintains very good read performance but perhaps less than optimal write performance. Also, the security of the data is much better with this method because even if the battery backup fails, there is a smaller window for data corruption than with write-back caching.

2.1.4.2 Write-Back Caching

This is the most popular caching method today. Write-back caching employs a lazy write mechanism in which data are not written synchronously on the disk when the data block is written to the cache. The primary advantage of this scheme is that bursty data writes are evened out, thus improving performance.

2.2   Redundant Array of Independent Disks (RAID)

In the 1980s, when disk drives began to decrease in price and improve in reliability, a group of three University of California at Berkeley professors realized that they could make a bunch of off-the-shelf disks perform as well or better than a single large expensive disk (SLED). At that time, for performance and reliability, you still needed to spend a lot of money on proprietary drives to attach to your mainframes and minicomputers. The introduction of smaller, standard drives built on a large scale began to emulate the big drives in what became known as a redundant array of independent disks (RAID).[1] These devices have all but replaced the big, proprietary drives for high-end systems. An entire industry has been built around RAID technology, accounting for billions of dollars in sales each year. Compaq is a major player in this market.

2.2.1   RAID Terminology

Before we move any further into our discussion of RAID, let's define a few terms that we will need later on in the text.

A **RAID device** is any highly intelligent controller that implements some or all parts of the RAID specifications. One example of such a device connected to a Tru64 UNIX system is Compaq's StorageWorks HSZ family of storage controllers.[2] These controllers connect to your

Alpha system with a SCSI interface and offer features such as dual-redundancy, spare device management, battery backup, and intelligent manageability. There are other popular brands available as well that can be used successfully with Tru64 UNIX.

Fundamental to our discussion of RAID is **striping**, which is a method of concatenating multiple drives into one logical storage unit. Striping involves partitioning each drive's storage space into stripes that may be as small as one sector (512 bytes) or as large as several megabytes. These stripes are then interleaved in a round-robin fashion, so that the combined space is composed of alternating stripes from each drive. In effect, the storage space of the drives is shuffled like a deck of cards. The type of application environment you have determines whether large or small stripes should be used. A typical stripe size is 128 or 256 blocks (64 or 128 kilobytes). In HSZ terminology, a stripe is also known as a "chunk," thus the "CHUNKSIZE" keyword is used to alter the default stripe size.

Parity is a simple mechanism by which data can be verified for correctness when written to a device. When the number of all the "on" bits is counted, an additional bit is added to the existing bits to make the resulting sum of all the bits even or odd. Thus, there are two types of parity: even and odd. Odd parity means the sum of the number of bits, including the parity bit, is an odd number. Likewise, even parity means that the sum of the number of bits, including the parity bit, is an even number.

2.2.2   RAID Levels

Five theoretical levels of RAID were defined by the original work done at the University of California at Berkeley: RAID 1 through RAID 5. Some of these levels are never seen in practice because they offer little difference from the common levels. Each of these RAID levels offers different performance or redundancy features and each has different tradeoffs in its implementation. Later on, RAID 0 and RAID 0+1 levels were created to add some features that were missing from the original theory. RAID levels 2, 3, and 4 are rarely, if ever, seen in practice, but we include them here for completeness. The following is a list of each RAID level and its definition:

- RAID 0: Also known as striping, RAID level 0 is not redundant, hence it does not truly fit the RAID paradigm. In level 0, data are split across drives, resulting in higher data throughput. Because no redundant information is stored, performance is very good, but the failure of any disk in the array results in data loss. In Figure 2–1, we give an example of a fictitious 768-byte RAID 0 logical unit consisting of two stripes and created from three disks.

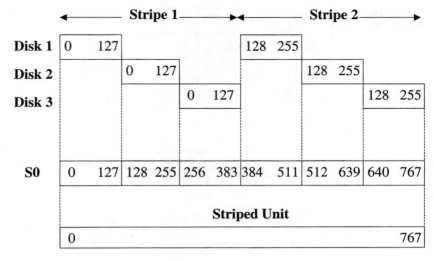

FIGURE 2–1
RAID 0 Logical Unit

- RAID 1: This level provides redundancy by writing all data to two or more drives. The performance of a level 1 array tends to be faster on reads and slower on writes compared to a single drive, but if either drive fails, no data are lost. This is a good entry-level redundant system because only two drives are required. On the other hand, because the data are completely duplicated, the cost per megabyte is the highest of any of the RAID levels. This level is commonly referred to as **mirroring**. In Figure 2-2, we have an example of two disks (D1 and D2) representing a total size of 1024 blocks mirrored to another two disks (D3 and D4) of identical size.

- RAID 0+1: This level was never referred to in the original Berkeley paper but is a logical extension of it. This is the combination of mirroring and striping, and provides complete redundancy and performance improvement using striping for each duplicated copy of the data. The cost per megabyte for this RAID level is the same as for RAID 1, but the performance tends to be better. In Figure 2–3, we have an example of a three-disk stripe (D1, D2, and D3) mirrored to another three-disk stripe (D4, D5, and D6). This example is called **mirrored stripes**, which is one of the two types of RAID 0+1. The other type is known as **striped mirrors**, which has the advantage of being able to take two single-drive failures without loss of the unit. The latter situation would be preferable in many cases if the RAID controller supports it.

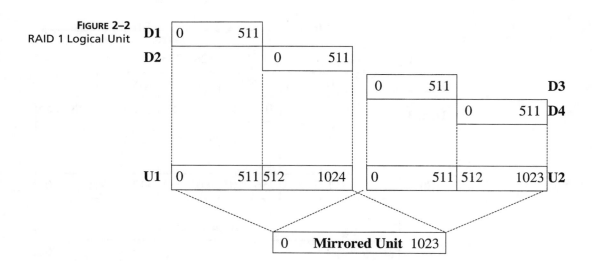

FIGURE 2–2
RAID 1 Logical Unit

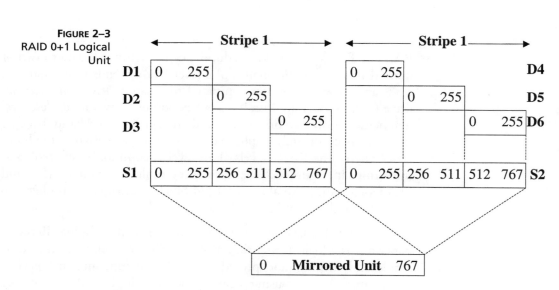

FIGURE 2–3
RAID 0+1 Logical
Unit

- RAID 2: This level uses Hamming error correction codes and is intended for use with drives that do not have built-in error detection. All SCSI drives support built-in error detection, so this level is of little benefit when using SCSI drives. Thus, you will never see this RAID level implemented in the real world.

- RAID 3: This level stripes data at a byte level across several drives, with parity stored on one drive. It is otherwise similar to level 4. Byte-level striping requires hardware support for efficient use.

- RAID 4: This level stripes data at a block level across several drives, with parity stored on one drive. The parity information allows recovery from the failure of any single drive. The performance of a level 4 array is very good for reads (the same as level 0). Writes, however, require that parity data be updated each time. This process slows small random writes, in particular, although large writes or sequential writes are fairly fast. Because only one drive in the array stores redundant data, the cost per megabyte of a level 4 array can be fairly low.

- RAID 5: This level is similar to level 4 but distributes parity among the drives. This function can speed small writes in multiprocessing systems because the parity disk does not become a bottleneck. Because parity data must be skipped on each drive during reads, however, the performance for reads tends to be considerably lower than a level 4 array. The cost per megabyte is the same as for level 4.

2.2.3   Hardware vs. Software RAID

With the changes in LSM implemented in Tru64 UNIX 5.0, you'll find a considerable blurring of the lines in terms of what can (and should) be done with respect to RAID in hardware and/or software. As usual, there are tradeoffs to consider when deciding whether to implement RAID in software or hardware. When implementing RAID in hardware and software, usually one must choose between the three main factors of performance, complexity, and flexibility. Any change in one of these factors could cause a detrimental impact on the others. The following list includes some tips gained through extensive experience and is designed to help guide you when deciding on a hardware or software RAID solution.

1.   As a general rule, the highest performing RAID should be implemented in hardware (smart controller firmware), but greater flexibility is gained by implementing RAID using a volume manager like LSM. Therefore, when performance is the primary factor, try to implement RAID in hardware as much as possible. Not only does this scenario provide the best performance, but it also reduces the complexity of the solution. Any reduction of complexity in the system is a real plus when considering the work required by the system administration staff to deal with device failures. Complex systems can and do fail in unpredictable ways, so simpler tends to be better. On the other hand, if flexibility is the primary objective, then software RAID would be the clear choice.

2.   Don't overimplement RAID. We have many options to choose from between LSM, hardware RAID controllers, and AdvFS file

striping. Therefore, it would be easy to implement RAID at the wrong level and unintentionally reduce performance, increase complexity, or reduce availability. For example, if mirroring were implemented at the hardware level and between devices in LSM, then there would be almost no improvement in availability gained at the expense of disk space. Another foolish example is a stripe set implemented on a hardware RAID controller, which can be carved into pieces that can then be striped again using LSM. This additional striping would actually increase write performance, rather than improving it as was intended. This is like double-compressing a file because we hope to get a smaller file the second time around. The usual result may actually be a larger file. The same thing can happen with RAID implementations. Too much of a good thing can actually have the opposite effect.

3. Be careful to implement RAID at the appropriate level. For example, prior to version 5.0, LSM would not support RAID 5, but only RAID levels 0, 1, and 0+1. It is important, however, to distinguish the difference between what can be done and what should be implemented. We believe the cases in which software RAID 5 should be implemented are limited. LSM implementation of RAID level 5 has low overhead and provides redundancy, but we don't recommend using software-based RAID 5 for servers on which I/O performance is an important factor. In those cases, hardware RAID 5 should be used to maximize performance and reduce complexity.

4. Combining software and hardware RAID may be the best option in some cases. For example, some amount of redundancy is not available with hardware RAID (e.g., mirroring across busses), so a software solution may be the only option.

2.3   Tru64 UNIX Device Management

This section introduces the concepts required to understand devices in Tru64 UNIX. For the most part, Tru64 UNIX is similar to other UNIX vendors is some ways and is very different in others. Understanding these similarities and differences is important so that a thorough coverage of the file systems is possible. We begin rather generically with an overview of device management, but our end goal is to delve into an in-depth discussion of those devices used in disk device management because they are used in file systems management as well.

We discuss both pre-5.0 and 5.0 device naming and structure here because Tru64 UNIX 5.0 supports both types. Also, all users of pre-5.0 systems are not expected to immediately migrate to 5.0 structure, so the pre-5.0 information is helpful to those users who haven't migrated yet. In the cases where pre-5.0 is discussed, it is so noted; otherwise, it is assumed that we are discussing 5.0 behavior.

Beginning with 5.0, Tru64 UNIX device management was changed dramatically not only from the user's perspective since the naming scheme changed, but also in the kernel. Two main reasons predicated the changes: (1) to enable TruCluster 5.0 Single System Image (SSI), which means that disk and tape devices are seen consistently across the entire cluster, and (2) to allow SCSI Wide device and fibre channel support. In order to support these new requirements, the old device-naming scheme was changed.

2.3.1 Devices in Tru64 UNIX

As with any UNIX operating system, the Tru64 UNIX system device files are located in the /dev directory in the root file system. Device files represent the user-level process "handle" into the device drivers that control various hardware devices on the system. The device drivers are each assigned a major number, which uniquely defines it to the kernel. The major number is an offset into one of two tables, known as the **switch tables**, that define the operations that are permissible on the devices. We have two switch tables because one is for character devices (cdevsw[]) and one is for block devices (bdevsw[]). As we know, it is possible to have a single device with both a character device file and a block device file associated with it, but those operations that are supported are different, and thus the code to perform those operations is also different.

Each device special file in Tru64 UNIX is assigned a unique 32-bit device number (dev_t in <sys/types.h>) that consists of the combination of the major and minor numbers. In Figure 2–4, we show an example of what the major and minor numbers look like for a SCSI disk drive. The major number for any device special file is an offset into the block or character switch table. This is how the operating system determines which driver to associate with that device. The minor number is a driver-specific number that the driver uses to find a particular device of that class. In our example shown in Figure 2–4, we show how the SCSI disk minor number is calculated from the bus, target, LUN and partition. Similarly, SCSI tape device is shown in Figure 2–5.

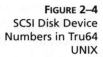

FIGURE 2–4
SCSI Disk Device
Numbers in Tru64
UNIX

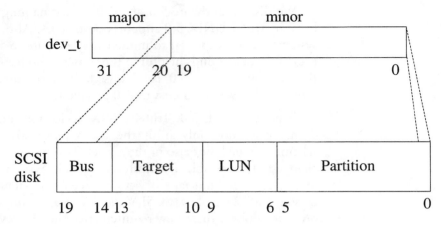

FIGURE 2–5
SCSI Tape Device
Numbers in
Tru64 UNIX

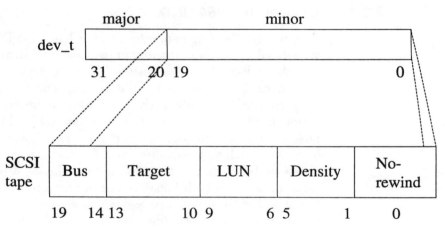

2.3.1.1   Device Special Files

The SCSI disk devices naming on Tru64 UNIX has traditionally followed the Berkley Standard Distribution (BSD™) standard conventions. The older device-naming scheme was severely limited in some important ways. Primarily, the old scheme could not be adapted for use in a Single System Image (SSI) cluster environment.[3] Therefore, for a cluster to behave as a single system, the devices must be cluster-wide, rather than local. The BSD-style SCSI disk devices were named based on a formula that includes the local bus and target numbers. There is simply no way to make this number unique for all nodes in the cluster. Second, the SCSI 3 standard, as discussed earlier in this chapter, supports up to 64 LUNs per device. This could not be accommodated with the older conventions.

Device naming in Tru64 UNIX 5.0 has changed significantly from the BSD-derived naming of prior versions. We illustrate the differences for several of the typical device types you may find on your system in Table 2–1. For example, the disk device format has changed as follows:

Old format:

```
/dev/rz[L]DP
/dev/rrz[L]DP
```

New format:

```
/dev/disk/dskXP
/dev/rdisk/dskXP
```

where the mnemonics above refer to the following:

L = The logical unit number (LUN): This is optional for LUN 0 devices. If LUNs are supported for the device, this is a letter from a through h representing LUN 0 through 7.

D = Device number: This number is unique to a system and is based on the formula (bus# × 8) + target#.

P = Partition: This is a lowercase letter from a to h representing the first through eighth partition.

X = The cluster-wide unique device number

TABLE 2–1 Device Special Files for Tru64 UNIX 4.x and 5.x Versions

V4.x DEVICE	V5.x DEVICE	DESCRIPTION
/dev/rz[x]	/dev/disk/dsk[x]	SCSI disk block special device
/dev/rrz[x]	/dev/rdisk/dsk[x]	SCSI disk character special device[4]
/dev/rmt[x]	/dev/tape/tape_d[x]	SCSI tape character device
/dev/fd[x]	/dev/disk/floppy[x]	Floppy block special device
/dev/rfd[x]	/dev/rdisk/floppy[x]	Floppy character special device
/dev/rz[x]	/dev/disk/cdrom[x]	CD-ROM block special device
/dev/rrz[x]	/dev/rdisk/cdrom[x]	CD-ROM character special device
/dev/re[x]	/dev/disk/re[x]	SWXCR block special device
/dev/rre[x]	/dev/rdisk/re[x]	SWXCR character special device
/dev/ra[x]	N/A	RA block special device
/dev/rra[x]	N/A	RA character special device

As discussed in Chapter 1, character device special files are used for reading from and writing to those devices that must be accessed one character at a time. Some examples of this type of device are a terminal (tty) or a SCSI tape (tz) device. On the other hand, block devices must be accessed one disk block (512 bytes) at a time. The block devices that you'll see every day are your disk devices such as SCSI hard and CD-ROM disks (rz), floppy (fd), SWXCR™ RAID devices (re), and RA-series disks (ra). In this section, we discuss some of these different devices (disks and tapes).

SCSI Disks.   SCSI disks are the most common device for storing and retrieving files on a computer system. On a Tru64 UNIX system, the SCSI disks are normally contained in a shelf or are internally mounted in a system cabinet.

Example:

Here is an example of the use of the *ls(1)* to examine the block and character device files for a single disk (target #4) on the second bus of a Tru64 UNIX 4.0x system. We also show the output from *file(1)* that gives more detailed information about the device, such as the bus, target, and LUN, as well as the disk type (RZ56) and soft and hard errors (if there are no errors, then that information is omitted).

```
# cd /dev
# ls -l *rz12*
crw-------  1 root    system    8,20480 Feb 11 08:39 rrz12a
crw-------  1 root    system    8,20481 Aug 14 1998 rrz12b
crw-------  1 root    system    8,20482 Dec 18 1998 rrz12c
crw-------  1 root    system    8,20483 Aug 14 1998 rrz12d
crw-------  1 root    system    8,20484 Aug 14 1998 rrz12e
crw-------  1 root    system    8,20485 Aug 14 1998 rrz12f
crw-------  1 root    system    8,20486 Aug 14 1998 rrz12g
crw-------  1 root    system    8,20487 Aug 14 1998 rrz12h
brw-------  1 root    system    8,20480 Aug 14 1998 rz12a
brw-------  1 root    system    8,20481 Aug 14 1998 rz12b
brw-------  1 root    system    8,20482 Aug 14 1998 rz12c
brw-------  1 root    system    8,20483 Aug 14 1998 rz12d
brw-------  1 root    system    8,20484 Aug 14 1998 rz12e
brw-------  1 root    system    8,20485 Aug 14 1998 rz12f
brw-------  1 root    system    8,20486 Aug 14 1998 rz12g
brw-------  1 root    system    8,20487 Aug 14 1998 rz12h

# file rrz12a
rrz12a: character special (8/20480) SCSI #1 RZ56 disk #96
(SCSI ID #4) (SCSI LUN #0)
```

Example:

Here, we duplicate the information provided in the previous example, but for a Tru64 UNIX 5.x system. This device is located on bus #2, target #6 at LUN 0 and is an RZ28D device type. Once again, there are no soft or hard errors on the device.

```
# cd /dev

# ls -l *disk/dsk46*
brw-------  1 root    system  19,593 Mar 15 11:04 disk/dsk46a
brw-------  1 root    system  19,595 Mar 15 11:04 disk/dsk46b
brw-------  1 root    system  19,597 Mar 15 11:04 disk/dsk46c
brw-------  1 root    system  19,599 Mar 15 11:04 disk/dsk46d
brw-------  1 root    system  19,601 Mar 15 11:04 disk/dsk46e
brw-------  1 root    system  19,603 Mar 15 11:04 disk/dsk46f
brw-------  1 root    system  19,605 Mar 15 11:04 disk/dsk46g
brw-------  1 root    system  19,607 Mar 15 11:04 disk/dsk46h
crw-------  1 root    system  19,594 Mar 15 11:04 rdisk/dsk46a
crw-------  1 root    system  19,596 Mar 15 11:04 rdisk/dsk46b
crw-------  1 root    system  19,598 Mar 15 11:04 rdisk/dsk46c
crw-------  1 root    system  19,600 Mar 15 11:04 rdisk/dsk46d
crw-------  1 root    system  19,602 Mar 15 11:04 rdisk/dsk46e
crw-------  1 root    system  19,604 Mar 15 11:04 rdisk/dsk46f
crw-------  1 root    system  19,606 Mar 15 11:04 rdisk/dsk46g
crw-------  1 root    system  19,608 Mar 15 11:04 rdisk/dsk46h

# file rdisk/dsk46a
rdisk/dsk46a:  character special (19/594) SCSI #2 RZ28D disk
#1 (SCSI ID #6) (SCSI LUN #0)
```

SCSI Tapes.   As you can see in Table 2–1, in addition to SCSI disk devices changing names in 5.0, the SCSI tape devices also changed device naming.

Example:

This example shows the tape device files for the first tape device on a Tru64 UNIX version 4.0x system.

```
# cd /dev

# ls -l *rmt0*
crw-rw-rw-  1 root    system   9,1031 Feb 11 08:43 nrmt0a
crw-rw-rw-  1 root    system   9,1027 Feb 11 14:32 nrmt0h
crw-rw-rw-  1 root    system   9,1025 Mar 19 02:59 nrmt0l
crw-rw-rw-  1 root    system   9,1029 Feb 11 08:43 nrmt0m
crw-rw-rw-  1 root    system   9,1030 Feb 11 08:43 rmt0a
crw-rw-rw-  1 root    system   9,1026 Feb 11 08:43 rmt0h
crw-rw-rw-  1 root    system   9,1024 Feb 11 08:43 rmt0l
crw-rw-rw-  1 root    system   9,1028 Feb 11 08:43 rmt0m

# file rmt0h
rmt0h: character special (9/1026) SCSI #0 TLZ04 19 tape #0
(SCSI ID #1) (SCSI LUN #0) errors = 199/0 61000_bpi
```

2.3.1.2   Multipath and Multibus

Two SCSI device features that have recently come onto the scene are **multipath** and **multibus**. These are similar but not identical terms of which you need to be aware. The first term, multipath, refers to the ability to connect more than one adapter to the same storage unit. The Tru64 UNIX operating system has been designed to automatically determine whether the same storage unit is connected via multiple adapters (paths) and to appropriately coordinate access to it.

The second term, multibus, which is similar to and is often confused with multipath, is different. Multipath is the general term that means that multiple adapters are connected to the same storage. Multibus, however, is a more specific term that refers to the capability of those storage devices to connect to multiple independent busses. Multibus is one way in which multipath can be implemented.

This multipath/multibus capability can be used to increase availability and, in most cases, performance as well. Most configurations can eliminate the single point of failure of the SCSI bus, whereas other configurations retain that single point of failure. Multipath configurations can contain paths to storage that use either multiple adapters connected to a single bus or multiple adapters connected to separate busses. Each different configuration provides its own availability and performance benefits.

For disk devices, multiple paths can be used not only for failover but also to balance the load to the device. For tape devices, multiple paths are used only for failover the next time you open the device. The upshot is that this mechanism provides automatic failover of disk I/O during an adapter failure, whereas tape failover requires the application to restart and resynchronize with the device. Therefore, tape devices are less fault-tolerant than disks.

The term **single path active** refers to devices that are single-ported, or if multiported, can only be accessed from one port at a time. Devices of this genre include tapes, CD-ROMs, and single-spindle disks. The load for these types of devices can be split across the multiple busses, and those busses are available for failover, but the I/O for a given logical unit uses only one of the paths at a time. Thus, with a single path active device, no parallelism can be achieved.

2.3.1.3   Automatic Device Determination

Many of the newer SCSI devices available are assigned two different unique pieces of information to identify them. This information is stored in the SCSI device in two places and is accessible by the SCSI inquiry command. The first piece of information is an ASCII string provided by the manufacturer, and the second is a guaranteed worldwide unique identifier. When a device is first accessed or at initial system boot, these unique identifiers are examined and used to build what the Tru64 UNIX system recognizes as a device's worldwide identifier (WWID).

In Tru64 UNIX, when an identical WWID is detected via different access paths in a multipath environment, that device is recognized to be the same device. When I/O is ready for a particular device, the disk driver examines the I/O already queued for that device and sends the current I/O to the path with the queue that contains the fewest entries. Thus, all paths to a device are used to spread the I/O load on the system.

Many older devices cannot be used for multipath because they do not contain either of the unique device identifiers needed. In that case, the operating system simply takes these devices' bus address, target number, and LUN, and appends them to create a type of unique ID for the system to use. Using this scheme, because the bus address would be different along each path in a multipath, a single device would have two different WWIDs. Therefore, the device looks like two totally different devices to the system.

2.3.2   Partition Table and Disk Label

The **partition table** is a logical representation of the layout of the blocks on a Tru64 UNIX disk. These eight logical partitions are named "a" though "h," as shown in Figure 2–6. All of the partition sizes and offsets can be changed from the default to suit the user's needs; however, by convention, the "a" partition is used for the root file system and starts at block 0 of the disk. The "c" partition is the entire disk, by default, with a starting block of 0 and a size equal to that of the entire disk. The diagram shown in Figure 2–6 represents the default partition layout of a Tru64 UNIX partition table.

2.3.2.1   The Disk Label

Each disk on a system may contain a disk label, which provides detailed information about the geometry of the disk and the partitions into which the disk is divided. The disk label should be non-existent when the disk is formatted and may be initialized and changed later with the *disklabel(8)* command. The system disk driver and the bootstrap program use this information to determine how to boot from the drive and where to find the file systems on the disk partitions. The file system employs additional

FIGURE 2–6
Tru64 UNIX Default
Partition Table

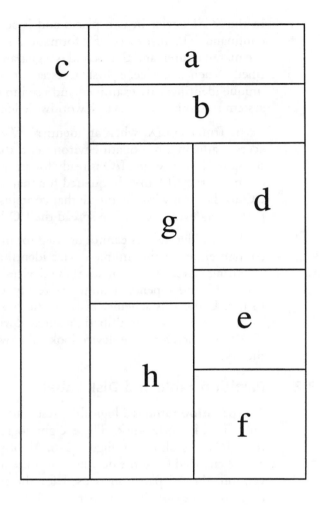

information in order to use the disk most efficiently and to locate important file system information. The description of each partition contains
an identifier for the partition type (standard file system, swap area, etc.).
The file system updates the in-core copy of the label if it contains incomplete information about the file system.

The label is usually located in block 0. There is a specific offset from
the beginning of the block, to allow room for the initial boot block. The
disk block containing the label is normally made read-only so that it is
not accidentally overwritten by disk-to-disk copies or swap operations.
Modifications to the label block may only be performed by the *diskla-
bel(8)* command, which utilizes a special *ioctl(2)* call.

The offset of a partition usually cannot be changed or made smaller while it is open. One exception to this rule is that any change is allowed if the disk is not labeled and you are trying to write an initial label on the disk. The initial label for a disk or disk pack must be installed by writing to the raw disk. All of these operations are normally done using the *disklabel(8)* program.

Example:

This is a Tru64 UNIX version 4.0x example of how you can use the *disklabel(8)* command to examine a disk's partition table and other information in its disk label.

```
# disklabel -r rz0

# /dev/rrz0a:
type: SCSI
disk: RZ1BB-BA
label:
flags: dynamic_geometry
bytes/sector: 512
sectors/track: 86
tracks/cylinder: 16
sectors/cylinder: 1376
cylinders: 3045
sectors/unit: 4110480
rpm: 7200
interleave: 1
trackskew: 9
cylinderskew: 54
headswitch: 0        # milliseconds
track-to-track seek: 0 # milliseconds
drivedata: 0

8 partitions:
#      size   offset   fstype[fsizebsizecpg]
 a:  262144        0   4.2BSD 1024 8192 16  # (Cyl.   0 - 190*)
 b:  780816   262144    swap                # (Cyl. 190*- 757*)
 c: 4110480        0   unused    0    0     # (Cyl.   0 - 2987*)
 d:       0        0   unused    0    0     # (Cyl.   0 - -1)
 e:       0        0   unused    0    0     # (Cyl.   0 - -1)
 f:       0        0   unused    0    0     # (Cyl.   0 - -1)
 g: 2097152  1042960   4.2BSD 1024 8192 16  # (Cyl. 757*- 2282*)
 h:  970368  3140112   4.2BSD 1024 8192 16  # (Cyl. 2282*- 2987*)
```

2.3.2.2   The /etc/disktab File

The /etc/disktab database describes disk geometries and disk partition characteristics. For Tru64 UNIX, this file is rarely, if ever, used anymore. It was once used to initialize the disk label on the disk and for creating UFSs (using *newfs(8)*) on LSM volumes. With dynamic geometry drives, however, specifying static information about disk geometry is no longer needed. Some system utilities, such as *disklabel(8)*, can actually query the device to determine information about it. In ULTRIX[5] and other older UNIX variants, the /etc/disktab is used primarily by *newfs(8)* for obtaining disk geometry information to create the new file system.

The format of the /etc/disktab file is patterned after the /etc/termcap terminal database. Entries in an /etc/disktab file consist of several colon-separated fields. The first entry for each disk gives the names that are known for the disk, separated by vertical bar characters. The last name given has traditionally been a long name that fully identifies the disk. The following list indicates the normal values stored for each disk entry:

```
Name    Type   Description
ty      str    Type of disk (for example, removable, winchester)
dt      str    Type of controller (for example, SMD, ESDI, floppy)
ns      num    Number of sectors per track
nt      num    Number of tracks per cylinder
nc      num    Total number of cylinders on the disk
sc      num    Number of sectors per cylinder, nc*nt default
su      num    Number of sectors per unit, sc*nc default
se      num    Sector size in bytes, DEV_BSIZE default
sf      bool   Controller supports bad144-style bad sector forwarding
rm      num    Rotation speed, rpm, default 3600
sk      num    Sector skew per track, default 0
cs      num    Sector skew per cylinder, default 0
hs      num    Headswitch time, usec, default 0
ts      num    One-cylinder seek time, usec, default 0
il      num    Sector interleave (n:1), default 1
d[0-4]  num    Drive-type-dependent parameters
bs      num    Boot block size, default BBSIZE
sb      num    Superblock size, default SBSIZE
ba      num    Block size for partition 'a' (bytes)
bd      num    Block size for partition 'd' (bytes)
be      num    Block size for partition 'e' (bytes)
bf      num    Block size for partition 'f' (bytes)
bg      num    Block size for partition 'g' (bytes)
bh      num    Block size for partition 'h' (bytes)
fa      num    Fragment size for partition 'a' (bytes)
fd      num    Fragment size for partition 'd' (bytes)
fe      num    Fragment size for partition 'e' (bytes)
ff      num    Fragment size for partition 'f' (bytes)
fg      num    Fragment size for partition 'g' (bytes)
fh      num    Fragment size for partition 'h' (bytes)
oa      num    Offset of partition 'a' in sectors
ob      num    Offset of partition 'b' in sectors
oc      num    Offset of partition 'c' in sectors
od      num    Offset of partition 'd' in sectors
oe      num    Offset of partition 'e' in sectors
of      num    Offset of partition 'f' in sectors
og      num    Offset of partition 'g' in sectors
```

```
oh    num    Offset of partition 'h' in sectors
pa    num    Size of partition 'a' in sectors
pb    num    Size of partition 'b' in sectors
pc    num    Size of partition 'c' in sectors
pd    num    Size of partition 'd' in sectors
pe    num    Size of partition 'e' in sectors
pf    num    Size of partition 'f' in sectors
pg    num    Size of partition 'g' in sectors
ph    num    Size of partition 'h' in sectors
ta    str    Partition type of partition 'a'
             (4.2BSD file system, swap, etc.)
tb    str    Partition type of partition 'b'
tc    str    Partition type of partition 'c'
td    str    Partition type of partition 'd'
te    str    Partition type of partition 'e'
tf    str    Partition type of partition 'f'
tg    str    Partition type of partition 'g'
th    str    Partition type of partition 'h'
```

Example:

This is an example of an entry for a disk (the rz23 type) in an /etc/disktab file.

```
rz23|RZ23|DEC RZ23 Winchester:\
    :ty=winchester:dt=SCSI:ns#33:nt#8:nc#776:\
    :oa#0:pa#40960:ba#8192:fa#1024:\
    :ob#40960:pb#58498:bb#8192:fb#1024:\
    :oc#0:pc#204864:bc#8192:fc#1024:\
    :od#99458:pd#35135:bd#8192:fd#1024:\
    :oe#134593:pe#35135:be#8192:fe#1024:\
    :of#169728:pf#35136:bf#8192:ff#1024:\
    :og#99458:pg#105406:bg#8192:fg#1024:\
    :oh#134593:ph#70271:bh#8192:fh#1024:
```

2.3.3 Boot Process

Booting your Tru64 UNIX system is a complex process. In this section, we provide a rough idea of what happens with respect to the file systems in the process of booting a Tru64 UNIX system. The hope is that this explanation can assist you with troubleshooting any file system–related boot problems that crop up.

Firmware. The first step in the boot process of Tru64 UNIX begins at the Alpha system console. The default boot device and other parameters can be specified to qualify what can happen when the system boots. In addition, the boot command can be entered at the console prompt to begin the boot process.

The primary boot blocks. The first block of the boot disk is read, and the primary boot block is loaded into memory. This file system type independent boot block finds and loads the secondary boot blocks.

The secondary boot blocks. The secondary boot blocks, which are specific to the file system type, are loaded into memory. They understand enough about the file system to find the kernel loader file on the root file system and execute it.

The kernel loader. The kernel loader's job is to find and load the kernel (/vmunix) into memory. The kernel loader is called osf_boot and must be present in the root directory for the system to successfully boot and load the kernel.

The kernel. The kernel file (/vmunix) is the heart of the UNIX operating system. The kernel executes the key operating system services, such as memory and process management and I/O processing. It also plays a key role in file systems administration and buffer management, which you see later in this book.

The init process and /etc/inittab. Following the loading and starting of the kernel, the first true process to be started on the system is init. Init's job is to read the /etc/inittab file and perform the instructions located in that file. With respect to the file systems, this file starts LSM, mounts file systems, and starts the update daemon. Update performs a *sync(2)* every 30 seconds in order to flush any dirty buffers (modified pages) out to the persistent storage.

Checking and mounting disks and LSM volumes. As discussed in Chapter 1, the *bcheckrc(8)* script reads the /etc/fstab file and performs the steps required to get local file systems mounted so the rest of the startup scripts can be executed. This process may include starting up LSM and checking quotas, if necessary.

2.4   Useful Storage Tools

Tru64 UNIX has several useful tools that can be used to find out more information or to perform certain tasks for the system storage. If you are trying to make your file systems perform well, you should know how to use these tools. In this section, we provide an overview and examples of some of these tools.

2.4.1 The SCSI CAM Utility

The *scu(8)* tool is one of the most helpful utilities for dealing with SCSI devices on your system. The term SCU actually stands for SCSI CAM utility and provides many vital functions, such as the following:

- examining device inquiry information

- formatting disks

- managing disk defects

- loading new drive firmware

- reading and writing mode pages

You will probably never need most of the features that *scu(8)* provides, but keep it in mind whenever you need to do something to a SCSI device.

Example:

This Tru64 UNIX version 4.0x system example shows how you can look at SCSI devices with *scu(8)*. This system has a shared bus because there is another "processor"-type device on bus 16.

```
# scu
scu> scan edt
Scanning all available buses, please be patient...

scu> sho edt

CAM Equipment Device Table (EDT) Information:

  Device: RZ28D    Bus: 0, Target: 0, Lun: 0, Type: Direct Access
  Device: RZ28M    Bus: 0, Target: 1, Lun: 0, Type: Direct Access
  Device: RZ29L-AA Bus: 0, Target: 3, Lun: 0, Type: Direct Access
  Device: TLZ06    Bus: 0, Target: 4, Lun: 0, Type: Sequential Access
  Device: RRD46    Bus: 0, Target: 5, Lun: 0, Type: Read-Only Direct Access
  Device: RZ26     Bus: 0, Target: 6, Lun: 0, Type: Direct Access
  Device: RZ29L-AS Bus: 16, Target: 1, Lun: 0, Type: Direct Access
  Device: RZ26N    Bus: 16, Target: 2, Lun: 0, Type: Direct Access
  Device: DEC R01 A11 Bus: 16, Target: 6, Lun: 7, Type: Processor
```

Example:

This is a simple Tru64 UNIX version 5.x example of the output from *scu(8)*, with only a few direct-connected SCSI drives and no shared bus. Notice that the output from the command has changed significantly from our last example.

```
# scu
scu> scan edt
Scanning all available buses, please be patient...
```

```
scu> show edt

CAM Equipment Device Table (EDT) Information:

Bus/Target/Lun Device Type ANSI Vendor ID  Product ID  Revision N/W
----------- ----------- ------ ---------- ---------- --------
    0  1  0  Direct   SCSI-2 DEC    RZ26  (C) DEC   392A  N
    0  2  0  Direct   SCSI-2 DEC    RZ26  (C) DEC   392A  N
    0  3  0  Direct   SCSI-2 DEC    RZ26  (C) DEC   392A  N
    0  4  0  CD-ROM   SCSI-2 DEC    RRD42 (C) DEC   4.5d  N
```

Example:

This is a more complex version 5.x example of the output from *scu(8)*, with HSZ drives, non-LUN-0 drives, and a shared bus.

```
scu> scan edt
Scanning all available buses, please be patient...

scu> show edt

CAM Equipment Device Table (EDT) Information:

Bus/Target/Lun Device Type ANSI Vendor ID  Product ID  Revision N/W
----------- ----------- ------ ---------- ---------- --------
    0  0  0  Direct   SCSI-2 DEC    RZ26L (C) DEC   442D  N
    0  1  0  Direct   SCSI-2 DEC    RZ26  (C) DEC   T392  N
    0  2  0  Direct   SCSI-2 DEC    RZ28M (C) DEC   0616  N
    0  3  0  Direct   SCSI-2 DEC    RZ28M (C) DEC   0616  N
    0  6  0  CD-ROM   SCSI-2 DEC    RRD43 (C) DEC   1084  N
    1  2  1  Direct   SCSI-2 DEC    HSZ40     V32Z  W
    1  2  2  Direct   SCSI-2 DEC    HSZ40     V32Z  W
    1  2  4  Direct   SCSI-2 DEC    HSZ40     V32Z  W
    1  3  0  Direct   SCSI-2 DEC    HSZ40     V32Z  W
    1  3  1  Direct   SCSI-2 DEC    HSZ40     V32Z  W
    1  3  2  Direct   SCSI-2 DEC    HSZ40     V32Z  W
    1  3  4  Direct   SCSI-2 DEC    HSZ40     V32Z  W
    1  3  5  Direct   SCSI-2 DEC    HSZ40     V32Z  W
```

Example:

In this example, we show how you can set the focus of the *scu(8)* command to one of the devices on the system. This task is often completed to examine or set information for only that device. Otherwise, *scu(8)* will complain because it cannot issue some commands to all of the devices on the system (nor would you want it to). This example shows how to examine the mode pages for a device.

```
scu> scan edt
Scanning all available buses, please be patient...

scu> show edt

CAM Equipment Device Table (EDT) Information:
Bus/Target/Lun Device Type ANSI Vendor ID  Product ID  Revision N/W
```

```
----------- ----------- ------ --------- ---------- --------
0 5 0  CD-ROM  SCSI-2 DEC   RRD47    (C) DEC  1206  N
2 1 0  Direct  SCSI-2 DEC   RZ1DF-CB (C) DEC  0371  W
2 2 0  Direct  SCSI-2 DEC   RZ1CB-CS (C) DEC  0844  W
2 3 0  Direct  SCSI-2 DEC   RZ1CB-CS (C) DEC  0844  W
2 4 0  Direct  SCSI-2 DEC   RZ1CF-CF (C) DEC  1614  W
2 5 0  Direct  SCSI-2 DEC   RZ1CB-CS (C) DEC  0844  W
2 6 0  Direct  SCSI-2 DEC   RZ1CF-CF (C) DEC  1614  W
3 1 0  Direct  SCSI-2 DEC   RZ1DF-CB (C) DEC  0371  W
3 3 0  Direct  SCSI-2 DEC   RZ1CB-CS (C) DEC  0844  W
3 4 0  Direct  SCSI-2 DEC   RZ1CF-CF (C) DEC  1614  W
3 5 0  Direct  SCSI-2 DEC   RZ1CB-CS (C) DEC  0844  W
3 6 0  Direct  SCSI-2 DEC   RZ1CF-CF (C) DEC  1614  W
scu> set nexus bus 2 target 5 lun 0
Device: RZ1CB-CS, Bus: 2, Target: 5, Lun: 0, Type: Direct Access

scu> show mode

Mode Parameters (Current Values):

Mode Parameter Header:

        Mode Data Length: 155
           Medium Type: 0 (Default Medium Type)
   Device Specific Parameter: 0x10 (Supports DPO & FUA bits)
     Block Descriptor Length: 8

Mode Parameter Block Descriptor:

        Density Code: 0
   Number of Logical Blocks: 8380080
     Logical Block Length: 512
scu> sho pages code 1

Read-Write Error Recovery Parameters (Page 0x1 - Current Values):

Mode Parameter Header:

        Mode Data Length: 23
           Medium Type: 0 (Default Medium Type)
   Device Specific Parameter: 0x10 (Supports DPO & FUA bits)
     Block Descriptor Length: 8

Mode Parameter Block Descriptor:

        Density Code: 0
   Number of Logical Blocks: 8380080
     Logical Block Length: 512

Page Header / Data:
           Page Code: 0x1
       Parameters Savable: Yes
           Page Length: 10
             Byte 2: 0xe4
             Byte 3: 0x51
             Byte 4: 0x40
             Byte 5: 0
             Byte 6: 0
```

```
Byte 7: 0
Byte 8: 0x2e
Byte 9: 0
Byte 10: 0xff
Byte 11: 0xff
```

2.4.2   Gathering I/O Statistics with *iostat(8)*

The *iostat(8)* utility is used for looking at the I/O throughput to terminals and disk devices on your system. Similar to the other "stat" tools, *iostat(8)* allows you to specify an interval in which you get one line of output for each interval and for a specific number of intervals. You can also specify the devices on which you want *iostat(8)* to report. See Table 2–2 for a description of each of the fields in the *iostat(8)* output.

TABLE 2–2   Column Definitions for the *iostat(8)* Tool

COLUMN HEADING	DESCRIPTION
tin	The average number of characters per second read in from the terminal over the specified interval.
tout	The average number of characters per second written out to the terminal over the specified interval.
bps (disk)	The number of bytes transferred per second during the specified interval.
tps (disk)	The number of transactions completed to the specified device over the specified interval.
cpu us	The average percentage of CPU time spent in user mode over the specified interval.
cpu ni	The average percentage of CPU time spent at nice (lower) priority over the specified interval.
cpu sy	The average percentage of CPU time spent in system mode over the specified interval.
cpu id	The average percentage of CPU time spent idle over the specified interval.

Example:

In this example, we examine the I/O throughput statistics for three disks (i.e., dsk5, dsk6, and dsk7), with a five-second interval time. Because no count parameter was specified, the tool continuously reports at the same interval until it is interrupted.

```
# iostat dsk5 dsk6 dsk7 5
tty       dsk5      dsk6      dsk7      cpu
tin tout bps tps bps   tps bps tps us ni sy id
  0  39   0   0  183   365   0   0  10  0 18 72
  0  13   0   0  182   364   0   0  10  0 19 70
  0  13   0   0  171   343   0   0  10  0 17 73
  1  25   0   0   10    20   0   0   1  0  3 96
  8  21   0   0    0     0   0   0   0  0  2 98
  0  14   0   0 2547    80   0   0   3  0  7 90
  0  13   0   0 2233    70   0   0   2  0  5 93
  0  13   0   0 2246    70   0   0   2  0  5 93
  0  21   0   0 1235    39   0   0   1  0  4 95
  9  22   0   0  141     2   0   0   1  0  4 95
  0  13   0   0 2367    37   0   0   2  0  4 93
  0  13   0   0 2150    34   0   0   2  0  4 94
  0  13   0   0 2060    32   0   0   2  0  4 94
  0  13   0   0 2150    34   0   0   2  0  5 92
  0  13   0   0 2150    34   0   0   2  0  4 94
  0  21   0   1  998    16   0   0  23  0  5 72
^C
```

2.4.3 The *disklabel(8)* Command

In Tru64 UNIX, the *disklabel(8)* command can be used to examine and alter the partition table. Additionally, *disklabel(8)* can be used to write new boot blocks onto a disk.

Example:

As mentioned in the section on the disk label, the *disklabel(8)* command has the following output when using the tool to examine a disk's label:

```
# disklabel -r dsk1
# /dev/rdisk/dsk1c:
type: SCSI
disk: BB00921B91
label:
flags: dynamic_geometry
bytes/sector: 512
sectors/track: 168
tracks/cylinder: 20
sectors/cylinder: 3360
cylinders: 5273
sectors/unit: 17773524
rpm: 7207
interleave: 1
trackskew: 48
cylinderskew: 52
headswitch: 0       # milliseconds
track-to-track seek: 0 # milliseconds
drivedata: 0
```

```
8 partitions:
#       size    offset   fstype[fsize bsizecpg]  # NOTE: values not exact
a:    262144         0   AdvFS                    # (Cyl.   0 -  78*)
b:    262144    262144    swap                    # (Cyl.  78*- 156*)
c:17773524         0   unused    0       0        # (Cyl.   0 - 5289*)
d: 5749745    524288   unused    0       0        # (Cyl. 156*- 1867*)
e:  5749745   6274033   unused    0       0       # (Cyl. 1867*- 3578*)
f:  5749746  12023778   unused    0       0       # (Cyl. 3578*- 5289*)
g: 1433600    524288   AdvFS                      # (Cyl. 156*- 582*)
h:15815636  1957888   LSMsimp                     # (Cyl. 582*- 5289*)
```

This reflects the output for a disk on a Tru64 UNIX version 5.0A system.

2.4.4   The *file(1)* Command

We discussed the use of the *file(1)* in Chapter 1 for looking at information about files on a file system. The *file(1)* command is also a handy tool for getting a quick idea of whether a device is responding or not. If the *file(1)* command is executed on the raw "a" partition and as the root user on the system, then it performs a SCSI inquiry command to the device. The purpose of the inquiry is to ask the device to report information about itself, such as its type and a few other details. If the device does not respond, then that is an indication that something is wrong with the device that deserves further investigation. This may mean the device is powered off or, if it's a disk, it won't spin up for some reason. A disk drive will generally try to spin itself up on an inquiry, and if it fails to do so, will report an error.[6]

Example:

This example shows the output from the *file(1)* command executed on a Tru64 UNIX version 5.0A system on all the raw disks on the system. As you can see, you will get some good information from the command. One disk below, dsk4, is not available because it doesn't report its inquiry data. The device was pulled from the slot in the storage shelf and thus could not respond to the inquiry.

```
# cd /dev/rdisk

# file d*a
dsk0a: character special (19/18) SCSI #0 RZ26L disk #0 (SCSI ID #0) (SCSI LUN #0)
dsk10a: character special (19/194) SCSI #1 HSZ40 disk #12 (SCSI ID #2) (SCSI LUN #1)
dsk11a: character special (19/210) SCSI #1 HSZ40 disk #13 (SCSI ID #2) (SCSI LUN #2)
dsk12a: character special (19/226) SCSI #1 HSZ40 disk #14 (SCSI ID #3) (SCSI LUN #5)
dsk1a: character special (19/34) SCSI #0 RZ26 disk #1 (SCSI ID #1) (SCSI LUN #0)
dsk2a: character special (19/50) SCSI #0 RZ28M disk #2 (SCSI ID #2) (SCSI LUN #0)
dsk3a: character special (19/66) SCSI #0 RZ28M disk #3 (SCSI ID #3) (SCSI LUN #0)
dsk4a: character special (19/98)
dsk5a: character special (19/114) SCSI #1 HSZ40 disk #6 (SCSI ID #3) (SCSI LUN #0)
dsk6a: character special (19/130) SCSI #1 HSZ40 disk #7 (SCSI ID #3) (SCSI LUN #1)
```

```
dsk7a: character special (19/146) SCSI #1 HSZ40 disk #0 (SCSI ID #3) (SCSI LUN #2)
dsk8a: character special (19/162) SCSI #1 HSZ40 disk #10 (SCSI ID #2) (SCSI LUN #4)
dsk9a: character special (19/178) SCSI #1 HSZ40 disk #11 (SCSI ID #3) (SCSI LUN #4)
```

2.4.5   The Device Special File Manager [*dsfmgr(8)*]

The device special file manager, *dsfmgr(8)*, provides management of the device special files on a single system or cluster. This tool was introduced in Tru64 UNIX version 5.0 to specifically manage changes to the devices. Using this utility, you can perform the following functions:

- Add entries into the three different databases.

- Remove existing entries from the databases.

- Create device directories.

- Delete an existing entry from one of the databases.

- Delete a device special file on a particular node in a cluster.

- Create new device special files on a particular node in a cluster.

- Create and delete device special files with the "old" device-naming scheme.

- Exchange the device special files for the named cluster nodes.

- Move the device special file for one named cluster node to another.

- Verify device information.

- Display information from the databases.

Under normal circumstances, the device special file utility runs automatically during system boot. All devices are polled by the hardware management service to determine if any devices were added since the system was last booted. If any new devices are found, then the device special files are created with no manual intervention. As a system administrator, you may need to run the utility manually to perform some or all of the following functions:

- Create device special files according to the "old" naming format.

- Re-create or reassign device names, such as when a device fails and must be replaced.

- Examine or verify the device special file data, if device files or databases are lost or corrupted.

Device driver developers and vendors may also need to use the *dsfmgr(8)* utility to create an environment for developing and testing a device driver, or for adding new classes of devices to a system. Additional capabilities are available, such as the following:

- Create and add a new class of devices, or remove an existing device from the database.

- Create or delete the class directories under the /dev directory.

- Create or delete device special files according to the revised naming convention, and any required class directories, if they do not already exist.

- Create device special files according to the legacy (rz*, tz*) naming convention.

- Display the contents of the existing database entries and device special file assignments.

Example:

This example illustrates how you can use the *dsfmgr(8)* tool to examine all of the data in the current database. For a system with a lot of devices, this output can be quite long. Some of the output below has been removed for the sake of brevity.

```
# dsfmgr -s
dsfmgr: show all datum for system at /

Device Class Directory Default Database:
   # scope mode name
  -- ----- ---- -----------
   1  l    0755 .
   2  l    0755 none
   3  c    0755 cport
   4  c    0755 disk
   5  c    0755 rdisk
   6  c    0755 tape
   7  c    0755 ntape
   8  c    0755 changer

Category to Class-Directory, Prefix Database:
   # category         sub_category   type       directory   iw t mode prefix
  -- ---------        -----------    ------     ---------    ------------------
   1 disk             cdrom          block      disk         1 b 0600 cdrom
   2 disk             cdrom          char       rdisk        1 c 0600 cdrom
   3 disk             floppy         block      disk         1 b 0600 floppy
   4 disk             floppy         char       rdisk        1 c 0600 floppy
   5 disk             floppy_fdi     block      disk         1 b 0666 floppy
   6 disk             floppy_fdi     char       rdisk        1 c 0666 floppy
   7 disk             generic        block      disk         1 b 0600 dsk
   8 disk             generic        char       rdisk        1 c 0600 dsk
   9 media_changer    generic        *          changer      1 c 0666 mc
  10 parallel_port    printer        *          .            1 c 0666 lp
  11 port             control        sgeneric   .            0 c 0600 scp
  12 port             control        storage    cport        1 c 0600 scp
  13 pseudo           kevm           *          .            0 c 0600 kevm
  14 tape             *              norewind   ntape        1 c 0666 tape
```

```
  15   tape             *               rewind    tape         1 c 0666 tape
  16   terminal         hardwired       *         .            2 c 0666 tty
  17   *                *               *         none         1 c 0000 unknown
```

Device Directory Tree:
```
     9  8 drwxr-xr-x 6 root    system    8192 Mar 30 13:49 /dev/.
  1786  8 drwxr-xr-x 2 root    system    8192 Jan 20 09:25 /dev/none
  1674  8 drwxr-xr-x 2 root    system    8192 Jan 20 09:22 /dev/cport
  1676  8 drwxr-xr-x 2 root    system    8192 Jan 20 09:22 /dev/disk
  1730  8 drwxr-xr-x 2 root    system    8192 Jan 20 09:22 /dev/rdisk
  1788  8 drwxr-xr-x 2 root    system    8192 Jan 20 09:25 /dev/tape
  1790  8 drwxr-xr-x 2 root    system    8192 Jan 20 09:25 /dev/ntape
  1792  8 drwxr-xr-x 2 root    system    8192 Jan 20 09:25 /dev/changer
```

Dev Nodes:
```
  1794  0 crw------- 1 root    system    78,1048575 Jan 20 09:25 /dev/scp_scsi
  1795  0 crw------- 1 root    system    80,    0 Jan 20 09:25 /dev/kevm
  1796  0 crw------- 1 root    system    80,    2 Jan 20 09:25 /dev/kevm.pterm
  1797  0 crw-rw-rw- 1 root    system    35,    0 Jan 20 09:25 /dev/tty00
  1798  0 crw-rw-rw- 1 root    system    35,    1 Jan 20 09:25 /dev/tty01
  1799  0 crw-rw-rw- 1 root    system    34,    0 Jan 20 09:25 /dev/lp0
  1679  0 brw------- 1 root    system    19,   33 Jan 20 09:22 /dev/disk/dsk0a
  1733  0 crw------- 1 root    system    19,   34 Jan 20 09:22 /dev/rdisk/dsk0a
  1680  0 brw------- 1 root    system    19,   35 Jan 20 09:22 /dev/disk/dsk0b
  1734  0 crw------- 1 root    system    19,   36 Jan 20 09:22 /dev/rdisk/dsk0b
  1681  0 brw------- 1 root    system    19,   37 Jan 20 09:22 /dev/disk/dsk0c
  1735  0 crw------- 1 root    system    19,   38 Mar 11 16:24 /dev/rdisk/dsk0c
  1682  0 brw------- 1 root    system    19,   39 Jan 20 09:22 /dev/disk/dsk0d
  1736  0 crw------- 1 root    system    19,   40 Jan 20 09:22 /dev/rdisk/dsk0d
  1683  0 brw------- 1 root    system    19,   41 Jan 20 09:22 /dev/disk/dsk0e
  1737  0 crw------- 1 root    system    19,   42 Jan 20 09:22 /dev/rdisk/dsk0e
  1684  0 brw------- 1 root    system    19,   43 Jan 20 09:22 /dev/disk/dsk0f
  1738  0 crw------- 1 root    system    19,   44 Jan 20 09:22 /dev/rdisk/dsk0f
  1685  0 brw------- 1 root    system    19,   45 Jan 20 09:22 /dev/disk/dsk0g
  1739  0 crw------- 1 root    system    19,   46 Jan 20 09:22 /dev/rdisk/dsk0g
  1686  0 brw------- 1 root    system    19,   47 Jan 20 09:22 /dev/disk/dsk0h
  1740  0 crw------- 1 root    system    19,   48 Jan 20 09:22 /dev/rdisk/dsk0h
  1687  0 brw------- 1 root    system    19,   49 Jan 20 09:22 /dev/disk/dsk1a
  1741  0 crw------- 1 root    system    19,   50 Jan 20 09:22 /dev/rdisk/dsk1a
  1688  0 brw------- 1 root    system    19,   51 Jan 20 09:22 /dev/disk/dsk1b
  1742  0 crw------- 1 root    system    19,   52 Jan 20 09:22 /dev/rdisk/dsk1b
  1689  0 brw------- 1 root    system    19,   53 Jan 20 09:22 /dev/disk/dsk1c
```

[snip]

```
  1725  0 brw------- 1 root    system    19, 125 Jan 20 09:22 /dev/disk/dsk5g
  1779  0 crw------- 1 root    system    19, 126 Jan 20 09:22 /dev/rdisk/dsk5g
  1726  0 brw------- 1 root    system    19, 127 Jan 20 09:22 /dev/disk/dsk5h
  1780  0 crw------- 1 root    system    19, 128 Jan 20 09:22 /dev/rdisk/dsk5h
  1727  0 brw-r--r-- 1 root    system    19,   1 Jan 20 09:22 /dev/disk/floppy0a
  1781  0 crw-r--r-- 1 root    system    19,   2 Jan 20 09:22 /dev/rdisk/floppy0a
  1728  0 brw-r--r-- 1 root    system    19,   5 Jan 20 09:22 /dev/disk/floppy0c
  1782  0 crw-r--r-- 1 root    system    19,   6 Jan 20 09:22 /dev/rdisk/floppy0c
  1677  0 brw------- 1 root    system    19,   17 Jan 20 09:22 /dev/disk/cdrom0a
  1731  0 crw------- 1 root    system    19,   18 Jan 20 09:22 /dev/rdisk/cdrom0a
  1678  0 brw------- 1 root    system    19,   21 Jan 20 09:22 /dev/disk/cdrom0c
  1732  0 crw------- 1 root    system    19,   22 Jan 20 09:22 /dev/rdisk/cdrom0c
```

Old Device Nodes:
```
  1799  0 crw-rw-rw- 1 root    system    34,   0 Jan 20 09:25 /dev/lp0
```

Example:

The following example shows you how to use the device special file utility to verify the device database and correct any errors. This function can be useful if you suspect that the database may have become corrupted or it gets out of sync with the actual hardware on the system.

```
# dsfmgr -V -F -v

dsfmgr -V -F -v
 Secure Session Lock. At Thu Mar 30 21:10:20 2000
dsfmgr: verify with fix all datum for system at /

Default File Tree:
  OK.

Device Class Directory Default Database:
  OK.

Device Category to Class Directory Database:
  OK.

Dev directory structure:
  OK.

Device Status Files:
  OK.

Dev Nodes:
  OK.

 Release Session Lock at Thu Mar 30 21:10:20 2000
```

2.4.6   The Hardware Manager Utility [*hwmgr(8)*]

The hardware manager utility, *hwmgr(8)*, was introduced in Tru64 UNIX version 5.0 and is designed to work with the kernel hardware management module. The purpose of the tool is to enable you to manage hardware components and the hardware subsystems that maintain information about hardware components. A hardware component can be a storage peripheral, such as a disk or a tape, or a system component, such as a CPU or a bus. You can use the *hwmgr(8)* utility to manage hardware components on either a single system or on a cluster. As you can see, this tool is powerful and can perform many tasks unrelated to device management. Therefore, we examine only the tool's device management functions here.

The *hwmgr(8)* utility provides two types of commands: internal and generic. Internal commands do not contain a subsystem identifier on the command line. Generic commands are characterized by a subsystem identifier after the command name.

The examples in this section are primarily concerned with two components: (1) The "component" subsystem references all hardware devices specified in the binary /etc/dec_hwc_ldb and /etc/dec_hwc_cdb databases; these databases contain information on all hardware components currently registered with hardware management. (2) The "scsi" subsystem references all SCSI devices in the binary /etc/dec_scsi_db database. The SCSI database contains entries for all devices managed by the SCSI CAM architecture.

Example:

Here, we show how to use *hwmgr(8)* to list all the devices on a simple Tru64 UNIX system.

```
# hwmgr -view devices
HWID:      DSF Name  Model      Location
------------------------------------------------------------
   13:  /dev/disk/dsk0c    RZ26  bus-0-targ-1-lun-0
   14:  /dev/disk/dsk1c    RZ26  bus-0-targ-2-lun-0
   15:  /dev/disk/dsk2c    RZ26  bus-0-targ-3-lun-0
   16:  /dev/disk/cdrom0c  RRD42 bus-0-targ-4-lun-0
   17:  /dev/disk/floppy0c RX23  bus-0-targ-5-lun-0
```

Example:

This example shows the same *hwmgr(8)* command as in the previous example, but it is being run on a system with more devices to illustrate the multibus differences between the two. This is a nonclustered system, although if it were clustered the results would be the same.

```
# hwmgr -view devices
HWID:          DSF Name  Model          Location
------------------------------------------------------------
   15:  /dev/disk/floppy0c 3.5in  fdi0-unit-0
   33:  /dev/disk/dsk10c HSZ40  bus-1-targ-2-lun-1
   31:  /dev/disk/dsk8c  HSZ40  bus-1-targ-2-lun-4
   32:  /dev/disk/dsk9c  HSZ40  bus-1-targ-3-lun-4
   34:  /dev/disk/dsk11c HSZ40  bus-1-targ-2-lun-2
   35:  /dev/disk/dsk12c HSZ40  bus-1-targ-3-lun-5
   20:  /dev/disk/dsk0c  RZ26L  bus-0-targ-0-lun-0
   21:  /dev/disk/dsk1c   RZ26  bus-0-targ-1-lun-0
   22:  /dev/disk/dsk2c  RZ28M  bus-0-targ-2-lun-0
   23:  /dev/disk/dsk3c  RZ28M  bus-0-targ-3-lun-0
   24:  /dev/disk/cdrom0c RRD43  bus-0-targ-6-lun-0
   26:  /dev/disk/dsk5c  HSZ40  bus-1-targ-3-lun-0
   27:  /dev/disk/dsk6c  HSZ40  bus-1-targ-3-lun-1
   28:  /dev/disk/dsk7c  HSZ40  bus-1-targ-3-lun-2
```

Example:

This is a single-system example of the "hwmgr –show scsi." The cluster member version is in a subsequent example. You'll notice in this output there are no multipath devices because all ones are shown in the "NUM PATH" column.

```
# hwmgr -show scsi
```

	SCSI		DEVICE	DEVICE	DRIVER	NUM	DEVICE	FIRST
HWID:	DEVICEID	HOSTNAME	TYPE	SUBTYPE	OWNER	PATH	FILE	VALID PATH
18: 1		ruby	disk	none	0	1	dsk1	[0/1/0]
22: 5		ruby	disk	none	2	1	dsk4	[0/2/0]
23: 6		ruby	disk	none	0	1	dsk5	[0/3/0]
24: 7		ruby	disk	none	2	1	dsk6	[0/4/0]
25: 8		ruby	disk	none	2	1	dsk7	[0/6/0]
57: 4		ruby	cdrom	none	0	1	cdrom0	[1/0/0]
65: 0		ruby	disk	none	0	1	dsk43	[2/0/0]
66: 2		ruby	disk	none	0	1	dsk47	[2/1/0]
67: 3		ruby	disk	none	0	1	dsk45	[2/2/0]
68: 9		ruby	disk	none	0	1	dsk46	[2/6/0]
69: 10		ruby	disk	none	0	1	dsk44	[2/3/0]
70: 11		ruby	disk	none	2	1	dsk48	

Example:

This shows use of the hwmgr –show scsi command on a cluster member. As we alluded to in one of our previous examples, the default is used to show only those devices local to this system.

```
# hwmgr -view cluster
Member ID    State   Member HostName
---------    -----   ---------------
   1          UP     ping.zk3.dec.com (localhost)
   2          UP     pong.zk3.dec.com

# hwmgr -show scsi -type disk
```

	SCSI	DEVICE	DEVICE	DRIVER	NUM	DEVICE	FIRST	
HWID:	DEVICEID	HOSTNAME	TYPE	SUBTYPE	OWNER	PATH	FILE	VALID PATH
60: 1		ping	disk	none	0	1	dsk0	[1/0/0]
61: 2		ping	disk	none	0	1	dsk1	[2/1/0]
62: 3		ping	disk	none	0	1	dsk2	[2/2/0]
63: 4		ping	disk	none	0	1	dsk3	[2/3/0]
64: 5		ping	disk	none	2	1	dsk4	[2/4/0]
65: 6		ping	disk	none	2	2	dsk5	[2/5/0]
66: 7		ping	disk	none	2	1	dsk6	[2/6/0]
67: 8		ping	disk	none	0	1	dsk7	[3/1/0]
68: 9		ping	disk	none	2	1	dsk8	[3/3/0]
69: 10		ping	disk	none	2	1	dsk9	[3/4/0]
70: 11		ping	disk	none	0	1	dsk10	[3/5/0]
71: 12		ping	disk	none	2	1	dsk11	[3/6/0]

```
# hwmgr -show scsi -type disk -member pong
```

HWID:	SCSI DEVICEID	DEVICE HOSTNAME	DEVICE TYPE	DRIVER SUBTYPE	NUM OWNER	DEVICE PATH	FIRST FILE	VALID PATH
61:	2	pong	disk	none	2	1	dsk1	[2/1/0]
62:	3	pong	disk	none	0	1	dsk2	[2/2/0]
63:	4	pong	disk	none	0	1	dsk3	[2/3/0]
64:	5	pong	disk	none	2	1	dsk4	[2/4/0]
65:	6	pong	disk	none	0	1	dsk5	[2/5/0]
66:	7	pong	disk	none	2	1	dsk6	[2/6/0]
67:	16	pong	disk	none	2	1	dsk7	[3/1/0]
68:	17	pong	disk	none	2	1	dsk8	[3/3/0]
69:	18	pong	disk	none	2	1	dsk9	[3/4/0]
70:	19	pong	disk	none	2	1	dsk10	[3/5/0]
71:	20	pong	disk	none	2	1	dsk11	[3/6/0]

2.5   Summary

We have discussed much of the background information you need to understand and work with devices on Tru64 UNIX. With this knowledge, you can set up your devices such that they allow your file systems to perform well. Also, you can use some of this information later to tune your file systems to perform better on the devices. Some of the tools and techniques introduced to you will be useful in troubleshooting your file system. For example, the first question to ask when analyzing a failed file system problem will most likely be: "Have you experienced any hardware problems?"

In the next section, we cover the next layer in the I/O subsystem hierarchy: the Logical Storage Manager. We utilize some of the information covered in this chapter, in the LSM chapter. In particular, the sections on RAID concepts are appropriate when discussing the software RAID product, LSM.

Notes

1.   The concept, as it was originally proposed, was called Redundant Array of *Inexpensive* Disks before the early vendors realized that they were charging too much for the arrays to call them inexpensive. In a remarkable display of newspeak, the industry decided that rather than lower the price, they would simply change the name.

2.   The HSZ designation refers to a "hierarchical storage" device with a SCSI interface.

3. The TruCluster product that began shipping with Tru64 UNIX
    5.0a is the first generally shipped product using the new device-
    naming convention. TruCluster 1.x used the old standard and was
    simply a failover product. Version 5.0a clustering was a vast
    improvement over the 1.x versions.

4. The reason why dsk was chosen for the root name of a disk instead
    of disk is to avoid confusion with "disk" device names used by
    LSM in the /etc/vol directory.

5. ULTRIX is a 4.2BSD-based UNIX that ran on older Digital Equip-
    ment Corporation hardware such as the VAX and MIPS™ systems.

6. An error on a SCSI device is usually indicated with a return of
    CHECK CONDITION. When this message occurs, another
    command is required to get the actual error code from the device.

3

Logical Storage Manager

Random chance seems to have
operated in our favor.
— *Mr.Spock* in *The Doomsday Machine*

In the previous chapter, we discussed the lowest layer in the I/O subsystem. Later, in Chapter 4, we begin the discussion of the file system layers that the system users usually see. This chapter is a discussion of a piece that the users rarely see because it falls between these two layers. Located between the disk device driver and the file system layers is an optional product known as the Logical Storage Manager (LSM). The LSM provides a mechanism in Tru64 UNIX for creating and managing storage containers known as *logical volumes*. A logical volume behaves to the upper layers in the I/O subsystem as either a normal UNIX block or character device. The logical volumes are a powerful method for managing storage in Tru64 UNIX. Not only can volumes be of an arbitrary size, but they also can be organized such that redundancy or performance of the volume is enhanced. LSM supports software RAID levels 0, 1, and 0+1 in Tru64 UNIX versions prior to 5.0. Beginning with version 5.0, RAID level 5 was also added for increased levels of redundancy.

All this power does come at a price. Although the LSM imposes little overhead on the system, it is not free. In addition, management of LSM can be complicated, and there is a steep learning curve to become proficient. Many LSM users report that they set it up once and it works well until there is a problem or a change is needed. At that time, little problems can become big problems. Even with these few shortcomings, LSM is an essential part of any Tru64 UNIX administrator's storage management strategy. The bottom line is that the product is powerful and useful; our goal here is to increase readers' knowledge so that management and troubleshooting of LSM will be a snap.

3.1   Logical Storage Manager Concepts

Our stated goal of this chapter is to increase readers' knowledge of LSM for the specific intention of making use of the product easier. Therefore, to understand how the LSM works, we need to define some terminology and describe its architecture. This section discusses these LSM fundamentals.

3.1.1   LSM Architecture

The LSM contains several components that cooperate to provide storage services to the upper layers of the operating system. As we saw in the previous two chapters, LSM fits between the file systems (if one exists) and the physical storage devices. If no file system is being used, then the application layer interfaces directly with the LSM layer through its block special devices. An overview of the LSM architecture can be found in Figure 3–1. The architecture consists of several components, including the LSM daemons, a kernel driver, and a set of device special files. The relationship among the components is shown in the figure, and we describe the components in greater detail in the rest of this section.

FIGURE 3–1
LSM Architecture

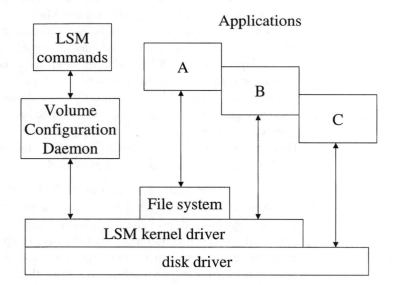

3.1.1.1   LSM Daemons

The LSM architecture consists of three basic types of daemons: the volume configuration daemon, the volume extended I/O daemons, and the

LSM error daemons. Each of these daemons has its own function within the architecture that we describe as follows.

The volume configuration daemon, also known as **vold**, performs several functions in the LSM architecture, such as:

1. Manages the interaction between the LSM commands and the LSM kernel driver.

2. Maintains the changes to the LSM configuration.

3. Responds to asynchronous events that occur to the configuration.

Only one volume configuration daemon should exist in each properly configured LSM environment in any Tru64 UNIX system. Although more than one vold process can be present for short periods, this is not the norm.

The LSM volume configuration daemon has three states (or modes) in which it operates: boot mode, running, or stopped. The method for determining its current state is by using the "voldctl mode" command. We discuss the *voldctl(8)* command more completely later in this chapter.

After the volume configuration daemon, the extended I/O daemons, also known as the **voliod** daemons, handle the following functions:

1. Takes care of some extended I/O functions without requiring the calling process to block.

2. Deals with the interface to part of the kernel driver called the **volspec driver.**

3. Starts, and interfaces with, LSM error daemons to deal with error recovery for the LSM volumes.

4. Allows the LSM device driver to schedule writes to the volumes if they have block change logging (BCL) enabled.

3.1.1.2 Kernel Driver

The LSM kernel driver does most of the "heavy lifting" for the architecture. More specifically, the LSM kernel driver performs the function of translating blocks located in the logical volumes into physical disk blocks. This task is difficult because the logical volumes can be organized in many different ways. The main reasons why the LSM architects decided that the translation would be handled in the kernel is speed and security. Performing this function in the kernel is faster than using a user-level thread because it reduces the amount the data transfer between user and kernel modes. The kernel also performs its operations in an uninteruptible fashion, which eliminates any opportunity for data corruption.

3.1.1.3   Device Special Files

The LSM utilizes device special files of two main types. The first is a series of four device files used by the various LSM daemons that interact with the kernel. These device files are all character special device type and have the major number of 41 associated with them. The second type of device special file associated with LSM are the most visible part of the architecture: the character and block special files that represent the logical volumes. We discuss both of these categories of device special files in this section. The following example shows the four device special files in the /dev directory on the Tru64 UNIX 4.x system.

```
# cd /dev
# ls -l vol?*
crw-r--r--  1 root    system  41, 0 May 12 1999 volconfig
crw-r--r--  1 root    system  41, 1 Jul 23 1998 volevent
crw-r--r--  1 root    system  41, 3 Jul 23 1998 volinfo
crw-r--r--  1 root    system  41, 2 Jul 23 1998 voliod
```

In a 5.x system, the volinfo file has been replaced by voltrace. The name has changed, but the functionality remains the same.

```
# ls -l vol?*
crw-r--r--  1 root    system  41, 0 Feb 21 13:23 volconfig
crw-r--r--  1 root    system  41, 3 Feb 21 13:23 volinfo
crw-r--r--  1 root    system  41, 2 Feb 21 13:23 voliod
crw-r--r--  1 root    system  41, 1 Feb 21 13:23 voltrace
```

TABLE 3–1   Logical Storage Manager Device Special Files

DEVICE FILE NAME	MINOR NUMBER	VERSION	DESCRIPTION
volconfig	0	4.x, 5.x	Used by the vold to get information or to perform certain configuration changes.
volevent	1	4.x	Used to perform kernel tracing.
voltrace	1	5.x	See volevent.
voliod	2	4.x, 5.x	Used by the voliod daemons to retrieve and change kernel status.
volinfo	3	4.x, 5.x	Used by the different LSM utilities to get information about the configuration.

In addition to these special LSM device files, the volumes are also accessed through device special files located in the /dev/vol directory. The volumes, which can be referenced directly by the end user, have a major number of 40 associated with them. When a volume is created, two device special files with the same major and minor number are created to access the device. The first is a character device, which is referenced by a name of the format /dev/rvol/{disk group}/{volume}. In addition, the format for the volume's block special device name is /dev/vol/{disk group}/{volume}. The root disk group also creates its device special files for each in the /dev/rvol and /dev/vol, respectively, for easier access.

```
# cd /dev/vol
# ls -lR
total 8
drwxr-xr-x  2 root    system   8192 Feb 21 13:24 rootdg
brw-------  1 root    system  40, 0 Feb 21 13:24 rootvol
brw-------  1 root    system  40, 1 Feb 21 13:24 swapvol
brw-------  1 root    system  40, 5 Feb 21 13:24 usrvol

./rootdg:
total 0
brw-------  1 root    system  40, 0 Feb 21 13:24 rootvol
brw-------  1 root    system  40, 1 Feb 21 13:24 swapvol
brw-------  1 root    system  40, 5 Feb 21 13:24 usrvol

# cd /dev/rvol
# ls -lR
total 8
drwxr-xr-x  2 root    system   8192 Feb 21 13:24 rootdg
crw-------  1 root    system  40, 0 Feb 21 13:24 rootvol
crw-------  1 root    system  40, 1 Feb 21 13:24 swapvol
crw-------  1 root    system  40, 5 Feb 21 13:24 usrvol

./rootdg:
total 0
crw-------  1 root    system  40, 0 Feb 21 13:24 rootvol
crw-------  1 root    system  40, 1 Feb 21 13:24 swapvol
crw-------  1 root    system  40, 5 Feb 21 13:24 usrvol
```

As this example shows, the directory tree for both /dev/vol and /dev/rvol trees are identical except that the type of the device special file is block or character depending on which directory it falls under.

3.1.1.4 LSM Terminology

This section introduces some of the terminology associated with LSM volumes. Because the jargon associated with logical volumes can be a bit difficult to understand, we start out by explaining the terms and how they relate to each other pictorially. The first step is to examine a diagram of a typical LSM volume. Figure 3–2 shows the layout of a generic LSM volume called vol01.

As you can see from the diagram, there are four primary LSM objects:

- **disk:** The lowest-level object in the LSM, the disk is an entire disk device, a single disk partition, or an encapsulated file system.

FIGURE 3–2
Generic LSM Volume

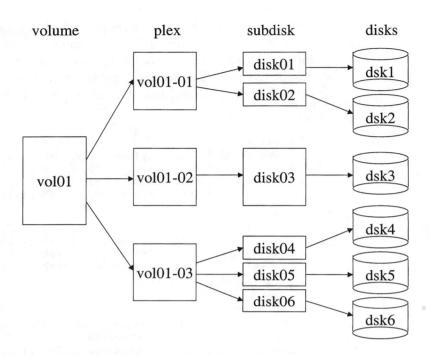

- **subdisk:** A set of contiguous blocks in a block device that can be used to construct plexes.

- **plex:** A single copy of a mirrored volume. A plex can be either striped, RAID 5, or concatenated.

- **volume:** A virtual block device that can be used for raw storage or to contain a file system just like any real block device, but which contains part, all, or multiple block devices.

The disks, subdisks, plexes, and volumes in an LSM configuration are organized into logical groupings known as **disk groups**. Each disk group, as shown in Figure 3–3, has a common configuration database and is managed somewhat independently from the other disk groups in an LSM configuration. For example, when creating logical volumes, you can only choose disks that make up the volume from one particular disk group. You cannot choose some disks from one group and some from another for a single LSM volume. In addition, all of the disks in a disk group can be brought online at the same time using the import function. Conversely, the deport function brings all of the disks in the disk group offline.

Every LSM configuration has at least one disk group known as the root disk group or rootdg. The rootdg can never be deported and must

FIGURE 3–3
Logical Storage
Manager Disk
Groups

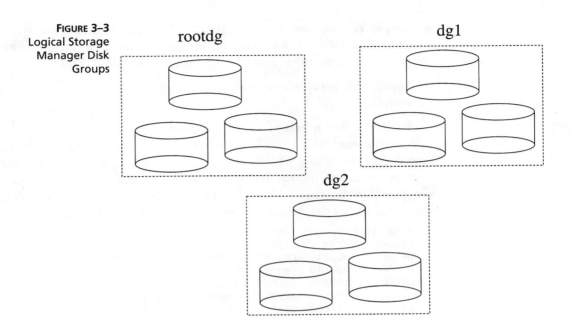

FIGURE 3–3 Logical Storage Manager Disk Groups

always have at least one valid configuration copy and one log associated with it specified in the /etc/volboot file. When the volume configuration daemon starts, it examines the volboot file for one valid configuration copy in the disk's private region. Without this information, the daemon cannot be started and LSM will not operate properly. The rootdg's configuration database contains information about the configuration of all of the other disk groups. For this reason, it is a good idea to have multiple rootdg private regions and configurations copies listed in the volboot file. We discuss later how to manage the volboot file with the *voldctl(8)* command and how to manage configuration copies in private regions of disks.

Disk group configuration copies and logs are stored in the private region of the disks in the disk group. Some disks have private regions but others do not. The organization of the private and public region for a disk in an LSM configuration tells how you refer to the disk. A disk's public and private region can be organized in the following three ways:

- **sliced:** A disk that has been dedicated entirely for LSM use and that contains both a public and private region. The public region is located on the "g" partition of the disk, and the private region is on the "h" partition.

- **simple:** A single partition of a disk that has been dedicated for use by LSM. The public and private regions are contained within the single partition, rather than in different partitions like sliced disks.

- **nopriv:** An encapsulated disk that has no private region associated with it.

Each disk that is part of an LSM configuration has a disk access (da) record associated with it that is usually the same as the disk name. The da record that contains a partition can be either a simple or nopriv type; however, sliced da records are referred to by just the disk name without the partition attached. The following sample output from *voldisk(8)* command shows the da records under the "DEVICE" heading:

```
# voldisk list
DEVICE    TYPE      DISK      GROUP      STATUS
dsk0a     nopriv    root01    rootdg     online
dsk0b     nopriv    swap01    rootdg     online
dsk0d     simple    dsk0d     rootdg     online
dsk0g     nopriv    usr01     rootdg     online
dsk6      sliced    dsk6      rootdg     online
```

The example also shows that another name is associated with these disks under the "DISK" heading. These names are called the disk media (dm) records for the disks. The system administrator assigns this name when the disk is placed into a disk group. Thus, the name assigned is arbitrary and can be changed. LSM was designed this way so that disks can be easily swapped from one device to another without having to change any of the upper-level LSM information (volumes and subdisks). This flexibility is one of the features that LSM provides that is not available when simply using a disk partition on which to place your file systems or raw disks.

The usage type of an LSM volume refers to how the volume will be used after it has been created. The volume's usage type defines the set of commands that can be used on the volume and generally, to define its expected use. When creating logical volumes, you have one of two common choices for usage type, either the "gen" or "fsgen" type. The "gen" usage type is used when a volume will not be used for a file system, and "fsgen" is used just for file systems.

Two other less common usage types exist: "root" and "swap" types. As the name implies, a volume with root usage type is used strictly to contain the system's root volume. The swap usage type is used only for the system's primary swap. These types are usually assigned only when you are encapsulating the system disk. The *volencap(8)* command or installation procedure does this work for you. Secondary swap areas that you wish to add into the LSM should be set up as "gen" type.

3.1.2 LSM Command Structure

The LSM has three main interfaces that can be employed to accomplish its various tasks: (1) command-line interface, (2) menu-based interface, and (3) graphical user interface. The menu-based interface, known as the *voldiskadm(8)*, is a script-based front-end to the commands. The graphical user interface (GUI) to the LSM is also called the *dxlsm(8X)*. As with most things in UNIX, there is more than one way to accomplish a given job; LSM is no exception to this rule. The latter two interfaces are user-friendly front-ends that simply execute the commands. We believe the best way to learn LSM is by understanding the commands, rather than the GUI or menu-based interfaces. Only by studying how the commands work can you truly master the LSM; therefore, we will only cover the command interface in this chapter.

The command-line-driven interface is divided into two classes of commands: top-down commands and bottom-up commands. The former are so called because they operate on the logical volumes and work their way down to the physical disks. The bottom-up commands operate on the disks and work their way up to the volume level. The bottom-up commands tend to be more powerful and require greater skill in order to use them. On the other hand, the top-down commands perform a lot of the work for you and don't allow you to specify all the possible options, but they don't require as much skill to use. Tables 3–2 and 3–3 are an overview of some of the commands that fall into each of the two categories.

TABLE 3–2 Top-Down Logical Storage Manager Commands

COMMAND	DESCRIPTION
volassist	Performs many functions on logical volumes. Used to create, mirror, move, grow, shrink, and back up LSM volumes.
volsetup	An interactive script that performs all functions necessary to set up LSM on a system. Creates the device special files, initializes the volboot file, adds entries into the inittab file, and adds the first rootdg disk.
voldiskadm	A menu-based interface to LSM that allows you to perform many of the necessary functions.
volsave	Makes a backup copy of the LSM configuration data so it can be recovered in case of disaster.
volrestore	Recovers the LSM configuration data from the previously saved information.
volencap	Takes an existing file system and places it under LSM control.
volrootmir	Mirrors a system disk that has previously been encapsulated.

TABLE 3–2   Top-Down Logical Storage Manager Commands (Continued)

COMMAND	DESCRIPTION
voldisksetup	An interactive script that places a disk or partition under LSM control.
volmirror	Used to mirror the volumes on a disk or change or display the default mirroring policies.
volevac	Evacuates all of the LSM volumes from a given disk.
volrecover	Reattaches stale plexes automatically.
volwatch	Monitors the LSM configuration and notifies users by e-mail when exceptions occur.

TABLE 3–3   Bottom-Up Logical Storage Manager Commands

COMMAND	DESCRIPTION
volmake	Creates new subdisk, plex, and volume configuration records.
volsd	Performs operations on subdisks, such as associating, disassociating, splitting, joining, and moving.
volinstall	Sets up the initial LSM configuration.
voldisk	Performs many functions on LSM disks, such as initializing, defining, online, offline, remove, list, clear, import, and check.
voldg	Performs management functions for the LSM disk groups, such as initializing, importing, deporting, add disk, remove disk, list, free, and flush.
volplex	Performs operations on LSM plexes, such as attaching, detaching, disassociating, copying, snapshot management, and moving.
voldisksetup	Used to set up a disk or partition for use with LSM.
volume	Performs operations on LSM volumes, such as initializing, setting read policy, starting, stopping, resynchronizing, maintaining, and setting attributes.
volprint	Gives LSM configuration information.
voledit	Alters records in the LSM configuration database.
volmend	Corrects some problems in LSM configuration records.
voldctl	Controls the volume configuration daemon.
volinfo	Reports on the accessibility and usability of LSM volumes.
volstat	Reports on LSM volume performance statistics.
volnotify	Reports on LSM events and configuration changes.
voltrace	Traces certain operations on LSM volumes.

3.1.3   Installing and Setting Up LSM

This section gives the steps to follow in order to install LSM on a Tru64 UNIX system from scratch. If some of the steps have already been performed on your system, then you can skip down to the next step to be performed.

1.   Install the LSM subsets.

2.   Load the LSM license.

3.   Build LSM into the kernel.

4.   Set up the initial LSM configuration.

5.   Set up other disk groups and LSM volumes.

The Tru64 UNIX installation procedure, beginning in version 5.0, allows the user to choose to set up LSM on the system disk. If this option has been chosen, steps 1 through 4 may be omitted.

3.1.3.1   Install the LSM Subsets

The first step toward making your LSM system operational is to install the base subsets. Table 3–4 shows all of the LSM subsets that can be installed. The LSM base subsets consist of OSFLSMBASExxx and OSFLSMBINxxx. With these two subsets installed, most of the basic LSM functions can be performed. If the LSM GUI is desired, then the additional subset to install is OSFLSMX11xxx. Prior to Tru64 UNIX version 5.0, additional subsets were needed in order to obtain additional functionality such as mirroring and striping. If the system is being set up to perform functions covered by the LSM advanced utilities, then an additional two subsets (OSFLSMBINCOMxxx and OSFLSMBINOB-JECTxxx) must also be installed. In Tru64 UNIX 5.0 and higher, those two subsets are obsolete.

TABLE 3–4   Logical Storage Manager Subsets

SUBSET	DESCRIPTION
OSFLSMBASExxx	Logical Storage Manager (System Administration)
OSFLSMBINxxx	Logical Storage Manager Kernel Modules (Kernel Build Environment)
OSFLSMBINCOMxxx	Logical Storage Manager Kernel Header and Common Files (Kernel Build Environment)
OSFLSMBINOBJECTxxx	Logical Storage Manager Kernel Objects (Kernel Software Development)
OSFLSMX11xxx	Logical Storage Manager GUI (System Administration)

If any or all of the subsets are not installed, then you must get the operating system CD out and install them using the *setld(8)* tool. See the man page for *setld(8)* for additional information on how to install new subsets.

3.1.3.2   Load the LSM License

Once the subsets have been verified, the next step in the process is to install the license, if appropriate. The LSM-OA license is required if you want your system to take advantage of the additional features provided by the advanced utilities. If the license is not installed and active, then even if the subsets are installed, those features cannot be used on the system. You must use the *lmf(8)* utility to verify the active license. If not registered and active, then the LSM advanced utilities will not be accessible.

3.1.3.3   Build LSM into the Kernel

The next step is to verify that LSM is built into the system's kernel. If this is not the case, then LSM will not work because the kernel components will not be accessible to the LSM daemons. One way to determine if the currently running kernel has LSM components built into it is to execute the following script:

```
 1 #!/bin/ksh
 2
 3 KERNEL="/vmunix"
 4 if [ -n "${1}" ]; then
 5   KERNEL="${1}"
 6 fi
 7
 8 if [ "'nm ${KERNEL} | grep volinfo'X" != "X" ]; then
 9   echo "LSM is configured in ${KERNEL} kernel."
10 fi
```

If this script does not report that LSM is configured in the kernel, then you need to update the kernel configuration file and build a new kernel. LSM kernel components are included if the following two lines are included in the Tru64 UNIX system's kernel configuration file (/sys/conf/<SYSTEMNAME>).

For Tru64 UNIX pre-5.0, the following lines are needed:

```
pseudo-device   lsm      1
pseudo-device   lsm_ted  0
```

For Tru64 UNIX 5.0 systems, these two entries are required:

```
pseudo-device   lsm        1
pseudo-device   lsm_vmted  0
```

Once the kernel configuration file has been verified, then you can build a new kernel using the *doconfig(8)* command. Once completed, *doconfig(8)* will advise you to copy the new kernel into the root directory and then reboot.

3.1.3.4 Set Up the Initial LSM Configuration

The next step in the process for setting up your LSM configuration is actually a series of three ministeps: (1) create the LSM device special files, (2) initialize the volboot file, and (3) update the /etc/inittab file and add an initial rootdg disk with a configuration database. Three primary methods can be used to accomplish this step with the command-line interface.

1. ***Top-down:*** Using *volsetup(8)*, you simply provide an initial disk or partition to be added into your rootdg disk group. If a disk is provided, then the disk will be sliced, and if a partition is given, then it will be simple. That would take care of all the steps needed to set up the system for LSM use.

    The following example shows how to set up LSM, making its first disk dsk0:

    ```
    # volsetup dsk0
    LSM: Creating Logical Storage Manager device special files.
    Checking for an existing LSM configuration

    Initialize vold and the root disk group:
    Add disk dsk0 to the root disk group as dsk0:
    Addition of disk dsk0 as dsk0 succeeded.
    Initialization of vold and the root disk group was successful.
    volwatch daemon started - mail only
    ```

2. ***Bottom-up:*** This approach is by far the most complex and is really unnecessary because *volsetup(8)* does all the work for you. We think it is important to understand the bottom-up steps, however, in case you run into problems and end up in a troubleshooting situation. Basically, the bottom-up steps are the following:

■ *Volinstall(8)* creates the four character device files in /dev and updates the /etc/inittab file so that LSM is started on system boot.

■ Voliod, a minimum of two are started. More voliod daemons will be started if more than one CPU is configured.

■ Vold is started in disabled mode.

■ *Voldctl(8)* initializes the /etc/volboot file.

■ The disk label is edited.

- *Voldisk(8)* initializes the private region of the disk.

- *Voldg(8)* adds the disk to the rootdg disk group.

- *Voldctl(8)* adds the disk to the volboot file.

- *Voldctl(8)* sets the vold daemon to enabled mode.

3. **System disk encapsulation**: Beginning in Tru64 UNIX 4.0, the LSM configuration could be initialized by encapsulating the system disk and rebooting. Prior versions required the user to use *volsetup(8)* first, which would temporarily sacrifice a partition or disk somewhere else on your system to hold the initial rootdg configuration database. Then, once the encapsulation was completed, the initial disk could be removed. In addition, beginning in Tru64 UNIX 5.0, the system can be installed from the operating system CD with LSM on the system disk. The system disk encapsulation is accomplished using the *volencap(8)* command. We discuss system disk encapsulation in greater detail later in this chapter.

3.1.3.5 Set Up Other Disk Groups and LSM Volumes

Adding more disks to any LSM configuration is a simple process. First, you need to make sure that the disk is not in use by another facility. As discussed in Chapter 2, this task is usually accomplished by simply checking the disk's label and making sure that all of the partitions are marked as "unused." If only a single partition is to be used, then you only need to check the partition you want to use and any overlapping partitions. If the disk is new, then you will need to put a default disk label on it using the *disklabel(8)* command. If the disk has been used for any purpose before, has some partitions that are not marked "unused," and you know it is not in use anymore, then we recommend you zero out the existing label and put a new default label on it. This way you can start cleanly.

Now, once you have the label issues worked out, you are ready to add the disk into LSM. As usual, we have a choice of using one of three procedures in order from easiest to most difficult:

1. **Top-down:** Use the *voldiskadd(8)* utility, which will prompt you for which disk group to add the disk into. If the disk group does not already exist, then you will be prompted whether the new disk group should be created or not. If so, it will do that for you. In true top-down fashion, you need to know very little to be successful.

2. **Bottom-up:** The *voldisksetup(8)* command is not interactive, and you will need to provide some command-line inputs to set up the

disk the way you want. If you want, you can specify the size of the public and private regions, and information about the number of configuration copies and log you want to be included.

3. *Real Bottom-up:* You can also use the *voldisk(8)* and *voldg(8)* commands to add in additional disks, but you need to understand what you're doing to be successful.

Of these three options, we think the first option will meet your needs most of the time. As you gain experience with the LSM tools and utilities, you may decide to venture into bottom-up commands.

3.1.4 LSM Versions and History

Over time, LSM has evolved and new versions have been rolled out. For the most part, the LSM version you have is not generally known, but we include them in Table 3–5 in order to give readers an idea of what features have been included in what versions.

TABLE 3–5 Logical Storage Manager Version History

LSM VERSION	LSM KERNEL VERSION	TRU64 UNIX VERSION	MAJOR FEATURES
1.0	4	2.0	Initial port of Veritas Volume Manager™ code. Product included on Complementary Products CD.
1.1	4	3.0	SMP. Product included on OS CD.
1.2	4	3.2	Boot disk encapsulation and mirroring.
1.2A	4	3.2c	Bug fixes.
4.0	4	4.0	International support, larger supported limits, volsave/ volrestore configurations.
7.0	7	5.0	RAID 5, Dirty Region Logging, auto-configuration.

The kernel version can be determined by examining the volinfo.version parameter using the kernel debugger. The LSM version for most Tru64 UNIX versions is documented in the /usr/include/vxvm/lsm_version.h file. It is the value associated with the definition of LSM_VERSION.

3.2 Creating Logical Volumes

Now that you've added your disks into LSM, it is time to decide on the size and what kind of logical volumes you need to create. This decision is totally up to you, but you will want to keep in mind the RAID information presented in Chapter 2 and then map that information to your particular requirements. Some of the things you will need to know to make your decisions include the following:

- *The read/write ratio of the application(s).* If the ratio is greater than one, then mirroring is a good option. If the ratio is less than one, then striping is helpful. If the ratio is close to one, then RAID 0+1 would be the better way to go.

- *Size, number, and frequency of file updates.* A few large files have a totally different performance characteristic than many small files.

- *Whether file systems or raw will be used.* If file systems are to be used, then management is at the file system level. The raw option puts more management on LSM.

- *Redundancy requirements.* If complete redundancy is required, then mirroring and RAID 5 fits the bill.

- *Cost.* Although disks continue to get bigger and cheaper all the time, you need to keep in mind that mirroring uses double the number of disks as a nonmirrored solution. RAID 5 is better than mirroring because it provides almost the same redundancy, with only N+1 disks.

- *Excess CPU cycles.* RAID 5 may be a nice solution for redundancy, but it comes at a cost of compute time for the parity calculations. Using LSM to create your RAID solution is flexible and easy to implement on-the-fly; however, you need to decide if you have enough extra CPU cycles on your system that will not be available for your applications.

So, now that you've decided what you need, we now go over the different options you have available. We begin our discussion in this section by covering the three types of plexes available in Tru64 UNIX version 5.0 and later. You must completely understand these concepts in order to create your volumes appropriately. Creating volumes is the goal of this section.

3.2.1   Concatenated Plex

As previously discussed, plexes are built out of subdisks. The first type of plex you can create is also the simplest. The **concatenated plex** means that blocks in the subdisks are placed end to end. Figure 3–4 illustrates how a concatenated plex is created from three different subdisks. The subdisks in the example come from three different disk partitions. Here, the disk partitions are dsk10d, dsk11e, and dsk12f, and the subdisks are named dsk10d-01, dsk11e-01, and dsk12f-01, respectively. To make this example simpler, we have made these three partitions of an equal size of 256 disk blocks. In order to make it a concatenated plex, the blocks are laid out end to end. The order of the blocks used in the plex is arbitrary and depends on the way the plex was created. A top-down approach would make the order of the layout in whatever way the tool decided to do it, whereas a bottom-up approach would let you have total control. Let's explore both approaches now to illustrate the difference.

FIGURE 3–4
LSM Concatenated
Plex

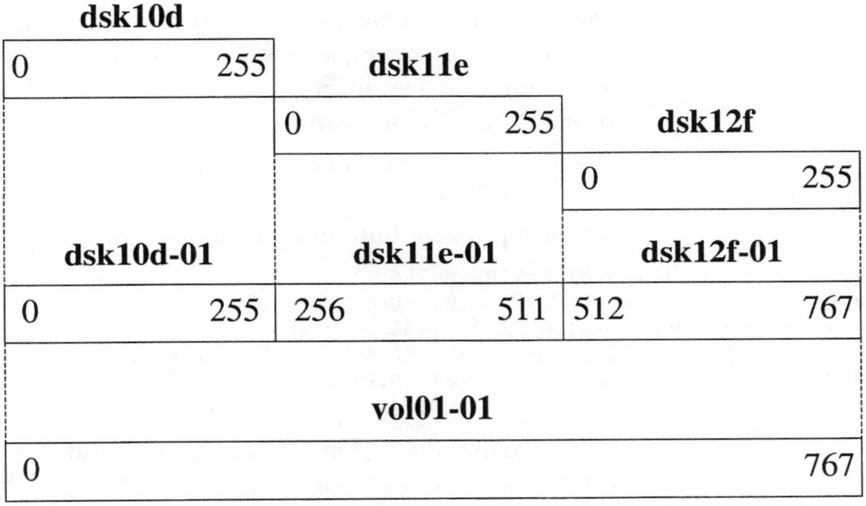

The top-down command used to create a concatenated plex like we have shown in our example is the following:

```
# volassist –Ufsgen make vol01 768 dsk10d dsk11e dsk12f
```

The *volassist(8)* command actually creates a concatenated volume with a single plex because *volassist(8)* creates only volumes. This example illustrates some of the limitations of the top-down approach. You don't have a finer granularity of control as you do with bottom-up commands. Although the power of the top-down approach is apparent—because you can create an entire volume with a single command—this method may not be adequate to meet your needs in every instance. Thus, the two approaches are available. Now, let's explore one set of bottom-up commands we use to perform the same function.

```
# volmake sd dsk10d-01 dsk10d,0,256
# volmake sd dsk11e-01 dsk11e,0,256
# volmake sd dsk12f-01 dsk12f,0,256
```

```
# volmake plex vol01-01 sd=dsk10d-01,dsk11e-01,dsk12f-01 layout=concat
# volmake -Ufsgen vol vol01 plex=vol01-01
# volume start
```

3.2.2   Striped Plex

Our discussion in Chapter 2 should have given you a good idea that a striped plex implements RAID 1 in software using the LSM. If a simple, striped volume is desired, then you need a volume containing a single, striped plex. In this case, the plex has no meaning; it just presents the striped blocks to the volume as is. If mirroring is desired, then you need to create two or more plexes up to a maximum of eight. Going back to our example, shown in Figure 3–5, the top-down command to create a striped volume is the following:

```
# volassist make vol01 768 layout=stripe stwidth=128 dsk10d
  dsk10e dsk11f
```

and the equivalent bottom-up commands are:

```
# volmake sd dsk10d-01 dsk10d,0,256
# volmake sd dsk11e-01 dsk11e,0,256
# volmake sd dsk12f-01 dsk12f,0,256
# volmake plex vol01-01 sd=dsk10d-01,dsk11e-01,dsk12f-01 layout=stripe stwidth=128
# volmake -Ufsgen vol vol01 plex=vol01-01
# volume start
```

Notice that the commands are not very different between the striped plex case and the concatenated plex case from the last section. The differences being that you must specify the layout and the stripe width for the plex. This example specifies a stripe width of 128 blocks across the three subdisks. The figure shows this difference more dramatically than we can state here, so take a moment and study it before moving on to the next section.

Example:

In this example, we want to create a striped volume called volstripe, which spans 5 disks, uses the default stripe width of 128 blocks, and is 200 stripes in size. Thus, the first operation we need to perform is to calculate what the volume size will be for this volume, in units of disk blocks. The calculation of the volume size is made using the following formula:

```
vol_size = num_subdisks * stripe_width * num_stripes
         = 5 * 128 * 200
         = 128000
```

After that, because we've already identified which disks will be used for the striped volume, we can move on to creating the volume using volassist.

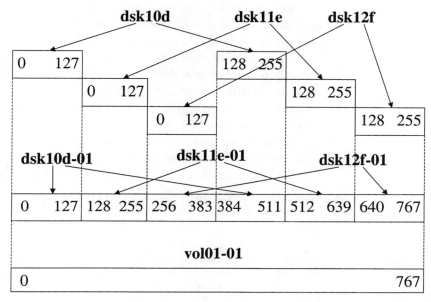

FIGURE 3–5
LSM Striped Plex

```
# volassist make volstripe 128000 layout=stripe disk01 disk02 disk03 disk04 disk05
# volprint -Aht
Disk group: rootdg

DG NAME          NCONFIG        NLOG    MINORS   GROUP-ID
DM NAME          DEVICE         TYPE    PRIVLEN  PUBLEN  STATE
V  NAME          USETYPE        KSTATE  STATE    LENGTH  READPOL    PREFPLEX
PL NAME          VOLUME         KSTATE  STATE    LENGTH  LAYOUT     NCOL/WID   MODE
SD NAME          PLEX           DISK    DISKOFFS LENGTH  [COL/]OFF  DEVICE     MODE

dg rootdg        default        default 0        949521863.1026.ruby.alf.dec.com

dm disk01        dsk7c          simple  4096     4106368 -
dm disk02        dsk10          sliced  4096     8375968 -
dm disk03        dsk11          sliced  4096     8375968 -
dm disk04        dsk35          sliced  4096     8375968 -
dm disk05        dsk33          sliced  4096     8375968 -

v  volstripe     fsgen          ENABLED ACTIVE   128000  SELECT     volstripe-01
pl volstripe-01  volstripe      ENABLED ACTIVE   128000  STRIPE     5/128      RW
sd disk05-01     volstripe-01 disk05   0        25600   0/0        dsk33      ENA
sd disk04-02     volstripe-01 disk04   960      25600   1/0        dsk35      ENA
sd disk03-02     volstripe-01 disk03   50016    25600   2/0        dsk11      ENA
sd disk01-03     volstripe-01 disk01   150016   25600   3/0        dsk7c      ENA
sd disk02-03     volstripe-01 disk02   150016   25600   4/0        dsk10      ENA
```

3.2.2.1   Calculating Striped Volume Size

This last example brings up a point with respect to striped volumes that we'd like to explore in greater depth. That is, the calculation of the size of a striped volume is rarely this simple. Normally, we don't know what the number of stripes is ahead of time. Typically, an administrator setting up a striped volume knows how many disks are available and the stripe width, but not the number of stripes. If we don't make this calculation correctly, then *volassist(8)* may or may not complain, but you may also have just created a nonoptimal volume. The *volassist(8)* will create the plex, if possible at the next integral stripe width size and allow the volume to be only the size you specified. In our example, we chose an arbitrary size that we knew would not fit into an integral stripe width. Here's what the resulting volume looks like:

```
# volassist make volbroken 654321 layout=stripe disk01 disk02 disk03 disk04 disk05

# volprint -Aht
Disk group: rootdg

DG NAME            NCONFIG        NLOG      MINORS   GROUP-ID
DM NAME            DEVICE         TYPE      PRIVLEN  PUBLEN    STATE
V  NAME            USETYPE        KSTATE    STATE    LENGTH    READPOL    PREFPLEX
PL NAME            VOLUME         KSTATE    STATE    LENGTH    LAYOUT     NCOL/WID MODE
SD NAME            PLEX           DISK      DISKOFFS LENGTH    [COL/]OFF DEVICE     MODE

dg rootdg          default        default   0                 949521863.1026.ruby.alf.dec.com

dm disk01          dsk7c          simple    4096     4106368   -
dm disk02          dsk10          sliced    4096     8375968   -
dm disk03          dsk11          sliced    4096     8375968   -
dm disk04          dsk35          sliced    4096     8375968   -
dm disk05          dsk33          sliced    4096     8375968   -

v  volbroken       fsgen          ENABLED   ACTIVE   654321    SELECT     volbroken-01
pl volbroken-01    volbroken      ENABLED   ACTIVE   654720    STRIPE     5/128    RW
sd disk01-01       volbroken-01   disk01    0        130944    0/0        dsk7c      ENA
sd disk02-01       volbroken-01   disk02    0        130944    1/0        dsk10      ENA
sd disk03-01       volbroken-01   disk03    0        130944    2/0        dsk11      ENA
sd disk05-01       volbroken-01   disk05    0        130944    3/0        dsk33      ENA
sd disk04-01       volbroken-01   disk04    0        130944    4/0        dsk35      ENA
```

If you try to create a volume at the maximum size of the volume, *volassist(8)* will give you an error because it cannot create a striped volume at the next larger integral stripe width size. Let's say for simplicity's sake that we want to create a striped volume with four of the disks listed above: disk02, disk03, disk04, and disk05. We chose these disks because they are all the same size; having different sized disks in a striped volume complicates the math. We will look at the more complex case later on. So, here we have:

```
# bc
8375968*4
33503872
```

```
# volassist make volbroken2 33503872 layout=stripe disk02 disk03 disk04 disk05
lsm:volassist: ERROR: Cannot allocate space for 33503872 block volume
```

Therefore, we must have an even number of stripes in our volume size in order to get an optimal volume. Usually, we know the size of the disks we want to stripe, and we want to calculate the biggest striped volume we can create on it and not waste space. So, here's how we do that:

Start with the volprint output:

```
# volprint -Aht
Disk group: rootdg
```

DG NAME	NCONFIG	NLOG	MINORS	GROUP-ID			
DM NAME	DEVICE	TYPE	PRIVLEN	PUBLEN	STATE		
V NAME	USETYPE	KSTATE	STATE	LENGTH	READPOL	PREFPLEX	
PL NAME	VOLUME	KSTATE	STATE	LENGTH	LAYOUT	NCOL/WID	MODE
SD NAME	PLEX	DISK	DISKOFFS	LENGTH	[COL/]OFF	DEVICE	MODE
dg rootdg	default	default	0	949521863.1026.ruby.alf.dec.com			
dm disk01	dsk7c	simple	4096	4106368	–		
dm disk02	dsk10	sliced	4096	8375968	–		
dm disk03	dsk11	sliced	4096	8375968	–		
dm disk04	dsk35	sliced	4096	8375968	–		
dm disk05	dsk33	sliced	4096	8375968	–		

```
# bc
33503872/(4*128)
65437
65437*4*128
33503744

# volassist make volbroken2 33503744 layout=stripe disk02 disk03 disk04 disk05

# volprint -Aht
Disk group: rootdg
```

DG NAME	NCONFIG	NLOG	MINORS	GROUP-ID			
DM NAME	DEVICE	TYPE	PRIVLEN	PUBLEN	STATE		
V NAME	USETYPE	KSTATE	STATE	LENGTH	READPOL	PREFPLEX	
PL NAME	VOLUME	KSTATE	STATE	LENGTH	LAYOUT	NCOL/WID	MODE
SD NAME	PLEX	DISK	DISKOFFS	LENGTH	[COL/]OFF	DEVICE	MODE
dg rootdg	default	default	0	949521863.1026.ruby.alf.dec.com			
dm disk01	dsk7c	simple	4096	4106368	–		
dm disk02	dsk10	sliced	4096	8375968	–		
dm disk03	dsk11	sliced	4096	8375968	–		
dm disk04	dsk35	sliced	4096	8375968	–		
dm disk05	dsk33	sliced	4096	8375968	–		
v volbroken2	fsgen	ENABLED	ACTIVE	33503744	SELECT	volbroken2-01	
pl volbroken2-01	volbroken2	ENABLED	ACTIVE	33503744	STRIPE	4/128	RW
sd disk02-01	volbroken2-01	disk02	0	8375936	0/0	dsk10	ENA
sd disk03-01	volbroken2-01	disk03	0	8375936	1/0	dsk11	ENA
sd disk05-01	volbroken2-01	disk05	0	8375936	2/0	dsk33	ENA
sd disk04-01	volbroken2-01	disk04	0	8375936	3/0	dsk35	ENA

```
# voldg free
GROUP       DISK        DEVICE      TAG       OFFSET       LENGTH     FLAGS
rootdg      disk01      dsk7c       dsk7      0            4106368    -
rootdg      disk02      dsk10       dsk10     8375936      32         -
rootdg      disk03      dsk11       dsk11     8375936      32         -
rootdg      disk04      dsk35       dsk35     8375936      32         -
rootdg      disk05      dsk33       dsk33     8375936      32         -
```

This succeeds and creates an optimal volume; therefore, let's look at the calculation we completed previously. We come up with a formula for the case when all the disks are the same size.

```
num_stripes = trunc[(num_vols * vol_size)/(num_vols * stripe_width)]
```

which we can now just plug into our simple volume size formula from before:

```
vol_size = num_subdisks * stripe_width * num_stripes
```

Finally, we need to be able to handle the case where the volumes are not all the same size. If you try to simply create a striped volume using all of the space, even though it is an integral stripe width size, it will fail as follows:

```
# bc
8375968*4 + 4106368
37610240

# volassist make volbroken2 37610240 layout=stripe disk01 disk02 disk03 disk04 disk05
lsm:volassist: ERROR: Cannot allocate space for 37610240 block volume
```

So, the tweak we need to incorporate into our formula is that the integral number of stripes needs to fit on the smallest volume in the stripe. Our resulting calculations and volume turn out to look like the output as follows:

```
# bc
5*4106368
20531840
20531840/(5*128)
32081
32081*5*128
20531840

# volassist make volcorrect 20531840 layout=stripe disk01 disk02 disk03 disk04 disk05

# volprint -Aht
Disk group: rootdg

DG NAME          NCONFIG       NLOG     MINORS    GROUP-ID
DM NAME          DEVICE        TYPE     PRIVLEN   PUBLEN    STATE
V  NAME          USETYPE       KSTATE   STATE     LENGTH    READPOL    PREFPLEX
PL NAME          VOLUME        KSTATE   STATE     LENGTH    LAYOUT     NCOL/WID MODE
SD NAME          PLEX          DISK     DISKOFFS  LENGTH    [COL/]OFF DEVICE    MODE
```

```
dg rootdg        default       default    0949521863.1026.ruby.alf.dec.com

dm disk01        dsk7c         simple     4096     4106368     -
dm disk02        dsk10         sliced     4096     8375968     -
dm disk03        dsk11         sliced     4096     8375968     -
dm disk04        dsk35         sliced     4096     8375968     -
dm disk05        dsk33         sliced     4096     8375968     -

v  volcorrect fsgen          ENABLED  ACTIVE  20531840 SELECT    volcorrect-01
pl volcorrect-01 volcorrect  ENABLED  ACTIVE  20531840 STRIPE5/128        RW
sd disk01-01  volcorrect-01 disk01  0      4106368    0/0     dsk7c  ENA
sd disk02-01  volcorrect-01 disk02  0      4106368    1/0     dsk10  ENA
sd disk03-01  volcorrect-01 disk03  0      4106368    2/0     dsk11  ENA
sd disk05-01  volcorrect-01 disk05  0      4106368    3/0     dsk33  ENA
sd disk04-01  volcorrect-01 disk04  0      4106368    4/0     dsk35  ENA

# voldg free
GROUP          DISK         DEVICE       TAG        OFFSET      LENGTH      FLAGS
rootdg         disk02       dsk10        dsk10      4106368     4269600     -
rootdg         disk03       dsk11        dsk11      4106368     4269600     -
rootdg         disk04       dsk35        dsk35      4106368     4269600     -
rootdg         disk05       dsk33        dsk33      4106368     4269600     -
```

Fortunately, it worked, but we have wasted some space here. The best thing you can do from this point is to create another striped volume with the four remaining disks.

```
# bc
4*4269600
17078400
17078400/(4*128)
33356
33356*4*128
17078272

# volassist make volcorrect2 17078272 layout=stripe disk02 disk03 disk04 disk05

# volprint -Aht
Disk group: rootdg

DG NAME          NCONFIG      NLOG        MINORS     GROUP-ID
DM NAME          DEVICE       TYPE        PRIVLEN    PUBLEN     STATE
V  NAME          USETYPE      KSTATE      STATE      LENGTH     READPOL    PREFPLEX
PL NAME          VOLUME       KSTATE      STATE      LENGTH     LAYOUT     NCOL/WID MODE
SD NAME          PLEX         DISK        DISKOFFS   LENGTH     [COL/]OFF DEVICE    MODE

dg rootdg        default      default     0          949521863.1026.ruby.alf.dec.com

dm disk01        dsk7c        simple      4096       4106368     -
dm disk02        dsk10        sliced      4096       8375968     -
dm disk03        dsk11        sliced      4096       8375968     -
dm disk04        dsk35        sliced      4096       8375968     -
dm disk05        dsk33        sliced      4096       8375968     -

v  volcorrect fsgen          ENABLED  ACTIVE  20531840 SELECTvolcorrect-01
pl volcorrect-01 volcorrect  ENABLED  ACTIVE  20531840 STRIPE5/128RW
sd disk01-01  volcorrect-01 disk010    4106368 0/0           dsk7c ENA
```

```
sd  disk02-01  volcorrect-01 disk02    0          4106368    1/0    dsk10    ENA
sd  disk03-01  volcorrect-01 disk03    0          4106368    2/0    dsk11    ENA
sd  disk05-01  volcorrect-01 disk05    0          4106368    3/0    dsk33    ENA
sd  disk04-01  volcorrect-01 disk04    0          4106368    4/0    dsk35    ENA
v   volcorrect2fsgen           ENABLED  ACTIVE  17078272   SELECT volcorrect2-01
pl  volcorrect2-01 volcorrect2ENABLED ACTIVE17078272      STRIPE 4/128   RW
sd  disk02-02  volcorrect2-01 disk02   4106368 4269568    0/0    dsk10    ENA
sd  disk03-02  volcorrect2-01 disk03   4106368 4269568    1/0    dsk11    ENA
sd  disk05-02  volcorrect2-01 disk05   4106368 4269568    2/0    dsk33    ENA
sd  disk04-02  volcorrect2-01 disk04   4106368 4269568    3/0    dsk35    ENA

# voldg free
GROUP        DISK        DEVICE      TAG       OFFSET     LENGTH    FLAGS
rootdg       disk02      dsk10       dsk10     8375936    32        -
rootdg       disk03      dsk11       dsk11     8375936    32        -
rootdg       disk04      dsk35       dsk35     8375936    32        -
rootdg       disk05      dsk33       dsk33     8375936    32
```

Now, we've done about the best we can, given the circumstances. If we replaced the smaller disk with one of the same size, then we could make one large striped volume and most likely be optimal as well.

3.2.3   RAID 5 Plex

The ability to create RAID 5 plexes is one of the most important features added to LSM in Tru64 UNIX 5.0. It is also one of the more complicated aspects, so we attempt to make it easier to understand and implement. As you should know from our discussion in Chapter 2, RAID 5 is really just a special case of a striped plex. We see that the following is a simple top-down command for creating a RAID 5 plex:

```
# volassist make vol01 768 layout=raid5 dsk10d dsk11e dsk12f
```

and the equivalent bottom-up commands are:

```
# volmake sd dsk10d-01 dsk10d,0,256
# volmake sd dsk11e-01 dsk11e,0,256
# volmake sd dsk12f-01 dsk12f,0,256
# volmake plex vol01 layout=raid5 stwidth=128 sd=dsk10d-01,dsk11e-01,dsk12f-01
# volmake -Ufsgen vol vol01 plex=vol01-01
# volume start
```

Example:

Here is an example showing you how to use *volassist(8)* to create a RAID 5 logical volume.

```
# voldg free
GROUP        DISK        DEVICE      TAG       OFFSET     LENGTH   FLAGS
rootdg       disk01      dsk7c       dsk7      0          4106368   -
rootdg       disk02      dsk10       dsk10     0          8375968   -
rootdg       disk03      dsk11       dsk11     0          8375968   -
rootdg       disk04      dsk35       dsk35     0          8375968   -
rootdg       disk05      dsk33       dsk33     960        8375008   -
```

```
# volassist make volraid 100000 disk01 disk02 disk03 disk04 layout=raid5

# volprint -Aht
Disk group: rootdg
```

DG	NAME		NCONFIG	NLOG	MINORS	GROUP-ID			
DM	NAME		DEVICE	TYPE	PRIVLEN	PUBLEN	STATE		
V	NAME		USETYPE	KSTATE	STATE	LENGTH	READPOL	PREFPLEX	
PL	NAME		VOLUME	KSTATE	STATE	LENGTH	LAYOUT	NCOL/WID	MODE
SD	NAME		PLEX	DISK	DISKOFFS	LENGTH	[COL/]OFF	DEVICE	MODE
dg	rootdg default	default 0		949521863.1026.ruby.alf.dec.com					
dm	disk01		dsk7c	simple	4096	4106368	–		
dm	disk02		dsk10	sliced	4096	8375968	–		
dm	disk03		dsk11	sliced	4096	8375968	–		
dm	disk04		dsk35	sliced	4096	8375968	–		
dm	disk05		dsk33	sliced	4096	8375968	–		
v	volraid		raid5	ENABLED	ACTIVE	100032	RAID	–	
pl	volraid-01		volraid	ENABLED	ACTIVE	100032	RAID	3/32	RW
sd	disk01-01		volraid-01	disk01	0	50016	0/0	dsk7c	ENA
sd	disk02-01		volraid-01	disk02	0	50016	1/0	dsk10	ENA
sd	disk03-01		volraid-01	disk03	0	50016	2/0	dsk11	ENA
pl	volraid-02		volraid	ENABLED	LOG	960	CONCAT	–	RW
sd	disk04-01		volraid-02	disk04	0	960	0	dsk35	ENA

3.2.4   Creating Mirrored Volumes

Setting up mirrored volumes is a simple matter of creating a volume with a single plex, attaching a plex of equal size to the first, and allowing the two to synchronize. Once they have synchronized, the second plex will have an exact copy of the data from the first plex. As shown in Figure 3–6, you can have up to eight plexes mirrored together in a single LSM volume. The most important thing in order for the plexes to be mirrored is that the size has to be the same. The composition of the plexes can be either striped or concatenated. So, a striped plex can be mirrored with a concatenated plex. Either of the plexes could be made from one hundred disks or one; it doesn't matter.

3.2.4.1   Simple Mirroring

There are two approaches to creating a simple LSM mirror: top-down and bottom-up. The top-down method uses either the *volassist(8)* or *volmirror(8)* commands. The former is by far the most common method.

Example:

This example uses the top-down approach, which shows how to create a simple mirror of two concatenated plexes using *volassist(8).*

```
# volassist make volmirror 100000 disk01

# volassist mirror volmirror disk02
```

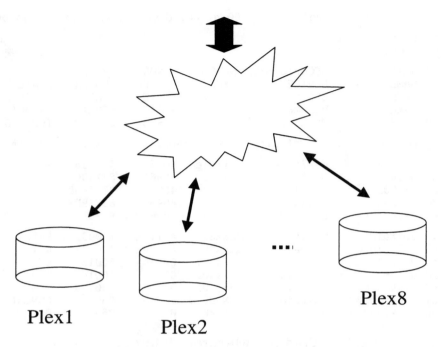

Figure 3–6
LSM Extended
Mirrored Volume

Plex1

Plex2

Plex8

```
# volprint -Aht
Disk group: rootdg

DG NAME           NCONFIG       NLOG    MINORS   GROUP-ID
DM NAME           DEVICE        TYPE    PRIVLEN  PUBLEN   STATE
V  NAME           USETYPE       KSTATE  STATE    LENGTH   READPOL  PREFPLEX
PL NAME           VOLUME        KSTATE  STATE    LENGTH   LAYOUT   NCOL/WID MODE
SD NAME           PLEX          DISK    DISKOFFS LENGTH   [COL/]OFF DEVICE  MODE

dg rootdg         default       default 0                949521863.1026.ruby.alf.dec.com

dm disk01         dsk7c         simple  4096     4106368 -
dm disk02         dsk10         sliced  4096     8375968 -
dm disk03         dsk11         sliced  4096     8375968 -
dm disk04         dsk35         sliced  4096     8375968 -
dm disk05         dsk33         sliced  4096     8375968 -

v  volmirror      fsgen         ENABLED ACTIVE   100000   SELECT   -
pl volmirror-02   volmirror     ENABLED ACTIVE   100000   CONCAT   -        RW
sd disk02-02      volmirror-02  disk02  50016    100000   0        dsk10    ENA
pl volmirror-01   volmirror     ENABLED ACTIVE   100000   CONCAT   -        RW
sd disk01-02      volmirror-01  disk01  50016    100000   0        dsk7c    ENA

[snip]
```

Example:

This Tru64 UNIX 4.0 example shows how to create a simple mirrored volume from an existing volume using bottom-up commands. We have included the extra *volprint(8)* output so you can see what things look like between the steps. We use the same disk for both plexes in this example, but in real life you most likely wouldn't want to do that.

```
# voldisk list
DEVICE            TYPE          DISK       GROUP      STATUS
rz6               sliced        rz6        rootdg     online

# volprint -ht
DG NAME           GROUP-ID
DM NAME           DEVICE        TYPE       PRIVLEN    PUBLEN     PUBPATH
V  NAME           USETYPE       KSTATE     STATE      LENGTH     READPOL    PREFPLEX
PL NAME           VOLUME        KSTATE     STATE      LENGTH     LAYOUT     ST-WIDTH MODE
SD NAME           PLEX          PLOFFS     DISKOFFS LENGTHDISK-NAMEDEVICE

dg rootdg         893785171.1025.sunny.alf.dec.com

dm rz6            rz6           sliced     1024       2049820    /dev/rrz6g

v  voltest        fsgen         ENABLED    ACTIVE     500000     SELECT     -
pl voltest-01     voltest       ENABLED    ACTIVE     500000     CONCAT     -        RW
sd rz6-01         voltest-01    0          0          500000     rz6        rz6

# voldg free
GROUP             DISK          DEVICE     TAG        OFFSET     LENGTH     FLAGS
rootdg            rz6           rz6        rz6        500000     1549820    -
homedg            rz130         rz130      rz130      16000000   1772484    -

# volmake sd rz6-02 rz6,500000,500000

# volprint -ht
DG NAME           GROUP-ID
DM NAME           DEVICE        TYPE       PRIVLEN    PUBLEN     PUBPATH
V  NAME           USETYPE       KSTATE     STATE      LENGTH     READPOL    PREFPLEX
PL NAME           VOLUME        KSTATE     STATE      LENGTH     LAYOUT     ST-WIDTH MODE
SD NAME           PLEX          PLOFFS     DISKOFFS   LENGTH     DISK-NAMEDEVICE

dg rootdg         893785171.1025.sunny.alf.dec.com

dm rz6            rz6           sliced     1024       2049820    /dev/rrz6g

sd rz6-02         -             -          500000     500000     rz6        rz6

v  voltest        fsgen         ENABLED    ACTIVE     500000     SELECT     -
pl voltest-01     voltest       ENABLED    ACTIVE     500000     CONCAT     -        RW
sd rz6-01         voltest-01    0          0          500000     rz6        rz6

# volmake plex voltest-02 sd=rz6-02

# volprint -ht
DG NAME           GROUP-ID
DM NAME           DEVICE        TYPE       PRIVLEN    PUBLEN     PUBPATH
V  NAME           USETYPE       KSTATE     STATE      LENGTH     READPOL    PREFPLEX
PL NAME           VOLUME        KSTATE     STATE      LENGTH     LAYOUT     ST-WIDTH MODE
SD NAME           PLEX          PLOFFS     DISKOFFS   LENGTH     DISK-NAMEDEVICE

dg rootdg         893785171.1025.sunny.alf.dec.com

dm rz6            rz6           sliced     1024       2049820    /dev/rrz6g
```

```
pl voltest-02      -             DISABLED -500000 CONCAT    -        RW
sd rz6-02          voltest-02    0        500000  500000    rz6      rz6

v  voltest         fsgen         ENABLED  ACTIVE  500000    SELECT   -
pl voltest-01      voltest       ENABLED  ACTIVE  500000    CONCAT   -         RW
sd rz6-01          voltest-01    0        0       500000    rz6      rz6

#  volplex att voltest voltest-02

#  volprint -ht
DG NAME            GROUP-ID
DM NAME            DEVICE        TYPE     PRIVLEN PUBLEN  PUBPATH
V  NAME            USETYPE       KSTATE   STATE   LENGTH  READPOL PREFPLEX
PL NAME            VOLUME        KSTATE   STATE   LENGTH  LAYOUT  ST-WIDTH MODE
SD NAME            PLEX          PLOFFS   DISKOFFS LENGTH DISK-NAMEDEVICE

dg rootdg          893785171.1025.sunny.alf.dec.com

dm rz6             rz6           sliced   1024    2049820 /dev/rrz6g

v  voltest         fsgen         ENABLED  ACTIVE  500000    SELECT   -
pl voltest-01      voltest       ENABLED  ACTIVE  500000    CONCAT   -         RW
sd rz6-01          voltest-01    0        0       500000    rz6      rz6
pl voltest-02      voltest       ENABLED  ACTIVE  500000    CONCAT   -         RW
sd rz6-02          voltest-02    0        500000  500000    rz6      rz6
```

3.2.4.2 System Disk Mirroring

One of the most popular uses for LSM is for making a mirrored system disk. The reason you would consider implementing this capability is to be able to rapidly recover from a system disk failure. In most cases, when one of the mirrored system disks fails, the system continues on as if nothing happened. In this section, we explore this powerful capability that LSM provides and how to best set it up so that it will be available to you when disaster strikes. We have developed the following process by which you can completely mirror your system disk using LSM:

1. Perform some preencapsulation steps. If you are already using LSM on your system, then you want to do a *volsave(8)* to save the configuration. Next, make a complete backup of your system disk using *vdump(8)* before doing anything else. Verify that the backup is complete and can be restored correctly and save this tape in a safe place. Also, check out your system disk and make sure you are not already using LSM on it anywhere.

2. Identify an unused disk with at least the same number of blocks as the original system disk. A disk of the same type as the original system disk is the best. You can try to span controllers to improve performance; however, you want to use only local busses for both of the mirrors. Avoid using shared busses, which will cause problems with the TruCluster software.

3. Queue up the encapsulation of the entire system disk with *volen-cap(8)*. If successful, you can proceed to the next step. Otherwise, you need to follow the directions given to correct the problem before proceeding.

4. Reboot the system. This step will complete the process of encapsulation. When complete, all of the partitions will be included into LSM as volumes.

5. Prepare the second disk for mirroring by putting a default disk label on it. Then, edit the label using the "c" partition as your handle and make sure the root partition size matches the size of the root on the original system disk. The swap "b" partition size must be the size of the swap area on the original, plus 1024 blocks.

6. Mirror the entire system disk to the new disk using *volrootmir(8)*. This process will take some time because the system will begin synchronizing the plexes of each volume. How long it takes depends on the speed of your CPU and the size of the system disk.

7. Perform some postmirroring steps. Do a *volsave(8)* and *vdump(8)* of the system disk again, as we did in step 1. Save this tape in a safe place.

Example:

Here, we show a Tru64 UNIX 4.0x example of a complete system disk encapsulation and mirroring. This system disk includes a root, swap, /usr, and /usr/var file system on the disk rz1. We will be mirroring to rz0, which is an unused disk of the same type as the original disk. Both are rz28-type disks, which meet the size requirements.

```
# file /dev/rrz[01]a
/dev/rrz0a:character special (8/0) SCSI #0 RZ28D disk #0 (SCSI ID #0) (SCSI LUN
#0)
/dev/rrz1a:character special (8/1024) SCSI #0 RZ28M disk #8 (SCSI ID #1) (SCSI LUN
#0)

# df /
Filesystem         512-blocks  Used    Available Capacity  Mounted on
root_domain#root   262144      184836  63616     75%       /

# showfdmn root_domain

Id                Date Created            LogPgs  Domain Name
3516a170.000d0029 Mon Mar 23 12:52:48 1998  512   root_domain

Vol  512-Blks  Free    % Used  Cmode  Rblks  Wblks  Vol Name
1L   262144    63616   76%     on     256    256    /dev/rz1a

# volencap rz1

Setting up encapsulation for rz1.
```

```
- Creating simple disk rz1d to ensure rootdg has a boot disk config area.
- Partition rz1a is the root partition which requires 2 passes
to encapsulate and the temporary use of a free partition.
- Using partition rz1e for temporary root encapsulation.
- Creating nopriv disk for primary swap device rz1b.
- Creating nopriv disk for rz1g.
- Creating nopriv disk for rz1h.

The following disks are queued up for encapsulation or use by LSM.
You must reboot the system to perform the actual encapsulations.
rz1d rz1a rz1e rz1b rz1g rz1h

# reboot
```

Then, the system will reboot three times while it configures for LSM on the system disk on its own. When the system finally comes up for the last time, the entire system disk will be encapsulated.

```
# volprint -Aht
Disk group: rootdg
```

DG	NAME	GROUP-ID						
DM	NAME	DEVICE	TYPE	PRIVLEN	PUBLEN	PUBPATH		
V	NAME	USETYPE	KSTATE	STATE	LENGTH	READPOL	PREFPLEX	
PL	NAME	VOLUME	KSTATE	STATE	LENGTH	LAYOUT	ST-WIDTH	MODE
SD	NAME	PLEX	PLOFFS	DISKOFFS	LENGTH	DISK-NAME	DEVICE	
dg	rootdg		893785171.1025.sunny.alf.dec.com					
dm	rz1a	rz1a	nopriv	0	262144	/dev/rrz1a		
dm	rz1b	rz1b	nopriv	0	779792	/dev/rrz1b		
dm	rz1d	rz1d	simple	1024	0	/dev/rrz1d		
dm	rz1g	rz1g	nopriv	0	2097152	/dev/rrz1g		
dm	rz1h	rz1h	nopriv	0	970368	/dev/rrz1h		
dm	rz2	rz2	sliced	1024	8379040	/dev/rrz2g		
dm	rz3	rz3	sliced	1024	2049820	/dev/rrz3g		
dm	rz6	rz6	sliced	1024	2049820	/dev/rrz6g		
v	rootvol	root	ENABLED	ACTIVE	262144	ROUND	–	
pl	rootvol-01	rootvol	ENABLED	ACTIVE	262144	CONCAT	–	RW
sd	rz1a-01	rootvol-01	0	0	262144	rz1a	rz1a	
v	swapvol	swap	ENABLED	ACTIVE	779792	ROUND	–	
pl	swapvol-01	swapvol	ENABLED	ACTIVE	779792	CONCAT	–	RW
sd	rz1b-01	swapvol-01	0	0	779792	rz1b	rz1b	
v	vol-rz1g	fsgen	ENABLED	ACTIVE	2097152	SELECT	–	
pl	vol-rz1g-01	vol-rz1g	ENABLED	ACTIVE	2097152	CONCAT	–	RW
sd	rz1g-01	vol-rz1g-01	0	0	2097152	rz1g	rz1g	
v	vol-rz1h	fsgen	ENABLED	ACTIVE	970368	SELECT	–	
pl	vol-rz1h-01	vol-rz1h	ENABLED	ACTIVE	970368	CONCAT	–	RW
sd	rz1h-01	vol-rz1h-01	0	0	970368	rz1h	rz1h	

```
# voldisk list
DEVICE TYPE      DISK      GROUP      STATUS
rz1a   nopriv    rz1a      rootdg     online
rz1b   nopriv    rz1b      rootdg     online
```

```
rz1d    simple     rz1d      rootdg    online
rz1g    nopriv     rz1g      rootdg    online
rz1h    nopriv     rz1h      rootdg    online
rz2     sliced     rz2       rootdg    online
rz3     sliced     rz3       rootdg    online
rz6     sliced     rz6       rootdg    online
```

At this point, the encapsulation process has been completed successfully. The next step is to mirror this disk over to rz0 using *volrootmir(8)*.

```
# volrootmir -a rz0

Mirroring system disk rz1 to disk rz0.

This operation will destroy all contents on disk rz0.
The partition map from rz1 will be copied to rz0 and
all volumes associated with rz1 will be mirrored.

Do you want to continue with this operation? (y or n) y

Initializing rz0.

Mirroring rootvol to rz0a.
Mirroring swapvol to rz0b.
Mirroring vol-rz1g to rz0g.
Mirroring vol-rz1h to rz0h.

# volprint -Aht
Disk group: rootdg
```

DG	NAME	GROUP-ID					
DM	NAME	DEVICE	TYPE	PRIVLEN	PUBLEN	PUBPATH	
V	NAME	USETYPE	KSTATE	STATE	LENGTH	READPOL	PREFPLEX
PL	NAME	VOLUME	KSTATE	STATE	LENGTH	LAYOUT	ST-WIDTH MODE
SD	NAME	PLEX	PLOFFS	DISKOFFS	LENGTH	DISK-NAMEDEVICE	

dg	rootdg893785171.1025.sunny.alf.dec.com							
dm	rz0a	rz0a	nopriv	0	262144	/dev/rrz0a		
dm	rz0b	rz0b	nopriv	0	779792	/dev/rrz0b		
dm	rz0d	rz0d	simple	1024	0	/dev/rrz0d		
dm	rz0g	rz0g	nopriv	0	2097152	/dev/rrz0g		
dm	rz0h	rz0h	nopriv	0	970368	/dev/rrz0h		
dm	rz1a	rz1a	nopriv	0	262144	/dev/rrz1a		
dm	rz1b	rz1b	nopriv	0	779792	/dev/rrz1b		
dm	rz1d	rz1d	simple	1024	0	/dev/rrz1d		
dm	rz1g	rz1g	nopriv	0	2097152	/dev/rrz1g		
dm	rz1h	rz1h	nopriv	0	970368	/dev/rrz1h		
dm	rz2	rz2	sliced	1024	8379040	/dev/rrz2g		
dm	rz3	rz3	sliced	1024	2049820	/dev/rrz3g		
dm	rz6	rz6	sliced	1024	2049820	/dev/rrz6g		
v	rootvol	root	ENABLED	ACTIVE	262144	ROUND	-	
pl	rootvol-01	rootvol	ENABLED	ACTIVE	262144	CONCAT	-	RW
sd	rz1a-01p	rootvol-01	0	0	16	rz1a	rz1a	
sd	rz1a-01	rootvol-01	16	16	262128	rz1a	rz1a	
pl	rootvol-02	rootvol	ENABLED	ACTIVE	262144	CONCAT	-	RW
sd	rz0a-01p	rootvol-02	0	0	16	rz0a	rz0a	

```
sd  rz0a-01rootvol-0216      16          262128      rz0a        rz0a

v   swapvol        swap      ENABLED     ACTIVE      779792      ROUND       -
pl  swapvol-01     swapvol   ENABLED     ACTIVE      779792      CONCAT      -           RW
sd  rz1b-01        swapvol-01  0         0           779792      rz1b              rz1b
pl  swapvol-02     swapvol   ENABLED     ACTIVE      779792      CONCAT      -           RW
sd  rz0b-01        swapvol-02  0         0           779792      rz0b        rz0b

v   vol-rz1g       fsgen     ENABLED     ACTIVE      2097152     SELECT      -
pl  vol-rz1g-01    vol-rz1g  ENABLED     ACTIVE      2097152     CONCAT      -           RW
sd  rz1g-01        vol-rz1g-01  0        0           2097152     rz1g        rz1g
pl  vol-rz1g-02    vol-rz1g  ENABLED     ACTIVE      2097152     CONCAT      -           RW
sd  rz0g-01        vol-rz1g-02  0        0           2097152     rz0g        rz0g

v   vol-rz1h       fsgen     ENABLED     ACTIVE      970368      SELECT      -
pl  vol-rz1h-01    vol-rz1h  ENABLED     ACTIVE      970368      CONCAT      -           RW
sd  rz1h-01        vol-rz1h-01  0        0           970368      rz1h        rz1h
pl  vol-rz1h-02    vol-rz1h  ENABLED     ACTIVE      970368      CONCAT      -           RW
sd  rz0h-01        vol-rz1h-02  0        0           970368      rz0h        rz0h

# voldisk list
DEVICE TYPE        DISK      GROUP       STATUS
rz0a   nopriv      rz0a      rootdg      online
rz0b   nopriv      rz0b      rootdg      online
rz0d   simple      rz0d      rootdg      online
rz0g   nopriv      rz0g      rootdg      online
rz0h   nopriv      rz0h      rootdg      online
rz1a   nopriv      rz1a      rootdg      online
rz1b   nopriv      rz1b      rootdg      online
rz1d   simple      rz1d      rootdg      online
rz1g   nopriv      rz1g      rootdg      online
rz1h   nopriv      rz1h      rootdg      online
rz2    sliced      rz2       rootdg      online
rz3    sliced      rz3       rootdg      online
rz6    sliced      rz6       rootdg      online

# voldctl list
Volboot file
version: 3/1
seqno:0.47
hostid:jackson
entries:
disk rz6 type=sliced
disk rz2 type=sliced
disk rz3 type=sliced
disk rz1d type=simple
disk rz0d type=simple
```

Next, it is important to update the console variable "bootdef_dev" to include both disks "DKA0,DKA100" so that if the first disk is unavailable on boot, the console will automatically try to boot from the second disk.

The final step in the process of mirroring the system disk is to run some checks. First, you want to make sure you can boot from each disk independently. That involves starting from the console mode, pulling one disk out, and booting from the other. Make sure you complete that process for both disks. Next, you want to make sure that the mirroring will work correctly if one of the disks fails. So, you should pull one disk and monitor that the plexes fail out properly. Try it both ways. When both of those tests are complete, you should feel confident that the system disk will survive most disasters.

It is important that you keep in mind some of the downsides of LSM system disk mirroring. One of the biggest drawbacks is that LSM system disk mirroring can make recovery much more complex in the case of corruption of key files. This is the case where you cannot rely on either mirror in the rootvol volume. In this case, you would need to recover from system disk backups that you previously made using *vdump(8)*, perform some cleanup, and redo the system disk encapsulation process. It is advisable to consider a hardware RAID solution for a system disk, rather than using LSM because of the potential lost production time should this type of event occur. With a hardware RAID solution, you can skip the cleanup and reencapsulation, and get the system back faster. A hardware-only mirroring or RAID system must be carefully designed to avoid single points of failure at the controller.

3.3 Managing Logical Volumes

Once you've set up your initial LSM configuration and set up some simple volumes, you need to know more information about how to manage them. This section covers lots of good information and advice on how to perform various functions with your LSM configuration, including how to gather information, perform consistent backups, grow and shrink logical volumes, monitor LSM for problems, save and restore your LSM configuration information, and modify plex and volume information.

3.3.1 Gathering Information

One of the most important things you need to know how to do with LSM is how to gather information about the state of the system. In this section, we do not attempt to be exhaustive in our coverage, but we discuss the most important data-gathering commands and flags that we think are the most useful.

3.3.1.1   Voldisk list

One of the most helpful commands for gathering data on your LSM configuration is the voldisk list command. There are two ways to use this command for gathering information. First, this command is useful for finding out which disks have been added to which disk group, what their disk access and disk media names are, what type of disk they are, and what their status is.

Example:

This is a Tru64 UNIX version 4.0x example of one way to use voldisk list to find out information about the disks in an LSM configuration.

```
# voldisk list
DEVICE  TYPE     DISK    GROUP       STATUS
rz10h   simple   rz10h   rootdg      online
rz43    sliced   -       -           online
rz50    sliced   rz50    scratchdg   online
rz51    sliced   rz51    scratchdg   online
rzb41   sliced   -       -           online
rzb49   sliced   rzb49   dg1         online
rzb50   sliced   rzb50   scratchdg   online
rzb51   sliced   rzb51   scratchdg   online
rzc50   sliced   rzc50   scratchdg   online
rzc51   sliced   rzc51   scratchdg   online
rzd50   sliced   rzd50   scratchdg   online
rzd51   sliced   rzd51   scratchdg   online
rze42   sliced   rze42   dg_22       online
rze50   sliced   rze50   scratchdg   online
rze51   sliced   rze51   scratchdg   online
rzf42   sliced   -       -           online
rzf50   sliced   rzf50   scratchdg   online
rzf51   sliced   rzf51   scratchdg   online
```

Example:

Here, we have a 5.0x case of the use of voldisk list similar to what we saw in the previous example.

```
# voldisk list
DEVICE  TYPE     DISK    GROUP    STATUS
dsk1    sliced   -       -        unknown
dsk4    sliced   -       -        unknown
dsk5    sliced   -       -        unknown
dsk6    sliced   -       -        unknown
dsk7c   simple   disk01  rootdg   online
dsk10   sliced   disk02  rootdg   online
dsk11   sliced   disk03  rootdg   online
dsk12   sliced   -       -        unknown
dsk33   sliced   disk05  rootdg   online
dsk35   sliced   disk04  rootdg   online
```

The second way you can use voldisk list is by passing a disk access name to it. This step gives detailed information about the disk itself, such as its name, its identifier, flags, public and private region information, and configuration database and log information. This information is helpful if you are trying to find out which disks have configuration copies, for example.

Example:

This example illustrates the use of voldisk list in another way that tells us more information about the disk itself on a Tru64 UNIX 4.0x system.

```
# voldisk list rz131
Device:    rz131
devicetag: rz131
type:      sliced
hostid:
disk:      name= id=940528112.2701.maxx.alf.dec.com
group:     name=dg2 id=910373995.1149.maxx.alf.dec.com
flags:     online ready private
pubpaths:  block=/dev/rz131g char=/dev/rrz131g
privpaths: block=/dev/rz131h char=/dev/rrz131h
version:   1.1
iosize:    512
public:    slice=6 offset=16 len=17772484
private:   slice=7 offset=0 len=1024
update:    time=950286500 seqno=0.92
headers:   0 248
configs:   count=1 len=726
logs:      count=1 len=110
Defined regions:
config  priv  17-   247[ 231]: copy=01 offset=000000
config  priv  249-  743[ 495]: copy=01 offset=000231
log     priv  744-  853[ 110]: copy=01 offset=000000
```

Example:

We examine an LSM disk dsk33 in this example. This is clearly a 5.0x system, and we see similar information as we saw in the 4.0x case in the previous example.

```
# voldisk list dsk33
Device:    dsk33
devicetag: dsk33
type:      sliced
hostid:    ruby.alf.dec.com
disk:      name=disk05 id=951756807.1567.ruby.alf.dec.com
group:     name=rootdg id=949521863.1026.ruby.alf.dec.com
flags:     online ready autoimport imported
pubpaths:  block=/dev/disk/dsk33g char=/dev/rdisk/dsk33g
privpaths: block=/dev/disk/dsk33h char=/dev/rdisk/dsk33h
version:   2.1
iosize:    min=512 (bytes) max=2048 (blocks)
public:    slice=6 offset=16 len=8375968
private:   slice=7 offset=0 len=4096
update:    time=951756814 seqno=0.5
```

```
headers:     0 248
configs:     count=1 len=2993
logs:        count=1 len=453
Defined regions:
config  priv   17-    247[ 231]: copy=01 offset=000000 enabled
config  priv  249-   3010[ 2762]: copy=01 offset=000231 enabled
log     priv  3011-  3463[ 453]: copy=01 offset=000000 enabled
```

Unfortunately, the volume configuration daemon must be running in order for this command to provide any useful output. Therefore, if the vold is not running for some reason, you will not be able to get information using voldisk list. The message you will receive is "voldisk: Volume daemon is not accessible," and the command will not succeed.

3.3.1.2 Volprint

The most useful command to gather information about the state of the LSM is the volprint command. So much information and various formats are available that it would take a long time to cover them completely. The reference page is good for an exhaustive coverage. We simply cover some of the most useful aspects of the tool.

The most frequent use of *volprint(8)* is to get a complete list of all of the disk groups, volumes, plexes, subdisks, and disks. We also get states and sizes for all of those LSM records. The following few examples illustrate the kinds of information you get from *volprint(8)*.

Example:

This example shows the result of running the *volprint(8)* tool on a 5.0x system. In this example, we have a simple configuration and only a single disk group. The single volume in the rootdg disk group is called voltest, and both the volume and its plex (voltest-01) have the state of ENABLED. This means that the volume is ready and able to perform useful work.

```
# volprint -Aht
Disk group: rootdg
```

DG	NAME	NCONFIG	NLOG	MINORS	GROUP-ID		
DM	NAME	DEVICE	TYPE	PRIVLEN	PUBLEN	STATE	
V	NAME	USETYPE	KSTATE	STATE	LENGTH	READPOL	PREFPLEX
PL	NAME	VOLUME	KSTATE	STATE	LENGTH	LAYOUT	NCOL/WID
MODE							
SD	NAME	PLEX	DISK	DISKOFFS	LENGTH[COL/]OFF	DEVICEMODE	
dg	rootdg	default	default	0	949521863.1026.ruby.alf.dec.com		
dm	disk01	dsk7c	simple	4096	4106368	–	
dm	disk02	dsk10	sliced	4096	8375968	–	

```
dm  disk03      dsk11       sliced    4096    8375968    -
dm  disk04      dsk35       sliced    4096    8375968    -
dm  disk05      dsk33       sliced    4096    8375968    -

v   voltest     fsgen       ENABLED   ACTIVE  204800     SELECT    -
pl  voltest-01  voltest     ENABLED   ACTIVE  204800     CONCAT    -    RW
sd  disk01-01   voltest-01  disk01    0       204800     0         dsk7cENA
```

Example:

This busy example shows how the *volprint(8)* command can be used to examine the Tru64 UNIX 4.0x system. Here, we note that three disk groups exist besides rootdg.

```
# volprint -Aht
Disk group: rootdg
```

DG	NAME	GROUP-ID					
DM	NAME	DEVICE	TYPE	PRIVLEN	PUBLEN	PUBPATH	
V	NAME	USETYPE	KSTATE	STATE	LENGTH	READPOL	PREFPLEX
PL	NAME	VOLUME	KSTATE	STATE	LENGTH	LAYOUT	ST-WIDTH MODE
SD	NAME	PLEX	PLOFFS	DISKOFFS	LENGTH	DISK-NAMEDEVICE	

```
dg  rootdg      899300893.1025.durnik.zk3.dec.com

dm  rz10h       rz10h       simple    2048    176008     /dev/rrz10h
```

```
Disk group: dg_22
```

DG	NAME	GROUP-ID					
DM	NAME	DEVICE	TYPE	PRIVLEN	PUBLEN	PUBPATH	
V	NAME	USETYPE	KSTATE	STATE	LENGTH	READPOL	PREFPLEX
PL	NAME	VOLUME	KSTATE	STATE	LENGTH	LAYOUT	ST-WIDTH MODE
SD	NAME	PLEX	PLOFFS	DISKOFFS	LENGTH	DISK-NAMEDEVICE	

```
dg  dg_22       946475757.5759.durnik.zk3.dec.com

dm  rze42       rze42       sliced    1024    8376988    /dev/rrze42g

v   dg_22_vol000 fsgenENABLED ACTIVE   8376988  ROUND      -
pl  dg_22_pl000  dg_22_vol000 ENABLEDACTIVE8376988 CONCAT  -          RW
sd  dg_22_sd000  dg_22_pl000  0        0        8376988    rze42    rze42
```

```
Disk group: dg1
```

DG	NAME	GROUP-ID					
DM	NAME	DEVICE	TYPE	PRIVLEN	PUBLEN	PUBPATH	
V	NAME	USETYPE	KSTATE	STATE	LENGTH	READPOL	PREFPLEX
PL	NAME	VOLUME	KSTATE	STATE	LENGTH	LAYOUT	ST-WIDTH MODE
SD	NAME	PLEX	PLOFFS	DISKOFFS	LENGTH	DISK-NAMEDEVICE	

```
dg  dg1         946487984.5836.durnik.zk3.dec.com

dm  rzb49       rzb49       sliced    1024    4108430    /dev/rrzb49g

v   dg1_vol000  fsgen       ENABLED   ACTIVE  4108430    ROUND     -
pl  dg1_pl000   dg1_vol000  ENABLED   ACTIVE  4108430    CONCAT    -    RW
sd  dg1_sd000   dg1_pl000   0         0       4108430    rzb49    rzb49
```

```
Disk group: scratchdg
```

DG	NAME	GROUP-ID					
DM	NAME	DEVICE	TYPE	PRIVLEN	PUBLEN	PUBPATH	
V	NAME	USETYPE	KSTATE	STATE	LENGTH	READPOL	PREFPLEX
PL	NAME	VOLUME	KSTATE	STATE	LENGTH	LAYOUT	ST-WIDTH MODE
SD	NAME	PLEX	PLOFFS	DISKOFFS	LENGTH	DISK-NAME DEVICE	
dg	scratchdg	952434680.5989.durnik.zk3.dec.com					
dm	rz50	rz50	sliced	1024	8376988	/dev/rrz50g	
dm	rz51	rz51	sliced	1024	8376988	/dev/rrz51g	
dm	rzb50	rzb50	sliced	1024	8376988	/dev/rrzb50g	
dm	rzb51	rzb51	sliced	1024	8376988	/dev/rrzb51g	
dm	rzc50	rzc50	sliced	1024	8376988	/dev/rrzc50g	
dm	rzc51	rzc51	sliced	1024	8376988	/dev/rrzc51g	
dm	rzd50	rzd50	sliced	1024	8376988	/dev/rrzd50g	
dm	rzd51	rzd51	sliced	1024	8376988	/dev/rrzd51g	
dm	rze50	rze50	sliced	1024	8376988	/dev/rrze50g	
dm	rze51	rze51	sliced	1024	8376988	/dev/rrze51g	
dm	rzf50	rzf50	sliced	1024	8376988	/dev/rrzf50g	
dm	rzf51	rzf51	sliced	1024	8376988	/dev/rrzf51g	
v	volscratch	fsgen	ENABLED	ACTIVE	100523856	SELECT-	
pl	volscratch-01	volscratch	ENABLED	ACTIVE	100523856	CONCAT - RW	
sd	rz50-01	volscratch-01	0	0	8376988	rz50	rz50
sd	rz51-01	volscratch-01	8376988	0	8376988	rz51	rz51
sd	rzb50-01	volscratch-01	16753976	0	8376988	rzb50	rzb50
sd	rzb51-01	volscratch-01	25130964	0	8376988	rzb51	rzb51
sd	rzc50-01	volscratch-01	33507952	0	8376988	rzc50	rzc50
sd	rzc51-01	volscratch-01	41884940	0	8376988	rzc51	rzc51
sd	rzd50-01	volscratch-01	50261928	0	8376988	rzd50	rzd50
sd	rzd51-01	volscratch-01	58638916	0	8376988	rzd51	rzd51
sd	rze50-01	volscratch-01	67015904	0	8376988	rze50	rze50
sd	rze51-01	volscratch-01	75392892	0	8376988	rze51	rze51
sd	rzf50-01	volscratch-01	83769880	0	8376988	rzf50	rzf50
sd	rzf51-01	volscratch-01	92146868	0	8376988	rzf51	rzf51

In order to decode some of the state information, we refer you to Tables 3–6 and 3–7, which describe the volume and plex states, respectively. With knowledge of the plex or volume state, it is possible to devise a recovery plan or set of steps to clean up any failures that may occur.

TABLE 3–6   LSM Volume State Fields

VOLUME STATE	DESCRIPTION
EMPTY	The volume is not yet initialized. This is the initial state for volumes created by volmake.
CLEAN	The volume has been stopped and the contents for all plexes are consistent. A volume start will get it to the ACTIVE state.
ACTIVE	The volume has been started and is running normally, or was running normally when the system was stopped. If the system crashes in this state, then the volume may require plex consistency recovery.

TABLE 3–6   LSM Volume State Fields (Continued)

VOLUME STATE	DESCRIPTION
NEEDSYNC	This volume requires recovery. This is typically set after a system failure to indicate that the plexes in the volume may be inconsistent, so that they require recovery (see the discussion of the resynchronization operation in *volume(8)*).
SYNC	Plex consistency recovery is currently being done on the volume. Volume resync sets this state when it starts to recovery plex consistency on a volume that was in the NEEDSYNC state.

TABLE 3–7   LSM Plex State Fields

PLEX STATE	DESCRIPTION
EMPTY	The plex is not yet initialized. This state is set when the volume state is also EMPTY.
CLEAN	The plex was running normally when the volume was stopped. The plex will be enabled without requiring recovery when the volume is started.
ACTIVE	The plex is running normally on a started volume. The plex condition flags (NODAREC, REMOVED, RECOVER, and IOFAIL) may apply if the system is rebooted and the volume restarted.
STALE	The plex was detached, either by volplex det or by an I/O failure. Volume start will change the state for a plex to STALE if any of the plex condition flags are set.STALE plexes will be reattached automatically, when starting a volume, by calling "volplex att."
OFFLINE	The plex was disabled by the volmend off operation. See our discussion of *volmend(8)* for more information.
SNAPATT	This snapshot plex is being attached by the volassist snapstart operation. When the attach is complete, the state for the plex will be changed to SNAPDONE. If the system fails before the attach completes, then the plex and all of its subdisks will be removed.
SNAPDONE	This snapshot plex created by volassist snapstart is fully attached. A plex in this state can be turned into a snapshot volume with volassist snapshot. See our discussion of *volassist(8)* for more information. If the system fails before the attach completes, then the plex and all of its subdisks will be removed.
SNAPTMP	This snapshot plex is being attached by the volplex snapstart operation. When the attach is complete, the state for the plex will be changed to SNAPDIS. If the system fails before the attach completes, then the plex will be dissociated from the volume.
SNAPDIS	This snapshot plex created by volplex snapstart is fully attached. A plex in this state can be turned into a snapshot volume with volplex snapshot. See our discussion of *volplex(8)* for more information. If the system fails before the attach completes, then the plex will be dissociated from the volume.

TABLE 3–7   LSM Plex State Fields (Continued)

PLEX STATE	DESCRIPTION
TEMP	This plex is being associated and attached to a volume with volplex att. If the system fails before the attach completes, then the plex will be dissociated from the volume.
TEMPRM	This plex is being associated and attached to a volume with volplex att. If the system fails before the attach completes, then the plex will be dissociated from the volume and removed. Any subdisks in the plex will be kept.
TEMPRMSD	This plex is being associated and attached to a volume with volplex att. If the system fails before the attach completes, then the plex and its subdisks will be dissociated from the volume and removed.

TABLE 3–8   LSM Plex Read Policies

POLICY	DESCRIPTION
Round	This is also known as the round-robin plex read policy. The reads to that volume will be evenly distributed I/O read requests between all plexes of that volume in order. The reads are distributed by alternating read requests to each plex in a volume. This is the default.
Prefer	This is also known as the preferred plex policy. This policy designates a specific plex of a particular volume to be used for I/O read requests. You would use this policy if one of the plexes is on a device that you know will always be the best performing out of all the plexes in the volume.
Select	The default plex read policy is based on the plex associations to that volume. If the volume contains a single, enabled, striped plex, then the default is to prefer that plex. For any other association, the default is to use a round-robin policy.

3.3.1.3   Voldg free

This command is helpful for determining where to find free space on each disk and in each disk group. When you are ready to make a new volume or volumes and you get errors, you can find out why by checking out the free space available.

Example:

This example shows how to use the "voldg free" command to find out what disks have free space on them.

```
# voldg free
GROUP    DISK     DEVICE   TAG      OFFSET    LENGTH    FLAGS
rootdg   disk01   dsk7c    dsk7     204800    3901568   -
rootdg   disk02   dsk10    dsk10    0         8375968   -
rootdg   disk03   dsk11    dsk11    0         8375968   -
rootdg   disk04   dsk35    dsk35    0         8375968   -
rootdg   disk05   dsk33    dsk33    0         8375968   -
```

3.3.1.4 Voldg list

The "voldg list" command gives a complete list of all the disk groups, their status, and the disk group identifier.

Example:

```
# voldg list
NAMESTATEID
rootdgenabled908801308.1025.maxx.alf.dec.com
sysdgenabled941468336.2725.maxx.alf.dec.com
homedgenabled942154027.2746.maxx.alf.dec.com
```

3.3.1.5 Voldctl list

This command lists out the contents of the /etc/volboot file in a formatted fashion. You need to use this command when you want to know why the volume daemon will not start, for example. Make sure all disks in the rootdg disk group that have a configuration copy are listed in this file.

Example:

This Tru64 UNIX 4.0x example shows the output from the voldctl list command.

```
# voldctl list
Volboot file
version: 3/1
seqno:0.38
hostid:jackson
entries:
  disk rz6 type=sliced
  disk rz132 type=sliced
  disk rz133 type=sliced
  disk rz2 type=sliced
  disk rz3 type=sliced
  disk rz129 type=sliced
  disk rz130 type=sliced
  disk rz131 type=sliced
```

Example:

This Tru64 UNIX 5.0x example shows the output from the voldctl list command.

```
# voldctl list
Volboot file
version: 3/1
seqno:0.9
hostid:ruby.alf.dec.com
entries:
  disk dsk7c type=simple privoffset=16
  disk dsk10 type=sliced
  disk dsk11 type=sliced
```

```
disk dsk33 type=sliced
disk dsk35 type=sliced
```

Now we know how to look around and gather information about our LSM configuration. These commands will be invaluable to you in a troubleshooting situation, so we suggest that you keep them in your arsenal.

3.3.2 Backing Up LSM Volumes

One of the biggest challenges facing any UNIX system administrator is how to get a good, consistent backup of your dynamic file systems without taking the system down for an extended period. Fortunately, Tru64 UNIX has several methods for achieving this goal. If you are using primarily AdvFSs, then the clone fileset is the best option for making a consistent backup. We recommend this option for most AdvFS sites, and we discuss it in greater detail in Chapter 6.

LSM also includes the capability for making consistent backups by creating a special mirrored copy of a plex called a **snapshot**. One of the drawbacks is that you need to have enough storage available in the same disk group as the volumes that you wish to back up. LSM snapshots are also not appropriate for large multivolume domains. Regarding the use of snapshots, we recommend you consider using them under the following conditions:

- You need a completely consistent backup.

- You are backing up a UFS.

- You are trying to back up smaller, single-volume AdvFS file domains.

- You have enough extra space in the same disk group to store the snapshot for any volume.

- You can take the file system offline for a short time (like in the middle of the night).

We have developed the following procedure for a complete single-volume backup using volassist:

1.   Create a snapshot plex for an existing LSM volume as follows:

      ```
      # volassist snapstart <volume>
      ```

      This can be done at any time prior to the time you will be starting your snapshot operation.

2.   When the snapstart operation is complete and the plex is in a SNAPDONE state, select a convenient time to complete the snapshot operation. You will want to inform users of the upcoming

snapshot and warn them to stop using that file system during that time. You may want to *umount(8)* or use *fuser(8)* on the file system to ensure that it is clean.

```
# umount /<mount_point>
```

or

```
# fuser -k -c /<mount_point>
```

3. Create a snapshot volume that reflects the original volume as follows:

```
# volassist snapshot <volume> <snapshot_volume>
```

Once the snapshot is complete, you can resume normal use of the volume. In the case of a UFS or AdvFS, it can be remounted.

4. How you proceed for this step will depend on whether you are working with UFS or AdvFS. The steps will be completely different for each.

    ■ If you are backing up UFS, you need to use *fsck(8)* on the volume to clean the temporary volume's contents.

```
# fsck -p /dev/rvol/<disk_group>/<snapshot_volume>
```

    ■ For AdvFS, you need to create a temporary directory and symbolic link(s) in /etc/fdmns.

```
# cd /etc/fdmns
# mkdir <new_domain>
# cd <new_domain>
# ln -s /dev/vol/<disk_group>/<snapshot_volume>
```

5. Create a new mount point or identify an existing directory for the temporary mount.

```
# mkdir /<new_mount_point>
```

Mount the snapshot on a temporary location to check the integrity and use for the backup.

    ■ For AdvFS, you must use the "-o dual" flag to the *mount(8)* command, or the mount will fail. See our *mount(8)* discussion in Chapter 6 for details on this option.

```
# mount -o dual <new_domain#fileset> /<new_mount_point>
```

    ■ For UFS, a regular mount should be fine.

```
# mount /dev/vol/<disk_group>/<snapshot_volume>
    /<new_mount_point>
#
```

6. Copy the temporary volume to tape, or to some other appropriate backup media. For example, a UFS on the temporary volume could be backed up with the following command:

```
# vdump -0uf <tape_device> -D /<new_mount_point>
```

7. After the backup has been completed, you have some cleanup to do. First, unmount the file system, then remove the file system (for AdvFS), and finally remove the temporary volume.

```
# umount /<new_mount_point>
# rmfdmn -f <new_domain>
# volume stop <snapshot_volume>
# voledit -rf rm <snapshot_volume>
```

At this point, you will be right back where you started, except you will have a consistent backup tape of the file system. You should be able to take this procedure and use it at your site. So, now let's look at some examples showing how we did with it and what some of the volumes look like at each step.

Example:

This example shows how to use the previous procedure to make a consistent backup of a UFS.

```
# df -k /test
Filesystem                   1024-blocks Used   Available Capacity Mounted on
/dev/vol/rootdg/voltest 98479       27585  61046     32%      /test
# volassist snapstart voltest disk02

# volprint -Aht
Disk group: rootdg

DG  NAME         NCONFIG     NLOG        MINORS      GROUP-ID
DM  NAME         DEVICE      TYPE        PRIVLEN     PUBLEN      STATE
V   NAME         USETYPE     KSTATE      STATE       LENGTH      READPOL   PREFPLEX
PL  NAME         VOLUME      KSTATE      STATE       LENGTH      LAYOUT    NCOL/WID MODE
SD  NAME         PLEX        DISK        DISKOFFS LENGTH[COL/]OFF DEVICEMODE

dg   rootdg     default    default   0           949521863.1026.ruby.alf.dec.com

dm   disk01     dsk7c      simple    4096        4106368-
dm   disk02     dsk10      sliced    4096        8375968-
dm   disk03     dsk11      sliced    4096        8375968-
dm   disk04     dsk35      sliced    4096        8375968-
dm   disk05     dsk33      sliced    4096        8375968-

v    voltest    fsgen                 ENABLED     ACTIVE      204800      SELECT    -
pl   voltest-01 voltest               ENABLED     ACTIVE      204800      CONCAT    -      RW
sd   disk01-01  voltest-01  disk01    0           204800      0           dsk7c    ENA
pl   voltest-02 voltest               ENABLED     SNAPDONE    204800      CONCAT    -      WO
sd   disk02-01  voltest-02  disk02    0           204800      0           dsk10ENA

# fuser -k -c /test
```

```
# volassist snapshot voltest volsnapshot

# volprint -Aht

Disk group: rootdg

DG  NAME            NCONFIG       NLOG       MINORS    GROUP-ID
DM  NAME            DEVICE        TYPE       PRIVLEN   PUBLEN     STATE
V   NAME            USETYPE       KSTATE     STATE     LENGTH     READPOL   PREFPLEX
PL  NAME            VOLUME        KSTATE     STATE     LENGTH     LAYOUT    NCOL/WID MODE
SD  NAME            PLEX          DISK       DISKOFFS  LENGTH     [COL/]OFF DEVICEMODE

dg   rootdg    default    default   0        949521863.1026.ruby.alf.dec.com

dm   disk01    dsk7c     simple     4096     4106368-
dm   disk02    dsk10     sliced     4096     8375968-
dm   disk03    dsk11     sliced     4096     8375968-
dm   disk04    dsk35     sliced     4096     8375968-
dm   disk05    dsk33     sliced     4096     8375968-

v    volsnapshot    fsgen              ENABLED   ACTIVE    204800    ROUND     -
pl   volsnapshot-01 volsnapshot ENABLED   ACTIVE    204800    CONCAT    -    RW
sd   disk02-01      volsnapshot-01 disk02 0  204800    0         dsk10     ENA

v    voltest    fsgen              ENABLED   ACTIVE    204800    SELECT    -
pl   voltest-01 voltest        ENABLED   ACTIVE    204800    CONCAT    -    RW
sd   disk01-01  voltest-01     disk01     0         204800    0         dsk7cENA

# fsck -p /dev/vol/rootdg/volsnapshot
/sbin/ufs_fsck -p /dev/vol/rootdg/volsnapshot
/dev/rvol/rootdg/volsnapshot: 3 files, 27585 used, 70894 free (14 frags, 8860
blocks, 0.0% fragmentation)
/dev/rvol/rootdg/volsnapshot: Filesystem '/dev/rvol/rootdg/volsnapshot' Tru64
UNIX UFS v.3 UFS

# mount /dev/vol/rootdg/volsnapshot /mnt

# df /mnt
Filesystem                    512-blocks  Used   Available  Capacity   Mounted on
/dev/vol/rootdg/volsnapshot  196958      55170  122092     32%        /mnt

# vdump -0uf /dev/tape/tape_d0 -D /mnt
path: /mnt
dev/fset : /dev/vol/rootdg/volsnapshot
type: ufs
vdump: Date of last level 0 dump: the start of the epoch
vdump: Dumping directories
vdump: Dumping 28223520 bytes, 1 directories, 2 files
vdump: Dumping regular files
vdump: Status at Sat Mar4 12:02:58 2000
vdump: Dumped 28223520 of 28223520 bytes; 100.0% completed
vdump: Dumped 1 of 1 directories; 100.0% completed
vdump: Dumped 2 of 2 files; 100.0% completed
vdump: Dump completed at Sat Mar4 12:02:58 2000

# umount /mnt

# volume stop volsnapshot

# voledit -rf rm volsnapshot
```

Example:

This example shows how to use the previous procedure to make a consistent backup of an AdvFS that is sitting on top of an LSM volume.

```
# df -k /test
Filesystem      1024-blocks  Used    Available Capacity  Mounted on
test_dmn#test   102400       27584   70576     29%       /test

# volassist snapstart voltest disk02

# volprint -Aht
Disk group: rootdg

DG  NAME           NCONFIG       NLOG      MINORS      GROUP-ID
DM  NAME           DEVICE        TYPE      PRIVLEN     PUBLEN     STATE
V   NAME           USETYPE       KSTATE    STATE       LENGTH     READPOL    PREFPLEX
PL  NAME           VOLUME        KSTATE    STATE       LENGTH     LAYOUT     NCOL/WID MODE
SD  NAME           PLEX          DISK      DISKOFFS    LENGTH     [COL/]OFF DEVICEMODE

dg   rootdg        default       default   0           949521863.1026.ruby.alf.dec.com

dm   disk01        dsk7c         simple    4096        4106368-
dm   disk02        dsk10         sliced    4096        8375968-
dm   disk03        dsk11         sliced    4096        8375968-
dm   disk04        dsk35         sliced    4096        8375968-
dm   disk05        dsk33         sliced    4096        8375968-

v    voltest       fsgen         ENABLED   ACTIVE      204800     SELECT     -
pl   voltest-01    voltest       ENABLED   ACTIVE      204800     CONCAT     -     RW
sd   disk01-01     voltest-01    disk01    0           204800     0          dsk7cENA
pl   voltest-02    voltest       ENABLED   SNAPDONE    204800     CONCAT     -     WO
sd   disk02-01     voltest-02    disk02    0           204800     0          dsk10ENA

# fuser -k -c /test

# volassist snapshot voltest volsnapshot

# volprint -Aht

Disk group: rootdg

DG  NAME           NCONFIG       NLOG      MINORS      GROUP-ID
DM  NAME           DEVICE        TYPE      PRIVLEN     PUBLEN     STATE
V   NAME           USETYPE       KSTATE    STATE       LENGTH     READPOL    PREFPLEX
PL  NAME           VOLUME        KSTATE    STATE       LENGTH     LAYOUT     NCOL/WID MODE
SD  NAME           PLEX          DISK      DISKOFFS    LENGTH     [COL/]OFF DEVICEMODE

dg   rootdg        default       default   0           949521863.1026.ruby.alf.dec.com

dm   disk01        dsk7c         simple    4096        4106368-
dm   disk02        dsk10         sliced    4096        8375968-
dm   disk03        dsk11         sliced    4096        8375968-
dm   disk04        dsk35         sliced    4096        8375968-
dm   disk05        dsk33         sliced    4096        8375968-

v    volsnapshot   fsgen         ENABLED   ACTIVE      204800     ROUND      -
pl   volsnapshot-01 volsnapshot  ENABLED   ACTIVE      204800     CONCAT     -     RW
sd   disk02-01     volsnapshot-01 disk02 0  204800     0          dsk10      ENA
```

```
v   voltest      fsgen        ENABLED   ACTIVE   204800   SELECT    -
pl  voltest-01   voltest      ENABLED   ACTIVE   204800   CONCAT    -     RW
sd  disk01-01    voltest-01   disk01    0        204800   0         dsk7cENA
# cd /etc/fdmns

# mkdir snap_dmn

# cd snap_dmn

# ln -s /dev/vol/rootdg/volsnapshot
```

Note here that if you try to mount the snapshot file system while the original is mounted, you will receive an error. The reason for the error is that the domain identifier for the two file systems will be duplicated, which is not valid. You cannot activate two file systems with the same domain identifier.

```
# mount snap_dmn#test /mnt
snap_dmn#test on /mnt: I/O error
```

And, with the correct option to the mount command, the domain mounts correctly after a brief delay to update internal structures.

```
# mount -o dual snap_dmn#test /mnt
Dual mounting a split mirror AdvFS filesystem.
This takes a short while to update the domain's ID.
```

```
# df -k /mnt
Filesystem    1024-blocks Used  Available CapacityMounted on
snap_dmn#test 102400      27584 70576     29%      /mnt
```

```
# vdump -0uf /dev/tape/tape_d0 -D /mnt
path: /mnt
dev/fset : snap_dmn#test
type: advfs
advfs id : 0x38c14520.00013a5e.1
vdump: Date of last level 0 dump: the start of the epoch
vdump: Dumping directories
vdump: Dumping 28239904 bytes, 1 directories, 4 files
vdump: Dumping regular files

vdump: Status at Sat Mar4 12:19:56 2000
vdump: Dumped 28239904 of 28239904 bytes; 100.0% completed
vdump: Dumped 1 of 1 directories; 100.0% completed
vdump: Dumped 4 of 4 files; 100.0% completed
vdump: Dump completed at Sat Mar4 12:19:56 2000
```

```
# umount /mnt
```

```
# rmfdmn snap_dmn
rmfdmn: remove domain snap_dmn? [y/n] y
rmfdmn: domain snap_dmn removed.
```

```
# volume stop volsnapshot
```

```
# voledit -rf rm volsnapshot
```

3.3.3   Growing and Shrinking LSM Volumes

One of the most common calls into the Compaq Customer Support Center for LSM is something like: "I grew my LSM volume, but my file system doesn't show the additional space." The response to that question will always be that the UFSs and AdvFSs are not able to dynamically grow to take advantage of this new space.So, that is the expected behavior. Unfortunately, this response doesn't always make the caller happy, but it is the reality of the situation. In order to take advantage of the LSM feature that allows logical volumes to grow and shrink, you need to back up the file system first, then resize the logical volume, then remake the file system and restore from your backup. It's not fun, but that is the procedure. If you are using AdvFS, rather than growing the logical volume, you can dynamically add space by creating a new volume and adding it to the existing file system. If you want to understand how to do that, we refer you to Chapter 6, where we cover the *addvol(8)* command.

Now that we've covered that ground, let's look at how you can increase or decrease the size of a logical volume. The primary top-down command to do this (again) is *volassist(8)*. The important keywords for increasing the size of a logical volume are *growby* and *growto*, and the keywords for reducing it are *shrinkby* and *shrinkto*. You need to keep in mind that changing the size of a logical volume has an effect on the file system that is using it. You can cause problems, for example, if you reduce the size of a volume that is in use by a file system and those blocks are used in another logical volume later on. The result will eventually be corruption of both file systems that are now overlapping. The result of increasing the size of the logical volume with a file system on it is to simply waste space. The following two examples illustrate the use of the "volassist growby" and "volassist growto" commands.

Example:

This example shows how you can use *volassist(8)* to increase the size of a logical volume by 100,000 blocks. We also show that even though the size of the volume increased, the size of the AdvFS using that volume did not change. You must use the '-f' flag if you want to use this keyword to *volassist(8)*.

```
# volprint -Aht
Disk group: rootdg
DG  NAME        NCONFIG       NLOG        MINORS      GROUP-ID
DM  NAME        DEVICE        TYPE        PRIVLEN     PUBLEN      STATE
V   NAME        USETYPE       KSTATE      STATE       LENGTH      READPOL     PREFPLEX
PL  NAME        VOLUME        KSTATE      STATE       LENGTH      LAYOUT      NCOL/WID MODE
```

```
SD  NAME         PLEX        DISK        DISKOFFS   LENGTH      [COL/]OFF DEVICEMODE

dg   rootdg     default    default    0          949521863.1026.ruby.alf.dec.com

dm disk01dsk7csimple40964106368-
dm   disk02      dsk10      sliced      4096       8375968-
dm   disk03      dsk11      sliced      4096       8375968-
dm   disk04      dsk35      sliced      4096       8375968-
dm   disk05      dsk33      sliced      4096       8375968-

v    voltest      fsgen            ENABLED   ACTIVE    204800    SELECT    -
pl   voltest-01   voltest          ENABLED   ACTIVE    204800    CONCAT    -    RW
sd   disk01-01    voltest-01   disk01    0         204800    0         dsk7cENA
```

```
# voldg free
GROUP     DISK        DEVICE      TAG       OFFSET    LENGTH      FLAGS
rootdg    disk01      dsk7c       dsk7      204800    3901568     -
rootdg    disk02      dsk10       dsk10     0         8375968     -
rootdg    disk03      dsk11       dsk11     0         8375968     -
rootdg    disk04      dsk35       dsk35     0         8375968     -
rootdg    disk05      dsk33       dsk33     0         8375968     -
```

```
# df -k /test
Filesystem     1024-blocks   Used    Available Capacity Mounted on
test_dmn#test  102400        27584   70576     29%       /test
```

```
# volassist -f growby voltest 100000
```

```
# volprint -Aht
Disk group: rootdg

DG  NAME         NCONFIG     NLOG        MINORS     GROUP-ID
DM  NAME         DEVICE      TYPE        PRIVLEN    PUBLEN      STATE
V   NAME         USETYPE     KSTATE      STATE      LENGTH      READPOL   PREFPLEX
PL  NAME         VOLUME      KSTATE      STATE      LENGTH      LAYOUT    NCOL/WID MODE
SD  NAME         PLEX        DISK        DISKOFFS   LENGTH      [COL/]OFF DEVICEMODE

dg   rootdg     default    default    0          949521863.1026.ruby.alf.dec.com

dm   disk01      dsk7c      simple      4096       4106368-
dm   disk02      dsk10      sliced      4096       8375968-
dm   disk03      dsk11      sliced      4096       8375968-
dm   disk04      dsk35      sliced      4096       8375968-
dm   disk05      dsk33      sliced      4096       8375968-

v    voltest      fsgen            ENABLED   ACTIVE    304800    SELECT    -
pl   voltest-01   voltest          ENABLED   ACTIVE    304800    CONCAT    -    RW
sd   disk01-01    voltest-01   disk01    0         304800    0         dsk7cENA
```

```
# df -k /test
Filesystem     1024-blocks   Used    Available Capacity Mounted on
test_dmn#test  102400        27584   70576     29%       /test
```

```
# showfdmn test_dmn

Id    Date CreatedLogPgs Version   Domain Name
38c1436f.000d81adSat Mar4 12:10:07 20005124 test_dmn

Vol 512-Blks Free    % Used Cmode Rblks   Wblks   Vol Name
1L  204800   141152  31%    on    65536   65536   /dev/vol/rootdg/voltest
```

Example:

In this example, we grow a logical volume to the size 500,000 blocks using *volassist(8)*.

```
# volassist -f growto voltest 500000

# volprint -Aht
Disk group: rootdg
```

DG	NAME	NCONFIG	NLOG		MINORS	GROUP-ID			
DM	NAME	DEVICE	TYPE		PRIVLEN	PUBLEN	STATE		
V	NAME	USETYPE	KSTATE		STATE	LENGTH	READPOL	PREFPLEX	
PL	NAME	VOLUME	KSTATE		STATE	LENGTH	LAYOUT	NCOL/WID	MODE
SD	NAME	PLEX	DISK		DISKOFFS	LENGTH	[COL/]OFF	DEVICEMODE	
dg	rootdg	default	default	0	949521863.1026.ruby.alf.dec.com				
dm	disk01	dsk7c	simple	4096	4106368-				
dm	disk02	dsk10	sliced	4096	8375968-				
dm	disk03	dsk11	sliced	4096	8375968-				
dm	disk04	dsk35	sliced	4096	8375968-				
dm	disk05	dsk33	sliced	4096	8375968-				
v	voltest	fsgen	ENABLED		ACTIVE	500000	SELECT	-	
pl	voltest-01	voltest	ENABLED		ACTIVE	500000	CONCAT	-	RW
sd	disk01-01	voltest-01	disk01		0	500000	0	dsk7cENA	

```
# df -k /test
Filesystem      1024-blocks  Used     Available CapacityMounted on
test_dmn#test   102400       27584    70576     29%      /test
```

Example:

Here, we show how the voltest logical volume can be reduced in size using the shrinkby keyword for *volassist(8)*. Notice that the size of the file system on the volume is unaffected.

```
# volassist -f shrinkby voltest 120000

# volprint -Aht
Disk group: rootdg
```

DG	NAME	NCONFIG	NLOG		MINORS	GROUP-ID			
DM	NAME	DEVICE	TYPE		PRIVLEN	PUBLEN	STATE		
V	NAME	USETYPE	KSTATE		STATE	LENGTH	READPOL	PREFPLEX	
PL	NAME	VOLUME	KSTATE		STATE	LENGTH	LAYOUT	NCOL/WID	MODE
SD	NAME	PLEX	DISK		DISKOFFS	LENGTH	[COL/]OFF	DEVICEMODE	
dg	rootdg	default	default	0	949521863.1026.ruby.alf.dec.com				
dm	disk01	dsk7c	simple	4096	4106368-				
dm	disk02	dsk10	sliced	4096	8375968-				
dm	disk03	dsk11	sliced	4096	8375968-				
dm	disk04	dsk35	sliced	4096	8375968-				
dm	disk05	dsk33	sliced	4096	8375968-				
v	voltest	fsgen		ENABLED	ACTIVE	380000	SELECT	-	

```
pl  voltest-01    voltest        ENABLED     ACTIVE    380000      CONCAT    -    RW
sd  disk01-01     voltest-01     disk01      0         380000      0              dsk7cENA
# df -k /test
Filesystem        1024-blocks    Used        Available Capacity   Mounted on
test_dmn#test     102400         27584       70576     29%         /test
```

Example:

This is another example of how a logical volume can be reduced in size. This time, we use the shrinkto keyword to the *volassist(8)* command. Throughout all of these changes, the file system remains unchanged.

```
# volassist -f shrinkto voltest 204800

# volprint -Aht
Disk group: rootdg

                    DG NAMENCONFIGNLOGMINORSGROUP-ID
DM  NAME            DEVICE         TYPE        PRIVLEN   PUBLEN     STATE
V   NAME            USETYPE        KSTATE      STATE     LENGTH     READPOL   PREFPLEX
PL  NAME            VOLUME         KSTATE      STATE     LENGTH     LAYOUT    NCOL/WID MODE
SD  NAME            PLEX           DISK        DISKOFFS  LENGTH     [COL/]OFF DEVICEMODE

dg  rootdg          default        default     0         949521863.1026.ruby.alf.dec.com

dm  disk01          dsk7c          simple      4096      4106368    -
dm  disk02          dsk10          sliced      4096      8375968    -
dm  disk03          dsk11          sliced      4096      8375968    -
dm  disk04          dsk35          sliced      4096      8375968    -
dm  disk05          dsk33          sliced      4096      8375968    -

v                   voltest        fsgen       ENABLED   ACTIVE     204800SELECT-
pl                  voltest-01     voltest     ENABLED   ACTIVE     204800CONCAT-RW
sd                  disk01-01      voltest-01disk01      0          2048000dsk7cENA

# df -k /test
Filesystem        1024-blocks    Used        Available Capacity   Mounted on
test_dmn#test     102400         27584       70576     29%         /test
```

3.3.4   Keeping an Eye on Things

All by itself, you will find that the LSM will work reliably for a long time. Every so often, you come across a site where the customer has a mirrored volume, but one of the disks has failed and the customer was not aware of the problem. LSM simply did its job silently and only logged something in the log, but the system kept on running normally. The *volwatch(8)* and *volnotify(8)* facilities were specifically designed for those situations. They work together to inform you of events and problems that occur with LSM.

The *volwatch(8)* facility is a script that monitors the LSM, waiting for exception events to occur. It then sends an e-mail to the default user of root, or to those users specified on the command line.

The *volnotify(8)* command displays events related to disk and configuration changes, as managed by the LSM configuration daemon. *Volnotify(8)* displays requested event types until killed by a signal, until a given number of events have been received, or until a given number of seconds has passed.

3.3.5   Saving and Restoring LSM Configurations

One of the problems you may run into with the LSM is what to do if the configuration is lost. How do you get back the LSM configuration without making the situation worse by messing around with commands? The *volsave(8)* and *volrestore(8)* commands were designed to solve this problem. If you save your configuration ahead of time, using the *volsave(8)* command, then you can later use *volrestore(8)* to bring it back. These commands were first introduced with LSM in Tru64 UNIX version 4.0.

Example:

Here, we show the *volsave(8)* command in operation on a 4.0x system.

```
# volsave
LSM configuration being saved to /usr/var/lsm/db/LSM.20000307105432.jackson

LSM configuration saved successfully to /usr/var/lsm/db/LSM.20000307105432.jackson
# ls -lR /usr/var/lsm/db
total 8
dr-xr-x---   3 root system 8192 Mar 7 10:54 LSM.20000307105432.jackson

/usr/var/lsm/db/LSM.20000307105432.jackson:
total 11
-r--r-----   1 root system 231 Mar   7 10:54 header
dr-xr-x---   2 root system 8192 Mar 7 10:54 rootdg.d
-r--r-----   1 root system 512 Mar   7 10:54 volboot
-r--r-----   1 root system 699 Mar   7 10:54 voldisk.list

/usr/var/lsm/db/LSM.20000307105432.jackson/rootdg.d:
total 4
-r--r-----   1 root system 3823 Mar 7 10:54 allvol.DF
```

Example:

This example illustrates how to use *volrestore(8)* to find out information about the saved LSM configuration. This command is helpful if you want to verify the configuration you are planning to restore before you go about doing so.

```
# volrestore -l
LSM Configuration Save Utility Version 1.
Configuration Information stored in directory
/usr/var/lsm/db/LSM.20000307143011.jackson
```

```
Created at Tue Mar 7 14:30:17 EST 2000 on HOST jackson.alf.dec.com

LSM Configuration for Diskgroup rootdg.

dm  rz129       rz129       sliced      1024      17772484   /dev/rz129g
dm  rz130       rz130       sliced      1024      17772484   /dev/rz130g
dm  rz131       rz131       sliced      1024      17772484   /dev/rz131g
dm  rz132       rz132       sliced      1024      17772484   /dev/rz132g
dm  rz133       rz133       sliced      1024      8379040    /dev/rz133g
dm  rz2         rz2         sliced      1024      8379040    /dev/rz2g
dm  rz3         rz3         sliced      1024      2049820    /dev/rz3g
dm  rz6         rz6         sliced      1024      2049820    /dev/rz6g

v   volbig      fsgen       ENABLED     ACTIVE    91947656   SELECT-
pl  volbig-01   volbig      ENABLED     ACTIVE    91947656   CONCAT-RW
sd  rz129-01    volbig-01   0           0         17772484   rz129rz129
sd  rz130-01    volbig-01   17772484 0  17772484  rz130      rz130
sd  rz131-01    volbig-01   35544968 0  17772484  rz131      rz131
sd  rz132-01    volbig-01   53317452 0  17772484  rz132      rz132
sd  rz133-01    volbig-01   71089936 0  8379040   rz133      rz133
sd  rz2-01      volbig-01   79468976 0  8379040   rz2        rz2
sd  rz3-01      volbig-01   87848016 0  2049820   rz3        rz3
sd  rz6-01      volbig-01   89897836 0  2049820   rz6        rz6
```

Example:

This example shows how you can recover your Tru64 UNIX version 4.0x LSM configuration after having restored from a backup tape. Use *volsetup(8)* to initially set up LSM, then use *volrestore(8)* to get the old configuration back. The final step is to start the volumes. In this case, there is only one volume, which is easy-to-use *volume(8)*, but if you have a complicated setup, then you would probably want to use *volrecover(8)* to bring the volumes and plexes back to the ENABLED state.

```
# volsetup -o force rz2

Approximate maximum number of physical disks that will be managed by LSM ? [10]

Initialize vold and the root disk group:

Add disk rz2 to the root disk group as rz2:
Addition of disk rz2 as rz2 succeeded.

Initialization of vold and the root disk group was successful.

# volrestore

Using LSM configuration from /usr/var/lsm/db/LSM.20000308093919.jackson
Created at Wed Mar 8 09:39:21 EST 2000 on HOST jackson.alf.dec.com

Would you like to continue ? [y,n,q,?] (default: n) y

Working .

Restoring rootdg

Checking volbig
```

The following volumes in diskgroup rootdg cannot be
started. Refer to LSM documentation on how to set
the plex states before starting the volumes.

volbig

```
# volprint -Aht
Disk group: rootdg
```

DG	NAME	GROUP-ID					
DM	NAME	DEVICE	TYPE	PRIVLEN	PUBLEN	PUBPATH	
V	NAME	USETYPE	KSTATE	STATE	LENGTH	READPOL	PREFPLEX
PL	NAME	VOLUME	KSTATE	STATE	LENGTH	LAYOUT	ST-WIDTH MODE
SD	NAME	PLEX	PLOFFS	DISKOFFS	LENGTH	DISK-NAME DEVICE	
dg	rootdg	952525597.1025.jackson.alf.dec.com					
dm	rz2	rz2	sliced	1024	8379040	/dev/rrz2g	
dm	rz3	rz3	sliced	1024	2049820	/dev/rrz3g	
dm	rz6	rz6	sliced	1024	2049820	/dev/rrz6g	
v	volbig	fsgen	DISABLED	EMPTY	8379040	SELECT	-
pl	volbig-01	volbig	DISABLED	EMPTY	8379040	CONCAT	- RW
sd	rz2-01	volbig-01	0	0	8379040	rz2	rz2

```
# volume start volbig

# volprint -Aht
Disk group: rootdg
```

DG	NAME	GROUP-ID					
DM	NAME	DEVICE	TYPE	PRIVLEN	PUBLEN	PUBPATH	
V	NAME	USETYPE	KSTATE	STATE	LENGTH	READPOL	PREFPLEX
PL	NAME	VOLUME	KSTATE	STATE	LENGTH	LAYOUT	ST-WIDTH MODE
SD	NAME	PLEX	PLOFFS	DISKOFFS	LENGTH	DISK-NAME DEVICE	
dg	rootdg	952525597.1025.jackson.alf.dec.com					
dm	rz2	rz2	sliced	1024	8379040	/dev/rrz2g	
dm	rz3	rz3	sliced	1024	2049820	/dev/rrz3g	
dm	rz6	rz6	sliced	1024	2049820	/dev/rrz6g	
v	volbig	fsgen	ENABLED	ACTIVE	8379040	SELECT	-
pl	volbig-01	volbig	ENABLED	ACTIVE	8379040	CONCAT	- RW
sd	rz2-01	volbig-01	0	0	8379040	rz2	rz2

3.3.6   Changing Volume and Plex Attributes

The *voledit(8)* command is used to set or change the attributes for various
objects in LSM configuration records. Only those attributes that do not
depend on volume usage types can be modified with this utility. In particular, setting the length and logging type for a volume requires use of
the volume set operation.

The *volmend(8)* utility is used to correct some simple configuration record problems. You can perform certain usage-type-dependent operations on subdisks, plexes, and volumes.

The *volume(8)* command with the set keyword can be used for operations that can set attributes that depend on usage types. In particular, setting the length and logging type for a volume requires use of the volume set operation.

3.3.7 LSM Startup

Starting up LSM can happen in one of several ways that all start with the *lsmbstartup(8)* script. This script is called from inittab or *bcheckrc(8)* for starting LSM up at boot time, or you can use *lsmbstartup(8)* from the command line. Several other auxiliary scripts perform various functions in the startup process, which occur as follows:

- *bcheckrc(8):* As we discussed in Chapter 2, this main script checks and mounts all the file systems in the /etc/fstab. One of the things this script does is checks for the existence of the /etc/vol/volboot file. If that file exists, then the script checks that the mode of the vold daemon is "not-running." If so, then *bcheckrc(8)* executes *lsmbstartup(8).*

- *lsmbstartup(8):* This main LSM startup script is called from inittab or *bcheckrc(8).* It is mainly just a front-end for the vol-startup script. It performs some checks to make sure LSM is not already running and so forth. The last thing it does is call *vol-startup.*

- *vol-startup:* This script performs a few more checks. It makes sure voliod and vold exist and are executable programs. Then, the script enables the vold daemon, and if the mode is changed to "enabled," it runs a *volrecover(8)* to enable any stale plexes in the background.

- *volstartup(8):* This script is used on the command line to start or restart the vold and voliod daemons. We believe the preferred method for starting up LSM is by using *lsmbstartup(8).*

- *vol-reconfig:* This script checks to see if any encapsulations are pending, and if so, executes them on boot. It runs out of the inittab file.

The following /etc/inittab entries are important to starting up LSM properly. They must be listed in the correct sequence as shown or you may experience strange problems:

```
lsmr:s:sysinit:/sbin/lsmbstartup -b </dev/console >/dev/console 2>&1 ##LSM
lsm:23:wait:/sbin/lsmbstartup -n </dev/console >/dev/console 2>&1 ##LSM
vol:23:wait:/sbin/vol-reconfig </dev/console >/dev/console 2>&1 ##LSM
fs:23:wait:/sbin/bcheckrc < /dev/console > /dev/console 2>&1
```

If you wish to work with LSM in single-user mode, then you can either execute *bcheckrc(8)* or *lsmbstartup(8)* directly from the command-line prompt. Which method you choose depends on your goals. If you are simply trying to get all the local file systems mounted and some of them are using LSM volumes, then just use *bcheckrc(8)*; however, if you just want LSM started and no file systems, or selective file systems, you'll want to use *lsmbstartup(8)* first. This command is handy for trouble-shooting file systems problems in single-user mode.

3.4   Undocumented *volprivutil(8)* Tool

One difficulty with troubleshooting LSM is that most of the tools for gathering useful information simply do not work unless the vold is running. There will be times when either the daemon cannot start, or it has become hung and you need to get some information. The *volprivutil(8)* utility is an undocumented command that can be useful. It has several different keywords that allow it to give information about a disk or to change disk access records in the configuration database. The *volprivutil(8)* command can also read a copy of the private region from a disk that was copied using *dd(1)* on another system.

4.0x Syntax:

```
volprivutil scan device-pathname
volprivutil list device-pathname
volprivutil set device-pathname attribute ...
volprivutil dumplog device-pathname [copy]
volprivutil [-cf] dumpconfig device-pathname [copy]
```

5.0x Syntax:

```
volprivutil [-o privoffset] scan device-pathname
volprivutil [-o privoffset] list device-pathname
volprivutil [-o privoffset] set device-pathname attribute ...
volprivutil [-o poffs] [-1] dumplog device-pathname [copy-number]
volprivutil [-o poffs] [-cf] [-C path-to-voldump] dumpconfig
device-pathname [copy-number]
```

TABLE 3–9   Keywords for the *volprivutil(8)* Command

KEYWORD	DESCRIPTION
scan	Scans the private region for information and prints it out. Similar to the list keyword but with slightly different output.
list	Lists the contents of the private region in much the same way and with the same output format that voldisk list uses.

TABLE 3–9   Keywords for the *volprivutil(8)* Command (Continued)

KEYWORD	DESCRIPTION
set	Sets an attribute value to a specific value. This is dangerous and should be used with caution.
dumplog	Reads a disk kernel log and prints out the entries. It will print the first copy by default.
dumpconfig	Reads a disk configuration copy and prints out the entries. It will print the first copy by default.

Example:

This example shows how you can list the contents of a disk's private region on a 4.0x system using *volprivutil(8)*.

```
# /usr/sbin/volprivutil list /dev/rrz2h
hostid:jackson.alf.dec.com
diskid:952525598.1028.jackson.alf.dec.com
group:name=rootdg id=952525597.1025.jackson.alf.dec.com
version: 1.1
iosize:512
public:slice=6 offset=16 len=8379040
private: slice=7 offset=0 len=1024
update:time: 952546346seqno: 0.7
headers: 0 248
configs: count=1 len=726
logs:count=1 len=110
tocblks: 0
tocs:1/1023
Defined regions:
configpriv17-247[231]: copy=01 offset=000000
configpriv249-743[495]: copy=01 offset=000231
logpriv744-853[110]: copy=01 offset=000000
```

Example:

This example shows how you can list the contents of a disk's private region on a 5.0x system using *volprivutil(8)*.

```
# /usr/lib/lsm/bin/volprivutil list /dev/rdisk/dsk10h
diskid:951332577.1398.ruby.alf.dec.com
group:name=rootdg id=949521863.1026.ruby.alf.dec.com
flags:private autoimport
hostid:ruby.alf.dec.com
version: 2.1
iosize:512
public:slice=6 offset=16 len=8375968
private: slice=7 offset=0 len=4096
update:time: 951404365seqno: 0.7
headers: 0 248
configs: count=1 len=2993
logs:count=1 len=453
```

```
tocblks: 0
tocs:1/4095
Defined regions:
config priv  17-    247[ 231]: copy=01 offset=000000 enabled
config priv  249-  3010[2762]: copy=01 offset=000231 enabled
log     priv 3011- 3463[453]: copy=01 offset=000000 enabled
```

Example:

This example shows how to use the "dumpconfig" keyword to obtain formatted records from the first configuration copy of the private region on a disk.

```
# /usr/lib/lsm/bin/volprivutil dumpconfig /dev/rdisk/dsk10h
#Config copy 01

#Header nblocks=11972 blksize=128 hdrsize=512
#flags=0x100 (CLEAN)
#version: 4/1
#dgname: rootdg dgid: 949521863.1026.ruby.alf.dec.com
#config: tid=0.1798 nvol=1 nplex=1 nsd=1 ndm=5 nda=4
#pending: tid=0.1798 nvol=1 nplex=1 nsd=1 ndm=5 nda=4
#
#Block    4: flag=# x ref=0  offset=1     frag_size=0
#Block    5: flag=# x ref=0  offset=2     frag_size=0
#Block    6: flag=# x ref=0  offset=3     frag_size=0
#Block    7: flag=# x ref=0  offset=741   frag_size=0
#Block    8: flag=# x ref=0  offset=6     frag_size=0
#Block   10: flag=# x ref=0  offset=721   frag_size=0
#Block   11: flag=# x ref=0  offset=256   frag_size=0
#Block   12: flag=# x ref=0  offset=742   frag_size=0
#Block   14: flag=# x ref=0  offset=663   frag_size=0
#Block   16: flag=# x ref=0  offset=743   frag_size=0
#Block   18: flag=# x ref=0  offset=549   frag_size=0
#Block   19: flag=# x ref=0  offset=664   frag_size=0
#Block   21: flag=# x ref=0  offset=666   frag_size=0
#
#Record  1: type=#  x flags=# x gen_flags=# x size=43
#Blocks: 4
dadsk7c
 comment="
 type=simple
 info="privoffset=16
 rid=0.1067
 online=on
 update_tid=0.1068
#Record 2: type=#    x flags=# x gen_flags=# x size=58
#Blocks: 5
dgrootdg
 comment="
 putil0="
 putil1="
 putil2="
 dgid=949521863.1026.ruby.alf.dec.com
```

```
                  rid=0.1025
                  update_tid=0.1026
                  nconfig=default
                  nlog=default
                  base_minor=0
#Record 3: type=#    x flags=# x gen_flags=# x size=30
#Blocks: 6
dadsk10
 comment="
 type=sliced
 info="
 rid=0.1400
 online=on
 update_tid=0.1401
#Record 6: type=#    x flags=# x gen_flags=# x size=30
#Blocks: 8
dadsk11
 comment="
 type=sliced
 info="
 rid=0.1407
 online=on
 update_tid=0.1408
#Record 256: type=# x flags=# x gen_flags=# x size=30
#Blocks: 11
dadsk33
 comment="
 type=sliced
 info="
 rid=0.1569
 online=on
 update_tid=0.1570
#Record 741: type=# x flags=# x gen_flags=# x size=77
#Blocks: 7
volvoltest
 use_type=fsgen
 fstype="AdvFS
 comment="
 putil0="
 putil1="
 putil2="
 state="ACTIVE
 writeback=on
 writecopy=off
 specify_writecopy=off
 pl_num=1
 start_opts="
 read_pol=SELECT
 minor=5
 user=root
 group=system
 mode=0600
 log_type=REGION
 len=204800
```

```
                log_len=0
                update_tid=0.1798
                rid=0.1742
                detach_tid=0.0
                active=off
                forceminor=off
                badlog=off
                recover_checkpoint=0
                sd_num=0
                sdnum=0
                kdetach=off
                storage=off
                applrecov=off
                recover_seqno=0
               #Record 742: type=# x flags=# x gen_flags=# x size=52
               #Blocks: 12
               plex voltest-01
                comment="
                putil0="
                putil1="
                putil2="
                layout=CONCAT
                sd_num=1
                state="ACTIVE
                update_tid=0.1798
                rid=0.1744
                vol_rid=0.1742
                detach_tid=0.0
                noerror=off
                kdetach=off
                stale=off
                ncolumn=0
               #Record 743: type=# x flags=# x gen_flags=# x size=59
               #Blocks: 16
               sddisk01-01
                comment="
                putil0="
                putil1="
                putil2="
                dm_offset=0
                pl_offset=0
                len=204800
                update_tid=0.1798
                rid=0.1746
                plex_rid=0.1744
                dm_rid=0.1080
                minor=1048575
                detach_tid=0.0
                column=0
                mkdevice=off
                subvolume=off
                stale=off
                kdetach=off
                relocate=off
```

```
#Record 549: type=#  x flags=#  x gen_flags=#  x size=64
#Blocks: 18
dmdisk05
 comment="
 putil0="
 putil1="
 putil2="
 diskid=951756807.1567.ruby.alf.dec.com
 last_da_name=dsk33
 rid=0.1571
 removed=off
 spare=off
 failing=off
 update_tid=0.1716
#Record 663: type=#  x flags=#  x gen_flags=#  x size=64
#Blocks: 14
dmdisk04
 comment="
 putil0="
 putil1="
 putil2="
 diskid=949592467.1096.ruby.alf.dec.com
 last_da_name=dsk35
 rid=0.1460
 removed=off
 spare=off
 failing=off
 update_tid=0.1769
#Record 664: type=#  x flags=#  x gen_flags=#  x size=64
#Blocks: 19
dmdisk01
 comment="
 putil0="
 putil1="
 putil2="
 diskid=949592023.1065.ruby.alf.dec.com
 last_da_name=dsk7c
 rid=0.1080
 removed=off
 spare=off
 failing=off
 update_tid=0.1769
#Record 666: type=#  x flags=#  x gen_flags=#  x size=64
#Blocks: 21
dmdisk03
 comment="
 putil0="
 putil1="
 putil2="
 diskid=951332637.1405.ruby.alf.dec.com
 last_da_name=dsk11
 rid=0.1409
 removed=off
 spare=off
```

```
failing=off
update_tid=0.1769
#Record 721: type=# x flags=# x gen_flags=# x size=64
#Blocks: 10
dmdisk02
 comment="
 putil0="
 putil1="
 putil2="
 diskid=951332577.1398.ruby.alf.dec.com
 last_da_name=dsk10
 rid=0.1402
 removed=off
 spare=off
 failing=off
 update_tid=0.1794
```

Example:

Here is an example that shows how you can dump out the log information for an LSM disk using *volprivutil(8)*.

```
# /usr/lib/lsm/bin/volprivutil dumplog /dev/rdisk/dsk10h
LOG #01
BLOCK 0: KLOG 0 : COMMIT tid=0.1797
BLOCK 0: KLOG 1 : DIRTY rid=0.1742

# /usr/lib/lsm/bin/volprivutil -l dumplog /dev/rdisk/dsk10h
LOG #01
#BLOCK 0: tid=0.0 seqno=3 (len=453)
BLOCK 0: KLOG 0 : COMMIT tid=0.1797
BLOCK 0: KLOG 1 : DIRTY rid=0.1742
#BLOCK  1: tid=0.0 seqno=0 (len=453)
#BLOCK  2: tid=0.0 seqno=0 (len=453)
#BLOCK  3: tid=0.0 seqno=0 (len=453)
#BLOCK  4: tid=0.0 seqno=0 (len=453)
#BLOCK  5: tid=0.0 seqno=0 (len=453)
#BLOCK  6: tid=0.0 seqno=0 (len=453)
#BLOCK  7: tid=0.0 seqno=0 (len=453)
#BLOCK  8: tid=0.0 seqno=0 (len=453)
#BLOCK  9: tid=0.0 seqno=0 (len=453)
#BLOCK 10: tid=0.0 seqno=0 (len=453)
#BLOCK 11: tid=0.0 seqno=0 (len=453)
#BLOCK 12: tid=0.0 seqno=0 (len=453)

[snip]

#BLOCK 124: tid=0.0 seqno=0 (len=453)
#BLOCK 125: tid=0.0 seqno=0 (len=453)
#BLOCK 126: tid=0.0 seqno=0 (len=453)
#BLOCK 127: tid=0.0 seqno=0 (len=453)
```

3.5   Tuning LSM

Tuning LSM can be tricky business. Most of the time, the performance issues can be corrected either at the file system level or the device level. Tuning the LSM involves monitoring the performance of your configuration and making corrections as needed. The best tool for monitoring the performance of the LSM configuration is the *volstat(8)* command, which we discuss in greater detail in this section. We also cover how to configure your system for better mirror synchronization performance. Finally, we discuss a new feature called enhanced round-robin scheduling, which you can use to improve mirrored read performance.

3.5.1   The *volstat(8)* Tool

The *volstat(8)* tool is useful for determining how the LSM volumes are performing under loaded environment. We find that in situations where LSM is involved, *volstat(8)* eclipses *iostat(8)* for useful I/O information.

Syntax:

```
volstat [-g diskgroup] [-i interval] [-c count] [-f format][-r] [-psvd] [object...]
```

TABLE 3–10   Flags for the *volstat(8)* Command

FLAG	DESCRIPTION
object	The LSM object about which to gather statistics.
-g diskgroup	Specifies the LSM disk group we wish to examine.
-i interval	Specifies the time interval in seconds between which to print volume statistics.
-c count	Specifies the number of intervals for which to print statistics.
-f format	Specifies the format for the desired statistics. The default format is "s."
s	Prints information about reads and writes.
a	Prints information about atomic operations performed (for mirrored volumes only).
v	Prints information about verified reads and writes (for mirrored volumes only).
c	Prints information about corrected reads and writes (for mirrored and RAID 5 volumes only).
f	Prints information about failed reads and writes.
b	Prints information about read-writeback mirror consistency recovery operations (for mirrored volumes only).
F	Prints information about full-stripe writes (for RAID5 volumes only).

TABLE 3–10   Flags for the *volstat(8)* Command (Continued)

FLAG		DESCRIPTION
	M	Print information about read-modify-writes.
	W	Prints information about reconstruct writes.
	R	Prints information about reconstruct reads.
	O	Prints information about VOL_R5_ZERO operations.
	S	Prints information about VOL_R5_RESYNC operations.
	C	Prints information about VOL_R5_RECOVER operations.
	V	Prints information about VOL_R5_VERIFY operations.
-r		Resets counters instead of printing statistics.
-p		Displays information for plexes associated with the specified object.
-s		Displays information for the subdisks associated with the specified object.
-v		Displays information for volumes associated with the specified object.
-d		Displays information for the disks associated with the specified object.

Example:

This example is an illustration of using *volstat(8)* to monitor a logical volume while the UFS on it is in the process of being restored from a backup tape. In this case, the writes dominate the reads.

```
# volstat -i 5 -c 10
                             OPERATIONS       BLOCKS      AVG TIME(ms)
 TYP NAME                    READ  WRITE   READ    WRITE   READ  WRITE
 Wed Mar  8 22:43:38 2000
 vol volbig                   281  10490   3748   410129    7.7  644.9

 Wed Mar  8 22:43:43 2000
 vol volbig                     0    183      0     3654    0.0  714.4

 Wed Mar  8 22:43:48 2000
 vol volbig                     0     14      0     1792    0.0   22.6

 Wed Mar  8 22:43:53 2000
 vol volbig                     0     13      0     1664    0.0   26.7

 Wed Mar  8 22:43:58 2000
 vol volbig                     0     14      0     1792    0.0   26.2

 Wed Mar  8 22:44:03 2000
 vol volbig                     0     13      0     1664    0.0   30.0

 Wed Mar  8 22:44:08 2000
 vol volbig                     0     18      0     1744    0.0   33.5
```

```
Wed Mar   8 22:44:13 2000
vol volbig                          0      13      0     1524   0.0    32.8

Wed Mar   8 22:44:18 2000
vol volbig                          0      19      0     2432   0.0    25.3

Wed Mar   8 22:44:23 2000
vol volbig                          0      20      0     2560   0.0    21.3
```

Example:

This example shows how to use *volstat(8)* to monitor a logical volume while the UFS file system on it is relatively busy.

```
# volstat -i 5 -c 10 volsmall
                        OPERATIONS        BLOCKS        AVG TIME(ms)
TYP NAME               READ  WRITE     READ    WRITE    READ   WRITE

Thu Mar   9 22:50:57 2000
vol volsmall            685  29009     6687   281927    22.9    23.5

Thu Mar   9 22:51:02 2000
vol volsmall            322    338      322     3042    15.5    28.8

Thu Mar   9 22:51:07 2000
vol volsmall            346    374      346     3374    14.3    26.5

Thu Mar   9 22:51:12 2000
vol volsmall            320    355      320     3202    15.5    27.8

Thu Mar   9 22:51:17 2000
vol volsmall            358    371      358     3318    13.9    26.4

Thu Mar   9 22:51:22 2000
vol volsmall            358    342      358     3092    13.9    25.7

Thu Mar   9 22:51:27 2000
vol volsmall            358    340      358     3060    13.9    28.9

Thu Mar   9 22:51:32 2000
vol volsmall            310    337      310     3040    16.0    26.1

Thu Mar   9 22:51:37 2000
vol volsmall            318    336      318     3012    15.7    30.4

Thu Mar   9 22:51:42 2000
vol volsmall            326    331      326     2986    15.2    29.8
```

Example:

Here, we illustrate how you can reset the *volstat(8)* counters and then use *volstat(8)* to examine the disk statistics. These statistics can be helpful for determining which disks are busy and which aren't. We can also see how an individual disk is performing. In this case, we realize that we are doing a lot more reads than writes to the disk on average. Mirroring the disk can help improve the overall performance of the application.

```
# volstat -r
# volstat -d
                OPERATIONS        BLOCKS         AVG TIME(ms)
TYP NAME       READ  WRITE    READ  WRITE      READ   WRITE
dm rz2          48      1     6144     16      68.5    11.7
dm rz3           0      0        0      0       0.0     0.0
dm rz6           0      0        0      0       0.0     0.0
```

We really haven't begun to scratch the surface of what the *volstat(8)* command is capable of doing. We can't possibly cover it all here. Therefore, you will have to look over the options and determine through experimentation what data gathering you need. After the data-gathering phase is complete, you can determine how you can tune the configuration to improve performance.

3.5.2 Improving Mirror Synchronization Performance

One way to improve performance of the LSM mirror resynchronization is by implementing a logging feature. The one you choose will be based on the version of Tru64 UNIX you are running. In version 4.0x, we have block change logging (BCL), and in 5.0, the concept of dirty region logging (DRL) was introduced. Each logging feature is designed to reduce mirrored volume synchronization time. We describe the features of each in the following sections.

3.5.2.1 Block Change Logging

- During a write to a mirrored volume, the changes are logged on a per-block basis in the block change log.

- When an I/O is complete, the entry is flushed from the log.

- After a crash, only changed blocks need to be resynchronized instead of the entire volume.

- Write performance can be impacted if the log becomes full. Some pending I/Os must complete so it can release the log space before more writes can occur.

3.5.2.2 Dirty Region Logging

- Enables fast mirror recovery after a failure with little impact to write performance.

- During a write to a mirrored volume, the appropriate region(s) in the volume is marked as "dirty" in its dirty region log.

■ After a crash, only the "dirty regions" within the volume need to be resynchronized or recovered instead of the entire volume.

3.5.2.3 BCL vs. DRL

■ DRL logs mirrored-writes when the region has not already been logged as dirty. Reduces logging overhead while still providing fast mirroring recovery.

■ DRL associates an additional plex (logging plex) with the volume. You can associate logging subdisks instead (similar to BCL).

■ When upgrading from 4.0x to 5.0, the two formats are not compatible. Therefore, only a BCL of two or more blocks will automatically be converted. BCL of one block requires a manual process to convert.

DRL performance improvement can be striking. Tests performed with random 8 kilobyte writes to 24 gigabyte mirrored volume, with each plex being three-way striped and a default log size of 26 blocks, have shown that resynchronization drops from more than 170 minutes to a little more than 30 seconds. Keep in mind that performance of other I/O-intensive activities will be severely impacted until the resynchronization is complete. Based on this data, the case for using DRL is clear.

3.5.3 Enhanced Round-Robin Scheduling

The goal of this Tru64 UNIX 5.0 enhancement[1] is to increase the performance of sequential reads by taking advantage of disk read-ahead cache. This performance enhancement introduces a new round-robin mode, whereby the difference between the last block read and the next block to read is compared to a new tunable parameterlsm_V_ROUND_enhance_proximity. If the difference is less than or equal to the parameter, then we read from the same plex. This enhancement is an attempt by the LSM software to take advantage of disk caching and increasing the chance that the block will result in a cache hit. The result should be improved sequential read performance. The two new tunable parameters added by this enhancement are:

■ lsm_V_ROUND_enhanced: This variable activates the new enhanced round-robin read policy if it is set to 1 (TRUE).Otherwise, the policy is deactivated. The default value is 1 (TRUE).

■ lsm_V_ROUND_enhance_proximity: This variable provides the proximity in which the last read and new read most lie in an attempt to read data from the disk's cache by reading from the same plex. The variable can be adjusted from 0 to 4096. The default value for this parameter is 512.

Testing has shown that by implementing this enhanced round-robin algorithm, and appropriately tuning the proximity value, you can come close to reaching the performance of the preferred plex algorithm with sequential reads. The test results show that the improvement can come close to 10 percent. Naturally, your own mileage may vary.

You can set up your own test for both round-robin and preferred plex settings of a mirrored LSM volume using commands similar to the following:

```
# volstat -r
# time dd if=/dev/rvol/rootdg/vol01 of=/dev/null bs=512k&
# volstat -i 1 -vd vol01
```

In this way, you can test different values for the proximity parameter in your own environment and see if you get a performance improvement. Even better would be to use your own application instead of *dd(1)*.

3.6   Summary

Simply put, troubleshooting the LSM is an art. It simply cannot always be scientifically explained why some people appear to have "the touch" in this area and others obviously don't. Clearly, after many years of experience working with this product, this is the case. Some people can work magic and clear up any problem with LSM. They simply know the product so well that they can make it do anything they need it to do. Those people are the very few LSM wizards, and if you aren't one of them, then you want to be talking to one when something goes wrong. In their hands, you will be assured that you will not lose data. In this chapter, we have attempted to give you some insight into their knowledge.

At this point, we begin our in-depth discussion of the major file systems in the following chapters.

Notes

1.   This enhancement has been included in some 4.0x releases and is available for others by patch kit.

4

Tru64 UNIX File Systems Architecture

> It takes considerable knowledge just
> to realize the extent of your own ignorance.
> — *Thomas Sowell*

Up to this point, we have discussed primarily the storage subsystem and Logical Storage Manager layers. In this chapter, we cover the design of the Tru64 UNIX file system, the layer that sits between the user level and each supported file system type.

We begin by covering the virtual file system, including the structures and operations defined by this standard. Next, we give details of the caches that Tru64 UNIX employs to assist with speeding up access to the file systems. Finally, we finish up this chapter with a discussion of the system call interface and the most common system calls used for file I/O.

4.1   Introduction

As we stated previously, Tru64 UNIX supports many different types of file systems. In this chapter, we describe how this is accomplished internally by the operating system. The virtual file system (VFS) is a layer that exists between the user layer and each supported type of file system. This layer of abstraction offers a great deal of power to the user. A user layer program does not need to understand the details of how to write a file for example, but only how to use the *write(2)* system call. As long as the system call conforms to the POSIX.1 standard, the program will be completely portable between any file system type that supports the semantic. Naturally, the *write(2)* will fail on a file system type that doesn't support that function. One such example might be the compact disc read-only memory file system (CDFS). Because CDFS is always read-only, it can never be made to perform that function.

Among the standards that Tru64 UNIX conforms to is the Institute of Electrical and Electronics Engineers (IEEE) standard 1003.1-1990 (operating system interface). This standard is more commonly referred to as POSIX.1 (IEEE 1990).[1] It defines a set of interfaces to the operating system known as functions. Because the standard defines interfaces rather than implementation, no distinction is made between system calls and library functions. Thus, this chapter is really a discussion of how Tru64 UNIX implements its conformity to the POSIX.1 standard.

4.2   The Virtual File System

The **virtual file system (VFS)** was first proposed back in the mid-1980s in a paper by S. R. Kleinman of Sun Microsystems (Kleinman 1986) as a mechanism for supporting simultaneous file systems types on a single UNIX system. The concept was key to Sun's design for the network file system (NFS), which allowed data to be easily shared among a group of computers. Prior to that time, UNIX systems had a direct, monolithic interface to the inode as described by Maurice J. Bach (Bach 1986). This made it difficult to plug in any new file system types and support them simultaneously. Subsequently, the VFS interface was modified and expanded in the UNIX community, so that today it is difficult to find a UNIX implementation that does not support it[2]; Tru64 UNIX is no exception.

The two main internal structures used to support VFS are the virtual inode and the mount table. Each of these structures and the set of VFS operations that can be performed on them are discussed in the following sections.

4.2.1   The Virtual Node

The **vnode**, or virtual node, is an in-memory data structure used in the implementation of the VFS to refer to an open file (an in-memory inode for UFS). As previously stated, the vnode allows the VFS in the Tru64 UNIX system to support multiple file system types such as UFS, AdvFS, CDFS, and NFS. The primary data structure used by the VFS for accessing files is the vnode structure.

The vnode structure consists of two basic sections, as shown in Figure 4–1. First is the file system–independent portion, which contains information such as the reference count for this vnode and the type of file to which this vnode refers. The definition of this information is contained in the include file <sys/vnode.h>. The second section of the vnode information is the file system–dependent portion. This part is appended to the end of the vnode structure and can be referenced by the address of its v_data field. For example, the file system–dependent part for UFS is the inode, for AdvFS it is called the BfNode, and for NFS it is the rnode. Table 4-1 provides a complete list of the fields in the vnode structure.

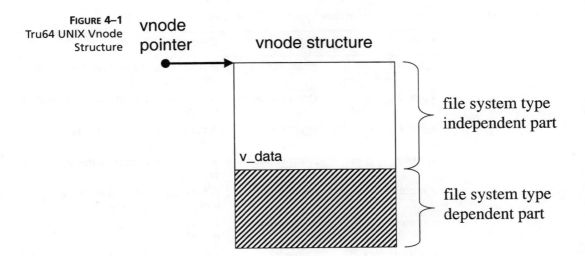

FIGURE **4–1**
Tru64 UNIX Vnode
Structure

The following example illustrates how to examine a vnode using the kernel debugger.

TABLE **4–1**   The Fields in the vnode Structure

FIELD	DATA TYPE	DESCRIPTION
v_lock	simple_lock	A simple lock ensuring multiprocessor exclusion for access to this vnode
v_flag	u_int	The vnode flags (i.e., VROOT). See Table 4–2 for a complete list of flags.
v_usecount	uint_t	Reference count indicating the number of users of this vnode
v_holdcnt	int	Page and buffer references
v_aux_lockers	u_int	Semaphore. Zero if free
v_shlockc	u_short	Count of shared locks
v_exlockc	u_short	Count of exclusive locks
v_lastr	off_t	Last read (read ahead)
v_id	u_long	Capability identifier
v_type	vtype	The vnode type. The possible values are: VNON, VREG, VDIR, VBLK, VCHR, VLNK, VSOCK, VFIFO, VBAD
v_tag	vtagtype	Type of the file system–specific portion of the vnode. The possible values are: VT_NON, VT_UFS, VT_NFS, VT_MFS, VT_S5FS, VT_CDFS, VT_DFS, VT_EFS, VT_PRFS, VT_MSFS, VT_FFM, VT_FDFS, VT_ADDON, VT_DVDFS

TABLE 4–1   The Fields in the vnode Structure (Continued)

FIELD	DATA TYPE	DESCRIPTION
v_mount	struct mount*	A pointer to the mount structure to which this vnode belongs
v_op	struct vnodeops*	A pointer to the set of valid operations for this vnode
v_freef	struct vnode*	A forward pointer to the list of free vnodes
v_freeb	struct vnode*	A backward pointer to the list of free vnodes
v_mountf	struct vnode*	A forward pointer to the list of mounted file systems
v_mountb	struct vnode**	A backward pointer to the list of mounted file systems
v_buflists_lock	simple lock	A simple lock protecting the clean and dirty block list heads
v_cleanblkhd	struct buf *	A pointer to the head of the clean block list
v_dirtyblkhd	struct buf*	A pointer to the head of the dirty block list
v_ncache_time	u_int	A timestamp indicating the last cache activity
v_free_time	u_int	A timestamp indicating the time this vnode is on the free list
v_output_lock	simple lock	A simple lock protecting the v_numoutput and v_outflag fields
v_numoutput	int	The number of writes that are in progress
v_outflag	u_int	The output flags
v_cache_lookup_refs	u_int	The number of cache lookup references
v_rdcnt	u_short	The count of readers
v_wrcnt	u_short	The count of writers
v_mountedhere	struct mount*	Pointer to the mounted VFS
v_un vu_socket	struct socket*	A UNIX IPC socket pointer
v_un vu_specinfo	struct specinfo*	A device specinfo structure pointer
v_un vu_fifonode	struct fifonode*	A pipe and fifo structure pointer
v_object	struct vm_ubc_object*	Virtual memory object used for this vnode
v_secattr	secinfo_t*	The security attributes of this vnode
v_data	v_data[1]	A placeholder for the file system–specific data

Table 4–2 Possible Values for the v_flags Field in the vnode Structure

Flag	Value	Description
VROOT	0x0001	This vnode refers to the root of its file system.
VTEXT	0x0002	This vnode references a pure text prototype. This flag is obsolete.
VXLOCK	0x0004	This vnode is locked in order to change its underlying type.
VXWANT	0x0008	A process is waiting for this vnode.
VEXLOCK	0x0010	The v_lock is an exclusive lock.
VSHLOCK	0x0020	The v_lock is a shared lock.
VLWAIT	0x0040	A process is waiting on shared or exclusive lock.
VXFSYNCING	0x0080	This vnode is being fsynced. In Tru64 UNIX 5.0a, this flag has been removed.
VMOUNTPOINT	0x0100	A file system is or will soon be mounted on this directory.
VINACTIVATING	0x0200	A vnode release (vrele) is in progress on this object.
VFLOCK	0x0400	This vnode is locked for first fifo open.
VFWAIT	0x0800	A process is waiting for fifo open.
VSYSTEM	0x1000	This vnode is being used by the kernel.
VENF_LOCK	0x2000	Mandatory file locking is enabled for this vnode.
VLOCKS	0x4000	An fcntl file locks exist on this file.
VSWAP	0x8000	Swapping is allowed for this vnode.
VCOBJECT	0x10000	Creating vnode object.
VCWAIT	0x20000	Waiting for create to complete.
V_PRIVATE	0x40000	Private DFS vnode; don't place on free chain.
V_CONVERTED	0x80000	Vnode has been converted for VFS+ usage.
V_AUD_VALID	0x100000	V_AUD_SELECT and V_AUD_SELECT bits are valid.
VIOERROR	0x200000	A write error has occurred on the file referenced by this vnode.
VNEEDRECLAIM	0x400000	The revoke/clearalias routine has been called on this vnode. This flag was removed in Tru64 UNIX 5.0A and is superceded by VREVOKED below.
V_AUD_SELECT	0x800000	This vnode object is selected for data access auditing.
V_AUD_DESELECT	0x1000000	This vnode object is bypassed for data access auditing.

TABLE 4–2   Possible Values for the v_flags Field in the vnode Structure (Continued)

FLAG	VALUE	DESCRIPTION
VREVOKED	0x8000000	This vnode has been revoked by clearalias.
VMLD	0x10000000	Vnode is a multilevel directory.
VXENIX	0x20000000	Xenix file locks on file (only valid for i386).
VDUP	0x40000000	Duplicate this vnode on *open(2)*. Normally used for the File Descriptor File System (FDFS).
VCOVERED	0x80000000	This is a CFS flag, specifying that the vnode is covered.

Example:

This example shows how to examine a vnode on a Tru64 UNIX system using the kernel debugger, *kdbx(8)*. For purposes of this example, we assume that the kernel space address we are using is valid. The goal here was simply to give an example of how to examine both the file system–independent information and then based on that, the file system–dependent portions of a vnode. This technique is helpful for troubleshooting a problem on a running system or for examining a crash dump. In either case, we would be looking for a problem or inconsistency with the data.

```
(kdbx) p *(struct vnode *)0xfffffc01cfe12000
struct {
  v_lock = struct {
    sl_data = 0x4b945c
    sl_info = 0x0
    sl_cpuid = 0x0
    sl_lifms = 0x0
  }
  v_flag = 0x100        ⇐ a VMOUNTPOINT – See Table 4–2
  v_usecount = 0x1
  v_aux_lockers = 0x0
  v_shlockc = 0x0
  v_exlockc = 0x0
  v_lastr = 0xffffffffffffffff
  v_id = 0x31f6
  v_type = VDIR          ⇐ this vnode points to a directory – See Table 4–1
  v_tag = VT_UFS         ⇐ and it is a UFS – See Table 4–1
  v_mount = 0xfffffc01cf7ac8c0
  v_op = 0xfffffc000066a030
  v_freef = (nil)
  v_freeb = (nil)
  v_mountf = 0xfffffc01cfb83e00
  v_mountb = 0xfffffc01cfe12250
  v_buflists_lock = struct {
    sl_data = 0x4b20ec
    sl_info = 0x0
    sl_cpuid = 0x0
```

```
      sl_lifms = 0x0
  }
  v_cleanblkhd = 0xfffffc00015c3e88
  v_dirtyblkhd = (nil)
  v_ncache_time = 0xbd42e
  v_free_time = 0x1f4
  v_output_lock = struct {
    sl_data = 0x4b834c
    sl_info = 0x0
    sl_cpuid = 0x0
    sl_lifms = 0x0
  }
  v_numoutput = 0x0
  v_outflag = 0x0
  v_cache_lookup_refs = 0x1
  v_rdcnt = 0x0
  v_wrcnt = 0x0
  v_mountedhere = 0xfffffc01d2832500
  v_un = union {
    vu_socket = (nil)
    vu_specinfo = (nil)
    vu_fifonode = (nil)
  }
  v_object = (nil)
  v_secattr = (nil)
  v_data = "¨"
}
```

From this information, we know a few things about the file that this vnode is referencing. First, because of the v_tag field, we see that this file resides on a UFS from the VT_UFS value. Second, we see that this is a directory file from the v_type field, which is VDIR. Also, this is a mount point directory because the v_flag field has the VMOUNTPOINT flag set. Given this information, we can format the address of the v_data field as an in-memory inode, and we obtain the following:

```
(kdbx) p *(struct inode *)&(*(struct vnode
*)0xfffffc01cfe12000).v_data
struct {
  i_chain = {
    [0] 0xfffffc00002180a8
    [1] 0xfffffc01d2bd72b8
  }
  i_vnode = 0xfffffc01cfe12000    ⇐ this should be the vnode address
                                    we started with

  i_devvp = 0xfffffc01ff542e00
  i_flag = 0x0
  i_dev = 0x2800000
  i_number = 0xa780
  i_fs = 0xfffffffe00a1b000
  i_diroff = 0x0
  i_endoff = 0x0
  i_dirstamp = 0x0
```

```
i_din = struct {
  di_mode = 0x41ed
  di_nlink = 0x2
  di_uid = 0x0
  di_gid = 0x0
  di_qsize = 0x200
  di_atime = 0x336c136b
  di_atspare = 0xbb7ed
  di_mtime = 0x3346f518
  di_mtspare = 0x26d70
  di_ctime = 0x3346f518
  di_ctspare = 0x2c520
  di_Mun = union {
    di_Mb = struct {
      Mb_db = {
        [0] 0x2c248
        [1] 0x0
        [2] 0x0
        [3] 0x0
        [4] 0x0
        [5] 0x0
        [6] 0x0
        [7] 0x0
        [8] 0x0
        [9] 0x0
        [10] 0x0
        [11] 0x0
      }
      Mb_ib = {
        [0] 0x0
        [1] 0x0
        [2] 0x0
      }
    }
    di_Msymlink = "HÂ"
  }
  di_flags = 0x0
  di_blocks = 0x2
  di_gen = 0x33470261
  di_proplb = 0x0
  di_spare = {
    [0] 0x0
    [1] 0x0
    [2] 0x0
  }
}
i_dquot = {
  [0] (nil)
  [1] (nil)
}
i_delayoff = 0x0
i_delaylen = 0x0
i_consecreads = 0x2
i_clusterlbn = 0x0
```

```
       i_clustersz = 0x0
       i_prop1boff = 0x0
       i_io_lock = struct {
         l_lock = struct {
           sl_data = 0x2a1cfc
           sl_info = 0x0
           sl_cpuid = 0x0
           sl_lifms = 0x0
         }
         l_caller = 0x497e6c
         l_wait_writers = 0x0
         l_readers = 0x0
         l_flags = '^@'
         l_lifms = '\200'
         l_info = 0x0
         l_lastlocker = 0xfffffc01d5955080
       }
       i_iodone = struct {
         ev_slock = struct {
           sl_data = 0x298acc
           sl_info = 0x0
           sl_cpuid = 0x0
           sl_lifms = 0x0
         }
         ev_event = 0x4959b4
         ev_waiter = 0x0
       }
       i_incore_lock = struct {
         sl_data = 0x4975cc
         sl_info = 0x0
         sl_cpuid = 0x0
         sl_lifms = 0x0
       }
     }
```

Now that we have shown you what a vnode is, in the next section we give you the operations that are defined for it.

4.2.2   Vnode Operations

As part of the vnode interface, a set of logical operations on the vnodes has also been defined. These operations can be seen in the <sys/vnode.h> header file, and we have summarized the routines and their called macros in Table 4–3. Whenever a vnode operation is performed in the kernel, rather than calling the routine directly, the kernel file system developers use a macro. The macro provides an abstraction so that if the underlying mechanisms need to be changed to accommodate a new type of file system, then the macro ensures that the correct action is performed and avoids many changes to the VFS and underlying type-specific file system layers.

Example:

A kernel developer wishes to issue a file system type–independent file open. Table 4–3 tells her she wants to use the VOP_OPEN() predefined macro. We see that from <sys/vnode.h>, the VOP_OPEN() macro is defined as follows:

```
#define VOP_OPEN(vpp,f,c,r)
_VOP_(vn_open,(*vpp),((vpp),(f),(c)),(r))
#define _VOP_(f,v,arg,r)                          \
MACRO_BEGIN                                        \
    if (!MOUNT_FUNNEL((v)->v_mount)) {            \
        (r) = (*((v)->v_op->f))arg;               \
    } else {                                       \
        unix_master();                            \
        (r) = (*((v)->v_op->f))arg;               \
        unix_release();                           \
    }                                              \
MACRO_END
```

The kernel developer wishes to use this macro to open a file after calling namei() to get the vnode pointer. Therefore, she simply specifies the VOP_OPEN() with a pointer to the vnode, some arguments (file mode and credentials), and the a variable to hold the return status code. Her end result is a call that looks something like this:

```
VOP_OPEN( &vp, FREAD | FWRITE, ndp->ni_cred, error );
```

Where the valid file modes (FREAD, FWRITE, etc.) are defined in <sys/fcntl.h>.

TABLE 4–3   Valid vnode Operations

MACRO	ROUTINE	DESCRIPTION
VOP_LOOKUP	vn_lookup()	Converts a component of a pathname to a pointer to a vnode.
VOP_CREATE	vn_create()	Creates a new regular file and returns a vnode pointer to it.
VOP_MKNOD	vn_mknod()	Creates a new device special file and returns a vnode pointer to it.
VOP_OPEN	vn_open()	Performs any open protocol on a file referenced by a given vnode pointer.
VOP_CLOSE	vn_close()	Performs any close protocol on a file referenced by a given vnode pointer.
VOP_ACCESS	vn_access()	Checks access permissions for a file referenced by the given vnode pointer.
VOP_GETATTR	vn_getattr()	Gets attributes for a file pointed to by the file referenced by the given vnode pointer.

Table 4-3   Valid vnode Operations (Continued)

MACRO	ROUTINE	DESCRIPTION
VOP_SETATTR	vn_setattr()	Sets attributes for a file pointed to by the file referenced by the given vnode pointer.
VOP_READ	vn_read()	Reads from a file referenced by the given vnode pointer.
VOP_WRITE	vn_write()	Writes to a file referenced by the given vnode pointer.
VOP_IOCTL	vn_ioctl()	Performs an ioctl on a given file referenced by the given vnode pointer.
VOP_SELECT	vn_select()	Performs a select on a given file referenced by the given vnode pointer.
VOP_MMAP	vn_mmap()	Maps a file system object pointed to by the file referenced by the given vnode pointer.
VOP_FSYNC	vn_fsync()	Writes out all the cached information for the file referenced by the given vnode pointer.
VOP_SEEK	vn_seek()	Performs a seek into a file referenced by the given vnode pointer.
VOP_REMOVE	vn_remove()	Removes the file by name in a given directory referenced by a given vnode pointer.
VOP_LINK	vn_link()	Links the file referenced by the given vnode pointer to a given target name in a given target directory.
VOP_RENAME	vn_rename()	Renames the file with a given name in a directory referenced by a given vnode pointer to the given target directory name.
VOP_MKDIR	vn_mkdir()	Creates a new directory with a given name in a directory referenced by the given vnode pointer.
VOP_RMDIR	vn_rmdir()	Removes a directory with a given name from a directory referenced by a given vnode pointer.
VOP_SYMLINK	vn_symlink()	Creates a new symbolic link from the path with the given name to the given target name in a directory referenced by the given vnode pointer.
VOP_READDIR	vn_readdir()	Reads entries from a directory referenced by a given vnode pointer.
VOP_READLINK	vn_readlink()	Reads a symbolic link using a given vnode pointer.

TABLE 4–3   Valid vnode Operations (Continued)

MACRO	ROUTINE	DESCRIPTION
VOP_ABORTOP	vn_abortop()	Aborts operation. Called after namei() when a create or delete doesn't actually finish.
VOP_INACTIVE	vn_inactive()	The file referenced by the given vnode pointer is no longer referenced by the vnode layer.
VOP_RECLAIM	vn_reclaim()	Reclaims the vnode referenced by the given pointer so it can be used for other purposes.
VOP_BMAP	vn_bmap()	Maps the given logical block number in the file referenced by the given vnode pointer to a physical block number and physical device.
VOP_STRATEGY	vn_strategy()	Blocks an oriented interface to read or write a logical block from a file into or out of a buffer.
VOP_PRINT	vn_print()	Prints out the contents of file system–specific information from a file referenced by the given vnode pointer.
VOP_PGRD	vn_pgrd()	Reads a specific file system page from a file referenced by the given vnode.
VOP_PGWR	vn_pgwr()	Writes a specific file system page to a file referenced by the given vnode.
VOP_SWAP	vn_swap()	Swaps to the device special file referenced by the given vnode.
VOP_BREAD	vn_bread()	Buffered file read. Returns a buffer pointer.
VOP_BRELSE	vn_brelse()	Releases the file buffer with no I/O needed.
VOP_LOCKCTL	vn_lockctl()	File lock control operations.
VOP_SYNCDATA	vn_syncdata()	Performs a sync operation for the file referenced by the given vnode.
VOP_LOCK	vn_lock()	Locks a file referenced by the given vnode.
VOP_GETPROPLIST	vn_getproplist()	Gets information about a property list referenced by the given vnode.
VOP_SETPROPLIST	vn_setproplist()	Sets information about a property list on a file referenced by the given vnode.
VOP_DELPROPLIST	vn_delproplist()	Deletes a property list on a file referenced by the given vnode.
VOP_PATHCONF	vn_pathconf()	Retrieves the file implementation details on a file referenced by a given vnode.

Example:

Our aim in this example is to give you an idea of how the object-oriented structure of vnodes works. We choose to examine the vnode for the directory that is being covered by the root file system. First, the code must examine the v_tag field in the vnode structure to determine on which type of file system the vnode resides. Second, the vnode operations contain pointers to the specific routines for that file system type. In this case, we find that the vn_open is pointing to the msfs_open() (AdvFS open) kernel routine.

```
(dbx) p (*rootfs.m_prev.m_vnodecovered).v_tag
VT_MSFS                    ⇐ this is an AdvFS vnode

(dbx) p (*rootfs.m_prev.m_vnodecovered.v_op).vn_open
0xffffffc0000454430   ⇐ the address of the vn_open routine

(dbx) (*rootfs.m_prev.m_vnodecovered.v_op).vn_open/i
[msfs_open:1939, 0xffffffc0000454430] ldq    t1, 0(a0)
```

You can see that the address for vn_open in this vnode is the msfs_open routine because the vnode we are examining is an AdvFS. Therefore, the correct routine will be called when an *open(2)* system call is issued to this vnode.

4.2.3   The Mount Table

The **mount table** is a systemwide, in-memory structure that contains information about the mounted file systems. The table actually consists of a doubly linked list starting at the root file system and containing mount structures, each referring to one of the mounted file systems on a particular Tru64 UNIX system. When the *mount(2)* system call is issued either by the system administrator using the *mount(8)* command, or by the system at boot time, a structure is allocated within the kernel and the new entry is added to the mount table–linked list. As file systems are mounted, the entries are always inserted into the list after the root, but before any others; however, when a file system is unmounted, it can be removed from anywhere. The root file system, once mounted, can never be unmounted short of shutting down the system.

Example:

A Tru64 UNIX system tool, *kdbx(8)*, contains a macro called mount, which traverses the mount table and gives a nice formatted output. The following shows a system before mounting a new file system:

```
(kdbx) mount
MOUNT          MAJ   MIN   VNODE          ROOTVP         TYPE       PATH        FLAGS
===========  =====  ====  =============  =============  ========  ==========  ==========
k0x07824d80                NULL           k0x0769afc0    msfs      /           loc
k0x07825980                k0x0122a480    k0x03993440    msfs      /var        loc
k0x07825680                k0x0768cfc0    k0x03993200    msfs      /usr        loc
k0x07825800    0     0     k0x03868d80    NULL           procfs    /proc
```

Then, we mount a new UFS on /mnt and see that the new file mount table entry has been inserted immediately following the root (/) entry.

```
(kdbx) mount
MOUNT          MAJ   MIN   VNODE          ROOTVP         TYPE       PATH        FLAGS
===========  =====  ====  =============  =============  ========  ==========  ==========
k0x07824d80                NULL           k0x039926c0    msfs      /           loc
k0x026d8a80    40    5     k0x02718000    k0x03992000    ufs       /mnt        loc
k0x07825980                k0x0122a480    k0x0398a240    msfs      /var        loc
k0x07825680                k0x0768cfc0    k0x03993200    msfs      /usr        loc
k0x07825800    0     0     k0x03868d80    NULL           procfs    /proc
```

The mount table is implemented as a circular, doubly linked list. The m_nxt field in the mount structure references the forward pointers, and the backward pointers are called m_prev. The pointer to the first entry is called rootfs, which is also the pointer to the root file system's table entry. The rootfs is a global kernel variable, so it can be referenced from any routine in the kernel. When traversing, you can begin from the rootfs and visit every entry by following the m_nxt fields, until the next entry to visit will be the rootfs entry again. At this point, you know you have visited every entry in the table. Conversely, you can traverse the mount table in the opposite direction by starting with the m_prev pointer from the rootfs entry and following each m_prev field until you reach the rootfs entry. When that happens, you know you have reached the end of the list.

Example:

An example of a Tru64 UNIX mount table is shown in Figure 4–2. This fictitious mount table consists of four file systems, each having a different file system type. The first entry in the table (the rootfs) is an AdvFS, the second is a UFS, the third is a NFS, and the fourth is a CDFS. Notice that pointers from the mount structure's m_data field point to the file system type–dependent data. The file system–dependent data has a different structure for each type.

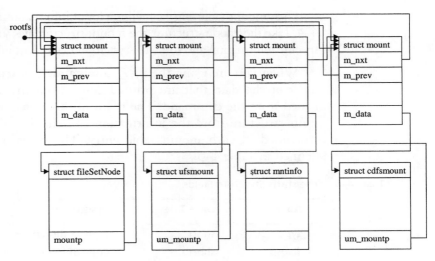

FIGURE 4–2
Tru64 UNIX Mount
Table Entries

TABLE 4–4   The mount Structure Fields

FIELD	DATA TYPE	DESCRIPTION
m_lock	simple lock	Lock providing multiprocessor exclusion to fields in this mount structure
m_flag	int	Mounts flags
m_funnel	int	Serializes (or funnel) access to this file system
m_next	struct mount*	The next file system in the mount table
m_prev	struct mount*	The previous file system in the mount table
m_op	struct vfsops*	The valid operations on this file system
m_vnodecovered	struct vnode*	The vnode on which this file system was mounted
m_mounth	struct vnode*	The list of referenced vnodes for this mounted file system
m_vlist_lock	simple lock	Lock used to protect access to the vnode list
m_exroot	uid_t	The exported mapping for uid 0
m_uid	uid_t	The user ID for the user who performed the mount
m_stat	struct nstatfs	The cache of file system statistics
m_nfs_errmsginfo	structure	Information used to control NFS server console error messages
m_tag	tag_t	Used for unlabeled file systems
m_unmount_lock	lock_data_t	Complex lock used for pathname/unmount synchronization

Each mount table entry contains a lot of information, as specified in Table 4–4. Like the vnode structure, the mount structure has some file system type–specific information and some file system–independent information.

When you are using the *df(1)* command, as discussed in Chapter 1, most of the data that are printed come from the *statfs(2)* system call issued from the command. The result of this system call is to populate a statfs structure from the information contained in the nstatfs structure contained in each mount table entry. The fields in this structure are defined in Table 4–5.

TABLE 4–5   The statfs Structure Fields

Field	Data Type	Description
f_type	short	Type of filesystem
f_flags	short	Copy of mount flags
f_fsize	int	Fundamental file system block size
f_bsize	int	Optimal transfer block size
f_blocks	int	Total data blocks in the file system. This may not represent the file system's size.
f_bfree	int	Free blocks in the file system
f_bavail	int	Free blocks available to nonroot users
f_files	int	Total file nodes in the file system
f_ffree	int	Free file nodes in the file system
f_fsid	fsid_t	The file system identifier
f_spare	int	Spare. Not used.
f_mntonname	char*	The directory on which this file system has been mounted
f_mntfromname	char*	The name of the mounted file system
mount_info	union mount_info	The mount arguments specific to the file system type that are passed to *mount(2)*

Example:

This example shows how to use *kdbx(8)* to examine a Tru64 UNIX 4.0x system's mount table starting at the root file system, referenced by the rootfs global kernel variable. All Tru64 UNIX systems have this kernel variable defined as the global pointer to the mount structure for the root file system.

```
(kdbx) p *rootfs
struct {
  m_lock = struct {
    sl_data = 0x0
```

```
            sl_info = 0x0
            sl_cpuid = 0x0
            sl_lifms = 0x0
          }
          m_flag = 0x5000
          m_funnel = 0x0
          m_next = 0xffffffff82f8ce80
          m_prev = 0xffffffff82efd960
          m_op = 0xfffffc00005ea890
          m_vnodecovered = (nil)
          m_mounth = 0xffffffff8aed9c00
          m_vlist_lock = struct {
            sl_data = 0x0
            sl_info = 0x0
            sl_cpuid = 0x0
            sl_lifms = 0x0
          }
          m_exroot = 0x0
          m_uid = 0x0
          m_stat = struct {
            f_type = 0x1
            f_flags = 0x5000
            f_fsize = 0x400
            f_bsize = 0x2000
            f_blocks = 0xf6ff
            f_bfree = 0x2665
            f_bavail = 0xdb1
            f_files = 0x41fe
            f_ffree = 0x3ac7
            f_fsid = struct {
              val = {
                [0] 0x2800000
                [1] 0x1
              }
            }
          }
          f_spare = {
            [0] 0x0
            [1] 0x0
            [2] 0x0
            [3] 0x0
            [4] 0x0
            [5] 0x0
            [6] 0x0
            [7] 0x0
            [8] 0x0
          }
          f_mntonname = "/"
          f_mntfromname = "/dev/vol/rootdg/rootvol"
          mount_info = union {
            ufs_args = struct {
              fspec = (nil)
              exflags = 0x0
              exroot = 0x0
            }
```

```
nfs_args = struct {
  addr = (nil)
  fh = (nil)
  flags = 0x0
  wsize = 0x0
  rsize = 0x0
  timeo = 0x0
  retrans = 0x0
  hostname = (nil)
  acregmin = 0x0
  acregmax = 0x0
  acdirmin = 0x0
  acdirmax = 0x0
  netname = (nil)
  pathconf = (nil)
}
mfs_args = struct {
  name = (nil)
  base = (nil)
  size = 0x0
}
cdfs_args = struct {
  fspec = (nil)
  exflags = 0x0
  exroot = 0x0
  flags = 0x0
  version = 0x0
  default_uid = 0x0
  default_gid = 0x0
  default_fmode = 0x0
  default_dmode = 0x0
  map_uid_ct = 0x0
  map_uid = (nil)
  map_gid_ct = 0x0
  map_gid = (nil)
}
procfs_args = struct {
  fspec = (nil)
  exflags = 0x0
  exroot = 0x0
}
msfs_args = struct {
  id = struct {
    id1 = 0x0
    id2 = 0x0
    tag = 0x0
  }
}
ffm_args = struct {
  ffm_flags = 0x0
  f_un = union {
    ffm_pname = (nil)
    ffm_fdesc = 0x0
  }
```

```
        }
      }
    }
    m_data = 0xffffffff8adda900
    m_nfs_errmsginfo = struct {
      n_noexport = 0x0
      last_noexport = 0x0
      n_stalefh = 0x0
      last_stalefh = 0x0
    }
    m_unmount_lock = struct {
      l_lock = struct {
        sl_data = 0x0
        sl_info = 0x0
        sl_cpuid = 0x0
        sl_lifms = 0x0
      }
      l_caller = 0x2965fc
      l_wait_writers = 0x0
      l_readers = 0x0
      l_flags = '^@'
      l_lifms = '\200'
      l_info = 0x0
      l_lastlocker = 0xffffffff82fcda40
    }
  }
```

The mechanics of mounting multiple file system types is quite interesting and bears discussing. In our basic discussion of the *mount(8)* command in Chapter 1, we glossed over what was going on "under the hood" that allowed the mount command to mount each file system type.

We did not mention in our earlier discussion that the *mount(8)* command itself handles much of the option processing, but it may also use a helper program that is called by *mount(8)* to handle additional option processing before issuing the *mount(2)* system call. Some file system types are handled internally by *mount(8)*, whereas the rest are handled by a helper program. For example, when you mount a UFS, it is done by *mount(8)* itself; however, when you mount an AdvFS, the *mount(8)* command executes the mount_advfs helper program.

The operation to mount a file system in the VFS is an object-oriented operation. The *mount(2)* system call, when issued by the mount command (or one of its helpers), does all of the dirty work of building the mount table entry as we discussed before. The *mount(2)* calls the vfs_mount() routine by way of the VFS_MOUNT macro. The vfs_mount() routine then determines which type of file system is to be mounted and calls the appropriate file system type–specific code with the appropriate arguments. For example, when mounting a UFS, the ufs_mount() routine is called by vfs_mount().

Example:

Here, we examine the mount operation for the vfs_mount() pointer and discover that an AdvFS mount operation will be performed.

```
(dbx) p *(*rootfs).m_op
struct {
  vfs_mount = 0xfffffc0000450b50  ⇐ this is the specific mount routine
  vfs_start = 0xfffffc0000452700
  vfs_unmount = 0xfffffc0000452710
  vfs_root = 0xfffffc0000452be0
  vfs_quotactl = 0xfffffc0000452c60
  vfs_statfs = 0xfffffc0000453070
  vfs_sync = 0xfffffc0000453250
  vfs_fhtovp = 0xfffffc0000453950
  vfs_vptofh = 0xfffffc0000453a20
  vfs_init = 0xfffffc0000453a50
  vfs_mountroot = 0xfffffc00004506d0
  vfs_swapvp = 0xfffffc0000454310
  vfs_smoothsync = 0xfffffc00004540b0
}

(dbx) 0xfffffc0000450b50/i
[msfs_mount:2454, 0xfffffc0000450b50]    lda   sp, -192(sp)
```

In the next section, we discuss the other VFS operations that can be performed on a file system in Tru64 UNIX.

4.2.4   VFS Operations

A mount structure's valid operations are also known as the VFS operations. When a VFS operation is required, the Tru64 UNIX kernel calls a set of C language macros that are defined to call its corresponding VFS kernel routine. Table 4–6 lists the macros and corresponding kernel routines, as well as a description of their intended function. As with the vnode operations, the macros for VFS operations are used to make it easier to modify the code. The macro defines the operation, and the routine is an implementation detail that can be changed.

TABLE 4–6   Virtual File System Operations

MACRO	ROUTINE	DESCRIPTION
VFS_MOUNT	vfs_mount()	Mounts a virtual file system.
VFS_START	vfs_start()	Makes a file system operational, if necessary.
VFS_UNMOUNT	vfs_unmount()	Unmounts a virtual file system.
VFS_ROOT	vfs_root()	Returns the root vnode for this file system.

TABLE 4–6   Virtual File System Operations (Continued)

MACRO	ROUTINE	DESCRIPTION
VFS_QUOTACTL	vfs_quotactl()	Performs operations associated with quotas.
VFS_STATFS	vfs_statfs()	Returns file system statistics. The information returned is contained in a statfs structure.
VFS_SYNC	vfs_sync()	Writes out all cached file system information for a virtual file system.
VFS_FHTOVP	vfs_fhtovp()	Returns the vnode pointer that corresponds to the given file handle.
VFS_VPTOFH	vfs_vptofh()	Returns the file handle that corresponds to the given vnode pointer.
VFS_MOUNTROOT	vfs_mountroot()	Mounts the file system as the system's root file system.
VFS_SWAPVP	vfs_swapvp()	Sets up for swapping to a file. Note this feature is not supported in Tru64 UNIX.

4.2.5   VFS Tuning Parameters

The VFS subsystem contains a substantial number of parameters, which are listed in Table 4–7. These parameters can be seen by issuing the following command:

```
# sysconfig -q vfs
```

We discuss some of these attributes in subsequent sections of this chapter and Chapter 5. We'll refer you to those discussions rather than rehashing that information here. We refer you to the *sys_attrs_vfs(5)* reference page for more information.

TABLE 4–7   Virtual File System sysconfig Parameters

PARAMETER	DESCRIPTION	V4	V5
name-cache-size name_cache_size	This is a namei cache parameter, see section 4.3.2.	X	X
name-cache-hash-size name_cache_hash_size	This is a namei cache parameter, see section 4.3.2.	X	X
buffer-hash-size buffer_hash_size	Size of the hash chain table for the metadata buffer cache.	X	X
special-vnode-alias-tbl-size special_vnode_alias_tbl_size	Size of the special vnodes alias table for vnodes of character or block special device files	X	X
bufcache	The size in percentage of system memory to size the metadata buffer cache. The default value is 3%.	X	X

TABLE 4–7   Virtual File System sysconfig Parameters (Continued)

PARAMETER	DESCRIPTION	V4	V5
bufpages	The number of pages to reserve for buffers. If this attribute is set, it overrides the value of the bufcache attribute.	X	X
path-num-max path_num_max	This is the size of the pathname zone for pathname lookup buffers.	X	X
sys-v-mode sys_v_mode	This is an obsolete System V parameter.	X	X
ucred-max ucred_max	This is an obsolete parameter.	X	X
nvnode	This is a vnode cache parameter, see section 4.3.3.	X	X
max-vnodes max_vnodes	This is a vnode cache parameter, see section 4.3.	X	X
min-free-vnodes min_free_vnodes	This is a vnode cache parameter, see section 4.3.3.	X	X
vnode-age vnode_age	This is a vnode cache parameter, see section 4.3.3.	X	X
namei-cache-valid-time namei_cache_valid_time	This is a namei cache parameter, see section 4.3.2.	X	X
max-free-file-structures max_free_file_structures	This is an obsolete parameter.	X	X
max-ufs-mounts max_ufs_mounts	This is the maximum number of UFS or MFS mounts.	X	X
vode-deallocation-enable vnode_deallocation_enable	This is a vnode cache parameter, see section 4.3.3.	X	X
pipe-maxbuf-size pipe_maxbuf_size	The maximum number of bytes that is buffered per pipe.	X	X
pipe-single-write-max	The maximum size of a single write to a pipe.	X	
pipe-databuf-size pipe_databuf_size	The number of bytes in each data pipe buffer.	X	X
pipe-max-bytes-all-pipes pip_max_bytes_all_pipes	The maximum number of bytes reserved for all pipes.	X	X
noadd-exec-access noadd_exec_access	When enabled, does not allow creation of new executable files.	X	X
fifo-do-adaptive fifo_do_adaptive	This attribute is used to disable the pipe code that attempts to batch writes to a pipe and then deliver this data in a single call to a reader.	X	X
nlock_record	The maximum number of record locks that can be held by one process. This limit prevents lock structures for a process from consuming too much kernel memory.		X

TABLE 4–7 Virtual File System sysconfig Parameters (Continued)

PARAMETER	DESCRIPTION	V4	V5
smoothsync-age smoothsync_age	This is a smooth sync parameter, see section 4.5.2.	X	X
io-throttle-shift io_throttle_shift	This is an I/O throttling parameter, see section 4.5.2.	X	X
io_throttle_static	This is an I/O throttling parameter, see section 4.5.2.[3]		X
io-throttle-maxmzthruput io_throttle_maxmzthruput	This is an I/O throttling parameter, see section 4.5.2.	X	X
revoke_tty_only	A value that determines whether the *revoke(2)* system call can invalidate file descriptors on block special devices.		X
strict_posix_osync	A value that enables (1) or disables (0) strict POSIX conformance to clearing dirty file status for O_SYNC operations.		X

4.3   The File System Caches

Tru64 UNIX uses several file system caches to speed up operation of the system. **Cache** is a term used to describe high-speed storage that acts as a buffer between the fast system and slower storage devices. This kind of buffer has been used in many operating systems, including UNIX, for many years in an attempt to mitigate the effects of using slower storage. In this case, the high-speed storage we are referring to is a portion of the memory of the system, and the slower speed storage is magnetic storage or disks.

Three main file system caches are used in Tru64 UNIX to speed up the operation of the VFS: (1) the namei cache (2) the unified buffer cache (UBC) and (3) the vnode cache. Each of these caches has tunable parameters associated with them. We discuss each of these in the following sections.

4.3.1   The Unified Buffer Cache

The Tru64 UNIX operating system utilizes the UBC to hold the actual file data, which includes both reads and writes from conventional file activity and page faults from memory mapped file sections. The UBC and the virtual memory subsystem share and compete for all of the main memory and utilize the same physical pages. This sharing means that all available physical memory can be used for both buffering I/O and for the address space of the process. The UBC contains only file data; it does not directly contain file system metadata. UFS metadata is contained in the metadata buffer cache, and AdvFS metadata is stored in the AdvFS cache.

Prior to Tru64 UNIX version 5.1, the AdvFS carved its cache out of the UBC, but managed it by itself. In order to understand the prior version behavior, we refer you to the discussion in Chapter 7 about AdvFS tuning parameters for details. In version 5.1, the separate AdvFS cache is eliminated because the AdvFS blocks and metadata are managed by the UBC, rather than managed independently. This change results in a significant performance improvement because of reduced overhead and complexity. Also, the AdvFS cache is no longer limited as it was before, so AdvFS can utilize any UBC blocks that are available directly.

You can examine the performance statistics of the UBC on a Tru64 UNIX 4.0x system by using the kernel debugger and looking at the vm_perf global. In version 5.0x, this has been changed to a per-processor structure, so you'll need to do a little more work to look at the UBC. We show these steps in the following examples.

Example:

This Tru64 UNIX version 4.0x example shows you how to use the kernel debugger to examine the virtual memory statistics, including the UBC.

```
(kdbx) pd vm_perf
struct {
  vpf_pagefaults = 296270
  vpf_kpagefaults = 3415
  vpf_cowfaults = 86194
  vpf_cowsteals = 15646
  vpf_zfod = 66528
  vpf_kzfod = 3415
  vpf_pgiowrites = 0
  vpf_pgwrites = 0
  vpf_pgioreads = 58311
  vpf_pgreads = 0
  vpf_swapreclaims = 0
  vpf_taskswapouts = 0
  vpf_taskswapins = 0
  vpf_vmpagesteal = 0
  vpf_vmpagewrites = 0
  vpf_vmpagecleanrecs = 0
  vpf_vplmsteal = 0
  vpf_vplmstealwins = 0
  vpf_vpseqdrain = 180765
  vpf_ubchit = 5777
  vpf_ubcalloc = 360778
  vpf_ubcpushes = 0
  vpf_ubcpagepushes = 0
  vpf_ubcdirtywra = 0
```

```
        vpf_ubcreclaim = 0
        vpf_ubcpagesteal = 0
        vpf_ubclookups = 368255
        vpf_ubclookuphits = 7477
        vpf_reactivate = 479
        vpf_allocatedpages = 14221
        vpf_vmwiredpages = 1261
        vpf_ubcwiredpages = 1224
        vpf_mallocpages = 750
        vpf_totalptepages = 398
        vpf_contigpages = 79
        vpf_rmwiredpages = 0
        vpf_ubcpages = 7495
        vpf_freepages = 692
        vpf_vmcleanpages = 0
        vpf_swapspace = 42224
    }
```

In addition, in version 4.0x, the UBC internal variables and kernel tunable parameters can be examined using the kernel debugger as follows:

```
(dbx) pd ubc_pages
7495
(dbx) pd ubc_maxpages
7496
(dbx) pd ubc_maxpercent
50
(dbx) pd ubc_borrowlimit
2998
(dbx) pd ubc_borrowpercent
20
(dbx) pd ubc_minpages
1499
(dbx) pd ubc_minpercent
10
```

Example:

This example shows how you can use the kernel debugger on a Tru64 UNIX 5.0x system to examine the UBC information. In this case, we are assuming only one **memory affinity domain** (MAD), which would be the case for any UMA (Non-NUMA) systems. NUMA systems have more than one MAD associated; therefore, you will need to know which one to examine and fill in the value for the '0' below.

```
(dbx) pd vm_mads[0].md_ubc
struct {
  ubc_lru_lock = 0
  ubc_lru = 0xfffffc0000eeb3a0
  ubc_lru_count = 5664
  ubc_pages_lock = 0
  ubc_pages = 5664
```

```
      ubc_minpages = 3071
      ubc_maxpages = 30713
      ubc_wiredpages = 1599
      ubc_seqdrain = 15356
      ubc_seqpercent = 10
      ubc_borrowlimit = 6142
      ubc_iocount_lock = 0
      ubc_iocount = 0
      ubc_buffers = 256
      ubc_dirty_lock = 0
      ubc_dirty_pages = 0
      ubc_dirty_min = 307
      ubc_dirty_limit = 566
      ubc_dirty_wra = 5
      ubc_dirty_pcnt = 10
      ubc_dirty_seconds = 1
      ubc_ffl = 1
      ubc_cache_free = 1
      ubc_pagesteal = 24
      ubc_active = 0
      ubc_dirty_thread = 0xfffffc000f2dc000
}
```

As with any performance exercise, tuning the UBC can be tricky. Most of the time, the default values are sufficient, but other times they may not be. We see in Figure 4–3 how the UBC sizing parameters and the value of the equivalent kernel variables (given in pages) are related to one another. You can change the default values of the UBC tuning parameters in the vm subsystem of your system's /etc/sysconfigtab. These parameters are defined as follows:

- **ubc_minpercent:** This is the minimum percentage of physical memory to which the system will allow the UBC to shrink. The default value is 10 percent of the managed physical memory.

- **ubc_maxpercent:** This is the maximum percentage of managed physical pages to which the system will allow the UBC to grow. The default is 100 percent of a Tru64 UNIX system's managed memory.

- **ubc_borrowpercent:** This is the percentage of the physical managed memory to which the system will trim the UBC down when the total available physical memory gets low. The default is 20 percent of the physical memory. See Figure 4–3 to understand this attribute's relationship to the other attributes.

- **vm_ubcpagesteal:** This is the minimum percentage of physical memory that the UBC must hold before the system can begin stealing pages. The default is 24 percent of physical memory.

- **vm_ubcfilemaxdirtypages:** In the context of an application thread, the number of pages that must be dirty (modified) before the update daemon starts writing them. This value is for internal use only and should not be modified. The default value is −1.

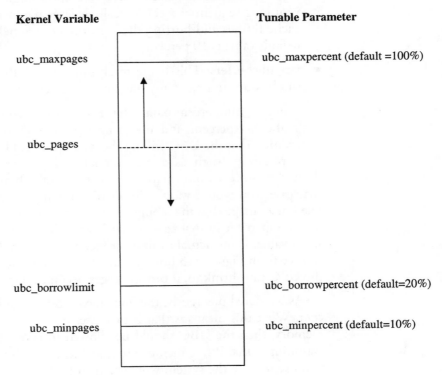

Kernel Variable   **Tunable Parameter**

ubc_maxpages   ubc_maxpercent (default =100%)

ubc_pages

ubc_borrowlimit   ubc_borrowpercent (default=20%)

ubc_minpages   ubc_minpercent (default=10%)

- **vm_ubcdirtypercent:** When the number of modified UBC least recently used (LRU) list pages exceeds the value of the vm_ubcdirtypercent attribute, the virtual memory subsystem rewrites to swap space with the oldest modified UBC LRU pages. The default value of the vm_ubcdirtypercent attribute is 10 percent of the total UBC LRU pages.

- **ubc_maxdirtywrites:** In order to minimize the impact of sync when rewriting UBC pages, the ubc_maxdirtywrites attribute specifies the maximum number of disk writes that the kernel can perform each second. The default value is five disk writes per second.

- **vm_ubcseqstartpercent:** This is the percentage of physical memory above which the system recognizes that a sequential file access is in progress. The system begins stealing pages from the UBC LRU list to satisfy its demand for pages. The default value is 50 percent.

- **vm_ubcseqpercent:** This is the maximum percent of physical memory in the UBC that can be used to cache a single file. This is to prevent long sequential access to a single large file from causing excessive cache flushes and hurting the performance of the entire system. The default value is 10 percent.

- **vm_ubcbuffers:** This is the total number of UBC I/O requests that can be outstanding at any one time. The default value is 256 buffers.

The ubc_minpercent parameter is sometimes reduced in conjunction with ubc_maxpercent and ubc_borrowpercent if there is a reasonable expectation that the UBC will not be well utilized. This can be the case if an application (such as a commercial database product) utilizes raw devices to store its information, which generally bypasses the UBC. In that case, you would want to limit the growth of the UBC in order to maximize usage by the application. The advantage of lowering the ubc_minpercent in that case is that it will allow the UBC to shrink to a small value, if the actual utilization meets the lowered expectations. You can see from Figure 4–3 how this attribute is the smallest value to which the UBC can shrink to, if process pages become scarce.

As we stated previously, the ubc_maxpercent default value is 100 percent. What this means is that if processes do not need the available free memory, then the UBC should be allowed to take advantage of it. The reasoning is that if free memory is available, then why not let the file system use it since the system will later trim back the UBC if the processes need it. In reality, the UBC never uses anything close to 100 percent of the memory because the processes are normally using it; however, the free list may become very short if there is a spike in file system activity.

One school of thought is that ubc_maxpercent should be lowered on many systems in order to prevent the UBC from growing too large and causing the system to spend too much time reclaiming memory. The theory is that if the UBC on your system is allowed to grow such that it uses a lot of memory (which it has a tendency to do when there is a lot of file system activity), then your system may waste its cycles needlessly trimming the cache. You may want to consider tuning back this value, in that case. In addition, if your system is primarily a database server using raw disk, it will not need to have a large UBC. In that case, you can safely reduce it.

No matter which camp you sit in, it is prudent to examine the operation of your system and tune it accordingly, if necessary. Generalizations almost never apply in your situation. It is important to know the options and tradeoffs and to make your decisions based on the way they impact your operation.

4.3.2 The File Name to Vnode Translation (namei) Cache

The **namei cache** stores recently used file system pathnames and matches them with their respective vnodes. It also stores inode (or tag) information for files that were referenced but not found. Having this information in the cache substantially reduces the amount of searching that is needed to perform pathname translations.

The namei cache has a two-stage structure such that there are basically two ways to find a particular entry in the cache. The first method is a sequential search, visiting every node until you either reach the correct one or you've visited every node and deduced that the entry is not in the cache. Clearly, this method is inefficient, and the time to search increases linearly with the size of the list. A search of the list in this way would follow the doubly linked LRU list by the nc_nxt field in the forward direction or the nc_prev pointers in the reverse direction. The second method for finding the correct entry in the namei cache is using the hash table. Using a special hashing algorithm, the search is narrowed down to only a few entries in one of the buckets rather than the entire list. Both mechanisms are shown pictorially in Figure 4–4.

The structure of a namei cache entry is defined in <sys/namei.h> as follows:

```
struct namecache {
struct namecache *nc_forw;   /* hash chain forward pointer */
struct namecache *nc_back;   /* hash chain backward pointer */
struct namecache *nc_nxt;   /* LRU chain */
struct namecache **nc_prev;  /* LRU chain */
struct vnode *nc_dvp;        /* vnode of parent of name */
u_long nc_dvpid;             /* capability number of nc_dvp */
struct vnode *nc_vp;         /* vnode the name refers to */
u_long nc_vpid;              /* capability number of nc_vp */
u_long nc_time;              /* last cache activity time */
char  nc_nlen;               /* length of name */
char  nc_name[NCHNAMELEN];   /* segment name */
struct nchash *nc_hash_chain; /* header of my hash chain */
u_int nc_lru_dist;           /* LRU append counter when put on end */
};
```

LRU list

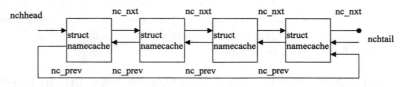

Hash list

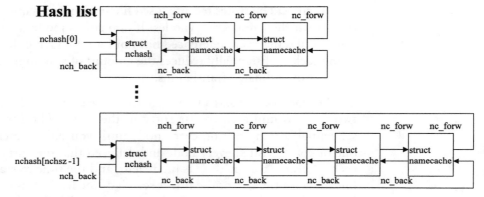

Example:

This example shows how you can examine the first two namei cache LRU
list entries on a running system using the kernel debugger.

```
(dbx) pd *namecache
struct {
  nc_forw = 0xfffffc0000b00040
  nc_back = 0xfffffc0000b00040
  nc_nxt = 0xfffffc0000b9db10
  nc_prev = 0xfffffc0000b81c68
  nc_dvp = (nil)
  nc_dvpid = 693082
  nc_vp = (nil)
  nc_vpid = 694056
  nc_time = 777237
  nc_nlen = 12
  nc_name = "vfragpg.8.gz"
  nc_hash_chain = (nil)
  nc_lru_dist = 469205
}

(dbx) p *(*namecache).nc_nxt
struct {
  nc_forw = 0xfffffc0000b9db10
  nc_back = 0xfffffc0000b9db10
  nc_nxt = 0xfffffc0000b20890
  nc_prev = 0xfffffc0000b00050
  nc_dvp = (nil)
```

```
    nc_dvpid = 694687
    nc_vp = (nil)
    nc_vpid = 694704
    nc_time = 777238
    nc_nlen = '^P'
    nc_name = "fs_mkfset.cb.tcl"
    nc_hash_chain = (nil)
    nc_lru_dist = 469955
}
```

Tuning the namei cache is a process that consists of monitoring the miss rate and changing parameters to make it perform more effectively. In 4.0x, monitoring is simply a matter of examining the nchstats using the kernel debugger. In 5.0x, this global structure has been changed to be a processor-specific structure. You want to calculate the miss rate using these values and make sure that this value is less than 20 percent. The following formula will give you the miss rate for a Tru64 UNIX system.

```
                        ncs_miss * 100
miss rate = -------------------------------------
                ncs_goodhits + ncs_neghits + ncs_miss
```

Example:

This example shows how to examine the namei cache statistics on a running 4.0x system using the kernel debugger.

```
(kdbx) pd nchstats
struct {
  ncs_goodhits = 965881
  ncs_neghits = 7813
  ncs_badhits = 663
  ncs_falsehits = 19721
  ncs_miss = 30999
  ncs_long = 94
  ncs_pass2 = 0
  ncs_2passes = 0
  ncs_dirscan = 0
}
```

For this example, we see that the miss rate is good, by our 20 percent standard.

```
miss rate = (30999 × 100)/(965881 + 7813 + 30999) = 3%
```

Example:

This example illustrates how you can examine the namei cache statistic on a running 5.0x system using the kernel debugger. This example assumes that only one **processor affinity group** (PAG) exists, and therefore, only one MAD exists as well.

```
(dbx) pd (*processor_ptr[0]).nchstats
```

```
struct {
  ncs_goodhits = 2870625
  ncs_neghits = 142115
  ncs_badhits = 347467
  ncs_falsehits = 122521
  ncs_miss = 391127
  ncs_long = 2067
  ncs_badtimehits = 11414
  ncs_collisions = 20
  ncs_unequaldups = 0
  ncs_pad = {
    [0] 0
    [1] 0
    [2] 0
  }
}
```

Even though this miss rate is higher than our previous example, it still falls within our acceptable range.

```
miss rate = (391127 × 100)/(2870625 + 142115 + 391127) = 11%
```

If you wish to make name lookup operations faster, then you need to increase the number of entries in the namei cache. The recommended method to do this is by increasing the value of the maxusers attribute or by increasing the value of the name_cache_size attribute. Increasing the value of maxusers or name_cache_size allocates more system resources for the kernel's use; however, it also increases the amount of physical memory consumed by the kernel. Even on a system with a large amount of memory, this is really not significant when weighed against the performance that can be gained. The namei cache *sysconfig(8)* parameters are:

- **name_cache_size:** The number of namei cache entries to set aside for the namei cache. The default value is 150 for 24 MB systems and (2 × nvnode × 11/10) for 32 MB or larger memory systems. This parameter is not dynamic; a reboot is required to change the value.

- **name_cache_hash_size:** This is the size of the namei cache hash table maintained in memory for quick cache lookups. The namei cache uses a hashing algorithm to speed up searches in the cache. The attribute sizes the hash table, which can improve lookup speed, if appropriately sized. The default is the smaller of name_cache_size/8 or 8192.

- **namei_cache_valid_time:** The number of seconds that a namei cache entry can remain in the cache before it is discarded. The default is 30 seconds for 24 MB systems and 1200 seconds for 32 MB and larger memory systems.

4.3.3   The Vnode Cache

The **vnode cache** is used to keep track of recently used vnodes on the system. When a vnode is no longer being used, it remains in the cache for awhile, in case it is needed again. The time that the vnode remains in the cache is referred to as the **vnode age**. At some point, the vnode becomes too old and is removed from the cache.

You can monitor the vnode cache by examining the vnode_stats information on the running system. This is easily done on a 4.0x system by using the kernel debugger and printing the vnode_stats structure. In version 5.0 and higher, you must look at the per-processor vnode statistics kept there.

Example:

This example shows you how to examine the vnode statistics on a running Tru64 UNIX 4.0x system using the kernel debugger.

```
(dbx) pd vnode_stats
struct {
  vn_allocations = 6338
  vn_deallocations = 3359
  vn_recycled = 571319
  vn_getnewcalls = 575462
  vn_getlock = 0
  vn_vgetcalls = 4663699
  vn_vgetfree = 2696854
  vn_freecalls = 3322983
  vn_failget = 0
  vn_waitvxlock = 0
  vn_inactivating = 0
  vn_transitioning = 0
  vn_faildeallocs = 518596
  rev_number = 3
}
```

Example:

This example shows how to examine the per-processor vnode statistics on a running Tru64 UNIX 5.0x system using the kernel debugger.

```
(dbx) p (*processor_ptr[0]).vnode_stats
struct {
  vn_allocations = 56708
  vn_recycled = 2233935
  vn_getnewcalls = 2262467
  vn_getlock = 0
  vn_vgetcalls = 8721484
  vn_vgetfree = 2133794
  vn_freecalls = 4785861
  vn_failget = 0
```

```
vn_waitvxlock = 0
vn_inactivating = 0
vn_transitioning = 0
vn_prim_deallocs = 28175
vn_sec_deallocs = 25531
vn_failed_prim_deallocs = 0
vn_failed_sec_deallocs = 1814774
vn_pad = {
  [0] 0
  [1] 0
  [2] 0
  [3] 0
  [4] 0
  [5] 0
  [6] 0
  [7] 0
  [8] 0
}
}
```

You can tune the vnode cache by altering a few of the parameters in /etc/sysconfigtab. Those that apply to the vnode table are the following:

- **max_vnodes:** The value of this vfs subsystem parameter determines the size of the vnode table (see Figure 4–5). The default value of the max_vnodes attribute is 5 percent of memory. The max_vnodes attribute is dynamically changeable, so it can be modified without rebooting the system.

- **nvnodes:** This is an obsolete parameter. It is effectively replaced by max_vnodes and vnode_age. The default value is calculated based on the following formula: nproc + (2 × maxusers) + 128.

- **min_free_vnodes:** This is the minimum number of free vnodes on the free list. If the number of vnodes on the free list is less than the value of the min_free_vnodes parameter, then vnodes are removed. The minimum value for this parameter is 150 for 24 MB systems and nvnodes for 32 MB and larger memory systems.

- **vnode_age:** The amount of time, in seconds, that a vnode can remain on the free list before it is removed. The default value is 2 seconds for 24 MB systems and 120 seconds for 32 MB and larger memory systems.

- **vnode_deallocation_enable:** A value that enables (1) or disables (0) vnode deallocation. Enabling vnode deallocation decreases memory usage because it returns to the system the memory allocated to vnodes. On the other hand, disabling it forces the system to use a static vnode pool. With static vnode pool, the namei_cache_valid_time is not used. The default value is 1 (enabled).

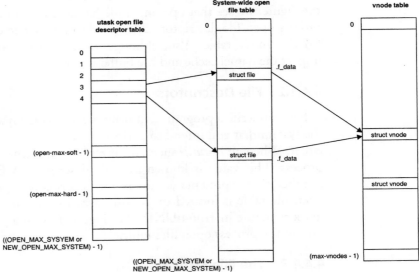

4.4   The System Call Interface

The first exposure programmers usually get to the VFS is through the system call interface to it. A detailed description of all of the system calls can be found in Section 2 of the Tru64 UNIX reference pages, but we attempt to provide a representative sample to show you how these calls affect the use of the file system by regular users. We do this by introducing some example code written specifically to exploit them.

4.4.1   Opening, Closing, and Creating Files

In this section, we discuss some of the most important system calls for setting up and tearing down the structures for files. They are used for creating, opening, and closing files.

4.4.1.1   Open(2) and creat(2)

The *open(2)* and *creat(2)* system calls[4] establish a relationship between the file, named by the path parameter, and a file descriptor. The opened file descriptor must be used by subsequent I/O functions, such as *read(2)*, *write(2)*, and *stat(2)*, to access or manipulate that file. The *open(2)* sets up several structures in kernel and process memory so that subsequent operations can be performed on the file using its file descriptor. The state of kernel structures following an *open(2)* can be seen by looking at Figure 4–5. In this figure, we see that opening a file has an effect on three tables: (1) the process open file descriptor table, (2) the systemwide open file table, and (3) the vnode table. Also, although we don't show it here, it may also impact the namei cache and the buffer cache.

4.4.1.2   File Descriptors

When you write a program that utilizes the *open(2)* system call, it informs the system that you intend to perform I/O or in some other way manipulate it. When an *open(2)* succeeds, it returns an integer back to the calling process. This value is known as a file descriptor. A **file descriptor** is a number that represents an index into a process's open files table. The open file table is located in the user area in standard UNIX and in the utask structure in Tru64 UNIX. See Figure 4–5 for a pictorial representation of the process open files table.

4.4.1.3   The File Structure

Another object that can be created when an *open(2)*, *creat(2)*, or *pipe(2)* system call is issued is called a **file structure**. If that file has not already been opened by another process, then a new entry will be added into the system-wide open files table. On the other hand, if another process had already performed an operation that previously added the open files table entry, then the new operation would simply increment the reference count, rather than creating a new entry. The file structure is defined in <sys/file.h> as follows:

```
struct file {
    udecl_simple_lock_data(,f_incore_lock)
    int    f_flag;        /* see below */
    uint_t f_count;        /* reference count */
    int    f_type;        /* descriptor type */
    int    f_msgcount;        /* references from message queue */
    struct ucred *f_cred;      /* descriptor's credentials */
    struct fileops {
        int    (*fo_read)();
        int    (*fo_write)();
        int    (*fo_ioctl)();
        int    (*fo_select)();
        int    (*fo_close)();
    } *f_ops;
    caddr_t f_data;           /* vnode, socket, etc. */
    union {               /* offset or next free file struct */
        off_t     fu_offset;
        struct file   *fu_freef;
```

```
              } f_u;
              uint_t f_io_lock;        /* i/o lock (low half of thread ptr) */
              int   f_io_waiters;      /* number of waiters on i/o lock */
          };
```

Program 4–1

The create.c program is a simple example of how to use the *open(2)*, *creat(2),* and *close(8)* system calls. Although this program is really not visibly doing much, there's quite a bit going on in the kernel.

```
1 /*
2  * create.c - Demonstrate the creat(2)/open(2)/close(2) system calls
3  *
4  * Written By: Steven Hancock, Copyright © 1996, 2000
5  * Written on: 16-Aug-1996
6  * Last Updated: 15-Mar-2000
7  */
8
9 #include <stdio.h>
10 #include <sys/stat.h>
11 #include <sys/types.h>
12 #include <errno.h>
13 #include <fcntl.h>
14
15 #define FILENAME "test_file"
16 #define FILEMODE 0644
17
18 main(int argc,char *argv[])
19 {
20   int fd;
21
22   if((fd = open(FILENAME,O_RDONLY)) < 0) {
23     if(errno != ENOENT) {
24       perror("open");
25       exit(1);
26     }
27   }
28   else {
29     fprintf(stderr,"File %s exists. I cannot create it.\n",FILENAME);
30     close(fd);
31     exit(2);
32   }
33
34   if((fd = creat(FILENAME, FILEMODE)) < 0) {
35     perror("creat");
36     exit(3);
37   }
38
39   close(fd);
40 }
```

In a sample run of this program, we see that the first time it executes, the program checks to see if it can open the file for read-only access in line 22. If the *open(2)* fails (upon failure, we get a negative status return back from the *open(2)* call), then we drop to line 23, where we check the errno value returned. If the errno is ENOENT, which means that the file does not exist, then we can continue processing at line 34 in the program. There, we execute a *creat(2)* to create the file; a file descriptor is returned and placed into the fd variable. After successfully creating the file, we drop to line 39, which closes it again. A successful run of the program returns a status code of 0.

```
# ls test_file
test_file not found

# ./create

# echo $status
0

# ls test_file
test_file
```

In the second run of the program, the *open(2)* in line 22 succeeds (upon success, we get a 0 return status back), then we skip to line 28 to execute the else part of the if-then-else structure. If that happens, then we report that the file exists and we cannot create it; we close the file and exit with a status code of 2.

```
# ./create
File test_file exists. I cannot create it.

# echo $status
2
```

The returned file descriptor is the lowest file descriptor not previously open for that process. No process can have more than the hard limit, defined by OPEN_MAX_HARD, of file descriptors opened simultaneously. OPEN_MAX_HARD is defined in the #include file <sys/param.h> as 4096 file descriptors. The soft limit is also defined by the variable OPEN_MAX_SOFT and has a default value of 4096 as well. These values can be further limited by the system administrator using the /etc/sysconfigtab with entries such as the following:

```
proc:
open-max-soft = 1024
open-max-hard = 4000
```
And reboot for the new values to be effective.

Program 4–2:

The maxopen.c program is simply designed to reach the per-process maximum number of open files. It does this by opening the same file in read-only mode for up to 5000 times, or until it reaches the limit, whichever comes first.

```
1  /*
2    maxopen.c - Program to demonstrate the max number of open files.
3
4    Written By: Steven Hancock, Copyright © 2000
5    Written on: 15-Mar-2000
6    Last Updated: 15-Mar-2000
7  */
8
9  #include <stdio.h>
10 #include <sys/stat.h>
11 #include <sys/types.h>
12 #include <errno.h>
13 #include <fcntl.h>
14
15 #define FILENAME "test_file"
16 #define MAXFILES 5000
17
18 main(int argc,char *argv[])
19 {
20   int fd[MAXFILES],
21     i;
22
23   for(i = 0;i < MAXFILES;i++) {
24     if((fd[i] = open(FILENAME,O_RDONLY)) < 0) {
25       if(errno != EMFILE) {
26         perror("open");
27         exit(1);
28       }
29       else {
30         printf("opened file %d times.\n",i);
31         printf("last fd: %d\n",fd[i-1]);
32         exit(0);
33       }
34     }
35     if(!i)
36       printf("first fd: %d\n",fd[i]);
37   }
38   printf("opened file %d times.\n",i);
39 }
```

On a sample run of this program, we see that the output comes back quickly that the first available file descriptor is 3. This makes sense because the three standard file descriptors remain open for this process. The stdin, stdout, and stderr file descriptors are already utilizing numbers

0, 1, and 2 before this program runs. The program continues to run until it gets a failed status return from the *open(2)* system call at line 24. When that happens, we check to see if the errno is EMFILE, which indicates that we have reached our soft per-process open file limit. If so, we print the information about the last successful open we performed (thus, the "i-1" is used in the *printf(3)* at line 31).

```
# ./maxopen
first fd: 3
opened file 1021 times.
last fd: 1023
```

Finally, we confirm that the soft per-process limit is 1024 on this system. Therefore, our example program has hit the appropriate limit.

```
# sysconfig -q proc | grep open
open-max-soft = 1024
open-max-hard = 4000
```

4.4.1.4 Close(2)

A program issues a *close(2)* system call when it no longer wishes to have an association with that file. The descriptor for the file to be disassociated is given to *close(2)* as a parameter. The kernel removes the file descriptor, but it may not remove the entries in the systemwide open file table or vnode table. If there are other references to the open file structure, then the count is reduced by one. The vnode structure may also have additional references. If the reference count is 2 or greater, then it is simply reduced by one. Only when the reference count drops to 0 are the file and vnode structures actually removed from memory.

If the file had been previously unlinked, but remained open, then the *close(2)* may complete the process of removing accessibility of the file on-disk. The prior *unlink(2)* had performed the on-disk operations to remove the file, but the existing references maintained the existence of the file on-disk. The file is simply not accessible to any new references because the directory entry, which makes the association between a file's name and its inode, has been removed. When all file descriptors associated with an open file are closed, the systemwide open file structure is freed. If the link count of the file is 0 when all file descriptors associated with the file have been closed, then the in-memory data structures associated with the file are freed and the file is no longer accessible. See Program 4–3 for an example of this mechanism in action.

4.4.2   Removing Files

The *unlink(2)* system call removes the directory entry specified by the path parameter. If the entry is a hard link (meaning the reference count is >1), then it decrements the link count of the file referenced by the link.

When all links to a file are removed and no process has the file open or mapped, all resources associated with the file are reclaimed, and the file is no longer accessible. If one or more processes have the file open or mapped when the last link is removed, then the link is removed before the *unlink(2)* function returns, but the removal of the file contents is postponed until all open or map references to the file are removed. If the path parameter names a symbolic link, then the symbolic link itself is removed but not the file to which it is pointing.

A process must have write access to the parent directory of the file to be unlinked with respect to all access policies. Upon successful completion, the *unlink(2)* function marks for update the st_ctime and st_mtime fields of the directory that contained the link. If the file's link count is not 0, then the st_ctime field of the file is also marked for update. Program 4–3 gives an example of the *unlink(2)* system call.

Program 4–3:

The unlink.c program shown here is designed to illustrate that the open and unlinked file is only accessible to the processes that have the file open before the unlink. After that, the directory entry no longer exists for other processes.

```
 1 /*
 2   unlink.c - Program to demonstrate the unlink(2) system call
 3
 4    Written By: Steven Hancock, Copyright © 1996, 2000
 5    Written on: 16-Aug-1996
 6    Last Updated: 03-Apr-2000
 7 */
 8
 9 #include <stdio.h>
10 #include <sys/stat.h>
11 #include <sys/types.h>
12 #include <fcntl.h>
13 #include <errno.h>
14
15 #define FILENAME "test_file"
16
17 main(int argc, char *argv[])
18 {
19   int fd, fd2, error;
20   struct stat *buf;
```

```
21
22   printf("Opening file %s.\n", FILENAME);
23
24   if((fd = open(FILENAME, O_RDONLY)) < 0) {
25     perror("open");
26     exit(1);
27   }
28
29   printf("Unlinking file %s.\n", FILENAME);
30
31   if((error = unlink(FILENAME)) < 0) {
32     perror("unlink");
33     exit(2);
34   }
35
36   buf = (struct stat *)malloc(sizeof(struct stat));
37   if(buf == NULL) {
38     fprintf(stderr,"malloc failed");
39     exit(3);
40   }
41
42   printf("Attempting to stat(2) the file.\n");
43   if((fd2 = stat(FILENAME, buf)) < 0) {
44     perror("stat");
45   }
46
47   printf("Closing file %s.\n",FILENAME);
48
49   close(fd);
50   free(buf);
51 }
```

The following example shows two sample runs of the program. In the first case, the file test_file doesn't exist, so the *open(2)* fails. In the second case, the test_file exists and can be opened and unlinked.

```
$ ./unlink
Opening file test_file.
open: No such file or directory

$ touch test_file

$ ./unlink
Opening file test_file.
Unlinking file test_file.
Attempting to stat(2) the file.
stat: No such file or directory
Closing file test_file.
```

The "No such file or directory" return from *open(2)* or *stat(2)* is caused by an errno of ENOENT, which means that the entry doesn't exist in the current directory.

4.4.3 Gathering File Statistics

The *stat(2)* system call is used to obtain details about the file with a name given by the path parameter. Access permission for the named file is not relevant, but all directories listed in the pathname leading to the file must be searchable. As discussed in Chapter 1, the stat information comes from the inode of the file on disk. When the file information is read, it is written into an area specified by the buffer parameter, which is a pointer to a stat structure, defined in <sys/stat.h> and described in Table 4–8.

TABLE 4–8 The Fields of the stat Structure

FIELD	DATA TYPE	DESCRIPTION
st_dev	dev_t	ID of the device containing a directory entry for this file. File serial number plus the device ID uniquely identify the file within the system.
st_ino	ino_t	The file's unique inode or tag number
st_mode	mode_t	The file's mode bits (see Table 4–9)
st_nlink	nlink_t	The count of the number of links
st_uid	uid_t	The user ID of the file's owner
st_gid	gid_t	The group ID of the file's group owner
st_rdev	dev_t	The ID of the device, if this is a character or block special file
st_size	off_t	The file size, in bytes
st_atime	time_t	The time of last access of the file (see Chapter 1 for discussion of the atime)
st_spare1	int	Filler
st_mtime	time_t	The time of last data modification (see Chapter 1 for discussion of the mtime)
st_spare2	int	Filler
st_ctime	time_t	The time of last file status change (see Chapter 1 for discussion of the ctime)
st_spare3	int	Filler
st_blksize	uint_t	The size of block of the file
st_blocks	int	The number of blocks allocated for the file
st_flags	uint_t	The user-defined flags for the file
st_flags	uint_t	The user-defined flags for the file
st_gen	uint_t	The file's generation number

The values of the mode_t information are defined in <sys/mode.h> as shown in Table 4–9.

TABLE 4–9   File Mode Values

Symbol	Bits (Octal)	Description
S_ISUID	0004000	Sets user ID on execution (see Chapter 1 for a discussion of SUID bit).
S_ISGID	0002000	Sets group ID on execution (see Chapter 1 for a discussion of SGID bit).
S_IRWXU	0000700	Reads, writes, and executes permissions for the file object's owner.
S_IRUSR	0000400	Reads permission for the file object's owner.
S_IWUSR	0000200	Writes permission for the file object's owner.
S_IXUSR	0000100	Executes/searches permissions for the file object's owner.
S_IRWXG	0000070	Reads, writes, and executes permissions for the file object's group owner.
S_IRGRP	0000040	Reads permissions for the file object's group owner.
S_IWGRP	0000020	Writes permissions for the file object's group owner.
S_IXGRP	0000010	Executes/searches permissions for the file object's group owner.
S_IRWXO	0000007	Reads, writes, and executes permissions for other users of the file.
S_IROTH	0000004	Reads permissions for the "other" users of the file.
S_IWOTH	0000002	Writes permissions for the "other" users of the file.
S_IXOTH	0000001	Executes/searches permissions for the "other" users of the file.

There are two alternative *stat(2)* functions: the *fstat(2)* and the *lstat(2)*. The former has the same semantics as the *stat(2)* system call but uses a file descriptor to reference the file, rather than the pathname. You can think of the *stat(2)* as being a combination of an *open(2)* with an *fstat(2)* and a *close(2)* in a single system call. The *lstat(2)* has different behavior than *stat(2)* or *fstat(2)* when used with a symbolic link. The *lstat(2)* gives information about the symbolic link, whereas the other two system calls follow the link and provide statistics about the file to which it refers.

Program 4–4:

The stat.c program, shown as follows, demonstrates how the *lstat(2)* can be used to gather statistics about a file called test_file.

```
1 /*
```

```
 2   stat.c - Program to demonstrate the lstat(2) system call
 3
 4   Written By: Steven Hancock, Copyright © 1996, 2000
 5   Written on: 1-Aug-1996
 6   Last Updated: 03-Apr-2000
 7 */
 8
 9 #include <sys/stat.h>
10 #include <sys/types.h>
11 #include <fcntl.h>
12 #include <time.h>
13
14 #define FILENAME "test_file"
15
16 main(int argc, char argv[])
17 {
18   int fd;
19   struct stat *buf;
20   char st_atime[64], st_ctime[64], st_mtime[64];
21
22   buf = (struct stat *)malloc(sizeof(struct stat));
23
24   if((fd = lstat(FILENAME,buf)) < 0) {
25    perror("lstat");
26    exit(1);
27   }
28
29   printf("File statistics for %s\n",FILENAME);
30   printf("Inode: %d, Mode: %0004o, Type: ",buf->st_ino,
31          buf->st_mode & 0x0FFF);
32
33   switch( buf->st_mode & S_IFMT ) {
34    case S_IFDIR:
35      printf("directory\n");
36      break;
37    case S_IFREG:
38      printf("regular\n");
39      break;
40    case S_IFLNK:
41      printf("symbolic link\n");
42      break;
43    case S_IFCHR:
44      printf("character special\n");
45      break;
46    case S_IFBLK:
47      printf("block special\n");
48      break;
49    case S_IFSOCK:
50      printf("socket\n");
51      break;
52    case S_IFIFO:
53      printf("FIFO\n");
54      break;
55    default:
56      printf("unknown\n");
```

```
57  }
58
59  printf("Num links: %d\n",buf->st_nlink);
60  printf("UID: %d, GID: %d\n",buf->st_uid,buf->st_gid);
61  printf("File size: %d\n",buf->st_size);
62  printf("atime: %sctime: %smtime: %s",ctime(&buf->st_atime),
63        ctime(&buf->st_ctime), ctime(&buf->st_mtime));
64
65  free(buf);
66  close(fd);
67 }
```

The following sample run shows the stat program output when it is run on a directory file.

```
$ ls -lid test_file
307244 drwxr-xr-x  2 139   100      512 Apr 3 11:05 test_file

$ ./stat
File statistics for test_file
Inode: 307244, Mode: 0755, Type: directory
Num links: 2
UID: 139, GID: 100
File size: 512
atime: Mon Apr 3 11:05:18 2000
ctime: Mon Apr 3 11:05:18 2000
mtime: Mon Apr 3 11:05:18 2000
```

Another sample run shows how the *lstat(2)* system call gives information about a symbolic link itself rather than the file to which it points.

```
$ ls -l test_file
lrwxrwxrwx 1 139   100      6 Apr 3 11:35 test_file -> stat.c

$ ./stat
File statistics for test_file
Inode: 821861, Mode: 0777, Type: symbolic link
Num links: 1
UID: 139, GID: 100
File size: 6
atime: Mon Apr 3 11:35:42 2000
ctime: Mon Apr 3 11:35:42 2000
mtime: Mon Apr 3 11:35:42 2000
```

4.4.4 Reading and Writing Files

In this section, we discuss the system calls that allow you to retrieve data blocks from a file or put data blocks into a file. All of the I/O to and from storage are handled by the *read(2)* and *write(2)* system calls. The file I/O is normally handled by these two system calls in a sequential manner. The *lseek(2)* system call is used to position the file pointer (the fu_offset field in the file structure) so that random access to a file is possible.

4.4.4.1 Read(2)

The *read(2)* system call attempts to read a specified number of data bytes from the file associated with its file descriptor parameter. The data are read into a preallocated buffer pointed to by its buffer parameter. Because the *read(2)* requires a file descriptor for its parameter, the file must have already been opened using *open(2)* or created with *creat(2)*.

The number of bytes read is returned from the system call upon success. If the return from the *read(2)* is –1, then the function has failed. The errno will be set to indicate the error that occurred.

4.4.4.2 Write(2)

The *write(2)* system call attempts to write a specified number of data bytes to the file associated with the file descriptor parameter. The data are written to the file from the buffer pointed to by the buffer parameter.

Upon success, the return from the *write(2)* will be the number of bytes actually written to the file. If a –1 is returned, then the function has failed and the errno will be set to indicate the error.

4.4.4.3 Lseek(2)

The *lseek(2)* system call sets the file offset within an open file to a specified value. The first parameter to *lseek(2)* is the file descriptor of the open file, the second parameter is the offset into the file, and the third parameter, known as *whence*, determines how the offset is to be interpreted.

A successful return from *lseek(2)* returns the byte offset within the file to which the file pointer was set. If the system call fails, then a –1 is returned and the errno is set to indicate the error.

The *lseek(2)* system call allows the file offset to be set beyond the end of existing data in the file. If data are later written at this point, then subsequently reading data in the gap returns bytes with the value 0 until data are actually written into the gap. By itself, the *lseek(2)* system call does not extend the size of the file. A *write(2)* must follow the *lseek(2)* in order to extend the file past its existing endpoint. As discussed in Chapter 1, this is the way in which sparse files can be created.

4.5   New Features of VFS

In Tru64 UNIX 5.0, a few new features were added to the VFS layer to support new functionality or to improve performance of the file systems. In this section, we discuss some of those new features.

4.5.1   The Cluster File System

Beginning with Tru64 UNIX and TruCluster Server 5.0A,[5] a new abstraction layer has been added to the interface between the POSIX layer and the file system layer (AdvFS, CDFS, UFS). This abstraction layer, known as the **cluster file system** (CFS), is completely transparent to the user and applications on a cluster system, except that all file systems are seen by all systems in a cluster. We won't endeavor to cover clusters in great depth here, but we introduce a few concepts that will enhance readers' appreciation for what the CFS is and why it is special.

In a standalone system, there is no way to discern the existence of the CFS. Even so, it still exists in a single system as well as in a multisystem cluster. In fact, a single system with TruCluster installed is really just a cluster with only one member. CFS maintains its cache coherency with assistance from the **distributed lock manager** (DLM). The DLM piece does not exist without having TruCluster installed.

Another important piece is the **device request dispatcher** (DRD). The new DRD is similar to the distributed raw disk from TruCluster 1.x; however, it exists for all disk and tape devices in the cluster, not just those shared disks for which an association has been made. Furthermore, unlike the DRD of TCR version 1.X (which was a client/server implementation), the DRD can allow for simultaneous access by all members on the same shared bus via direct-access I/O (DAIO), although private bus devices would still be served. The shared device-naming scheme cannot be disabled. In addition, the new Tru64 UNIX device-naming scheme discussed in Chapter 2 is required to make it work. Once you think about this, you'll understand that CFS could not exist without the new global naming conventions. In fact, as discussed in Chapter 2, CFS was one of the main drivers of the new device-naming scheme.

The mount table in a cluster shows all file systems mounted on each system to all systems in the cluster. So, file systems created and mounted on devices that are shared or nonshared will only be mounted to one member of the cluster but will be seen by all members. This is not controllable; file systems cannot be made local and will always be seen by all members. Care should be taken to ensure that data that are meant to be local are not inadvertently made read-write accessible to other systems in the cluster.

Example:

This is an example of a *df(1)* command output from a two-member Tru-Cluster. You'll notice that the file systems from both of the members are visible from this system.

```
# df
Filesystem        512-blocks        Used   Available   Capacity   Mounted on
cluster_root#root     262144      159820       90672        64%    /
root2_domain#root     262144       85568      165392        35%    /cluster/members/
member2/boot_partition
root1_domain#root     262144       85442      164752        35%    /cluster/members/
member1/boot_partition
cluster_usr#usr      8690144     1231044     7427936        15%    /usr
cluster_var#var      8690144       45662     8632784         1%    /var
/proc                      0           0           0       100%    /proc
```

4.5.2   Leveling Cache Flush Performance

Since very early in the development of caching in UNIX, the update daemon has operated in the same manner as it has today. Every 30 seconds, the daemon runs and executes a *sync(2)* system call to flush all of the dirty buffers to disk. This mechanism works well for most systems, but others with a large amount of volatile data can have a "pausing" of their system while the cache is flushed.

The **smooth sync** and **I/O throttling** features were first introduced in Tru64 UNIX 5.0[6] in order to address the problem of systems "pausing" when large numbers of dirty pages were flushed to disk during each pass of the update daemon. In the case of very large and very active UFSs and AdvFSs, the system "pauses" could be frequent and disruptive to the operation of the rest of the system.

Smooth syncing allows each dirty page to age for a specified time period before being written out to disk. This allows more opportunity for frequently modified pages to be found in the cache, thus decreasing the overall I/O load on the system. In addition, pages are queued to a device only after having aged sufficiently, rather than being flushed by the update daemon. Therefore, cache flushes in which large numbers of dirty pages become locked on the device queue are minimized.

In addition, the I/O throttling feature addresses the problem of locking dirty pages on the device queue. It enforces a limit on the number of delayed I/O requests allowed to be on the device queue at any one time. The result of this constraint is to allow the system to be more responsive to any synchronous requests added to the device queue. This may also decrease the duration of process stalls for specific dirty buffers since pages continue to remain available until placed on the device queue.

Four /etc/sysconfigtab parameters were added with this capability. These are discussed as follows.

- **smoothsync_age:** This is the number of seconds that a page ages before becoming eligible for being flushed to disk via the smooth sync mechanism. A value of 30 corresponds to the mechanism provided by the traditional UNIX update daemon. Increasing this value increases the exposure of lost data should the system crash; however, it also decreases overall I/O load on the system by allowing the dirty data to remain in cache longer. On many systems, data must always be kept up-to-date; these are prime candidates for an increased smoothsync_age. This parameter can be adjusted from 0 (off) up to 300, and the default value is 30.

- **io_throttle_shift:** The greater the number of requests on an I/O device queue, the longer the time required to process those requests and make those pages and devices available. The number of concurrent delayed I/O requests on an I/O device queue can be throttled by setting the io_throttle_shift tunable. The throttle value is based on this tunable and the calculated I/O completion rate, and is proportional to the time required to process the I/O device queue. Table 4–10 shows the correspondence between io_throttle_shift values and the time to process the device queue. The valid range for this tunable is from –4 to 4 inclusive. The default value of io_throttle_shift is 1.

TABLE 4–10   Io-throttle-shift to Process Time Conversions

IO-THROTTLE-SHIFT	TIME TO PROCESS DEVICE QUEUE (SEC)
-4	0.0625
-3	0.125
-2	0.25
-1	0.5
0	1
1	2
2	4
3	8
4	16

- **io_throttle_static:** This sets the internal I/O throttle value to an absolute, nonzero value rather than a formula like we have with io_throttle_shift. The default value is 0, which means we follow the io_throttle_shift method for calculating I/O throttle values.

- **io-maxmzthruput:** This parameter trades off maximizing I/O throughput against maximizing the availability of dirty pages. It is a Boolean value, which can be either 1 (on) or 0 (off). The default value of io_maxmzthruput is 1. If your environment is particularly sensitive to delays in accessing sets of frequently used dirty pages, then you might consider setting this attribute to 0.

In order to activate smooth sync, the following lines must be present in the /etc/inittab file immediately following the line containing "update." This enables smooth sync on transitions into multiuser mode and disables smooth sync on transition into single-user mode.

```
smsync:23:wait:/sbin/sysconfig -r vfs smoothsync-age=30 > /
dev/null 2>&1
smsyncS:Ss:wait:/sbin/sysconfig -r vfs smoothsync-age=0 > /
dev/null 2>&1
```

Also, for smooth sync to be active on selected file systems, you must update your /etc/fstab entries for the UFSs to enable the selected mount options. The two options are smsync2 and throttle, as we discussed in Chapter 1. The following example shows how you can set this up:

Example:

To activate smooth sync and I/O throttling on an existing file system called /dev/vol/volbig, we edit the fstab and change the following line from

```
/dev/vol/volbig /usr/staff/k2 ufs rw 0 2
```

to

```
/dev/vol/volbig /usr/staff/k2 ufs rw,smsync2,throttle 0 2
```

Then, just remount the file system for it to take effect. Any changes you make to the smooth sync or I/O throttling parameters will be manifest on this file system. Otherwise, the normal update behavior will be seen.

4.6   Summary

In this chapter, we have discussed the virtual file system. Most modern UNIX systems utilize this powerful feature because it allows them to implement many different file system types on the same system, each utilizing the normal POSIX interface. Tru64 UNIX follows this standard and implements it in much the same way as the other vendors do.

In the next chapter, we move into our first fully supported, general-purpose file system type known as the UNIX File System.

Notes

1.   In order to see what standards your version of Tru64 UNIX conforms to, see the *standards(5)* reference page.

2.   One of the exceptions is Compaq's (formerly Digital's) ULTRIX operating system. ULTRIX used the gnode interface, which was a competitor to Sun's vnode in the 1980s. Today, ULTRIX can still be found at customer sites, but it is no longer fully supported by the company.

3.   This parameter is introduced in Tru64 UNIX 5.0A, rather than 5.0.

4.   The origin of *creat(2)* with the missing "e" is not widely known; however, according to Kernighan and Pike (1984), Ken Thompson was interviewed at about the time UNIX was beginning to gain some commercial success, and he was asked if he would do anything differently if he were redesigning it. After a pause, Ken stated: "I'd spell creat(2) with an e."

5.   The hooks are there in Tru64 UNIX 5.0; however, TruCluster Server 5.0 was never generally released to customers. Version 5.0a was the first generally released version to include all of the pieces to fully support the cluster file system.

6.   The fix was also available for UFS in certain 4.0x versions and by patch kit. The AdvFS smooth sync feature was first available in Tru64 UNIX 5.0.

5

UNIX File System

> Imagination is more important than knowledge.
> — *Albert Einstein*

In this chapter, we cover the UNIX file system (UFS),[1] which is the first of two general-purpose, local file system types (the second being AdvFS) that are fully supported in all versions of Tru64 UNIX.

We begin this chapter by discussing the history of UFS. Then, we cover some of the file system's on-disk structure details as well as some of the in-memory structures. Next, we discuss some of the tools available for creating, tuning, and examining UFSs. Also, we cover the tools for troubleshooting and repairing corrupted file systems. We include brief coverage of backups and quotas, concluding with information about the memory-based UFS.

5.1   Brief History of UFS

The UFS has been around in various forms since version 7 of UNIX. We endeavor here to provide readers with some historical perspective in order to enhance their understanding of how the system has evolved over time and some of the design decisions that were made. This information provides a basis for describing how the file system behaves today.

This section first discusses the original file system for UNIX and the newer file system based on work done with the Berkeley fast file system (FFS).[2]

5.1.1   The Traditional UNIX File System

The traditional UFS looked and behaved almost identically to how it looks and behaves today from the end user's perspective. The original UNIX system was implemented on Digital Equipment Corporation PDP-8™ hardware and evolved over time to VAX™, MIPS, and many other non-Digital platforms. One of the things that made UNIX successful was the fact that the operating system was portable. As the UNIX system's popularity grew, it started to become apparent that the performance and reliability of the file system was not keeping up with the user's requirements.

Some of the features of the implementation of the "old" file system were:

- Fixed-size blocks (512 bytes each)
- Single copy of the superblock located at a fixed location
- File system I/O buffered by the kernel
- No alignment constraints on data transfers
- All operations appear to be synchronous
- No symbolic links

Generally, the old file system was simple and performed the work it was designed to do adequately. It provided a hierarchical mechanism for storing user files and a measure of protection of privacy between users; however, the file system was likely to become fragmented over time because of the small block size, which severely impacted performance. Also, the file system was likely to become corrupted if the system crashed for any reason. This could easily happen because some operations were not ordered in such a way as to allow inconsistencies to be cleaned up. The lack of block alignment constraints also led to inconsistent file updates.

5.1.2   The Berkeley Fast File System

The original work done at the University of California at Berkeley and described in McKusick et al. (1984) determined that both the performance and reliability could be improved without changing the basic file system interface. Therefore, existing programs would not have to be modified to accommodate the improvements.

Researchers found that the problems with the file system's performance were not caused by the interface's design, but simply that the implementation was suboptimal. It was found that when the size of the file system block was doubled from 512 to 1024, a linear improvement in performance could be gained. The researchers showed that this trend continued even with page sizes at 2048 and 4096, so they decided on the latter of these two figures for the default page size.

Another performance problem was that over time, the "old" file system free space became fragmented, thus requiring many disk seeks to access a single file. Thus, the file system design was changed to improve the locality of file placement references in order to minimize seek latency. On the other hand, a larger block size also led to more wasted space. The design was improved to include the concept of a fragment, so that smaller files and pieces of files could be stored more efficiently. We'll discuss fragments in greater detail later in this chapter.

The reliability was also improved by ordering the modification of critical information on the file system so that functions could either be completed or repaired cleanly by a program after a system crash. Some operations were made atomic and aligned on a block boundary so files could be written and updated without risking corruption.

Other improvements made in the FFS were as follows:

- Long file names were added. The "old" file system supported file names up to 14 characters. The limit was made arbitrary.

- File locking was added.

- Symbolic links were added as a file type.

- The rename function was added to the kernel to make it atomic.

- Quotas were added.

5.2   Layout of UFS On-Disk Structure

Based on the changes introduced in the Berkeley FFS, the general on-disk structure of the UFS is shown in Figure 5–1.

FIGURE 5–1
UNIX File System On-Disk Structure

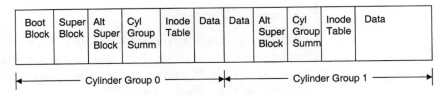

5.2.1   The Inode

The **inode** is the focus of file system activity on a UFS. Each inode has an associated number and describes an individual file on the file system. Each possible file in the file system has one inode. File systems have a maximum number of inodes; therefore, a file system can contain only a set maximum number of files. The maximum number of inodes is calculated using a formula that depends on the size of the file system.

Inode 0 cannot be used, and the first inode (inode 1) is unnamed and unused. Inode 1 was originally used for bad block replacement, but it has not been used for that purpose for some time. The second inode (inode 2) must correspond to the root directory for the file system. All other files in the file system are under the file system's root directory. After inode 2, the system can assign any inode to any file and can assign any data block to any file. The inodes and blocks are not allocated in any particular order, although they generally start at 3 and increase sequentially.

If an inode is assigned to a file, then the inode can contain the following information:

- File type
- File owner
- Protection information
- Link count
- Size of the file in bytes
- Last file accessed date (atime)
- Last file modification date (mtime)
- Last inode modification time (ctime)
- Pointers to data blocks

Figure 5–2 pictorially shows the structure of an inode in a Tru64 UFS. As you can see, there are 12 direct blocks and one each of single, double, and triple indirect blocks.

Example:

Compaq's supported maximum UFS size is 1 TB; however, the theoretical maximum size is larger. But, how is this number calculated? As an exercise to a group of seminar students, we posed the following questions regarding the theoretical size of the UFS following the presentation of the diagram in Figure 5–2.

Questions:

What is the theoretical maximum size of a file that can be stored using the following four cases:

a)   Strictly direct pointers

b)   Direct and single indirect pointers

FIGURE 5–2
UFS Inode Structure

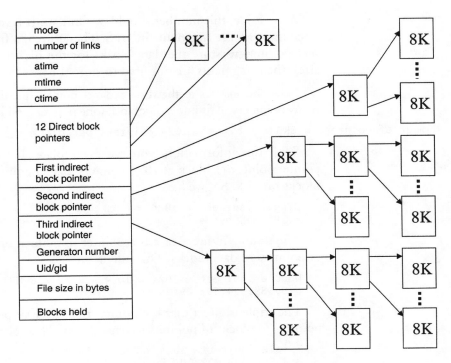

c)   Direct, single, and double indirect pointers

d)   Direct, single, double, and triple indirect pointers

Assume Tru64 UNIX parameters (8-kilobyte blocks, 12 direct pointers, etc). HINT: the size of a pointer is 64 bits.

Answers:

The first important piece of information to know in order to answer these questions is that the maximum size of a UFS is actually bounded at the top end by the maximum file size. This concept implies that the inode is a key structure to understanding this limit. For now, we assume that no other factors limit the theoretical maximums at this time, other than the direct and indirect pointers in an individual inode.

As we have discussed, the Tru64 UNIX inode contains 15 pointers: 12 direct and one each of single, double, and triple indirect pointers. Because direct pointers point directly to data blocks (or fragments) on disk, and because data blocks are a fixed 8 kilobytes, the maximum size of a file using only direct blocks will be:

```
Direct = 12 × 8 KB = 96 KB
```

As an aside, this number should be familiar: It is the maximum size of a file that can use fragments in UFS. Therefore, if a file is using the indirect pointers to store the data blocks for the file (it is >96 kilobytes in size), then fragments are not used to store the file.

Now, the answers to the three indirect pointer questions depend on how many pointers will fit into a disk block (one pointer is 64 bits, or 8 bytes):

```
Number of pointers = 8KB ÷ 8 bytes = 1024 pointers per block
```

With this information, you can extrapolate that one single indirect pointer points to a block of 1024 pointers that all point to other 8-kilobyte blocks on disk. So, we have:

```
Single indirect = 1024 × 8 KB = 8 MB
8,388,608 bytes
```

The double indirect case is a pointer to a block of pointers to blocks of pointers to data blocks. This calculation is:

```
Double indirect = 1024 × 1024 × 8 KB = 8 GB
= 8,589,934,592 bytes
```

The triple indirect case is a pointer to a block of pointers to blocks of pointers to blocks of pointers to data blocks. This calculation is:

```
Triple indirect= 1024 × 1024 × 1024 × 8 KB = 8 TB
= 8,796,093,022,208 bytes
```

Now, to answer the questions, keep in mind that to get to the single indirect pointer, the file would have to have used the first 12 direct pointers, or 96 KB. The same goes for the double indirect, in which the single and direct pointers must have been used before getting to the double indirect pointer; the same goes for the triple indirect pointer as well.

So, the answers are:

a)   96 KB = 98,304 bytes

b)   8 MB + 96 KB = 8,486,912 bytes

c)   8 GB + 8 MB + 96 KB = 8,598,421,504 bytes

d)   8 TB + 8 GB + 8 MB + 96 KB = 8,804,691,443,712 bytes

It is really not practical to make a file system this large because the time to *fsck(8)* or back it up would be prohibitively long. Enter AdvFS . . .

5.2.2   Superblocks

The first block of every UFS is called the **superblock** and contains information that describes the parameters of the file system. More specifically, it contains the following information:

- Total size of the file system (in blocks)
- Number of blocks reserved for inodes
- Name of the file system
- Device identification
- Date of the last superblock update
- Head of the free-block list, which contains all of the free blocks (the blocks available for allocation) in the file system. When new blocks are allocated to a file, they are obtained from the free-block list. When a file is deleted, its blocks are returned to the free-block list.
- List of free inodes, which is the partial listing of inodes available to be allocated to newly created files.

The superblock is a critical structure in the UFS. Without it there would not be a file system. Because it is so critical, the *newfs(8)* command allocates several backup or alternate superblocks that can be used for recovery should the primary (block 1) become unreadable. These backup superblocks are allocated when the file system is created using the *newfs(8)* command and are listed to the screen at that time. One backup superblock is allocated per cylinder group at varying offsets within each cylinder group. That is done so that the loss of a single platter in the disk should not destroy all the backup superblocks. You can use *newfs(8)* with the '-N' qualifier to get a printout of the backup superblock list for a particular file system. You can use *fsck(8)* with the '-b' switch to use an alternate superblock to clean a file system for use.

Example:

Here's an example of a superblock as shown from *fsdb(8)*:

```
> :sb
   super block:
magic 11954  format dynamic time  Fri Aug 23 12:36:44 1996
nbfree 65474  ndir  11   nifree 13423  nffree 36
ncg   44   ncyl 698   size  552438 blocks 535173
bsize 8192  shift  13   mask 0xffffe000
fsize 1024  shift  10   mask 0xfffffc00
frag  8    shift  3    fsbtodb 1
cpg   16   bpg  1584  fpg  12672  ipg   3008
minfree 10%  optim  time maxcontig 8   maxbpg 2048
rotdelay 0ms  headswitch 0us trackseek 0us  rps   60
ntrak 16   nsect 99  npsect 99   spc   1584
trackskew 0   interleave 1
nindir 2048  inopb 64   nspf 2
sblkno 16   cblkno 24   iblkno 32   dblkno 408
sbsize 2048  cgsize 3072  cgoffset 56   cgmask 0xfffffff0
csaddr 408   cssize 1024  shift  9    mask 0xfffffe00
cgrotor 41   fmod 0    ronly 0
```

5.2.3   Cylinder Groups

A **cylinder group** is a list of a fixed number of consecutive cylinders in a
disk partition. Each cylinder group contains bookkeeping information
that includes a redundant copy of the superblock, space for inodes, a bitmap describing available blocks in the cylinder group, and summary
information describing the usage of data blocks within the cylinder
group. The bitmap of available blocks in the cylinder group replaces the
traditional file system's free list. For each cylinder group, a static number
of inodes is allocated at file system creation time. The default policy is to
allocate one inode for each 4096 bytes of space in the cylinder group,
with the expectation that this amount will be far greater than will ever be
needed. This is sometimes not enough inodes to store a large number of
smaller files, however, and you may run out of inodes before all of the
space is utilized.

The motivation for the existence of cylinder groups is to create clusters of inodes that are spread over the disk, instead of locating them all at
the beginning. The file system is designed to allocate file blocks close to
the inodes that describe them to avoid long seeks between getting the
inode and getting its associated data. Also, when the inodes are spread
out, there is less chance of losing them all due to a single disk failure.

Example

Here's an example cylinder group from *fsdb(8):*

```
> :cg
cg 1:
magic   90255  tell   c74000  time   Fri Aug 16 19:59:10 1996
cgx     1      ncyl   16      niblk 3008 ndblk  12672
nbfree  1523   ndir   1       nifree 0    nffree 0
rotor   7912   irotor 3007    frotor 7912
frsum   0      0      0       0      0     0      0
sum of frsum: 0
iused: 0-3007
free:  8-15, 24-71, 504-7911, 7952-12671
b:
 c0:  (43)    4 6 6 5 5 6 6 5
 c1:  (99)    13 12 13 12 12 13 12 12
 c2:  (99)    13 12 13 12 12 13 12 12
 c3:  (99)    13 12 13 12 12 13 12 12
 c4:  (99)    13 12 13 12 12 13 12 12
 c5:  (99)    13 12 13 12 12 13 12 12
 c6:  (99)    13 12 13 12 12 13 12 12
 c7:  (99)    13 12 13 12 12 13 12 12
 c8:  (99)    13 12 13 12 12 13 12 12
 c9:  (98)    13 12 13 12 12 13 11 12
 c10: (95)    12 11 12 11 12 13 12 12
```

```
c11:  (99)    13 12 13 12 12 13 12 12
c12:  (99)    13 12 13 12 12 13 12 12
c13:  (99)    13 12 13 12 12 13 12 12
c14:  (99)    13 12 13 12 12 13 12 12
c15:  (99)    13 12 13 12 12 13 12 12
```

5.2.4 Fragments

The main problem with using larger blocks in file systems is that most UFSs contain primarily small files. A uniformly large block size on an average system wastes space in the file system. One of the primary results from McKusick et al.'s study (1984) was that as the block size increases, the waste rises quickly to an intolerable 45.6 percent waste with 4-kilobyte file system blocks. Wasted space was defined to be the percentage of disk space not containing user data. Conversely, another key conclusion was that smaller blocks were much less wasteful, but performance suffered.[3] A compromise solution is to allow larger block sizes but to use a smaller data structure to store the pieces that don't constitute an entire block.

A **fragment** in a UFS is a partial data block that is used to hold the parts of files that are too small to fit into a complete data block. This fragment can be a small file that is smaller than a complete file system page or a portion of a file that exceeds an integral number of file system pages. Any file that is larger than 96 kilobytes in size will not use fragments because the assumption is that a file that size will grow.

Data are laid out such that larger blocks can be transferred in a single disk operation, greatly increasing file system throughput. A file in a UFS is composed of 8-kilobyte file system pages and is not changeable. This compares to 1024 in the "old" UNIX file system: Disk accesses will thus transfer up to eight times as much information per disk transaction. In large files, several blocks may be allocated from the same cylinder, so that even larger data transfers are possible before a seek is required.

For large blocks to be used without significant waste, small files must be used more efficiently. This efficiency is obtained in UFS by allowing the division of a single file system block into one or more fragments. The fragment size is specified at the time that the file system is created; each file system block optionally can be broken into one, two, four, or eight fragments, each of which is addressable. The lower bound on the fragment size is 1024 bytes in Tru64 UNIX. In other vendors' UFS implementations, however, the lower bound of the fragment size is constrained by the disk sector size of 512 bytes. The block map associated with each cylinder group records the space available in a cylinder group in fragments; to determine whether a block is available, the system examines aligned fragments.

To change the fragment size, you use the '-f' switch to the *newfs(8)* command during the file system creation. Here's an example of creating a new file system:

```
# newfs -f 2048 /dev/rdisk/dsk2g rz29
```

The '-b' flag is obsolete for the *newfs(8)* command in Tru64 UNIX. In order to simplify the code and optimize access to the file system data, it was decided to use a fixed-size file system block of 8192 bytes. One of the consequences of this decision was to render the '-b' flag to *newfs(8)* ineffective. Thus, in our example above, the '-b' flag is not specified because the only possible value that you could give is 8192.

The superblock's "frag" field defines the number of fragments that can be stored in a single file system block. This means that the possible values that you can specify for the fragment size in Tru64 UNIX can be 1024, 2048, 4096, and 8192 bytes based on the possible "frag" values of 8, 4, 2, and 1. This has been true since the early days of the FFS. In ULTRIX UFS, which closely resembles the original Berkeley FFS, the block size is not fixed and can be either 4096 or 8192 bytes. Therefore, the valid range of sizes for a fragment that can be given to the '-f' flag depends on the block size. For example, if the block size is specified (using the '-b' flag) as 4096, then the possible range for the '-f' flag is 512, 1024, 2048, and 4096. Thus, in ULTRIX UFS, the '-f' and '-b' flags to *newfs(8)* are used in conjunction with each other to define the file system. In the old days, the FFS was referred to by the way the file system was configured. An FFS that was created with a 4096-byte block and a 512-byte fragment size, was a 4k/512 file system.

5.2.5   Boot Blocks

The first block of every UFS (block 0) is reserved for a boot, or initialization, program. This block is known as the **primary boot block**. When the system boots, it looks at the primary boot block to load the boot program and to decide which file system type is located on the root. Once this happens, if the system determines that a UFS root file system exists, it begins reading the **secondary boot blocks** loaded in disk blocks 1 to 15. The secondary boot blocks for AdvFS are physically located in disk blocks 64 to 95.

In Tru64 UNIX, the *disklabel(8)* command is used to write the boot block to a disk. The following is an example for writing a new default disk label to a disk with UFS boot blocks:

```
# disklabel -wr -t ufs dsk20c rzxx
```

The bootstrap programs that are used by the *disklabel(8)* command are located in the /mdec directory. The names of the bootstrap programs can be specified in the /etc/disktab file. If they are not specified, however, then the default names use either the {type}boot syntax for the primary bootstrap or the boot{type} syntax for the secondary bootstrap. The "type" is the type of disk, such as rz or re. For example, the names are /mdec/rzboot and /mdec/bootrz for a UFS rz-type disk. If you specify the "-t advfs" option, then the default names use either the {type} boot.advfs syntax for the primary bootstrap or the boot{type}.advfs syntax for the secondary bootstrap, for example, /mdec/rzboot.advfs and /mdec/bootrz.advfs.

If the '-t' flag is not specified, then the default is to write UFS boot blocks. If AdvFS boot blocks are desired, then the "-t advfs" option should be used to write them.

5.2.6 In-Memory vs. On-Disk Structures

It is important to distinguish at this point the difference between the in-memory structures and the on-disk structures in the UFS. Inodes that exist on-disk are read into cache only when the file system is mounted and the inode has been referenced. When an inode exists on an unmounted file system, it does not have an in-memory equivalent. An in-memory inode, which is also referred to as an in-core inode, is defined by the inode structure. On the other hand, the on-disk inode, referred to as the permanent inode, is defined by the dinode structure. As you recall from Chapter 4, we discussed the vnode and the way the inode information is appended to the vnode information following the v_data field. This is the in-core inode information.

5.3 Tools and Techniques

So far, we've discussed mainly the theory behind the UFS but not much in the way of practical knowledge. In this section, we cover the tools and techniques available to the system administrator for creating, managing, and troubleshooting UFSs.

The first thing most administrators need to accomplish after installing a new system is to set up new file systems for users and application software. We include a discussion here of the method to set up new Tru64 UFSs and tune them to perform appropriately.

5.3.1   Creating a New UNIX File System

The *newfs(8)* command (pronounced new-fiss) is used in Tru64 UNIX for creating UFSs. Unlike AdvFS, most of the structure of the UFS is static and is laid down on disk at the time it is created. Therefore, it is important to understand the parameters involved in setting up and tuning a new file system as well as how the file system will be used upfront. Although for most applications the defaults for these parameters are sufficient, sometimes they are not. If not, the penalty for not choosing proper parameters upfront could be severe. If you poorly tune your file system, then the performance could suffer or you could end up with a lot of wasted space.

Syntax:

```
newfs [-N] [options] device [disk-type]
```

TABLE 5–1   Flags for the *newfs(8)* Command

FLAGS	DESCRIPTION
device	The name of the device special file on which to create a UFS.
disk-type	The type of disk on which the file system will be created.
-N	Displays the file system parameters without really creating the file system. This is useful for finding alternate superblocks to recover the file system. See the *fsck(8)* section of this chapter and Appendix C for details on UFS recovery.
-b block_size	The block size of the file system in bytes. Note that the block size is fixed at 8 KB. This flag is obsolete in Tru64 UNIX.
-f frag_size	The fragment size of the file system in bytes. The fragment size must be a power of two fractional size of a file system block. The possible values are 1024, 2048, 4096, and 8192. The default value is 1024, which equates to eight fragments per file system block.
-m minfree	The percentage of space reserved from nonroot users. The minfree value is also known as the minimum free space threshold. The default value is 10 percent. See the *tunefs(8)* section of this chapter for more details on how to set this option.
-o opt_preference	This flag can be set to one of two possible values: "space" or "time." This means that the file system can either attempt to minimize the time spent allocating blocks, or try to minimize the space fragmentation on the disk. If the value of minfree is less than 10 percent, then the default is to optimize for space; if the value of minfree is greater than or equal to 10 percent, then the default is to optimize for time. See the *tunefs(8)* section of this chapter for more details on how to modify this flag.

TABLE 5–1 Flags for the *newfs(8)* Command (Continued)

FLAGS	DESCRIPTION
-a maxcontig	This specifies the maximum number of contiguous blocks (cluster) that are laid out before forcing a rotational delay (see the –d option). The default value is 8. See the *tunefs(8)* section in this chapter for more details on how to modify this flag.
-d rotdelay	This specifies the expected time (in milliseconds) to service a transfer completion interrupt and initiate a new transfer on the same disk. The default is 4 milliseconds. See the *tunefs(8)* section of this chapter for more details on how to modify this flag.
-e maxbpg	This indicates the maximum number of blocks that any single file can allocate out of a cylinder group before it is forced to begin allocating blocks from another cylinder group. The default is about one-quarter of the total blocks in a cylinder group. See the *tunefs(8)* section of this chapter for more details on how to modify this flag.
-i # bytes/inode	This flag specifies the desired density of inodes in the file system. The default is to create an inode for each 4096 bytes of data space. If fewer inodes are desired, then a larger number should be used; to create more inodes, a smaller number should be given. Creating a new file system with too few inodes can result in running out of space prematurely, but specifying too many inodes wastes space.
-c # cylinders/group	The number of cylinders per cylinder group in a file system. The default value is 16. If you specify an inode density that is too small, you may be forced by *newfs(8)* to alter this value.
-s size	The size of the file system in disk blocks (512 bytes/block).
-r revolutions/minute	The speed of the disk in revolutions per minute (RPM).
-S sector-size	The size of a sector in bytes (almost always 512 bytes).
-u sectors/track	The number of sectors per track available for data allocation by the file system. This does not include sectors reserved at the end of each track for bad block replacement (see the '-p' flag).
-t # tracks/cylinder	The number of tracks per cylinder available for data allocation by the file system.
-p spare_sectors/track	Spare sectors (bad sector replacements) are physical sectors that occupy space at the end of each track. They are not counted as part of the sectors per track (-u) because they are not available to the file system for data allocation.

TABLE 5–1   Flags for the *newfs(8)* Command (Continued)

FLAGS	DESCRIPTION
-x spare_sectors/cyl	Spare sectors (bad sector replacements) are physical sectors that occupy space at the end of the last track in the cylinder. They are deducted from the sectors per track (-u) of the last track of each cylinder because they are not available to the file system for data allocation.
-l interleave	Used to describe perturbations in the media format to compensate for a slow controller. Interleave is physical sector interleave on each track, specified as the denominator of the ratio: sectors read/sectors passed over. Thus, an interleave of 1/1 implies contiguous layout, whereas 1/2 implies that logical sector 0 is separated by one sector from logical sector 1.
-k sector0-skew/track	Used to describe perturbations in the media format to compensate for a slow controller. Track skew is the offset of sector 0 on track N relative to sector 0 on track N-1 on the same cylinder.

We would like to note that although some of the flags in Table 5–1 set vitally important file system parameters, others (beginning with the '-r' flag) are never used. The options we are referring to are those that depend on knowledge of the disk technology that no longer applies. Because many UFSs are no longer resting on a simple hard disk and could be on either a RAID device or a logical volume, the disk architecture–specific flags no longer apply. The defaults for these flags should be used.

Example:

This example illustrates how to use *newfs(8)* to create a new file system using entirely the default values. We also show that once the file system is mounted, you can calculate the minfree percentage based on the sizes reported from *df(1)*. Minfree is one of the parameters you may choose to tune in your file system based on the usage you expect.

```
# newfs /dev/vol/vol03 rz28
Warning: calculated sectors per cylinder (1584) disagrees with disk label (0)
Warning: 190 sector(s) in last cylinder unallocated
/dev/rvol/vol03:    424322 sectors in 268 cylinders of 16 tracks, 99
sectors
     207.2MB in 17 cyl groups (16 c/g, 12.38MB/g, 3008 i/g)
super-block backups (for fsck -b #) at:
32, 25488, 50944, 76400, 101856, 127312, 152768, 178224,
203680, 229136, 254592, 280048, 305504, 330960, 356416, 381872,
405536,

# mount /dev/vol/vol03 /mnt

# df /mnt
```

```
Filesystem      512-blocks  Used  Available  Capacity  Mounted on
/dev/vol/vol03  410960      2     369862     1%        /mnt
# bc
(410960 - 369862) * 100)/410960
10
```

Here, we calculate that the minfree value is set to the default by using a calculation based on the output from *df(1)*.

Example:

This is another example of using *newfs(8)*, but this time we change the minfree value from the default of 10 percent to 5 percent. You will notice that *newfs(8)* reports that with a minfree value of 5 percent, it is setting the optimization preference from time to space for you (the default is time). This was done because when the file system is more than 90 percent full, frags will be needed to optimize free space usage. An optimization preference of time does not use frags and speeds up access. If this is not desired, then you may need to specify that you want the optimization preference to be set to time. See Table 5–1 for an explanation of how to do that.

```
# newfs -m 5 /dev/vol/vol03 rz28
Warning: changing optimization to space because minfree is less than 10%
Warning: calculated sectors per cylinder (1584) disagrees with disk label (0)
Warning: 190 sector(s) in last cylinder unallocated
/dev/rvol/vol03:    424322 sectors in 268 cylinders of 16 tracks, 99
sectors
     207.2MB in 17 cyl groups (16 c/g, 12.38MB/g, 3008 i/g)
super-block backups (for fsck -b #) at:
32, 25488, 50944, 76400, 101856, 127312, 152768, 178224,
203680, 229136, 254592, 280048, 305504, 330960, 356416, 381872,
405536,

# mount /dev/vol/vol03 /mnt

# df /mnt
Filesystem      512-blocks  Used  Available  Capacity  Mounted on
/dev/vol/vol03  410960      2     390410     1%        /mnt

# bc
((410960 - 390410) * 100)/410960
5

# umount /mnt

# dumpfs /dev/vol/vol03 | more
magic    11954  format   dynamic time  Thu Aug 29 13:54:36 1996
nbfree   25683  ndir     1       nifree  51133     nffree   15
ncg      17     ncyl     268     size    212161    blocks   205480
bsize    8192   shift    13      mask    0xffffe000
fsize    1024   shift    10      mask    0xfffffc00
frag     8      shift    3       fsbtodb 1
```

cpg	16	bpg	1584	fpg	12672	ipg	3008
minfree	5%	optim	space	maxcontig	8	maxbpg	2048
rotdelay	0ms	headswitch	0us	trackseek	0us	rps	60
ntrak	16	nsect	99	npsect	99	spc	1584
trackskew	0	interleave	1				
nindir	2048	inopb	64	nspf	2		
sblkno	16	cblkno	24	iblkno	32	dblkno	408
sbsize	2048	cgsize	3072	cgoffset	56	cgmask	0xfffffff0
csaddr	408	cssize	1024	shift	9	mask	0xfffffe00
cgrotor	0	fmod	0	ronly	0	clean	3

The *dumpfs(8)* output verifies that the minfree value has been set to the desired value of 5 percent.

Example:

Here is an example of how to use *newfs(8)* to create a 44 MB UFS using the *newfs(8)* tool. The system administrator knows that this file system will be used for a Usenet News feed and will need a large number of very small files. This usage means that the system administrator has to account for a larger number of inodes than will be generated for the file system by default. This cannot be changed later, so the inodes need to be allocated upon file system creation. If the defaults are used, then the file system will run out of inodes long before it runs out of disk space. If that happens, the only thing that can be done to recover is to back it up, remake the file system with the correct parameters, and restore it.

The average file size for the Usenet News articles has been calculated to be around 200 bytes each; therefore, the "-i 200" flag is used. For more discussion about setting up Usenet News servers, refer to Chapter 8.

```
# newfs -i 200 /dev/vol/volbig
Warning: Bytes per inode restrict cylinders per group to 3.
Warning: 3448 sector(s) in last cylinder unallocated
/dev/rvol/volbig:    91947656 sectors in 22449 cylinders of 32 tracks, 128 sectors
    44896.3MB in 7483 cyl groups (3 c/g, 6.00MB/g, 20864 i/g)
super-block backups (for fsck -b #) at:
32, 12448, 24864, 37280, 49696, 62112, 74528, 86944,
99360, 111776, 124192, 136608, 149024, 161440, 173856, 186272,
198688, 211104, 223520, 235936, 248352, 260768, 273184, 285600,
298016, 310432, 322848, 335264, 347680, 360096, 372512, 384928,
393248, 405664, 418080, 430496, 442912, 455328, 467744, 480160,
492576, 504992, 517408, 529824, 542240, 554656, 567072, 579488,
591904, 604320, 616736, 629152, 641568, 653984, 666400, 678816,
691232, 703648, 716064, 728480, 740896, 753312, 765728, 778144,
786464, 798880, 811296, 823712, 836128, 848544, 860960, 873376,
885792, 898208, 910624, 923040, 935456, 947872, 960288, 972704,
985120, 997536, 1009952, 1022368, 1034784, 1047200, 1059616, 1072032,
1084448, 1096864, 1109280, 1121696, 1134112, 1146528, 1158944, 1171360,
1179680, 1192096, 1204512, 1216928, 1229344, 1241760, 1254176, 1266592,
1279008, 1291424, 1303840, 1316256, 1328672, 1341088, 1353504, 1365920,
```

```
1378336, 1390752, 1403168, 1415584, 1428000, 1440416, 1452832, 1465248,
1477664, 1490080, 1502496, 1514912, 1527328, 1539744, 1552160, 1564576,
1572896, 1585312, 1597728, 1610144, 1622560, 1634976, 1647392, 1659808,
1672224, 1684640, 1697056, 1709472, 1721888, 1734304, 1746720, 1759136,
1771552, 1783968, 1796384, 1808800, 1821216, 1833632, 1846048, 1858464,

[snip]

91325472, 91337888, 91350304, 91362720, 91375136, 91387552, 91399968, 91412384,
91424800, 91437216, 91449632, 91462048, 91474464, 91486880, 91499296, 91511712,
91524128, 91536544, 91548960, 91561376, 91573792, 91586208, 91598624, 91611040,
91619360, 91631776, 91644192, 91656608, 91669024, 91681440, 91693856, 91706272,
91718688, 91731104, 91743520, 91755936, 91768352, 91780768, 91793184, 91805600,
91818016, 91830432, 91842848, 91855264, 91867680, 91880096, 91892512, 91904928,
91917344, 91929760, 91942176,

# dumpfs /dev/vol/volbig
magic       11954  format      dynamic  time  Mon Mar 6 15:48:40 2000
nbfree      3292286 ndir       1        nifree     156125309   nffree 14
ncg         7483   ncyl        22449    size       45973828    blocks 26338303
bsize       8192   shift       13       mask       0xfffffe000
fsize       1024   shift       10       mask       0xffffffc00
frag        8      shift       3        fsbtodb    1
cpg         3      bpg         768      fpg        6144 ipg  2  0864
minfree     10%    optim       time     maxcontig  8    maxbpg  2048
rotdelay    0ms    headswitch  0us      trackseek  0us  rps     60
ntrak       32     nsect       128      npsect     128  spc     4096
trackskew   0      interleave  1
nindir      2048   inopb       64       nspf       2
sblkno      16     cblkno      24       iblkno     32   dblkno  2640
sbsize      2048   cgsize      4096     cgoffset   64   cgmask  0xffffffe0
csaddr      2640   cssize      119808   shift      9    mask    0xffffffe00
cgrotor     0      fmod        0        ronly      0    clean   3

[snip]
```

The result of the *newfs(8)* is to create a file system that can hold more than 156 million files, each with an average size of 200 bytes.

5.3.2 Tuning the On-Disk Structure of a UNIX File System

The *tunefs(8)* command (pronounced like tune-a-fish) changes the dynamic, tunable parameters of a UFS located in the superblock. The tool does not alter any data on the file system; it only affects the way future writes are handled. The flags that you specify indicate which parameters are to be changed. The following items can be changed using *tunefs(8)*:

- The maximum number of contiguous blocks that will be written in one transfer (the cluster size)

- The rotational delay between groups of blocks in a file

- The maximum number of blocks that any single file can allocate out of a single cylinder group at one time

- The percentage of free space on the file system that is held back from use by the nonroot users

- The optimization preference

This tool works on mounted and active file systems as well as those that are unmounted; however, the superblock for a mounted file system is cached in memory, so changes made while a file system is mounted will be clobbered the next time the buffers are synchronized. If you attempt to make changes to a mounted root file system, the system must be rebooted for those changes to be effective.

Syntax:

```
tunefs [-a maxcontig] [-d rotdelay] [-e maxbpg] [-m minfree]
[-o optim] file_system
```

TABLE 5–2   Flags for the *tunefs(8)* Command

FLAGS	DESCRIPTION
file_system	The block special device that specifies an existing UFS to tune.
-a maxcontig	This flag specifies the maximum number of contiguous blocks that will be laid out before forcing a rotational delay (see the '-d' flag). The default value is 8. File systems that reside on devices that utilize device drivers that can chain several buffers together in a single transfer should set this flag to the maximum chain length. The authors have had no occasion to tune this value on a running system.
-d rotdelay	This flag specifies the expected number of milliseconds that it will take to service a transfer completion interrupt and initiate a new transfer on the same disk. It is used to decide how much rotational spacing to place between successive blocks in a file.
-e maxbpg	Indicates the maximum number of blocks that any single file can allocate out of a cylinder group before it is forced to begin allocating blocks from another cylinder group. Typically, this value is set to about one-quarter of the total blocks in a cylinder group. The intent is to prevent any single file from using up all of the blocks in a single cylinder group, thus degrading access times for all files subsequently allocated in that cylinder group. The effect of this limit is to cause big files to do long seeks more frequently than if they were allowed to allocate all the blocks in a cylinder group before seeking elsewhere. If you have a file system with exclusively large files, this parameter should be set higher to improve performance.

TABLE 5–2   Flags for the *tunefs(8)* Command (Continued)

FLAGS	DESCRIPTION
-m minfree	Specifies the percentage of space held back from normal users; the minimum free space threshold. The default value used is 10 percent. This value can be set to 0; however, up to a factor of 3 in throughput will be lost over the performance obtained at a 10 percent threshold. Note that if the value is raised above the current usage level, users will be unable to allocate files until enough files have been deleted to get under the higher threshold.
-o opt_preference	The file system can either try to minimize the time spent allocating blocks, or it can attempt to minimize the space fragmentation on the disk. If the value of minfree (see above) is less than 10 percent, then the file system should optimize for space to avoid running out of full-sized blocks. For values of minfree greater than or equal to 10 percent, fragmentation is unlikely to be problematic, and the file system can be optimized for time.

Example:

Here, we show how to use *tunefs(8)* to change the minfree value dynamically when the file system is mounted and online.

```
# newfs /dev/vol/rootdg/voltest
Warning: 3808 sector(s) in last cylinder unallocated
/dev/rvol/rootdg/voltest:    500000 sectors in 123 cylinders of 32 tracks, 1s
   244.1MB in 8 cyl groups (16 c/g, 32.00MB/g, 7680 i/g)
super-block backups (for fsck -b #) at:
32, 65696, 131360, 197024, 262688, 328352, 394016, 459680,

# mount /dev/vol/rootdg/voltest /test

# df /test
Filesystem                   512-blocks  Used  Available  Capacity  Mounted on
/dev/vol/rootdg/voltest      484350      2     435912     1%        /test

# tunefs -m 2 /dev/rvol/rootdg/voltest
minimum percentage of free space changes from 10% to 2%
should optimize for space with minfree < 10%

# dumpfs /dev/rvol/rootdg/voltest | grep minfree
minfree 2%   optim  time  maxcontig 8    maxbpg 2048
```

Example:

This example shows how the *tunefs(8)* command can be used to change the optimization preference for an existing and unmounted UFS.

```
# dumpfs /dev/vol/vol03 | grep minfree
minfree 5%   optim  space  maxcontig 8     maxbpg 2048

# tunefs -o time /dev/vol/vol03
```

```
                optimization preference changes from space to time
                should optimize for space with minfree < 10%

                # dumpfs /dev/vol/vol03 | grep minfree
                minfree 5%   optim  time  maxcontig 8   maxbpg 2048
```

The *tunefs(8)* reference page has historically mentioned that you can tune a file system, but you cannot tune a fish.[4] I'm not sure why they removed it from the Tru64 main page, but we mention it here in order to lobby for its return.

5.3.3   Examining UFS On-Disk Structures

The *dumpfs(8)* command prints out very detailed superblock and cylinder group information for the specified UFS(s) or special device. This command is useful for getting information about the file system block size and minimum free space percentage, for example. If the file system is mounted, then you must specify the raw device.

Syntax:

```
                dumpfs filesystem ... | device
```

TABLE 5–3   Flags for the *dumps(8)* Command

FLAGS	DESCRIPTION
filesystem	The name of the file system(s) about which to dump information.
device	The device containing the file system about which to dump information.

Example:

Here, we have a *dumpfs(8)* example on the Tru64 UNIX 4.0 system. You'll notice that the superblock information comes first in the output, then the cylinder groups follow.

```
# dumpfs /dev/rrz9g
magic      11954   format     dynamic  time      Thu Aug 1 11:26:45 1996
nbfree     138804  ndir       711      nifree    352631     nffree    1972
ncg        144     ncyl       2299     size      1562965    blocks    1514562
bsize      8192    shift      13       mask      0xffffe000
fsize      1024    shift      10       mask      0xfffffc00
frag       8       shift      3        fsbtodb   1
cpg        16      bpg        1360     fpg       10880      ipg       2560
minfree    10%     optim      time     maxcontig 8         maxbpg    2048
rotdelay   0ms     headswitch 0us      trackseek 0us       rps       60
ntrak      16      nsect      85       npsect    85         spc       1360
trackskew  0       interleave 1
nindir     2048    inopb      64       nspf      2
sblkno     16      cblkno     24       iblkno    32         dblkno    352
```

```
sbsize      2048     cgsize      3072     cgoffset  48        cgmask   0xfffffff0
csaddr      352      cssize      3072     shift     9         mask     0xfffffe00
cgrotor     24       fmod        0        ronly     0         clean    0
blocks available in each of 8 rotational positions
cylinder number 0:
  position 0:   0  11  16  27  32  43  48  59  64  75  80
  position 1:   1   6  17  22  33  38  49  54  65  70  81
  position 2:   7  12  23  28  39  44  55  60  71  76
  position 3:   2  13  18  29  34  45  50  61  66  77  82
  position 4:   3   8  19  24  35  40  51  56  67  72  83
  position 5:   9  14  25  30  41  46  57  62  73  78
  position 6:   4  15  20  31  36  47  52  63  68  79  84
  position 7:   5  10  21  26  37  42  53  58  69  74
cs[].cs_(nbfree,ndir,nifree,nffree):
    (1253,6,2465,9)    (1282,6,2547,2)    (1270,6,2506,25)   (1229,6,2517,24)
    (1047,1,2055,13)   (1294,6,2537,7)    (860,6,2504,30)    (0,1,2138,18)
    (701,6,2545,7)     (652,4,2406,3)     (734,2,2260,84)    (662,6,2477,9)
    (600,3,2292,5)     (544,4,2281,18)    (899,6,2522,0)     (874,6,2523,7)
    (965,6,2529,23)    (782,6,2469,5)     (950,2,2313,72)    (702,3,2062,7)
[Snip...]
    (1301,5,2544,3)    (1176,5,2500,11)   (857,5,2474,5)     (998,5,2509,7)
    (671,5,2478,5)     (1154,5,2532,21)   (1088,5,2516,4)    (707,5,2480,42)
cylinders in last group 11
blocks in last group 935
  cg 0:
    magic    90255    tell      6000     time     Wed May 29 21:00:59 1996
    cgx      0        ncyl      16       niblk    2560       ndblk    10880
    nbfree   1253     ndir      6        nifree   2465       nffree   9
    rotor    848      irotor    94       frotor   816
    frsum    1        2         0        1        0          0        0
    sum of frsum: 9
    iused: 0-94
    free:  823, 830-831, 838-839, 844-847, 856-10879
    b:
  c1: (63)    8  8  8  8  8  8  8  7
  c2: (85)   11 11 10 11 11 10 11 10
  c3: (85)   11 11 10 11 11 10 11 10
  c4: (85)   11 11 10 11 11 10 11 10
  c5: (85)   11 11 10 11 11 10 11 10
  [Snip...]
```

TABLE 5–4 Field Descriptions for Superblock Output from *dumpfs(8)*

FIELD	DESCRIPTION
magic	The superblock magic number
format	The rotational table format. The two possible values are static or dynamic. Static is the original 4.2 BSD format.
time	The last time the superblock was written
sblkno	The address of superblock in the file system
cblkno	The offset of cylinder block in the file system
iblkno	The offset of inode blocks in the file system

TABLE 5–4   Field Descriptions for Superblock Output from *dumpfs(8)* (Continued)

FIELD	DESCRIPTION
dblkno	The offset of first data after the cylinder group
cgoffset	The cylinder group offset within the cylinder
cgmask	Bit mask used to calculate mod ntrak
size	The total number of blocks in the file system
dsize	The number of data blocks in the file system
ncg	The number of cylinder groups in the file system
bsize	The size of basic blocks in the file system. In Tru64 UNIX, this is fixed at 8192 bytes.
fsize	The size of fragment blocks in the file system
frag	The number of fragments in a block in the file system
minfree	The minimum percentage of free blocks in order to disallow non-root users from writing to the file system
rotdelay	The number of milliseconds for optimal next block
rps	The number of disk revolutions per second
bmask	The "blkoff" calculation of block offsets
fmask	The "fragoff" calculation of fragment offsets
bshift	The "lblkno" calculation of logical block number
fshift	The "numfrags" calculated number of fragments
maxcontig	The maximum number of contiguous blocks
maxbpg	The maximum number of blocks per cylinder group
fragshift	The block to fragment shift
fsbtodb	The file system block to data block shift constant
sbsize	The actual size of the superblock
csmask	csum block offset
csshift	csum block number
nindir	The number of indirect pointers in a file system block
inopb	The number of inodes in a secondary storage block
nspf	Number of disk sectors per frag
optim	Optimization preference. The possible values are "space" and "time."
npsect	Number of sectors per track including spares
interleave	The hardware sector interleave
trackskew	Sector 0 skew per track
headswitch	The head switch time in microseconds
trkseek	The track-to-track seek in microseconds
csaddr	The block address of the cylinder group summary area
cssize	The total size of the cylinder group summary area

TABLE 5–4   Field Descriptions for Superblock Output from *dumpfs(8)* (Continued)

FIELD	DESCRIPTION
cgsize	The cylinder group size
ntrak	The number of tracks per cylinder
nsect	The number of sectors per track
spc	The number of sectors per cylinder
ncyl	The total number of cylinders in the file system
cpg	The number of cylinders per cylinder group
ipg	The number of inodes per cylinder group
fpg	The number of fragments per group multiplied by the frag value
cstotal	The cylinder group summary information
fmod	A flag used to indicate whether the superblock has been modified
clean	A flag used to indicate whether the file system has been unmounted cleanly
ronly	A flag used to indicate whether the file system is mounted read-only
fsmnt	The name that the file system is mounted on
cgrotor	The last cylinder group searched

TABLE 5–5   Field Descriptions for Cylinder Group Output from *dumpfs(8)*

FIELD	DESCRIPTION
magic	The cylinder group magic number
time	The time the cylinder group information was last written
cgx	We are this numbered cylinder group
ncyl	The number of cylinders in this cylinder group
niblk	The number of inode blocks in this cylinder group
ndblk	The number of data blocks in this cylinder group
ndir	The number of directories in this cylinder group
nbfree	The number of free blocks in this cylinder group
nifree	The number of free inodes in this cylinder group
nffree	The number of free inodes in this cylinder group
rotor	The position of the last used block
frotor	The position of the last used frag
irotor	The position of the last used inode
frsum	The counts of the available frags
b	The free block positions
iused	The used inode map
free	The free block map

5.4   Detecting and Correcting Problems

The UFS has been around for a long time and thus has a reputation for being stable. Even when problems do crop up, a lot of knowledge about what can be done to correct the problem is available, and the tools are good. On the other hand, when severe problems appear, as they still do, it is important to understand the tools for detecting and correcting them.

5.4.1   The UFS Structure Checker

The premier tool for detecting and correcting file system corruption is the file system structure checker, *fsck(8)*. When a Tru64 UNIX system boots up, it runs *bcheckrc(8)*, which executes a *fsck(8)* on each UFS specified in /etc/fstab prior to mounting it. If the file system was cleanly unmounted before the boot, then it will not need to do anything, the file system will be mounted, and the process moves on. If the file system was not cleanly unmounted, however, *fsck(8)* will be run using the '-p' flag. This mode of operation for *fsck(8)* is also known as **preen mode**. In preen mode, *fsck(8)* makes some corrections that are safe to make without user interaction. This mode has been shown to be perfectly fine for most cases, and the correction occurs so that the boot process can continue on. In other cases, this process will not result in a file system that is mountable when the process is complete. In those cases, the boot process will stop in single-user mode and manual interaction will be required.

The *fsck(8)* tool performs an enormous number of checks on a UFS and can take a long time to run for large file systems. That's why for large file systems, Compaq recommends using AdvFS. Rapid recovery is one of the major advantages of that file system over the UFS. Appendix C contains a complete description of what *fsck(8)* does and how it does it.

Syntax:

```
fsck [options] [filesystem...]
```

TABLE 5–6   Flags for the *fsck(8)* Command

FLAGS	DESCRIPTION
filesystem	The name of the file system to be checked.
-b block	Uses the specified block number as the superblock for the file system. Block 32 is commonly the first of the alternate superblocks.
-c	If the file system is in the old (static table) format, then the tool will convert it to the new (dynamic table) format. If the file system is in the new format, then this flag converts it to the old format, provided that the old format can support the file system configuration.

TABLE 5–6   Flags for the *fsck(8)* Command (Continued)

FLAGS	DESCRIPTION
	In interactive mode, *fsck(8)* lists the direction of the conversion and asks if the conversion should be done. The format of a file system can be determined from the output from the *dumpfs(8)* command.
-l number	Limits the number of parallel checks to the number specified. By default, the limit is the number of disks running one process per disk. If a smaller limit is given, then the disks are checked using a round-robin-type schedule, one file system at a time.
-m mode	Uses the mode specified in octal as the permission bits to use when creating the lost-and-found directory rather than the default 777. In particular, systems that do not want to have lost files accessible by all users on the system should use a more restrictive set of permissions, such as 700.
-n	Answers "no" to every prompt except for the "CONTINUE?" prompt. The flag does not write to the lost-and-found directory in the file system. If you do not have write permission on the file system, then *fsck(8)* defaults to the behavior of the '-n' flag.
-o	Unconditionally checks the file system even if it has been unmounted cleanly.
-p	Preen mode. Noninteractively corrects the following file system inconsistencies: nonreferenced inodes, link counts in inodes that are too large, missing blocks in the free map, blocks in the free map that are also in files, and wrong counts in the superblock.
-v	Verbose mode. Causes more extensive messages to be displayed during the file system checks.
-y	Answers "yes" to every prompt. This flag should be used with caution because the file system data can be left in an inconsistent state.

Example:

The following example illustrates the use of the *fsck(8)* command to check and correct a UFS using one of the alternate superblocks located on block 722,336.

```
# fsck -b 722336 /dev/vol/rootdg/vol06
/sbin/ufs_fsck -b 722336 /dev/vol/rootdg/vol06
Alternate super block location: 722336
** /dev/rvol/rootdg/vol06
** Last Mounted on
** Phase 1 - Check Blocks and Sizes
** Phase 2 - Check Pathnames
** Phase 3 - Check Connectivity
** Phase 4 - Check Reference Counts
** Phase 5 - Check Cyl groups
1 files, 1 used, 484366 free (14 frags, 60544 blocks, 0.0%
fragmentation)

UPDATE STANDARD SUPERBLOCK? [yn] y

***** FILE SYSTEM WAS MODIFIED *****
```

Normally, it would not be necessary to do this, but if the primary superblock is corrupted, then this mechanism can correct the problem. If you happen to have saved the list of alternate superblocks from the time that the file system was created, then you can use that information as shown in this example. If not, you can try to use block 32, which is almost always the first alternate. In addition, you can also use the *newfs(8)* command with the '–N' flag, which won't create a new file system but will report on the list of locations for alternate superblocks in the file system only if it were to actually create one. This should give the list of alternate superblocks on the actual file system; however, you should be aware that it is possible for this information to be incorrect if some of the disk geometry–related file system parameters were altered at the time the file system was created. Although you should know that this is possible, it is rarely the case in practice. If you created the file system, you would know whether this was the case or whether defaults were used.

5.4.2   Miscellaneous File System Checker Tools

Three UFS checker tools predate *fsck(8)* and, according to their reference pages, are "obsoleted" by it. The tools we are referring to are *icheck(8)*, *dcheck(8)*, and *ncheck(8)*. We have found these tools to be useful for file system recovery, even where it was appropriate to use *fsck(8)*. Therefore, we are covering them here.

5.4.2.1   The *icheck(8)* Command

The *icheck(8)* command is the file system storage consistency checker. It is replaced by fsck for the most part, but it does provide some interesting data and statistics in its output.

The standard output from *icheck(8)* includes a report of the following items:

- The total number of files and the numbers of regular, directory, block special, character special, and fifo files

- The total number of blocks in use and the numbers of single and double indirect blocks and directory blocks (currently the tool does not count triple indirect blocks as the reference page currently states)

- The number of free blocks

- The number of blocks missing; that is, not in any file or in any free map

A list of block numbers follows the '-b' option, and whenever any of the named blocks turns up in a file, a diagnostic is produced.

Syntax:

```
icheck [-b numbers] [filesystem]
```

TABLE 5–7 Flags for the *icheck(8)* Command

FLAGS	DESCRIPTION
Filesystem	The name of the file system on which to perform the inode check.
-b numbers	Specifies the number of the block or blocks to check.

Example:

This example shows how *icheck(8)* can give useful information about the file system, such as the number of files of different types, and so forth.

```
# icheck /dev/vol/vol01
/dev/vol/vol01:
files   12 (r=11,d=1,b=0,c=0,sl=0,sock=0,fifo=0)
used  16502 (i=2,ii=0,b=2057,f=30)
free 518671 (b=64832,f=15)
missing 0
```

Example:

Here, we see the use of *icheck(8)* to look at specific block numbers to determine what is located on those blocks. This tool can be useful if BBRs (or bad blocks) have been reported on those blocks and you want to determine what file may have become corrupted.

```
# icheck -b 100 101 102 103 /dev/vol/vol01
/dev/vol/vol01:
100 arg; frag 2 of 8, inode=128, class=inodes 128-192
101 arg; frag 2 of 8, inode=128, class=inodes 128-192
102 arg; frag 3 of 8, inode=128, class=inodes 128-192
103 arg; frag 3 of 8, inode=128, class=inodes 128-192
files   12 (r=11,d=1,b=0,c=0,sl=0,sock=0,fifo=0)
used  16502 (i=2,ii=0,b=2057,f=30)
free 518671 (b=64832,f=15)
missing 0
```

5.4.2.2 The *dcheck(8)* Command

The *dcheck(8)* command reads the directories in a file system and compares the link-count in each inode with the number of directory entries by which it is referenced. To get optimum performance, specify the raw version of the special file because the inode list will be read in large chunks. If you run *dcheck(8)* on a large file system, it can take a long time to complete.

Syntax:

```
dcheck [-i numbers] [filesystem]
```

TABLE 5–8   Flags for the *dcheck(8)* Command

FLAGS	DESCRIPTION
filesystem	The name of the file system to check.
-i numbers	Specified with a list of inode numbers. If a specified inumber is found in a directory, then the dcheck command displays the inumber, the inode number of the directory, and the name of the entry.

Example:

We show here how the *dcheck(8)* tool is used to list out all of the inode numbers of each file and the number of entries in which this file appears.

```
# dcheck /dev/vol/vol01
/dev/vol/vol01:
    entries link cnt
2     303    10
3008  26     2
3009  25     1
3010  25     1
3011  25     1
3012  25     1
3013  25     1
3014  25     1
3015  25     1
3016  25     1
3017  25     1
3018  25     1
3019  25     1
3020  25     1
3021  25     1
3022  25     1
3023  25     1
3024  25     1
3025  25     1
3026  25     1
[Snip...]
```

5.4.2.3 The *ncheck(8)* Command

The *ncheck(8)* command with no options generates a list of all files on every specified file system. The list includes the pathname and the corresponding inode number of each file. A slash dot follows the name of each directory file.

Issuing the command with the "-i numbers" option reduces the report to only those files with inode numbers. Issuing the command with the -a option allows for the printing of the names dot and dot dot, which are ordinarily suppressed. Issuing the command with the -s option reduces the report to special files and files with set-user-ID mode. This flag is intended to discover concealed violations of security policy.

The *ncheck(8)* utility can be used with either UFS or AdvFS. For a UFS, each file system parameter must be a character device special file (for example, /dev/disk/dsk3c). You can also specify an AdvFS fileset by entering a standard AdvFS domain#fileset designation.

Syntax:

```
ncheck [-i numbers] [-asm] filesystems ...
```

TABLE 5–9   Flags for the *ncheck(8)* Command

FLAGS	DESCRIPTION
Filesystem	The name of the file system or file systems to check.
-I numbers	Reduces the report to only those files with i-numbers numbers.
-a	Allows printing of the names dot and dot dot, which are ordinarily suppressed.
-m	Allows printing of the mode, UID, and GID of files. This flag takes effect only if either the '-i' or the '-s' flag is also specified on the command line.
-s	Reduces the report to special files and files with set-user-ID mode.

Example:

Here, we show use of the *ncheck(8)* command on a UFS. The listing gives the name of every file and its inode number. Be aware that this output can be exceedingly long if large numbers of files exist on the file system.

```
# ncheck /dev/vol/vol01
/dev/vol/vol01:
3      /#.mrg...login
4      /#.mrg..DXsession
5      /DXsession
6      /DXsession.PreMRG
7      /DXterm
8      /genvmunix
9      /osf_boot
10     /quota.group
11     /quota.user
12     /real.profile
13     /vmunix
```

5.4.3   Removing a UFS File By Its Inode Number

The *clri(8)* command is used to repair file system corruption by removing a file from a UFS using its inode number.

The *clri(8)* command writes zeros on the inodes with the decimal inode numbers on the specified file system. After *clri(8)* has finished its work, any blocks in the affected file are defined as "missing" when you run *icheck(8)* on the file system. You'll need to use a tool such as *fsck(8)* to actually clean up the missing files.

The primary purpose of this tool is to remove a file that does not appear in any directory. If you use the command to remove an inode that does appear in a directory, take care to track down the entry and remove it. Otherwise, when the inode is reallocated to some new file, the old entry will still point to that file. If you then remove the old entry, you will destroy the new file, and the new entry will again point to an unallocated inode. Consequently, the entire cycle repeats itself.

Syntax:

```
clri file_system inode_number ...
```

TABLE 5–10   Flags for the *clri(8)* Command

FLAGS	DESCRIPTION
file_system	The name of the file system from which to clear the file.
inode_number	The inode number of the file to clear.

Example:

This example shows how to use *clri(8)* to remove a single file with the inode number 7 from an unmounted file system.

```
# ncheck /dev/vol/vol01
/dev/vol/vol01:
3    /#.mrg...login
4    /#.mrg..DXsession
5    /DXsession
6    /DXsession.PreMRG
7    /DXterm
8    /genvmunix
9    /osf_boot
10   /quota.group
11   /quota.user
12   /real.profile
13   /vmunix

# clri /dev/vol/vol01 7
clearing 7

# mount /dev/vol/vol01 /test
/dev/vol/vol01 on /test: Dirty file system

# fsck /dev/vol/vol01
/sbin/ufs_fsck /dev/vol/vol01
** /dev/rvol/vol01
```

```
** Last Mounted on /test
** Phase 1 - Check Blocks and Sizes
** Phase 2 - Check Pathnames
UNALLOCATED I=7 OWNER=root MODE=0
SIZE=0 MTIME=Dec 31 19:00 1969
NAME=/DXterm

REMOVE? [yn] y

** Phase 3 - Check Connectivity
** Phase 4 - Check Reference Counts
** Phase 5 - Check Cyl groups

FREE BLK COUNT(S) WRONG IN SUPERBLK
SALVAGE? [yn] y

BLK(S) MISSING IN BIT MAPS
SALVAGE? [yn] y

SUMMARY INFORMATION BAD
SALVAGE? [yn] y

11 files, 16496 used, 518677 free (13 frags, 64833 blocks,
0.0% fragmentation)

***** FILE SYSTEM WAS MODIFIED *****

# mount /dev/vol/vol01 /test

# ls /test

#.mrg...login   DXsession.PreMRG quota.group    vmunix

#.mrg..DXsession genvmunix    quota.user
DXsession    osf_boot    real.profile
```

Example:

This example shows how, even if a tool like *clri(8)* is used improperly, to remove the root directory inode (inode 2) of the file system, and the *fsck(8)* tool will correct the problem later on.

```
# mount /dev/vol/vol03 /test

# ls /test

# ls -la /test
total 9
drwxr-xr-x  2 root    system     512 Aug 21 11:24 .
drwxr-xr-x 23 root    system    8192 Aug 8 17:30 ..

# umount /test

# clri /dev/vol/vol03 2
clearing 2

# mount /dev/vol/vol03 /test
/dev/vol/vol03 on /test: Dirty file system

# fsck /dev/vol/vol03
/sbin/ufs_fsck /dev/vol/vol03
```

```
** /dev/rvol/vol03
** Last Mounted on /test
** Phase 1 - Check Blocks and Sizes
** Phase 2 - Check Pathnames
ROOT INODE UNALLOCATED
ALLOCATE? [yn] y

** Phase 3 - Check Connectivity
** Phase 4 - Check Reference Counts
** Phase 5 - Check Cyl groups
FREE BLK COUNT(S) WRONG IN SUPERBLK
SALVAGE? [yn] y

BLK(S) MISSING IN BIT MAPS
SALVAGE? [yn] y

SUMMARY INFORMATION BAD
SALVAGE? [yn] y

1 files, 1 used, 205479 free (7 frags, 25684 blocks, 0.0%
fragmentation)

***** FILE SYSTEM WAS MODIFIED *****

# mount /dev/vol/vol03 /test

# ls -la /test
total 9
drwxr-xr-x  2 root    system    1024 Aug 21 11:28 .
drwxr-xr-x 23 root    system    8192 Aug 8 17:30 ..
```

5.4.4   The UFS Debugger

One of the most complex and powerful tools for examining and changing UFS on-disk structures is the file system debugger, or *fsdb(8)*. The *fsdb(8)* command can be used to repair a damaged file system after a crash. It has conversions to translate block and inode numbers into their corresponding disk addresses. Also included are mnemonic offsets to access different parts of an inode. These offsets greatly simplify the process of correcting control block entries or descending the file system tree.

Syntax:

```
fsdb [options] special
```

TABLE 5–11   Flags for the *fsdb(8)* Command

FLAGS	DESCRIPTION
special	The special device for the file system to be debugged.
-o	Overrides some error conditions. The *fsdb(8)* command contains several error-checking routines to verify inode and block addresses. These can be disabled if necessary by using the '-o' option.
-p'string'	Sets prompt to 'string.'
-w	Opens the file system for write access. The default is for read-only access.

Security is a concern when using the *fsdb(8)* command. Because *fsdb(8)* reads the raw disk, it is able to circumvent normal file system security. Extreme caution is advised in determining its availability on the system. Suggested permissions are 500, owned by bin. Note that in order to modify any portion of the disk, *fsdb(8)* must be invoked with the '-w' option. The default is read-only access.

The syntax for the *fsdb(8)* tool is very adb-like and was adopted to promote the use of *fsdb(8)* through familiarity. Unfortunately, adb is not a familiar tool in Tru64 UNIX because *dbx(8)* or *ladebug(8)* are the main debuggers used. Therefore, users who are not familiar with adb will need to learn its syntax to use *fsdb(8)* effectively. The adb-like syntax has been retained mainly for historical reasons. The *fsdb(8)* tool came to Tru64 UNIX from its ULTRIX/VAX and BSD heritage, which used adb as their primary system debugger. The dbx debugger was introduced in ULTRIX/MIPS and was retained with Tru64 UNIX.

The *fsdb(8)* command uses hexadecimal numbers by default; however, you can control how data are displayed or accepted using the "base" command. Once set, all input defaults to this base and all output is shown in this base. The base can be overridden temporarily for input by preceding hexadecimal numbers with '0x', preceding decimal numbers with '0t', or octal numbers with '0'. Hexadecimal numbers beginning with a-f or A-F must be preceded with '0x' to distinguish them from commands.

Several global values are maintained by *fsdb(8)*: the current base (referred to as base); the current address (referred to as dot); the current inode (referred to as inode); the current count (referred to as count); and the current type (referred to as type). Most commands use the preset value of dot in their execution.

Disk addressing by *fsdb(8)* is at the byte level; however, *fsdb(8)* offers many commands to convert a desired inode, directory entry, block, superblock, and so on to a byte address. Once the address has been calculated, *fsdb(8)* records the result in dot.

Example:

As our first example, we start simply with an illustration of how to maneuver within the tool and print out various structures. So, we enter the following command to begin a read-only session debugging the /dev/vol/rootdg/vol06 file system.

```
# /usr/sbin/fsdb /dev/vol/rootdg/vol06
fsdb of /dev/vol/rootdg/vol06 (Read only) -- last mounted on /mnt
```

The first thing we usually do upon entering the tool is set our context. Here, we start with inode number 2, which we know exists because it is the root inode for any file system.

```
> 2:inode
```

Then, we can print out the inode information in a nicely structured fashion. The dot command is used for printing information based on our current context.

```
> .
i#: 2       md: d---rwxr-xr-x uid: 0          gid: 0
ln: e       bs: 2      sz : 200
db#0: 3e8
    accessed: Wed Oct 27 20:43:50 1999
    modified: Wed Oct 27 20:44:31 1999
    created : Wed Oct 27 20:44:31 1999

>
i#: 3       md: ----rw-r--r-- uid: 0          gid: 0
ln: 1       bs: 3e90      sz : 7d0000
db#0: 3f0    db#1: 3f8    db#2: 400    db#3: 408
db#4: 410    db#5: 418    db#6: 420    db#7: 428
db#8: 430    db#9: 438    db#a: 440    db#b: 448
ib#0: 1ad38
    accessed: Wed Oct 27 20:44:30 1999
    modified: Wed Oct 27 20:48:35 1999
    created : Wed Oct 27 20:48:35 1999

>
i#: 4       md: l---rwxrwxrwx uid: 0          gid: 0
ln: 1       bs: 0      sz : 6
symlink: ../var
    accessed: Tue Oct 26 07:42:07 1999
    modified: Tue Oct 26 07:42:07 1999
    created : Tue Oct 26 07:42:08 1999
```

To exit the tool, enter the following command:

```
> :q
```

Example:

In this example, we show how to examine directory entries on a UFS. Using the ":ls" command, you can specify a directory to look at. Keep in mind that the directory specified may look like an absolute path but is relative to the root of this file system.

```
> :ls /
/:
./        cluster/   lbin/    opt/         test.out
../       dt/        lib/     preserve@    var@
bin/      examples/  local/   sbin/
ccs/      include/   man@     share/
```

Once there, subsequent use of the <Return> key (or +, -) advances to subsequent entries.

```
> 2:ino; 0:dir?d
i#: 2          .
>  .
Point #1
i#: 2          .
>
Point #1
i#: 2          ..
>
Point #1
i#: 1e00       local
>
Point #1
i#: 4          var
>
Point #1
i#: 3c00       bin
```

Example:

Now, we want to examine the superblock in a formatted fashion, rather than just the inode information. The ":sb" command is used for this purpose as follows:

```
# fsdb /dev/vol/vol01
fsdb of /dev/vol/vol01 (Read only) -- last mounted on /test
> :sb
    super block:
magic      11954    format     dynamic  time        Thu Aug 29 13:38:33 1996
nbfree     64365    ndir       12       nifree      13419        nffree  38
ncg        44       ncyl       698      size        552438       blocks  535173
bsize      8192     shift      13       mask        0xffffe000
fsize      1024     shift      10       mask        0xfffffc00
frag       8        shift      3        fsbtodb     1
cpg        16       bpg        1584     fpg         12672        ipg     3008
minfree    10%      optim      time     maxcontig   8            maxbpg  2048
rotdelay   0ms      headswitch 0us      trackseek   0us          rps     60
ntrak      16       nsect      99       npsect      99           spc     1584
trackskew  0        interleave 1
nindir     2048     inopb      64       nspf        2
sblkno     16       cblkno     24       iblkno      32           dblkno  408
sbsize     2048     cgsize     3072     cgoffset    56           cgmask 0xfffffff0
csaddr     408      cssize     1024     shift       9            mask   0xfffffe00
cgrotor    1        fmod       0        ronly  0
blocks available in each of 8 rotational positions
cylinder number 0:
    position 0:   0  13  19  25  31  44  50  56  62  75  81  87 93
    position 1:   1   7  20  26  32  38  51  57  63  69  88  94
    position 2:   2   8  14  27  33  39  45  58  64  70  76  82 95
    position 3:   3   9  15  21  34  40  46  52  71  77  83  89
```

```
position 4:    10  16  22  28  47  53  59  65  78  84  90  96
position 5:     4  17  23  29  35  41  54  60  66  72  85  91 97
position 6:     5  11  30  36  42  48  61  67  73  79  92  98
position 7:     6  12  18  24  37  43  49  55  68  74  80  86
cs[].cs_(nbfree,ndir,nifree,nffree):
   (401,3,2991,8) (1521,1,0,0) (442,0,0,0) (1518,1,2007,4)
   (1535,0,0,0) (1284,1,0,0) (1535,0,0,0) (1535,0,0,0)
   (1535,0,0,0) (1535,0,0,0) (1535,0,0,0) (1535,0,0,0)
   (1535,0,0,0) (1535,0,0,0) (1535,0,0,0) (1535,0,0,0)
   (1535,0,0,0) (1535,0,0,0) (1535,0,0,0) (1535,0,0,0)
   (1535,0,0,0) (1535,0,0,0) (1535,0,0,0) (1535,0,0,0)
   (1535,0,0,0) (1535,0,0,0) (1535,0,0,0) (1535,0,0,0)
   (1535,0,0,0) (1535,0,0,0) (1535,0,0,0) (1535,0,0,0)
   (1535,0,0,0) (1535,0,0,0) (1533,1,818,6) (1532,1,2007,4)
   (1532,1,2007,4) (1520,1,0,0) (1534,1,582,7) (893,1,3007,5)
cylinders in last group 10
blocks in last group 990
> :cg
>

cg 1:
magic      90255    tell      c74000    time      Thu Aug    29         13:34:55 1996
cgx        1        ncyl      16        niblk     3008       ndblk      12672
nbfree     1521     ndir      1         nifree    0          nffree     0
rotor      7912     irotor    3007      frotor    7912
frsum      0        0         0         0         0          0          0
sum of frsum: 0
iused: 0-3007
free:   24-55, 64-71, 504-7911, 7952-12671
b:
   c0: (41)     4 4 6 5 5 6 6 5
   c1: (99)     13 12 13 12 12 13 12 12
   c2: (99)     13 12 13 12 12 13 12 12
   c3: (99)     13 12 13 12 12 13 12 12
   c4: (99)     13 12 13 12 12 13 12 12
   c5: (99)     13 12 13 12 12 13 12 12
   c6: (99)     13 12 13 12 12 13 12 12
   c7: (99)     13 12 13 12 12 13 12 12
   c8: (99)     13 12 13 12 12 13 12 12
   c9: (98)     13 12 13 12 12 13 11 12
  c10: (95)     12 11 12 11 12 13 12 12
  c11: (99)     13 12 13 12 12 13 12 12
  c12: (99)     13 12 13 12 12 13 12 12
  c13: (99)     13 12 13 12 12 13 12 12
  c14: (99)     13 12 13 12 12 13 12 12
  c15: (99)     13 12 13 12 12 13 12 12
>:q
```

5.4.5   Improving UFS Performance

You can make some changes to improve the performance of your UFS, other than the parameters to *newfs(8)* and *tunefs(8)*. These changes involve examining some of the internal counters maintained by the kernel and using `/etc/sysconfigtab` to tweak some kernel parameters. We discuss both of these steps in this section.

5.4.5.1 UFS Fragmentation

One of the most popular questions that comes up with respect to performance on a UFS is, "How do I defragment my file systems?" The answer to this question is that the design of UFS precludes most of the problems with fragmentation encountered with other file system types. On the other hand, UFS is susceptible to inefficiency with cluster reads and writes. In UFS parlance, a **cluster** is a contiguous group of file system pages that are read from or written to the disk at the same time in order to improve performance.

To check UFS cluster efficiency using *dbx(8)*, you examine the ufs_clusterstats structure to see how efficiently the system is performing cluster read and write transfers. You can also examine cluster reads and writes separately with the ufs_clusterstats_read and ufs_clusterstats_write structures.

Example:

This is an example of examining UFS cluster statistics on a Tru64 UNIX 4.0 system.

```
(kdbx) p ufs_clusterstats
struct {
  full_cluster_transfers = 56358
  part_cluster_transfers = 366639
  non_cluster_transfers = 799768
  sum_cluster_transfers = {
    [0] 0
    [1] 799768
    [2] 194713
    [3] 77833
    [4] 35587
    [5] 25573
    [6] 24191
    [7] 8742
    [8] 56358
    [9] 0
  }
}
(kdbx) p ufs_clusterstats_read
struct {
  full_cluster_transfers = 55761
  part_cluster_transfers = 365610
  non_cluster_transfers = 778715
  sum_cluster_transfers = {
```

```
      [0] 0
      [1] 778715
      [2] 194096
      [3] 77673
      [4] 35471
      [5] 25496
      [6] 24147
      [7] 8727
      [8] 55761
      [9] 0
  }
}

(kdbx) p ufs_clusterstats_write
struct {
  full_cluster_transfers = 597
  part_cluster_transfers = 1029
  non_cluster_transfers = 21055
  sum_cluster_transfers = {
    [0] 0
    [1] 21055
    [2] 617
    [3] 160
    [4] 116
    [5] 77
    [6] 44
    [7] 15
    [8] 597
    [9] 0
  }
}
```

The number of pages in a cluster in Tru64 UNIX is 8 (or 64 kilobytes) pre-5.0a and 32 (or 256 kilobytes) in 5.0a and higher. This change, along with some UBC improvements, has shown to make over a tenfold increase in performance for sequential access to large files (files that don't completely fit into cache).

Example:

This example shows the ufs_clusterstats structure in a Tru64 UNIX 5.0 system with 32 entries in the sum_cluster_transfers field.

```
(dbx) pd ufs_clusterstats
struct {
  full_cluster_transfers = 0
  part_cluster_transfers = 9637
  non_cluster_transfers = 19047
  sum_cluster_transfers = {
    [0] 0
    [1] 19047
    [2] 2076
    [3] 1257
```

```
          [4]  854
          [5]  587
          [6]  429
          [7]  372
          [8]  4062
          [9]  0
          [10] 0
          [11] 0
          [12] 0
          [13] 0
          [14] 0
          [15] 0
          [16] 0
          [17] 0
          [18] 0
          [19] 0
          [20] 0
          [21] 0
          [22] 0
          [23] 0
          [24] 0
          [25] 0
          [26] 0
          [27] 0
          [28] 0
          [29] 0
          [30] 0
          [31] 0
          [32] 0
          [33] 0
      }
  }
```

5.4.5.2 Buffer Cache

The metadata buffer cache (or bufcache) contains UFS file metadata—superblocks, inodes, indirect blocks, directory blocks, and cylinder group summaries. The bufcache parameter, as discussed in Chapter 4, is used to size the traditional buffer cache. The default is 3 percent of physical memory. This value can sometimes be too small and needs to be increased, or it needs to be decreased if the metadata buffer cache is not being utilized. The lowest value to which you can set the parameter is 1 percent. You might want to lower this value to 1 percent, if UFS is not being used on the system at all. We discuss here how you can use the kernel debugger to examine the cache efficiency and make corrections, if needed.

To check the metadata buffer cache, use the kernel debugger to examine the bio_stats structure on a running system or crash dump. If the miss rate is high, then you may want to raise the value of the bufcache attribute. Unfortunately, in Tru64 UNIX prior to version 4.0, this parameter is only changeable with a kernel rebuild. On the other hand, it can be changed in /etc/sysconfigtab in version 4.0 and higher. Thus, in recent versions, only a reboot is required.

The miss rate can be calculated as follows:

```
                       getblk_misses
miss rate = ---------------------------
               getblk_misses + getblk_hits
```

Ideally, you want to get the miss rate to be less than 3 percent. If, after making this calculation, you discover that the miss rate is greater than 3 percent, then you should consider increasing the bufcache parameter value. The authors have not seen too many instances where this was needed.

Example:

This example shows how to use the kernel debugger, *kdbx(8)*, to examine the buffer cache statistics in a running Tru64 UNIX kernel.

```
(kdbx) p bio_stats
struct {
  getblk_hits = 749312
  getblk_misses = 1817
  getblk_research = 0
  getblk_dupbuf = 0
  getnewbuf_calls = 1843
  getnewbuf_buflocked = 0
  vflushbuf_lockskips = 0
  mntflushbuf_misses = 0
  mntinvalbuf_misses = 0
  vinvalbuf_misses = 0
  allocbuf_buflocked = 0
  ufssync_misses = 0
}

(kdbx) pd (1817*100)/(1817+749312)
0
```

Clearly, this system is not active with respect to the UFS. On an active system, you would see a much larger number for each of the fields in the bio_stats structure. Even so, the miss rate is less than 1 percent, which is within our acceptable range.

5.5   Backing Up and Restoring UFSs

A backup strategy is critically important to properly manage your Tru64 UNIX system. It is possible for a bad block or some other hardware problem to suddenly cause files to become corrupted and need to be restored from backups. It is rather common that a system user inadvertently removes a file from the system that needs to be restored later. In these instances, your backup strategy will be tested. This section describes the two backup solutions for the UFS that ship with the base operating system.

In this book, we provide all the troubleshooting assistance we possibly can; however, if all else fails, you must have a good backup so that you can remake the file system and restore it to a known good state.

5.5.1   The *dump(8)* and *restore(8)* Commands

The *dump(8)* and *restore(8)* commands have been around for a long time and are specifically designed to be used with the UFS. This makes these tools the logical candidates for use with your UFS backup strategy; however, they have begun to show their age. We believe that *vdump(8)* and *vrestore(8)* should be used instead because their features make them a better choice for now and into the future than *dump(8)* and *restore(8)*.

5.5.2   The *vdump(8)* and *vrestore(8)* Commands

The *vdump(8)* and *vrestore(8)* commands can be used for UFS, AdvFS, and NFS. We cover the use of these tools in some detail in Chapter 6, so we refer you to that discussion. Even though we discuss these commands as they are used with the AdvFS, we think the usage is close enough for you to completely understand how these tools can also be used to implement your backup strategy for UFS.

5.6   Quotas

If you manage a system with two or more users sharing a single file system, you probably already understand the usefulness of quotas. The main benefit of setting quotas is for those cases where you cannot control your users' behavior using the standard methods of peer pressure and intimidation, and their productivity is being affected. There will always be those people who will never take the time to clean up after themselves. The advent of ever larger and cheaper disk farms makes the task of policing disk space that much more difficult.

Quotas are most frequently used to limit usage on a UFS on a user-by-user basis. This section shows how to set up and manage quotas on your UFSs.

5.6.1   How Quotas Work

You can apply quotas to file systems to establish a limit on the number of blocks and inodes (or files) that a user or group of users can allocate. You can set a separate quota for each user or group of users on each file system.

File systems can have both soft and hard file limits. When a hard limit is reached, no more disk space allocations or file creations that would exceed the limit are allowed. The soft limit may be exceeded for a period known as the grace period. If the soft limit is exceeded for an amount of time that exceeds the **grace period**, then no more disk space allocations or file creations are allowed until enough disk space is freed or enough files are deleted to bring the disk space usage or number of files below the soft limit.

5.6.2   Enabling Quotas

To activate quotas on a UFS, perform the following steps:

1. Configure the kernel to include the following line in the system configuration file:

    ```
    options  QUOTA
    ```

2. Edit the /etc/fstab file to add the userquota and groupquota options in the fourth field for those file systems on which you wish to enable quotas. The former would be used to enable user quotas and the latter is used for group quotas. See our discussion in Chapter 1 for the syntax for setting file system options in /etc/fstab.

3. The next step is to run the *quotacheck(8)* command to create the user and group quota files and to populate the usage data. For a large file system with lots of usage, the *quotacheck(8)* step can take some time.

4. Next, you should use *edquota(8)* to activate the quota editor and to create an entry for each user. The editor you will be using is specified with the EDITOR environment variable.

5. Use the *quotaon(8)* command to activate the quota system.

6. To check and enable disk quotas during the next system boot, use the following command to set the disk quota configuration variable:

    ```
    # /usr/sbin/rcmgr set QUOTA_CONFIG yes
    ```

7. To turn off quotas, use the *quotaoff(8)* command.

5.6.3   Setting Quotas

Once quotas have been enabled for a particular UFS, they must be set for each user. The following example shows how this is accomplished.

Example:

This example shows how quotas are established and set by the system administrator. In this case, hard and soft quotas are set for the user "hancock" to 200 and 500 blocks, respectively. Initially, the quotas for the user were set to 0, when the *quotacheck(8)* command is issued. Later, the quotas are set manually, using the *edquota(8)* command.

```
# quotacheck /dev/vol/vol01
Creating quota file /test/quota.user
Creating quota file /test/quota.group

# edquota hancock
[dumps you into vi editor...]
Quotas for user hancock:
/test: blocks in use: 0, limits (soft = 0, hard = 0)
    inodes in use: 0, limits (soft = 0, hard = 0)

[Change to...]

Quotas for user hancock:
/test: blocks in use: 0, limits (soft = 200, hard = 500)
    inodes in use: 0, limits (soft = 20, hard = 50)
```

5.7   UFS Tuning Parameters

The UFS system configuration subsystem (viewable with sysconfig -q ufs) contains a set of parameters that can be used to tune the system. Table 5–12 gives a summary of the parameters and a description of each.

TABLE 5–12   UFS sysconfigtab Parameters

PARAMETER	DESCRIPTION	V4	V5
inode-hash-size inode_hash_size	The number of entries in the inode lookup LRU hash table.	X	X
create-fastlinks create_fastlinks	Enables or disables whether fastlinks can be created or not.	X	X
ufs-blkpref-lookbehind ufs_blkpref_lookbehind	Range of blocks behind the current block location through which to search for a free block to allocate for an indirect block write operation.	X	X
nmount	This parameter is obsolete and is replaced by the max-ufs-mounts parameter in the vfs subsystem.	X	X

TABLE 5–12   UFS sysconfigtab Parameters (Continued)

PARAMETER	DESCRIPTION	V4	V5
ufs_lockholdmax	The maximum number of file locks that can be held by a single user.		X
ufs_object_safety	This parameter restricts how a stale UFS object can be reused. The default value of 0 doesn't restrict reuse, whereas a non-zero value requires that blocks must be cleared before they can be reused. There is a serious performance penalty for using this feature.		X

5.8   Memory-Based UFS

MFS is a memory-based version of the UFS. The *mfs(8)* command is used to build a memory file system. When the file system is unmounted, mfs exits, and the contents of the file system are lost. If mfs is sent a signal while running, for example during system shutdown, then it attempts to unmount its corresponding file system. The parameters for mfs are almost the same as those for *newfs(8)*. For a memory file system, the special device file provides only a set of configuration parameters, including the size of the virtual memory segment to allocate. If the special device file is omitted, then you must specify the segment size. The special device file is usually the primary swap area because that is where the file system is backed up when free memory gets low and the memory supporting the file system has to be paged.

Example:

You can enable /tmp as a memory file system by adding an entry in the /etc/fstab file as shown here. This creates a 10 MB memory file system, mounted on /tmp:

```
# cat /etc/fstab
root_domain#root    /    advfs rw 0 1
/proc       /proc  procfs rw 0 0
usr_domain#usr /usr  advfs rw 0 2
usr_domain#var /var  advfs rw 0 2
-s20480      /tmp  mfs rw 1 0

# df -k /tmp
Filesystem   1024-blocks   Used  Available  Capacity  Mounted on
mfs:224      9791          1     8810       0%        cluster/members/member0/tmp
```

Note that the contents of /tmp will be lost whenever a reboot or unmount is performed; however, for a file system like /tmp where everything is transient, this should not be a big problem.

The inode equivalent for the MFS referenced in the v_data field, is called the mfsnode and is defined in <ufs/mfsnode.h> as follows:

```
struct mfsnode {
    struct vnode *mfs_vnode;      /* vnode associated with this mfsnode */
    caddr_t mfs_baseoff;          /* base of file system in memory */
    long mfs_size;                /* size of memory file system */
    pid_t  mfs_pid;               /* our process id */
    struct buf *mfs_buflist;      /* list of I/O requests */
    task_t mfs_task;              /* our task */
    int    mfs_numthreads;        /* number of threads started */
    long   mfs_spare[4];
};
```

See our discussion in Chapter 4 that describes how to examine the file system type specific information in a vnode structure.

5.9 Summary

The UFS is one of the two general-purpose file systems supported by Tru64 UNIX. We have covered the on-disk and in-memory structures of UFS and the tools for managing it. Although the UFS has been around for quite a long time, it is still a viable file system type and continues to be used at many Tru64 UNIX sites around the world.

Notes

1. The acronym UFS has been used in other texts to stand for the unified file system, which is another term that refers to the UNIX file system, based on the Berkeley fast file system. Here, when we refer to UFS we are using it as a shorthand for the UNIX file system.

2. This file system is sometimes referred to as just the fast file system (FFS). The Berkeley part is so-named because the original file system improvement work was done at the University of California at Berkeley. In addition, these changes were incorporated into the Berkeley standard distribution (BSD) of UNIX in version 4.2.

3. More up-to-date results can be found in Irlam (1993). The results of this data suggest that file sizes are increasing, thus the wastage is less pronounced in the 4-kilobyte block (fragment) size (12.3 percent), but larger (61.2 percent) with a 16-kilobyte block size. With an 8-kilobyte block size, such as is used with the Tru64 UNIX UFS, the wasted space was 29.4 percent.

4. See BSD (1994) in the *tunefs(8)* reference page. This humorous statement has been included since the early days of the BSD distribution, and many UNIX-based systems still carry it today.

Advanced File System: The Basics

> Man's mind stretched to a new idea
> never goes back to its original dimensions.
> — *Oliver Wendell Holmes*

This chapter is a discussion of one of the most powerful and useful parts of the Tru64 UNIX system—the Advanced File System (AdvFS). If you are familiar only with the UNIX file system (UFS) from either Tru64 UNIX or another vendor's UNIX, then you will need to learn some concepts to fully appreciate AdvFS. The first question that is often asked concerning the AdvFS by those unfamiliar with it is: "UFS has been around for so many years and continues to work well, so why do I need AdvFS?" This question is answered simply that AdvFS offers powerful features that are not and will never be available in UFS. The authors believe that AdvFS is essential for those users with large file systems (and they get bigger every day) and 24-hour, year-round uptime requirements. UFS does not provide the features necessary for managing very large file systems. In addition, AdvFS was designed from the beginning, like Tru64 UNIX, to be a 64-bit file system. Thus, large file systems have always been supported, and the theoretical limits of AdvFS will not be reached for quite some time.

6.1   AdvFS Features and Concepts

AdvFS is enormously powerful compared to UFS. Unlike UFS, AdvFS separates the directory hierarchy layer of the file system from the physical storage access layer. The directory hierarchy handles file naming and the POSIX file system interface such as opening and reading files. The physical storage layer handles write-ahead logging, file allocation, and physical disk I/O functions.

The advantage of this separation is that it allows you to manage the physical storage of files separately from the directory hierarchy. For example, you can move a file's data blocks from one disk to another within a storage domain without changing its pathname, or you can force a single file to span multiple disk volumes in order to improve performance of the entire file system.

We think you'll find many useful and interesting features of AdvFS as we continue our discussions in this chapter. This section, in particular, gives a high-level overview of some concepts with which you should be familiar in order to get the most from your AdvFS. We also list those features that are most important to know about and that are not available in UFS, or even in some competing products.[1]

6.1.1   File Domain and Fileset

As we just pointed out, the two-layer structure is the cornerstone of AdvFS and its unique design. Supporting the design are three new file system concepts: the **file domain,** the **fileset,** and the **volume**. The interrelationship between these elements of an AdvFS file domain can be found in Figure 6–1.

FIGURE 6–1
AdvFS Domain
Components

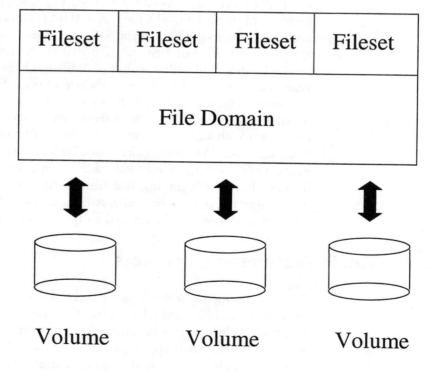

6.1.1.1   File Domain

A file domain is a pool of storage to which you can add and remove volumes dynamically as the user requirements for the storage change. An

AdvFS volume is any element that behaves like a read-write UNIX block device. For example, a volume can be a single disk partition, an entire disk, or an aggregate volume provided by the Logical Storage Manager (LSM). For the purpose of this discussion, a disk is any device that presents itself to the operating system as a single device and can be disklabeled as a single disk. This could be a RAID or other block special device, which encompasses many other disks "under the hood." The maximum number of volumes that can be included in a file domain is 256. In practice, far fewer than that number are ever needed.

6.1.1.2   Fileset

A fileset follows the logical structure of a traditional UFS. To the UNIX user, it is a hierarchy of directories and files, just like any other file system. The fileset is also the entity that you mount. AdvFS goes beyond UFS, by allowing you to create multiple filesets that share a common pool of storage within a file domain.

A fileset is similar to a file system in the following ways:

- You can mount filesets like you can mount file systems.

- Filesets are units on which you enable quotas.

- Filesets are units that you back up.

Filesets offer the following features that are not provided by file systems:

- You can clone a fileset and back it up while users are still accessing the original.

- A fileset can span several disks in a file domain.

Follow these guidelines for creating and using filesets:

- You can create an unlimited number of filesets per system; however, the number of filesets you can simultaneously mount is limited to 512.

- The more filesets that you establish, the greater your flexibility. On the other hand, a greater number of filesets increases your management overhead.

6.1.2   Transaction Log

The AdvFS employs a **transaction log** to ensure the integrity of the file system. This differs from UFS, which uses ordered writes and a file system checker program to ensure data integrity. The transaction log performs **write-ahead logging** so that modifications to the **metadata** (file structure information) are completely written to a transaction log before the actual changes are written to disk. The log, which is implemented as a circular file buffer, ensures that the file system is not left in an inconsistent state after an unexpected system crash. By default, only metadata changes are logged for performance reasons. As the root user, you can change logging on a per-file basis, thus data writes can be logged for those files as well as for metadata.

The transaction log for a file domain is initiated at the time the domain is created. The first time the file domain is activated, 4 MB (512 eight-kilobyte pages) of storage is allocated for the log. Only one transaction log exists per domain, thus in a multivolume domain only one of the volumes contains the log. For most domains, the default log size is sufficient; however, very busy or large domains may require that the log size be increased.

After a system crash, AdvFS consults the transaction log to determine which file system transactions have completed. All completed transactions are committed to disk, and uncompleted transactions are undone. The number of uncommitted records in the log, not the amount of data in the file system, dictates the speed of recovery. This means that recovery usually takes only a few seconds. Traditional UFSs rely on the *fsck(8)* utility to recover from a system failure. As we saw in Chapter 5, *fsck(8)* can literally take hours to check and repair a large UFS. Thus, for large file systems, AdvFS is a must.

6.1.3   Extent-Based Allocation

The AdvFS uses a fixed-size **page** consisting of 8 kilobytes (or 16 disk blocks). It will attempt, whenever possible, to write each file to disk as a set of contiguous pages known as an **extent**. In other words, a single extent consists of storage from a single file that is physically adjacent on a disk volume. When storage is added to a file in AdvFS, it is grouped in extents rather than in the UFS method to allocate one block at a time.

An **extent map** is a description of all of a file's extents, which are physically located on a particular AdvFS volume. A file can have multiple extent maps associated with it when it occupies more than one volume in a domain. Or, it can have only a single extent map when all of its data blocks are located on a single volume. Clearly, the maximum number of extent maps that a file can have is equal to the number of volumes in the domain. The minimum number of extent maps that a file can have is zero because a file that is smaller than a single page has no extents, thus no extent map.

Contiguous placement of the pages means that the I/O subsystem is as efficient as possible. When a file consists of many smaller extents, then the I/O subsystem must work much harder to read or write that file and file system performance suffers. Defragmenting, which is the process of coalescing many smaller extents into fewer (ideally, one) larger extents, can reverse this effect. Thus, the end result of the defragment process on all of the files on a file system is to improve performance.

6.1.4   Fragments

Files, or pieces of files, that are smaller than 8K are allocated from one of the **fragment** (or frag) lists. There are 8 frag lists for 1K to 7K sized file fragments and the free list. As we have said, files that are smaller than 8K do not contain any extents. Therefore, they do not have extent maps associated with them.

6.1.5   File Storage Allocation

Files on an active file system will continually grow and shrink. Their space requirements change over time. To maintain contiguous file placement without overallocating space on the disk, AdvFS uses a unique file storage allocation scheme. Each time a file is appended, AdvFS adds pages to the file by preallocating one-fourth of the file size, up to 16 pages. If a large write requires file space, then AdvFS attempts to allocate up to 256 contiguous pages. When a file is closed, excess preallocated space is truncated, and space is returned to the free list.

In a single-volume domain, file allocation is simple because all of the storage is allocated from the one volume; however, for file domains with more than one volume, storage allocation is less straightforward. New files on multivolume domains are allocated in round-robin fashion across volumes. Once a volume becomes more than 86 percent full, it is no longer used for new file allocation. Then, once all volumes are more than 86 percent full, round-robin allocation resumes until the volumes are completely full. When existing files are appended, storage is allocated on the volume on which the file was initially allocated, until the volume is full.

When a new volume is added to a file domain, it is added to the storage allocation sequence together with the other volumes. Files are allocated to the new volume in turn.

6.2   Getting Started with AdvFS

This section covers some of the basics of how to install, create, and mount AdvFS for use on your Tru64 UNIX system. Then, we discuss how to remove those file systems.

6.2.1   Installing AdvFS

Before you can begin setting up an AdvFS, you must make sure the following subsets are loaded and built into the running kernel:

```
OSFADVFSxxx     POLYCENTER AdvFS (System Administration)
OSFADVFSBINxxx  POLYCENTER AdvFS Kernel Objects (Kernel Build Environment)
```

Use the *setld(8)* command to check for the existence of these subsets and to load them if they are not installed.

In addition, the AdvFS kernel objects will be included in a built kernel if you ensure that the kernel option for AdvFS is included into the kernel configuration file. This file is called /sys/conf/<SYSTEMNAME>. The following line needs to be included:

```
options    MSFS
```

After adding the MSFS option,[2] use the *doconfig(8)* command to rebuild the kernel. Once the kernel has been successfully rebuilt, copy it to the root directory and reboot the system for the change to take effect.

Conversely, if AdvFS is not used or needed for a particular system, then eliminating the MSFS option from the kernel configuration file and rebuilding and rebooting from the kernel will eliminate the kernel objects from being included. This task could be performed to reduce the size of the kernel. Keep in mind that if AdvFS is not built into the kernel and AdvFSs are used on the system, those file systems will not be mountable when booted from that custom kernel. This could render your system unbootable from that kernel if AdvFS is used for your system's root file system.

6.2.2   Setting Up an AdvFS

Once the subsets are installed and the kernel option is enabled for AdvFS, we can now create file systems. Creating an AdvFS requires four steps.

1.   Create a file domain.

2.   Create a fileset.

3.   Create the mount point.

4.   Mount the fileset.

You must have root privilege to perform these functions.

6.2.2.1 Making a File Domain

The first step in creating an AdvFS is to make a file domain. The *mkfdmn(8)* command is used to create a single-volume file domain. As we stated earlier, a file domain is a pool of storage used for creating file systems. The domain is now referred to by its domain name rather than by the device.

You should be aware that if you are trying to make a new AdvFS on a device that had previously held one, and that file system was not removed according to the instructions in section 6.2.3, then you will receive an error message and the operation will fail. This feature is designed to prevent you from destroying your file systems unintentionally. If you really intend to do this because you know the file system is no longer in use, then you can override this protection using the '–o' flag to *mkfdmn(8)*. See section 6.2.3 for instructions for removing an AdvFS.

Syntax:

New: mkfdmn [-F] [-1 num_pages] [-o] [-r] [-x num_pages]
[-V3 | -V4] [-p num_pages] device_special domain

Old: mkfdmn [-F] [-1 num_pages] [-o] [-p num_pages] [-r]
[-t type] [-x num_pages] special domain

TABLE 6–1 Flags for the *mkfdmn(8)* Command

FLAG	DESCRIPTION	V4	V5
device_special	The block special device name, such as /dev/disk/dsk3c, of the first AdvFS volume used to create the file domain.	X	X
domain	The name of the new file domain you wish to create.	X	X
-F	This flag is used to ignore overlapping partition or block warnings.	X	X
-o	This flag is used to overwrite an existing file domain, allowing you to re-create the domain structure.	X	X
-r	Specifies the file domain as the root domain. This prevents multiple volumes in the root domain. AdvFS supports only one volume in the root domain.	X	X
-V3 I -V4	AdvFS on-disk version used to create the new domain. V4 is the new Tru64 UNIX 5.0 on-disk structure and V3 is the pre-5.0 version. The default is to use V4, if neither is specified.		X

TABLE 6–1   Flags for the *mkfdmn(8)* Command (Continued)

FLAG	DESCRIPTION	V4	V5
-t type	This option was retired in Tru64 UNIX 5.0 and is no longer used. Previously, this flag enabled you to define the disk type of the initial volume. This action was necessary only if the disk had not already been labeled with the *disklabel(8)* utility.	X	
-x num_pages	This sets the number of pages by which the bitfile metadata table (BMT) grows.	X	X
-p num_pages	Sets the number of pages to preallocate for the first extent in the bitfile metadata table (BMT).	X	X
-l num_pages	Sets the number of pages in the log file. AdvFS rounds this number up to a multiple of four. This switch was added in Tru64 UNIX 4.0D.	X	X

The two required parameters are the block special device name and the domain name, which must be unique. The following example shows the syntax for creating an AdvFS domain using a disk partition.

Example:

```
# mkfdmn /dev/disk/dsk2c domain1
```

You can also specify an LSM volume with the *mkfdmn(8)* command, for example:

Example:

```
# mkfdmn /dev/vol/publicdg/vol-01 domain2
```

Almost any name is completely acceptable as a domain name. The typical convention is to use the word domain in the domain name; however, this is not required. If AdvFS is used for the root and /usr file systems, then these are typically called root_domain and usr_domain, respectively. During a system installation, if AdvFS is chosen for those file systems or for factory installation, then those names will be used.

6.2.2.2   Creating a Fileset

A file domain is not really usable without at least one fileset. You can use the *mkfset(8)* command to create a fileset in a file domain. A file domain can contain many filesets, all of which share the domain's underlying storage. This provides a way to logically partition storage into multiple file systems without wasting space by dedicating it to each one.

Syntax:

```
mkfset domain setname
```

TABLE 6-2   Flags for the *mkfset(8)* Command

FLAG	DESCRIPTION
domain	Specifies the name of an existing file domain.
setname	Specifies the name of the fileset to be created in the specified file domain.

You do not have to name the fileset the same as its mount point directory; however, it is a common convention. For example, if the mount point is /u01, then you can name the fileset u01 (the directory name without the leading /).

Example:

This simple example shows how to use the *mkfset(8)* command to create two filesets in a single AdvFS file domain called efs_dmn.

```
# mkfset efs_dmn efs
# mkfset efs_dmn efs2
```

You can create multiple filesets within a file domain. Each fileset within a file domain can be either mounted or unmounted independently of the other filesets in the file domain.

6.2.2.3   Mounting AdvFS

As with UFS, if the mount point directory does not already exist, then you can create it using the *mkdir(1)* command. Then you can use the *mount(8)* command to mount a fileset. The syntax for mounting AdvFS often throws people off at first because it is a bit different from UFS. We cover the AdvFS-specific aspects of *mount(8)* here for completeness; however, we refer you to our general discussion in Chapter 1 for information related to other file systems.

Syntax:

```
mount [-t advfs] [-o dual] domain#fileset directory
```

TABLE 6-3   *Mount(8)* Flags that Pertain to the AdvFS

FLAGS	DESCRIPTION
domain	The name of the file domain to be mounted
fileset	The name of the fileset to be mounted
directory	The mount point directory
-t advfs	The type of file system to be mounted. In the case of AdvFS, specifies AdvFS (not required).
-o dual	This flag allows a fileset to be mounted even if it has the same domain ID as a file system that is already mounted. This flag was added in Tru64 UNIX 4.0E.

Example:

This example shows two alternate syntaxes for mounting an AdvFS from the command line with superuser privileges.

```
# mount -t advfs domain1#users /usr/users
```

The '-t' switch is optional, so the following alternative syntax is also acceptable.

```
# mount domain1#users /usr/users
```

The pound sign character between the file domain and fileset is a required part of the mount syntax. In this way, the fileset to be mounted from within a domain can be specified. Be careful not to confuse its use with a comment when reading the fstab file. Comments in the fstab file are still delimited by the pound sign character.

Example:

This example shows a real Tru64 UNIX 5.0 fstab file with AdvFS. One of the entries (the test_domain one) has been commented out.

```
# cat /etc/fstab
root_domain#root         /       advfs   rw  0 1
/proc                    /proc   procfs  rw  0 0
usr_domain#usr           /usr    advfs   rw  0 2
usr_domain#var           /var    advfs   rw  0 2
#test_domain#test        /test   advfs   rw  0 2
```

Example:

This example illustrates how to perform a split-mirror mount of an AdvFS domain j_dmn using an LSM volume named voltest1 with two plexes. This technique, available in Tru64 UNIX V4.0E and higher, is an alternative to clone fileset backups.

```
# df /j
Filesystem   512-blocks   Used   Available   Capacity   Mounted on
j_dmn#j      200000       32     191472      1%         /j

# showfdmn j_dmn

      Id          Date Created LogPgs Domain Name
37f2c69e.000a920a Wed Sep 29 22:10:38 1999    512 j_dmn

  Vol       512-Blks     Free    %     Used   Cmode  Rblks Wblks    Vol Name
   1L       200000       191472  4%    on     128    128   /dev/vol/rootdg/
voltest1

# volprint -ht voltest1
```

```
DG NAME        GROUP-ID
DM NAME        DEVICE        TYPE      PRIVLEN   PUBLEN  PUBPATH
V  NAME        USETYPE       KSTATE    STATE     LENGTH  READPOL    PREFPLEX
PL NAME        VOLUME        KSTATE    STATE     LENGTH  LAYOUT     ST-WIDTH  MODE
SD NAME        PLEX          PLOFFS    DISKOFFS  LENGTH  DISK-NAME  DEVICE

v  voltest1    fsgen         ENABLED   ACTIVE    200000  SELECT     -
pl voltest1-01 voltest1      ENABLED   ACTIVE    200000  CONCAT     -         RW
sd rz3-03      voltest1-01   0         6291456   200000  rz3        rz3
pl voltest1-02 voltest1      ENABLED   ACTIVE    200000  CONCAT     -         RW
sd rz3-04      voltest1-02   0         6491456   200000  rz3        rz3

# umount /j

# volplex dis voltest1-02

# volprint -ht voltest1
DG NAME       GROUP-ID
DM NAME        DEVICE        TYPE      PRIVLEN   PUBLEN  PUBPATH
V  NAME        USETYPE       KSTATE    STATE     LENGTH  READPOL    PREFPLEX
PL NAME        VOLUME        KSTATE    STATE     LENGTH  LAYOUT     ST-WIDTH  MODE
SD NAME        PLEX          PLOFFS    DISKOFFS  LENGTH  DISK-NAME  DEVICE

v  voltest1    fsgen         ENABLED   ACTIVE    200000  SELECT     -
pl voltest1-01 voltest1      ENABLED   ACTIVE    200000  CONCAT     -         RW
sd rz3-03      voltest1-01   0         6291456   200000  rz3        rz3

# volmake -Ufsgen vol voltest2 plex=voltest1-02

# volume start voltest2

# volprint -ht voltest2
DG NAME        GROUP-ID
DM NAME        DEVICE        TYPE      PRIVLEN   PUBLEN  PUBPATH
V  NAME        USETYPE       KSTATE    STATE     LENGTH  READPOL    PREFPLEX
PL NAME        VOLUME        KSTATE    STATE     LENGTH  LAYOUT     ST-WIDTH  MODE
SD NAME        PLEX          PLOFFS    DISKOFFS  LENGTH  DISK-NAME  DEVICE

v  voltest2    fsgen         ENABLED   ACTIVE    200000  ROUND      -
pl voltest1-02 voltest2      ENABLED   ACTIVE    200000  CONCAT     -         RW
sd rz3-04      voltest1-02   0         6491456   200000  rz3        rz3

# cd /etc/fdmns

# mkdir j2_dmn

# cd j2_dmn

# ln -s /dev/vol/rootdg/voltest2 rootdg.voltest2

# cd /etc/fdmns

# mount j_dmn#j /j

# mount j2_dmn#j /mnt
j2_dmn#j on /mnt: I/O error

# mount -o dual j2_dmn#j /mnt
Dual mounting a split-mirror AdvFS filesystem.
This takes a short while to update the domain's ID.
```

```
# df /j
Filesystem        512-blocks    Used      Available Capacity   Mounted on
j_dmn#j           200000        32        191472    1%         /j

# df /mnt
Filesystem        512-blocks    Used      Available Capacity   Mounted on
j_dmn#j           200000        32        191472    1%         /mnt
```

This example shows one of the three common ways you can perform a split-mirror mount. We also discussed another way to do a split-mirror mount in Chapter 3 with our coverage of LSM's snapshot capability. In that chapter, we provide a more extensive example of how you may do a backup using LSM snapshot and a split-mirror mount. The third method for split-mirror mount is by breaking a mirror at the RAID controller level. We don't cover that procedure in this text, but simply make you aware that this is possible.

6.2.3   Removing an AdvFS

Occasionally, a device or devices containing an AdvFS need to be reused for another purpose. In order to reuse devices that had been used by an AdvFS, it is a good idea to make sure the file system is completely removed. This good system administration practice will prevent future problems. Some problems that you could avoid are either putting a swap space in the middle of an existing file system or wasting disk space because you didn't realize that a partition was available on a device.

The steps to follow to remove an AdvFS completely are as follows:

1.   Unmount the file system.

2.   Remove the filesets (optional).

3.   Remove the domain.

You must have root privileges to perform these operations.

6.2.3.1   Unmounting an AdvFS

Use the *umount(8)* command to unmount any AdvFS. Note that a file system will not unmount if it has open files on it. All open files have to be closed before the unmount will succeed. If you attempt to unmount a file system that has open files, you will receive the error message "device busy," and the unmount will fail.

Syntax:

```
umount file_system... | directory...
```

TABLE 6–4 AdvFS Flags for the *umount(8)* Command

FLAG	DESCRIPTION
file_system	The AdvFS (domain#fileset) to be unmounted
directory	The mount point directory of the AdvFS to be unmounted

Example:

This example shows how to use the unmount command to unmount an AdvFS.

```
# df /junk
Filesystem         512-blocks  Used  Available Capacity  Mounted on
junk_domain#junk   2197152     42    2187504   1%         /junk
# umount /junk
```

6.2.3.2 Removing Filesets

The *rmfset(8)* command is used for removing AdvFS filesets for a given domain. This step is technically not required for removing a file system. You should be aware, however, that using *rmfset(8)* will result in removal of all the files on the fileset.

Syntax:

```
rmfset [-f] domain setname
```

TABLE 6–5 Flags for the *rmfset(8)* Command

FLAG	DESCRIPTION
domain	Specifies the name of an existing file domain
setname	Specifies the name of the fileset to be deleted from the specified file domain
-f	Do not prompt for confirmation. This is useful when writing scripts that use *rmfset(8)*.

Example:

The following example shows how to use the *rmfset(8)* command to remove the fileset "junk" from the domain "junk_domain." This is the domain's only fileset.

```
# showfsets junk_domain
junk
    Id            : 343a4ca6.000010c5.1.8001
    Files         :    0, SLim=    0, HLim=    0
    Blocks (512)  :    0, SLim=    0, HLim=    0
    Quota Status  : user=off group=off
```

```
# rmfset junk_domain junk
rmfset: remove fileset junk? [y/n] y

# showfsets junk_domain
showfsets: domain 'junk_domain' has no filesets
```

6.2.3.3 Removing File Domains

The *rmfdmn(8)* utility is used to remove an existing file domain. If you attempt to remove a file domain without first unmounting all of its filesets, then an error message will be returned and the domain will not be removed.

Syntax:

```
rmfdmn [-f] domain
```

TABLE 6–6   Flags for the *rmfdmn(8)* Command

FLAG	DESCRIPTION
domain	The name of a file domain to remove
-f	Do not prompt for confirmation. The default is to prompt for confirmation.

Example:

This simple example illustrates usage of the *rmfdmn(8)* command to remove a domain called "junk_domain." Because we did not specify the '-f' option, the tool required our approval before proceeding.

```
# rmfdmn junk_domain
rmfdmn: remove domain junk_domain? [y/n] y
rmfdmn: domain junk_domain removed.

# showfsets junk_domain
showfsets: can't show set info for domain 'junk_domain'
showfsets: error = No such file or directory
```

In Tru64 UNIX version 4.0, the *rmfdmn(8)* command was moved to the base AdvFS subset from the advanced AdvFS utilities (see section 6.4). Therefore, if you are using a version of the operating system prior to 4.0, then you must install and activate the Advanced Utilities in order to use this utility. If you do not have that, then you can simply perform the steps that the *rmfdmn(8)* command would follow. Assuming that all of the filesets are already unmounted, those steps are as follows:

1.   Remove the directory and links from /etc/fdmns for this domain. You also want to remove the lock file for that domain from /etc/fdmns, if this is a Tru64 UNIX 4.0 or greater system. The lock file has a name like .advfslock_<domain>.

2. If the volume is a disk partition, then edit the disk label and set the partition fstype field to "unused." If it's a multivolume file domain, then you must do this for all of the volumes. If any of the file domain's volumes are LSM logical volumes, then this step can be omitted for those volumes. (You need to decide if you want to remove the logical volume too or use it as-is for something else.)

3. Write zeros over the file system's magic number. This step is optional and requires extreme care because it will prevent some file system utilities from recognizing the partition as belonging to an AdvFS. (See our discussion of *advscan(8)* later in this chapter.) You can do this with *dd(1)* on the first 64 blocks of each raw partition or logical volume.

Once you have completed these steps, the partition is totally removed from AdvFS and can be used for something else, including a new AdvFS.

Example:

This example shows how to follow our procedure for removing a file domain completely without using *rmfdmn(8)*. In this case, our domain "stuff_domain" is using a logical volume rather than a disk partition.

```
# df /stuff
Filesystem          512-blocks  Used   Available Capacity  Mounted on
stuff_domain#stuff  100000      18480  67920     22%       /stuff

# umount /stuff

# rm -rf /etc/fdmns/stuff_domain

# rm /etc/fdmns/.advfslock_stuff_domain

# /sbin/advfs/advscan -g rootdg

Scanning devices   /dev/rvol/rootdg

Partition       Domain Id

rootdg.vol_stuff   38cda603.00017970    V3, dismounted
                1 volume in domain

       Created        Mon Mar 13 21:37:55 2000
       Last mount      Fri Mar 17 09:35:40 2000
# dd if=/dev/zero of=/dev/rvol/vol_stuff bs=512 count=64
64+0 records in
64+0 records out

# /sbin/advfs/advscan -g rootdg

Scanning devices   /dev/rvol/rootdg

Partition       Domain Id
```

6.3   Managing Advanced File Systems

In addition to creating and removing AdvFSs, several activities are involved in properly managing them. This section discusses the tasks and special commands that can be used to accomplish those activities. We begin by covering ways for getting more information about AdvFSs and files. Then we move into backup and restoring data, managing quotas, and using the /etc/fdmns directory to perform maintenance tasks. We also cover the finer details of additional and advanced AdvFS commands.

6.3.1   Getting Information About AdvFS

The first step to managing the AdvFS is to find out information about the file system and how it is configured. This section gives a detailed explanation of the most useful tools available for gathering information about AdvFSs. You should understand and be familiar with these tools before you need them. Just as with the UFS tools we discussed in the previous chapter, their usefulness will not be apparent until you have a need for the information they provide.

6.3.1.1   Displaying File Domain Information

The *showfdmn(8)* command is used to show details of the attributes of a file domain and its volumes. If no filesets in the domain are mounted, then you cannot get meaningful information from the *showfdmn(8)* command and an error message will be returned. Therefore, you cannot get information from *showfdmn(8)* if at least one fileset in the domain cannot be mounted for some reason.

Syntax:

```
showfdmn [-k] domain
```

TABLE 6–7   Flags for the *showfdmn(8)* Command

FLAGS	DESCRIPTION
domain	The domain to display information about.
-k	Displays the block counts in kilobytes instead of the default 512-byte blocks.

Example:

Here is an example of a simple, single-volume domain. The /usr file is used here for illustration purposes.

```
# showfdmn usr_domain

       Id              Date Created              LogPgs   Version    Domain Name
36b0147f.000473f0   Thu Jan 28 02:40:47 1999    512      4          usr_domain

Vol    512-Blks      Free      % Used   Cmode    Rblks    Wblks    Vol Name
  1L   1522464       128080    92%      on       16384    16384    /dev/
vol/rootdg/usrvol
```

Example:

The following is an example of *showfdmn(8)* output for a multivolume domain. In this case, the domain has three LSM volumes.

```
# showfdmn test_dmn

       Id              Date Created              LogPgs   Domain Name
33c3a315.0001bec1   Wed Jul 9 10:41:25 1997     512      test_dmn

Vol   512-Blks    Free      % Used   Cmode   Rblks   Wblks      Vol Name
  1L    424323    382992    10%      on      128     128     /dev/vol/vol03
  2    1104876   1104624    0%       on      128     128     /dev/vol/vol01
  3     424323    424160    0%       on      128     128     /dev/vol/vol02
      --------------------  ------
      1953522   1911776     2%
```

Example:

The following is an example of *showfdmn(8)* output when there are no mounted filesets.

```
# umount /test

# showfdmn test_domain

       Id              Date Created              LogPgs   Version    Domain Name
37c008e8.0004c330   Sun Aug 22 09:27:52 1999    512      4          test_domain
showfdmn: unable to display volume info; domain not active

# mount test_domain#test /test

# showfdmn test_domain | more

       Id              Date Created              LogPgs   Version    Domain Name
37c008e8.0004c330   Sun Aug 22 09:27:52 1999    512      4          test_domain

Vol    512-Blks     Free      % Used   Cmode    Rblks    Wblks    Vol Name
  1L  2 046736     2038208    0%       on       16384    16384    /dev/vol/ste-
vedg/vol01
```

The *showfdmn(8)* command display is divided into two different sections: the domain attributes section and the volume attributes section. The two sections are each summarized in the following two tables.

TABLE 6–8 Domain Attributes from the *showfdmn(8)* Command

FIELD	DESCRIPTION
Id	Unique hexadecimal number that identifies a file domain
Date Created	Day, month, and time that the file domain was created
LogPgs	Number of eight-kilobyte pages in the transaction log of the specified file domain
Version	The internal on-disk structure version of this domain. If the domain was created pre-5.0, then this will have the number 3. If it was created in version 5.0 or later, then it will have the number 4. Tru64 UNIX 5.0 or later can mount pre-5.0 domains, but additional features will not be supported. This field is new in 5.0.
Domain Name	Name of the file domain

TABLE 6–9 Volume Attributes from the *showfdmn(8)* Command

FIELD	DESCRIPTION
Vol	Volume number within the file domain; an L next to the number indicates that the volume contains the transaction log
512-Blks	Size of the volume in 512-byte blocks
Free	Number of blocks in a volume that are available for use
% Used	Used percentage of volume space currently allocated to files or metadata
Cmode	I/O consolidated mode; default mode is on
Rblks	Maximum number of 512-bytes blocks read from the volume at one time
Wblks	Maximum number of 512-byte blocks written to the volume at one time
Vol Name	Name of the special device for the volume

Readers may notice that the *showfdmn(8)* has no option to display information for all domains on the system at once. A technique can be employed to display this information, thus it is not necessary to add an option of this kind. In order to display information for all of the domains on a system, enter the following sequence of commands:

```
# cd /etc/fdmns
# showfdmn *
```

The /etc/fdmns directory contains a subdirectory for each file domain created by mkfdmn. Keep in mind that the *showfdmn(8)* command displays only information for mounted AdvFSs. It is possible that domains that are not mounted will be referenced in the /etc/fdmns directory and will not have information displayed.

6.3.1.2 Displaying Fileset Information

Use the *showfsets(8)* command to show the attributes of the filesets in a domain. The fileset does not have to be mounted to use the showfsets command.

Syntax:

```
showfsets [-b | q] [-k] domain [fileset...]
```

TABLE 6–10 Flags for the *showfsets(8)* Command

FLAG	DESCRIPTION
domain	The full pathname of the file domain
fileset	The name of one or more filesets for which to display information
-b	This flag lists only the names of the filesets in a specified domain.
-q	This flag displays quota limits for filesets in a specified domain.
-k	This flag displays the total number of blocks and the number of free blocks in terms of one-kilobyte blocks instead of the default 512-byte blocks.

Example:

This example illustrates the use of the *showfsets(8)* command to examine full information about the filesets in a multifileset domain.

```
# showfsets var_domain

var
    Id            : 33e9e4ea.000714dc.1.8001
    Files         :     5, SLim=    0, HLim=    0
    Blocks (512) :     0, SLim=    0, HLim=    0
    Quota Status : user=off group=off

tmp
    Id            : 33e9e4ea.000714dc.2.8001
    Clone is      : clone_tmp
    Files         :     2, SLim=    0, HLim=    0
    Blocks (512) :    32, SLim=    0, HLim=    0
    Quota Status : user=off group=off

local
    Id            : 33e9e4ea.000714dc.3.8001
    Files         :   185, SLim=    0, HLim=    0
    Blocks (512) : 49260, SLim=    0, HLim=    0
    Quota Status : user=off group=off

clone_tmp
    Id            : 33e9e4ea.000714dc.4.8001
    Clone of      : tmp
    Revision      : 1
```

The *showfsets(8)* command displays the following fields for each fileset:

TABLE 6–11   Standard Fields Displayed for the *showfsets(8)* Command

Field	Description
Id	A combination of the file domain identifier and an additional set of numbers that identify the fileset within the file domain
Clone is	Specifies which fileset is the clone for this fileset, if applicable.
Clone of	Specifies which fileset this fileset is a clone of, if applicable.
Revision	Specifies the number of times you revised a clone fileset. For example, if you re-create a clone fileset of the same parent fileset three times, then the revision value is 3.
Files	Specifies the number of files in the fileset and current soft and hard quota limits.
Blocks	Specifies the number of blocks currently in use by a mounted fileset and the current soft and hard quota limits.
Quota Status	Specifies which quota types are enabled (enforced).

The *showfsets(8)* command with the '-q' flag set displays block and file information for a specified domain or for one or more named filesets in the domain. The characteristics of a named fileset are shown in the following table:

TABLE 6–12   Quota Fields Displayed for the *showfsets(8)* Command

Field	Description
BF	Specifies the block usage limits. A plus character in this field means that the soft block usage is exceeded; an asterisk means that the hard limit is reached.
Block (512) Limits	Specifies the number of blocks used, the soft limit (the number of blocks that can be exceeded for a period of time), the hard limit (the number of blocks that cannot be exceeded), and the grace period (the remaining time for which the soft limit may be exceeded).
File Limits	Specifies the number of files used, the soft and hard file limits for the fileset, and the grace period remaining.

Example:

This simple example shows how to use the showfsets command to examine the fileset quotas using the '-q' flag. In this case, we have exceeded the block usage hard and soft limits for the fileset quotas.

```
# showfsets -q efs_dmn
            Block (512) limits        File limits
Fileset BF  used   soft  hard grace used soft  hard grace
efs     *-  23744 2000  6000 none 3    1000 3000
```

Example:

This is another example of examining quotas using *showfsets(8)*. Here, the block quotas are within the hard limit but have exceeded the soft limit.

```
# showfsets -q efs_dmn
              Block (512) limits        File limits
Fileset BF used  soft hard grace   used  soft hard grace
efs     +-  23744 2000 50000 none 3      1000 3000
```

6.3.1.3 Displaying File Information

You can use the *showfile(8)* command to display information about a file in the AdvFS. The *showfile(8)* command displays the attributes of one or more AdvFS files. The command also displays the extent map of each file. An extent is a contiguous area of disk space that the file system allocates to a file. Simple files have one extent map; striped files have an extent map for every stripe segment.

You can list AdvFS attributes for an individual file or the contents of a directory. Although the *showfile(8)* command lists both AdvFS and non-AdvFS files, the command displays meaningful information for AdvFS files only.

Syntax:

```
showfile [-x] file_name ...
```

TABLE 6–13   Flags for the *showfile(8)* Command

FLAGS	DESCRIPTION
file_name	The name of the file or files to examine
-x	Displays the full storage allocation map (extent map) for files in an AdvFS.

Example:

This example shows how to use *showfile(8)* to examine a file's AdvFS attributes.

```
# showfile perl5
    Id    Vol PgSz Pages XtntType Segs SegSz Log Perf File
    e.8001 1   16   103   simple   **   **    off 100% perl5
```

The *showfile(8)* command displays the following fields for each fileset.

TABLE 6–14   Standard Fields Displayed for the *showfile(8)* Command

FIELD	DESCRIPTION
Id	A combination of the "tag" number and a generation number that is unique to the file
Vol	The volume number that this file's primary metadata resides on. The data extents of the file can reside on another volume.
PgSz	The page size in 512-byte blocks
Pages	The number of pages allocated to the file
XtntType	The extent type can be simple, which is a regular AdvFS file special extents; stripe, which is a striped file; symlink, which is a symbolic link to a file; UFS, NFS, and so on.
Segs	The number of stripe segments per striped file, which is the number of volumes a striped file crosses. (Applies only to stripe type.)
SegSz	The number of pages per stripe segment. (Applies only to stripe type.
Log (I/O)	The data logging option is async, sync, or ftx. The *chfile(8)* command can be used to alter this value. This field changed in V5.0 and is discussed in greater detail in section 6.3.5.3 in this book.
Perf	The efficiency of file extent allocation, expressed as a percentage of the optimal extent layout. A high percentage, such as 100 percent, indicates that the AdvFS I/O system has achieved optimal efficiency. A low percentage indicates the need for file defragmentation.
File	The name of the file being examined

Example:

This example illustrates use of showfile with the '-x' switch to examine a file's extent map and other attributes.

```
# showfile -x perl5

    Id    Vol PgSz Pages XtntType Segs SegSz Log Perf File
   e.8001 1   16   103   simple    **   **   off 100% perl5

    extentMap: 1
      pageOff        pageCnt    vol    volBlock      blockCnt
         0           103         1     14256         1648
      extentCnt: 1
```

The additional fields displayed using the '-x' switch to *showfile(8)* are described in Table 6–15.

TABLE 6–15   Extent Map Fields Displayed for the *showfile(8)* Command

FIELD	DESCRIPTION
extentMap	A number that specifies which extent map is being examined. Whereas a simple file has one extent map, a striped file has more than one extent map.
PageOff	The starting page number of the extent

TABLE 6–15   Extent Map Fields Displayed for the *showfile(8)* Command

FIELD	DESCRIPTION
PageCnt	The number of eight-kilobyte pages in the extent
Vol	The location of the extent
VolBlock	The starting block number of the extent
BlockCnt	The number of 512-byte blocks in the extent
ExtentCnt	The total number of extents in the extent map

Example:

In Chapter 4, we discussed how a sparse file is created using the *lseek(2)* system call. This example shows how a normal user can create a sparse file using *dd(1)* and examine the extent map for the file on an AdvFS. The extent map contains "holes" or data that are not mapped on disk. Interestingly, in this case, the blocks are actually contiguous with one another physically on disk but not logically in the file.

```
$ dd if=/dev/zero of=test bs=512 count=16
16+0 records in
16+0 records out

$ dd if=/dev/zero of=test bs=512 count=16 oseek=100000
16+0 records in
16+0 records out

$ ls -ls test
16 -rwxrwxr-x  1 hancock crash1  51208192 Mar 31 14:30 test

$ showfile -x test

    Id      Vol PgSz Pages XtntType Segs SegSz I/O   Perf File
23c.8018 1   16   2     simple   **    **   async 50%  test

    extentMap: 1
      pageOff       pageCnt     vol     volBlock     blockCnt
         0             1         1      7141440        16
       6250            1         1      7141456        16
      extentCnt: 2
```

6.3.1.4   Displaying Metadata Information

It may occasionally become necessary to display the metadata for a given domain. This task can be accomplished using the showfile command and a hidden directory known as .tags (the .tags directory and its contents is covered in greater detail later in Chapter 7). This directory is found in the mount point directory for each mounted fileset in each domain. A more complete discussion of metadata is covered later in Chapter 7. For now, you should just be aware that the *showfile(8)* command can be used to examine metadata.

Example:

One of the metadata files that exists for each volume in a domain is called the bitfile metadata table (BMT). To look at the BMT for the first volume of a domain, you want to examine the file with a (–6) tag associated with it. Normally, the positive tags with values greater than 5 are associated with normal files on the file systems (tags 1 through 5 are special). The following example shows how this is done.

```
# cd /test/.tags

# showfile -x M-6

    Id      Vol PgSz Pages XtntType Segs  SegSz I/O  Perf File
fffffffa.000011 6   1    simple   **    **    ftx  100% M-6

  extentMap: 1
    pageOff  pageCnt   vol  volBlock  blockCnt
      0        1        1     32        16
    extentCnt: 1
```

6.3.2   Backup and Restore

The primary utility for making backups in AdvFS is the *vdump(8)* command, and the primary utility for restoring from backups made with *vdump(8)* is *vrestore(8)*. Although using the *dump(8)* and *vdump(8)* commands is similar (not identical), the tape format is not the same. The *vrestore(8)* command can also be used to restore files from an archive tape made using the *dump(8)* command, but not vice versa.

The *vdump(8)* and *vrestore(8)* commands offer several additional features that are not available with the traditional UNIX backup utilities *dump(8)* and *restore(8)*:

- They support AdvFS, UFS, and NFS.

- They allow you to back up individual subdirectories by using the '–D' flag.

- They write the data in a compressed format by using the '–c' flag, reducing storage, and running faster on slow backup devices.

It is not our intention here to rehash backup and recovery strategies because this topic is well covered in Chapter 1 and in other texts. The reader should consult Cheek (1999) for a more thorough coverage of backup and recovery strategies in Tru64 UNIX. Here, we review the *vdump(8)* and *vrestore(8)* tools (along with the remote equivalents) and their capabilities. Readers must decide on their own how these tools will meet their specific requirements. Later in this chapter, we also revisit backups and the use of clone filesets to give readers a greater appreciation for the capabilities of the AdvFS for online backups and recovery.

The *rvdump(8)* and *rvrestore(8)* tools are new to Tru64 UNIX version 5.0. The discussion that follows may not be applicable to pre-5.0 systems. In order to emulate the *rvdump(8)* functionality in older versions, a command similar to the following has been widely used for years:

```
vdump -b 60 -f - -D <dir> | rsh <host> [<user>]
dd of=<tape> bs=60k
```

Where <dir>, <host>, <user>, and <tape> are user-supplied values defined as follows:

dir: The directory to be backed up using vdump to the remote tape.

host: The host name of the system that has the tape drive. This host must be resolvable by sending to a valid IP address on the network.

user: The user name used to log into the remote host. This user must have write privileges to the tape device. If user is omitted, then root user will be used.

tape: The name of the remote tape device.

Example:

This example shows how this command can be used to back up the /usr file system on a Tru64 UNIX 5.0 system to a tape drive on a Tru64 UNIX 4.0F system.

```
# vdump -b 60 -f - -D /usr | rsh jack2 dd of=/dev/rmt0h
bs=60k
path      : /usr
dev/fset  : usr_domain#usr
type      : advfs
advfs id  : 0x36b0147f.000473f0.1
vdump: Date of last level 0 dump: the start of the epoch
vdump: Dumping directories
vdump: Dumping 526542936 bytes, 906 directories, 26807 files
vdump: Dumping regular files

vdump: Status at Tue Sep 14 11:04:05 1999
vdump: Dumped 105347174 of 526542936 bytes; 20.0% completed
vdump: Dumped 14 of 906 directories; 1.5% completed
vdump: Dumped 1021 of 26807 files; 3.8% completed

[snip]

vdump: Status at Tue Sep 14 11:24:20 1999
vdump: Dumped 481916231 of 526542936 bytes; 91.5% completed
vdump: Dumped 629 of 906 directories; 69.4% completed
vdump: Dumped 22283 of 26807 files; 83.1% completed
```

```
vdump: Status at Tue Sep 14 11:27:28 1999
vdump: Dumped 528391185 of 526542936 bytes; 100.4% completed
vdump: Dumped 906 of 906 directories; 100.0% completed
vdump: Dumped 26807 of 26807 files; 100.0% completed
vdump: Dump completed at Tue Sep 14 11:27:28 1999
0+208309 records in
8455+0 records out
```

So, this example is one way to accomplish remote backups using an older method. We now discuss the new tool shipped with version 5.0 and show how the same thing can be accomplished more easily.

6.3.2.1   Backups with {r}vdump(8)

This section covers the *vdump(8)* and *rvdump(8)* commands.

Syntax:

```
{r}vdump –h | –V | –w
vdump [-0..9] [-CDNPUquv] [-F num_buffers] [-T tape_num]
[-b size] [-f device] [-x num_blocks] path
rvdump [-0..9] [-CDNUquv] [-F num_buffers] [-T tape_num]
[-b size] [-f nodename:device] [-x num_blocks] path
```

TABLE 6–16   Flags for the *vdump(8)* and *rvdump(8)* Commands

FLAG	DESCRIPTION	V4	V5
path	The name of the full path to an AdvFS fileset to backup. When used with '–D' flag, this represents a directory.		
-b size	The number of one-kilobyte blocks per record in the saveset. The default is 60 with a valid range of 2 through 64 blocks. The value of this option also determines the size of a buffer.	X	X
-C	Compresses the data as it is backed up, which minimizes the saveset size.	X	X
-D	Performs a level 0 backup on the specified subdirectory. This option overrides any backup level specification in the command. With this option specified, the user and group quota files and the fileset quotas are not backed up.	X	X
-f {nodename:}device	Specifies the destination of the saveset. For *vdump(8)*, the local destination can be a device, a file, or, when the hyphen character is specified, standard output. For *rvdump(8)*, the mandatory specification is nodename:device to specify the remote machine name that holds the device or file.	X	X

TABLE 6–16 Flags for the *vdump(8)* and *rvdump(8)* Commands (Continued)

FLAG	DESCRIPTION	V4	V5
-F num_buffers	The number of in-memory buffers to use. The default is 8, with a valid range of 2 through 64 buffers. The size of a buffer is determined by the value of the '-b' option.	X	X
-h	This flag displays usage help for the command.	X	X
-N	This flag specifies not to rewind a tape storage device.	X	X
-P	This flag is new in Tru64 UNIX 5.0. Using this flag, command will produce a backward-compatible saveset that can be read by earlier versions of the *vrestore(8)* command. Some features that didn't previously exist, such as large UIDs, will be lost.		X
-q	Quiet mode. Prints messages for errors only, not informational messages.	X	X
-T tape_num	The starting number for the first tape. The default is 1. The tape number is used only to prompt the operator to load another tape in the drive.	X	X
-u	Puts a timestamp entry into /etc/vdumpdates corresponding with the start of the backup.	X	X
-U	Do not unload a tape device.	X	X
-v	Very verbose mode. Prints the name of each file as it is being backed up.	X	X
-V	Prints the current version of the command.	X	X
-w	Prints the filesets that have not been backed up within one week.	X	X
-x num_blocks	Performs an "exclusive or" (XOR) operation on each of the blocks specified by num_blocks as they are written to the saveset. The results are written to the saveset as an XOR block, which immediately follows the blocks. *Vrestore(8)* uses this block to recover one of the blocks in the group in the event of a read error. The default is 8, with a valid range of 1 through 32 blocks.	X	X
-0..9	Backup level. A 0 causes the entire fileset (or directory tree) to be backed up to the storage device. The default is 9.	X	X

Example:

In this example, we perform the same operation as in the last example but show how you would accomplish this using the new *rvdump(8)* tool. Naturally, the performance of any remote backup solution depends greatly on the network's speed and usage level.

```
# rvdump -f jack2:/dev/rmt0h -D /usr
Trying to establish connection to host jack2 using username
root...
path        : /usr
dev/fset    : usr_domain#usr
type        : advfs
advfs id    : 0x36b0147f.000473f0.1
rvdump: Date of last level 0 dump: the start of the epoch
rvdump: Dumping directories
rvdump: Dumping 526542936 bytes, 906 directories, 26807 files
rvdump: Dumping regular files

rvdump: Status at Tue Sep 14 11:41:11 1999
rvdump: Dumped 104914394 of 526542936 bytes; 19.9% completed
rvdump: Dumped 14 of 906 directories; 1.5% completed
rvdump: Dumped 1012 of 26807 files; 3.8% completed

[snip]

rvdump: Status at Tue Sep 14 12:01:16 1999
rvdump: Dumped 467006548 of 526542936 bytes; 88.7% completed
rvdump: Dumped 621 of 906 directories; 68.5% completed
rvdump: Dumped 18000 of 26807 files; 67.1% completed

rvdump: Status at Tue Sep 14 12:05:17 1999
rvdump: Dumped 528391185 of 526542936 bytes; 100.4% completed
rvdump: Dumped 906 of 906 directories; 100.0% completed
rvdump: Dumped 26807 of 26807 files; 100.0% completed
rvdump: Dump completed at Tue Sep 14 12:05:17 1999
```

6.3.2.2 Restoring with *{r}vrestore(8)*

Syntax:

```
{r}vrestore -h | -V

{r}vrestore -t | -l [-f {nodename:}device]

{r}vrestore -i [-mqv] [-f {nodename:}device] [-D path] [-o opt]

{r}vrestore -x [-mqv] [-f {nodename:}device] [-D path] [-o opt] [file...]
```

TABLE 6–17   Flags for the *vrestore(8)* and *rvrestore(8)* Commands

FLAG	DESCRIPTION
file	The file or files to restore when using the '-x' option. All other options must precede any file names on the command line.

TABLE 6–17   Flags for the *vrestore(8)* and *rvrestore(8)* Commands (Continued)

FLAG	DESCRIPTION
-D path	The destination path of where to restore the files. Without the '-D' option, the files are restored to the current directory.
-f {nodename:}device	When an argument follows the '-f' option, it specifies either:
	For *restore(8)*, the name of the storage device that contains the archive set to be restored. The default device, if none is specified, is /dev/tape/tape0_d1.
	For *rvrestore(8)*, the mandatory specification is nodename:device to refer to the node's name and device that holds the archive set to be restored. There is no default device.
-h	This flag displays the usage for the command.
-I	Interactive mode. After reading directory information from the saveset, *vrestore(8)* provides a shell-like interface that allows you to select the files you want to restore. We continue our discussion of interactive mode later in this section.
-l	This flag lists the entire archive set's structure.
-m	Does not restore the ownership or mode information.
-q	Quiet mode. Prints messages of error severity or higher. It does not print informational messages.
-t	Prints out a long listing of all files contained in a saveset. The sizes of any AdvFS quota files are not shown.
-v	Verbose mode. Writes the name of each file read from the storage device to stdout as it is being restored.
-V	This flag shows the version of the command.
-x	Restores files from the archive set. You would use this command as an alternative to using the add and then restore commands in interactive mode.
-o opt	Specifies what action you wish the tool to take when a file already exists. The options are "yes" (always overwrite), "no," or "ask," and the default is "yes."

Example:

Here, we show how to use the *rvrestore(8)* command to restore from a remote backup tape.

```
# df .
Filesystem        512-blocks Used  Available Capacity Mounted on
test_domain#test 2046736    64    2038176   1%       /test

# rvrestore -x -f jack2:/dev/rmt0h
```

```
Trying to establish connection to host jack2 using username root...
rvrestore: Date of the vdump save-set: Tue Sep 14 11:34:26 1999
rvrestore: Save-set source directory : /usr

# df .
Filesystem        512-blocks Used  Available Capacity Mounted on
test_domain#test 2046736      1034330983504  52%      /test
```

6.3.2.3 Interactive Mode

The *vrestore(8)* command enters interactive mode when invoked with the '−i' flag. This mode allows you to selectively restore files from a specified archive set in a shell-like environment. The environment has several commands that you can issue to perform various functions and to navigate among the directories on the archive set. Some commands require an argument parameter, such as a subdirectory or one or more file names. Others use the current directory as the default when you do not specify an argument. You can also specify multiple file names, but they should be separated by spaces. If a file name contains the space character, you can use quotation marks around the entire file name to prevent *vrestore(8)* from confusing it with multiple different files. A file name that contains quotation marks should precede each quotation mark by a backslash. Here, we explain the valid commands available in interactive mode:

add file [**file ...**]: Adds the files in the archive set specified by arg to the list of files to be restored; only files and directories that have been added to the list will be restored. (See the example following this list.)

cd [**dir**]: Changes the current working archive set directory to the directory specified.

delete file [**file ...**]: This command deletes all files and their subdirectories specified from the list of files to be restored.

extract or restore: Restores any files that were previously selected by using the add command to the current destination directory. (See the example following this list.)

Help or ?: Displays help information for the interactive commands.

ls [**dir**]: Lists files in the current saveset directory or contents of the directory specified. Directory entries are appended with a slash character when viewed with ls command.

pwd: Prints out the current working directory in the archive set.

quit or exit: Leaves the interactive mode immediately. Any files or directories that have been added on the list of files to be restored and have not been extracted from the archive will be lost.

sh command: Escapes from the shell-like environment to run the specified UNIX command. It returns to interactive mode when the command is complete.

verbose: Verbose mode. The name of each file restored from the archive set will be displayed as it is extracted.

Example:

In this example, we illustrate an interactive restore using *vrestore(8)*. The root fileset is actually the second archive on our tape, so we must skip over the first archive. In this case, we have a bootable tape created using *btcreate(8)*, which will normally put the bootable portions at the front of the tape, leaving the *vdump(8)* archives for the rest.

We are looking to restore two files from the tape, the vmunix and rz1.label. First, you want to make sure that you are in the directory to which you wish to restore the files. In this case, we want them in /tmp and we will move them to the target location later. This is usually a good idea because you may want to compare your original file with your backup copy, in case you suspect corruption, for example.

```
# cd /tmp
# mt rewind
# mt -f /dev/nrmt0h fsf 1
# vrestore -i
vrestore: Date of the vdump save-set: Fri Mar 10 07:56:58
2000
(/) ls

.:
#.mrg...login                  #.mrg..DXsession
.Xauthority                    .advfs_hostlist
.asWedit-prefs                 .cshrc
.dt/                           .dtprofile
.elm/                          .login
.lsof_sunny                    .netscape/
.new...cshrc                   .new...login
.new...profile                 .new..DXsession
.profile                       .proto...cshrc
.proto...login                 .proto...profile
.proto..DXsession              .proto..DXsession.FailMRG
.proto..DXsession.PreMRG       .rhosts
.sh_history                    .sysman/
.tags                          .xsession-errors
```

```
DXsession                    DXsession.PreMRG
DXterm                       GENERIC
Mail/                        News/
O3D.out                      PCITMP1
PCITMP2:                     PCITMP3
backup/                      bin
cdrom/                       check_cd
core                         core.aseagent
crash/                       dev/
etc/                         genvmunix
guru/                        home/
j/                           junk/
kits/                        lib
master                       mbox
mdec/                        mnt/
mnt2/                        nsmail/
nsr                          opt/
osf_boot                     patches/
proc/                        quota.group
quota.user                   real.profile
rz1.label                    sbin/
shlib/                       subsys/
sys/                         tcb/
test/                        tmp/
usr/                         var
vmunix                       vmunix.pre_isp
webmnt/

(/) add vmunix

(/) add rz1.label

(/) ls

.:
#.mrg...login                #.mrg..DXsession
.Xauthority                  .advfs_hostlist
.asWedit-prefs               .cshrc
.dt/                         .dtprofile
.elm/                        .login
.lsof_sunny                  .netscape/
.new...cshrc                 .new...login
.new...profile               .new..DXsession
.profile                     .proto...cshrc
.proto...login               .proto...profile
.proto..DXsession            .proto..DXsession.FailMRG
.proto..DXsession.PreMRG     .rhosts
.sh_history                  .sysman/
.tags                        .xsession-errors
DXsession                    DXsession.PreMRG
DXterm                       GENERIC
Mail/                        News/
O3D.out                      PCITMP1
PCITMP2:                     PCITMP3
backup/                      bin
```

```
cdrom/                          check_cd
core                            core.aseagent
crash/                          dev/
etc/                            genvmunix
guru/                           home/
j/                              junk/
kits/                           lib
master                          mbox
mdec/                           mnt/
mnt2/                           nsmail/
nsr                             opt/
osf_boot                        patches/
proc/                           quota.group
quota.user                      real.profile
*rz1.label                      sbin/
shlib/                          subsys/
sys/                            tcb/
test/                           tmp/
usr/                            var
*vmunix                         vmunix.pre_isp
webmnt/

(/) restore

# ls -l vmunix rz1.label
-rw-r--r--  1 root   system   1058 Mar 7 16:04 rz1.label
-rwxr-xr-x  1 root   system   9427680 Mar 3 11:35 vmunix
```

Using *vdump(8)* and *vrestore(8)* on clone filesets is the same as for regular filesets, except the clone fset is normally removed immediately following the completion of the backup. Once a vrestore has been completed, the backup fileset will look identical to the fileset that was backed up at the time the clone was made. We discuss clone fileset backups in greater detail later in this chapter.

6.3.3 Managing Quotas

Quotas provide a useful way of tracking and controlling the amount of physical storage that each fileset consumes. Quota enforcement can be turned on for some, but not all, of a domain's filesets.

The AdvFS quota system is compatible with the Berkeley-style quotas of UFS we discussed in Chapter 5; however, the AdvFS quota system differs in several important ways:

- AdvFS differentiates between quota maintenance and quota enforcement.

- Quota maintenance tracks file and disk space usage for users and groups in the quota.user and quota.group files in the root directory of a fileset. These statistics are tracked whether or not quota enforcement is enabled.

- When quota enforcement is enabled, the AdvFS quota system enforces all quota limits set by the system administrator.

- The AdvFS quota system always maintains quota information. Unlike UFS, this function cannot be disabled.

- AdvFS supports fileset quotas, in addition to user and group quotas. This capability limits the amount of disk storage and number of files consumed by the fileset, which is useful when a file domain contains more than one fileset.

Similar to the Berkeley-style quota system, you can set soft and hard limits on the number of blocks and number of files. The soft limit can be exceeded for a specified grace period.

TABLE 6–18   AdvFS Quota Commands

COMMAND	FUNCTION
quot	Displays the number of blocks in the fileset that are owned by each user.
quota	Displays the user and group disk usage and quota limits.
quotacheck	Checks fileset quota consistency; filesets checked should be quiescent.
repquota	Summarizes user/group or fileset quotas.
edquota	Edits user and group quota limits, and grace period.
quotaon	Turns quota enforcement on; filesets specified must have entries in /etc/fstab and be mounted at the time.
quotaoff	Turns quota enforcement off.
chfsets	Changes block and file soft and hard limits for a fileset.
df	Displays the limits and actual number of blocks used by a fileset.
showfdmn	Displays space usage for the specified domain.
showfsets	Displays the file and block usage limits for the filesets in a domain.

6.3.4   Working with /etc/fdmns

A special directory, known as /etc/fdmns, has special significance with respect to managing and gathering information about AdvFS domains. This section discusses ways this directory can be used to manage your AdvFS.

6.3.4.1   What's in the /etc/fdmns Directory?

The /etc/fdmns directory contains two different items:

1.   Lock files (Tru64 UNIX 4.0 and higher) used to ensure exclusive access to the domains by the AdvFS utilities.

2. Subdirectories that are named for the AdvFS domains defined on the system. Within each subdirectory, a symbolic link (or more than one for multivolume domains) points to the block device file that contains the data for the AdvFS volume.

Example:

The following example shows a real /etc/fdmns directory on a Tru64 UNIX 5.0 system that contains three AdvFS file domains.

```
# cd /etc/fdmns
# ls -lR | more
total 24
-r--------  1 root    system       0 Jan 28 1999  .advfslock_fdmns
-r--------  1 root    system       0 Jan 28 1999  .advfslock_root_domain
-r--------  1 root    system       0 Feb 3 1999   .advfslock_test_domain
-r--------  1 root    system       0 Jan 28 1999  .advfslock_usr_domain
drwxr-xr-x  2 root    system    8192 Jan 28 1999  root_domain
drwxr-xr-x  2 root    system    8192 Aug 22 09:27 test_domain
drwxr-xr-x  2 root    system    8192 Jan 28 1999  usr_domain

./root_domain:
total 0
lrwxr-xr-x 1 root    system    23 Jan 28 1999 rootdg.rootvol -> /dev/vol/rootdg/rootvol

./test_domain:
total 0
lrwxr-xr-x 1 root    system    22 Aug 22 09:27 stevedg.vol01 -> /dev/vol/stevedg/vol01

./usr_domain:
total 0
lrwxr-xr-x 1 root    system    22 Jan 28 1999 rootdg.usrvol -> /dev/vol/rootdg/usrvol
```

6.3.4.2 Renaming AdvFS Domains

One common reason you would want to make changes to the contents of the /etc/fdmns directory is when you want to rename a domain to another name. Because no AdvFS command is available to accomplish this task, this technique is really the only way to do this. The procedure to rename an AdvFS domain is as follows:

1. Unmount the filesets, if necessary.

2. Move the directory file to a new name in the /etc/fdmns.

3. Remount the domain's filesets with the new name.

Example:

This example shows how to use the previous procedure to rename an AdvFS domain from the name "test_dmn" to "stuff_dmn."

```
# df | grep test_dmn
test_dmn#test          6000000    3714302    154384  97%  /mnt2

# umount /mnt2

# cd /etc/fdmns

# mv test_dmn stuff_dmn

# mount stuff_dmn#test /mnt2

# df | grep test_dmn

# df | grep stuff_dmn
stuff_dmn#test         6000000    3714302    154384  97%  /mnt2
```

6.3.4.3 Renaming AdvFS Volumes

Another reason to make changes to the contents of the /etc/fdmns direc-tory is when a device used for an AdvFS volume has changed in some way. For example, a device has changed names because of a bus or target relocation (Tru64 UNIX pre-5.0 device naming only) or an LSM volume has been renamed. Also, it occasionally becomes necessary in trouble-shooting situations to change the link from an encapsulated LSM volume back to the raw device. In these cases, the procedure is as follows:

1.   Unmount the filesets in the domain, if necessary.

2.   Remove the incorrect link in the /etc/fdmns/<domain_name> directory.

3.   Make a new symbolic link using the new name.

4.   Mount the filesets.

Example:

This example illustrates the technique used for renaming an LSM volume in an AdvFS domain from the name "vol05" to "vol06."

```
# df | grep efs_dmn
efs_dmn#efs          60000    23744    36256  39%  /efs

# umount /efs

# cd /etc/fdmns/efs_dmn

# ls -l
total 0
lrwxr-xr-x  1 root    system     14 Aug 18 09:58 rootdg.vol05 -> /dev/vol/rootdg/
vol05

# rm rootdg.vol05

# ln -s /dev/vol/rootdg/vol06 rootdg.vol06

# ls -l
```

```
total 0
lrwxrwxrwx 1 root  system   21 Oct 2 09:20 rootdg.vol06 -> /dev/vol/rootdg/vol06
# showfsets efs_dmn
efs
    Id           : 33f8551d.00064ecb.1.8001
    Clone is     : clone_efs
    Files        :        3, SLim=  1000, HLim=   3000
    Blocks (512) : 23744, SLim=  2000, HLim=   6000 grc=  none
    Quota Status : user=off group=off

clone_efs
    Id           : 33f8551d.00064ecb.2.8001
    Clone of     : efs
    Revision     : 1
```

6.3.4.4 Re-creating AdvFS Domains

Occasionally, there is a need to make the domain directory and link(s) to the device(s) by hand. Most of the time, you would use the *advscan(8)* tool for this purpose. This procedure is normally needed only when booting into standalone mode from the Tru64 UNIX CD-ROM or if you are writing a script to re-create a well-known AdvFS structure. The procedure to re-create the /etc/domain/<domainname> directory by hand is the following:

1. Change your current working directory to the /etc/fdmns directory.

2. Make a new subdirectory using the name you want to give to the domain.

3. Change your current working directory to this new subdirectory.

4. Create a symbolic link for each of the block special devices in the domain.

Example:

This example shows how to use standard UNIX commands to re-create the structure of the domain directory called "my_domain" containing a single LSM volume called "vol06" from the rootdg disk group.

```
# cd /etc/fdmns

# rm -rf efs_dmn

# mkdir my_domain

# cd my_domain

# ln -s /dev/vol/rootdg/vol06 rootdg.vol06

# showfsets my_domain
efs
```

```
    Id              : 33f8551d.00064ecb.1.8001
    Clone is        : clone_efs
    Files           :    0, SLim=    1000, HLim=    3000
    Blocks (512)    :    0, SLim=    2000, HLim=    6000
    Quota Status    : user=off group=off

clone_efs
    Id              : 33f8551d.00064ecb.2.8001
    Clone of        : efs
    Revision        : 1
```

6.3.5   Additional AdvFS Tasks

This section discusses some additional useful AdvFS commands. These commands are used to perform specialized tasks such as renaming filesets and changing certain attributes of files, filesets, and volumes.

6.3.5.1   Renaming Filesets

The *renamefset(8)* command assigns a new name to an existing fileset within a file domain. Before renaming a fileset, unmount the fileset and any existing fileset clones. After renaming a fileset, update the corresponding entries in the /etc/fstab file to reflect the name change.

Syntax:

```
renamefset domain old_set_name new_set_name
```

TABLE 6–19   Flags for the *renamefset(8)* Command

FLAGS	DESCRIPTION
Domain	The name of the file domain containing the fileset to rename
old_set_name	The fileset name to change
new_set_name	The new fileset name

Example:

This example shows how to rename a fileset using *renamefset(8)* in a domain called "junk_domain" from "junk" to "newjunk."

```
# showfsets junk_domain
junk
    Id              : 34608122.0008e32f.1.8001
    Files           :    0, SLim=    0, HLim=    0
    Blocks (512)    :    0, SLim=    0, HLim=    0
    Quota Status    : user=off group=off

# renamefset junk_domain junk newjunk

# showfsets junk_domain
newjunk
    Id              : 34608122.0008e32f.1.8001
```

```
Files        :    0, SLim=    0, HLim=    0
Blocks (512) :    0, SLim=    0, HLim=    0
Quota Status : user=off group=off
```

6.3.5.2 Changing Fileset Attributes

The *chfsets(8)* command enables you to change file usage limits and block usage limits. Filesets can have both soft and hard disk storage and file limits. When a hard limit is reached, no more disk space allocations or file creations, which would exceed the limit, are allowed. The soft limit may be exceeded for a specified period (called the grace period). The grace periods for the soft limits are set with the *edquota(8)* command.

Syntax:

```
chfsets [-F limit] [-f limit] [-B limit] [-b limit] domain [file_set . . .]
```

TABLE 6–20   Flags for the *chfsets(8)* Command

FLAGS	DESCRIPTION
domain	The name of the file domain for which to alter fileset attributes
file_set	The name of one or more filesets for which to alter attributes
-F limit	The file usage soft limit (quota) of the fileset
-f limit	The file usage hard limit (quota) of the fileset
-B limit	The block usage soft limit (quota) in 1K blocks of the fileset
-b limit	The block usage hard limit (quota) in 1K blocks of the fileset

Example:

The following is an example of how the *chfsets(8)* command returns an error if no filesets in the domain are mounted.

```
# chfsets -b 1000 -f 200 junk_domain newjunk
newjunk
        Id            : 34608122.0008e32f.1.8001
        File H Limit : 0 --> 200
        Block H Limit : 0 --> 1000
chfsets: At least one fileset in this domain must be mounted.

# showfsets junk_domain
newjunk
        Id            : 34608122.0008e32f.1.8001
        Files         : 0,  SLim= 0,   HLim= 0
        Blocks (512)  : 0,  SLim= 0,   HLim= 0
        Quota Status  : user=off group=off
```

Example:

This is a successful change of fileset block and file quotas using *chfsets(8)*.

```
# df /junk
Filesystem         512-blocks        Used    Available Capacity
Mounted on
var_domain#junk        2000            32        1968     2%
/junk

# showfsets var_domain
var
        Id             : 33f1e64d.000e20d2.1.8001
        Files          :     1105,  SLim= 0,   HLim= 0
        Blocks (512)   :   422064,  SLim= 0,   HLim= 0
        Quota Status   : user=off group=off

junk
        Id             : 33f1e64d.000e20d2.2.8001
        Files          :        2,  SLim= 0,   HLim= 0
        Blocks (512)   :       32,  SLim= 0,   HLim= 0
        Quota Status   : user=off group=off

# chfsets -b 1000 -f 200 var_domain junk

junk
        Id             : 33f1e64d.000e20d2.4.8001
        File H Limit : 0 --> 200
        Block H Limit: 0 --> 1000

# showfsets var_domain

var
        Id             : 33f1e64d.000e20d2.1.8001
        Files          :     1105,  SLim= 0,   HLim= 0
        Blocks (512)   :   422064,  SLim= 0,   HLim= 0
        Quota Status   : user=off group=off

junk
        Id             : 33f1e64d.000e20d2.2.8001
        Files          :        2,  SLim= 0,   HLim= 200
        Blocks (512)   :       32,  SLim= 0,   HLim= 2000
        Quota Status   : user=off group=off
```

6.3.5.3 Changing File Data Logging Attributes

The *chfile(8)* command enables you to change the characteristics of a file
with respect to the way it handles the problem of inconsistent data block
updates. As previously stated, by default, the file domain protects metadata writes from inconsistency by committing them atomically to its
transaction log. In addition, a file's data portion (non-metadata) is not
afforded the same protection by default. Thus, if a system failure causes
an incomplete data write, then the metadata are always consistent, but
the file may still contain old data. This event should be rare, but it could
happen. Some users cannot afford this possibility for a small subset of
critical data files. Therefore, AdvFS provides optional capabilities that can

reduce or eliminate this possibility if they are enabled using *chfile(8)*. A file that has either of the two write-consistency capabilities turned on will remain internally consistent in the event of a system crash.

The first of the two capabilities to which we have been referring is called **forced synchronous writes** and is enabled by setting the '-l' flag to *chfile(8)* to "on." Enabling this feature for a specific file causes the file to always be updated synchronously. This is equivalent to forcing the use of the O_SYNC flag to the *open(2)* system call when the file is opened. Thus, when a *write(2)* is made to the file, the system will not return a successful status until the entire write is made to the disk. If a complete write (metadata and all data blocks) cannot be performed, then a failure is returned.

The second of these features is known as **atomic write data logging** and is enabled by setting the '–L' flag to *chfile(8)* to "on." When this mode is enabled, write requests to a file remain asynchronous, but they are also written to the AdvFS log file. Thus, any uncommitted transactions will automatically be cleaned up upon the next domain activation, just like what occurs for uncommitted metadata changes. In other words, the file structure information and the file data will be written in a single transaction.

For example, if you are writing more than one 8K block to a file when the system crashes, the first block may be fully written. If you do not have atomic write data logging turned on, the file structure will be consistent, but the rest of the file may still contain old data. With atomic write data logging, all the new data are written to the transaction log, so in the event of a crash, the uncommitted transactions can be backed out to maintain the consistency of the file.

The downside of enabling either of these features is that they can slow system performance and cause the need to significantly increase the size of the domain's transaction log.

It is important to note that behavior of the '-l' flag has changed. Prior to Tru64 UNIX 5.0, when "chfile -l on" was applied to an AdvFS file, the behavior was not the same as it is in 5.0. Therefore, keep in mind that if you were used to the old behavior, it has changed.

Syntax:

```
chfile [-l on | off] [-L on|off] file_name ...
```

TABLE 6–21   Flags for the *chfile(8)* Command

FLAGS	DESCRIPTION
File_name	The name of the file for which to change attributes
-l on l off	Turns forced synchronous writes for the specified file on or off. By default, this feature is disabled for each file.
-L onloff	Turns atomic write data logging for the specified file on or off. By default, this feature is disabled for each file.

Example:

This example shows how to use the *chfile(8)* command to examine the data logging attributes for a file.

```
# ls -l
total 31632
-rw-r--r--  1 root    system  10788928 Aug 22 12:48 file1
-rwxr-xr-x  1 root    system  10788928 Aug 22 12:48 file2
-rwxr-xr-x  1 root    system  10788928 Aug 22 12:48 file3

# showfile *
    Id     Vol PgSz Pages XtntType  Segs SegSz    I/O Perf File
  2f4.80b0 1   16   1318  simple    **   ** async 0%   file1
  34c.8198 1   16   1318  simple    **   ** async 0%   file2
  2e1.8340 1   16   1318  simple    **   ** async 1%   file3

# chfile file?
I/O mode = normal asynchronous writes
I/O mode = normal asynchronous writes
I/O mode = normal asynchronous writes
```

Example:

This example shows how to use the *chfile(8)* command to alter the data logging attributes for a file.

```
# chfile -l on file2

# chfile -L on file3

# showfile *
    Id     Vol PgSz Pages XtntType  Segs SegSz I/O   Perf File
  2f4.80b0 1   16   1318  simple    **   **    async 0% file1
  34c.8198 1   16   1318  simple    **   **    sync  0% file2
  2e1.8340 1   16   1318  simple    **   **    ftx   % file3

# chfile file?
I/O mode = normal asynchronous writes
I/O mode = forced synchronous writes
I/O mode = atomic write data logging
```

For a file with atomic write data logging turned on, the system will not use frags when storing it in order to reduce overhead. Thus, files will always be sized as some even multiple of the AdvFS page size of 8K.

6.3.5.4 Changing Volume Attributes

The purpose of the *chvol(8)* command is to enable you to change some of the volume attributes of an active domain. The changes you can make with *chvol(8)* can be made on-the-fly while the domains are actively being used and will take effect immediately. Thus, *chvol(8)* is a good tool for making tuning adjustments that don't require a system reboot. A later section of this chapter covers more specific information on how to use *chvol(8)* for tuning in this way.

The *chvol(8)* command, when used without any flags, displays the current cmode and the I/O transfer parameters.

Syntax:

```
chvol [-l] [-r blocks] [-w blocks] [-t blocks] [-c on | off]
[-A] special domain
```

TABLE 6–22   Flags for the *chvol(8)* Command

FLAGS	DESCRIPTION
Special	The block special device name, such as /dev/disk/dsk5c, of the volume for which to change attributes
domain	The name of the file domain that contains the volume
-l	This flag, which is new in Tru64 UNIX version 5.0, displays the range of I/O transfer sizes, in 512-byte blocks. These values are calculated by the kernel, based on the disk's geometry. The rblks is the minimum, the maximum, and the preferred transfer size for reads, and the wblks is the minimum, the maximum, and the preferred transfer size for writes.
-r blocks	The maximum number of 512-byte blocks that the file system reads from the disk at one time
-w blocks	The maximum number of 512-byte blocks that the file system writes to the disk at one time
-t blocks	The maximum number of dirty, 512-byte blocks that the file system will cache in-memory (per volume in a domain). Dirty means that the data have been written by the application but the file system has cached it in memory so it has not yet been written to disk. The number of blocks must be in multiples of 16. The maximum value is 32,768, and the default (when a volume is added to a domain) is 768 blocks. For optimal performance, specify blocks in multiples of wblks (as specified by the '-w' option).
-c on l off	Turns I/O consolidation mode on or off.
-A	Activates a volume after an incomplete rmvol operation.

Example:

This pre-5.0 example shows how to change the read and write size parameters for one volume in a two-volume domain.

```
# showfdmn junk_domain

        Id              Date Created              LogPgs  Domain Name
34608122.0008e32f Wed Nov 5 09:22:26 1997  512      junk_domain

    Vol  512-Blks  Free     % Used  Cmode  Rblks  Wblks  Vol Name
    1L   2097152   2064416  2%      on     128    128    /dev/vol/vol01
    2    100000    75920    24%     on     128    128    /dev/vol/vol02
         --------- -------- ------
         2197152   2140336  3%
```

```
# chvol /dev/vol/vol01 junk_domain
rblks = 128 wblks = 128 cmode = on, thresh = 768
```

```
# echo "pd volinfo.max_io" | kdbx -k /vmunix | tail -1
128
```

```
# chvol -r 256 -w 256 /dev/vol/vol01 junk_domain
Warning: /dev/vol/vol02: Decreasing maximum read transfer
size to 65536 bytes
Warning: /dev/vol/vol02: Decreasing maximum write transfer
size to 65536 bytes
```

```
# chvol /dev/vol/vol01 junk_domain
rblks = 128 wblks = 128 cmode = on, thresh = 768
```

```
# chvol -r 64 -w 64 /dev/vol/vol02 junk_domain
```

```
# chvol /dev/vol/vol02 junk_domain
rblks = 64 wblks = 64 cmode = on, thresh = 768
```

```
# showfdmn junk_domain

        Id              Date Created              LogPgs  Domain Name
34608122.0008e32f Wed Nov 5 09:22:26 1997  512      junk_domain

    Vol  512-Blks  Free     % Used  Cmode  Rblks  Wblks  Vol Name
    1L   2097152   2064416  2%      on     128    128    /dev/vol/vol01
    2    100000    75920    24%     on     128    128    /dev/vol/vol02
         --------- -------- ------
         2197152   2140336  3%
```

Example:

This Tru64 UNIX version 5.0 example shows how to change the read and write size parameters for one of the volumes in a two-volume domain.

```
# showfdmn test_domain

        Id              Date Created            LogPgs  Version  Domain Name
37c008e8.0004c330  Sun Aug 22 09:27:52 1999  512     4        test_domain

  Vol  512-Blks    Free % Used Cmode Rblks Wblks Vol Name
  1L   2046736   2038208  0%    on    16384 16384 /dev/vol/stevedg/vol01
```

```
# chvol /dev/vol/stevedg/vol01 test_domain
rblks = 16384 wblks = 16384 cmode = on, thresh = 16384
```

```
# chvol -l /dev/vol/stevedg/vol01 test_domain
rblks: min = 16 max = 16384 pref = 16384
wblks: min = 16 max = 16384 pref = 16384

# echo "pd volinfo.max_io" | kdbx -k /vmunix | tail -1
16384

# chvol -r 2048 -w 1024 -t 32768 /dev/vol/stevedg/vol01 test_domain

# chvol /dev/vol/stevedg/vol01 test_domain
rblks = 2048 wblks = 1024 cmode = on, thresh = 32768
```

6.3.5.5 Locating AdvFS Partitions On Disk

In section 6.3.4, we discussed a manual technique for re-creating the domain and volume information in the /etc/fdmns directory. The procedure we outlined can be used when you have moved disks to a new system, have moved disks around in a way that has changed device numbers (pre-Tru64 UNIX 5.0), have lost track of the location of the domains, or have reconfigured LSM disks or volumes. Unfortunately, this technique had the shortcoming that you needed to know what the structure of the domains was in order to re-create it; however, what can you do if you don't know what the structure was? This is where *advscan(8)* becomes a handy tool. It can be used to find and correct (if requested) pieces of AdvFS domains on disk partitions and in LSM disk groups. *Advscan(8)* can repair the following inconsistencies in the /etc/fdmns directory:

1. The entire /etc/fdmns directory

2. A single file domain subdirectory

3. One or more individual links from a file domain subdirectory

The *advscan(8)* command can examine a list of disks and disk groups, and search all partitions and volumes in each in order to determine which partitions on a disk were part of an AdvFS file domain. You can run the *advscan(8)* command to rebuild all or part of your /etc/fdmns directory automatically, or you can rebuild it manually by supplying the names of the partitions in a file domain.

If '-g' option is used, the partitions are listed in the order they are found on the disk. Otherwise, the partitions are listed as they are grouped in file domains.

The '-r' option to *advscan(8)* can be used to repair file domain information (directories and links) from the /etc/fdmns. This is handy when you don't know what disks were in the domains or what domains existed on which volumes. According to the documentation, it is still recommended that you keep a hard-copy record of the /etc/fdmns directory. This is a good idea, although a good backup will suffice.

The algorithm used by *advscan(8)* to determine if a partition or LSM volume is part of an AdvFS domain is to read the on-disk structures as follows:

- The first two eight-kilobyte pages of a partition or LSM volume to find the file domain information, such as domain ID.

- The disk label to determine if any overlapping partitions exist.

- The boot block to determine if the partition contains AdvFS boot blocks.

The *advscan(8)* command displays the date the domain was created (which will be the same as the domain ID), the on-disk structure version, and the last known or current state of the volume. This information is read directly from the volume's on-disk structure. Any inconsistencies in this information will be obvious by examining it and comparing.

Syntax:

```
advscan [-g] [-a] [-r] [-f domain_name] disks disk_group
```

TABLE 6–23   Flags for the *advscan(8)* Command

FLAGS	DESCRIPTION
disks	The name of the disk(s) to be scanned
disk_group	The LSM disk group(s) to be scanned
-g	Lists partitions in the order they are found on disk.
-a	Scans all disks found in any /etc/fdmns domain, as well as those in the command line.
-r	Re-creates missing domains. The domain name is created from the device name(s).
-f domain_name	Fixes the domain count and the links for the named domain.

Example:

This simple example shows how *advscan(8)* can be used to search a single LSM disk group, rootdg for AdvFS volumes. In this case, two volumes "vol01" and "vol02" were found to be part of a single domain. The domain ID is given; however, because the name association does not exist in /etc/fdmns, the name is reported as "*unknown*."

```
# /sbin/advfs/advscan rootdg

Scanning devices    /dev/rvol/rootdg
```

```
Found domains:

*unknown*
        Domain Id    34608122.0008e32f
        Created      Wed Nov 5 09:22:26 1997

        Domain volumes    2
        /etc/fdmns links   0

        Actual partitions found:
                rootdg.vol01*
                rootdg.vol02*
```

Example:

Here, we continue the previous example by using *advscan(8)* with the '-r' option to rebuild the associations in /etc/fdmns. Because the name was unknown, *advscan(8)* takes a guess at the name of domain_rootdg.vol01_rootdg.vol02. This guess is usually not the desired name, so this problem can easily be rectified by renaming the directory to the desired name for the domain.

```
# /sbin/advfs/advscan -r rootdg

Scanning devices    /dev/rvol/rootdg

Found domains:

*unknown*
        Domain Id    34608122.0008e32f
        Created      Wed Nov 5 09:22:26 1997

        Domain volumes    2
        /etc/fdmns links   0

        Actual partitions found:
                rootdg.vol01*
                rootdg.vol02*

Creating /etc/fdmns/domain_rootdg.vol01_rootdg.vol02/
    linking rootdg.vol01
    linking rootdg.vol02

# cd /etc/fdmns

# mv domain_rootdg.vol01_rootdg.vol02 junk_domain

# showfsets junk_domain
newjunk
    Id             : 34608122.0008e32f.1.8001
    Files          :    0, SLim=    0, HLim=    0
    Blocks (512)   :    0, SLim=    0, HLim=    0
    Quota Status   : user=off group=off
```

6.3.5.6 Moving or Changing the Size of the Transaction Log

A single transaction log per AdvFS file domain resides on one of the volumes in the domain. As discussed in section 6.3.1, the *showfdmn(8)* command can be used to determine the current location of the transaction log. In the *showfdmn(8)* command display, the letter "L" displays next to the volume number for the volume that contains the log. The transaction log can reside on any volume in the domain that has enough space to hold it. Of course, if there's only one volume in a domain, then the log cannot be moved. The command used to move the log between volumes in a file domain is *switchlog(8)*, which has two primary functions:

1.   Relocates the transaction log of the specified file domain to a different volume.

2.   Changes the size of the log while moving it.

Moving the transaction log within a multivolume file domain is typically done to place the log on a faster, a less congested, or a mirrored volume.

When removing the volume containing the log from a file domain using *rmvol(8)*, it is not necessary to explicitly move the transaction log to another volume. The transaction log will automatically be relocated to another volume.

Syntax:

```
switchlog [-l log-pages] domain_name volume_num
```

TABLE 6–24   Flags for the *switchlog(8)* Command

FLAG	DESCRIPTION
-l log_pages	The number of eight-kilobyte pages to size the log. This flag is undocumented in 4.0 and higher versions, although it still works. It is still a useful feature, but it is planned for retirement in some future release.
domain_name	The name of an existing file domain to examine
volume_num	The number of the new volume to use for the log

For 4.0x versions and higher, the *mkfdmn(8)* command can be used to create a domain with a larger transaction log size. Therefore, the switchlog –l may not be needed if the goal is simply to create a domain with a larger transaction log than the default (4 MB). (See the section in this chapter where we discuss the *mkfdmn(8)* command in greater detail.)

Example:

This example shows how to use the *switchlog(8)* command to move the transaction log in domain "test_domain" from volume 1 to 3. The *showfdmn(8)* command is used before and after to verify that the log movement occurred. The size of the log remains consistent at 512 pages.

```
# showfdmn test_domain

        Id            Date Created              LogPgs   Domain Name
354614cd.0006d4dc   Tue Apr 28 13:41:33 1998    512      test_domain

Vol   512-Blks    Free    % Used   Cmode   Rblks   Wblks        Vol Name
 1L    100000    91536      8%       on      128     128    /dev/vol/vol01
 2     100000    99872      0%       on      128     128    /dev/vol/vol02
 3     100000    99872      0%       on      128     128    /dev/vol/vol03
 4     100000    99872      0%       on      128     128    /dev/vol/vol04
       ----------  ----------  ------
       400000    391152      2%

# /sbin/advfs/switchlog test_domain 3

# showfdmn test_domain

        Id            Date Created              LogPgs   Domain Name
354614cd.0006d4dc   Tue Apr 28 13:41:33 1998    512      test_domain

Vol   512-Blks    Free    % Used   Cmode   Rblks   Wblks        Vol Name
 1     100000    91536      8%       on      128     128    /dev/vol/vol01
 2     100000    99872      0%       on      128     128    /dev/vol/vol02
 3L    100000    91680      8%       on      128     128    /dev/vol/vol03
 4     100000    99872      0%       on      128     128    /dev/vol/vol04
       --------------------  ------
       400000    382960      4%
```

Example:

Here, we give an example that shows how to use the *switchlog(8)* command to move the transaction log from one volume to another in a domain. In addition, we use the '-l' switch to alter the size of the log. This example also illustrates how the showfile command shows how to examine the log before and after the *switchlog(8)* command is executed. Notice that the log has a different metadata tag associated with it before and after it is moved from one volume to another. This happens because the tag value is a function of the volume index (tag = $M - ((6 \times vol) + 3)$). We discuss calculating the metadata tag values in greater detail in Chapter 7.

```
# showfdmn test_domain

        Id            Date Created              LogPgs   Domain Name
354614cd.0006d4dc   Tue Apr 28 13:41:33 1998    512      test_domain

Vol   512-Blks    Free    % Used   Cmode   Rblks   Wblks        Vol Name
 1     100000    91536      8%       on      128     128    /dev/vol/vol01
 2     100000    99872      0%       on      128     128    /dev/vol/vol02
 3L    100000    91680      8%       on      128     128    /dev/vol/vol03
 4     100000    99872      0%       on      128     128    /dev/vol/vol04
       ----------  ----------  ------
       400000    382960      4%

# showfile -x /mnt/.tags/M-21
        Id Vol PgSz Pages XtntType Segs SegSz I/O  Perf File
fffffeb.0000  3  16   512  simple   **    **  async 100% M-21
```

```
    extentMap: 1
      pageOff  pageCnt    vol  volBlock  blockCnt
        0       512     3     112      8192
      extentCnt: 1
```

```
# /sbin/advfs/switchlog -l 4096 test_domain 2
```

```
# showfdmn test_domain
```

```
        Id                Date Created              LogPgs   Domain Name
354614cd.0006d4dc    Tue Apr 28 13:41:33 1998      4096     test_domain

Vol  512-Blks     Free    % Used  Cmode  Rblks  Wblks        Vol Name
 1    100000     91536      8%      on    128    128    /dev/vol/vol01
2L    100000     34336     66%      on    128    128    /dev/vol/vol02
 3    100000     91680      8%      on    128    128    /dev/vol/vol03
 4    100000     99872      0%      on    128    128    /dev/vol/vol04
     ----------  ----------  ------
      400000    317424     21%
```

```
# showfile -x /mnt/.tags/M-15
```

```
        Id     Vol          PgSz   Pages   XtntType  Segs  SegSz   I/O   PerfFile
fffffff1.0000    2      16   4096   simple      **     **   async   99%    M-15
      extentMap: 1
        pageOff      pageCnt    vol    volBlock    blockCnt
            0          1250      2         112       20000
         1250          1250      2       20112       20000
         2500          1250      2       40112       20000
         3750           346      2       60112        5536
      extentCnt: 4
```

```
# /sbin/advfs/switchlog -l 512 test_domain 1
```

```
# showfdmn test_domain
```

```
        Id                Date Created              LogPgs   Domain Name
354614cd.0006d4dc    Tue Apr 28 13:41:33 1998       512     test_domain

Vol  512-Blks     Free    % Used  Cmode  Rblks  Wblks        Vol Name
1L    100000     91536      8%      on    128    128    /dev/vol/vol01
 2    100000     34336     66%      on    128    128    /dev/vol/vol02
 3    100000     91680      8%      on    128    128    /dev/vol/vol03
 4    100000     99872      0%      on    128    128    /dev/vol/vol04
     ----------  ----------  ------
      400000    317424     21%
```

6.4   Using AdvFS Advanced Utilities

Prior to Tru64 UNIX version 5.0, many of the useful utilities for managing AdvFS were part of a separately licensed product known as the AdvFS Advanced Utilities. When referring to these utilities in this and later chapters, keep in mind that these functions are included with the base AdvFS operating system subset (OSFADVFS500).

6.4.1 Installing the Advanced Utilities

In order to use the AdvFS Advanced Utilities on a pre-5.0 system, the following subsets must be installed:

AFAADVANCEDxxx	POLYCENTER Advanced File System Advanced Utilities (General Applications)
AFAADVDAEMONxxx	POLYCENTER Advanced File System Daemon (General Applications)[3]
AFAADVGUIxxx	POLYCENTER Advanced File System Graphical User Interface (General Applications)
AFAADVMANxxx	POLYCENTER Advanced File System Advanced Utilities Reference Pages (General Applications)

The best location to find the correct Advanced Utilities version for the operating system version desired is from its Associated Products CD-ROM volume 2.

In addition, use of the AdvFS Advanced Utilities requires an additional license. Two possible licenses that are acceptable for allowing this capability are the ADVFS-UTILITIES license or a NAS 200 or higher license that has been properly activated.

6.4.2 Managing AdvFS Volumes

In the simplest case, an AdvFS exists on only a single volume. For this situation, there is not much to managing the domain because the choices regarding where different files and metadata reside are limited to only one volume. Once you add one or more volumes, then choices open up and management becomes a necessity. The commands discussed in this section are dedicated to assisting you to manage volumes and place items on them.

6.4.2.1 Adding Volumes

A newly created file domain consists of one volume, which can be a disk partition or an LSM logical volume. The *addvol(8)* utility enables you to dynamically increase the size of the domain by adding additional volumes. You can add volumes immediately after creating a file domain, or you can wait until the filesets within the domain require additional space.

Syntax:

```
addvol [-F ] type] [-x num_pages] [-p num_pages] special domain
```

TABLE 6–25   Flags for the *addvol(8)* Command

FLAG	DESCRIPTION
special	The special device name, such as /dev/disk/dsk4c, of the disk that you are adding to the file domain
domain	The name of the file domain
-F	Ignores overlapping partition or block warnings.
-x num_pages	Sets the number of pages by which the bitmap metadata table size grows. This flag is obsolete with domains created with on-disk version 4 or greater.
-p num_pages	Sets the number of pages to preallocate for the bitmap meta-data table. This flag is obsolete with domains created with on-disk version 4 or greater.

Example:

This example shows how to add two additional volumes to a domain using the *addvol(8)* command.

```
# showfdmn test_dmn

        Id              Date Created              LogPgs   Domain Name
33c3a315.0001bec1   Wed Jul 9 10:41:25 1997      512      test_dmn

Vol  512-Blks   Free    % Used  Cmode  Rblks   Wblks   Vol Name
 1L    424323  365440     14%     on     128     128   /dev/vol/vol03

# addvol /dev/vol/vol01 test_dmn

# showfdmn test_dmn

        Id              Date Created              LogPgs   Domain Name
33c3a315.0001bec1   Wed Jul 9 10:41:25 1997      512      test_dmn

Vol  512-Blks     Free    % Used  Cmode  Rblks   Wblks   Vol Name
 1L    424323   365440      14%     on     128     128   /dev/vol/vol03
 2    1104876  1104624       0%     on     128     128   /dev/vol/vol01
       ----------------- ------
       1529199  1470064       4%

# addvol /dev/vol/vol02 test_dmn

# showfdmn test_dmn

        Id              Date Created              LogPgs   Domain Name
33c3a315.0001bec1   Wed Jul 9 10:41:25 1997      512      test_dmn

Vol  512-Blks     Free    % Used  Cmode  Rblks   Wblks   Vol Name
 1L    424323   365440      14%     on     128     128   /dev/vol/vol03
 2    1104876  1104624       0%     on     128     128   /dev/vol/vol01
 3     424323   424160       0%     on     128     128   /dev/vol/vol02
       ----------------- ------
       1953522  1894224       3%
```

6.4.2.2 Removing Volumes

The *rmvol(8)* utility enables you to take a single volume out of an existing multivolume file domain. When you attempt to remove a volume, the files automatically migrate from that volume to other volumes in the file domain. Thus, it could take some time for the *rmvol(8)* to complete. The user must ensure that enough space is available in the remaining volumes to hold the files that are migrated from the removed volume. If there isn't enough space, then the *rmvol(8)* will not succeed and will print an error message. Only one of the migration utilities—*balance(8)*, *migrate(8)*, *rmvol(8)*, and *defragment(8)*—can be used on a domain at a time.

Syntax:

```
rmvol [-f] [-v] special domain
```

TABLE 6–26 Flags for the *rmvol(8)* Command

FLAG	DESCRIPTION
Special	The block special device name, such as /dev/disk/dsk5c, of the volume that you are removing from the file domain
domain	The name of the file domain
-f	Forces the removal of a volume that contains one or more stripe segments without first requesting confirmation.
-v	Verbose mode. Displays messages that describe which files are moved off the specified volume. Using this flag slows the rmvol process.

Example:

The following example shows how to remove a volume from a domain.

```
# rmvol /dev/vol/vol03 test_dmn
rmvol: Removing volume '/dev/vol/vol03' from domain 'test_dmn'
rmvol: Removed volume '/dev/vol/vol03' from domain 'test_dmn'

# showfdmn test_dmn
        Id              Date Created              LogPgs  Domain Name
33c3a315.0001bec1  Wed Jul 9 10:41:25 1997       512     test_dmn

Vol  512-Blks    Free  % Used  Cmode  Rblks  Wblks  Vol Name
2L   1104876   1078736     2%     on    128    128  /dev/vol/vol01
 3    424323    424096     0%     on    128    128  /dev/vol/vol02
     ----------  -------  ------
     1529199   1502832     2%
```

6.4.2.3 Balancing Usage Between AdvFS Volumes

The *balance(8)* utility attempts to evenly distribute the used space between volumes in a multivolume domain on a percentage basis. The goal is to improve file system performance by evening out the distribution of future file allocations. The best way to determine whether running *balance(8)* is necessary is to use the *showfdmn(8)* command to examine the percentage of used space on each volume. If this information shows you that the volumes are out of balance, then you need to run *balance(8)* on the domain.

You should run the *balance(8)* utility when adding or removing a volume because these procedures cause file distribution to become uneven. When you plan to run both the *defragment(8)* and *balance(8)* utilities on the same domain, run the *defragment(8)* utility before running the *balance(8)* utility. The *defragment(8)* utility often improves the balance of free space, thus enabling the *balance(8)* utility to run more quickly.

An important restriction is that the *balance(8)* command can only be used to balance usage on volumes in a file domain for which all filesets are mounted. If you try to balance volumes in an active file domain that includes unmounted filesets, then the system displays an error message indicating that a fileset is unmounted and the balance will fail. Only one of the migration utilities—*balance(8)*, *migrate(8)*, *rmvol(8)*, and *defragment(8)*—can be used on a domain at a time.

Syntax:

```
balance [-v] domain
```

TABLE 6–27   Flags for the *balance(8)* Command

FLAG	DESCRIPTION
Domain	The name of the file domain
-v	Verbose mode. Displays information about which files are being moved to different volumes. Selecting this flag slows down the balance procedure.

Example:

The following example illustrates the use of the *balance(8)* command.

```
# showfdmn test_dmn

        Id              Date Created              LogPgs  Domain Name
33c3a315.0001bec1  Wed Jul 9 10:41:25 1997        512    test_dmn

Vol  512-Blks     Free  % Used  Cmode  Rblks  Wblks  Vol Name
 1    424323    424160     0%     on     128    128   /dev/vol/vol03
2L   1104876   1074912     3%     on     128    128   /dev/vol/vol01
 3    424323    382384    10%     on     128    128   /dev/vol/vol02
     ----------  -------  ------
     1953522   1881456     4%
```

```
# balance test_dmn
balance: Balancing domain 'test_dmn'
balance: Balanced domain 'test_dmn'

# showfdmn test_dmn
```

Id	Date Created	LogPgs	Domain Name
33c3a315.0001bec1	Wed Jul 9 10:41:25 1997	512	test_dmn

Vol	512-Blks	Free	% Used	Cmode	Rblks	Wblks	Vol Name
1	424323	406608	4%	on	128	128	/dev/vol/vol03
2L	1104876	1057648	4%	on	128	128	/dev/vol/vol01
3	424323	417200	2%	on	128	128	/dev/vol/vol02
	-------	-------	----				
	1953522	1881456	4%				

6.4.2.4 Migrating Files to Other AdvFS Volumes

The migrate utility moves the specified page or pages of a file to a new location within the file domain. Because no read-write restrictions are imposed when using this command, you can migrate a file while users are reading it, writing to it, or both. File migration is transparent to users.

When you run the migrate utility with only the '-p' and '-n' flags, the utility attempts to allocate the destination pages contiguously. If not enough free, contiguous destination blocks are available, then the utility attempts to allocate the pages to the next available blocks on the same volume. If not enough destination blocks are available on the same volume, then the utility moves the file to the next available volume or volumes.

You can use the migrate utility to move heavily accessed files or pages of files to a different volume in the file domain. Use the '-d' flag to indicate a specific volume. Also, you can use the utility to defragment a specific file because the migrate utility defragments a file whenever possible. Only one of the migration utilities—*balance(8)*, *migrate(8)*, *rmvol(8)*, and *defragment(8)*—can be used on a domain at a time.

Syntax:

```
migrate [-p offset] [-n count] [-s index] [-d index] filename
```

TABLE 6–28 Flags for the *migrate(8)* Command

FLAG	DESCRIPTION
filename	The name of the file to migrate
-p offset	The page offset of the first page to migrate. The first page of the file is page 0. The default page offset is 0.
-n count	The number of pages to migrate, starting at the page offset value. If you do not specify the '-n' flag, then the migrate command migrates pages from the offset value to the end of the file.

TABLE **6–28**   Flags for the *migrate(8)* Command (Continued)

FLAG	DESCRIPTION
-s index	The index of the source volume (the volume from which the pages are migrated). You can determine the volume index, which is the number associated with each volume, by using the showfile '-x' command. Also, you must use this flag to move pages of a striped file, a segment of the striped file that resides on one volume, to another volume.
-d index	The index of the destination volume (the volume to which the pages are migrated). You can determine the volume index, which is the number associated with each volume, by using the showfile '-x' command. If you do not specify the '-d' flag, then the pages are moved to any volume or volumes with available space.

Example:

The following is an example of using the *migrate(8)* utility to move a file's data blocks from volume 3 to volume 1 in a domain.

```
# showfdmn test_dmn

         Id                Date Created                LogPgs   Domain Name
33c3a315.0001bec1   Wed Jul 9 10:41:25 1997      512     test_dmn

Vol  512-Blks     Free  % Used   Cmode   Rblks   Wblks   Vol Name
 1     424323   387568      9%      on     128     128   /dev/vol/vol03
 2L   1104876  1094240      1%      on     128     128   /dev/vol/vol01
 3     424323   399648      6%      on     128     128   /dev/vol/vol02
      -------------------- ------
      1953522  1881456      4%

# showfile -x vmunix

     Id    Vol   PgSz   Pages  XtntType   Segs   SegSz   Log   Perf    File
   6.8001    2     16    1097    simple     **      **    off   100%  vmunix

   extentMap: 1
     pageOff    pageCnt    vol   volBlock   blockCnt
        0         1097      3      70784      17552
   extentCnt: 1

# migrate -s 3 -d 1 vmunix

# showfile -x vmunix

     Id    Vol   PgSz   Pages  XtntType   Segs   SegSz   Log   Perf    File
   6.8001    2     16    1097    simple     **      **    off   100%  vmunix

   extentMap: 1
     pageOff    pageCnt    vol   volBlock   blockCnt
        0         1097      1      36752      17552
   extentCnt: 1

# showfdmn test_dmn

         Id                Date Created                LogPgs   Domain Name
33c3a315.0001bec1   Wed Jul 9 10:41:25 1997      512     test_dmn
```

```
Vol  512-Blks      Free  % Used   Cmode    Rblks    Wblks   Vol Name
 1     424323    370016     13%      on      128      128   /dev/vol/vol03
 2L   1104876   1094240      1%      on      128      128   /dev/vol/vol01
 3     424323    417200      2%      on      128      128   /dev/vol/vol02
     ------------------- ------
      1953522   1881456      4%
```

6.4.2.5   Striping Files Across AdvFS Volumes

The *stripe(8)* command allows you to spread the I/O load across multiple volumes in an AdvFS domain. The stripe utility will change a zero-length file (a file with no data written to it yet) to be spread evenly across several volumes within a file domain. As data are appended to the file, the data are spread across the volumes. AdvFS determines the number of pages per stripe segment and alternates the segments among the disks in a sequential pattern.

Existing, nonzero-length files cannot be striped using the *stripe(8)* utility. To stripe an existing file, perform the following steps:

1.   Create a new, zero-length file.

2.   Use the stripe utility to stripe the new file.

3.   Copy the contents of the file you want to stripe into the new striped file.

4.   After copying the file, you can delete the nonstriped file.

5.   Rename the striped file to the old file name.

Once a file is striped, you cannot use the stripe utility to modify the number of disks that a striped file crosses. To change the volume count of a striped file, perform the following steps:

1.   Create a new, zero-length file.

2.   Use *stripe(8)* to stripe the new file with a different volume count.

3.   Copy the contents of the first file into the second file.

4.   After copying the file, delete the first file.

5.   Rename the new file to the old name.

Syntax:

```
stripe -n count filename
```

TABLE 6–29   Flags for the *stripe(8)* Command

FLAG	DESCRIPTION
filename	The name of a zero-sized file to stripe
-n count	The number of volumes the striped file crosses. The number of volumes must be greater than one.

Example:

The following is an example of how to stripe a file in AdvFS.

```
# showfdmn test_dmn

        Id                 Date Created              LogPgs   Domain      Name
33c3a315.0001bec1   Wed Jul 9 10:41:25 1997      512      test_dmn

Vol  512-Blks       Free   % Used   Cmode    Rblks    Wblks    Vol  Name
 1     424323     406608      4%       on      128      128    /dev/vol/vol03
2L    1104876    1057648      4%       on      128      128    /dev/vol/vol01
 3     424323     417200      2%       on      128      128    /dev/vol/vol02
     -------------------- ------
      1953522    1881456      4%

# showfile -x vmunix

    Id    Vol   PgSz   Pages   XtntType    Segs    SegSz    Log   Perf     File
 6.8001    2     16    1097    simple       **      **     off   100%    vmunix

  extentMap: 1
    pageOff  pageCnt   vol   volBlock   blockCnt
       0       1097     1     36752      17552
    extentCnt: 1

# stripe -n 3 vmunix
stripe: advfs_set_bf_attributes failed --- E_ALREADY_STRIPED (-1182)

# touch vmunix2

# showfile -x vmunix2

    Id     Vol   PgSz   Pages   XtntType    Segs    SegSz    Log   Perf     File
 29.8001    2     16      0     simple       **      **     off   100%   vmunix2

  extentMap: 1
    pageOff  pageCnt    vol  volBlock  blockCnt
    extentCnt: 0

# stripe -n 3 vmunix2

# showfile -x vmunix2

    Id     Vol   PgSz   Pages   XtntType    Segs    SegSz    Log   Perf     File
 29.8002    2     16      0     simple        3       8     off   100%  vmunix2

  extentMap: 1
    pageOff  pageCnt  volIndex  volBlock  blockCnt
    extentCnt: 0

  extentMap: 2
    pageOff  pageCnt  volIndex  volBlock  blockCnt
    extentCnt: 0

  extentMap: 3
    pageOff  pageCnt  volIndex  volBlock  blockCnt
    extentCnt: 0

# cat vmunix >> vmunix2
```

```
# showfile -x vmunix2
     Id      Vol    PgSz   Pages  XtntType   Segs   SegSz   Log   Perf     File
  29.8002     1       16    1097    stripe      3       8   off   100%  vmunix2

  extentMap: 1
    pageOff  pageCnt  volIndex   volBlock   blockCnt
        0       8        3         88336      5888
       24       8
       48       8
       72       8
       96       8
      120       8

[snip]

      984       8
     1008       8
     1032       8
     1056       8
     1080       8
    extentCnt: 1

  extentMap: 2
    pageOff  pageCnt  volIndex   volBlock   blockCnt
        8       8        2         67008      5888
       32       8
       56       8
       80       8
      104       8

[snip]

      992       8
     1016       8
     1040       8
     1064       8
     1088       8
    extentCnt: 1

  extentMap: 3
    pageOff  pageCnt  volIndex   volBlock   blockCnt
       16       8        1         54304      5776
       40       8
       64       8
       88       8
      112       8

[snip]

      976       8
     1000       8
     1024       8
     1048       8
     1072       8
     1096       1

# showfdmn test_dmn
```

```
     Id              Date Created              LogPgs   Domain      Name
33c3a315.0001bec1   Wed Jul 9 10:41:25 1997    512     test_dmn

Vol  512-Blks      Free  % Used  Cmode   Rblks   Wblks    Vol Name
 1    424323     400832     6%     on      128     128    /dev/vol/vol03
2L   1104876    1051760     5%     on      128     128    /dev/vol/vol01
 3    424323     411312     3%     on      128     128    /dev/vol/vol02
     -------------------- ------
     1953522    1863904     5%
```

```
# rm vmunix
```

```
# mv vmunix2 vmunix
```

6.4.3   Backups Revisited

When we looked at backups previously, the functionality of the *vdump(8)* and *vrestore(8)* commands were roughly the same as for *dump(8)* and *restore(8)*. Now, we discuss how to greatly improve the backup capability of the AdvFS, by introducing the idea of a clone fileset.

6.4.3.1   Cloning Filesets

The *clonefset(8)* utility enables you to perform online backups of active files by making a read-only copy (clone) of an active fileset. Once you create and mount a clone fileset, you can back up the clone using the *vdump(8)* command or another supported backup utility (the dump command is not supported for use with AdvFS). Note that the clonefset utility clones only AdvFS filesets; it does not clone UFS filesets.

A clone fileset is a read-only snapshot of fileset data structures (metadata). When you clone a fileset, the utility copies only the structure of the original fileset, not its data. When you modify files in the original fileset, the file system copies the original pages to the clone fileset. In this way, the clone fileset contents remain the same as when you first created it.

You can create new versions of a clone fileset, but you can maintain only one clone per fileset at a time. You can remove an existing clone fileset just like you remove any regular fileset, by using the *rmfset(8)* command.

Syntax:

```
clonefset domain fileset clonename
```

TABLE 6–30   Flags for the *clonefset(8)* Command

FLAG	DESCRIPTION
domain	The name of the domain
fileset	The name of the original fileset that the clonefset utility will clone
clonename	The name of the read-only fileset created by the clonefset utility

Example:

This example shows how to use vdump and clones to make clean, consistent backups.

```
# df /mnt
Filesystem          512-blocks     Used    Available   Capacity   Mounted on
test_dmn#test         1953504      34992     1876640       2%        /mnt

# ls /mnt
.tags    quota.group quota.user  vmunix    vmunix.old

# showfsets test_dmn
test
    Id              : 33c3a315.0001bec1.1.8001
    Files           :      4, SLim=    0, HLim=    0
    Blocks (512)    : 34992, SLim=    0, HLim=    0
    Quota Status    : user=off group=off

# clonefset test_dmn test clone_test

# showfsets test_dmn
test
    Id              : 33c3a315.0001bec1.1.8001
    Clone is        : clone_test
    Files           :      4, SLim=    0, HLim=    0
    Blocks (512)    : 34992, SLim=    0, HLim=    0
    Quota Status    : user=off group=off

clone_test
    Id              : 33c3a315.0001bec1.2.8002
    Clone of        : test
    Revision        : 2

# mount test_dmn#clone_test /mnt2

# df /mnt2
Filesystem          512-blocks     Used    Available   Capacity   Mounted on
test_dmn#clone_test   1953504      76816     1876688       4%        /mnt2

# ls /mnt2
.tags    quota.group quota.user  vmunix    vmunix.old
```

At this point, the clone backup looks identical to the original. No changes have been made to the original fileset. Now, we show that if a file is removed from the original fileset, it will not be removed from the clone. This file will be backed up with the clone fileset as long as the backup is done before removing it.

```
# cd /mnt

# ls
.tags    quota.group quota.user  vmunix    vmunix.old

# rm vmunix.old

# ls
```

```
.tags    quota.group quota.user  vmunix
# cd /mnt2
# ls
.tags    quota.group quota.user  vmunix    vmunix.old
```

Now we see that if a file is created on the original fileset, the new file will not show up on the clone fileset. Therefore, this new file will not be backed up with the clone.

```
# cd /mnt
# touch stuff.txt
# ls
.tags    quota.group quota.user  stuff.txt  vmunix
# cd /mnt2
# ls
.tags    quota.group quota.user  vmunix    vmunix.old
```

Example:

This example picks up from where the previous example left off. The clone fileset is backed up using the *vdump(8)* command, and the clone fileset is removed.

```
# vdump -0f /dev/nrmt0h -D /mnt2
path       : /mnt2
dev/fset   : test_dmn#clone_test
type       : advfs
advfs id   : 0x33c3a315.0001bec1.2
vdump: Date of last level 0 dump: the start of the epoch
vdump: Dumping directories
vdump: Dumping 17900880 bytes, 1 directories, 4 files
vdump: Dumping regular files

vdump: Status at Tue Aug 12 09:28:18 1997
vdump: Dumped 17900880 of 17900880 bytes; 100.0% completed
vdump: Dumped 1 of 1 directories; 100.0% completed
vdump: Dumped 4 of 4 files; 100.0% completed
vdump: Dump completed at Tue Aug 12 09:28:18 1997

# umount /mnt2

# rmfset test_dmn clone_test
rmfset: remove fileset clone_test? [y/n] y

# showfsets test_dmn
test
    Id            : 33c3a315.0001bec1.1.8001
    Files         :      4, SLim=    0, HLim=   0
    Blocks (512)  : 17584, SLim=    0, HLim=   0
    Quota Status  : user=off group=off
```

Now, we'll take the backup tape and restore it to another domain and fileset.

```
# mkfdmn /dev/vol/temp_vol temp_dmn

# mkfset temp_dmn test

# showfsets temp_dmn
test
    Id            : 33f0661b.0002a848.1.8001
    Files         :    0, SLim=    0, HLim=    0
    Blocks (512) :    0, SLim=    0, HLim=    0
    Quota Status : user=off group=off

# cd /test

# ls
.tags    quota.group quota.user

# vrestore -xf /dev/rmt0h -D /test
vrestore: Date of the vdump save-set: Tue Aug 12 09:25:45 1997

# ls
.tags    quota.group quota.user  vmunix    vmunix.old
```

It is important not to create and mount a clone fileset if the available disk space for the file domain is less than 5 percent of the total. When a file domain runs out of disk space, the file system loses its ability to maintain the consistency of files within clone filesets. On very busy file systems, where many files are created or modified, 5 percent may still be too conservative. There must be enough room to store the additional copy of the metadata and the copied data blocks of any new or modified files for the duration of the existence of the clone.

You should make sure that you remove a fileset immediately after it is no longer needed in order to prevent problems. If you keep a clone fileset around too long, and the fileset is active, then you will eventually see a message similar to the following in your syslog file:

```
Feb 18 05:46:13 karagoz vmunix: WARNING: advfs cannot copy-on-write data to a
clone file.

Feb 18 05:46:13 karagoz vmunix: WARNING: encountered the following error:
ENO_MORE_BLKS (-1040)

Feb 18 05:46:13 karagoz vmunix: WARNING: do not continue using the clone fileset.

Feb 18 05:46:13 karagoz vmunix: WARNING: original fileset: name = sc24d4, id =
37e76778.0004ec69.00000001.8001

Feb 18 05:46:14 karagoz vmunix: WARNING: clone fileset: name = clone_b825, id =
37e76778.0004ec69.00000002.8029

Feb 18 05:46:14 karagoz vmunix: WARNING: file id = 000003fd.8002

Feb 18 05:46:14 karagoz vmunix:
```

```
Feb 18 05:46:14 karagoz vmunix: WARNING: original fileset: name = sc24d4, id =
37e76778.0004ec69.00000001.8001

Feb 18 05:46:14 karagoz vmunix: WARNING: clone fileset: name = clone_b825, id =
37e76778.0004ec69.00000002.8029

Feb 18 05:46:14 karagoz vmunix: WARNING: file id = 000003fd.8002

Feb 18 05:46:14 karagoz vmunix:
```

If this happens, you will not be able to create or modify files on any of the filesets in the domain. If you receive a file system full message, then you may have a clone fileset that needs to be removed like this one.

6.4.4   Managing Trashcans

Trashcans are the mechanism employed by the AdvFS to implement the file undelete functionality. Thus, trashcans are special directories designated by the system administrator to be used as a temporary holding place for files that are deleted. In order for this to occur automatically, the system administrator must make an association of a special directory (called a trashcan directory) to the directory from which the files will be deleted. This association is made using the *mktrashcan(8)* command and removed with the *rmtrashcan(8)* command. The *shtrashcan(8)* command shows whether a directory has a trashcan association or not.

6.4.4.1   Making Trashcans

To make an association of a directory to a trashcan, use the *mktrashcan(8)* command.

Syntax:

```
mktrashcan trashcan directory [directory ...]
```

TABLE 6–31   Flags for the *mktrashcan(8)* Command

FLAG	DESCRIPTION
trashcan	The directory that will contain files that are deleted from attached directories. Whenever you delete a file in the specified directory, the file system automatically moves the file to the trashcan directory.
directory	Specifies one or more directories, designated by the user, which will be attached to the trashcan.

Example:

This example illustrates how to attach a trashcan directory called "trashcan" to another directory called "stuff."

```
# pwd
/mnt
# ls
.tags stuff
# mkdir trashcan
# ls
.tags    stuff    trashcan
# chmod a+w trashcan
# mktrashcan trashcan stuff
  'trashcan' attached to 'stuff'
```

Example:

Now, we give an example of how files that are removed from the attached directory are moved into the trashcan directory when a file is deleted.

```
# ls
.tags    stuff    trashcan
# cd stuff
# ls DILBERT
DILBERT
# rm DILBERT
# ls DILBERT
DILBERT not found
# ls /mnt/trashcan
DILBERT
```

6.4.4.2 Removing Trashcan Associations

Trashcan directory associations can be removed using the *rmtrashcan(8)* command.

Syntax:

```
rmtrashcan directory [directory...]
```

TABLE 6–32   Flags for the *rmtrashcan(8)* Command

FLAG	DESCRIPTION
trashcan	The directory that contains files that were deleted from attached directories. Whenever you delete a file in the specified directory, the file system automatically moves the file to the trashcan directory.
directory	The directory that you attach to a trashcan directory.

Example:

This example shows how to use the *rmtrashcan(8)* command to remove a trashcan association.

```
# rmtrashcan /mnt/stuff
  '/mnt/stuff' detached
```

6.4.4.3   Displaying Information About Trashcans

The *shtrashcan(8)* command is used to determine if a directory has a trashcan attachment or not.

Syntax:

```
shtrashcan directory [directory...]
```

TABLE 6–33   Flags for the *shtrashcan(8)* Command

FLAG	DESCRIPTION
directory	The directory you want to examine for trashcan attachment

Example:

In this example, we illustrate how to use the *shtrashcan(8)* command to file out if a directory had a trashcan attachment.

```
# shtrashcan /mnt/stuff
  '/mnt/trashcan' attached to '/mnt/stuff'
```

Example:

In this second example, we see that *shtrashcan(8)* can be used with wildcards to examine all or some of the directories. Notice that *shtrashcan(8)* ignores any nondirectories such as file1, file2, and file3 here.

```
# ls -l
total 48
-rw-r--r--  1 hancock wkull      0 Aug 25 21:18 file1
-rw-r--r--  1 hancock wkull      0 Aug 25 21:18 file2
-rw-r--r--  1 hancock wkull      0 Aug 25 21:18 file3
drwxr-xr-x  2 hancock wkull   8192 Aug 25 21:09 stuff1
drwxr-xr-x  2 hancock wkull   8192 Aug 25 21:09 stuff2
drwxr-xr-x  2 hancock wkull   8192 Aug 25 21:09 stuff3
drwxr-xr-x  2 hancock wkull   8192 Aug 25 21:09 trashcan1
drwxr-xr-x  2 hancock wkull   8192 Aug 25 21:09 trashcan2
drwxr-xr-x  2 hancock wkull   8192 Aug 25 21:09 trashcan3

# shtrashcan *
  '/usr/staff/k2/hancock/test/trashcan1' attached to 'stuff1'
  '/usr/staff/k2/hancock/test/trashcan2' attached to 'stuff2'
  '/usr/staff/k2/hancock/test/trashcan3' attached to 'stuff3'
```

```
shtrashcan: 'trashcan1' has no trashcan
shtrashcan: 'trashcan2' has no trashcan
shtrashcan: 'trashcan3' has no trashcan
```

6.4.5   Defragmenting AdvFS Domains

Any system that dynamically allocates storage like AdvFS inevitably becomes fragmented over time. As we discussed previously, a file is considered fragmented when it consists of more than one uncontiguous segment. A highly fragmented file has a very large number of segments. A segment is one or more contiguous file system blocks. The author has seen individual files with greater than 50,000 extents. The performance of access to these files was, understandably, abysmal. In one case, the /vmunix file was so fragmented that the system was simply not able to read it and boot properly. It is very important for optimal system performance to make sure that files are as contiguous as possible. The easiest and most convenient way to accomplish this is by defragmenting domains regularly.

The *defragment(8)* utility is available for defragmenting AdvFS domains. The utility is designed to be used while the domains are active and in use; however, performance may suffer considerably if you choose to do so. Your users may let you know when they can no longer get their work done because a defragment is in progress! Therefore, we recommend running it during periods of low system activity. Beginning in Tru64 UNIX 4.0D, a script called *defragcron(8)* was provided, which assists in automating the defragmenting process. *Defragcron(8)* runs the AdvFS *defragment(8)* utility over all the domains or a given set of file domains. This script has been added to the default crontab entry for root. By default, this script will defragment all file domains every night between 1 a.m. and 5 a.m., local time. Of course, you can and will want to change this crontab entry to suit your needs. Defragmenting every night is way too frequent for most systems. By default, *defragcron(8)* is disabled.

The *defragment(8)* utility was added to the base operating system in Tru64 UNIX 4.0D in the AdvFS base subset (OSFADVFS) and no longer requires the AdvFS Advanced Utilities license. Only one of the migration utilities—*balance(8)*, *migrate(8)*, *rmvol(8)*, and *defragment(8)* —can be used on a domain at a time.

Syntax:

```
defragment [-e] [-n] [-t time] [-T time] [-v] [-V] domain
```

TABLE 6–34   Flags for the *defragment(8)* Command

FLAG	DESCRIPTION
domain	The name of the file domain you want to defragment
-e	Ignores errors and continues, if possible.
-n	Don't perform defragmentation. If used along with the '-v' flag, it will display only statistics about the file domain.
-t time	An approximate number of minutes for the *defragment(8)* utility to run. The utility will run until the specified time has expired, then it may continue until the current operation is complete, if necessary.
-T time	The exact number of minutes for the *defragment(8)* utility to run. Once the time has elapsed, *defragment(8)* stops.
-v	Verbose mode. Displays statistics on the amount of fragmentation in the file domain and information on the progress of the defragment procedure.
-V	Very verbose mode. Displays the same information as the '-v' flag plus each operation the defragment utility performs on each file.

The *defragment(8)* command requires that all filesets in the file domain be mounted. If you try to defragment an active file domain that includes unmounted filesets, then the system displays an error message indicating that a fileset is unmounted.

To determine the amount of file fragmentation in a file domain before using the defragment utility, issue the defragment command with the '-v' and '-n' flags. This command provides the fragmentation information without starting the defragment utility.

Example:

This example shows how to use *defragment(8)* with verbose output on a domain called "test_domain."

```
# defragment -v test_domain
defragment: Defragmenting domain 'test_domain'
Pass 1; Clearing
 Volume 1: area at block    13104 (   1296 blocks): 94% full
 Volume 2: area at block      112 (  52032 blocks): 28% full
 Volume 3: area at block      112 (  11424 blocks): 98% full
 Volume 4: area at block      112 (    800 blocks):  0% full
 Volume 5: area at block      112 (   5456 blocks): 87% full
 defragment: Defragmentation of striped files is not implemented.
 Domain data as of the start of this pass:
  Extents:                    44
  Files w/extents:            42
  Avg exts per file w/exts:   1.05
```

```
        Aggregate I/O perf:     100%
        Free space fragments:    32
                       <100K    <1M    <10M    >10M
         Free space:    0%       0%     0%      99%
         Fragments:     23       3      0       6
```

Filling

```
Pass 2; Clearing
 Volume 1: area at block   13104 (  1296 blocks): 94% full
 Volume 2: area at block     112 ( 52032 blocks): 28% full
 Volume 3: area at block     112 ( 11424 blocks): 98% full
 Volume 4: area at block     112 (   800 blocks):  0% full
 Volume 5: area at block      12 (  5456 blocks): 87% full
 Domain data as of the start of this pass:
  Extents:           42
  Files w/extents:        42
  Avg exts per file w/exts: 1.00
  Aggregate I/O perf:     100%
  Free space fragments:    32
                 <100K    <1M    <10M    >10M
   Free space:    0%       0%     0%      99%
   Fragments:     23       3      0       6
```

Filling

```
Pass 3; Clearing
 Volume 1: area at block   13104 (  1296 blocks): 94% full
 Volume 2: area at block     112 ( 52032 blocks): 28% full
 Volume 3: area at block     112 ( 11424 blocks): 98% full
 Volume 4: area at block     112 (   800 blocks):  0% full
 Volume 5: area at block      12 (  5456 blocks): 87% full
 Domain data as of the start of this pass:
  Extents:           42
  Files w/extents:        42
  Avg exts per file w/exts: 1.00
  Aggregate I/O perf:     100%
  Free space fragments:    32
                 <100K    <1M    <10M    >10M
   Free space:    0%       0%     0%      99%
   Fragments:     23       3      0       6
```

Filling

```
 Current domain data:
  Extents:           42
  Files w/extents:        42
  Avg exts per file w/exts: 1.00
  Aggregate I/O perf:     100%
  Free space fragments:    32
                 <100K    <1M    <10M    >10M
   Free space:    0%       0%     0%      99%
   Fragments:     23       3      0       6
defragment: Defragmented domain 'test_domain'
```

Example:

This example shows how to use the *defragment(8)* tool to gather fragmentation statistics for a domain with three filesets. Here, we see that if all of the filesets are not mounted, then the *defragment(8)* will not succeed. Once the third one is mounted, the *defragment(8)* proceeds.

```
# df
Filesystem          512-blocks       Used   Available    Capacity    Mounted on
root_domain#root       262144     182204       70800         73%     /
/proc                       0          0           0        100%     /proc
usr_domain#usr        1522464    1034346      127664         90%     /usr
usr_domain#var        1522464     327762      127664         72%     /var

# defragment -vn usr_domain
defragment: Gathering data for domain 'usr_domain'
defragment: Fileset not mounted
defragment: Domain name: usr_domain, fileset name: tmp
defragment: Can't mount bitfilesets
defragment: Can't gather data for domain 'usr_domain'

************** PROGRAM ABORT **************

defragment: Unable to open domain /etc/fdmns/usr_domain

# showfsets usr_domain
usr
    Id           : 36b0147f.000473f0.1.8001
    Files        :    24627, SLim=     0, HLim=     0
    Blocks (512) : 1034346, SLim=     0, HLim=     0
    Quota Status : user=off group=off

var
    Id           : 36b0147f.000473f0.2.8001
    Files        :      979, SLim=     0, HLim=     0
    Blocks (512) :   327762, SLim=     0, HLim=     0
    Quota Status : user=off group=off

tmp
    Id           : 36b0147f.000473f0.3.8001
    Files        :        5, SLim=     0, HLim=     0
    Blocks (512) :        0, SLim=     0, HLim=     0
    Quota Status : user=off group=off

# mount usr_domain#tmp /mnt

# defragment -vn usr_domain
defragment: Gathering data for domain 'usr_domain'
 Current domain data:
  Extents:                    23789
  Files w/extents:             7559
  Avg exts per file w/exts:    3.15
  Aggregate I/O perf:           12%
  Free space fragments:          90
                <100K    <1M    <10M    >10M
  Free space:    32%     68%     0%      0%
  Fragments:      57      33      0       0
```

6.5 Summary

This chapter was a basic discussion of the AdvFS. We began with important features and concepts of the powerful file system. Then, we detailed all of the tasks and commands in both the base and Advanced Utilities subsystems. As usual, we gave examples for each command or technique to illustrate the main points. We also gave a presentation of the AdvFS Advanced Utilities, which were a separate product from the base operating system prior to Tru64 UNIX 5.0. These utilities provide many of the features needed for online management of large file systems.

The AdvFS is powerful, yet complex. It is an essential part of any large-scale file system in Tru64 UNIX. After reading this chapter, you should see clear advantages of the AdvFS over UFS for large and continuous operations. Many of the routine maintenance operations can be accomplished while the file system is actively being used. You should also understand that large and complex file systems require periodic maintenance to remain at optimal performance.

In the next chapter, we continue our discussion of advanced topics in AdvFS on Tru64 UNIX systems.

Notes

1. Some competing log-based products with which the author is familiar are the JFS™ in AIX™ from IBM, VxFS from Veritas, and XFS from SGI.

2. The reason this option is known as MSFS instead of ADVFS is historical. Because the original name for what we now call the AdvFS was the mega-safe file system, this abbreviation remains in some contexts. Be careful not to confuse the reference to the AdvFS with the memory file system, which is often abbreviated MFS. Although the name of the file system was changed some time ago, you'll still find references to the old name.

3. The AdvFS daemon is only useful if the graphical user interface (GUI) is going to be used either locally or on a remote system.

7

Advanced File System:
Advanced Topics

> The inherent vice of capitalism is the unequal sharing of blessings; the
> inherent virtue of socialism is the equal sharing of miseries.
> — *Sir Winston Churchill*

In the last chapter, we were concerned primarily with introducing you to the Advanced File System (AdvFS) and its commands. Our discussion of the new concepts should provide you with enough information to be successful with most of the tasks you will encounter in the day-to-day administration of this powerful file system. This chapter is intended to move you to the next level of understanding by introducing some advanced topics in AdvFS. We begin by discussing troubleshooting, including the theory behind on-disk structures, file tags, metadata, and the tools used for recovering from file system corruption. Then, we move on to techniques and tools for monitoring and tuning your AdvFS.

7.1   Troubleshooting

As with any file system, your AdvFS is bound to have problems from time to time. Although AdvFS tends to be quite robust, no file system can fully protect you in case of a hardware failure or a malicious system user. Your skills and knowledge will be tested the most at those times. Thus, troubleshooting is one of the most important and most difficult tasks you will perform as a Tru64 UNIX administrator.

In previous sections, we simply provided hints of some of the vital concepts we discuss here. Now, the time has come to cover these topics in greater depth. By understanding these concepts, you will gain the knowledge you need to tackle tough issues when they occur. We begin with an in-depth discussion of file tags.

7.1.1   File Tags

Up to this point we've touched a bit on file tags, but we haven't really explored them in any depth. In this section, we provide a detailed explanation of a file's tag and how this knowledge can be used to gather additional helpful information about an AdvFS using some of the Advanced Utilities. Although we cover the concepts here, we explore these utilities in greater detail in Appendix B.

7.1.1.1   Ordinary File Tags

Every file on an AdvFS has a unique number assigned to it known as its **tag**. The tag is somewhat like the inode number assigned to all files in a UFS. In fact, you can examine an ordinary file's tag number in the same way that you can find a UFS file's inode number.

```
# ls -li
total 2888
 364 drwxr-xr-x  2 root   system     8192     Nov 13 1998 old
 362 -rw-r--r--  1 root   system   295523     Oct 24 1997 ufs_handout.doc
 363 -rw-r--r--  1 root   system  2643013     Oct 24 1997 ufs_handout.ps
```

As stated previously, the first column of this output from the *ls(1)* command is the inode number for UFS, but for AdvFS this output represents the tag number. Note that you really can't tell from this output whether this file lies on a UFS or an AdvFS. For the average system user, it really doesn't matter, but for this discussion it is significant. Using the *showfile(8)* command, we can look at the same files and see the same information in the "Id" column.

```
# showfile *
     Id     Vol  PgSz  Pages  XtntType  Segs  SegSz  I/O    Perf  File
  16c.8001   2   16    1      simple    **    **     ftx    100%  old
  16a.8001   2   16    37     simple    **    **     async  100%  ufs_handout.doc
  16b.8001   2   16    323    simple    **    **     async  100%  ufs_handout.ps
```

Two main differences exist between the tag number given in *showfile(8)* and that given by *ls(1)*. The first is that the number is given as a hexadecimal. The second difference is that an additional number is given to the right of the decimal point, also in hex, that denotes the 32-bit **sequence number** of the file. Whenever an ordinary file is created on an AdvFS, it is assigned a unique file tag number in the range from 6 to $(2 \wedge 32)$ −1 from the tag free list. Tag numbers with the high bit set (8000 hex) are considered to be in use. If this is the first time this tag number is being used, then the tag sequence number is assigned a value of 8001 (hex) or 32,769 (decimal). This means that the tag is in use and it is the first one assigned. If this file tag is being reused, then the sequence number is incremented as the tag is taken off the free list.

Example:

In this example, we show how ordinary file tags are reused and the sequence number is incremented.

```
# touch test
# showfile test
    Id      Vol  PgSz  Pages  XtntType  Segs  SegSz  I/O    Perf  File
 3286.8002  3    16    0      simple    **    **     async  100%  test

# rm test

# touch test2

# showfile test2
    Id      Vol  PgSz  Pages  XtntType  Segs  SegSz  I/O    Perf  File
 3286.8003  1    16    0      simple    **    **     async  100%  test2

# rm test2

# touch test3

# showfile test3
    Id      Vol  PgSz  Pages  XtntType  Segs  SegSz  I/O    Perf  File
 3286.8004  2 1  6     0      simple    **    **     async  100%  test3
```

When the sequence number reaches the maximum value of 0xFFFE (hex) or 65,534 (decimal), the tag number is known as a **dead tag** and can never be reused again on that file system. Thus, there are 32,765 possible sequence numbers for each tag.

Example:

In order to prove that the tag really goes away, we developed a script called "dead_tag." When the following script is run until it completes on a quiescent AdvFS, it will produce a dead tag. Below, we show the script itself and some example output from a run of it.

```
 1 #!/bin/ksh
 2
 3 ITAG=""
 4 NTAG=""
 5 FILE=test1
 6
 7 touch ${FILE}
 8 ITAG=`showfile ${FILE} | tail -1 | awk -F. '{print $1}'
 9 NTAG=${ITAG}
10 while [ "X${ITAG}" = "X${NTAG}" ]
11 do
12    rm $FILE
13    touch ${FILE}
14    showfile ${FILE} | tail -1 | awk '{print $1}'
15    NTAG=`showfile ${FILE} | tail -1 | awk -F. '{print $1}'
```

```
16 done
17
18 print "Tag ${ITAG} is now a dead tag."
```
```
./dead_tag
5a5e.8001
5a5e.8002
```
```
[snip]
```
```
5a5e.fffb
5a5e.fffc
5a5e.fffd
5a5e.fffe
5a5d.8009
Tag 5a5e is now a dead tag.
```

7.1.1.2 The .tags Directory

When an AdvFS fileset is created, it contains a .tags pseudo directory in its root directory. This directory is immutable (i.e., it cannot be deleted or renamed and its permissions cannot be changed) and it doesn't actually contain anything (you cannot create files in it). In addition, the .tags directory can only be accessed by the root user.

The .tags directory is another way to access files via their tag number rather than via their file name. As stated previously, one way to obtain a file's tag is via the 'ls -i' command, which executes a *stat(2)* system call.

The .tags concept was originally implemented for use by a now defunct product known as **hierarchical storage manager (HSM)**[1] because it needed a way to open files via their tag. Over time, the .tags directory has turned out to be useful for other purposes. For example, *verify(8)* utilizes the .tags directory, as do other AdvFS utilities like *shfragbf(8)* and *tag2name(8)*. We cover the latter two utilities and other commands in Appendix B.

7.1.1.3 Special Reserved Tags

As mentioned previously, the .tags directory does not contain any files. When the AdvFS subsystem receives a request to open a file in .tags, for example "/usr/.tags/1," it knows that this is a special request, so it doesn't look for a file named "1" as it would in any other directory; instead, it opens the file with tag 1. This explains why you don't see anything when you issue a command like "ls /usr/.tags," but a command like "ls -li /usr/.tags/1" yields the following result:

```
1 ----------  0 root   system  74317824 Dec 31 1969
/usr/.tags/1
```

Each fileset has a set of special predefined tags as shown in Table 7–1.

TABLE 7–1   Special Reserved Tags

TAG	DESCRIPTION
1	Fragment file
2	Fileset's root directory
3	.tags directory
4	User quota file
5	Group quota file

Of all these, the fragment file does not have a corresponding real file name; therefore, you must specify .tags/1 when using *shfragbf(8)*.

7.1.1.4 Metadata Tags

In addition to ordinary tags and special reserved tags, metadata tags are also used to access a domain's metadata. This is where the power of the file tags really lies. Metadata tags always begin with the letter 'M' in order to differentiate them from ordinary file tags. Within the metadata file tag class, there are two types: the negative type and the positive type. The positive type of metadata tag is reserved for fileset tags and is discussed in the next section. Here, we cover the negative type of metadata tag, which consists of the following metadata files:

- For each domain, we have one transaction log, one root tag directory, and multiple fileset tag directories (one for each existing fileset).

- For each volume, we have one bitfile metadata table (BMT), one reserved BMT, one storage bitmap (SBM), and one miscellaneous metadata file (contains the fake superblock and the boot blocks).

The transaction log, root tag directory, BMT, storage bitmap, and miscellaneous metadata file all have special reserved tags. These can be calculated as shown in the Tables 7–2 and 7–3.

TABLE 7–2   Metadata Tags (pre-Tru64 UNIX 5.0)

METADATA TAG	TAG CALCULATION	VOLUME 1 EXAMPLE
BMT tag	M – (6 × (volume number))	M-6
SBM tag	M – (6 × (volume number + 1))	M-7
Root tag directory tag	M – (6 × (volume number + 2))	M-8
Log tag	M – (6 × (volume number + 3))	M-9
Misc metadata tag	M – (6 × (volume number + 5))	M-11

TABLE 7–3   Metadata Tags (Tru64 UNIX 5.0)

METADATA TAG	TAG CALCULATION	VOLUME 1 EXAMPLE
Reserved BMT tag	M – (6 × (volume number))	M-6
SBM tag	M – (6 × (volume number + 1))	M-7
Root tag directory tag	M – (6 × (volume number + 2))	M-8
Log tag	M – (6 × (volume number + 3))	M-9
BMT tag	M – (6 × (volume number + 4))	M-10
Misc metadata tag	M – (6 × (volume number + 5))	M-11

Example:

Once again, to access domain metadata via .tags, you need to precede the tag with an "M." So, we can do the following:

```
# ls -ls M-6 M-7 M-8 M-9 M-10 M-11
9224 ----------  0 root   system   9445376 Dec 31 1969  M-10
  32 ----------  0 root   system     32768 Dec 31 1969  M-11
   8 ----------  0 root   system      8192 Dec 31 1969  M-6
  16 ----------  0 root   system     16384 Dec 31 1969  M-7
   8 ----------  0 root   system      8192 Dec 31 1969  M-8
4096 ----------  0 root   system   4194304 Dec 31 1969  M-9

# showfile M-6 M-7 M-8 M-9 M-10 M-11
      Id      Vol  PgSz  Pages  XtntType  Segs  SegSz  I/O    Perf  File
fffffffa.0000   1   16     1    simple    **    **     ftx    100%  M-6
fffffff9.0000   1   16     2    simple    **    **     ftx    100%  M-7
fffffff8.0000   1   16     1    simple    **    **     ftx    100%  M-8
fffffff7.0000   1   16   512    simple    **    **     async  100%  M-9
fffffff6.0000   1   16  1153    simple    **    **     ftx     50%  M-10
fffffff5.0000   1   16     4    simple    **    **     ftx     50%  M-11
```

This command gives the sizes of the metadata files in the .tags directory. Note, you must explicitly give the metadata tag name to obtain this output. A wildcard-based *ls(1)* would return nothing.

For the transaction log, you can use *showfdmn(8)* to determine which volume contains the log. The root tag directory is only on one disk, but there is no easy way to determine which disk contains it (except via *ls(1)* in .tags, it will report "file does not exist").

7.1.1.5   Fileset Tag

Fileset tag directories essentially describe the files in a fileset (in fact, they are used to open files by their tag, so .tags can be thought of as the directory name of the fileset's tag directory; but not quite because tag directories have a different structure from normal file system directories). The tag of a fileset's tag directory can be obtained via the *showfsets(8)* command.

Example:

```
# showfsets usr_domain

usr
    Id              : 36b0147f.000473f0.1.8001
    Files           :   24628, SLim=    0, HLim=    0
    Blocks (512) : 1034390, SLim=    0, HLim=    0
    Quota Status : user=off group=off

var
    Id              : 36b0147f.000473f0.2.8001
    Files           :     949, SLim=    0, HLim=    0
    Blocks (512) :  327380, SLim=    0, HLim=    0
    Quota Status : user=off group=off

tmp
    Id              : 36b0147f.000473f0.3.8001
    Files           :       2, SLim=    0, HLim=    0
    Blocks (512) :      32, SLim=    0, HLim=    0
    Quota Status : user=off group=off
```

The tag for a fileset is the third number in the 'Id' for that fileset. So, here 'usr' has tag 1, 'var' has a tag of 2, and 'tmp' has tag 3. Note that fileset tags are relative the domain, so they do not conflict with file tags. So, we can look at the fileset tag directories for filesets 'usr', 'var', and 'tmp' as follows:

```
# cd /usr/.tags

# ls -ls M1 M2 M3
256     ----------  0 root    system  262144 Dec 31 1969 M1
64      ----------  0 root    system   65536 Dec 31 1969 M2
64      ----------  0 root    system   65536 Dec 31 1969 M3

# showfile M1 M2 M3
    Id      Vol  PgSz  Pages  XtntType  Segs  SegSz  I/O  Perf  File
  1.8001     1    16    32    simple     **    **    ftx   17%  M1
  2.8001     1    16     8    simple     **    **    ftx  100%  M2
  3.8001     1    16     8    simple     **    **    ftx  100%  M3
```

The previous examples use only the *ls(1)* and *showfile(8)* commands; however, other commands can be used. For example, other AdvFS-specific on-disk tools are also available (e.g., *vods(8)*, *vbmtpg(8)*, or *nvbmtpg(8)* will display the BMT to examine metadata). We provide a detailed discussion of all of the AdvFS Advanced Utilities in Appendix B. The following example shows how the *vods(8)* command uses the BMT metadata file (M-6) as one of its parameters.

Example:

As an example, we use an older tool called *vods(8)* to look at a portion of the BMT on volume 1. You'll notice that this domain is a megaVersion 3 (on-disk version), which means that we are probably looking at a file system on a Tru64 UNIX 4.0x system.

```
$ /usr/field/vods /usr/.tags/M-6 0

PAGE LBN   0 megaVersion  3 nextFreePg  0 freeMcellCnt 19 pageId  0
nextfreeMCId cell  9 page  0
================================================================================

CELL  0  nextVdIndex   1 linkSegment   0  tag,bfSetTag: -6,  -2
nextMCId cell  4 page  0
================================================================================

RECORD 0 bcnt 92 version 0    type  2 BSR_ATTR
state 3 BSRA_VALID
bfPgSz 16
transitionId 0
cloneId 0
cloneCnt 0
maxClonePgs 0
deleteWithClone 0
outOfSyncClone 0
cl.dataSafety 2 BFD_FTX_AGENT
cl.reqServices 0
cl.optServices 0
cl.extendSize 0
cl.s_shelfPri 0
cl.s_readAhead 0
cl.acl 0
cl.rsvd_sec1 0
cl.rsvd_sec2 0
cl.rsvd_sec3 0

RECORD 1 bcnt 80 version 0    type  1 BSR_XTNTS
type 0 BSXMT_APPEND
chainVdIndex 1
chainMCId cell  6 page  0
tertiaryVdIndex 0
tertiaryMCId cell  0 page  0
blksPerPage 16
segmentSize 0
delLink.nextMCId cell  0 page  0
delLink.prevMCId cell  0 page  0
delRst.mcid cell  0 page  0
delRst.vdIndex 0
delRst.xtntIndex 0
delRst.offset 0
delRst.blocks 0
xu.nwf.nwPgCnt 4
xu.nwf.nwrPage 0
xu.nwf.notWrit[0] 00000020
xu.nwf.notWrit[1] 00000002
xu.x.mcellCnt 4
xu.x.xCnt 2
xu.x.bsXA[ 0] bsPage  0 vdblk    32
xu.x.bsXA[ 1] bsPage  2 vdblk    -1
```

```
RECORD 2 bcnt 28 version 0    type  9 *** unknown ***
 80000000 80000000 00000000 01000000  ........ ........
 04000000 30000000          ....0...
[the rest of the output is omitted]
```

Metadata tags ("M") can be accessed from any of the mounted fileset's .tags directories because they are global to the domain. We discuss the meaning of each metadata file in section 7.1.3. The next section covers troubleshooting with the *advfs_err(4)* man page.

7.1.2 *Advfs_err(4)* man page

One of the first places you should consult when you receive an AdvFS error is the *advfs_err(4)* man page, which can be used to determine what the problem is and possibly provide a suggestion for how to fix it. This resource is often overlooked but can prove to be of great value.

Example:

The following example illustrates encountering an error when attempting to create a new clone fileset and looking up the error in the *advfs_err(4)* man page.

```
# clonefset efs_dmn clone_efs clone_clone_efs
clonefset: can't create clone file set 'clone_clone_efs' of set 'clone_efs' in '
clonefset: error = E_CANT_CLONE_A_CLONE (-1125)

# man 4 advfs_err
Reformatting page. Please wait... completed

advfs_err(4)                            advfs_err(4)

NAME

 advfs_err - Lists and describes error messages

[snip]

(-1125)
   E_CANT_CLONE_A_CLONE
   You cannot create a clone fileset from a clone fileset.

[snip]

# showfsets efs_dmn
efs
    Id              : 33f8551d.00064ecb.1.8001
    Clone is        : clone_efs
    Files           :    3, SLim=   1000, HLim=   3000
    Blocks (512)    : 23744, SLim=   2000, HLim=   6000 grc=  none
    Quota Status    : user=off group=off

clone_efs
    Id              : 33f8551d.00064ecb.2.8001
    Clone of        : efs
    Revision        : 1
```

Example:

The following example illustrates encountering an error when attempting to add a volume to an existing file domain and looking up the error in the *advfs_err(4)* man page.

```
# addvol -p 307600 /dev/vol/voltemp export_domain
bs_disk_init: disk is too small
addvol: error = ENO_MORE_BLKS (-1040)
addvol: Can't add volume '/dev/vol/voltemp' to domain
'export_domain'
```

```
# man advfs_err
Reformatting page. Please wait... completed
```

```
advfs_err(4)
```

```
[snip]
```

```
(-1040)
   ENO_MORE_BLKS
   The domain is out of disk space.
```

```
[snip]
```

7.1.3   AdvFS Metadata

In this section, we describe the different AdvFS metadata in greater detail. Naturally, we're not permitted to discuss internal workings of the AdvFS code, but our aim is to give you a flavor for the structural detail in order to aid in troubleshooting.

As we explained earlier, AdvFS is broken down into two layers: the **file access subsystem (FAS)** and the **bitfile access subsystem (BAS)**. The FAS is concerned with the POSIX interface, such as the directory hierarchy and system call access for reading and writing files. The BAS is responsible for bitfile manipulations, disk I/O, and volume and domain management. A **bitfile** is a generic file supported by the BAS onto which the FAS applies POSIX semantics implemented as an array of eight-kilobyte pages. The primary reason for this extra layer of abstraction is to facilitate migration of generic bitfiles between volumes without knowledge by the FAS layer. This is where most of the power of AdvFS lies. Most of the important features, such as adding and removing volumes, would not be possible without this separation.[2]

7.1.3.1   File Access Subsystem

The FAS layer of an AdvFS consists of the following three structures:

- Directories

- File attributes

- Quota files

The AdvFS directory structure is virtually identical to a UFS directory. An AdvFS directory size is always an even multiple of an eight-kilobyte page. When it is created, it is 8K in size and will always extend itself one page at a time. Each directory entry is 512 bytes (a disk block) in size and is structured as follows:

Tag Number   Entry Length   Name Length   Name tag + Seq #

Table 7–4 explains each of these fields in a directory. The first four fields are the same as for a UFS directory; however, some of the "padding" at the end includes a 64-bit tag + sequence number information, as discussed in section 7.1.1.1. This information is not there for a directory entry on a UFS.

TABLE 7–4   AdvFS Directory Entry Fields

FIELD	SIZE (BITS)	DATA TYPE	DESCRIPTION
Tag Number	32	integer	The tag number for the file
Entry Length	16	integer	The total size of the directory entry
Name Length	16	integer	The size of the file name for this directory entry
Name	variable	character	A character string for the directory entry name. The string is zero-padded to the nearest 32-bit boundary.
tag + sequence number	64	integer	The tag.sequence number for the file

Example:

The following example shows the first few entries using *showfile(8)* in a directory on an AdvFS and the hex dump of the directory itself. We have highlighted the tag + sequence number for the entry for file "test2.out" to illustrate how this information is stored.

```
# showfile .* *
    Id     Vol  PgSz  Pages  XtntType  Segs  SegSz  I/O    Perf  File
  c37.8036  1    16    1     simple    **    **     ftx    100%  .
  9bd.8001  1    16    1     simple    **    **     ftx    100%  ..
  c44.802f  1    16    2     simple    **    **     async  100%  getit
  b8a.8148  1    16    1     simple    **    **     async  100%  getit.c
  c56.83fc  1    16    2     simple    **    **     async  100%  readit
  6b.b209   1    16    1     simple    **    **     async  100%  readit.c
  27.c66e   1    16    1     simple    **    **     async  100%  test2.out
  c38.8050  1    16    299   simple    **    **     async  100%  verify_5.0
# cat . | od -hc | head -10
0000000   0c37 0000 0014 0001 002e 0000 0c37 0000
          7 \f \0 \0 024 \0 001 \0   .  \0 \0 \0   7 \f \0 \0
```

```
0000020   8036 0000  09bd 0000  0014 0002  2e2e 0000
     6 200 \0 \0 275 \t \0 \0 024 \0 002 \0  .  . \0 \0
0000040   09bd 0000  8001 0000  0027 0000  001c 0009
   275 \t \0 \0 001 200 \0 \0  ' \0 \0 \0 034 \0 \t \0
0000060   6574 7473  2e32 756f  0074 0000  0027 0000
     t  e  s  t  2  .  o  u  t \0 \0 \0  ' \0 \0 \0
0000100   c66e 0000  0b8a 0000  0018 0007  6567 6974
     n 306 \0 \0 212 \v \0 \0 030 \0 \a \0  g  e  t  I
```

The quota files in an AdvFS look like their UFS equivalents; however, they are always present and are immutable. You will also notice that the "quota.user" file always has the tag number of 4, and the "quota.group" file has the tag number of 5. These tag numbers are assigned upon file system creation and cannot be changed. See Table 7–1 for these and other special reserved file tags.

Example:

Here, we see the quota files on an AdvFS file domain + fileset. Although we don't show it here, each fileset in a domain has its own quota files.

```
# ls -lai
total 64
   2 drwxr-xr-x  6 root    system    8192 May 1 14:24 .
   2 drwxr-xr-x 35 root    system    8192 May 1 21:42 ..
   3 drwx------  2 root    system    8192 May 1 10:49 .tags
  16 dr-x------  2 root    system    8192 May 1 14:24 lost+found
   5 -rw-r-----  1 root    operator  8192 May 1 10:49
quota.group
   4 -rw-r-----  1 root    operator  8192 May 1 10:49 quota.user
   6 drwxrwxrwt  2 root    system    8192 May 1 10:51 test1
   7 drwxrwxrwt  3 root    system    8192 May 1 14:48 test2

# df -k .
Filesystem     1024-blocks     Used  Available Capacity Mounted
on
steve_domain#steve   250000       48     245712   0% /steve

# showfsets steve_domain
steve
    Id            : 390d993e.01038d3c.1.8001
    Files       :    13, SLim=    0, HLim=    0
    Blocks (512) :   96, SLim=    0, HLim=    0
    Quota Status : user=off group=off
```

The quota files are sparse and can seem to take up quite a bit of space on an AdvFS. The reason this happens is that for every user ID or group ID on the system, AdvFS automatically sets aside an entry in the quota files. Thus, very large values for the UID or GID are written into the file at a point quite far from the beginning of the file. Because these files are sparse, the impact should be minimal. As we have seen, sparse files do not allocate all of their blocks on the file system, thus they are not really taking up the space they report.

7.1.3.2 Bitfile Access Subsystem

The BAS layer of an AdvFS domain consists of the following structures, one for each volume:

- Bitfile metadata table
- Reserved bitfile metadata table (new in Tru64 UNIX 5.0)
- Storage bitmap
- Misc bitfile

In addition, as previously discussed, each domain has one each of the following contained on one of its volumes.

- Transaction log
- Root tag directory

Now, we discuss each of these structures.

7.1.3.3 Bitfile Metadata Table (BMT)

The **bitfile metadata table** (BMT) is used to store bitfile metadata and is a critically important part of the AdvFS structure. In lay terms, the BMT stores information about files contained only on a single volume in an AdvFS file domain. In Figure 7–1, we show an example of a BMT for a volume in a file domain.

Structurally, the BMT consists of an array of eight-kilobyte pages, where each page consists of a header and an array of fixed-size mcells.

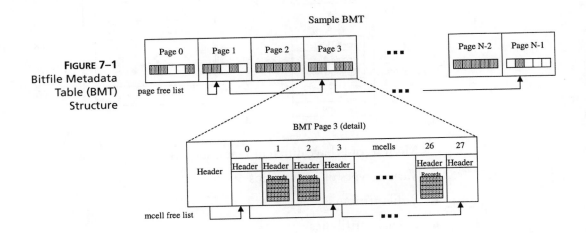

FIGURE 7–1
Bitfile Metadata
Table (BMT)
Structure

Each mcell contains one or more variable-length, typed records. Thus, the BMT bitfile has a three-level hierarchical structure:

- BMT pages
- BMT cells
- BMT records

The BMT is composed of **mcells**, or metadata cells, which are similar to inodes in the UFS. A single eight-kilobyte BMT page, as shown in Figure 7–2, is composed of a 16-byte header followed by 28 fixed-size (292 bytes each) mcells. One or more mcells can be linked to each other to describe a given bitfile, and the first mcell in the link is referred to as the **primary mcell**. Each mcell consists of variable-sized records describing attributes of the bitfile to which it refers.

FIGURE 7–2
BMT Page Structure

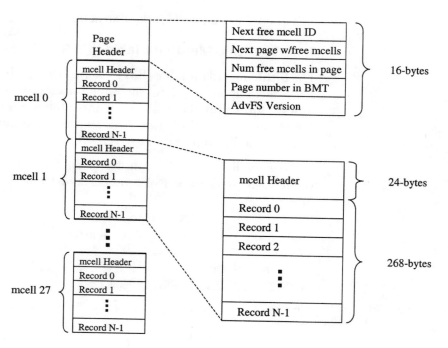

Mcell records have different types, such as:

- Various types of extent maps
- Bitfile attributes
- Domain attributes

- Virtual disk attributes

- Fragment attributes

- POSIX file statistics

- Symbolic link targets

The BMT is viewable on a mounted domain using the *showfile(8)* command, or with *vods(8)*, *vbmtchain(8)*, *vbmtpg(8)*, or *nvbmtpg(8)*. See Appendix B for a more detailed explanation of these tools and how they can be used.

Example:

One way to verify the structure we have discussed is to use the *nvbmtpg(8)* command to examine a specific mcell. This example shows mcell #2 on page 0 and volume 1 of the multivolume domain called "test_domain." This mcell has two records: the BSR_BFS_ATTR (bitfile set attributes) and BSR_SET_SHELVE_ATTR (the per bitfile set shelving attributes). Also, this is a Tru64 UNIX V5.x system because the megaVersion (on-disk version) is 4.

```
# df -k .
Filesystem      1024-blocks   Used  Available Capacity Mounted on
test_domain#test   250000       16    245520     0%    /test

# showfdmn test_domain

        Id                Date Created          LogPgs  Version  Domain Name
3803dad7.000cb9b5  Tue Oct 12 20:05:27 1999     512      4       test_domain

Vol  512-Blks    Free % Used Cmode Rblks Wblks Vol Name
 1L   100000    91488   9%    on  16384 16384 /dev/vol/rootdg/vol01
  2   100000    99888   0%    on  16384 16384 /dev/vol/rootdg/vol02
  3   100000    99888   0%    on  16384 16384 /dev/vol/rootdg/vol03
  4   100000    99888   0%    on  16384 16384 /dev/vol/rootdg/vol04
  5   100000    99888   0%    on  16384 16384 /dev/vol/rootdg/vol05
     ----------  ----------  ------
      500000     491040    2%

# cd /test/.tags
# /sbin/advfs/nvbmtpg -v M-10 0 2
=======================================================================
FILE "M-10"  BMT page 0
-----------------------------------------------------------------------
pageId 0 megaVersion 4
freeMcellCnt 19  nextFreePg -1  nextfreeMCId page,cell 0,9
-----------------------------------------------------------------------
CELL 2 linkSegment 1       bfSetTag -2 (fffffffe.0) tag 1 (1.8001)
next mcell volume page cell 0 0 0

RECORD 0  bCnt 220 version 0         BSR_BFS_ATTR (8)
bfSetId.domainId 3803dad7.cb9b5 (Tue Oct 12 20:05:27 1999)
bfSetId.dirTag 1 (1.8001)
```

```
fragBfTag 1 (1.8001)
nextCloneSetTag 0 (0.0)  origSetTag 0 (0.0)
nxtDelPendingBfSet 0 (0.0)
state BFS_READY  flags 0x0
cloneId 0  cloneCnt 0  numClones 0
fsDev 0xb559151f  freeFragGrps 0  oldQuotaStatus 0
uid 0  gid 1  mode 0744  setName "test"
fsContext[0], fsContext[1] 2.8001 (rootTag)
fsContext[2], fsContext[3] 3.8001 (tagsTag)
fsContext[4], fsContext[5] 4.8001 (userQuotaTag)
fsContext[6], fsContext[7] 5.8001 (groupQuotaTag)
fragGrps[0] firstFreeGrp  -1 lastFreeGrp  -1
fragGrps[1] firstFreeGrp  -1 lastFreeGrp  -1
fragGrps[2] firstFreeGrp  -1 lastFreeGrp  -1
fragGrps[3] firstFreeGrp  -1 lastFreeGrp  -1
fragGrps[4] firstFreeGrp  -1 lastFreeGrp  -1
fragGrps[5] firstFreeGrp  -1 lastFreeGrp  -1
fragGrps[6] firstFreeGrp  -1 lastFreeGrp  -1
fragGrps[7] firstFreeGrp  -1 lastFreeGrp  -1

RECORD 1  bCnt 36  version 0          BSR_SET_SHELVE_ATTR (17)
flags MSS_NO_SHELVE (0x4)
smallFile 5
readAhead 0
readAheadIncr 5
readAheadMax 50
autoShelveThresh 100
userId 0
shelf 0
```

7.1.3.4 Reserved Bitfile Metadata Table (RBMT)

In Tru64 UNIX 5.0, design changes were made to the on-disk structure to solve a difficult problem known as the BMT exhaustion problem, which we discuss in greater detail later in this chapter. The basic problem is caused by having a fixed-size BMT page 0, which is used to store mcells describing metadata files. In 5.0, the BMT page 0 contains metadata for only unreserved files; however, in prior versions, the BMT held metadata for both unreserved and reserved files. A **reserved file** in AdvFS is one of the metadata files we discussed earlier, whereas unreserved files are normal (non-metadata) user files. With a fixed-size BMT page 0 as in the previous design, the BMT eventually reaches a point where it can no longer expand. Thus, the expandable **reserved bitfile metadata table** (RBMT) replaces what was previously the fixed BMT page 0, effectively eliminating this problem. In the new design, the BMT is what we used to refer to as BMT page 1 and its extensions.

7.1.3.5 Storage Bitmap (SBM)

The storage bitmap (SBM) is an array of bits describing storage available and used on a given AdvFS volume. A clear bit indicates that a cluster[3] is unassigned and, conversely, a set bit means that a cluster is in use. A page of the SBM consists of eight-kilobyte pages, which yield 65,536 bits (minus overhead) for each page. The best method for examining the SBM on an AdvFS domain is by using one of the "new" domain examination tools known as *vsbmpg(8)*. Use of this tool is discussed in greater detail in Appendix B.

7.1.3.6 Fragment Bitfile

The fragment bitfile is used to keep track of free and used fragments in the file system. Because a page in an AdvFS consists of 8K, it would be a waste of space to store all smaller files in that size block. In addition, pieces of files that don't fit neatly into a full eight-kilobyte page are also put into a fragment. Thus, the fragment (similar to the frag used in UFS) is used in AdvFS to keep track of the smaller file bits. The logical structure of the fragment bitfile is a set of eight linked lists. The first list is the free list and consists of pointers to blocks that contain free frags. The second through eighth lists contain the fragment lists from 1-kilobyte to 7-kilobyte.

7.1.3.7 Transaction Log

The transaction log is a bitfile that allows an AdvFS domain to recover quickly from system interruptions. A single transaction log is maintained on one of the volumes in any AdvFS domain. The log consists of a circular list of log records, each of which has a unique logical sequence number assigned to it. Whenever a protected operation is performed in a domain, the log maintains records associated with the transaction. A protected operation would be anything that requires the entire transaction to either complete in its entirety or to abort (such as an update of a metadata structure). If the system crashes before the transaction has had a chance to complete, then the operation is rolled back the next time the domain is activated (e.g., one of the filesets is mounted).

The operation of the transaction log is complex and would take many pages to describe completely. You can examine the transaction log for a domain using tools described in Appendix B.

7.1.4 AdvFS On-Disk Structure

This section discusses the basics of the AdvFS on-disk structure. We first cover a little bit about the history and the previous on-disk versions that have existed. Then, we explain how the on-disk structure looks today.

7.1.4.1   On-Disk Structure Versions

AdvFS has been around for some time; however, its on-disk structure has not remained static and has continued to evolve. Table 7–5 shows the different on-disk structure versions[4] that have existed and which Tru64 UNIX versions utilized each. The latest changes were made in Tru64 UNIX version 5.0 and enabled some significant improvements.

TABLE 7–5   AdvFS On-Disk Versions

ON-DISK (MEGA)VERSION	TRU64 UNIX VERSION(S)	MAIN FEATURE
1	Field Test only	
2	1.0–2.x	Initial version
3	3.0–4.x	Changes to bitfile fragment format
4	5.0	Reserved BMT, 32-bit UID/GIDs and large quotas

7.1.4.2   Basic On-Disk Layout

The AdvFS on-disk structure is laid out as shown in Table 7–6 and Figure 7–3. This structure is the same for all volumes in a domain.

FIGURE 7–3
AdvFS On-Disk Structure

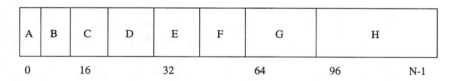

You'll note that if the virtual disk is not a system disk, then even though they exist, the boot blocks do not have any meaning. Also, the disk label may not be meaningful, particularly if the volume is a logical LSM volume.

TABLE 7–6   AdvFS On-Disk Structure Layout (Tru64 UNIX 5.0)

SECTION	BLOCKS	USAGE
A	0	Disk label
B	1 to 15	UFS boot blocks
C	16 to 19	Fake superblock
D	20 to 31	Unused
E	32 to 47	BMT page 0 (RBMT)
F	48 to 63	BMT page 1
G	61 to 95	AdvFS boot blocks (misc bitfile)
H	96+	BMT and file expansion

Example:

The AdvFS magic number that must be found at an offset of 1372 (decimal) into the fake superblock is 0x11081953[5] in hex. This number is used to validate whether an AdvFS exists on the device.

```
# df /export
Filesystem           512-blocks    Used    Available Capacity Mounted on
export_dmn#data      4099616       924348   3003104   24%     /export
# showfdmn export_dmn

         Id            Date Created             LogPgs  Domain Name
38a41e59.000f2cec  Fri Feb 11 09:36:09 2000     512    xport_dmn

Vol  512-Blks    Free   % Used Cmode Rblks  Wblks Vol Name
 1L  2049820  1492496    27%    on    128    128  /dev/vol/rootdg/volexport1
 2   2049820  1510608    26%    on    128    128  /dev/vol/rootdg/volexport2
     ---------- ---------- ------
     4099640   3003104    27%
# dd if=/dev/rvol/rootdg/volexport1 iseek=16 bs=512 count=3 | od -h
3+0 records in
3+0 records out
0000000 0000 0000 0000 0000 0000 0000 0000 0000
*
0002520 0000 0000 0000 0000 0000 0000 1953 1108
0002540 0000 0000 0000 0000 0000 0000 0000 0000
*
0003000
# dd if=/dev/rvol/rootdg/volexport2 iseek=16 bs=512 count=3 | od -h
3+0 records in
3+0 records out
0000000 0000 0000 0000 0000 0000 0000 0000 0000
*
0002520 0000 0000 0000 0000 0000 0000 1953 1108
0002540 0000 0000 0000 0000 0000 0000 0000 0000
*
0003000
```

7.2   Recovery

In this section, we discuss basic AdvFS troubleshooting techniques. We begin with recovery from domain panics, then move on to AdvFS I/O errors that you may sometimes see in the syslog files, cover some methods for dealing with corruption in an AdvFS domain, and finally finish up with discussions of the *verify(8)* and *salvage(8)* tools.

7.2.1   Domain Panics

In some instances, usually in the case of log or metadata write failure, the system takes a nonroot domain offline rather than panic. A **domain panic** prevents further access to the domain but allows filesets in the domain to be unmounted. Typically, an AdvFS domain panic signals a hardware problem; however, it may also indicate a software failure, particularly in a domain that contains critical system files, such as the root file system. AdvFS also periodically examines metadata, particularly after reading it from disk, and forces a domain panic if it detects corruption.

The benefit of an AdvFS domain panic is that it prevents further access by users to a single AdvFS file domain and allows the filesets in that domain to be unmounted and examined. In addition, all other AdvFS domains remain on line and in normal operation, unaffected by the domain panic. A domain panic message is logged with the following format:

```
AdvFS Domain Panic; Domain name Id domain_id
```

Normally, these domain panic messages are logged into the /var/adm/ messages file. Beginning in 4.0D, they are also logged into the /var/adm/ binary.errlog file.

Example:

This is an example of a domain panic message on a domain called "var_domain." It came from the messages file of a Tru64 UNIX 4.0x system.

```
AdvFS I/O error:
  Volume: /dev/rz1a
  Tag: 0xfffffffa.0000
  Page: 124
  Block: 11424
  Block count: 16
  Type of operation: Write
  Error: 5

bs_osf_complete: metadata write failed
AdvFS Domain Panic; Domain var_domain Id 0x32e4e8d9.00073ce0
AdvFS I/O error:
  Volume: /dev/rz1a
  Tag: 0xfffffff9.0000
  Page: 0
  Block: 112
  Block count: 16
  Type of operation: Read
  Error: 5
```

To recover an AdvFS domain from a domain panic, you need to collect as much information as you can about the condition of AdvFS filesets and metadata, in case you need to correct or document software problems for a problem report. Then, you need to take the steps that will let you run the *verify(8)* utility on the domain in an attempt to check the integrity of its filesets.

To recover from an AdvFS domain panic, we suggest you perform the following steps:

1. Use the *mount(8)* command to obtain a list of all the filesets in the domain. Then, use the *umount(8)* command to unmount all of the filesets in the domain. Note that the filesets in a domain must be unmounted to run the *verify(8)* utility that checks them. See the restrictions noted in the *verify(8)* reference page for more information.

2. If the problem is a hardware problem, then fix it before going to step 3.

3. Use *vfile(8)* or *savemeta(8)* to collect a copy of the on-disk meta-data in case a problem report is needed later.

4. Run the *verify(8)* utility on all of the filesets in the domain. See section 7.2.3 for information about how to run the *verify(8)* utility to detect and correct file system corruption.

5. If the *verify(8)* utility exits successfully, then mount all of the filesets you had unmounted in step 1. You can resume normal operations. If the *verify(8)* utility indicates that there is a problem and it cannot correct it, then recovery actions should be started.

6. If a failure prevents complete recovery, then you must first re-create the domain and restore the domain's data from backup media. Then, mount all of the restored filesets in the domain and resume normal operations. You should also file a problem report with Compaq.

7. As a last resort, if no current backup is available, the *salvage(8)* tool can be used to attempt to recover files from the damaged domain. See section 7.2.4 for an explanation of *salvage(8)*.

In some instances, it may be necessary to shut down the system to recover from a domain panic.

Beginning in Tru64 UNIX version 5.0, the behavior the system exhibits when a domain panic occurs has been changed. When *AdvfsDomainPanicLevel* is set to the default value of 1, a crash dump is created if a domain panic occurs in a domain that has any mounted filesets. When this parameter is set to 0, no crash dump is created during a domain panic. When set to 2, a crash dump is always created during a domain panic, whether or not the domain that took the panic has any mounted filesets. When set to 3, a domain panic is promoted to a system panic and the system crashes.

7.2.2   Interpreting AdvFS I/O Errors

Occasionally, you may run across an AdvFS I/O error message in /var/adm/messages with a format similar to the following:

```
AdvFS I/O error:
Domain#Fileset: <domain>#<fileset>
Mounted on: <directory>
Volume: <volume>
Tag: <tag_num>.<gen_num>
Page: <page_num>
Block: <block_num>
Block count: <block_count>
Type of operation: <type>
Error: <error>
To obtain the name of the file on which
the error occurred, type the command:
/usr/sbin/tag2name <directory>.tags/<tag_num>
```

These messages indicate that the AdvFS encountered a problem performing a standard UNIX system call and returned an error. The errors returned are typically an errno value, which can be found in the <sys/errno.h> header file. Table 7–7 describes the fields in an AdvFS I/O error message.

TABLE 7–7   AdvFS I/O Error Fields

FIELD	DESCRIPTION
domain	The name of the domain that received the error
fileset	The name of the fileset that received the error
directory	The mount point directory for the domain and fileset
volume	The name of the volume on which the file that had the error resided
tag_num	The tag number of the file that had an error. A negative number indicates a metadata tag.
gen_num	The sequence number of the file that had an error
page_num	The eight-kilobyte page that had the error
block_num	The starting 512-byte block that had the error
block_count	The number of 512-byte blocks in the bad page
type	The type of error received. This is either a read or write error.
error	The errno number received

With this information, you can use the *tag2name(8)* tool to determine the name of the file that has become corrupted (if it is not a metadata tag) and use this information to attempt recovery of the file or entire file system. See Appendix B for more information on *tag2name(8)*.

Example:

The following is an example of an AdvFS I/O error found in the messages file on a Tru64 UNIX system. The file turned out to be corrupt.

```
AdvFS I/O error:
  Domain#Fileset: CCS_domain#CCS
  Mounted on: /usr/CCS
  Volume: /dev/vol/rootdg/CCSvol
  Tag: 0x00007477.8001
  Page: 90
  Block: 2137344
  Block count: 32
  Type of operation: Write
  Error: 5
  To obtain the name of the file on which
  the error occurred, type the command:
  /sbin/advfs/tag2name /usr/CCS/.tags/29815
```

Once you see an AdvFS I/O error, you need to determine whether the file can be repaired or if the file system has to be recovered. One example of a corruption that was repaired using standard UNIX tools is described in Chapter 9. In many cases, the I/O error is associated with the on-disk block, and typical commands such as *mv(1)*, *cp(1)*, and *rm(1)* fail because of the underlying problem when accessing the file. So, re-creating the file system may be the only solution.

The first option is to restore the file system from known good backups. In some cases, this step is all that is required. In other cases, this option is not valid and recovering the file is a better solution, if possible. If all efforts to restore the file fail, then a couple of other options exist before re-creating the file system.

- *vdump(8)/vrestore(8):* When vdump(8) is used to back up the file, it will sometimes omit the bad file. Then, you re-create the file system and *vrestore(8)* re-creates from a clean file system.

- *verify(8):* Use the *verify(8)* utility to attempt to clean up the small corruption in-place. See section 7.2.3 for details on how to use *verify(8)*. The authors have not had great success using *verify(8)* to clean up small file and directory corruption like this, however. *Verify(8)* is much better for certain known metadata problems.

- *Temporarily work around the problem:* If the previous recovery fails, one possible workaround until another action can be scheduled is to move the bad file out of the way as follows:

```
# cd /mnt3/my_dir/
```

If all commands fail to help in replacing the file:

```
# sum bad.file          I/O Error, errno 6
# cp <file> bad.file    I/O Error, errno 6
# rm bad.file           I/O Error, errno 6
```

The following may isolate the file (by placing it in a unused directory):

```
# cd ..
# mv my_dir .trash_dir
# mkdir my_dir
# mv .trash_dir my_dir
```

In the next section, we discuss how to detect and correct AdvFS corruption using *verify(8)*.

7.2.3   Detecting and Correcting AdvFS Corruption

The *verify(8)* command checks on-disk structures such as the bitfile metadata table (BMT), the storage bitmaps, the tag directory, and the frag file for each fileset. It verifies that the directory structure is correct, that all directory entries reference a valid file (tag), and that all files (tags) have a directory entry. The *verify(8)* command checks the storage bitmap for double allocations and missing storage. It checks that all mcells in use belong to a bitfile and that all bitfiles have all of their mcells. The *verify(8)* command checks the consistency of free lists for mcells and tag directories. It checks that the mcells pointed to by tags in the tag directory match the corresponding mcells.

For each fileset in the specified file domain, the *verify(8)* checks the fragment file headers for consistency. In addition, for each file that has a fragment, the fragment file is checked to ensure that the fragment is marked as in use.

Syntax:

```
verify [-f|-d] [-v|-q] [-t] [-r] [-F] domain_name
```

TABLE 7–8   Flags for the *verify(8)* Command

FLAG	DESCRIPTION
domain_name	The name of the domain to be verified
-f	Creates a symbolic link to "fix" a lost file in the /mount_point/ lost+found directory; deletes any directory entries that do not have associated files; deletes files that have storage bitmap or extent map problems.
-d	Deletes lost files (that is, files with no directory entry).
-v	Prints file status information. Selecting this flag slows down the verify procedure.

TABLE 7–8   Flags for the *verify(8)* Command (Continued)

FLAG	DESCRIPTION
-q	Quiet mode. Prints minimal file status information.
-t	Displays the mcell totals.
-r	Checks the root file domain.
-F	Mounts the filesets of a file domain using the mount '-d' option if there is a mount failure of the file domain. Use this flag with caution.

Example:

This is an example of a *verify(8)* run on an uncorrupted file system.

```
# showfsets junk_domain
junk
    Id            : 34608122.0008e32f.1.8001
    Files         :    0, SLim=    0, HLim=   0
    Blocks (512)  :    0, SLim=    0, HLim=   0
    Quota Status  : user=off group=off

# mount junk_domain#junk /junk

# showfdmn junk_domain

        Id              Date Created              LogPgs   Domain Name
34608122.0008e32f   Wed Nov 5 09:22:26 1997       512     junk_domain

 Vol   512-Blks     Free     % Used  Cmode  Rblks  Wblks  Vol Name
  1L   2097152    2064416     2%      on     128    128   /dev/rvol/rootdg/vol1
  2     100000      75920    24%      on      64     64   /dev/rvol/rootdg/vol2
     ---------- ---------- ------
       2197152    2140336     3%

# umount /junk

# /sbin/advfs/verify junk_domain
+++ Domain verification +++

Domain Id 34608122.0008e32f

Checking disks ...

Checking storage allocated on disk /dev/rvol/rootdg/vol01

Checking storage allocated on disk /dev/rvol/rootdg/vol02

Checking mcell list ...

Checking mcell position field ...

Checking tag directories ...

+++ Fileset verification +++

+++ Fileset junk +++

Checking frag file headers ...
```

```
Checking frag file type lists ...

Scanning directories and files ...

Scanning tags ...

Searching for lost files ...
```

Example:

This is another example of a *verify(8)* run on an uncorrupted domain with the mcell totals displayed on a per-volume basis.

```
# /sbin/advfs/verify -t junk_domain
+++ Domain verification +++
Domain Id 34608122.0008e32f
Checking disks ...

Checking storage allocated on disk /dev/rvol/rootdg/vol01
display_mcell_totals: mcell count breakdown
  Inuse:21
    Primary:12
    Secondary:1
    Extent:6
    Other:2
    Bad:0
  Free:35
  Total:56

Checking storage allocated on disk /dev/rvol/rootdg/vol02
display_mcell_totals: mcell count breakdown
  Inuse:8
    Primary:6
    Secondary:0
    Extent:1
    Other:1
    Bad:0
  Free:48
  Total:56

Checking mcell list ...

Checking mcell position field ...

Checking tag directories ...

+++ Fileset verification +++

+++ Fileset junk +++

Checking frag file headers ...

Checking frag file type lists ...

Scanning directories and files ...

Scanning tags ...

Searching for lost files ...
```

7.2.4 Salvaging Corrupted AdvFS Domains

The *salvage(8)* tool recovers data from a fully or partially corrupted AdvFS domain. It ships as field test software with full documentation beginning with Tru64 UNIX version 4.0D. For recovery from AdvFS corruption prior to Tru64 UNIX version 4.0D (3.2C–4.0C), *salvage(8)* has been provided to customers on a case-by-case basis. For Tru64 UNIX versions before 3.2C, there is no recovery tool equivalent to *salvage(8)*.

The *salvage(8)* command does not fix AdvFS corruption in place in the way *fsck(8)* does for UFS. The *salvage(8)* tool must have enough disk space available in another directory on the system to hold all of the recovered files. As salvage runs, it re-creates the directory structure with all the files that it can recover from the original, corrupted file system. Files that are not recovered or that are only partially recovered are logged as such in the log. Partially recovered files are recovered with the .partial extension to their original location in the new directory structure, as long as you specify the '-p' option.

People are often confused about when or if *salvage(8)* should be used. There are no hard and fast rules, but as a guideline *salvage(8)* should be used only if the file system is unmountable because of massive corruption and current backups are not available. File systems that are mountable with just localized corruption should be cleaned up with *verify(8)*. With localized corruption, it is possible to direct *salvage(8)* to recover files from only a few directories. *Salvage(8)* has been successful in recovering most customer data, but it should not be a replacement for a sound backup strategy. Critical data should be appropriately backed up and restored, and *salvage(8)* should be used only as a last resort when there are no current backups to use to restore the re-created domain. Sometimes the best strategy is a full restore and an incremental *salvage(8)* to obtain any recently updated files.

Syntax:

```
New: salvage [-x | -p] [-1] [-S] [-v number] [-d time]
[-D directory] [-L path] [-o option] [-F format
[-f [archive]]] {-V special [-V special]... | domain} [fileset
[path]]
Old: salvage [-x | -p] [-1] [-S] [-v number] [-d time]
[-D directory] [-L path] [-o option] {-V special
[-V special...] | domain} [fileset [path]]
```

The new syntax is for salvage shipped with Tru64 UNIX version v4.0F and higher. Also, newer versions have been given out by Compaq support on a case-by-case basis. The flags for *salvage(8)* are covered in Table 7–9.

TABLE 7–9   Flags for the *salvage(8)* Command

FLAG	DESCRIPTION
domain	The name of the domain to be recovered. This is the domain name from /etc/fdmns.
fileset	The fileset to recover. This is the actual fileset name and not the mount point (unless they are the same). You can probably find this in /etc/fstab if you have entries in there for having the filesets mounted at boot time.
path	A path to recover (directory or single file). The path should be specified relative to the mount point of the fileset.
-x	Don't restore files that are only partially recoverable.
-p	Adds the .partial suffix to names of files that are only partially recoverable.
-l	Writes a message in the log file for every file recovered, with its status. (Default is summary and messages for partial and unrecovered files only.)
-S	Performs a sequential search of disk (this should be needed only when a massive amount of the metadata is destroyed). If *salvage(8)* reports that it cannot find any data or never completes, try using this flag.
-v number	Verbosity level for output. The possible values for this flag are: 0 = summary and errors. This is the default. 1 = lists partially recovered files, summary, and errors 2 = lists status of all files, summary, and errors
-d	Only files changed after this time should be recovered. The time format is the same as for the *at(1)* command: [[CC]YY]MMDDh-hmm[.SS], where CC is century, YY is last two digits of the year, MM is the month, DD is the day, hh is the hour, mm is minutes, and .SS is seconds. This commant is useful if you have a backup, but it is somewhat old. You can get the files that have changed since the backup.
-D directory	This flag specifies the destination directory to which the files will be recovered. If not specified, the default is cthe urrent working directory.
-L path	This flag specifies the directory and/or name for log file. The default is ./salvage.log.
-o	This flag is used to specify if *salvage(8)* should overwrite an existing file of the same name (takes "yes," "no," and "ask" as options).
-F format	This flag directs *salvage(8)* to recover files in an archive format instead of directly to a file system. The only legitimate value for format is tar.
-f [archive]	The name of the archive, if specified, or if a dash is specified, *salvage(8)* writes to standard output. If no archive is specified, the default is /dev/tape/tape0_d1.
-V	The volumes from which *salvage(8)* should recover data. If the domain is in /etc/fdmns, just specify the domain name in the command instead of using this switch. If not, you need to specify the block device using /dev/disk/dsknn format for each volume in the domain.

Because *salvage(8)* writes its recovered files to a different directory from the original, the '-f' flag should not be necessary in most cases. If you are recovering files to a directory containing files, then you should be sure to use this option to avoid problems.

If initial run of *salvage(8)* results in less than full recovery of all files, then it is worth trying to use sequential mode by specifying the "-S" switch as a last resort. This will result in a sequential scan of the file system looking for file system data and has been shown to be more successful in some cases than normal mode. On the other hand, the sequential mode can take much longer to run because it must visit all the blocks in the file system. Therefore, it is worth trying to use normal mode first on very large file systems and use sequential mode only if necessary.

The following two examples are real-world cases of *salvage(8)* runs on domains that were corrupted such that they were not mountable. In both cases, backups were not current and the data recovery was critical.

Example:

This is an example of scripted output as well as the salvage log file from an individual who ran *salvage(8)* to restore a corrupted file system and was completely successful. All of the lost files on the corrupted file system were completely recovered. This example should give you an idea of what the output from *salvage(8)* looks like when you run it.

```
sapcent:{/var/adm/crash}# salvage -p -l -v 2 -D /var/adm/crash/oracleGP1 GP11a1 fs1a1
salvage: Domain to be recovered 'GP11a1'
salvage: Fileset to be recovered 'fs1a1'
salvage: Volume(s) to be used '/dev/vol/GP1dg1/vol1a1'
salvage: Files will be restored to '/var/adm/crash/oracleGP1'
salvage: Logfile will be placed in '/var/adm/crash/oracleGP1/salvage.log'
salvage: Starting search of all filesets 21-Dec-1997 20:00:28
salvage: Starting search of fileset 'fs1a1'
salvage: Starting search of all volumes 21-Dec-1997 20:00:30
salvage: Starting search of volume '/dev/vol/GP1dg1/vol1a1'
salvage: Cleaning up memory structures for filesets 21-Dec-1997 20:00:30
salvage: Cleaning up memory structures for fileset tag 1
salvage: Loading file names for all filesets 21-Dec-1997 20:00:30
salvage: Loading file names on fileset 'fs1a1'
salvage: Starting recovery of all filesets 21-Dec-1997 20:00:33
salvage: Starting recovery of fileset 'fs1a1'
salvage: File './fs1a1' was successfully restored
salvage: File './fs1a1/.cshrc' was successfully restored
salvage: File './fs1a1/.dbenv_sapcent.csh' was successfully restored
salvage: File './fs1a1/.dbenv_sapcent.sh' was successfully restored
salvage: File './fs1a1/.kshrc' was successfully restored
salvage: File './fs1a1/.login' was successfully restored
salvage: File './fs1a1/.profile' was successfully restored
salvage: File './fs1a1/.sh_history_dev_ttyp0' was successfully restored
```

```
salvage: File './fs1a1/.sh_history_dev_ttyp1' was successfully restored
salvage: File './fs1a1/.tags' was successfully restored
salvage: File './fs1a1/64bo' was successfully restored
salvage: File './fs1a1/64bo/install' was successfully restored
salvage: File './fs1a1/64bo/install/64bo.ins' was successfully restored
salvage: File './fs1a1/64bo/install/64bo.map' was successfully restored
salvage: File './fs1a1/64bo/install/64bo.us' was successfully restored
salvage: File './fs1a1/64bo/install/64bo.vrf' was successfully restored
[snip]
```

The *salvage(8)* log for this recovery is shown as follows.

```
sapcent:{/var/adm/crash}# cat salvage.log

  Recovery of fileset fs1a1, fileset quotas:
Hard block limit = 0, soft block limit = 0
Hard file limit = 0, soft file limit = 0
./fs1a1 : 2 : successfully restored
./fs1a1/.cshrc : 171 : successfully restored
./fs1a1/.dbenv_sapcent.csh : 176 : successfully restored
./fs1a1/.dbenv_sapcent.sh : 175 : successfully restored
./fs1a1/.kshrc : 172 : successfully restored
./fs1a1/.login : 170 : successfully restored
./fs1a1/.profile : 173 : successfully restored
./fs1a1/.sh_history_dev_ttyp0 : 3803 : successfully restored
./fs1a1/.sh_history_dev_ttyp1 : 3804 : successfully restored
./fs1a1/.tags : 3 : successfully restored
./fs1a1/64bo : 3288 : successfully restored
./fs1a1/64bo/install : 3289 : successfully restored
./fs1a1/64bo/install/64bo.ins : 3293 : successfully restored

[snip]

./fs1a1/xa : 3300 : successfully restored
./fs1a1/xa/admin : 3312 : successfully restored
./fs1a1/xa/admin/xaview.sql : 3313 : successfully restored
./fs1a1/xa/doc : 3310 : successfully restored
./fs1a1/xa/doc/README.doc : 3311 : successfully restored
./fs1a1/xa/install : 3301 : successfully restored
./fs1a1/xa/install/catxa.orc : 3315 : successfully restored
./fs1a1/xa/install/partial.prd : 3303 : successfully restored
./fs1a1/xa/install/xa.ins : 3306 : successfully restored
./fs1a1/xa/install/xa.map : 3304 : successfully restored
./fs1a1/xa/install/xa.us : 3308 : successfully restored
./fs1a1/xa/install/xa.vrf : 3305 : successfully restored
./fs1a1/xa/xa.h : 3309 : successfully restored
5088 files processed, including 190 directories
4641 successfully recovered, 0 partially recovered
447 recovered larger, 0 unrecovered
0 had no attributes.
```

Example:

The following is an example of a run of *salvage(8)* to restore a corrupted file system that was not completely successful. The salvage.log file showed that all but four of the files were successfully restored.

```
# more salvage.log
  Recovery of fileset pharma_fs, fileset quotas:
Hard block limit = 0, soft block limit = 0
Hard file limit = 0, soft file limit = 0
./pharma_fs : 2 : successfully restored
./pharma_fs/.tags : 3 : successfully restored
./pharma_fs/bounds : 1070 : successfully restored
./pharma_fs/quota.group : 5 : successfully restored
./pharma_fs/quota.user : 4 : successfully restored
./pharma_fs/sapedi : 243 : successfully restored
./pharma_fs/sapedi/.$ADF$a.dml;5 : 287 : successfully restored
./pharma_fs/sapedi/.$ADF$account_check.lis;7 : 498 : successfully restored
./pharma_fs/sapedi/.$ADF$ap.lis;1 : 730 : successfully restored
./pharma_fs/sapedi/.$ADF$ar.com;2 : 301 : successfully restored
./pharma_fs/sapedi/.$ADF$ar.log;3 : 303 : successfully restored
./pharma_fs/sapedi/.$ADF$ar_r_aged_debt_by_due_date_type.lis;1 : 634 : success-
fully restored
./pharma_fs/sapedi/.$ADF$ar_r_aged_debt_sales.dml;1 : 628 : successfully restored
./pharma_fs/sapedi/.$ADF$ar_tr_type.dml;3 : 307 : successfully restored
./pharma_fs/sapedi/.$ADF$b.dml;2 : 309 : successfully restored
./pharma_fs/sapedi/.$ADF$batch.log;1 : 420 : successfully restored

[snip]

./pharma_fs.lost+found/tag_133 : 133 : successfully restored
./pharma_fs.lost+found/tag_134 : 134 : successfully restored
./pharma_fs.lost+found/tag_135.partial: 135 : partially recovered
   missing bytes 0 to 16383
./pharma_fs.lost+found/tag_137 : 137 : successfully restored
./pharma_fs.lost+found/tag_138 : 138 : successfully restored
./pharma_fs.lost+found/tag_139 : 139 : successfully restored

[snip]

./pharma_fs.lost+found/tag_92 : 92 : successfully restored
./pharma_fs.lost+found/tag_93 : 93 : successfully restored
./pharma_fs.lost+found/tag_94 : 94 : successfully restored
./pharma_fs.lost+found/tag_95 : 95 : successfully restored
./pharma_fs.lost+found/tag_96 : 96 : successfully restored
./pharma_fs.lost+found/tag_98 : 98 : successfully restored
./pharma_fs.lost+found/tag_99 : 99 : successfully restored
1135 files processed, including 6 directories
953 successfully recovered, 4 partially recovered
178 recovered larger, 0 unrecovered
1 had no attributes.
```

7.2.5 BMT Exhaustion

In Tru64 UNIX prior to version 5.0, it was possible to get an "out of space" error for user files before the AdvFS domain actually runs out of space. This problem, which is somewhat analogous to running out of inodes on a UFS, is generally known as the **BMT exhaustion problem**. On systems that consist primarily of small files (less than 8K) and regularly create and delete very large numbers (many hundreds of thousands) of these small files, AdvFS can run out of metadata space. Examples of systems that are prone to this problem are Usenet News servers and mail servers. In Tru64 UNIX 5.0, the way the BMT works has been redesigned to eliminate the possibility of exhaustion; however, because AdvFS version 3 domains can exist in 5.0, it is still important to understand these concepts.

There are basically two strategies for dealing with this issue: (1) fixing the problem after it has been encountered and (2) avoiding the problem by changing default domain parameters for the domain's volumes.

7.2.5.1   Strategy #1—Fix the Problem

The first strategy for fixing this problem is to attempt to clean up the BMT exhaustion after the fact. This process is often painful, but there are some reasonable strategies for cleaning it up. One thing to keep in mind is that although it is common to use the *defragment(8)* command to defragment files, this command is not capable of defragmenting metadata. Therefore, there are three common methods for dealing with the problem:

1. *Offline.* This method simply assumes that once the file domain is restored, the files are written to the disk and metadata extends itself in a contiguous fashion. This assumption is generally true for the files themselves as well. It might also be desirable to preallocate metadata when making the new file domain or adding volumes so that you can be sure that the BMT is contiguous. In Tru64 UNIX 4.0D and higher, preallocation may not be necessary because of the soft preallocation scheme. With this strategy, some downtime is required for that domain while the operation is in progress. Therefore, for large domains, your system could be down for awhile.

2. *Online.* This method can be accomplished while the domain is online and active, thus minimizing the impact on the domain users. The downside is that additional disk space needs to be available for the additional volume. This new volume needs to be large enough to hold all of the files and metadata that will migrate to it when the *rmvol(8)* command is executed. The amount of needed additional disk space can be lessened if multiple volumes are in the domain already. Thus, you simply need a volume that is at most the size of the largest volume in the domain already. Another downside is that your users will notice a performance impact while the file migrations are going on. You should plan to do this at a period of lower system activity in order to lessen the impact.

3.   *Conversion.* This method is for Tru64 UNIX 5.0 and higher only. You can convert your old domains from version 3 to version 4 on-disk structure. Unfortunately, this is not accomplished for you as in the past on-disk structure updates. It must be done by backing up the data, remaking the domain with *mkfdmn(8)* and *addvol(8)*, and restoring it. This could be done online with enough disk space and just pipe *vdump(8)* to *vrestore(8)* from one directory to another. This method also requires some downtime for the domain, just like in offline restoration.

Because the online method tends to be the most popular at high-profile sites, we focus on that one for now. The steps to follow for an online recovery from BMT exhaustion are:

1.   Identify a temporary volume that is large enough to hold the existing data and metadata. If the affected domain was constructed using mirrored LSM volumes, then the mirrors could easily be broken to make temporary volumes to add to the existing file domain.

2.   Gather some information about the domain.

a. First, find out the names and volume numbers for each of the volumes using *showfdmn(8)* as follows:

```
# showfdmn <domain>
```

Example:

In this example, we see that there is only a single volume in the export_domain domain. This volume number is 1, and the volume name is /dev/rz6c.

```
# showfdmn export_domain
```

Id	Date Created		LogPgs	Domain Name		
33f1c9d4.0000d5f0	Wed Aug 13 10:51:00 1997		512	export_domain		
Vol	512-Blks	Free	% Used	Cmode	Rblks	Wblks Vol Name
1L	2050860	797360	61%	on	256	256 /dev/rz6c

b. Second, find out one of the mount points for the domain as follows:

```
# df | grep <mount-point>
```

Example:

In this example, the mount point for this domain is called /export.

```
# df | grep export
export_dmn#data    6144000    2019522    2189104   48%  /export
```

3.   Next, use the volume information gathered in step #2 to find out how fragmented the BMT really is. Use the following commands:

```
# cd /<mount-pt>/.tags
# showfile -x M-(<vol #> * 6) | grep extentCnt
```

With this extent count number, if it's close to or at 683, then you are out of BMT space for that volume.

Example:

This is an example of how to use *showfile(8)* to quickly find the number of extents in each volume's BMT. Notice here that volume 1 has 683 extents.

```
# cd /export/.tags
# showfile -x M-6 | grep extentCnt
    extentCnt: 683
```

At this stage, while executing the *showfile(8)* commands for each volume, we'll need to record the "Pages" value for each volume as follows:

```
# showfile -x M-(<vol #> * 6)
```

Then, take all the "Pages" values for all the volumes and add them together to get the total usage for the BMT so far in eight-kilobyte pages. Take the total, double it, and divide by the number of expected volumes to use it for the next step.

Example:

This is an example of how to use *showfile(8)* to examine the full extent map of an exhausted BMT and gather the "Pages" number. In this case, it is 153,800. If we double this value, we get 307,600. We're only going to have one volume when we're done, so we only divide by 1 to get our final preallocation number of 307,600.

```
# showfile -x M-6
       Id      Vol  PgSz   Pages  XtntType  Segs  SegSz  I/O   Perf  File
ffffffffa.0000  1   16    153800  simple    **    **     ftx   100%  M-6

             extentMap: 1
               pageOff  pageCnt   vol   volBlock    blockCnt
                     0        2     1         32          32
                     2      128     1       9680        2048
                   130      128     1     112304        2048
                   258      128     1     228176        2048
                   386      128     1     316400        2048
                   514      128     1     411392        2048
                   642      128     1     502880        2048
                   770      128     1     707008        2048

           [snip]

             extentCnt: 683
```

```
# bc
153800*2
307600
```

4. Add the new volume from step #1 to the domain:

```
# addvol -p <2x usage/num vols> <block device> <domain>
```

Example:

Here, we show how to add in the new volume with a preallocated BMT using *addvol(8)* with the '-p' switch.

```
# advol -p 307600 /dev/vol/voltemp export_domain

# showfdmn export_domain
```

Id	Date Created	LogPgs	Domain Name
33f1c9d4.0000d5f0	Wed Aug 13 10:51:00 1997	512	export_domain

Vol	512-Blks	Free	% Used	Cmode	Rblks	Wblks	Vol Name
1L	2050860	797360	61%	on	256	256	/dev/rz6c
2	2087584	2087232	0%	on	128	128	/dev/vol/voltemp
	----------	----------	------				
	4138444	2884592	30%				

5. Remove and add the existing volumes one at a time. Each time the new volumes will be created with a larger preallocated BMT.

```
# rmvol <block device> <domain>
# addvol -p <(2x usage/<num vols>)> <block device> <domain>
```

6. When finished with all the original volumes, remove the last new temporary volume.

```
# rmvol <block device> <domain>
```

7. Finally, balance the volumes, if necessary as follows:

```
# balance <domain>
```

Once you have finished with this procedure, you will have expanded and balanced BMT. You should also be able to add many more new files to the domain.

7.2.5.2 Strategy #2—Avoid the Problem

To avoid this problem, preallocate the metadata immediately after the file domain is created and/or additional volumes are added.

For 3.x versions:

This can be done by writing a script (or C program) that creates and then deletes the estimated number of files that are expected to exist in the

AdvFS domain (the files created by the script should be empty). For example, the following ksh script preallocates metadata for 1000 files:

```
#!/bin/ksh

integer f=1000
  while ((f > 0))
  do
   touch prealloc_$f
   f=f-1
  done

rm prealloc_*
```

Needless to say, this is a long process for both the creation and later deletion of the zero-sized files. This can take many hours to complete for a large domain with many expected files. For some of the 3.x versions, you can request patches from Compaq that will add the '-x' and '-p' flags to *mkfdmn(8)* and *addvol(8)*. In that case, it is preferable to use those instead.

For 4.x versions:

Use the '-x' and '-p' switches to *mkfdmn(8)* and *addvol(8)* to increase the number of file system blocks (8K) to extend or preallocate the BMT, respectively.

For version 5.0 and higher:

If version 4 on-disk structure is used, then this problem has been completely eliminated by redesigning the way BMT is used and the introduction of the reserved BMT (RBMT). Otherwise, see the discussion for 4.x versions.

7.2.5.3   BMT Parameters

To set the BMT to grow by more than 128 pages each time additional metadata extents are needed, use the *mkfdmn(8)* command with the '-x' flag set to specify a number of pages greater than 128. You can increase the number of pages to any value; however, larger values tend to be less useful the larger they get. Table 7–10 shows suggested guidelines from the *mkfdmn(8)* reference page. The values on this table can be extrapolated linearly if more files are needed.

TABLE 7–10   Bitfile Metadata Table Extent Growth Values

NUMBER OF FILES	SUGGESTED BMT EXTENT SIZE (IN PAGES)	BMT SIZE (IN PAGES)
Less than 50,000	default (128)	3,600
100,000	256	7,200
200,000	512	14,400
300,000	768	21,600
400,000	1,024	28,800
800,000	2,048	57,600

If you make a file domain using the '-p' or '-x' flags to increase the BMT extent allocations, then you should use the same flag with the same number of pages when you add a volume to the file domain with the addvol command. See our previous discussion of the *addvol(8)* command for information about adding a volume to a file domain. Once again, we don't want extent growth to be out of balance across the different volumes in a domain.

Use a value in the -x num_pages argument that maintains the following ratio between the BMT extent size (the number of pages for the '-x' parameter) and the log file size (the number of pages for the '-l' parameter):

```
BMT extent size <= (log file size × 8184) / 4
```

It takes about one minute to process 5000 BMT extent size pages with the '-x' flag. A process that initiates a BMT extent size operation must take into account that a very large value for '-x' will take a long time to complete. Therefore, you might see a delay in your applications while this BMT expansion is in progress.

One question that often comes up is: "How do you find out what value of '-x' was used to *mkfdmn(8)* or *addvol(8)* for a particular volume?" You can use the following command to get the extent count value for a volume in a domain:

```
# /sbin/advfs/vbmtpg <volume> | grep bmtXntPgs
```

Example:

The following example illustrates how the '-x' flag was used to improve the performance of the BMT in a Tru64 UNIX 4.0B domain but failed to live up to the requirements.

Here, the system administrator followed the table in the *mkfdmn(8)* man page to create a two-volume domain with larger '-x' value so the BMT would be large enough to hold all the millions of files he intended to store on the domain. He calculated that he needed 2048 pages of BMT for each volume. Notice that he used the same value for the '-x' flag for each volume in the domain. This is not required, but it is a good idea to prevent an imbalance in the BMT usage between the volumes.

```
# mkfdmn -x 2048 /dev/vol/vol08 test_dmn
# mkfset test_dmn test
# addvol -x 2048 /dev/vol/vol09 test_dmn
# mount test_dmn#test /mnt2
# showfdmn test_dmn
```

```
      Id              Date Created              LogPgs   Domain Name
3404192a.000ef6a9    Wed Aug 27 08:10:18 1997   512      test_dmn

Vol  512-Blks      Free % Used  Cmode   Rblks   Wblks   Vol Name
 1L  3000000    2991136     0%     on     128     128   /dev/vol/vol08
 2   3000000    2999536     0%     on     128     128   /dev/vol/vol09
     ------------------- ------
     6000000    5990672     0%
# showfsets test_dmn
test
    Id               : 3404192a.000ef6a9.1.8001
    Files            :      2, SLim=    0, HLim=    0
    Blocks (512)     :     32, SLim=    0, HLim=    0
    Quota Status     : user=off group=off    0, HLim=    0
# showfile -x /mnt2/.tags/M-6

    Id         Vol  PgSz  Pages  XtntType  Segs  SegSz   Log    Perf   File
ffffffffa.0000   1   16     2    simple     **    **     ftx    100%   M-6
    extentMap: 1
      pageOff    pageCnt    vol   volBlock   blockCnt
            0          2      1         32         32
    extentCnt: 1
```

At this point, we have a brand-new domain with no files on it. The next few commands are executed after the usage on the domain has increased the number of files significantly. Here, we see more than 1.8 million files in the "test" fileset, comprising approximately 3.7 million blocks.

```
# showfsets test_dmn
test
    Id               : 3404192a.000ef6a9.1.8001
    Files            : 1806637, SLim=    0, HLim=    0
    Blocks (512) : 3714302, SLim=    0, HLim=    0
    Quota Status : user=off group=off
```

At this point, the customer is complaining that he can no longer create files on the domain, although there appears to be free space on it. We see that BMT on the second volume is exhausted, thus no more files can be created on it.

```
# showfile -x /mnt2/.tags/M-12 | grep extentCnt
    extentCnt: 683
# df /mnt2
Filesystem    512-blocks    Used Available Capacity Mounted on
test_dmn#test  6000000 3714302     154384      97%     /mnt2
```

So, the system administrator did some upfront domain maintenance on the domain so he could create more files than the default value of '-x' would have allowed; however, the exhaustion still eventually occurred. After investigating, he found that this resulted from the fragmentation that developed on the domain over time. Once the domain becomes fragmented, it really doesn't matter what value was used for '-x' because the BMT extent allocations have to come out of fragmented holes in the volume that are less likely to give the full '-x' value. This was the idea behind the introduction of the '-p' flag.

Example:

In this example, another system administrator calculated that in order to create all the files needed on the file system, a '-p' value of 108,576 was needed on a single-volume domain.

```
# mkfdmn -p 108576 /dev/vol/vol08 test_dmn

# mkfset test_dmn test

# mount test_dmn#test /mnt2

# showfile -x /mnt2/.tags/M-6
    Id         Vol PgSz   Pages XtntType  Segs SegSz  Log Perf File
ffffffa.0000    1   16  108578   simple    **    **   ftx 100% M-6

  extentMap: 1
    pageOff  pageCnt  vol  volBlock  blockCnt
       0        2      1      32        32
       2     108576    1     848     1737216
  extentCnt: 2
```

The previous command showed that the BMT was preallocated as requested. The BMT page 2 size should be the same as the value used for the '-p' parameter. In this case it is. As the file system fills up, we see that the BMT still expands itself past the second extent.

```
# showfsets test_dmn
test
    Id              : 3402ecde.00017d5f.1.8001
    Files           :    1561757, SLim=    0, HLim=   0
    Blocks (512)    :    3210838, SLim=    0, HLim=   0
    Quota Status    : user=off group=off    0, HLim=   0

# showfile -x /mnt2/.tags/M-6
    Id Vol PgSz Pages XtntType Segs SegSz Log Perf File
ffffffa.0000  1  16 112034  simple   **    ** ftx 100% M-6

  extentMap: 1
    pageOff  pageCnt  vol   volBlock   blockCnt
       0        2      1      32         32
       2     108576    1     848      1737216
    108578   128      1    4973408     2048
    108706   128      1    5757968     2048
    108834   128      1    1830368     2048
    108962   128      1    2223296     2048
    109090   128      1    2616096     2048
    109218   128      1    3009024     2048
    109346   128      1    3401952     2048
    109602   128      1    4187680     2048
    109730   128      1    4580608     2048
    109858   128      1     960816     2048
```

```
    109986  128    1    2353664    2048
    110114  128    1    3139232    2048
    110242  128    1    3532080    2048
    110370  108    1    2748096    1728
    110478  13     1    3707984    208
    110491  7      1    3708960    112
    110498  107    1    5910848    1712
    110605  19     1    3892272    304
    110624  2      1    3892592    32
    110626  105    1    5629344    1680
    110731  15     1    4060048    240
[snip]
    111650  89     1    3141280    1424
    111739  39     1    5383664    624
    111778  89     1    3177360    1424
    111867  39     1    5556256    624
    111906  88     1    4450688    1408
    111994  40     1    5740320    640
    extentCnt: 54
```

As the usage continues to increase, we see that the BMT once again becomes exhausted and no more files can be created on the domain. Clearly, the system administrator's calculation was low. He should have used a larger value for '-p' because at least 112,034 was needed.

```
# showfile -x /mnt2/.tags/M-6 | grep extentCnt
    extentCnt: 683
# showfsets test_dmn
test
    Id           : 3402ecde.00017d5f.1.8001
    Files        : 1783161, SLim=    0, HLim=    0
    Blocks (512) : 3666042, SLim=    0, HLim=    0
    Quota Status : user=off group=off
```

Table 7–11 gives you a general idea for different cases, based on the values given to *mkfdmn(8)* or *addvol(8)* of '-x' and '-p', of what the extent map should look like assuming the domain does not become fragmented before filling out the BMT extent map.

TABLE 7–11 Example BMT Extent Map Allocations

EXTENT	DEFAULT	-x 1024	-P 20000	-x 2048 -P 30000
1	2	2	2	2
2	128	1024	20,000	30,000
3	128	1024	128	2048
4	128	1024	128	2048
. . .	. . .	. . .	. . .	. . .
. . .	. . .	. . .	. . .	. . .
683	128	1024	128	2048

Should the domain become fragmented before filling out the BMT extent map, then you'll see the size of the extents at some point after the second one will diminish and be smaller than the default (or the value specified using the '-x' switch). It is very difficult, if not impossible, to predict what those sizes will be because the file system attempts to find the largest hole it can to hold the extent. The size of this hole depends on the fragmentation of the file system at the time the system attempts to find the extent. The following is a discussion of the BMT parameters to the *mkfdmn(8)* command.

Example:

In this example, we have a domain called pdp_domain, which has a single volume in it. We would like to figure out what value was used for the '-x' and '-p' to *mkfdmn(8)* when this domain was created because we are planning to add a new volume to the domain and match up the parameters in the new volume with the existing one.

```
# showfdmn pdp_domain
        Id                Date Created            LogPgs  Domain Name
38d2e2b3.000c212e  Fri Mar 17 20:58:11 2000      512     pdp_domain

Vol   512-Blks    Free      % Used  Cmode  Rblks  Wblks  Vol Name
 1L   2000000   1831248       8%      on    128    128   /dev/vol/volpdp1170
```

So, here we use the *vbmtpg(8)* command to examine the bmtXtntPgs field in mcell 4 of the BMT using the following command:

```
# /sbin/advfs/vbmtpg /dev/rvol/volpdp1170 | grep bmtXtntPgs
bmtXtntPgs 4096
```

This directly gives us a '-x' value of 4096. So, can we now figure out the '-p' value? The answer is not so simple, but in this case the answer is yes. Let's look at the output from *showfile(8)* on the BMT itself for this volume.

```
# showfile -x /mnt/.tags/M-6
    Id          Vol  PgSz  Pages  XtntType  Segs  SegSz  I/O  Perf  File
ffffffa.0000    1    16   10002  simple     **    **    ftx  100%  M-6

  extentMap: 1
    pageOff      pageCnt   vol   volBlock   blockCnt
       0            2       1      32          32
       2          10000     1      368        160000
  extentCnt: 2
```

You'll notice that the second extent in the BMT is 10,000. Usually, based on Table 7–11, if this is not the same as the '-x' value, then it is probably the '-p' value. That, and the fact that we have no other BMT allocations, leads us to the conclusion that this is probably the '-p' value.

7.2.5.4   Soft BMT Preallocation

In Tru64 UNIX version 4.0D, the internal algorithm for allocating BMT and all the reserved files was changed to include a "reservation" or "soft preal-location" scheme. Using this algorithm, the file system will pre-reserve a certain amount of space that will be used for BMT expansion. Thus, as long as the space is not needed for storing files, it will remain available in case the BMT needs to expand. As the BMT expands, the effect on the BMT extent map is that it will look as if the '-p' switch was used to preallocate with a single large extent #2. Of course, when the reserved space is completely used, the volume will revert to expanding at the '-x' value. Although this greatly reduces the chance that BMT exhaustion will occur, it does not eliminate it.

Another caveat is that if this domain was a carryover created before upgrading to 4.0D or later, then this BMT preallocation scheme is not followed. So, in order to take advantage of this feature, domains must have been created or volumes added in 4.0D or later.

Although the reservation is for all reserved files, the BMT is the one most likely to grow. The initial reservation (one-fifth of the volume) is meant to be sufficient for the metadata needs of the entire volume, although if the reservation is used up, the expansion process proceeds as before.

7.3   Tuning

In this section, we cover some methods and commands used for improving the performance of your AdvFS. We start with a discussion of the *advfsstat(8)* tool. This utility is quite invaluable, but also very complex. After that, we go into the AdvFS tuning parameters that you can modify in the /etc/sysconfigtab file on your system. These parameters can also be difficult to understand, but we attempt to sort them out for you. Finally, we cover a few other ways in which performance can be improved, most of which we have already covered in other discussions. Two topics that are new to Tru64 5.0 are the direct I/O capability and the directory index hashing features. To get more information on the other areas, such as defragmenting, we refer you to those sections in which we discuss that topic.

7.3.1   Gathering AdvFS Statistics

The *advfsstat(8)* command displays a wide selection of AdvFS performance statistics. It reports many statistics in default units of one disk block (512 bytes) per interval, with the default interval being one second. We do not try to cover every detail of this command because it would take an entire book to be completely accurate and complete. We do, however, cover some of the more useful statistics and provide a few examples, which should enable you to become proficient in the tool for your own needs. For example, the volume and buffer cache statistics will be of great interest to anyone looking at tuning the system, but lock statistics are really only useful to those with access to Tru64 UNIX source code.

The following syntax can be used for *advfsstat(8)*, and Table 7–12 lists the valid flags for the tool:

Syntax:

```
advfsstat [options] [stats-type] domain
advfsstat [options] -f 0 | 1 | 2 domain fileset
```

TABLE 7–12   The Valid Flags for the *advfsstat(8)* Command

FLAG	DESCRIPTION
domain	Specifies the name of an existing domain for which you would like to gather AdvFS statistics.
fileset	Specifies the name of an existing fileset domain for which you would like to gather AdvFS statistics.
-I sec	Specifies the time interval (in seconds) between displays. The *advfsstat(8)* command collects and reports information for the specified interval only. If sec is omitted, then *advfsstat(8)* uses a default interval of one second.
-c count	Specifies the total number of reports. For example, setting the *advfsstat(8)* command flags '-i 1' and '-c 10' would produce 10 reports at one-second intervals. If count is omitted, then *advfsstat(8)* returns one report.
-s	Displays raw statistics for the interval.
-R	Displays the percent ratio of the returned statistics. (Use only with the '-b', '-p', or '-r' flags.)
-b	Displays the buffer cache statistics for the selected domain.
-f 0	Displays all fileset vnop statistics for the selected fileset.
-f 1	Displays all fileset lookup statistics for the selected fileset.
-f 2	Displays the common fileset vnode operations statistics.
-I 0	Displays the basic lock statistics.
-I 1	Displays the more detailed lock statistics.
-I 2	Displays very detailed lock statistics.
-n	Displays namei cache statistics.
-p	Displays buffer cache pin statistics.
-r	Displays buffer cache reference statistics.
-S	Displays smooth sync statistics. This flag is new in Tru64 UNIX version 5.0.
-v 0	Displays volume read-write statistics.

TABLE 7–12   The Valid Flags for the *advfsstat(8)* Command (Continued)

FLAG	DESCRIPTION
-v 1	Displays detailed volume statistics.
-v 2	Displays very detailed volume I/O queue statistics as a snapshot at the time the interval ends.
-v 3	Displays very detailed volume I/O queue statistics similar to '-v 2'; however, the output is everything put into the queue over the interval, rather than a snapshot. This flag is new in Tru64 UNIX version 5.0.
-B r	Displays BMT record read statistics.
-B w	Displays BMT record write and update statistics.

Depending on which flags you specify, the values that are displayed are defined to be those shown in Table 7–13. As you can see, some of the statistics are complicated to understand because they require you to know a lot about the internals of AdvFS in order to interpret them properly. In the many tables in this section, we attempt to give you the information you need to understand what the output is trying to tell you.

TABLE 7–13   *Advfsstat(8)* Output if No Flags are Specified

HEADING	DEFINITION
Deref	The number of times the reference has been decremented over the specified interval
Unpin	The number of times a page of memory was removed from cache over the specified interval
Lazy	The number of times a page was removed from the lazy queue in the cache over the specified interval
Refhit	The number of times a reference to the cache succeeded over the specified interval
Pinhit	The number of times a reference to a pinned page was successful over the specified interval
Log	The number of times a log flush succeeded over the specified interval
Ubchit	The number of unified buffer cache hits over the specified interval
UnpinMeta	The number of times a metadata file block flush succeeded over the specified interval
DerefMeta	The number of times a metadata reference was decremented over the specified interval
Refhitwait	The number of times a successful reference to the cache had to wait for I/O over the specified interval
Blocking	The number of times an unpin operation resulted in blocking waiting on an I/O over the specified interval

TABLE 7–13 *Advfsstat(8)* Output if No Flags are Specified (Continued)

HEADING	DEFINITION
Unconsol	The number of times unconsolidation was successful over the specified interval
UnpinFtx	The number of flyweight transaction unpin operations that were successful over the specified interval
DerefFtx	The number of references to flyweight transactions that were successful over the specified interval
R_ahead	The number of read-ahead buffers queued over the specified interval
Pinread	The number of pin reads over the specified interval
Clean	The number of unpin cleans over the specified interval
ConsolAbort	The number of attempts to consolidate that resulted in a failure over the specified interval
UnpinData	The number of unpin data hits over the specified interval
DerefData	The number of ref data hits over the specified interval
Disk	The incremental volume count over the specified interval
Reads	The number of reads on volume over the specified interval
Writes	The number of writes on volume over the specified interval
Rglobs	The number of consolidated reads on volume over the specified interval
AveRglob	The average number of consolidated reads on volume over the specified interval
Wglobs	The number of consolidated writes on volume over the specified interval
AveWgolb	The average number of consolidated writes on volume over the specified interval

Example:

This example shows a snapshot of the high-level statistics for a single domain called "staff." The definition of the different data points on this display can be found in Table 7–13.

```
# advfsstat staff
Domain   -832779971.833504- Stats -
Deref    48    Refhit     44    Refhitwait  0    R_ahead      0
Unpin    82    Pinhit     78    Pinhitwait  0    Pinreads     0
Lazy     73    Log         9    Blocking    0    Clean        0
               Ubchit      3    Unconsol    0    ConsolAbort  0
               UnpinMeta  54    UnpinFtx   69    UnpinData    4
               DerefMeta  40    DerefFtx   47    DerefData    1

Disk   Reads   Writes   Rglobs   AveRglob   Wglobs   AveWglob
----   -----   ------   ------   --------   ------   --------
  1       1        9        0          0        1         32
```

7.3.1.1 Buffer Cache Statistics

The buffer cache statistics are some of the most useful output from the *advfsstat(8)* tool. Table 7–14 gives the header definitions; however, the terminology may be a little difficult to understand. Therefore, we give the following reference for some terms we thought might be confusing.

- Ref: An attempt to reference a page in the cache.

- Pin: A page that was taken from the UBC and wired into the AdvFS cache.

- Unpin: A page that was unwired and returned to the UBC.

TABLE 7–14   *Advfsstat(8)* Buffer Cache Information (-b flag)

HEADING	DEFINITION
pin cnt	The total number of pins over the specified interval
pin hit	The number of pin hits over the specified interval
pin hitw	The number of pin hit waits over the specified interval
pin read	The number of pin reads over the specified interval
ref cnt	The total number of cache references over the specified interval
ref hit	The total number of references that resulted in a hit in the cache over the specified interval
ref hitw	The number of references that resulted in a hit in the cache but had to wait for I/O to complete
unpin lazy	The number of unpin operations used by the lazy queue over the specified interval
unpin blk	The number of unpin operations that blocked over the specified interval
unpin cln	The number of unpin cleans over the specified interval
unpin log	The number of unpin operations for the transaction log over the specified interval
ra	The number of read-ahead buffers queued over the specified interval
ubc	The number of hits into the unified buffer cache over the specified interval
cons un	The number of unconsolidated hits over the specified interval
cons abrt	The number of attempts to consolidate that failed over the specified interval

Example:

Here is an example of how you can use the *advfsstat(8)* tool to take two different looks into the buffer cache statistic of a specific domain called "test_domain." In the first set of statistics (headings are defined in Table 7–14), the data were mostly read from disk using read-ahead buffering, but very few hits in the UBC were made. In the second case, the performance was much better because of the UBC caching that was done for the data blocks. In that case, the data was almost completely read out of the cache with no disk accesses needed.

```
# advfsstat -b -c 10 test_domain
pin                   ref             unpin-type          misc      cons
cnt hit hitw read     cnt    hit  hitw lazy blk cln log   ra  ubc   un abrt
  1   1    0    0     127    119   12    1   0   0   0   103    7    0    0
  0   0    0    0     477    477   63    0   0   0   0   456    0    0    0
  0   0    0    0     469    469   62    0   0   0   0   448    0    0    0
  0   0    0    0     469    469   57    0   0   0   0   448    0    0    0
  1   1    0    0     689    687   46    1   0   0   0   664    0    0    0
  0   0    0    0     741    741   45    0   0   0   0   720    0    0    0
  1   1    0    0     159    158    8    1   0   0   0   121    0    0    0
  0   0    0    0      21     21    0    0   0   0   0     0    0    0    0
  0   0    0    0      21     21    0    0   0   0   0     0    0    0    0
  0   0    0    0      21     21    0    0   0   0   0     0    0    0    0
# advfsstat -b -c 10 test_domain
pin                   ref             unpin-type          misc      cons
cnt hit hitw read     cnt    hit  hitw lazy blk cln log   ra  ubc   un abrt
  2   2    0    0    1965   1960    0    2   0   0   0    0 1956    0    0
  1   1    0    0    1045   1044    0    1   0   0   0    0 1010    0    0
  1   1    0    0      56     53    0    1   0   0   0    0   50    0    0
  4   4    0    0    4577   4568    0    4   0   0   0    0 4553    0    0
  3   3    0    0    3686   3676    0    3   0   0   0    0 3666    0    0
  4   4    0    0    3637   3627    0    4   0   0   0    0 3603    0    0
  4   3    0    0    2989   2979    0    3   0   0   1    0 2971    0    0
  3   3    0    0    2989   2979    0    3   0   0   0    0 2970    0    0
  3   3    0    0    2989   2979    0    3   0   0   0    0 2970    0    0
  5   5    0    0    5028   5013    0    5   0   0   0    0 5022    0    0
```

What this example shows is how performance can be greatly improved by taking full advantage of the UBC cache. We discuss UBC tuning in Chapter 4, and we refer you there for more information on how to modify the behavior of your UBC.

7.3.1.2 Vnode Operation Statistics

You can also use the *advfsstat(8)* tool to keep track of the vnode operations performed on a fileset in a domain. Table 7–15 gives the heading definitions for the output from the tool in that case. We also refer you to our discussion of the vnode operations in Chapter 4, where we fully define these operations and their function.

TABLE 7–15   The *advfsstat(8)* Fileset Vnode Operations Information (-f 0 flag)

HEADING	DEFINITION
lookup	The number of file lookups over the specified interval
create	The number of file creates, *creat(2)*, over the specified interval
close	The number of file closes, *close(2)*, over the specified interval
getattr	The number of get file attributes over the specified interval.
setattr	The number of set file attributes over the specified interval
read	The number of file reads, *read(2)*, over the specified interval
write	The number of file writes, *write(2)*, over the specified interval.
mmap	The number of *mmap(2)* system calls over the specified interval
fsync	The number of file syncs, *fsync(2)*, over the specified interval.
syncdata	The number of data syncs over the specified interval
remove	The number of file removes, *unlink(2)*, over the specified interval
rename	The number of files renamed, *rename(2)*, over the specified interval
readdir	The number of directory reads, *readdir(3)*, over the specified interval
mkdir	The number of directories created, *mkdir(2)*, over the specified interval
rmdir	The number of removed directories, *rmdir(2)*, over the specified interval
symlink	The number of symbolic links created, *symlink(2)*, over the specified interval
readlink	The number of links read, *readlink(2)*, over the specified interval
link	The number of links created, *link(2)*, over the specified interval
bread	The number of buffer cache reads, *breads*, over the specified interval
brelse	The number of buffer cache releases, *brelse*, over the specified interval
page_write	The number of page writes over the specified interval
page_read	The number of page reads over the specified interval
getpage	The number of pages retrieved over the specified interval
putpage	The number of pages returned over the specified interval

TABLE 7–16   The *advfsstat(8)* Fileset Lookup Information (-f 1 flag)

HEADING	DEFINITION
lookup	The total number of file lookups performed over the specified interval
hit	The number of file lookup hits performed over the specified interval
hit %	The percentage of lookups that resulted in a cache hit over the specified interval
noent	The number of file lookup noents over the specified interval
noent %	The percentage of lookups that were noents over the specified interval
miss	The number of file lookups that were not found in the cache over the specified interval
miss %	The percentage of lookups that were not found in the cache over the specified interval

TABLE 7–17   The *advfsstat(8)* Common Fileset Vnode Operations Information (-f 2 flag)

HEADING	DEFINITION
lkup	The number of file lookups over the specified interval
crt	The number of file creates over the specified interval
geta	The number of get file attributes over the specified interval
read	The number of file reads over the specified interval
writ	The number of file writes over the specified interval
fsnc	The number of file syncs over the specified interval
dsnc	The number of data syncs over the specified interval
rm	The number of file removes over the specified interval
mv	The number of file renames over the specified interval
rdir	The number of directory reads over the specified interval
mkd	The number of make directories over the specified interval
rmd	The number of remove directories over the specified interval
link	The number of links created over the specified interval

7.3.1.3 AdvFS Lock Statistics

Many locks are used within AdvFS to maintain consistency of the data structures in a multiprocessor environment. Many of these locks can be observed using *advfsstat(8)*; however, an intimate knowledge of the internals of AdvFS is needed before the statistics begin to make sense. Most Tru64 UNIX systems administrators probably do not spend time analyzing the lock statistics. Therefore, we don't provide a great deal of explanation other than to give the column definitions in Tables 7–18 through 7–21.

TABLE 7–18   The *advfsstat(8)* Basic Lock Information (-l 0 flag)

HEADING	DEFINITION
mutex	The number of mutual exclusion (mutex) locks granted over the interval
wait	The number of times a thread needed to wait for a lock to be granted over the interval
sig	The number of signal locks granted over the specified interval
bcast	The number of broadcast locks granted over the specified interval

TABLE 7–19   The *advfsstat(8)* Lock Statistics (-l 1 or -l 2 flags)

HEADING	DEFINITION
wait	The number of times a thread needed to wait for a lock to be granted over the specified interval
rwait	The number of time a thread needed to wait more than once for a lock over the specified interval
signl	The number of signals on lock over the specified interval
bcast	The number of broadcasts on lock over the specified interval
lock	The number of locks over the specified interval

TABLE 7–20   The *advfsstat(8)* Lock Statistics (-l 1 flag)

HEADING	DEFINITION
mutex	Mutual exclusion locks (mutexes)
genLk	Generic locks
stateLk	State locks
shrLk	Shared locks. The "bcast" value is hard-coded to zero for shared locks.
excLk	Exclusive locks
bufStateLk	Buffer state locks. The "lock" value is hard-coded to zero.
pinBlkCv	Pin block condition variable. The "lock" value is hard-coded to zero.
bfFlushCv	Bit file flush condition variable. The "lock" value is hard-coded to zero.
ftxCv	Flyweight transactions condition variable. The "lock" value is hard-coded to zero.
msgQCv	Message queue condition variable. The "lock" value is hard-coded to zero.
total	Total number of locks. The "rwait" value is hard-coded to zero.

Specifying the '-l 2' flag repeats the table of lock statistics specified by the '-l 1' flag and adds the flags shown in Table 7–21.

TABLE 7–21 The *advfsstat(8)* Detailed Lock Statistics (-l 2 flag)

HEADING	DEFINITION
LOG_DESC	Log descriptors locks
LOG_READ_STREAM	Log read stream locks
BF_STATE	Bitfile state locks
BF_XTNT_MAP	Bitfile extents locks
BF_COW	Bitfile copy on write locks
BF_MCELL_LIST	Bitfile metadata cell list locks
BF_FLUSH	Bitfile flush locks
BUFFER	Buffer locks
BF_SET_TBL	Set table locks
BF_SET_TAG_DIR	Set tag directory locks
VD_STG_MAP	Virtual disk storage map locks
VD_MCELLS	Virtual disk metadata cell locks
VD_PAGE0_MCELLS	Virtual disk page zero metadata cell locks
VD_MIG_MCELLS	Virtual disk migrate metadata cell locks
VD_DEV_BUSY	Virtual disk device busy locks
VD_ACTIVE	Virtual disk active locks
VD_LAZY_BLOCK	Virtual disk lazy blocking locks
WIRED_FREE	Wired free locks
RAW_BUF_FREE	Raw buffer free locks
INIT	Initialization locks
FS_BF_GET	Fileset bitfile get locks
unused22	Not used
unused23	Not used
unused24	Not used
FS_CONTEXT_SEM	Fileset context SEM locks
DQ_LOCK	Disk quota locks
FILE_SET_LK	Fileset locks
DOMAIN_TBL	Domain table locks
BF_SET_STATE	Bitfile set state locks
SERVICE_CLASS_TBL	Service class table locks
BF_SHLV	Bitfile shelving locks
FS_FILE	Fileset file locks

TABLE 7–21   The *advfsstat(8)* Detailed Lock Statistics (-l 2 flag) (Continued)

HEADING	DEFINITION
ZAP_MCELLS	Delete metadata cell locks
MOVE_METADATA	Move metadata locks
MIG_TRUNC	Migrate truncation locks
DDL_ACTIVE	Deferred delete list active locks
DDL_ACTIVE_WAIT	Deferred delete list active wait locks
QUOTA_FILE_LOCK	Quota file locks
FRAG_BF	Fragment bitfile locks
BF_SET_SHLV	Bitfile set shelving locks
LKU_MSS_PQD	HSM shelving pseudo-queuer device locks
LKU_MSS_PQD_LOWPRI	HSM shelving pseudo-queuer

7.3.1.4   Namei Cache Statistics

The namei cache statistics can be obtained with *advfsstat(8)*, but as you may recall from our namei cache discussion in Chapter 4, you can also gather these statistics using the kernel debugger. The namei cache is used by all name lookups on any file system type on the Tru64 UNIX system. The primary benefit to monitoring these statistics with *advfsstat(8)* over *kdbx(8)* is the ability to do interval reporting. A secondary benefit is that a nonroot user can run *advfsstat(8)*, whereas only a root user can run the kernel debugger. The kernel debugger provides only a single snapshot each time you print them out. Therefore, this tool can be used to look at statistics that don't apply strictly to AdvFS. Table 7–22 gives the heading definitions for the namei cache statistics.

TABLE 7–22   The *advfsstat(8)* Namei Cache Statistics (-n flag)

HEADING	DEFINITION
goodh	The number of good hits or hits that resulted in data being read directly out of cache over the specified interval
negh	The number of negative hits or hits that are still usable over the specified interval
badh	The number of bad hits or hits that must be dropped over the specified interval
falsh	The number of false hits or hits with ID mismatch over the specified interval
miss	The number of cache misses over the specified interval

Example:

This example illustrates how you can use *advfsstat(8)* to gather the namei cache statistics on your system over a specified time interval.

```
$ advfsstat -n -i 5 -c 10 staff
goodh negh badh falsh miss
  347   9    0    0    0
  455  15    2    0    3
  259  13    3    0    3
  469  17    1    0    1
   94  11    0    0    0
  324  20    0    0    0
  264  14    1    0    1
  426  16    0    0    1
  207  13    2    0    2
  155  13    1    0    0
```

7.3.1.5 Cache Pins and Refs

This is another section in which the statistics won't make much sense without intimate knowledge of the inner workings of AdvFS. Tables 7–23 and 7–24 give the pin statistics and reference statistics, respectively. We refresh your memory on the terminology of references and pins as follows to help you interpret the data given in the two tables:

- *Ref:* An attempt to reference a page in the cache.

- *Pin:* A page that was taken from the UBC and wired into the AdvFS cache.

- *Unpin:* A page that was unwired and returned to the UBC.

TABLE 7–23 The *advfsstat(8)* Buffer Cache Pin Statistics (-p flag)

HEADING	DEFINITION
pin cnt	Total number of pins over the specified interval
pin hit	The number of pin hits over the specified interval
pin hitw	The number of pin hits for which a thread needed to wait
pin read	The number of pin reads over the specified interval
pin lazy	The number of unpin lazys over the specified interval
pin blk	The number of unpin blocks over the specified interval
pin cln	The number of unpin cleans over the specified interval
pin log	The number of unpin logs over the specified interval
data bsFtx	The number of bitfile access subsystem flyweight transactions over the specified interval
data fsFtx	The number of file access subsystem flyweight transactions over the specified interval
data other	The number of other flyweight transactions over the specified interval

TABLE 7–24   The *advfsstat(8)* Buffer Cache Reference Statistics (-r flag)

HEADING	DEFINITION
ref cnt	The total number of references over the specified interval
ref hit	The number of references that resulted in cache hits over the specified interval
ref hitw	The number of references that resulted in a cache hit but that still needed to wait for I/O to complete over the specified interval
data bsFtx	The number of bitfile access subsystem flyweight transactions over the specified interval
data fsFtx	The number of file access subsystem flyweight transactions over the specified interval
data other	The number of other flyweight transactions over the specified interval

7.3.1.6   Volume Statistics

The volume statistics gathered by *advfsstat(8)* are some of the most useful for identifying bottlenecks. Once a device that is particularly slow has been identified using this tool, then it may only take some rearranging of workload to relieve the congestion. On the other hand, it may take a complete redesign of the file system structure or some new hardware to resolve the bottleneck. Either way, you can use *advfsstat(8)* to help determine the problem so it can be corrected.

The volume statistics come in four flavors: basic ('-v 0'), detailed ('-v 1'), very detailed snapshot ('-v 2'), and very detailed totaled ('-v 3'). The last two types look the same, but the interpretation of the numbers is slightly different. The snapshot simply gives the numbers as they look at the end of the interval, whereas the totaled shows all of the I/Os over the entire interval.

TABLE 7–25   The *advfsstat(8)* Volume Read and Write Statistics (-v 0 flag)

HEADING	DEFINITION
rd	The number of reads on a volume over the specified interval
wr	The number of writes on a volume over the specified interval

Example:

Here, we are looking at the volume statistics at five-second intervals for a single-volume domain called "sap_data4." The data suggests that the activity on this volume is heavily weighted toward reads. The definitions for the different columns in the output are described in Table 7–25.

```
# advfsstat -v 0 -i 5 sap_data4
vol1
 rd wr
 50  0
152  3
101  6
122  7
207  0
165  0
 88  0
  7  3
 59  0
  4  0
```

TABLE 7–26   The *advfsstat(8)* Detailed Volume Statistics (-v 1 flag)

HEADING	DEFINITION
rd	The number of reads on a volume over a specified interval
rg	The number of consolidated reads on a volume over a specified interval
arg	The average number of consolidated reads on a volume over the specified interval
wg	The number of consolidated writes on a volume over the specified interval
awg	The average number of consolidated writes on a volume over the specified interval

Example:

In this example, we examine the detailed volume statistics at five-second intervals for the "sap_data4" domain. The more detailed output from the previous example gives the consolidated read and write information in order to determine whether there is locality to the I/Os. The definitions for the different columns in the output are described in Table 7–26.

```
# advfsstat -v 1 -i 5 sap_data4
vol1
 rd wr rg arg wg awg
 56  0 30 256  0   0
 96  0 41 256  0   0
 18  3  2 256  0   0
 20  1  4 256  0   0
 50  0 10 256  0   0
 94  2 16 256  0   0
140  0  6 256  0   0
 61  0 23 256  0   0
 82  0 43 250  0   0
 97  5 47 256  0   0
 32  0 12 256  0   0
 10  0  0   0  0   0
```

```
 6  2  0    0   0  0
10  0  0    0   0  0
 5  0  0    0   0  0
16  2  1  112   1 32
```

TABLE 7–27   The *advfsstat(8)* Volume I/O Queue Statistics (-v 2 or -v 3 flags)

HEADING	DEFINITION
rd	The number of reads on a volume over the specified interval
wr	The number of writes on a volume over the specified interval
rg	The number of consolidated reads on a volume over the specified interval
arg	The average number of consolidated reads on a volume over the specified interval
wg	The number of consolidated writes on a volume over the specified interval
awg	The average number of consolidated writes on a volume over the specified interval
blk	The number of blocking queue requests on a volume over the specified interval
wlz	The wait lazy queue is where modifications to advfs metadata, such as directory updates when files are created or deleted, file stat structures, file extents structures, etc., are placed until the log pages representing those changes go out to disk. To keep a transaction/log-based file system consistent, the logged changes to the metadata must be safely on disk before the actual metadata pages are written to disk. So, this *advfsstat(8)* column shows the number of modified metadata pages that will soon be written to disk.
rlz	The queue is the "ready" lazy queue, not the "read" queue as the man page states. That is the queue in which metadata pages are moved from the wait lazy queue once their log pages are out to disk, and where modifications to file data pages are placed. If an application does multiple write() syscalls to modify one file page, then each write() will not cause a disk I/O. Instead, the page will be placed on the ready lazy queue after one write() and taken back off that queue to satify the next write(). In this way, overall system I/O is reduced. Because write()s are asynchronous, this is where the pages are queued until sync time, or until the advfs threshold on the readyLazyQ is hit. The other use of this queue is to gather many I/Os so that ones for contiguous disk blocks can be consolidated together.
con	The consolidate queue is where I/O requests from the ready lazy queue are sorted for consolidation. Because the I/O is usually started right up after the sorting and consolidation is done, *advfsstat(8)* doesn't often catch anything on this queue.
dev	The device queue is the number of requests that advfs has handed to the disk driver for which the I/O interrupt has not come in. This is the driver queue depth from the advfs perspective.

Example:

This example shows how you may examine the volume I/O queue statistics for a domain called "sap_data4" containing a single volume called "vol1." There are two time periods when we were waiting for an interrupt from a device in order to pass the I/O to the device queue. The definitions for the different columns in the output are described fully in Table 7–27.

```
# advfsstat -v 2 -i 5 sap_data4
vol1
rd    wr    rg    arg    wg    awg    blk    wlz    rlz    con    dev
13    0     2     256    0     0      0      2      0      0      0
21    1     2     256    0     0      0      2      0      0      0
11    0     2     256    0     0      0      2      0      0      0
32    0     0     0      0     0      0      2      0      0      0
37    0     1     80     0     0      0      2      0      0      0
43    0     4     256    0     0      0      2      0      0      0
38    0     0     0      0     0      0      2      0      0      0
 9    3     0     0      0     0      0      0      2      0      0
 8    0     0     0      0     0      0      0      2      0      0
16    0     2     256    0     0      0      0      2      0      0
61    0     8     256    0     0      0      0      2      0      0
35    0     4     256    0     0      0      0      2      0      0
38    0     2     256    0     0      0      0      2      0      1
58    2     4     120    0     0      0      2      0      0      0
52    0     2     256    0     0      0      2      0      0      0
54    0     5     256    0     0      0      2      0      0      1
49    4     9     225    0     0      0      2      0      0      0
46    0     17    220    0     0      0      2      0      0      0
57    2     4     256    0     0      0      2      0      0      0
52    1     19    256    1     32     0      2      0      0      0
```

7.3.2   AdvFS Tuning Parameters

Several sysconfigtab parameters are available on your Tru64 UNIX system for tuning various aspects of the file system performance and features; however, these parameters are notoriously hard to understand and manipulate. This section is an attempt to correct that issue. Table 7–28 shows how these parameters have changed over time. Some new parameters have been added, and others have been removed. In addition, some of the parameters' default values and range of values have been changed. In this section, we discuss each of these parameters and their uses. The goal for Tru64 UNIX version 5.1 and beyond will be to reduce and eventually eliminate many of these parameters.

TABLE 7–28   Advanced File System sysconfigtab Parameters

PARAMETER	DEFAULT	MIN	MAX	4.0D	4.0F	5.0
AdvfsCacheMaxPercent	7	1	30	X	X	X
AdvfsMinFragGrps	16	3	8,191	X	X	
	16	3	8,388,637			X
AdvfsMaxFragGrps	48	4	8,192	X	X	
	48	4	8,388,637			X
AdvfsAccessMaxPercent	25	5	95	X		
	80	5	95		X	X
AdvfsPreallocAccess	128	128	65,536	X	X	X
AdvfsAccessCleanupPercent	33	5	95		X	X
AdvfsMinFreeAccess	128	1	100,000			X
AdvfsMaxFreeAccessPercent	80	5	95			X
AdvfsSyncMmapPages	1	0	1	X	X	X
AdvfsMaxDevQLen	80	0	65,536	X		
	24	0	65,536		X	X
AdvfsFavorBlockingQueue	1	0	1	X	X	X
AdvfsReadyQLim	16,384	0	32,768	X	X	X
AdvfsDomainPanicLevel	1	0	32,768			X
AdvfsCacheHashSize	1,024	1,024	65,536		X	X

7.3.2.1 AdvfsPreallocAccess

AdvFS manages open files in the kernel using a specialized data entity known as an access structure. The *AdvfsPreallocAccess* sysconfig parameter value represents the initial number of these access structures to allocate in memory at boot time or when AdvFS is first initialized. Generally, the system needs a minimum number of these structures during system initialization. Your environment may also typically open a certain number of files even before the applications do any real work. So, the idea of *AdvfsPreallocAccess* is to give you a way to adjust the minimum number of these access structures upfront. For example, suppose that you know the system and its applications will typically open 2000 files, then you might want to increase *AdvfsPreallocAccess* to 2000. This would be a minimum, but AdvFS would still increase this amount if more than 2000 file access structures are needed during peak demand. *AdvfsAccessMaxPercent* limits the total amount of available system memory that AdvFS can allocate for AdvFS access structures. The reason for this limit is that AdvFS grows but does not shrink the number of access structures in V4.0 and earlier releases.

If the amount of memory of *AdvfsPreallocAccess* multiplied by the size of an access structure exceeds the *AdvfsAccessMaxPercent* limit, then AdvFS automatically decreases this preallocation limit so that it is less than or equal to the *AdvfsAccessMaxPercent* percent of available system memory. In other words, the maximum memory usage for access structures is limited by *AdvfsAccessMaxPercent*.

Environments that have lots of files being opened, such as some Internet sites, might consider increasing the *AdvfsPreallocAccess* parameter, as well as the *AdvfsAccessMaxPercent*. You should keep in mind, however, that AdvFS dedicates this system memory for access structures and will not release it. You need to factor memory requirements for other applications or user needs. Otherwise, you will run into a shortage of free memory.

7.3.2.2 AdvfsAccessMaxPercent and AdvfsAccessCleanupPercent

AdvFS uses access structures to keep information on all open files, devices, and directories in memory. Access structures for files that are no longer referenced are kept on two lists: a free list and a closed list. When the free list is empty and AdvFS needs a new access structure for a file, it can do one of two things: (1) allocate some more from the malloc pool, or (2) recycle some from the closed list to the free list. The *AdvfsAccessMaxPercent* and *AdvfsAccessCleanupPercent* are used to adjust the manner in which this process is done. *AdvfsAccessMaxPercent* is the percentage of the available kernel malloc pool beyond which AdvFS will not attempt to allocate more access structures. It is set by default to 80 percent, and valid values range from 5 to 95 percent. The malloc pool is approximately 25 percent of physical memory. Setting *AdvfsAccessMaxPercent* higher allows AdvFS to cache a greater number of access structures, but at the expense of removing malloc pool space from other uses and potentially causing some processes to run out of memory. Setting this value lower keeps AdvFS from consuming memory that might be required for other uses, but this is at the expense of waiting for some structures to be recycled. In its simplest form, this variable prevents AdvFS from using too much of the kernel malloc pool caching access structures. AdvFS monitors the number of access structures on the closed list and periodically recycles some from the closed list to the free list. An asynchronous background thread does this when *AdvfsAccessCleanupPercent* of all access structures are on the closed list. By default this value is set to 33 percent and can be adjusted from 5 percent to 95 percent. Reducing the value of *AdvfsAccessCleanupPercent* increases the frequency that the background thread will run and increases the likelihood that access structures will be on the free list. A side effect of reducing this value is that the amount of memory consumed for access lists grows more slowly than when this value is higher. Increasing the value of *AdvfsAccessCleanupPercent* reduces the frequency that the background thread runs and may yield a performance gain during normal operations, but give somewhat degraded performance during access-intensive operations such as *vdump(8)* and *du(1)*.

7.3.2.3 AdvfsCacheMaxPercent

The *AdvfsCacheMaxPercent* parameter sets the maximum percentage of physical memory that AdvFS will use for its buffer cache. This value can be set from 1 percent to 30 percent, with the default value of 7 percent. *AdvfsCacheMaxPercent* reduces the amount of memory available for the UBC, which might negatively impact overall system performance in some environments. In general, if the cache performance is low, then this parameter should be increased so that the performance rises above 95 percent (using advfsstat –b).

There have been cases in the 4.0x versions where lowering this value had a positive impact on system performance. This usually occurs when the system has a large amount of memory and the cache is continuously flushing. Cache flushes can take a very long time to complete if there is a large number of dirty buffers. Therefore, the answer is to reduce the number of buffers that will be flushed and subsequently speed things up. In version 5.0, the cache-flushing algorithms have been improved and this problem has been corrected. A kernel global variable, known as *flushvolcalls*, can be examined to determine if large numbers of cache flushes have occurred.

Example:

Here is a case in which we examine the cache flush counters on a poorly performing system and notice that elements 5 and 6 are quite high. If either of these values are above a few hundred, then you may need to consider tuning down this attribute.

```
(dbx) pd flushvolcalls
{
  [0] 0
  [1] 0
  [2] 0
  [3] 0
  [4] 0
  [5] 50389
  [6] 1193782
  [7] 0
  [8] 0
}
```

In addition to cache flushes, we have seen cases of systems where most of the I/O are large, sequential writes to an AdvFS. This could also be a case in which reducing the size of this parameter could be beneficial.

In Tru64 UNIX version 5.1, this parameter becomes obsolete because of changes made in the way the AdvFS cache is organized. AdvFS will no longer manage its own buffer headers; rather, it will let the UBC do that. This reduces unnecessary overhead from potentially looking in two places (the AdvFS cache and the UBC) for the same information. Although the parameter will continue to exist in version 5.1, it will be rendered ineffectual and will most likely be retired in a future revision.

7.3.2.4 AdvfsMinFragGrps and AdvfsMaxFragGrps

Each AdvFS fileset has its own fragment bitfile, which is used for small files and end-of-file fragments that are smaller than 8K. Each fragment bitfile logically consists of eight sections, one for each fragment size (1K, 2K, . . ., 7K), and a free list. Within each section is a linked list of 128K fragment groups. The actual file fragments are written inside one of the fragment groups. When all of the fragments within a fragment group are no longer needed, that group is moved to the free list.

When the number of groups on the free list reaches *AdvfsMaxFragGrps*, a message is sent to a kernel thread (bs_fragbf_thread) indicating which fileset fragment file has reached the limit. The bs_fragbf_thread then deallocates fragment groups from that fileset's free list until there are no more than *AdvfsMinFragGrps* on its list. This returns the file space back to the file system so that it can be used for other purposes.

The default value for *AdvfsMinFragGrps* is 16, and the default value for *AdvfsMaxFragGrps* is 48. What this means is that the bs_fragbf_thread truncates the free list from 48 groups (48 groups × 128K = 6 MB) to 16 groups (2 MB), returning 4 MB to the file system.

Valid values for *AdvfsMaxFragGrps* range from 4 to 8191. If set to the maximum value, the space consumed by unused fragment groups will grow to 1 GB per fileset before any space is deallocated and returned to the file system. Increasing this value might help if the filesets tend to have a lot of small files that are constantly created and deleted. This would prevent excessive deallocation and reallocation of space to the fragment bitfile at the expense of total disk storage available for other purposes within the filesets. Because this is a kernel variable, remember that all filesets on the system are treated in the same manner.

Valid values for *AdvfsMinFragGrps* are 3 to 8191 and must be less than the value set for *AdvfsMaxFragGrps* (sysconfig enforces this requirement). The same considerations used for setting *AdvfsMaxFragGrps* should be applied to this parameter as well.

7.3.2.5 AdvfsMaxDevQLen

The *AdvfsMaxDevQLen* sysconfig parameter was added to Tru64 UNIX 4.0 to handle the tradeoff between quick synchronous I/O response times and maximizing I/O throughput to AdvFS volumes. A default value of 80 was chosen as a compromise between these needs. Essentially, response time was favored over I/O throughput in choosing that default for general system workload environments. In version 4.0F and higher, the default value was lowered to 24 because it was believed that response times were too long in many cases. Because *AdvfsMaxDevQLen* applies to all AdvFS volumes in the system, you need to choose the value wisely if you plan to change it from the default.

The range is 0 and 1 to 65,536. Based on internal testing, a reasonable range is between 20 and 2000. Too low a value will hurt potential I/O throughput, and too high a value will cause excessively long user response times for synchronous I/O requests measured in seconds to minutes.

A value of 0 actually deactivates the AdvFS per-volume threshold, causing any and all I/O requests to immediately be issued to the disk whenever there is a sync request. We don't recommend that you choose this value.

If your environment is such that very few users or applications need to synchronously wait on I/O, then you might consider higher values up to 2000. We have seen this help; for example, when you have systems that generally write asynchronous data to files but rarely have users waiting for data.

A general formula for calculating response time would be the following: Response Time = AdvfsMaxDevQLen (Average I/O Latency

Example:

```
Response Time = 500 * 9 msec = 4500 ms = 4.5 sec
```

If your system environment contains mixed user applications or is sensitive to synchronous IO response times, we recommend that you use values less than 300. You will know that you have set the value of *Advfs-MaxDevQLen* too high when users complain about response times.

7.3.2.6 AdvfsFavorBlockingQueue

The *AdvFSFavorBlockingQueue* controls movement of I/O requests from consolidation queue to device queue. When enabled (the default), AdvFS first issues synchronous I/O. When disabled (set to 0), asynchronous I/O is flushed to disk, regardless of synchronous I/O. It is recommended that you use the default value of 1.

7.3.2.7 AdvfsSyncMmapPages

The *AdvfsSyncMmapPages* controls the behavior of *sync(2)* system calls and, consequently, the update daemon. The default value for *AdvfsSyncMmapPages* is 1, which means the asynchronous commit of dirty memory mapped file data to disk. If the value is set to 0, then modified data from the *write(2)* system call will be asynchronously written to disk but mmaped pages will not. What this means is that by setting this attribute to 0, any application using *mmap(2)* will need to flush its own buffers using *msync(2)*.

7.3.2.8 AdvfsReadyQLim

This new parameter was introduced in Tru64 UNIX version 4.0D. This attribute specifies the number of 512-byte blocks that can be on the ready lazy queue before the requests are moved to the device queue. The minimum value is 0, which disables buffering on the ready lazy queue. The maximum value is 32 KB, and the default value is 16 KB.

7.3.2.9 AdvfsDomainPanicLevel

This parameter is new for version 5.0. This parameter allows you to choose what action the system should take in the event that a domain panic occurs. The possible values of the attribute are listed in Table 7–29.

TABLE 7–29   AdvfsDomainPanicLevel Parameter Values

VALUE	MEANING
0	Do not create crash dumps for any file domains. This is the behavior in the event of domain panic pre-5.0.
1	Creates a crash dump only for a file domain with mounted filesets. This is the default behavior in Tru64 UNIX 5.0 and later.
2	Creates a crash dump for any file domains.
3	Promotes the domain panic to a system panic. The system will crash.

7.3.3   The *chvol(8)* Command

The *chvol(8)* command can be a useful tool for improving the I/O performance of the volumes in an AdvFS domain. The initial I/O transfer parameter for both reads and writes is a fixed value of 128 blocks in Tru64 UNIX before version 5.0. In version 5.0 and higher, the default value is set to whatever the maximum is that is supported by the underlying driver. This can be significant in cases like LSM where the only way to change the value is by patching the kernel. This becomes inconvenient for two reasons: (1) File systems must be remounted, or the system must be rebooted for the new value to take effect. This is not usually possible in a production environment. (2) The patched value will be lost whenever the kernel is rebuilt. What happens in this regard is that the system administrator often forgets what value has been set and then goes to install a patch or upgrade and the old value is lost. This usually results in a call to the customer support center and some wasted time for the customer. The 5.0 change eliminates both of these problems by allowing *chvol(8)* to change the value on-the-fly. Therefore, downtime is averted.

Once you change the I/O transfer parameters for a given volume with the '-r' flag or the '-w' flag, the parameters remain fixed until you change them. The underlying device driver limits the values for the I/O transfer parameters. Every device has a minimum and maximum value for the size of the reads and writes it can handle. If you set a value that is outside of the range that the device driver allows, then the device automatically resets the value to the largest or smallest it can handle. For example, for LSM volumes this value is based on a kernel parameter contained in the "volinfo.max_io" field. This value can be altered only using the kernel debugger, but not on-the-fly. See the real-world example in Chapter 9 for details and a full explanation of how this can be done.

By default, the I/O consolidation mode (cmode) is on. The cmode must be on for the I/O transfer parameters to take effect. You can use the '-c' flag to turn the cmode off, which sets the I/O transfer parameter to one page. In addition, for file system workloads that are heavily biased toward random writes, use the '-t' flag to increase the file system's dirty threshold. This may improve file write performance.

Example:

The following simple example shows how to examine and change the read, write, and threshold value using *chvol(8)*.

```
# showfdmn tst_dmn
        Id              Date Created              LogPgs   Domain Name
3662ad91.00002c20   Mon Nov 30 09:37:05 1998    512      tst_dmn

Vol   512-Blks   Free      % Used   Cmode   Rblks   Wblks   Vol Name
1L    200000     188656    6%       on      128     128     /dev/vol/dg3/voltst
# chvol /dev/vol/dg3/voltst tst_dmn
rblks = 128 wblks = 128 cmode = on, thresh = 16384

# chvol -r 256 -w 256 -t 32768 /dev/vol/dg3/voltst tst_dmn

# chvol /dev/vol/dg3/voltst tst_dmn
rblks = 256 wblks = 256 cmode = on, thresh = 32768
```

7.3.4 File Striping

File striping can be a serious option for improving the write performance to certain "hot" files on an AdvFS. For file striping to work, there must be more than one volume in the domain, and the file must be set up for striping using the *stripe(8)* command. This can be particularly true if the volumes are located on different controllers and different SCSI busses. Keep in mind that if the file system is already sitting on top of a striped LSM or hardware RAID volume, then file striping on top of that would most likely not add much to the situation. The file striping solution will also not be very useful if the file system contains many small files that change frequently. In that case, it would be impossible to try to use the *stripe(8)* command ahead of time.

Therefore, to summarize, file striping can be helpful and works best when:

- You have a few well-known "hot" files.

- The domain has more than one volume.

- The volumes are on separate controllers and busses.

- The write performance is more important than read performance.

  On the other hand, file striping will probably not be helpful if:

- The domain has only one volume.

- The domain has many fast-changing files.

- The LSM volumes or hardware RAID disks are already striped.

- Read performance is more important than write performance.

  If, based on the previous criteria, you have decided to set up file striping, see section 6.5.2.4 for more information and examples of how to use the *stripe(8)* command.

7.3.5   Log Placement

As previously discussed, there is only one transaction log on any domain, and any metadata changes must involve log writes. Therefore, the placement of the transaction log can have a big impact on the performance of the entire file system. The implication is that if the log is somehow placed onto the slowest volume in the domain, then the entire file system will be slowed down. Therefore, it is important to ensure that the log is put onto the fastest volume in the domain. We have already discussed how that can be accomplished using the *switchlog(8)* tool. We refer readers to that section of the chapter for more information on how to move the transaction log.

One suggestion that has been given with respect to log placement is that you can artificially reduce the I/O going to the log volume by filling it up. You can do this by migrating large static files that are not accessed very often over to it. Once you get the volume above 86 percent full, you can eliminate the non-log I/O to the volume until the other volumes become mostly full, too. It would be difficult to implement this strategy *a priori* without wasting space on the domain.

7.3.6   Use AdvFS Direct I/O to Speed Up Data Access

The normal operation for AdvFS is to use its cache to make subsequent reads of file system data more rapid. We saw this in our previous discussion of the AdvFS cache. Thus, caching is a big win for performance for most file system activity, assuming that the data can use the cache in an efficient manner. In other cases, programs either do not use cache effectively or perform their own internal caching. In those kinds of situations, the AdvFS cache may cause the application to perform poorly because of the overhead of managing an inefficient cache. In this case, direct I/O can help those programs and the overall system to perform better. Thus, when direct I/O is enabled for a file, read and write requests on it are executed to and from disk storage in a way that is similar to the way raw I/O is performed, bypassing AdvFS caching.[6] Based on internal Compaq studies, for a direct I/O-enabled file and when asynchronous I/O is utilized, the performance difference between direct I/O and raw is less than 3 percent.

If you wish to make the best use of the direct I/O feature, you should perform the following steps on an existing AdvFS[7]:

1.   Use a database or other program that can take advantage of the feature. Normally, a database program has its own caching feature that makes using the AdvFS cache unnecessary. These are excellent candidates for direct I/O. If your application does not have its

own cache and relies on the operating system for caching, then it will probably perform poorly.

2.   If you are writing a program, then you must open the file for direct I/O by using *open(2)* specifying the O_DIRECTIO flag.

Direct I/O cannot be used if either atomic write data logging or mmapping are used for the file. Therefore, if the file is already open for atomic write data logging or is mmapped, then calling the open function to initiate direct I/O will fail.

Although direct I/O will handle I/O requests of any byte size, the best performance will be observed when the requested byte size is aligned on file page boundaries and is evenly divisible into file system pages. Testing has shown that direct transfer from the user buffer to the disk is optimized in this configuration.

7.3.7   Defragmenting

As previously stated, a highly fragmented file system does not perform well. The fragments force the disks to perform many more seeks on different areas of the disk, which can be bad for performance. We suggest that you maintain a defragmenting regimen on your file systems so they can perform the best they possibly can. See our previous discussion of the *defragment(8)* and *defragcron(8)* tools for how this can be done.

7.3.8   Large Directory Speed Improvement

One problem seen by customers in Tru64 UNIX 4.0x with large, flat directory structures is that the time required to look up a file name in a directory that contained a large number of files became extremely long as the directory grew larger. The directory lookup was essentially a linear search that became quite noticeable when the number of files rose above around 10,000. This has been addressed in version 5.0 with a new directory lookup algorithm and supporting on-disk structure changes that utilize a B-tree algorithm. The result is to greatly improve directory lookup performance.

Example:

In one instance, a customer running Tru64 UNIX version 4.0D had a disk fail and replaced the drive, but the files needed to be restored from backups. Attempting to restore the file system took many hours because it contained a flat directory structure. Once the restore was complete, the problem no longer existed; however, it could be easily reproduced and reported, so a fix was put into the newer operating system revision. Because of the extent of the correction, a patch for 4.0D was not possible. A workaround was recommended to break the large directory up into a larger number of directories with fewer files in each. This task helped the customer speed up his normal access to the data in the short term. Also, in case he ever needed to restore the file system again in the future, the time to do it would be much less.

For those users who cannot redesign their directory structures, the workaround from the previous example would not be practical. One example of a file system that this could seriously impact is the /var/spool/mail directory on a large mail server. The *sendmail(8)* application will not let you change with the structure very much. Because this feature is available only if you have AdvFS V4 on-disk structures, and the workaround is not feasible, you would need to upgrade to 5.0 or greater and re-create your domains to take advantage of this feature. Upgrades can be difficult, but this is one feature that would make the job worth the effort.

7.4   Summary

This chapter was a discussion of advanced AdvFS topics, such as troubleshooting and tuning. This information should prove particularly helpful when faced with problems.

Keep in mind that in Chapter 9 on troubleshooting we present some case studies at real customer sites. Each case study used one or more specialized techniques for solving some type of real-world AdvFS problem. This chapter should provide you with much of the background you need to read and understand the discussion in Chapter 9. Also, as we mentioned on numerous occasions in this chapter, Appendix B has detailed information on the advanced tools you can use to perform operations on the AdvFS.

In the next chapter, we cover how to set up and configure Tru64 UNIX systems for various specialized applications.

Notes

1.   HSM was also known internally within Compaq/Digital as Ninja.

2.   Another reason why AdvFS has a two-layer structure was because it was once a design requirement to support other non-POSIX file

systems on top of the BAS (like VMS or MS-DOS). These requirements were never implemented.

3.   A cluster in AdvFS is a set of contiguous blocks. The default cluster
size is two disk blocks, or 1K.

4.   The on-disk structure was (and still is) called mega-version in defer-
ence to the fact that AdvFS used to have the moniker of the mega-
safe file system (MSFS).

5.   This number is the birthday of the original architect of AdvFS,
Christian Saether (Nov 11, 1958).

6.   In fact, Millsap (1992) specifically states that one of the "necessary
conditions" to consider using raw disk is the unavailability of a
direct I/O feature from the operating system.

7.   The Tru64 UNIX 5.0 *fstab(4)* reference page refers to the "Direc-
tIO" option; however, this is not implemented and will not work.
The page will be corrected in a future release.

File Systems Configuration and Tuning

The Constitution only gives people the
right to pursue happiness. You have to catch it yourself.
— *Benjamin Franklin*

Computer systems are increasingly being used to handle specialized functions, rather than for general-purpose computing like we used to see in the old days. We believe this trend works in our favor because a system that performs only one or a few tasks is much easier to tune to perform optimally than a general-purpose system. We have developed, over the course of many years, a set of instructions that you should follow to install and maintain your system in an optimal fashion. We are primarily concerned with file systems, so we do not cover the finer points of kernel tuning or network performance, but these steps are general enough to be applicable to a performance issue in those areas as well.

In this chapter, we give you some examples of the "standard" types of systems that we have seen at customer sites. We define four example system types: the Usenet News or e-mail server, the large database server, the Internet or Web server, and the NFS server. These examples will not be exactly like your system, but they should give you an idea of how to set up such a system and of what kinds of things you should be looking for in order to make the system perform well, for its assigned task.

8.1 Configuring Tru64 UNIX File Systems for Performance

There isn't any magic bullet for system tuning. In other words, we don't have a single set of parameters we can give you that will always give you the best performance. If we did, then many consultants would be out of work! The way your Tru64 system is tuned "out of the box" has been found through empirical testing to be appropriate for most customer applications and load requirements. Almost any system can benefit from some tuning or configuration adjustments, however, and the adjustment is a process, rather than a one-time task. You will need to constantly examine how the system performs and change things accordingly throughout the system's life.

Planning is the key to maintaining smooth file systems operation. The customer support center regularly gets frantic calls from customers whose systems are down and not performing well. The root cause of the problem was that the administrator did not follow the steps that we are about to give you. It usually turns out that the customers appropriately set up their systems but then never monitored and made adjustments as the workload changed. Or, the system was never sized for the task it was meant to handle. In that case, the customers need more memory, CPUs, or disks added with an additional cost. Or, they simply did not properly plan for disaster by testing their backups or disk-mirroring strategy, and it failed them at the wrong time.

We recommend that you use the following steps as a guideline in order to set up your file systems appropriately for a given task:

1. Identify your system's primary task or tasks. This should be a fairly easy job because you should have already decided on (or been asked to come up with) a new system to do a particular job. Therefore, this step will most likely have already been decided at the outset of the project.

2. Decide on an application program or programs that will be used to perform the function. This step will require some research on your part, unless a program has already been dictated by someone else. Sometimes you are constrained in this regard because you already know that your application uses only a particular database program. Even if you already "know" that, it doesn't hurt to look for other options.

3. Identify any special file systems requirements for the application. Some examples might be: Can the application take advantage of asynchronous I/O? Does the application vendor recommend against using file systems altogether? Will you need to create lots of smaller file systems or a few bigger ones? Does the application create lots of small files or fewer large files? Is this a 24-hour, year-round application?

4. Come up with a benchmark for your application with some sample data. Do not rely on vendor claims or standard benchmark information. The standard benchmarks will be totally unreliable for your application on your system with your expected workload.

5. Run your benchmark under load on a target system. The file systems should be set up as you would be setting them up for a real system because the configuration affects performance.

6. Monitor the system and tune it as required. This step lasts the longest and takes the most work on your part. You will need to continue to monitor and adjust as the workload changes.

After following these steps, you are ready for system setup and burn-in. You'll want to make sure that any kinks in the system that pop up in the first weeks of operation are dealt with swiftly. Once the real system is up and running, you should allow some time for initial problems to be worked out. We've found that once systems reach a steady state, they run very well under load for a long time.

8.2 Usenet News/Mail Server

We chose to discuss the Usenet News or e-mail server first mainly because that type of system seems to stretch the limits of its file systems the most. This type of system usually runs the *innd* or *sendmail* daemons as their applications, although some commercial applications perform these functions as well. These applications tend to receive a lot of data over the network (sometimes called a *newsfeed*) and store the data on the file system in lots of really small files on a single file system. The files will also be removed rapidly, thus they are dynamic in nature.

If we follow the procedure given in the last section, we find that the biggest problem is with step 3. We notice that these kinds of systems tend to have the following special characteristics:

1. Create and delete lots of small files.

2. Use lots of network I/O.

3. Have almost a 24-hour, year-round requirement.

4. Store their data almost exclusively on a single large file system.

For step 6 in our procedure, we see that the kinds of tuning problems this type of server tends to cause include:

1. Vnodes get used and reused often for both files and sockets. The fact that vnodes are used for both files and sockets can work to a disadvantage for a system like this because both are contending for resources at the same time. Appropriate care must be taken to tune

the VFS area. We refer you to Chapter 4 for our discussion of vnode monitoring and tuning parameters. You should be most concerned with the vnode aging and hashing information.

2. Data are difficult to cache because they change so often. In a really busy system, the update daemon still comes along every 30 seconds to sync the file systems. This task can cause the system to appear to freeze because so must dirty data in the cache needs to be flushed. The smooth sync capability, which we discussed in Chapter 4, can be used to help smooth out the data flushing. We discussed AdvFS cache tuning parameters in Chapter 7 and UFS and VFS cache tuning in Chapters 5 and we refer you to those sections for details about setting parameters.

3. Inodes or tags may be exhausted if maintenance is not performed. Because the applications will be using so many inodes or tags on the file system, the default number will almost certainly not be appropriate and will need to be increased. If you are using AdvFS, you will want to read the section in Chapter 7 where we discussed the BMT exhaustion problem. For UFS, the *newfs(8)* command can be used to increase the number of inodes for a particular file system. You will want to read the section in Chapter 5 on the *newfs(8)* command. In Tru64 UNIX version 5.0 AdvFS, several new features can help this problem tremendously. We suggest that you refer to the sections in Chapter 7 where we discussed the RBMT and indexed directories.

4. Fragmentation will almost surely become an issue. As time goes on, you may notice that the performance of the system gets worse, if defragmenting is not performed on a regular basis. For AdvFS, the *defragment(8)* command and *defragcron(8)* are helpful tools for defragmenting the file systems. In the case of UFS, we discussed fragmentation ways to monitor and correct the problem in Chapter 5.

5. On this type of system, backups are difficult, if not impossible. A News server database changes so often that backups often miss some of the files. Also, because you can usually re-create lost files from their "upstream" server, backups may not really be necessary. With an e-mail server, you also can miss backing up files. Unfortunately, however, the data are not re-creatable and messages may be lost forever in a corruption situation. There isn't much of a solution to this problem, unless you want to perform backups all the time. If you can spare enough disks, a disk-to-disk backup strategy

could work well here. We recommend nightly backups using clone filesets for critical mail servers at an absolute minimum. Naturally, this strategy will require you to use AdvFS.

8.3   A Database Server

A database server, as we refer to it, is a large back-end system that runs one of the commercially available database engines such as Oracle, Sybase, or Informix. Many of these big high-end database servers tend to run as the back-end to an enterprise application, such as an Enterprise Resource Planning (ERP) solution; however, the application servers tend to be on a mid-range server over the network. Some of the larger ERP solution vendors are SAP™, Baan™, Oracle Financials™, and People-Soft™. In addition to ERP, another possible use for a big database server is data warehousing. These servers tend to be very big, even by database server standards.

If we follow the procedure given in the last section, we find that the biggest problem is with step 3. We notice that these kinds of systems tend to have the following special characteristics:

1.   If file systems are used, they create fewer large files.

2.   In many cases, raw I/O is used to gain performance.

3.   Have a strict 24-hour, year-round requirement. Reliability and stability are the most important watch words for a large, enterprise data server. System downtime tends to be very expensive.

4.   Store their data in many larger file systems.

5.   Cache efficiency is normally good, unless a new database create is in progress.

6.   Reliable backups are an absolute must.

For step 6 in our procedure, we see that the kinds of tuning problems this type of server tends to cause include:

1.   Lots of memory is needed to appropriately cache file systems data. Frequent cache flushing is usually not a problem because everything is designed to stay in memory all the time. A new database creation can throw the cache out of whack for a short period, but that should correct itself quickly. We discussed AdvFS cache tun-

ing parameters in Chapter 6 and UFS and VFS cache tuning in Chapters 5 and 4. We refer you to those sections for details about setting parameters.

2.   If raw disks are used, then caches can be tuned down very low. You'll want to allow as much memory as possible to be used by the database software to do its own caching.

3.   Fragmentation is usually not an issue even if file systems are used because the files are not growing or changing storage requirements in any way. The database software is internally managing the file.

4.   Do not use sparse files to store database files because they will grow in size over time as the files are updated. Database programs usually do not understand how to deal with a file system full error, which can be catastrophic. We discussed sparse files in Chapter 1.

5.   Backups can be difficult because databases tend to have many table files, all of which must be consistent with each other or the backup is worthless. Also, if raw disks are used to store the databases, then the only system tool you have to perform a backup is *dd(1)*. With *dd(1)*, it will be nearly impossible to independently verify that you are getting a correct backup. Database vendors usually have their own software for backing things up. You are best off using the method recommended by the vendor.

6.   Backups can cause their own problems because of the shear volume of data involved. You may find that without enough tape drives and throughput available, a nightly backup could take longer than 24 hours to complete. The two strategies we have seen to handle this issue are to either throw more tape drives at the problem or to alter the backup strategy (e.g., try non-full backups).

7.   Do not use NFS mounted file systems to store database files. This is particularly true for NFS loopback mounting because caches are attempting to handle two file system blocks for the same data. This procedure wastes time and memory, and you will experience abysmal performance.

8.   LSM may be needed to carve out space for raw database tables. If raw disks are used, then each "disk" tends to be a single table space. Therefore, you may need to make many table spaces, which can only be done efficiently by using LSM. This task can also be

completed with an intelligent disk controller like an HSZ, but this can be clumsy compared with LSM. We discussed how to create and manage logical volumes in Chapter 3.

9. The direct I/O feature of AdvFS version 5.0 and higher is useful for those cases in which you'd like to get very close to the performance of raw I/O but still have the manageability of file systems. See our discussion in Chapter 7 for more detail on this useful capability.

10. System disk mirroring is a must for absolute redundancy. This can be done using either LSM or, more preferably, an intelligent disk controller, such as an HSZ. System disk mirroring using LSM is discussed in Chapter 3, and controller-based mirroring is covered in Chapter 2. Refer to those chapters for discussion about setting up mirroring.

8.4 Internet or E-Commerce Server

An Internet server is mainly a *web, ftp, gopher, wais,* or some other related application. A lot of sites today are using freeware tools such as Apache and Washington University's ftp daemon (wuftpd) to run their web servers. Some packages (e.g., Netscape Commerce Server) out there perform this function as well.

If we follow the procedure given in the last section, we find that the biggest problem is with step 3. We notice that these kinds of systems tend to have the following special characteristics:

1. They hold lots of small files but are usually static.

2. Use lots of network I/O.

3. Have almost a 24-hour, year-round requirement.

4. Usually store their data on larger file systems.

5. Backups are very important.

For step 6 in our procedure, we see that the kinds of tuning problems this type of server tends to cause include:

1. More than any other problem, vnode exhaustion will happen on busy servers. Because vnodes are used and reused often for both files and sockets, your system may run into a shortage of a critical

resource during peak usage. Appropriate care must be taken to tune the VFS area to allow for an appropriate number and aging of vnodes on the system. We refer you to Chapter 4 for our discussion of vnode monitoring and tuning parameters. You should be most concerned with the vnode aging and hashing information.

2.   Data caching can be a problem depending on the amount of data on the server. Usually, a steady state will be reached as long as enough memory is available. All bets are off, though, if the server has uneven traffic load. This situation can be problematic for the system to deal with, but the cache should hit a steady state after a short period. Bursty traffic tends to be dealt with by the caches, so the more memory, the better. We discussed AdvFS cache tuning parameters in Chapter 7 and UFS and VFS cache tuning in Chapters 5 and 4. We refer you to those sections for details about setting parameters.

3.   Inodes or tags may be exhausted if maintenance is not performed. Because the applications will be using so many inodes or tags on the file system, the default number will almost certainly not be appropriate and will need to be increased. If you are using AdvFS, you will want to read the section in Chapter 7 where we discussed the BMT exhaustion problem. For UFS, the *newfs(8)* command can be used to increase the number of inodes for a particular file system. You will want to read the section in Chapter 5 on the *newfs(8)* command. In Tru64 UNIX version 5.0 AdvFS, several new features can help this problem tremendously. We suggest that you refer to the sections in Chapter 7 where we discussed the RBMT and indexed directories.

4.   Fragmentation may become an issue. As time goes on, you may notice that the performance of the system gets worse, if defragmenting is not performed on a regular basis. For AdvFS, the *defragment(8)* command and *defragcron(8)* are helpful tools for defragmenting the file systems. In the case of UFS, we discussed ways to reduce or eliminate fragmentation in Chapter 5.

5.   Backups are critical but shouldn't be difficult. For a regular web server, the data do not change very often, so a regular backup schedule should be implemented. In the case of an e-commerce server, the back-end database will host the critical data, but some critical files may still reside on the web server. Most big e-commerce sites implement some sort of redundant web server solution such

as round-robin packet routing, so a single node being offline does not cause a significant problem. Use the *vdump(8)* tool with LSM snapshots (UFS or AdvFS) or clone filesets (AdvFS only) for your backup solution.

8.5 Network File System Server

An network file system (NFS) server is typically used to store and retrieve files for users' workstations or compute servers on a network. Therefore, they typically serve up file systems for other nodes.

If we follow the procedure given in the last section, we find that the biggest problem is with step 3. We notice that these kinds of systems tend to have the following special characteristics:

1. The workload mix is difficult to predict.

2. Use lots of network I/O.

3. Have almost a 24-hour, year-round requirement.

4. Storage mix is workload-dependent.

5. Quotas and/or ACLs may be very important.

6. Users can use up space and never release it.

7. Security can be an issue.

For step 6 in our procedure, we see that the kinds of tuning problems this type of server tends to cause include:

1. Data are difficult to cache because the workload mix can change and spikes may be experienced. In a really busy system, the update daemon still comes along every 30 seconds to sync the file systems. This task can cause the system to appear to freeze because so must dirty data in the cache needs to be flushed. The smooth sync capability, which we discussed in Chapter 4, can be used to help smooth out the data flushing. We discussed AdvFS cache tuning parameters in Chapter 7 and UFS and VFS cache tuning in Chapters 5 and 4. We refer you to those sections for details about setting parameters.

2. Inodes or tags may be exhausted if maintenance is not performed. Because the applications will be using so many inodes or tags on the file system, the default number will almost certainly not be appropriate and will need to be increased. If you are using AdvFS,

you will want to read the section in Chapter 7 where we discussed the BMT exhaustion problem. For UFS, the *newfs(8)* command can be used to increate the number of inodes for a particular file system. You will want to read the section in Chapter 5 on the *newfs(8)* command.

3. Fragmentation may become an issue. As time goes on, you may notice that the performance of the system gets worse, if defragmenting is not performed on a regular basis. For AdvFS, the *defragment(8)* command and *defragcron(8)* are helpful tools for defragmenting the file systems. In the case of UFS, we discussed fragmentation in Chapter 5.

4. Backups should be performed regularly. The best way to perform backups is by using vdump and either LSM snapshots (UFS or AdvFS) or clone filesets (AdvFS only). The former command would be used if a small downtime can be taken each night, and the latter command would be used if no downtime can be taken. You should see our discussions of LSM snapshots in Chapter 3 and of clone filesets in Chapter 6 for more information about these facilities.

5. Quotas may become necessary. You would want to use quotas if you want to control individual user usage by blocks or number of files. Both client and server need to agree on UIDs and GIDs for this feature to work properly. Network information service (NIS) can provide this capability and is often used in conjunction with NFS. We fully discussed setting up and managing quotas for UFS in Chapter 5 and AdvFS in Chapter 6.

6. Access control lists (ACLs) may be needed, depending on the complexity of the security environment. In addition, the NIS might be needed to create a common security environment for all the systems sharing files. Our ACL discussion is found in Chapter 1.

7. Prestoserve may help speed performance. A dedicated, persistent cache like prestoserve would be helpful for a very busy NFS server.

8.6   Summary

A specialized server can have its file systems tuned for optimal performance, if you keep in mind some of the information we've provided in this chapter. Chances are, your system will fall into one or more of these categories, and this information will provide a starting point for you to tune it.

9

File System Troubleshooting and Recovery

> Either I'm dead or my watch has stopped.
> — Final words of *Groucho Marx*

This chapter is a discussion of case studies of some complex file system problems and how they were resolved. We think the best way to discuss how to troubleshoot file system problems is by looking at examples and completely understanding what steps were followed and why. These case studies were derived from many years of experience in dealing with real customer problems. They are representative of the kinds of issues that some customers may experience.

9.1   Fixing a Corrupted AdvFS Directory

This is a real-world example of how a procedure was developed to remove a corrupted directory from an AdvFS domain. This procedure is only provided as an example, but we believe that it should be general enough to be used in other cases by people stuck with a small number of corrupted files or directories. In this case, a full restore of a large file system is not practical to clean up a minor problem such as this one.

As discussed in Chapter 5, the *clri(8)* command would be the best way to approach a problem such as this one if the corruption were on a UFS file system; however, for AdvFS there is no equivalent to *clri(8)*, therefore, another approach was needed for dealing with a corrupted directory. In the absence of a specialized tool, a procedure using standard tools was needed.

We begin with an individual who finds that he has a corrupted directory in one of his AdvFSs. He sent a scripted output of some file system commands, and this is what he found as a result:

```
                           # cd /usr/u4/web
                           # ls
aaccoswd    cccweb      dhhhsw      engweb      hgweb       otgweb      sehsweb
adm1web     circles     divweb      espaweb     iadvweb     physweb     swweb
apaweb      dbedweb     dspweb      eurodeaf    kdpweb      pkzweb      tcweb
aspweb      deafeyes    dzweb       extweb      kgweb       presweb     webclass
auditweb    deafway     eeoweb      fcsweb      lsguweb     psychweb    xx
caslweb     deweb       eliweb      gsaweb      ospweb      sbgweb

# cd xx

# ls
??????????????????????????????????????????????????????????????????????????????????

# file *
^C      ⇐ the file command hung, so he typed control-c to get the prompt back

# pwd
/usr/u4/web/xx

# cd ..

# ls -ld xx
drwx------  3 root    system   8192 Mar 31 13:07 xx

# pwd
/usr/u4/web

# rm -r xx
rm: xx/=A4=BF=A4=BF=A4=BF=A4=BF=A4=BF=A4=BF=A4=BF=A4=BF=A4=BF=A4=BF=A4=BF=A4=BF=
=A4=BF=A4=BF=A4=BF=A4=BF=A4=BF=A4=BF=A4=BF=A4=BF=A4=BF=A4=BF=A4=BF=A4=BF=A4=
=BF=A4=BF=A4=BF=A4: File name too long
rm: xx/ssion denied

# showfile -x /usr/u4/web/xx

     Id       Vol   PgSz   Pages  XtntType  Segs  SegSz   Log    Perf   File
8576.8009     1     16     1      simple    **    **      ftx    100%   xx

   extentMap: 1
     pageOff  pageCnt    vol    volBlock   blockCnt
        0            1     1     3032288          16
   extentCnt: 1
```

Thus, the symptoms of the corruption were that he couldn't list the contents of the directory "xx." In addition, the directory and its contents could not be removed using standard tools such as *rm(1)* or *rmdir(1)*. The ultimate goal was to remove this directory. The customer had a good backup and was willing to restore any lost files if he could just remove the corrupted directory and be sure of the integrity of the rest of the file system. He preferred not to take the time needed to restore the entire file system because it was large. Unfortunately, he had already attempted to use *verify(8)* to clean up the system, but he was not successful. Therefore, he required a better approach.

First, the directory file was readable, which helped by providing some additional information about the directory's contents. The benefit was that some additional evidence was derived about how the directory file was corrupted. The octal "220" values were known to be invalid, but it was not known for certain how this corruption occurred. It was speculated that the corruption was caused by bad blocks that were reported in the system's binary error log.

```
# cat xx | od -c
0000000    v  205   \0   \0  024   \0  001   \0    .   \0   \0   \0    v  205   \0   \0
0000020   \t  200   \0   \0  244  005   \0   \0  024   \0  002   \0    .    .   \0   \0
0000040  244  005   \0   \0  006  200   \0   \0   \0   \0   \0   \0  214   \0  004   \0
0000060    n    u    1    1   \0   \0   \0   \0    =   \f   \0   \0  200   \0   \0   \0
0000100   \0   \0   \0   \0    t   \0   \0   \0    .    1    o    g    i    n   \0   \0
0000120  212  206   \0   \0   \t  200   \0   \0   \0   \0   \0   \0  034   \0   \b   \0
0000140    .    p    r    o    f    i    1    e   \0   \0   \0   \0    y  205   \0   \0
0000160  006  200   \0   \0   \0   \0   \0   \0  024   \0  003   \0    b    i    n   \0
0000200    u  205   \0   \0  006  200   \0   \0   \0   \0   \0   \0  030   \0  004   \0
0000220    o    r    i    g   \0   \0   \0   \0    w  205   \0   \0  004  200   \0   \0
0000240   \0   \0   \0   \0  024   \0  003   \0    w    e    b   \0  022    1   \0   \0
0000260  002  200   \0   \0  253  006   \0   \0  334   \0  310   \0  220  220  220  220
0000300  220  220  220  220  220  220  220  220  220  220  220  220  220  220  220  220
*
0000600  220  220  220  220   \0   \0   \0   \0  253  006   \0   \0    %  200   \0   \0
0000620   \0   \0   \0   \0    p   \0   \0   \0   \0   \0  \\0   \0   \0   \0   \0   \0
0000640   \0   \0   \0   \0   \0   \0   \0   \0   \0   \0   \0   \0   \0   \0   \0   \0
*
```

[snip]

As a result of analyzing the available data, the following procedure was developed and successfully used to remove the corrupted directory file. The procedure works by writing zeros over the 16 disk blocks on which the directory resides so that *rmdir(1)* can be used to remove it. The *rmdir(1)* command normally cannot be used to remove directories that contain entries; however, *rmdir(1)* was effective here because after writing the zeros, the directory effectively contained no entries. The procedure included the following steps:

1. Find the corrupted directory or file. In this case, the directory was already identified as we showed previously.

2. Use *showfile(8)* to examine the extent map for the file or directory. As an example, we use a directory called "jjj" on a file domain mounted on "/tst."

```
# showfile -x /tst/jjj
    Id     Vol   PgSz   Pages   XtntType   Segs   SegSz   I/O  Perf File
  c.8002   1     16     1       simple     **     **      ftx  100% jjj
```

```
extentMap: 1
  pageOff   pageCnt    vol    volBlock    blockCnt
     0         1        1      131136      16
  extentCnt: 1
```

3. Record the "vol," "volBlock," and "blockCnt" values from the extent map because they will be needed later. In this case, the values are 1, 131136, and 16.

As illustrated in chapters 6 and 7, the number and sizes for each of the extents in an extent map can be more extensive than we show in our rather simplistic example. A directory that contained a large number of files may have more than one extent. Therefore, you may need to record the information for each extent for use in later steps of this procedure.

4. Find the block special device name for the volume(s) determined in step #2 using *showfdmn(8)*.

```
# showfdmn tst_dmn
         Id                 Date Created            LogPgs   Domain Name
3662ad91.00002c20    Mon Nov 30 09:37:05 1998      512        tst_dmn

Vol      512-Blks     Free     % Used   Cmode    Rblks    Wblks    Vol Name
 1L       200000     188640     6%        on      128      128     /dev/vol/dg3/voltst
```

5. Validate the correct data. Use *dd(1)* to read the directory file and pipe through *od(1)* to convert the data to ASCII character output. The parameters needed for the *dd(1)* will be the following:

   ▪ The "if" field will be the character special file corresponding to the volume found in step #3.

   ▪ The "bs" field will be 512.

   ▪ The "count" field will be the blockCnt value recorded in step #2.

   ▪ The "iseek" field will be the volBlock value recorded in step #2.

```
# dd if=/dev/rvol/dg3/voltst bs=512 count=16 iseek=131136 | od -c
0000000  \f  \0  \0   \0  024   \0  001   \0    .   \0   \0   \0   \f   \0   \0   \0
0000020  002 200  \0   \0  002   \0   \0   \0  024   \0  002   \0    .    .   \0   \0
0000040  002  \0  \0   \0  001  200   \0   \0   \0   \0   \0  330  001   \0   \0   \0
0000060  \0   \0  \0   \0   \0   \0   \0   \0   \0   \0   \0   \0   \0   \0   \0   \0
*
0001000  \0   \0  \0   \0   \0  002   \0   \0   \0   \0   \0   \0   \0   \0   \0   \0
0001020  \0   \0  \0   \0   \0   \0   \0   \0   \0   \0   \0   \0   \0   \0   \0   \0
*
0002000  \0   \0  \0  \\0   \0  002  \\0   \0  \\0   \0   \0   \0   \0   \0   \0   \0
0002020  \0   \0  \0   \0   \0   \0   \0   \0   \0   \0   \0   \0   \0   \0   \0   \0
*
[snip]
```

6. Next, unmount the file system to make sure there will be no unintended consequences.

```
# umount /tst
```

7. Write zeros over each of the extents in the directory file using *dd(1)* again like in step 4. The parameters needed for the *dd(1)* will be the following:

   - The "of" field will be the character special file corresponding to the volume found in step #3.

   - The "if" field will be /dev/zero.

   - The "bs" field will be 512.

   - The "count" field will be the blockCnt value recorded in step #2.

   - The "oseek" field will be the volBlock value recorded in step #2.

```
# dd if=/dev/zero of=/dev/rvol/dg3/voltst bs=512 count=16
oseek=131136
16+0 records in
16+0 records out
```

8. Next, remount the file system again.

```
# mount tst_dmn#tst /tst
```

9. Verify that the directory file still has an entry in its parent directory, so it will still be there but will contain no entries.

```
# ls /tst/jjj
# ls -la /tst/jjj
total 0
```

10. Remove the directory with the *rmdir(1)* command. The *rmdir(1)* will give an error message because the directory file is not valid. Recall that every valid directory file must have at least two entries "." and "..". The *rmdir(1)* succeeds, despite the error message.

```
# rmdir /tst/jjj
Invalid dir page detected by remove_dots
jjj tag 12.32770
```

11. The directory file is now removed. The files that were contained in the directory or any subdirectories will be lost; however, the file system integrity will be restored.

```
# ls /tst/jjj
/tst/jjj not found
# ls /tst
.tags    quota.group ttt     ttt3     txt34
fstab    quota.user  ttt2    txt1
```

The *verify(8)* command can be run using either the '-d' or '-f' flags after the final step in order to attempt to recover any files under the corrupted directory.

9.2   Detecting and Correcting Subtle AdvFS Metadata Corruption

Hardware problems can corrupt AdvFS metadata in strange and subtle ways. In this case study, we explore a Tru64 UNIX version 4.0D domain that became unmountable due to such a corruption. In this case, it was known that *verify(8)* could not be run because of the domain's very large size (230 gigabytes and 26 volumes). The domain was very active and couldn't be taken down for extended periods. Here, the system and domains had already been planned to be taken down for a short period in order to replace a failing RAID cache battery. The customer was experiencing hangs in the RAID controller because of problems with the cache battery. The domains were unmounted normally before shutting down the system.

When the system was booted back up, one domain "d00" would not mount. The error from the *mount(8)* command was E_VD_DMNATTR_DIFF, which indicated that there was an inconsistency in the domain attributes between the volumes.

```
# showfsets d00
showfsets: can't show set info for domain 'd00'
showfsets: error = E_VD_DMNATTR_DIFF (-1079)

# cd /etc/fdmns/d00

# ls -l
total 0
lrwxrwxrwx  1 root    system     12 Aug 30 08:36 rza129c -> /dev/rza129c
lrwxrwxrwx  1 root    system     12 Aug 30 08:36 rza130c -> /dev/rza130c
lrwxrwxrwx  1 root    system     12 Aug 30 08:36 rza131c -> /dev/rza131c
lrwxrwxrwx  1 root    system     12 Aug 30 08:36 rza132c -> /dev/rza132c
lrwxrwxrwx  1 root    system     12 Aug 30 08:36 rza137c -> /dev/rza137c
lrwxrwxrwx  1 root    system     12 Aug 30 08:36 rza138c -> /dev/rza138c
lrwxrwxrwx  1 root    system     12 Aug 30 08:36 rza139c -> /dev/rza139c
lrwxrwxrwx  1 root    system     12 Aug 30 08:36 rza140c -> /dev/rza140c
lrwxrwxrwx  1 root    system     12 Aug 30 08:36 rza145c -> /dev/rza145c
lrwxrwxrwx  1 root    system     12 Aug 30 08:36 rza146c -> /dev/rza146c
lrwxrwxrwx  1 root    system     12 Aug 30 08:36 rza147c -> /dev/rza147c
lrwxrwxrwx  1 root    system     12 Aug 30 08:36 rza148c -> /dev/rza148c
lrwxrwxrwx  1 root    system     12 Aug 30 08:36 rzb129c -> /dev/rzb129c
lrwxrwxrwx  1 root    system     12 Aug 30 08:36 rzb130c -> /dev/rzb130c
lrwxrwxrwx  1 root    system     12 Aug 30 08:36 rzb131c -> /dev/rzb131c
```

```
lrwxrwxrwx 1 root    system    12 Aug 30 08:36 rzb132c -> /dev/rzb132c
lrwxrwxrwx 1 root    system    12 Aug 30 08:36 rzb137c -> /dev/rzb137c
lrwxrwxrwx 1 root    system    12 Aug 30 08:36 rzb138c -> /dev/rzb138c
lrwxrwxrwx 1 root    system    12 Aug 30 08:36 rzb139c -> /dev/rzb139c
lrwxrwxrwx 1 root    system    12 Aug 30 08:36 rzb140c -> /dev/rzb140c
lrwxrwxrwx 1 root    system    12 Aug 30 08:36 rzb145c -> /dev/rzb145c
lrwxrwxrwx 1 root    system    12 Aug 30 08:36 rzb146c -> /dev/rzb146c
lrwxrwxrwx 1 root    system    12 Aug 30 08:36 rzb147c -> /dev/rzb147c
lrwxrwxrwx 1 root    system    12 Aug 30 08:36 rzb148c -> /dev/rzb148c
lrwxrwxrwx 1 root    system    12 Aug 30 08:36 rze132c -> /dev/rze132c
lrwxrwxrwx 1 root    system    12 Aug 30 08:36 rze140c -> /dev/rze140c
```

One tool that is often overlooked for diagnostic work is *advscan(8)*. Many people are aware that *advscan(8)* can be used to detect and correct problems in the /etc/fdmns directory, but because it must read and print out information from the volume's metadata, it can also be used to quickly determine if inconsistencies exist.

```
# /sbin/advfs/advscan -a -g
Scanning devices   /dev/rrz25 /dev/rrz26 /dev/rrza129 /dev/rrza130 /dev/rrza131
       /dev/rrza132 /dev/rrza137 /dev/rrza138 /dev/rrza139 /dev/rrza140
       /dev/rrza145 /dev/rrza146 /dev/rrza147 /dev/rrza148 /dev/rrzb129
       /dev/rrzb130 /dev/rrzb131 /dev/rrzb132 /dev/rrzb137 /dev/rrzb138
       /dev/rrzb139 /dev/rrzb140 /dev/rrzb145 /dev/rrzb146 /dev/rrzb147
       /dev/rrzb148 /dev/rrze132 /dev/rrze140 /dev/rrzc129 /dev/rrzc130
       /dev/rrzc131 /dev/rrzc132 /dev/rrzc137 /dev/rrzc138 /dev/rrzc139
       /dev/rrzc140 /dev/rrzc145 /dev/rrzc146 /dev/rrzc147 /dev/rrzc148
       /dev/rrzd129 /dev/rrzd130 /dev/rrzd131 /dev/rrzd132 /dev/rrzd137
       /dev/rrzd138 /dev/rrzd139 /dev/rrzd140 /dev/rrzd145 /dev/rrzd146
       /dev/rrzd147 /dev/rrzd148 /dev/rrze148

Partition      Domain Id

[snip]

/dev/rrza129c    344236a7.000a5605          V3, dismounted
                 26 volumes in domain
                 Created                    Mon Oct 13 10:56:39 1997
                 Last mount                 Thu Aug 19 14:53:20 1999

/dev/rrza130c    344236a7.000a5605          V3, dismounted
                 26 volumes in domain
                 Created                    Mon Oct 13 10:56:39 1997
                 Last mount                 Thu Aug 19 14:53:20 1999

/dev/rrza131c    344236a7.000a5605          V3, dismounted

                 Created                    Mon Oct 13 10:56:39 1997
                 Last mount                 Thu Aug 19 14:53:20 1999

/dev/rrza132c    344236a7.000a5605          V3, <= mounted should be "dismounted"

                 Created                    Mon Oct 13 10:56:39 1997
                 Last mount                 Thu May 13 10:47:46 1999
```

```
/dev/rrza137c      344236a7.000a5605      V3, dismounted

                   Created                Mon Oct 13 10:56:39 1997
                   Last mount             Thu Aug 19 14:53:20 1999

/dev/rrza138c      344236a7.000a5605      V3, dismounted

                   Created                Mon Oct 13 10:56:39 1997
                   Last mount             Thu Aug 19 14:53:20 1999

/dev/rrza139c      344236a7.000a5605      V3, dismounted

                   Created                Mon Oct 13 10:56:39 1997
                   Last mount             Thu Aug 19 14:53:20 1999

/dev/rrza140c      344236a7.000a5605      V3, dismounted

                   Created                Mon Oct 13 10:56:39 1997
                   Last mount             Thu Aug 19 14:53:20 1999

/dev/rrza145c      344236a7.000a5605      V3, dismounted

                   Created                Mon Oct 13 10:56:39 1997
                   Last mount             Thu Aug 19 14:53:20 1999

/dev/rrza146c      344236a7.000a5605      V3, dismounted

                   Created                Mon Oct 13 10:56:39 1997
                   Last mount             Thu Aug 19 14:53:20 1999

/dev/rrza147c      344236a7.000a5605      V3, dismounted

                   Created                Mon Oct 13 10:56:39 1997
                   Last mount             Thu Aug 19 14:53:20 1999

/dev/rrza148c      344236a7.000a5605      V3, dismounted

                   Created                Mon Oct 13 10:56:39 1997
                   Last mount             Thu Aug 19 14:53:20 1999

/dev/rrzb129c      344236a7.000a5605      V3, dismounted

                   Created                Mon Oct 13 10:56:39 1997
                   Last mount             Thu Aug 19 14:53:20 1999

/dev/rrzb130c      344236a7.000a5605      V3, dismounted

                   Created                Mon Oct 13 10:56:39 1997
                   Last mount             Thu Aug 19 14:53:20 1999

/dev/rrzb131c      344236a7.000a5605      V3, dismounted

                   Created                Mon Oct 13 10:56:39 1997
                   Last mount             Thu Aug 19 14:53:20 1999

/dev/rrzb132c      344236a7.000a5605      V3, dismounted

                   Created                Mon Oct 13 10:56:39 1997
                   Last mount             Thu Aug 19 14:53:20 1999

/dev/rrzb137c      344236a7.000a5605      V3, dismounted

                   Created                Mon Oct 13 10:56:39 1997
                   Last mount             Thu Aug 19 14:53:20 1999
```

/dev/rrzb138c	344236a7.000a5605	3, dismounted
	Created Last mount	Mon Oct 13 10:56:39 1997 Thu Aug 19 14:53:20 1999
/dev/rrzb139c	344236a7.000a5605	V3, dismounted
	Created Last mount	Mon Oct 13 10:56:39 1997 Thu Aug 19 14:53:20 1999
/dev/rrzb140c	344236a7.000a5605	V3, dismounted
	Created Last mount	Mon Oct 13 10:56:39 1997 Thu Aug 19 14:53:20 1999
/dev/rrzb145c	44236a7.000a5605	V3, dismounted
	Created Last mount	Mon Oct 13 10:56:39 1997 Thu Aug 19 14:53:20 1999
/dev/rrzb146c	344236a7.000a5605	V3, dismounted
	Created Last mount	Mon Oct 13 10:56:39 1997 Thu Aug 19 14:53:20 1999
/dev/rrzb147c	344236a7.000a5605	V3, dismounted
	Created Last mount	Mon Oct 13 10:56:39 1997 Thu Aug 19 14:53:20 1999
/dev/rrzb148c	344236a7.000a5605	V3, dismounted
	Created Last mount	Mon Oct 13 10:56:39 1997 Thu Aug 19 14:53:20 1999
/dev/rrze132c	344236a7.000a5605	V3, dismounted
	Created Last mount	Mon Oct 13 10:56:39 1997 Thu Aug 19 14:53:20 1999
/dev/rrze140c	344236a7.000a5605	V3, dismounted
	Created Last mount	Mon Oct 13 10:56:39 1997 Thu Aug 19 14:53:20 1999

[snip]

So, here we saw that one of the volumes in the domain, rz132c, was showing its state as "mounted." This state was confirmed using *vbmtpg(8)* and by examining the state field in the BSR_VD_ATTR record in mcell #4 in the BMT. The state field has a 1, which indicates a "mounted" state, whereas a 2 would indicate an "unmounted" state. The *vbmtpg(8)* utility reports the information as follows:

```
        # /sbin/advfs/vbmtpg /dev/rrza132c
PAGE LBN  32 megaVersion  3 nextFreePg  0 freeMcellCnt 17 pageId  0
nextfreeMCId page  0 cell  11
=======================================================================
```

[snip]

```
CELL  4  nextVdIndex   4 linkSegment   1  tag,bfSetTag:  -24,  -2
nextMCId  page  0 cell  6
=========================================================================
RECORD 0 bcnt 40 version 0    type  3 BSR_VD_ATTR
vdMntId: Thu May 13 10:47:46 1999
state 1 ⇐ this is the "mounted" volume state
vdIndex 4
jays_new_field 0
vdBlkCnt 17769177
stgCluster 2
maxPgSz 16
bmtXtntPgs 2048
serviceClass 1

RECORD 1 bcnt 24 version 0    type  4 BSR_DMN_ATTR
bfDomainId: Mon Oct 13 10:56:39 1997
maxVds 256
bfSetDirTag -2

[snip]
```

At this stage, the domain was effectively down and the customer had a backup, but the recovery would have taken a very long time on this domain with this amount of data. The problem was elevated to find a quick and creative solution because the corruption was localized and because the customer's data on the domain were apparently not affected. A specialized tool called "change_vdstate" was developed, and when delivered, it corrected this minor corruption. Once the tool was run, the *mount(8)* and *showfsets(8)* were successful.

```
# ./print_mcell_info /dev/rrza132c 2 | grep "Volume state:"
   Volume state: 1

# ./change_vdstate /dev/rrza132c 2
Changing vd state field from 1 to 2

# ./print_mcell_info /dev/rrza132c 2 | grep "Volume state:"
   Volume state: 2

# showfsets d00

fs00
   Id            : 344236a7.000a5605.1.8001
   Files         :    0, SLim=    0, HLim=    0
   Blocks (512)  :    0, SLim=    0, HLim=    0
   Quota Status  : user=off group=off

fs01
   Id            : 344236a7.000a5605.2.8001
   Files         :    0, SLim=    0, HLim=    0
   Blocks (512)  :    0, SLim=    0, HLim=    0
   Quota Status  : user=off group=off
```

Thanks to the quick response, the downtime on the system was limited, so the file system was back in service in a very short period.

9.3   Recovering a Medium-Complexity AdvFS and LSM Configuration

This case study is from an activity for a system administrator performing maintenance on a 1.x TruCluster system that has "offline" service. In Tru-Cluster parlance, this means that the service has been administratively taken down for some reason. When this occurs, the TruCluster software takes all of the storage for that service and makes it unavailable to any of the cluster members so that maintenance can be performed. Thus, the best way to make the file systems available is by mounting them by hand following the steps that TruCluster software follows to bring the service online. We are not trying to teach you TruCluster, but we simply use this example as a means of illustrating our point.

The first thing you need to know is what disks are involved, whether LSM is being used by the service, the LSM disk group, and what the AdvFS domain name was originally. This information is available from the ASE configuration database and should be known before continuing with this procedure. We are not trying to cover clustering here, so we will give you that information.

Service Name: sys

Disk: rz129

LSM: Yes

Disk Group: sys_dg

Domain name: sys_domain

With this information, let's find out what the state of the disk rz129 is with respect to LSM. We use the *voldisk(8)* command for this task.

```
# voldisk list
DEVICE    TYPE    DISK    GROUP     STATUS
rz129     sliced  -       -         offline
rz130     sliced  rz130   homedg    online
rz131     sliced  -       -         offline
rz132     sliced  -       -         offline
rz133     sliced  -       -         offline
rz6       sliced  rz6     rootdg    online
```

We see that the disk is offline. It must be online in order to proceed, so we perform the operation to bring the disk online with respect to LSM.

```
# voldisk online rz129
```

Next, we import the disk group so that the subdisks, plexes, and volume information are made available to the node on which we are working. The *volprint(8)* will succeed following the import for this LSM disk group.

```
# voldg import sysdg

# volprint -htg sysdg
DG NAME         GROUP-ID
DM NAME         DEVICE       TYPE      PRIVLEN    PUBLEN   PUBPATH
V  NAME         USETYPE      KSTATE    STATE      LENGTH   READPOL      PREFPLEX
PL NAME         VOLUME       KSTATE    STATE      LENGTH   LAYOUT       ST-WIDTH MODE
SD NAME         PLEX         PLOFFS    DISKOFFS   LENGTH   DISK-NAME    DEVICE

dg sysdg        941468336.2725.maxx.alf.dec.com

dm rz129        rz129        sliced    1024       17772484 /dev/rrz129g

v  volsys01     fsgen        DISABLED  ACTIVE     2000000  SELECT       -
pl volsys01-01  volsys01     DISABLED  ACTIVE     2000000  CONCAT       -RW
sd rz129-01     volsys01-01  0         0          2000000  rz129        rz129

v  volsys02     fsgen        DISABLED  ACTIVE     2000000  SELECT       -
pl volsys02-01  volsys02     DISABLED  ACTIVE     2000000  CONCAT       -RW
sd rz129-02     volsys02-01  0         2000000    2000000  rz129        rz129

v  volsys03     fsgen        DISABLED  ACTIVE     2000000  SELECT       -
pl volsys03-01  volsys03     DISABLED  ACTIVE     2000000  CONCAT       -RW
sd rz129-03     volsys03-01  0         4000000    2000000  rz129        rz129

v  volsys04     fsgen        DISABLED  ACTIVE     2000000  SELECT       -
pl volsys04-01  volsys04     DISABLED  ACTIVE     2000000  CONCAT       -RW
sd rz129-04     volsys04-01  0         6000000    2000000  rz129        rz129

v  volsys05     fsgen        DISABLED  ACTIVE     2000000  SELECT       -
pl volsys05-01  volsys05     DISABLED  ACTIVE     2000000  CONCAT       -RW
sd rz129-05     volsys05-01  0         8000000    2000000  rz129        rz129

v  volsys06     fsgen        DISABLED  ACTIVE     2000000  SELECT       -
pl volsys06-01  volsys06     DISABLED  ACTIVE     2000000  CONCAT       -RW
sd rz129-06     volsys06-01  0         10000000   2000000  rz129        rz129
```

Now, we must bring the volumes to the ENABLED state. The easiest way to do this is using the top-down command *volrecover(8)*.

```
# volrecover -sb

# volprint -htg sysdg

DG NAME         GROUP-ID

DM NAME         DEVICE       TYPE      PRIVLEN    PUBLEN   PUBPATH
V  NAME         USETYPE      KSTATE    STATE      LENGTH   READPOL      PREFPLEX
PL NAME         VOLUME       KSTATE    STATE      LENGTH   LAYOUT       ST-WIDTH MODE
SD NAME         PLEX         PLOFFS    DISKOFFS   LENGTH   DISK-NAME    DEVICE

dg sysdg        941468336.2725.maxx.alf.dec.com

dm rz129        rz129        sliced    1024       17772484 /dev/rrz129g
```

```
v   volsys01      fsgen           ENABLED    ACTIVE     2000000   SELECT     -
pl  volsys01-01   volsys01        ENABLED    ACTIVE     2000000   CONCAT     -    RW
sd  rz129-01      volsys01-01     0          0          2000000   rz129      rz129

v   volsys02      fsgen           ENABLED    ACTIVE     2000000   SELECT     -
pl  volsys02-01   volsys02        ENABLED    ACTIVE     2000000   CONCAT     -    RW
sd  rz129-02      volsys02-01     0          2000000    2000000   rz129      rz129

v   volsys03      fsgen           ENABLED    ACTIVE     2000000   SELECT     -
pl  volsys03-01   volsys03        ENABLED    ACTIVE     2000000   CONCAT     -    RW
sd  rz129-03      volsys03-01     0          4000000    2000000   rz129      rz129

v   volsys04      fsgen           ENABLED    ACTIVE     2000000   SELECT     -
pl  volsys04-01   volsys04        ENABLED    ACTIVE     2000000   CONCAT     -    RW
sd  rz129-04      volsys04-01     0          6000000    2000000   rz129      rz129

v   volsys05      fsgen           ENABLED    ACTIVE     2000000   SELECT     -
pl  volsys05-01   volsys05        ENABLED    ACTIVE     2000000   CONCAT     -    RW
sd  rz129-05      volsys05-01     0          8000000    2000000   rz129      rz129

v   volsys06      fsgen           ENABLED    ACTIVE     2000000   SELECT     -
pl  volsys06-01   volsys06        ENABLED    ACTIVE     2000000   CONCAT     -    RW
sd  rz129-06      volsys06-01     0          10000000   2000000   rz129      rz129
```

The next few steps have to do with the AdvFS domain and setting up the correct information in the /etc/fdmns directory so that the AdvFS tools will work properly.

```
# ls /etc/fdmns
.advfslock_bckup_domain    .advfslock_svc1_domain    home_domain
.advfslock_export_dmn      .advfslock_sys_domain     j2_dmn
.advfslock_fdmns           .advfslock_tst_dmn        j_dmn
.advfslock_home_domain     .advfslock_usr_domain     kits_domain
.advfslock_j_dmn           .advfslock_var_domain     root_domain
.advfslock_kits_domain     bckup_domain              usr_domain
.advfslock_root_domain     home                      var_domain

# cd /etc/fdmns

# /sbin/advfs/advscan -g sysdg
Scanning devices    /dev/rvol/sysdg

Partition       Domain Id

sysdg.volsys01 381dac69.000e5633   V3, dismounted
                                    4 volumes in domain

        Created     Mon Nov 1 10:06:17 1999
        Last mount  Mon Feb 28 20:02:34 2000

sysdg.volsys04 381dac69.000e5633   V3, dismounted

        Created     Mon Nov 1 10:06:17 1999
        Last mount  Mon Feb 28 20:02:34 2000

sysdg.volsys05 381dac69.000e5633   V3, dismounted

        Created     Mon Nov 1 10:06:17 1999
        Last mount  Mon Feb 28 20:02:34 2000
```

```
sysdg.volsys06 381dac69.000e5633  V3, dismounted

    Created     Mon Nov 1 10:06:17 1999
    Last mount  Mon Feb 28 20:02:34 2000
```

```
# /sbin/advfs/advscan -r sysdg
```

```
Scanning devices   /dev/rvol/sysdg
```

```
Found domains:
```

```
*unknown*
```

```
    Domain Id   381dac69.000e5633
    Created     Mon Nov 1 10:06:17 1999

    Domain volumes    4
    /etc/fdmns links    0
    Actual partitions found:
                sysdg.volsys01*
                sysdg.volsys04*
                sysdg.volsys05*
                sysdg.volsys06*
```

```
Creating /etc/fdmns/
domain_sysdg.volsys01_sysdg.volsys04_sysdg.volsys05_sysdg.v/
    linking sysdg.volsys01
    linking sysdg.volsys04
    linking sysdg.volsys05
    linking sysdg.volsys06
```

Now, we see that the *advscan(8)* command recovered the lost information in the /etc/fdmns, but the domain name it chose was not the same as the old volume name. We change the domain name by renaming this directory back to the original domain name.

```
# ls
.advfslock_bckup_domain
.advfslock_export_dmn
.advfslock_fdmns
.advfslock_home_domain
.advfslock_j_dmn
.advfslock_kits_domain
.advfslock_root_domain
.advfslock_svc1_domain
.advfslock_sys_domain
.advfslock_tst_dmn
.advfslock_usr_domain
.advfslock_var_domain
bckup_domain
domain_sysdg.volsys01_sysdg.volsys04_sysdg.volsys05_sysdg.volsys06
home
home_domain
j2_dmn
j_dmn
```

```
kits_domain
root_domain
usr_domain
var_domain

# mv domain_sysdg.volsys01_sysdg.volsys04_sysdg.volsys05_sysdg.volsys06
sys_domain

# ls
.advfslock_bckup_domain    .advfslock_sys_domain     j_dmn
.advfslock_export_dmn      .advfslock_tst_dmn        kits_domain
.advfslock_fdmns           .advfslock_usr_domain     root_domain
.advfslock_home_domain     .advfslock_var_domain     sys_domain
.advfslock_j_dmn           bckup_domain              usr_domain
.advfslock_kits_domain     home                      var_domain
.advfslock_root_domain     home_domain
.advfslock_svc1_domain     j2_dmn

# cd sys_domain

# ls -l
total 0
lrwxr-xr-x  1 root    system    23 Mar 2 16:32 sysdg.volsys01 -> /dev/vol
/sysdg/volsys01
lrwxr-xr-x  1 root    system    23 Mar 2 16:32 sysdg.volsys04 -> /dev/vol
/sysdg/volsys04
lrwxr-xr-x  1 root    system    23 Mar 2 16:32 sysdg.volsys05 -> /dev/vol
/sysdg/volsys05
lrwxr-xr-x  1 root    system    23 Mar 2 16:32 sysdg.volsys06 -> /dev/vol
/sysdg/volsys06
```

Once this procedure has been completed, we can use regular AdvFS tools to operate on the domain. Here, both *showfsets(8)* and *mount(8)* work fine on this domain.

```
# showfsets sys_domain
kits
    Id              : 381dac69.000e5633.1.8001
    Files           :    0, SLim=    0, HLim=    0
    Blocks (512)    :    0, SLim=    0, HLim=    0
    Quota Status    : user=off group=off

# mount sys_domain#kits /mnt

# df /mnt | more
Filesystem       512-blocks  Used     Available  Capacity  Mounted on
sys_domain#kits  8000000     5031502  2955904    63%       /mnt
```

When you get to this point, you are ready to perform any type of normal file system maintenance that may be required. One possible reason is to allow the database administrator to bring up the database without the users having access. As you can see, the previous steps could easily be scripted so that the process subsequently goes much smoother.

9.4   Troubleshooting and Correcting a Complex LSM Configuration

In this Tru64 UNIX version V4.0x case study, LSM volumes used for a raw database had somehow become inaccessible. The cause was initially unknown; however, it affected LSM volumes in two TruCluster services known as "baan_infx_p" and "baan_infx_s." The disk devices on which these volumes resided were no longer visible to LSM; however, further analysis showed that there wasn't a hardware problem with the disks, so recovery was possible.

When logging into the affected system, it was found that there were five drives in one of the disk groups and three in another in the "failed" state. This could be an indication of a hardware problem or, as was later discovered, the disk label had been inadvertently removed on the drives. It turned out that the system administrator was attempting to initialize some new drives and accidently destroyed the label on some of the active ones.

The following "voldisk list" and "volprint output" told the story for the two disk groups:

```
# voldisk list

DEVICE    TYPE      DISK     GROUP            STATUS
rz16      sliced    rz16     baan_infx_dg     online
rz17      sliced    rz17     sipros_infx_dg   online
rz25      sliced    rz25     sipros_infx_dg   online
rz32a     nopriv    rz32a    rootdg           online
rz32b     nopriv    rz32b    rootdg           online
rz32e     simple    rz32e    rootdg           online
rz32g     nopriv    rz32g    rootdg           online
rz37      sliced    rz37     rootdg           online
rz8a      nopriv    rz8a     rootdg           online
rz8b      nopriv    rz8b     rootdg           online
rz8e      simple    rz8e     rootdg           online
rz8g      nopriv    rz8g     rootdg           online
rz9c      simple    rz9c     rootdg           online
rzb16     sliced    rzb16    sipros_adfs_dg   online
rzb17     sliced    rzb17    baan_adfs_dg     online
rzb24     sliced    rzb24    sipros_adfs_dg   online
rzb25     sliced    rzb25    baan_adfs_dg     online
rzc17     sliced    -        -                offline
rzc25     sliced    rzc25    db_baan          online
rzd16     sliced    -        -                offline
rzd17     sliced    rzd17    db_baan          online
rzd24     sliced    -        -                offline
rzd25     sliced    -        -                offline
rze16     sliced    -        -                offline
```

```
rze17      sliced    rze17    supt_adfs_dg    online
rze24      sliced    rze24    supt_infx_dg    online
rze25      sliced    rze25    supt_infx_dg    online
-          -         rzd16    supt_infx_dg    failed was:rzd16
-          -         rzd24    supt_infx_dg    failed was:rzd24
-          -         rze16    supt_infx_dg    failed was:rze16
-          -         rzc16    baan_infx_dg    failed was:rzc16
-          -         rzc17    baan_infx_dg    failed was:rzc17
-          -         rzc24    baan_infx_dg    failed was:rzc24
-          -         rzd25    baan_infx_dg    failed was:rzd25
-          -         rz24     baan_infx_dg    failed was:rz24
# volprint -g baan_infx_dg -ht

DG  NAME         GROUP-ID
DM  NAME         DEVICE       TYPE     PRIVLEN   PUBLEN   PUBPATH
V   NAME         USETYPE      KSTATE   STATE     LENGTH   READPOL    PREFPLEX
PL  NAME         VOLUME       KSTATE   STATE     LENGTH   LAYOUT     ST-WIDTH MODE
SD  NAME         PLEX         PLOFFS   DISKOFFS  LENGTH   DISK-NAME  DEVICE

dg  baan_infx_dg 872015324.1276.brkdbpx08

dm  rz16         rz16         sliced   1024      41889100 /dev/rrz16g
dm  rz24         -            -        -         -        -
dm  rzc16        -            -        -         -        -
dm  rzc17        -            -        -         -        -
dm  rzc24        -            -        -         -        -
dm  rzd25        -            -        -         -        -

v   vol_rz16_01 gen           ENABLED  ACTIVE    4194304  SELECT     -
pl  pl-01        vol_rz16_01  ENABLED  ACTIVE    4194304  CONCAT     -      RW
sd  rz16-01      pl-01        0        0         4194304  rz16       rz16
pl  vol_rz16_01-01vol_rz16_01DISABLED NODEVICE  4194304  CONCAT     -      RW
sd  rz24-01      vol_rz16_01-010        0        4194304  rz24       -

v   vol_rz16_02 gen           ENABLED  ACTIVE    4194304  SELECT     -
pl  pl-02        vol_rz16_02  ENABLED  ACTIVE    4194304  CONCAT     -      RW
sd  rz16-02      pl-02        0        4194304   4194304  rz16       rz16
pl  vol_rz16_02-01 vol_rz16_02 DISABLED NODEVICE 4194304  CONCAT     -      RW
sd  rz24-02      vol_rz16_02-01 0       4194304   4194304  rz24       -

v   vol_rz16_03 gen           ENABLED  ACTIVE    4194304  SELECT     -
pl  pl-03        vol_rz16_03  ENABLED  ACTIVE    4194304  CONCAT     -      RW
sd  rz16-03      pl-03        0        8388608   4194304  rz16       rz16
pl  vol_rz16_03-01 vol_rz16_03 DISABLED NODEVICE 4194304  CONCAT     -      RW
sd  rz24-03      vol_rz16_03-01 0       8388608   4194304  rz24       -

v   vol_rz16_04 gen           ENABLED  ACTIVE    4194304  SELECT     -
pl  pl-04        vol_rz16_04  ENABLED  ACTIVE    4194304  CONCAT     -      RW
sd  rz16-04      pl-04        0        12582912  4194304  rz16       rz16
pl  vol_rz16_04-01 vol_rz16_04 DISABLED NODEVICE 4194304  CONCAT     -      RW
sd  rz24-04      vol_rz16_04-01 0       12582912  4194304  rz24       -

v   vol_rz16_05 gen           ENABLED  ACTIVE    4194304  SELECT     -
pl  pl-05        vol_rz16_05  ENABLED  ACTIVE    4194304  CONCAT     -      RW
sd  rz16-05      pl-05        0        16777216  4194304  rz16       rz16
pl  vol_rz16_05-01 vol_rz16_05 DISABLED NODEVICE 4194304  CONCAT     -      RW
sd  rz24-05      vol_rz16_05-01 0       16777216  4194304  rz24       -
```

```
v    vol_rz16_06 gen               ENABLED   ACTIVE    4194304   SELECT    -
pl   pl-06         vol_rz16_06 ENABLED   ACTIVE    4194304   CONCAT    -    RW
sd   rz16-06       pl-06       0         20971520  4194304   rz16      rz16
pl   vol_rz16_06-01vol_rz16_06DISABLED  NODEVICE  4194304   CONCAT    -    RW
sd   rz24-06       vol_rz16_06-010       20971520  4194304   rz24      -

v    vol_rz16_07 gen               ENABLED   ACTIVE    4194304   SELECT    -
pl   pl-07         vol_rz16_07 ENABLED   ACTIVE    4194304   CONCAT    -    RW
sd   rz16-07       pl-07       0         25165824  4194304   rz16      rz16
pl   vol_rz16_07-01vol_rz16_07DISABLED  NODEVICE  4194304   CONCAT    -    RW
sd   rz24-07       vol_rz16_07-010       25165824  4194304   rz24      -

v    vol_rz16_08 gen               ENABLED   ACTIVE    4194304   SELECT    -
pl   pl-08         vol_rz16_08 ENABLED   ACTIVE    4194304   CONCAT    -    RW
sd   rz16-08       pl-08       0         29360128  4194304   rz16      rz16
pl   vol_rz16_08-01vol_rz16_08DISABLED  NODEVICE  4194304   CONCAT    -    RW
sd   rz24-08       vol_rz16_08-010       29360128  4194304   rz24      -

v    vol_rz16_09 fsgen             ENABLED   ACTIVE    4194304   SELECT    -
pl   pl-17         vol_rz16_09 ENABLED   ACTIVE    4194304   CONCAT    -    RW
sd   rz16-09       pl-17       0         33554432  4194304   rz16      rz16
pl   pl-18         vol_rz16_09 DISABLED  NODEVICE  4194304   CONCAT    -    RW
sd   rz24-09       pl-18       0         33554432  4194304   rz24      -

v    vol_rzc16_01gen               DISABLED  NEEDSYNC  4194304   SELECT    -
pl   pl-09         vol_rzc16_01 DISABLED  NODEVICE  4194304   CONCAT    -    RW
sd   rzc16-01      pl-09       0         0         4194304   rzc16     -
pl   pl-13         vol_rzc16_01 DISABLED  NODEVICE  4194304   CONCAT    -    RW
sd   rzc24-01      pl-13       0         0         4194304   rzc24     -

v    vol_rzc16_02gen               DISABLED  NEEDSYNC  4177920   SELECT    -
pl   pl-10         vol_rzc16_02 DISABLED  NODEVICE  4177920   CONCAT    -    RW
sd   rzc16-02      pl-10       0         4194304   4177920   rzc16     -
pl   pl-14         vol_rzc16_02 DISABLED  NODEVICE  4177920   CONCAT    -    RW
sd   rzc24-02      pl-14       0         4194304   4177920   rzc24     -

v    vol_rzc17_01gen               DISABLED  NEEDSYNC  4194304   SELECT    -
pl   pl-11         vol_rzc17_01 DISABLED  NODEVICE  4194304   CONCAT    -    RW
sd   rzc17-01      pl-11       0         0         4194304   rzc17     -
pl   pl-15         vol_rzc17_01 DISABLED  NODEVICE  4194304   CONCAT    -    RW
sd   rzd25-01      pl-15       0         0         4194304   rzd25     -

v    vol_rzc17_02gen               DISABLED  NEEDSYNC  4177920   SELECT    -
pl   pl-12         vol_rzc17_02 DISABLED  NODEVICE  4177920   CONCAT    -    RW
sd   rzc17-02      pl-12       0         4194304   4177920   rzc17     -
pl   pl-16         vol_rzc17_02 DISABLED  NODEVICE  4177920   CONCAT    -    RW
sd   rzd25-02      pl-16       0         4194304   4177920   rzd25     -

# volprint -g supt_infx_dg -ht
DG   NAME          GROUP-ID
DM   NAME          DEVICE      TYPE      PRIVLEN   PUBLEN    PUBPATH
v    NAME          USETYPE     KSTATE    STATE     LENGTH    READPOL    PREFPLEX
pl   NAME          VOLUME      KSTATE    STATE     LENGTH    LAYOUT     ST-WIDTHMODE
sd   NAME          PLEX        PLOFFS    DISKOFFS  LENGTH    DISK-NAME  DEVICE

dg supt_infx_dg 873300082.1666.brkdbpx08

dm rzd16     -      -      -      --
```

```
dm rzd24     -        -       -      -       -
dm rze16     -        -       -      -       -
dm rze24     rze24    sliced  1024   8376988 /dev/rrze24g
dm rze25     rze25    sliced  1024   41878860 /dev/rrze25g

v  vol_rzd16_01 gen            ENABLED  ACTIVE    4194304  SELECT    -
pl pl-09        vol_rzd16_01 DISABLED NODEVICE  4194304  CONCAT    -    RW
sd rzd16-01     pl-09        0        0         4194304  rzd16     -
pl pl-15        vol_rzd16_01 ENABLED  ACTIVE    4194304  CONCAT    -    RW
sd rze24-01     pl-15        0        16        4194304  rze24     rze24

v  vol_rzd16_02 gen            ENABLED  ACTIVE    4177920  SELECT    -
pl pl-10        vol_rzd16_02 DISABLED NODEVICE  4177920  CONCAT    -    RW
sd rzd16-02     pl-10        0        4194304   4177920  rzd16     -
pl pl-16        vol_rzd16_02 ENABLED  ACTIVE    4177920  CONCAT    -    RW
sd rze24-02     pl-16        0        4194320   4177920  rze24     rze24

v  vol_rzd24_01 gen            DISABLED ACTIVE    4194304  SELECT    -
pl pl-11        vol_rzd24_01 DISABLED NODEVICE  4194304  CONCAT    -    RW
sd rzd24-01     pl-11        0        0         4194304  rzd24     -
pl pl-13        vol_rzd24_01 DISABLED NODEVICE  4194304  CONCAT    -    RW
sd rze16-01     pl-13        0        16        4194304  rze16     -

v  vol_rzd24_02 gen            DISABLED ACTIVE    4177920  SELECT    -
pl pl-12        vol_rzd24_02 DISABLED NODEVICE  4177920  CONCAT    -    RW
sd rzd24-02     pl-12        0        4194304   4177920  rzd24     -
pl pl-14        vol_rzd24_02 DISABLED NODEVICE  4177920  CONCAT    -    RW
sd rze16-02     pl-14        0        4194320   4177920  rze16     -

v  vol_rze25_01 gen            ENABLED  ACTIVE    4194304  SELECT    -
pl pl-01        vol_rze25_01 ENABLED  ACTIVE    4194304  CONCAT    -    RW
sd rze25-01     pl-01        0        0         4194304  rze25     rze25

v  vol_rze25_02 gen            ENABLED  ACTIVE    4194304  SELECT    -
pl pl-02        vol_rze25_02 ENABLED  ACTIVE    4194304  CONCAT    -    RW
sd rze25-02     pl-02        0        4194304   4194304  rze25     rze25

v  vol_rze25_03 gen            ENABLED  ACTIVE    4194304  SELECT    -
pl pl-03        vol_rze25_03 ENABLED  ACTIVE    4194304  CONCAT    -    RW
sd rze25-03     pl-03        0        8388608   4194304  rze25     rze25

v  vol_rze25_04 gen            ENABLED  ACTIVE    4194304  SELECT    -
pl pl-04        vol_rze25_04 ENABLED  ACTIVE    4194304  CONCAT    -    RW
sd rze25-04     pl-04        0        12582912  4194304  rze25     rze25

v  vol_rze25_05 gen            ENABLED  ACTIVE    4194304  SELECT    -
pl pl-05        vol_rze25_05 ENABLED  ACTIVE    4194304  CONCAT    -    RW
sd rze25-05     pl-05        0        16777216  4194304  rze25     rze25

v  vol_rze25_06 gen            ENABLED  ACTIVE    4194304  SELECT    -
pl pl-06        vol_rze25_06 ENABLED  ACTIVE    4194304  CONCAT    -    RW
sd rze25-06     pl-06        0        20971520  4194304  rze25     rze25

v  vol_rze25_07 gen            ENABLED  ACTIVE    4194304  SELECT    -
pl pl-07        vol_rze25_07 ENABLED  ACTIVE    4194304  CONCAT    -    RW
sd rze25-07     pl-07        0        25165824  4194304  rze25     rze25
```

```
v    vol_rze25_08 gen            ENABLED   ACTIVE   4194304   SELECT    -
pl   pl-08        vol_rze25_08 ENABLED   ACTIVE   4194304   CONCAT    -     RW
sd   rze25-08     pl-08          0         29360128 4194304   rze25     rze25

v    vol_rze25_09 fsgen          ENABLED   ACTIVE   4194304   SELECT    -
pl   pl-17        vol_rze25_09 ENABLED   ACTIVE   4194304   CONCAT    -     RW
sd   rze25-09     pl-17          0         33554432 4194304   rze25     rze25
```

Because the data appeared to be fine, the solution was to manually clean up the LSM disk failures. Once this task is completed, the mirrored volumes will be able to resynchronize from the good plex over to its mirror.

So, the first thing we want to do is to check the hardware status of the disks using the *file(1)* command on the character special device files. As discussed in Chapters 1 and 2, this command performs a SCSI inquiry command and returns useful data if the device is able to respond. In this case, the devices respond with the following:

```
# file /dev/rrzc16
/dev/rrzc16a:  character special (8/32896) SCSI #2 HSZ50-AX disk #130 (SCSI ID #0)
(SCSI LUN #2)

# file /dev/rrzc24a
/dev/rrzc24a:  character special (8/49280) SCSI #3 HSZ50-AX disk #194 (SCSI ID #0)
(SCSI LUN #2)
```

As previously stated, we suspected that the problem could either have been hardware or a disk label problem. Thus, because the drives were responding, the next step was to check the disk label to make sure there were no obvious problems. We encountered the following from *disklabel(8)*:

```
# disklabel -r rzc16
# /dev/rrzc16a:type: SCSI
disk: hsz40
label:
flags: dynamic_geometry
bytes/sector: 512
sectors/track: 113
tracks/cylinder: 20
sectors/cylinder: 2260
cylinders: 3707
sectors/unit: 8378028
rpm: 3600
interleave: 1
trackskew: 7
cylinderskew: 26
headswitch: 0              # milliseconds
track-to-track seek: 0    # milliseconds
drivedata: 0

8 partitions:
#         size    offset   fstype  [fsize bsize  cpg]
  a:     131072        0   unused       0      0        # (Cyl.   0 - 57*)
  b:     262144   131072   unused       0      0        # (Cyl.  57*- 173*)
```

```
c:      8378028         0   unused    0       0       # (Cyl.   0 - 3707*)
d:            0         0   unused    0       0       # (Cyl.   0 - -1)
e:            0         0   unused    0       0       # (Cyl.   0 - -1)
f:            0         0   unused    0       0       # (Cyl.   0 - -1)
g:      3992406    393216   unused    0       0       # (Cyl. 173*- 1940*)
h:      3992406   4385622   unused    0       0       # (Cyl. 1940*- 3707*)
```

This disk label had somehow been reset to the default; therefore, LSM cannot find the metadata from the private data region of this simple disk. Recall from our discussion in Chapter 3 of LSM simple disks that the 'g' partition normally contains the public data and the 'h' partition contains the private region. The private data partition should have an "fstype" of LSMpriv and the public area should be LSMpubl. In addition, the sizes and offsets of the partitions on this disk have clearly been changed back to the default values. Without this information being in place on the disk label, LSM cannot find the data it requires to bring this disk online. Therefore, it leaves the data in a "failed" state, as we saw in the output from the "voldisk list" command previously.

Next, we moved on to checking the hardware status of the two other failed disks.

```
# file /dev/rrzc17a
/dev/rrzc17a:  character special (8/33920) SCSI #2 HSZ50-AX disk #138 (SCSI ID #1)
(SCSI LUN #2)

# file /dev/rrzd25a
/dev/rrzd25a:  character special (8/50368) SCSI #3 HSZ50-AX disk #203 (SCSI ID #1)
(SCSI LUN #3)
```

Once again, the hardware is responding fine; however, in this case, the label was also fine for the two drives.

```
# disklabel -r /dev/rrzc17a
# /dev/rrzc17a:
type: SCSI
disk: hsz40
label:
flags: dynamic_geometry
bytes/sector: 512
sectors/track: 113
tracks/cylinder: 20
sectors/cylinder: 2260
cylinders: 3707
sectors/unit: 8378028
rpm: 3600
interleave: 1
trackskew: 7
cylinderskew: 26
headswitch: 0            # milliseconds
track-to-track seek: 0  # milliseconds
drivedata: 0
```

```
8 partitions:
#        size   offset   fstype   [fsize bsize  cpg]
  a:    131072        0   unused      0     0          # (Cyl.   0 -  57*)
  b:    262144   131072   unused      0     0          # (Cyl.  57*- 173*)
  c:   8378028        0   unused      0     0          # (Cyl.   0 - 3707*)
  d:         0        0   unused      0     0          # (Cyl.   0 - -1)
  e:         0        0   unused      0     0          # (Cyl.   0 - -1)
  f:         0        0   unused      0     0          # (Cyl.   0 - -1)
  g:   8377004        0   LSMpubl                      # (Cyl.   0 - 3706*)
  h:      1024  8377004   SMpriv                       # (Cyl. 3706*- 3707*)
# disklabel -r /dev/rrzd25a
# /dev/rrzd25a:
type: SCSI
disk: hsz40
label:
flags: dynamic_geometry
bytes/sector: 512
sectors/track: 113
tracks/cylinder: 20
sectors/cylinder: 2260
cylinders: 3707
sectors/unit: 8378028
rpm: 3600
interleave: 1
trackskew: 7
cylinderskew: 26
headswitch: 0               # milliseconds
track-to-track seek: 0      # milliseconds
drivedata: 0

8 partitions:
#        size   offset   fstype   [fsize bsize  cpg]
  a:    131072        0   unused      0     0          # (Cyl.   0 -  57*)
  b:    262144   131072   unused      0     0          # (Cyl.  57*- 173*)
  c:   8378028        0   unused      0     0          # (Cyl.   0 - 3707*)
  d:         0        0   unused      0     0          # (Cyl.   0 - -1)
  e:         0        0   unused      0     0          # (Cyl.   0 - -1)
  f:         0        0   unused      0     0          # (Cyl.   0 - -1)
  g:   8377004        0   LSMpubl                      # (Cyl.   0 - 3706*)
  h:      1024  8377004   LSMpriv                      # (Cyl. 3706*- 3707*)
# voldisk list | grep rzd25
rzd25      sliced      -           -            offline
-          -           rzd25       baan_infx_dg failed was:rzd25
# voldisk list | grep rzc17
rzc17      sliced      -           -            offline
-          -           rzc17       baan_infx_dg failed was:rzc17
```

These two drives were already in good shape, thus they could be brought online directly with no additional steps. The following "voldisk online" command will do the trick for these drives.

```
# voldisk online rzc17

# voldisk list | grep rzc17
rzc17          sliced    -           -              online
-              -         rzc17       baan_infx_dg failed was:rzc17
```

In addition, this member must also be added back to the disk group using the "voldg adddisk" command. This task was performed in order to make the drive completely accessible to the disk group.

```
# voldg -g baan_infx_dg -k adddisk rzc17

# voldisk list | grep rzc17
rzc17          sliced    rzc17       baan_infx_dg online
```

The two LSM volumes that rely on this drive are shown as follows in our *volprint(8)* output. Our last step using *voldg(8)* had brought one plex in each volume into the "ACTIVE" state.

```
# volprint -g baan_infx_dg -ht

[snip]

v   vol_rzc17_01 gen            DISABLED NEEDSYNC 4194304   SELECT    -
pl  pl-11        vol_rzc17_01 DISABLED ACTIVE   4194304   CONCAT    -      RW
sd  rzc17-01     pl-11        0        0        4194304   rzc17     rzc17
pl  pl-15        vol_rzc17_01 DISABLED NODEVICE 4194304   CONCAT    -      RW
sd  rzd25-01     pl-15        0        0        4194304   rzd25     -

v   vol_rzc17_02 gen            DISABLED NEEDSYNC 4177920   SELECT    -
pl  pl-12        vol_rzc17_02 DISABLED ACTIVE   4177920   CONCAT    -      RW
sd  rzc17-02     pl-12        0        4194304  4177920   rzc17     rzc17
pl  pl-16        vol_rzc17_02 DISABLED NODEVICE 4177920   CONCAT    -      RW
sd  rzd25-02     pl-16        0        4194304  4177920   rzd25     -

[snip]
```

With that, we were now able to start the logical volume "vol_rzc17_02" with only one plex active using the *volume(8)* command as follows:

```
# volume -g baan_infx_dg start vol_rzc17_02

# volprint -g baan_infx_dg vol_rzc17_02
TYPE NAME        ASSOC    KSTATE    LENGTH COMMENT
vol vol_rzc17_02 gen      ENABLED  4177920

# volprint -g baan_infx_dg -ht

[snip]

v   vol_rzc17_01 gen            DISABLED NEEDSYNC 4194304   SELECT    -
pl  pl-11        vol_rzc17_01 DISABLED ACTIVE   4194304   CONCAT    -      RW
sd  rzc17-01     pl-11        0        0        4194304   rzc17     rzc17
pl  pl-15        vol_rzc17_01 DISABLED NODEVICE 4194304   CONCAT    -      RW
sd  rzd25-01     pl-15        0        0        4194304   rzd25     -
```

```
v    vol_rzc17_02 gen            ENABLED  ACTIVE    4177920   SELECT    -
pl   pl-12         vol_rzc17_02 ENABLED  ACTIVE    4177920   CONCAT    -     RW
sd   rzc17-02      pl-12        0        4194304   4177920   rzc17     rzc17
pl   pl-16         vol_rzc17_02 DISABLED NODEVICE  4177920   CONCAT    -     RW
sd   rzd25-02      pl-16        0        4194304   4177920   rzd25     -
[snip]
```

Finally, we started the other volume that utilized disk rzc17, using the *volume(8)* command in the same way as before.

```
# volume -g baan_infx_dg start vol_rzc17_01
```

Now that we've completed those steps, these two volumes are completely accessible to the applications. This allows the database administrator to access the data while we continue to correct the problems. Next, we bring the other disk, rzd25, online to LSM and add it to the disk group just like we did for rzc17.

```
# voldisk online rzd25

# voldg -g baan_infx_dg -k adddisk rzd25

# voldisk list | egrep "rzc17|rzd25"
rzc17    sliced  rzc17    baan_infx_dg online
rzd25    sliced  rzd25    baan_infx_dg online

# volprint -ht -g baan_infx_dg

[snip]

v    vol_rzc17_01 gen            ENABLED  ACTIVE    4194304   SELECT    -
pl   pl-11         vol_rzc17_01 ENABLED  ACTIVE    4194304   CONCAT    -     RW
sd   rzc17-01      pl-11        0        0         4194304   rzc17     rzc17
pl   pl-15         vol_rzc17_01 DISABLED STALE     4194304   CONCAT    -     RW
sd   rzd25-01      pl-15        0        0         4194304   rzd25     rzd25

v    vol_rzc17_02 gen            ENABLED  ACTIVE    4177920   SELECT    -
pl   pl-12         vol_rzc17_02 ENABLED  ACTIVE    4177920   CONCAT    -     RW
sd   rzc17-02      pl-12        0        4194304   4177920   rzc17     rzc17
pl   pl-16         vol_rzc17_02 DISABLED STALE     4177920   CONCAT    -     RW
sd   rzd25-02      pl-16        0        4194304   4177920   rzd25     rzd25

[snip]
```

At this point, we were finished with those two disks and were now able to move on to some other cleanup work. The problems with rzc16 and rzd24 all happened because in troubleshooting, these drives had been totally removed from LSM using the "voldisk rm" command. The following procedure was used to recover from that problem.

```
# voldisk define rz24
voldisk: Unable to locate private and public regions in rz24 disklabel
# disklabel -r rz24
# /dev/rrz24a:
type: SCSI
```

```
disk: hsz40
label:
flags: dynamic_geometry
bytes/sector: 512
sectors/track: 113
tracks/cylinder: 20
sectors/cylinder: 2260
cylinders: 18535
sectors/unit: 41890140
rpm: 3600
interleave: 1
trackskew: 7
cylinderskew: 26
headswitch: 0              # milliseconds
track-to-track seek: 0    # milliseconds
drivedata: 0

8 partitions:
#         size     offset    fstype   [fsize bsize   cpg]
  a:     131072          0   unused        0     0          # (Cyl.    0 - 57*)
  b:     262144     131072   unused        0     0          # (Cyl.   57*- 173*)
  c:   41890140          0   unused        0     0          # (Cyl.    0 - 18535*)
  d:           0          0   unused        0     0          # (Cyl.    0 - -1)
  e:           0          0   unused        0     0          # (Cyl.    0 - -1)
  f:           0          0   unused        0     0          # (Cyl.    0 - -1)
  g:   20748462     393216   unused        0     0          # (Cyl.  173*- 9354*)
  h:   20748462  21141678    unused        0     0          # (Cyl. 9354*- 18535*)
```

This disk is a mirror to the one before that contained no LSM public or private information.

```
# disklabel -r rz16
# /dev/rrz16a:
type: SCSI
disk: hsz40
label:
flags: dynamic_geometry
bytes/sector: 512
sectors/track: 113
tracks/cylinder: 20
sectors/cylinder: 2260
cylinders: 18535
sectors/unit: 41890140
rpm: 3600
interleave: 1
trackskew: 7
cylinderskew: 26
headswitch: 0              # milliseconds
track-to-track seek: 0    # milliseconds
drivedata: 0

8 partitions:
#         size     offset    fstype   [fsize bsize   cpg]
  a:     131072          0   unused        0     0          # (Cyl.    0 - 57*)
  b:     262144     131072   unused        0     0          # (Cyl.   57*- 173*)
```

```
c:    41890140         0    unused    0      0    # (Cyl.  0 - 18535*)
d:           0         0    unused    0      0    # (Cyl.  0 - -1)
e:           0         0    unused    0      0    # (Cyl.  0 - -1)
f:           0         0    unused    0      0    # (Cyl.  0 - -1)
g:    41889116         0              LSMpubl     # (Cyl.  0 - 18535*)
h:        1024  41889116             LSMpriv      # (Cyl. 18535*- 18535*)
```

We used a handy technique here to save the label off a known good and correctly labeled drive and write it to the drive with the bad label. We can do this because any LSM mirror should be identical to another. In addition, drives that are the same size and that have been initialized into LSM in the same way have identical labels. Thus, this technique can be used even if the drives were not LSM mirrors.

```
# disklabel -r rz16 > /tmp/rz16.label
# disklabel -R rz24 /tmp/rz16.label
# disklabel -r rz24
# /dev/rrz24a:
type: SCSI
disk: hsz40
label:
flags: dynamic_geometry
bytes/sector: 512
sectors/track: 113
tracks/cylinder: 20
sectors/cylinder: 2260
cylinders: 18535
sectors/unit: 41890140
rpm: 3600
interleave: 1
trackskew: 7
cylinderskew: 26
headswitch: 0              # milliseconds
track-to-track seek: 0    # milliseconds
drivedata: 0

8 partitions:
#         size    offset    fstype   [fsize bsize   cpg]
a:      131072         0    unused    0      0    # (Cyl.  0 - 57*)
b:      262144    131072    unused    0      0    # (Cyl.  57*- 173*)
c:    41890140         0    unused    0      0    # (Cyl.  0 - 18535*)
d:           0         0    unused    0      0    # (Cyl.  0 - -1)
e:           0         0    unused    0      0    # (Cyl.  0 - -1)
f:           0         0    unused    0      0    # (Cyl.  0 - -1)
g:    41889116         0              LSMpubl     # (Cyl.  0 - 18535*)
h:        1024  41889116             LSMpriv      # (Cyl. 18535*- 18535*)
```

Once we completed the disk label recovery, the process proceeded as before with recovering the disks, plexes, and volumes.

```
# voldisk define rz24

# voldg -g baan_infx_dg -k adddisk rz24
```

```
# volprint -g baan_infx_dg -ht
```

DG	NAME	GROUP-ID				PUBPATH	
DM	NAME	DEVICE	TYPE	PRIVLEN	PUBLEN	PUBPATH	
V	NAME	USETYPE	KSTATE	STATE	LENGTH	READPOL	PREFPLEX
PL	NAME	VOLUME	KSTATE	STATE	LENGTH	LAYOUT	ST-WIDTH MODE
SD	NAME	PLEX	PLOFFS	DISKOFFS	LENGTH	DISK-NAME	DEVICE

dg	baan_infx_dg	872015324.1276.brkdbpx08					
dm	rz16	rz16	sliced	1024	41889100	/dev/rrz16g	
dm	rz24	rz24	sliced	1024	41889100	/dev/rrz24g	
dm	rzc16	-	-	-	-	-	
dm	rzc17	rzc17	sliced	1024	8376988	/dev/rrzc17g	
dm	rzc24	-	-	-	-	-	
dm	rzd25	rzd25	sliced	1024	8376988	/dev/rrzd25g	

```
[snip]
# disklabel -r rzd25
# /dev/rrzd25a:
type: SCSI
disk: hsz40
label:
flags: dynamic_geometry
bytes/sector: 512
sectors/track: 113
tracks/cylinder: 20
sectors/cylinder: 2260
cylinders: 3707
sectors/unit: 8378028
rpm: 3600
interleave: 1
trackskew: 7
cylinderskew: 26
headswitch: 0         # milliseconds
track-to-track seek: 0   # milliseconds
drivedata: 0

8 partitions:
#        size    offset   fstype  [fsize bsize  cpg]
 a:    131072         0   unused       0     0         # (Cyl.   0 -  57*)
 b:    262144    131072   unused       0     0         # (Cyl.  57*- 173*)
 c:   8378028         0   unused       0     0         # (Cyl.   0 - 3707*)
 d:         0         0   unused       0     0         # (Cyl.   0 -  -1)
 e:         0         0   unused       0     0         # (Cyl.   0 -  -1)
 f:         0         0   unused       0     0         # (Cyl.   0 -  -1)
 g:   8377004         0           LSMpubl           # (Cyl.   0 - 3706*)
 h:      1024   8377004           LSMpriv           # (Cyl. 3706*- 3707*)

# disklabel -r rzc16
# /dev/rrzc16a:
type: SCSI
disk: hsz40
label:
flags: dynamic_geometry
bytes/sector: 512
```

```
sectors/track: 113
tracks/cylinder: 20
sectors/cylinder: 2260
cylinders: 3707
sectors/unit: 8378028
rpm: 3600
interleave: 1
trackskew: 7
cylinderskew: 26
headswitch: 0              # milliseconds
track-to-track seek: 0    # milliseconds
drivedata: 0

8 partitions:
#         size    offset    fstype   [fsize bsize   cpg]
  a:     131072        0    unused        0     0    # (Cyl.    0 -   57*)
  b:     262144   131072    unused        0     0    # (Cyl.   57*-  173*)
  c:    8378028        0    unused        0     0    # (Cyl.    0 - 3707*)
  d:          0        0    unused        0     0    # (Cyl.    0 -   -1)
  e:          0        0    unused        0     0    # (Cyl.    0 -   -1)
  f:          0        0    unused        0     0    # (Cyl.    0 -   -1)
  g:    3992406   393216    unused        0     0    # (Cyl.  173*- 1940*)
  h:    3992406  4385622    unused        0     0    # (Cyl. 1940*- 3707*)
```

This is the same procedure as before, but the disk labels were corrupt on rzc16 and its mirror rzc24. We know, however, that these disks were partitioned the same as rzd25.

```
# disklabel -r rzd25 > /tmp/rzd25.label
# disklabel -R rzc16 /tmp/rzd25.label
# disklabel -R rzc24 /tmp/rzd25.label
```

The next step was to put all of these disks back into LSM and set them online using *voldisk(8)*.

```
# voldisk define rzc16
# voldisk define rzc24
# voldisk online rzc16
# voldisk online rzc24
```

Then we put disks back into the "baan_infx_dg" disk group using *voldg(8)* and take a look at the results with *volprint(8)*.

```
# voldg -g baan_infx_dg -k adddisk rzc16
# voldg -g baan_infx_dg -k adddisk rzc24

# volprint -g baan_infx_dg -ht

[snip]

v    vol_rzc16_01 gen            ENABLED  ACTIVE    4194304    SELECT     -
pl   pl-09        vol_rzc16_01   ENABLED  ACTIVE    4194304    CONCAT     -     RW
sd   rzc16-01     pl-09          0        0         4194304    rzc16      rzc16
pl   pl-13        vol_rzc16_01   DISABLED STALE     4194304    CONCAT     -     WO
sd   rzc24-01     pl-13          0        0         4194304    rzc24      rzc24
```

```
v   vol_rzc16_02 gen           DISABLED NEEDSYNC 4177920  SELECT     -
pl  pl-10         vol_rzc16_02 DISABLED ACTIVE   4177920  CONCAT     -     RW
sd  rzc16-02      pl-10        0        4194304  4177920  rzc16      rzc16
pl  pl-14         vol_rzc16_02 DISABLED STALE    4177920  CONCAT     -     RW
sd  rzc24-02      pl-14        0        4194304  4177920  rzc24      rzc24
```
                    [snip]

> At this point, we have completed all of the manual work for disk group "baan_infx_dg." The last step is to let the system recover the plexes by reattaching them. The best way to do that is by using the *volrecover(8)* command on this disk group only. We show the output from *ps(1)* and *volprint(8)* while the volrecover is doing its job as follows.

```
# volrecover -sb -g baan_infx_dg

# ps -ef | grep volplex
root     8   1 0.2  Oct 27 ??      0:59.67 vold -k -m boot
root  1333   1 0.0  Oct 27 ??      0:00.01 sh /usr/sbin/volwatch root
root  1344 1333 0.0  Oct 27 ??      0:00.01 sh /usr/sbin/volwatch root
root  1345 1344 0.0  Oct 27 ??      0:00.01 volnotify -f -w 15
root 19583   1 0.0  12:40:25 ??    0:00.01 volrecover -sb -g baan_infx_dg
root 19584 19583 2.1 12:40:25 ??    0:00.63 /etc/vol/type/gen/volplex -U gen -
g 872015324.1276.brkdbpx08 -- att vol_rz11
root 19585 19583 2.0 12:40:25 ??    0:00.63 /etc/vol/type/gen/volplex -U gen -
g 872015324.1276.brkdbpx08 -- att vol_rzc3
root 19587 19583 1.9 12:40:25 ??    0:00.65 /etc/vol/type/gen/volplex -U gen -
g 872015324.1276.brkdbpx08 -- att vol_rzc5
root 19596 18806 0.0 12:40:59 ttyp3  0:00.01 grep vol

# volprint -g baan_infx_dg -ht

[snip]

v   vol_rzc16_01 gen           ENABLED  ACTIVE   4194304  SELECT     -
pl  pl-09         vol_rzc16_01 ENABLED  ACTIVE   4194304  CONCAT     -     RW
sd  rzc16-01      pl-09        0        0        4194304  rzc16      rzc16
pl  pl-13         vol_rzc16_01 ENABLED  STALE    4194304  CONCAT     -     WO
sd  rzc24-01      pl-13        0        0        4194304  rzc24      rzc24

v   vol_rzc16_02 gen           ENABLED  ACTIVE   4177920  SELECT-
pl  pl-10         vol_rzc16_02 ENABLED  ACTIVE   4177920  CONCAT     -     RW
sd  rzc16-02      pl-10        0        4194304  4177920  rzc16      rzc16
pl  pl-14         vol_rzc16_02 DISABLED STALE    4177920  CONCAT     -     RW
sd  rzc24-02      pl-14        0        4194304  4177920  rzc24      rzc24

v   vol_rzc17_01 gen           ENABLED  ACTIVE   4194304  SELECT     -
pl  pl-11         vol_rzc17_01 ENABLED  ACTIVE   4194304  CONCAT     -     RW
sd  rzc17-01      pl-11        0        0        4194304  rzc17      rzc17
pl  pl-15         vol_rzc17_01 ENABLED  STALE    4194304  CONCAT     -     WO
sd  rzd25-01      pl-15        0        0        4194304  rzd25      rzd25

v   vol_rzc17_02 gen           ENABLED  ACTIVE   4177920  SELECT     -
pl  pl-12         vol_rzc17_02 ENABLED  ACTIVE   4177920  CONCAT     -     RW
sd  rzc17-02      pl-12        0        4194304  4177920  rzc17      rzc17
pl  pl-16         vol_rzc17_02 DISABLED STALE    4177920  CONCAT     -     RW
sd  rzd25-02      pl-16        0        4194304  4177920  rzd25      rzd25
```

Now that we've corrected the first disk group, the next step is to start fixing the "supt_infx_dg" disk group using a similar set of commands.

```
# volprint -g supt_infx_dg -ht
DG  NAME          GROUP-ID
DM  NAME          DEVICE        TYPE      PRIVLEN   PUBLEN    PUBPATH
V   NAME          USETYPE       KSTATE    STATE     LENGTH    READPOL    PREFPLEX
PL  NAME          VOLUME        KSTATE    STATE     LENGTH    LAYOUT     ST-WIDTH MODE
SD  NAME          PLEX          PLOFFS    DISKOFFS  LENGTH    DISK-NAME  DEVICE

dg  supt_infx_dg 873300082.1666.brkdbpx08
dm  rzd16    -        -       -       -      -
dm  rzd24    -        -       -       -      -
dm  rze16    -        -       -       -      -
dm  rze24    rze24    sliced  1024    8376988 /dev/rrze24g
dm  rze25    rze25    sliced  1024    41878860 /dev/rrze25g

v   vol_rzd16_01 gen             ENABLED   ACTIVE    4194304   SELECT     -
pl  pl-09         vol_rzd16_01 DISABLED  NODEVICE  4194304   CONCAT     -    RW
sd  rzd16-01      pl-09         0         0         4194304   rzd16      -
pl  pl-15         vol_rzd16_01 ENABLED   ACTIVE    4194304   CONCAT     -    RW
sd  rze24-01      pl-15         0         16        4194304   rze24      rze24

v   vol_rzd16_02 gen             ENABLED   ACTIVE    4177920   SELECT     -
pl  pl-10         vol_rzd16_02 DISABLED  NODEVICE  4177920   CONCAT     -    RW
sd  rzd16-02      pl-10         0         4194304   4177920   rzd16      -
pl  pl-16         vol_rzd16_02 ENABLED   ACTIVE    4177920   CONCAT     -    RW
sd  rze24-02      pl-16         0         4194320   4177920   rze24      rze24

v   vol_rzd24_01 gen             DISABLED  ACTIVE    4194304   SELECT     -
pl  pl-11         vol_rzd24_01 DISABLED  NODEVICE  4194304   CONCAT     -    RW
sd  rzd24-01      pl-11         0         0         4194304   rzd24      -
pl  pl-13         vol_rzd24_01 DISABLED  NODEVICE  4194304   CONCAT     -    RW
sd  rze16-01      pl-13         0         16        4194304   rze16      -

v   vol_rzd24_02 gen             DISABLED  ACTIVE    4177920   SELECT     -
pl  pl-12         vol_rzd24_02 DISABLED  NODEVICE  4177920   CONCAT     -    RW
sd  rzd24-02      pl-12         0         4194304   4177920   rzd24      -
pl  pl-14         vol_rzd24_02 DISABLED  NODEVICE  4177920   CONCAT     -    RW
sd  rze16-02      pl-14         0         4194320   4177920   rze16      -

v   vol_rze25_01 gen             ENABLED   ACTIVE    4194304   SELECT     -
pl  pl-01         vol_rze25_01 ENABLED   ACTIVE    4194304   CONCAT     -    RW
sd  rze25-01      pl-01         0         0         4194304   rze25      rze25

v   vol_rze25_02 gen             ENABLED   ACTIVE    4194304   SELECT     -
pl  pl-02         vol_rze25_02 ENABLED   ACTIVE    4194304   CONCAT     -    RW
sd  rze25-02      pl-02         0         4194304   4194304   rze25      rze25

v   vol_rze25_03 gen             ENABLED   ACTIVE    4194304   SELECT  -
pl  pl-03         vol_rze25_03 ENABLED   ACTIVE    4194304   CONCAT     -    RW
sd  rze25-03      pl-03         0         8388608   4194304   rze25      rze25

v   vol_rze25_04 gen             ENABLED   ACTIVE    4194304   SELECT     -
pl  pl-04         vol_rze25_04 ENABLED   ACTIVE    4194304   CONCAT     -    RW
sd  rze25-04      pl-04         0         12582912  4194304   rze25      rze25
```

```
v    vol_rze25_05 gen             ENABLED   ACTIVE    4194304    SELECT    -
pl   pl-05        vol_rze25_05 ENABLED   ACTIVE    4194304    CONCAT    -    RW
sd   rze25-05     pl-05           0         16777216  4194304    rze25     rze25

v    vol_rze25_06 gen             ENABLED   ACTIVE               4194304    SELECT  -
pl   pl-06        vol_rze25_06 ENABLED   ACTIVE    4194304    CONCAT    -    RW
sd   rze25-06     pl-06           0         20971520  4194304    rze25     rze25

v    vol_rze25_07 gen             ENABLED   ACTIVE    4194304    SELECT    -
pl   pl-07        vol_rze25_07 ENABLED   ACTIVE    4194304    CONCAT    -    RW
sd   rze25-07     pl-07           0         25165824  4194304    rze25     rze25

v    vol_rze25_08 gen             ENABLED   ACTIVE               4194304    SELECT  -
pl   pl-08        vol_rze25_08 ENABLED   ACTIVE    4194304    CONCAT    -    RW
sd   rze25-08     pl-08           0         29360128  4194304    rze25     rze25

v    vol_rze25_09 fsgen           ENABLED   ACTIVE    4194304    SELECT    -
pl   pl-17        vol_rze25_09 ENABLED   ACTIVE    4194304    CONCAT    -    RW
sd   rze25-09     pl-17           0         33554432  4194304    rze25     rze25

# voldisk list
DEVICE      TYPE       DISK       GROUP          STATUS
rz16        sliced     rz16       baan_infx_dg   online
rz17        sliced     rz17       sipros_infx_dg online
rz24        sliced     rz24       baan_infx_dg   online
rz25        sliced     rz25       sipros_infx_dg online
rz32a       nopriv     rz32a      rootdg         online
rz32b       nopriv     rz32b      rootdg         online
rz32e       simple     rz32e      rootdg         online
rz32g       nopriv     rz32g      rootdg         online
rz37        sliced     rz37       rootdg         online
rz8a        nopriv     rz8a       rootdg         online
rz8b        nopriv     rz8b       rootdg         online
rz8e        simple     rz8e       rootdg         online
rz8g        nopriv     rz8g       rootdg         online
rz9c        simple     rz9c       rootdg         online
rzb16       sliced     rzb16      sipros_adfs_dg online
rzb17       sliced     rzb17      baan_adfs_dg   online
rzb24       sliced     rzb24      sipros_adfs_dg online
rzb25       sliced     rzb25      baan_adfs_dg   online
rzc16       sliced     rzc16      baan_infx_dg   online
rzc17       sliced     rzc17      baan_infx_dg   online
rzc24       sliced     rzc24      baan_infx_dg   online
rzc25       sliced     rzc25      db_baan        online
rzd16       sliced     -          -              offline
rzd17       sliced     rzd17      db_baan        online
rzd24       sliced     -          -              offline
rzd25       sliced     rzd25      baan_infx_dg   online
rze16       sliced     -          -              offline
rze17       sliced     rze17      supt_adfs_dg   online
rze24       sliced     rze24      supt_infx_dg   online
rze25       sliced     rze25      supt_infx_dg   online
-           -          rzd16      supt_infx_dg   failed was:rzd16
-           -          rzd24      supt_infx_dg   failed was:rzd24
-           -          rze16      supt_infx_dg   failed was:rze16
```

```
# voldisk online rzd16
# voldisk online rzd24
# voldisk online rze16

# voldg -g supt_infx_dg -k adddisk rzd16
# voldg -g supt_infx_dg -k adddisk rzd24
# voldg -g supt_infx_dg -k adddisk rze16

# voldisk list
DEVICE      TYPE       DISK      GROUP            STATUS
rz16        sliced     rz16      baan_infx_dg     online
rz17        sliced     rz17      sipros_infx_dg   online
rz24        sliced     rz24      baan_infx_dg     online
rz25        sliced     rz25      sipros_infx_dg   online
rz32a       nopriv     rz32a     rootdg           online
rz32b       nopriv     rz32b     rootdg           online
rz32e       simple     rz32e     rootdg           online
rz32g       nopriv     rz32g     rootdg           online
rz37        sliced     rz37      rootdg           online
rz8a        nopriv     rz8a      rootdg           online
rz8b        nopriv     rz8b      rootdg           online
rz8e        simple     rz8e      rootdg           online
rz8g        nopriv     rz8g      rootdg           online
rz9c        simple     rz9c      rootdg           online
rzb16       sliced     rzb16     sipros_adfs_dg   online
rzb17       sliced     rzb17     baan_adfs_dg     online
rzb24       sliced     rzb24     sipros_adfs_dg   online
rzb25       sliced     rzb25     baan_adfs_dg     online
rzc16       sliced     rzc16     baan_infx_dg     online
rzc17       sliced     rzc17     baan_infx_dg     online
rzc24       sliced     rzc24     baan_infx_dg     online
rzc25       sliced     rzc25     db_baan          online
rzd16       sliced     rzd16     supt_infx_dg     online
rzd17       sliced     rzd17     db_baan          online
rzd24       sliced     rzd24     supt_infx_dg     online
rzd25       sliced     rzd25     baan_infx_dg     online
rze16       sliced     rze16     supt_infx_dg     online
rze17       sliced     rze17     supt_adfs_dg     online
rze24       sliced     rze24     supt_infx_dg     online
rze25       sliced     rze25     supt_infx_dg     online

# volrecover -sb -g supt_infx_dg

# volprint -g supt_infx_dg -ht | more
DG   NAME          GROUP-ID
DM   NAME          DEVICE        TYPE      PRIVLEN   PUBLEN    PUBPATH
V    NAME          USETYPE       KSTATE    STATE     LENGTH    READPOL    PREFPLEX
PL   NAME          VOLUME        KSTATE    STATE     LENGTH    LAYOUT     ST-WIDTH MODE
SD   NAME          PLEX          PLOFFS    DISKOFFS  LENGTH    DISK-NAME  DEVICE

dg supt_infx_dg 873300082.1666.brkdbpx08

dm rzd16    rzd16    sliced   1024     8376988 /dev/rrzd16g
dm rzd24    rzd24    sliced   1024     8376988 /dev/rrzd24g
dm rze16    rze16    sliced   1024     8376988 /dev/rrze16g
dm rze24    rze24    sliced   1024     8376988 /dev/rrze24g
dm rze25    rze25    sliced   1024    41878860 /dev/rrze25g
```

v	vol_rzd16_01	gen	ENABLED	ACTIVE	4194304	SELECT	–	
pl	pl-09	vol_rzd16_01	ENABLED	STALE	4194304	CONCAT	–	WO
sd	rzd16-01	pl-09	0	0	4194304	rzd16	rzd16	
pl	pl-15	vol_rzd16_01	ENABLED	ACTIVE	4194304	CONCAT	–	RW
sd	rze24-01	pl-15	0	16	4194304	rze24	rze24	
v	vol_rzd16_02	gen	ENABLED	ACTIVE	4177920	SELECT	–	
pl	pl-10	vol_rzd16_02	DISABLED	STALE	4177920	CONCAT	–	RW
sd	rzd16-02	pl-10	0	4194304	4177920	rzd16	rzd16	
pl	pl-16	vol_rzd16_02	ENABLED	ACTIVE	4177920	CONCAT	–	RW
sd	rze24-02	pl-16	0	4194320	4177920	rze24	rze24	
v	vol_rzd24_01	gen	ENABLED	ACTIVE	4194304	SELECT	–	
pl	pl-11	vol_rzd24_01	ENABLED	ACTIVE	4194304	CONCAT	–	RW
sd	rzd24-01	pl-11	0	0	4194304	rzd24	rzd24	
pl	pl-13	vol_rzd24_01	ENABLED	ACTIVE	4194304	CONCAT	–	RW
sd	rze16-01	pl-13	0	16	4194304	rze16	rze16	
v	vol_rzd24_02	gen	ENABLED	ACTIVE	4177920	SELECT	–	
pl	pl-12	vol_rzd24_02	ENABLED	ACTIVE	4177920	CONCAT	–	RW
sd	rzd24-02	pl-12	0	4194304	4177920	rzd24	rzd24	
pl	pl-14	vol_rzd24_02	ENABLED	ACTIVE	4177920	CONCAT	–	RW
sd	rze16-02	pl-14	0	4194320	4177920	rze16	rze16	
v	vol_rze25_01	gen	ENABLED	ACTIVE	4194304	SELECT	–	
pl	pl-01	vol_rze25_01	ENABLED	ACTIVE	4194304	CONCAT	–	RW
sd	rze25-01	pl-01	0	0	4194304	rze25	rze25	
v	vol_rze25_02	gen	ENABLED	ACTIVE	4194304	SELECT	–	
pl	pl-02	vol_rze25_02	ENABLED	ACTIVE	4194304	CONCAT	–	RW
sd	rze25-02	pl-02	0	4194304	4194304	rze25	rze25	
v	vol_rze25_03	gen	ENABLED	ACTIVE	4194304	SELECT	–	
pl	pl-03	vol_rze25_03	ENABLED	ACTIVE	4194304	CONCAT	–	RW
sd	rze25-03	pl-03	0	8388608	4194304	rze25	rze25	
v	vol_rze25_04	gen	ENABLED	ACTIVE	4194304	SELECT	–	
pl	pl-04	vol_rze25_04	ENABLED	ACTIVE	4194304	CONCAT	–	RW
sd	rze25-04	pl-04	0	12582912	4194304	rze25	rze25	
v	vol_rze25_05	gen	ENABLED	ACTIVE	4194304	SELECT	–	
pl	pl-05	vol_rze25_05	ENABLED	ACTIVE	4194304	CONCAT	–	RW
sd	rze25-05	pl-05	0	16777216	4194304	rze25	rze25	
v	vol_rze25_06	gen	ENABLED	ACTIVE	4194304	SELECT	–	
pl	pl-06	vol_rze25_06	ENABLED	ACTIVE	4194304	CONCAT	–	RW
sd	rze25-06	pl-06	0	20971520	4194304	rze25	rze25	
v	vol_rze25_07	gen	ENABLED	ACTIVE	4194304	SELECT	–	
pl	pl-07	vol_rze25_07	ENABLED	ACTIVE	4194304	CONCAT	–	RW
sd	rze25-07	pl-07	0	25165824	4194304	rze25	rze25	
v	vol_rze25_08	gen	ENABLED	ACTIVE	4194304	SELECT	–	
pl	pl-08	vol_rze25_08	ENABLED	ACTIVE	4194304	CONCAT	–	RW
sd	rze25-08	pl-08	0	29360128	4194304	rze25	rze25	
v	vol_rze25_09	fsgen	ENABLED	ACTIVE	4194304	SELECT	–	
pl	pl-17	vol_rze25_09	ENABLED	ACTIVE	4194304	CONCAT	–	RW
sd	rze25-09	pl-17	0	33554432	4194304	rze25	rze25	

We were able to completely recover from this failure with no loss of data by manipulating LSM metadata and manually correcting problems. LSM typically allows this level of troubleshooting and recovery with no data loss, but the correct knowledge and proper discipline is essential.

9.5   A Performance Improvement Case Involving AdvFS and LSM

In the following case study, we show you how *chvol(8)* is often used to increase the read and write I/O block size parameters. Unfortunately, because of the way the *chvol(8)* command works, you must change the LSM maximum I/O (the kernel parameter is "volinfo.max_io") parameter first, so that the AdvFS volume values can be changed. When an AdvFS domain is activated, the maximum values for the read and write I/O volume parameters supported by the underlying volume technology are read into memory.

What we mean here is that if, for example, the volume is an LSM local volume, then the value of the maximum throughput is also the maximum to which you can set the AdvFS volume parameter. In some hardware controller technology, you cannot change this value, so you are stuck with the supported maximum. One example of this is a SWXCR controller, which has a fixed maximum value for the I/O throughput of 64 kilobytes per transfer. This would make the SWXCR a poor choice for a high-performance database server.

Luckily, LSM allows you to change this parameter to a higher value. The unfortunate part is that if you want to take advantage of the dynamic nature of *chvol(8)*, then you must have thought about the LSM parameter change ahead of time. If you decide to make the change later, then you will have to remount the file system so that the new maximum transfer values for the volumes will be read. This procedure will allow *chvol(8)* to proceed without complaint. In many cases, remounting the file system requires some downtime of applications and users to make this happen. The other unfortunate thing about this parameter is that the only way to set it is by patching the kernel with the kernel debugger. The consequence of this requirement is that if for any reason the kernel is rebuilt later, the kernel will need to be patched again or the value will drop back to the default.

In addition to the maximum transfer parameter values, the current "dynamic" values set by *chvol(8)* (or default) are also stored in the volume structure. These values can be changed using *chvol(8)*, as long as the underlying controller supports it. In Tru64 UNIX versions before 5.0, the default value for this parameter is 128 blocks (64 kilobytes), which we find to be woefully low for many big databases. Here, we bump the value up to 2 kilobytes. The default value in 5.0 is 16 kilobytes, thus setting this LSM parameter will most likely not be needed anymore.

So, first let's examine the current value on a running LSM system, and we see that it is set to the default value.

```
(kdbx) p volinfo.max_io
128
```

In the following two commands, we both assign and patch the kernel using the kernel debugger. If you're familiar with the way in which the debugger works, then you know that the assign makes the in-memory value change and the patch changes the on-disk kernel. If you neglect to patch, then the value will be lost on the next reboot. On the other hand, if you don't do the assign, then the parameter change will not take effect until the next reboot. A reboot can be avoided by doing both of these operations at the same time.

```
(kdbx) assign volinfo.max_io=2048
2048

(kdbx) patch volinfo.max_io=2048
2048

(kdbx) p volinfo.max_io
2048
```

The file system we wish to change is called "tst_dmn#tst," and we see that it is already mounted.

```
# df | grep tst
tst_dmn#tst        200000    36   188656   1%  /tst

# showfdmn tst_dmn

        Id              Date Created          LogPgs  Domain Name
3662ad91.00002c20  Mon Nov 30 09:37:05 1998   512     tst_dmn

 Vol  512-Blks  Free    % Used  Cmode  Rblks  Wblks  Vol Name
 1L   200000   188656   6%      on     128    128    /dev/vol/dg3/voltst

# chvol /dev/vol/dg3/voltst tst_dmn
rblks = 128 wblks = 128 cmode = on, thresh = 16384

# chvol -r 256 -w 256 -t 32768 /dev/vol/dg3/voltst tst_dmn
Warning: /dev/vol/dg3/voltst: Decreasing maximum read transfer size to 65536 bytes
Warning: /dev/vol/dg3/voltst: Decreasing maximum write transfer size to 65536 bytes
```

Even though we have already changed the maximum transfer parameter for LSM, the value was not changed in the AdvFS volume structure because the domain was already activated. So, we must remount the file system in order for the maximum value to be changed in the volume structure for this domain.

```
# umount /tst

# mount tst_dmn#tst /tst

# chvol /dev/vol/dg3/voltst tst_dmn
rblks = 128 wblks = 128 cmode = on, thresh = 32768

# chvol -r 256 -w 256 -t 32768 /dev/vol/dg3/voltst tst_dmn

# chvol /dev/vol/dg3/voltst tst_dmn
rblks = 256 wblks = 256 cmode = on, thresh = 32768
```

Once we have completed the remounting, you see that the *chvol(8)* does not complain, and the parameters can now be increased up to a maximum of 4096. The performance of the file system will improve tremendously for large, sequential reads and writes.

9.6   Fsck Fails on a Large File System

In this case, the situation was that a Usenet News server running Tru64 UNIX 4.0F had gone down because of a power glitch. Upon reboot, a 400GB UFS could not be mounted because it was dirty, and the *fsck(8)* tool was failing with the following error:

```
/sbin/ufs_fsck /dev/rrz0c
** /dev/rrz0c
cannot alloc 200256002 bytes for lncntp
```

It was very likely that *fsck(8)* had never been successfully run on this file system because a normal shutdown unmounts the file system cleanly each time. Before the power outage, the system administrator had been very diligent about making sure that the system always shut down cleanly.

Now, if you refer to our discussion in Appendix C, you will discover that the "lncntp" is one of the bookkeeping structures used by *fsck(8)* to keep track of the inode link counts. It is allocated and populated in the setup phase of *fsck(8)* operation. The value that *fsck(8)* was attempting to allocate for this structure was known to be a function of two values from the file system's superblock ("fs_ncg" and "fs_ipg"). This value must be calculated to be approximately 200 MB because that is being reported in the previously listed error string. In addition, this allocation is being done by *fsck(8)* after allocating several other similarly calculated data structures. Clearly, the other allocations succeeded and this one failed.

A memory allocation fails in a user program such as this one for the following two common reasons:

1.   There is simply no more virtual memory (physical memory + swap) available on the system and we have eager mode swapping enabled.

2.   The per-process data size is set too small. Because we know that the default value for *per-proc-data-size* is 128 MB, this is a possibility.

The system reports that plenty of free memory and swap are available with eager mode swapping enabled. In addition, the *per-proc-data-size* is 250 MB and was increased to 350 MB, but we got the same error. Clearly, this was not a large enough value, but another reboot could not be tolerated on the production system. Thus, the file system was remade and restored from known good backups. Any further data from the file system that might have proved useful had been lost at this point. Later, it was calculated that 500 MB of virtual memory were needed by *fsck(8)* to be able to allocate all of the appropriate structures in the setup phase.

Meanwhile, analysis continued on the problem offline. The suggestion was made that the real problem could have been a corrupted primary superblock because *fsck(8)* uses the "fs_ncg" and "fs_ipg" values to perform its calculation of the "lncntp." This corruption was a possibility that could not be confirmed at this point. A *dumpfs(8)* or *fsdb(8)* printout of the superblock, if available, would have shown this problem very quickly.

With no more data from the file system to work with, the next best thing we could do was to attempt to reproduce the problem in the lab. The required amount of disk space was not readily available; however, it was probably not necessary as long as the superblock values could be duplicated under other circumstances. No special flags to *newfs(8)* had been used when creating the original 400GB file system (in particular '-i' and '-c'). Therefore, we guessed that we could simulate the symptoms with a very small '-i' value and a "somewhat" large file system (~91 million blocks). The following output is from the test performed on the laboratory system:

```
# newfs -i 200 /dev/vol/volbig
Warning: Bytes per inode restrict cylinders per group to 3.
Warning: 3448 sector(s) in last cylinder unallocated
/dev/rvol/volbig:    91947656 sectors in 22449 cylinders of 32 tracks, 128
sectors
    44896.3MB in 7483 cyl groups (3 c/g, 6.00MB/g, 20864 i/g)
super-block backups (for fsck -b #) at:
32, 12448, 24864, 37280, 49696, 62112, 74528, 86944,
99360, 111776, 124192, 136608, 149024, 161440, 173856, 186272,
```

```
198688, 211104, 223520, 235936, 248352, 260768, 273184, 285600,
[snip]

# dumpfs /dev/vol/volbig | more
magic       11954    format       dynamic time       Mon Mar 6 15:48:40 2000
nbfree      3292286 ndir         1       nifree     156125309        nffree    14
ncg         7483     ncyl         22449   size       45973828         blocks    26338303
bsize       8192     shift        13      mask       0xffffe000
fsize       1024     shift        10      mask       0xfffffc00
frag        8        shift        3       fsbtodb    1
cpg         3        bpg          768     fpg        6144      ipg      20864
minfree     10%      optim        time    maxcontig  8         maxbpg   2048
rotdelay    0ms      headswitch   0us     trackseek  0us       rps      60
ntrak       32       nsect        128     npsect     128       spc      4096
trackskew   0        interleave   1
nindir      2048     inopb        64      nspf       2
sblkno      16       cblkno       24      iblkno     32        dblkno   2640
sbsize      2048     cgsize       4096    cgoffset   64        cgmask   0xffffffe0
csaddr      2640     cssize       119808  shift      9         mask     0xffffffe00
cgrotor     0        fmod         0       ronly      0         clean    3
[snip]

# fsck /dev/vol/volbig
/sbin/ufs_fsck /dev/vol/volbig
** /dev/rvol/volbig
File system unmounted cleanly - no fsck needed

# fsck -o /dev/vol/volbig
/sbin/ufs_fsck -o /dev/vol/volbig
** /dev/rvol/volbig
cannot alloc 156125313 bytes for statemap

# sysconfig -q proc | grep data
per-proc-data-size = 134217728
max-per-proc-data-size = 1073741824
```

The output from *dumpfs(8)* and the error from *fsck(8)* are in agreement with the formula from the code. It is too large to allocate this much memory, given the default **per-process-data-size** of 128 MB.

After that, we increased the per-proc-data-size to the maximum and retried the *fsck(8)*, which then succeeded. So, we conclusively proved that the reason *fsck(8)* failed was because the per-process data size was simply too small. We also showed that it was unlikely that the superblock was corrupt. With this information, a problem report was opened to get this problem fixed in a future release.

9.7 Summary

We have shown you just a few advanced cases of troubleshooting file system issues on a Tru64 UNIX system. Volumes could be written to cover every issue on every aspect of the system. We simply provided a few representative studies, which should give you an idea of what you can do. With such complex environments being put together, the best hope for correcting problems as they arise is to have as much knowledge as possible about how the file systems work. Given what we have shown here, we hope that you will be able to apply the information we have provided to you in this text and correct many of the problems that you encounter.

Appendix A

Freeware Tools

This appendix is a discussion of freeware tools available to assist with troubleshooting file system problems on a Tru64 UNIX system. These tools are available from different sites on the Internet, to which we have tried to provide pointers, when possible. Any well-managed Tru64 UNIX system will have these tools installed and use them on a regular basis.

A.1   The lsof Utility

This utility is probably the most useful freeware tool for troubleshooting file system issues on any UNIX system, but in Tru64 in particular. It lists information about files that are open by the processes on a system. In many ways, this ability can be invaluable for troubleshooting why a file system might be full, for example. As discussed in Chapter 1, UNIX process can hold open files on a file system and unlink its directory entry, leaving no easy method to discover who is the culprit. Lsof does this in a much more readable fashion than does *fuser(8)*. You'll also find that the documentation that comes with lsof should answer most of your questions.

If you are looking for the latest distributed version of this tool, it is available via anonymous ftp from the host `vic.cc.purdue.edu`. You'll find the lsof distribution in the pub/tools/unix/lsof directory. If you want to use your web browser, that URL is:

```
ftp://vic.cc.purdue.edu/pub/tools/unix/lsof
```

What you will discover if you go to that site is source code that you can easily compile and install yourself. In addition, you will also find binaries for a bunch of supported UNIX and UNIX-like operating systems. As of this writing, 4.0D and 5.0 binary are available. The 4.0D version should work on Tru64 UNIX version 4.0D, E, F, and G. The 5.0 version should work correctly for Tru64 5.0 and higher.

A.2   The monitor Utility

Those users who are familiar with OpenVMS will find the monitor tool familiar. This is about the best tool we've seen that gives multiprocessor statistics in a regularly updated fashion. I recommend that anyone have a copy of it on their system. You can obtain monitor from the following URL:

```
ftp://gatekeeper.dec.com/pub/Digital/monitor.alpha.tar.Z
```

A.3   The vmubc Utility

This is an excellent X-based graphical tool for monitoring the memory usage of a Tru64 UNIX system. Unfortunately, as of this writing, the tool had not been ported to version 5.0 yet, but it is hoped that it will be ported soon. You can obtain vmubc from the following URL:

```
ftp://gatekeeper.dec.com/pub/Digital/vmubc.tar.Z
```

A.4   The collect Utility

Any good consultant keeps this tool in his or her "bag of tricks." As we have discussed, tools such as *iostat(8)* come with the Tru64 UNIX distribution that gives information about how the disks are performing. Collect does this and much more and provides recording and playback capabilities. Thus, you can gather the information online at the customer site and analyze the data later on another system back at the office. You can obtain collect at the following URL:

```
ftp://gatekeeper.dec.com/pub/Digital/collect/
```

In this directory, you will find a subset that you can download onto your system and install it using *setld(8)*.

A.5   The top Utility

Top is another tool, similar to monitor, that gives regularly updated information. What top provides is basically an ordered output from the *ps(1)* command. The benefit is a simple way to find out what processes are taking up all the CPU time on the system. The top utility can be obtained form the following URLs:

```
ftp://gatekeeper.dec.com/pub/Digital/top.tar.Z
```

```
ftp://gatekeeper.dec.com/pub/Digital/top.alpha.bin
```

This is where you can get both the source code to compile yourself and the binary for Tru64 UNIX.

A.6   The recover Tool

This is the closest thing to an undelete tool for UFS. The recover tool was written as an internal Compaq tool to use for recovering lost files on a UFS. You can obtain the source from the following site:

```
ftp://gatekeeper.dec.com/pub/sysadm/recover.tar.Z
```

You'll have to compile it yourself, but that is easy to do. A makefile is available for both ULTRIX on the Mips platform and Tru64 UNIX on Alpha.

Appendix B

Advanced AdvFS Commands

This appendix discusses several advanced AdvFS diagnostic tools in more detail. Most likely, these tools would not be used by the average Tru64 UNIX system administrator; however, you never know what tools will be useful. The nature of the problem you are trying to solve will dictate how best to troubleshoot it. Also, for completeness, we cover the rest of the tools here. Table B–1 is a summary of the utilities covered in this section.

TABLE B–1   Summary of Advanced AdvFS Commands

COMMAND	SECTION	V3.x	V4.x	V5.x
tag2name(8)	B.1	X	X	X
vfile(8)	B.2.1	X	X	X
vbmtchain(8)	B.2.2	X	X	X
vlogpg(8)	B.3.1	X	X	X
vbmtpg(8)	B.3.2	X	X	X
vfragpg(8)	B.3.3	X	X	X
vtagpg(8)	B.3.4	X	X	X
vlsnpg(8)	B.3.5	X	X	X
shfragbf(8)	B.3.6	X	X	X
nvbmtpg(8)	B.4.1			X
nvfragpg(8)	B.4.2			X
nvlogpg(8)	B.4.3			X
nvtagpg(8)	B.4.4			X
vsbmpg(8)	B.4.5			X
savemeta(8)	B.4.6	X	X	X
msfsck(8)	B.5.1	X	X	
vchkdir(8)	B.5.2	X	X	
vods(8)	B.5.3	X	X	
mssh(8)	B.5.4	X	X	X
logread(8)	B.5.5	X	X	
shblk(8)	B.6		X	X

451

B.1   *Tag2name(8)* Command

As discussed in Chapter 7, AdvFS identifies files internally by tag numbers. In some cases, error messages or diagnostic utilities specify a particular file by its tag number rather than by its file name. The *tag2name(8)* command can be used to convert this tag number to its file name on an AdvFS fileset.

To obtain the file name, specify the path to the desired tag number in the fileset's .tags directory as the argument to the *tag2name(8)* command. The full pathname of the corresponding file will be printed to standard out.

Syntax:

```
tag2name tags_directory/tag
```

TABLE B–2   Flags for the *tag2name(8)* Command

FLAG	DESCRIPTION
tags_directory	The full path of the AdvFS .tags directory for the mounted filesets in the domain that contains the corresponding file
tag	The AdvFS file tag number

Example:

This is an example of how tag2name(8) can be used to convert the tag number, shown with the ls(1) command, to the full pathname to the file.

```
# cd /export

# ls
.tags asWedit-2.5 photos.zip src2www
Mail.tar.gz cdrom quota.group stuff
T5.0-21r764.101 ftp quota.user tcr
WWW oldsrc src

# ls -li photos.zip
13153 -rw-r--r-- 1 root system 38148351 May 22 1997 photos.zip

# /sbin/advfs/tag2name /export/.tags/13153
/export/photos.zip
```

B.2   Metadata Examination Commands

These commands are used for examining or dumping out metadata information for files on AdvFS. As discussed in Chapter 7, each mcell location is described by three items:

1.   its volume

2.   the page within the BMT file located on that volume

3.   its cell within the BMT page

With most files, this information would be difficult to obtain from an unmounted domain; however, metadata files have fixed locations, so you can use *vfile(8)* to easily examine these files.

The primary mcell for the root tag directory is found in the BMT of the volume containing the log. To find this volume for a domain, use the *showfdmn(8)* or the *advscan(8)* command. The volume marked "L" contains the log. Certain metadata files are in fixed locations, as shown in Table B–3.

TABLE B–3   Fixed Mcell Locations for the AdvFS Metadata

PAGE	CELL	VOLUME	NOTES
Bitfile metadata table	0	0	every volume
Storage bitmap	0	1	every volume
Root tag directory	0	2	volume with log
Transaction log file	0	3	volume with log

B.2.1   The *vfile(8)* Command

Sometimes it is helpful when diagnosing AdvFS problems to dump out some of the special metadata files (BMT, SBM, etc.) on a domain. The *vfile(8)* command can be used to display the contents of a file from a domain with no mounted filesets. The file is identified by the location of its primary mcell.

Syntax:

```
vfile bmt_page cell special [special 2 ...]
```

TABLE B–4   Flags for the *vfile(8)* Command

FLAG	DESCRIPTION B
mt_page	Specifies the page within the BMT of the volume that contains the file's mcell.
cell	Specifies the cell of the BMT page that contains the file's mcell.
special	Specifies the volume on which the file's primary mcell is located.
special 2	Specifies the other volumes in this domain that may be accessed to follow the file's mcell chain.

Example:

The following example shows how to dump a copy of the transaction log into a file called "log."

```
# showfdmn test_domain

Id                          Date Created              LogPgs Domain Name
354614cd.0006d4dc Tue Apr 28 13:41:33 1998 4096    test_domain

Vol  512-Blks Free    % Used Cmode Rblks Wblks Vol Name
1    100000   69664   30%    on    128   128   /dev/vol/vol01
2L   100000   34352   66%    on    128   128   /dev/vol/vol02
3    100000   91664   8%     on    128   128   /dev/vol/vol03
4    100000   99872   0%     on    128   128   /dev/vol/vol04
--------------------------
     400000   295552 26%

# /sbin/advfs/vfile 0 3 /dev/vol/vol02 > log
```

Example:

The following example shows how to use the *vfile(8)* command to dump a copy of the BMT from volume 4 into a file named "bmt_vol4."

```
# showfdmn test_domain

Id                          Date Created              LogPgs Domain Name
354614cd.0006d4dc Tue Apr 28 13:41:33 1998 4096    test_domain

Vol  512-Blks Free    % Used Cmode Rblks Wblks Vol Name
1    100000   69664   30%    on    128   128   /dev/vol/vol01
2L   100000   34352   66%    on    128   128   /dev/vol/vol02
3    100000   91664   8%     on    128   128   /dev/vol/vol03
4    100000   99872   0%     on    128   128   /dev/vol/vol04
--------------------------
     400000   295552 26%

# /sbin/advfs/vfile 0 0 /dev/vol/vol04 > bmt_vol4
```

B.2.2   The *vbmtchain(8)* Command

The *vbmtchain(8)* utility displays metadata for a file. The file is described by the location of its primary mcell. Each mcell location is composed of three parts: volume, page within the BMT file located on that volume, and cell within the BMT page.

The *vbmtchain(8)* utility displays the attributes of the file including the time stamp, the extent map, and whether the file is a user directory or a data file.

Syntax:

```
vbmtchain bmt_page cell special [special 2...]
```

TABLE B–5   Flags for the *vbmtchain(8)* Command

FLAG	DESCRIPTION
bmt_page	The page within the BMT of the volume that contains the file's mcell
cell	The cell of the BMT page that contains the file's mcell
special	The volume on which the file's primary mcell is located
special 2	The other volumes in this domain that may be accessed to follow the file's mcell chain

Example:

The following example shows how *vbmtchain(8)* can be used to examine some of the attributes of the storage bitmap (SBM) on the second volume in an AdvFS domain.

```
# showfdmn test_domain

Id                    Date Created           LogPgs Domain Name
354614cd.0006d4dc Tue Apr 28 13:41:33 1998 4096    test_domain

Vol 512-Blks Free   % Used Cmode Rblks Wblks Vol Name
1   100000   69664  30%    on    128   128   /dev/vol/vol01
2L  100000   34352  66%    on    128   128   /dev/vol/vol02
3   100000   91664  8%     on    128   128   /dev/vol/vol03
4   100000   99872  0%     on    128   128   /dev/vol/vol04
--------------------------
    400000   295552 26%

# /sbin/advfs/vbmtchain 0 1 /dev/vol/vol02
VOL 2 LBN 32 BMT PAGE 0
========================================
CELL 1 nextVdIndex 0 linkSegment 0 tag,bfSetTag: -13, -2
nextMCId page 0 cell 0
========================================

RECORD 0 bcnt 92 version 0 type 2 BSR_ATTR
state 3 BSRA_VALID
bfPgSz 16
transitionId 0
cloneId 0
cloneCnt 0
maxClonePgs 0
deleteWithClone 0
outOfSyncClone 0
cl.dataSafety 2 BFD_FTX_AGENT
cl.reqServices 0
cl.optServices 0
cl.extendSize 0
cl.s_shelfPri 0
cl.s_readAhead 0
cl.acl 0
cl.rsvd_sec1 0
```

```
cl.rsvd_sec2 0
cl.rsvd_sec3 0

RECORD 1 bcnt 80 version 0 type 1 BSR_XTNTS
type 0 BSXMT_APPEND
chainVdIndex 0
chainMCId page 0 cell 0
tertiaryVdIndex 0
tertiaryMCId page 0 cell 0
blksPerPage 16
segmentSize 0
delLink.nextMCId page 0 cell 0
delLink.prevMCId page 0 cell 0
delRst.mcid page 0 cell 0
delRst.vdIndex 0
delRst.xtntIndex 0
delRst.offset 0
delRst.blocks 0
xu.nwf.nwPgCnt 1
xu.nwf.nwrPage 0
xu.nwf.notWrit[0] 00000060
xu.nwf.notWrit[1] 00000001
xu.x.mcellCnt 1
xu.x.xCnt 2
xu.x.bsXA[ 0] bsPage 0 vdblk 96
xu.x.bsXA[ 1] bsPage 1 vdblk -1
```

B.3   The "Old" Metadata Examination Commands

These commands are specialized commands used to examine certain metadata files on an AdvFS domain. Most of these have been superceded in Tru64 UNIX version 5.0 by the commands in section B.4. These tools are useless for looking at domains created with AdvFS V4 on-disk structure and higher.

B.3.1   The *vlogpg(8)* Command

The *vlogpg(8)* utility attempts to translate an eight-kilobyte-page part of a volume of an unmounted file system and formats it as a log page. The *vlogpg(8)* utility effectively replaced the undocumented *logread(8)* utility in V4.0 to display the pages and records needed to redo transactions that were in progress at the time of a crash.

Syntax:

```
vlogpg special [page_lbn]
```

TABLE B–6   Flags for the *vlogpg(8)* Command

FLAG	DESCRIPTION
special	The volume on which the log is located
page_lbn	The logical block number (LBN) within the volume to be formatted. The default value is zero.

Example:

Here is an example of a use of the *vlogpg(8)* command.

```
# showfdmn export_dmn | more

Id                      Date Created              LogPgs   Domain Name
364c5ee4.00021cf5 Fri Nov 13 11:31:32 1998       512      export_dmn

Vol    512-Blks Free   % Used Cmode Rblks  Wblks  Vol Name
1      2048000  726656 65%    on    128    128    /dev/vol/dg2/volexport
2L     2048000  746768 64%    on    128    128    /dev/vol/dg2/volexport2
3      2048000  712256 65%    on    128    128    /dev/vol/dg2/volexport3
       --------------------------
       6144000  218568064%

# cd /export/.tags

# showfile -x M-15

Id            Vol PgSz Pages XtntType Segs SegSz I/O    Perf File
ffffffff1.0000 2  16   512   simple   **   **    async  100% M-15

extentMap: 1
pageOff pageCnt vol volBlock blockCnt
0       512     2   12656    8192
extentCnt: 1

# /sbin/advfs/vlogpg /dev/vol/dg2/volexport2 12656
LOG PAGE LBN 12656 thisPageLSN 73018608
pgSafe 1 chkBit 0 curLastRec 1975 prevLastRec -1 pgType 3 BFM_FTXLOG
firstLogRec page 509 offset 0 lsn 73018392
================================================================

RECORD OFFSET 0 wordCnt 143 clientWordCnt 131 segment 0 lsn 73018608
nextRec page 0 offset 143 lsn 73018610
prevRec page 511 offset 1926 lsn 73018606
prevClientRec page 65535 offset 65535 lsn 0
firstSeg page 0 offset 0 lsn 73018608
----------------------------------------------------------------
01000000 01020100 199f2000 e45e4c36 ........ .. ..^L6
f51c0200 fd010000 182c5a04 0b000000 ........ .,.Z.....
20000000 20000000 00000000 e9320000 ...   ...2..
0200ffff e45e4c36 f51c0200 03000000 .....^L6 ........
01800000 51040000 23880000 e9320000 ....Q... #....2..
0200ffff e45e4c36 f51c0200 03000000 .....^L6 ........
```

```
01800000 51040000 23880000 feffffff  ....Q... #.......
00000000 03000000 01800000 01000000  ........ ........
02000000 a8020000 08000000 08000000  ........ ........
04000000 23880200 e9320000 55005400  ....#... .2..U.T.
feffffff 00000000 f4ffffff 00000000  ........ ........
97010000 03000000 00000000 10000000  ........ ........
5c0a0000 08000000 540a0000 24010000  /....... T...$...
eb320000 bf010000 01000000 97010018  .2...... ........
51040000 23880000 00000000 00000000  Q...#... ........
51040000 23880000 03000000 01800000  Q...#... ........
5c000200 01000000 10000000 199f2000  /....... ...... .
00000000 00000000 00000000 00000000  ........ ........
00000000 01000000 00000000 00000000  ........ ........
00000000 00000000 00000000 00000000  ........ ........
00000000 00000000 00000000 00000000  ........ ........
00000000 00000000 00000000 50000100  ........ ....P...
00000000 00000000 00000000 00000000  ........ ........
00000000 10000000 00000000 00000000  ........ ........
00000000 00000000 00000000 00000000  ........ ........
00000000 00000000 00006173 74207061  ........ ..ast pa
72616d65 74657220 6f6e206d 04000000  rameter on m....
51040000 20880000 a4810000 00000000  Q... ... ........
00000000 00000000 5b1e0000 00000000  ........ [.......
c6b0d537 08be6f29 c6b0d537 886b9c29  ...7..o) ...7.k.)
c6b0d537 0850ab29 00000000 70010000  ...7.P.) ....p...
01800000 00000000 00000000 01000000  ........ ........
00000000 04000000 04000020  ........ ...
```

RECORD OFFSET 143 wordCnt 84 clientWordCnt 72 segment 0 lsn 73018610
nextRec page 0 offset 227 lsn 73018612
prevRec page 0 offset 0 lsn 73018608
prevClientRec page 0 offset 0 lsn 73018608
firstSeg page 0 offset 143 lsn 73018610

```
01000000 01020200 199f2000 e45e4c36  ........ .. ..^L6
f51c0200 fd010000 182c5a04 05000000  ........ .,Z....
7c000000 00000000 00000000 51040000  |....... ....Q...
23880000 e45e4c36 f51c0200 03000000  #....^L6 ........
01800000 e9320000 1c000000 02005800  .....2.. ......X.
01000000 10000000 199f2000 00000000  ........ ........
00000000 00000000 00000000 00000000  ........ ........
01000000 00000000 00000000 00000000  ........ ........
00000000 00000000 00000000 00000000  ........ ........
00000000 00000000 feffffff 00000000  ........ ........
f4ffffff 00000000 97010000 01000000  ........ ........
700a0000 58000000 01000000 10000000  p...X... ........
199f2000 00000000 00000000 00000000  .. ..... ........
00000000 00000000 01000000 00000000  ........ ........
```

```
00000000 00000000 00000000 00000000 ........ ........
00000000 00000000 00000000 00000000 ........ ........
00000000 00000000 00000000 00000000 ........ ........

[snip]

RECORD OFFSET 1975 wordCnt 43 clientWordCnt 31 segment 0 lsn 73018674
nextRec page 65535 offset 65535 lsn 0
prevRec page 0 offset 1938 lsn 73018672
prevClientRec page 0 offset 1938 lsn 73018672
firstSeg page 0 offset 1975 lsn 73018674
--------------------------------------------------------------
01000000 02010300 209f2000 e45e4c36 ........ . ..^L6
f51c0200 fd010000 182c5a04 12000000 ........ .,Z.....
00000000 00000000 00000000 feffffff ........ ........
00000000 eeffffff 00000000 08000000 ........ ........
03000000 681b0000 04000000 701a0000 ....h... ....p...
00000000 641a0000 1c000000 04000000 ....d... ........
04010600 ffff0100 10000200 00000000 ........ ........
104a0600 01000000 ffffffff .J...... ....

END OF LOG PAGE LBN 12656 =================================================
pgType 3 BFM_FTXLOG
dmnId: Fri Nov 13 11:31:32 1998
=================================================================
```

B.3.2   The *vbmtpg(8)* Command

The *vbmtpg(8)* utility displays a complete, formatted page of the BMT for a mounted or unmounted domain. This is useful for debugging when some seemingly random file corruption has occurred.

Note that the *vbmtchain(8)* command displays all the mcells associated with a given file, whereas the *vbmtpg(8)* command displays a page of information. This page may contain information for more than one file and may not provide complete information on any file.

Syntax:

```
vbmtpg special [page_lbn]
```

TABLE B–7   Flags for the *vbmtpg(8)* Command

FLAG	DESCRIPTION
special	The volume on which the page is located
page_lbn	The LBN of the page to be examined. The default LBN is 32, which corresponds to BMT page 0.

Example:

The following pre-5.0 example shows formatted output of the BMT page 0 (the default) on one of the volumes in a domain.

```
# showfdmn test_domain

Id                      Date Created          LogPgs Domain Name
354614cd.0006d4dc Tue Apr 28 13:41:33 1998 4096    test_domain

Vol  512-Blks Free    % Used Cmode Rblks Wblks Vol Name
1    100000   69664   30%    on    128   128   /dev/vol/vol01
2L   100000   34352   66%    on    128   128   /dev/vol/vol02
3    100000   91664   8%     on    128   128   /dev/vol/vol03
4    100000   99872   0%     on    128   128   /dev/vol/vol04
     --------------------------
     400000   295552 26%

# /sbin/advfs/vbmtpg /dev/vol/vol01
PAGE LBN 32 megaVersion 3 nextFreePg 0 freeMcellCnt 22 pageId
0
nextfreeMCId page 0 cell 6
================================================================

CELL 0 nextVdIndex 1 linkSegment 0 tag,bfSetTag: -6, -2
nextMCId page 0 cell 4
================================================================

RECORD 0 bcnt 92 version 0 type 2 BSR_ATTR
state 3 BSRA_VALID
bfPgSz 16
transitionId 0

[snip]

CELL 4 nextVdIndex 0 linkSegment 1 tag,bfSetTag: -6, -2
nextMCId page 0 cell 0
================================================================

RECORD 0 bcnt 40 version 0 type 3 BSR_VD_ATTR
vdMntId: Tue Apr 28 13:43:07 1998
state 1
vdIndex 1
jays_new_field 0
vdBlkCnt 100000
stgCluster 2
maxPgSz 16
bmtXtntPgs 128
serviceClass 1

RECORD 1 bcnt 24 version 0 type 4 BSR_DMN_ATTR
bfDomainId: Tue Apr 28 13:41:33 1998
maxVds 256
bfSetDirTag -2

RECORD 2 bcnt 52 version 0 type 15 BSR_DMN_MATTR
seqNum 4
```

```
               delPendingBfSet 0
               uid 0
               gid 1
               mode 0744
               vdCnt 4
               recoveryFailed 0
               bfSetDirTag -8
               ftxLogTag -9
               ftxLogPgs 512

               CELL 5 nextVdIndex 0 linkSegment 0 tag,bfSetTag: -11, -2
               nextMCId page 0 cell 0
               ===============================================================
               RECORD 0 bcnt 92 version 0 type 2 BSR_ATTR
               state 3 BSRA_VALID
               bfPgSz 16
               transitionId 0
               cloneId 0
               cloneCnt 0
               maxClonePgs 0
               deleteWithClone 0
               outOfSyncClone 0
               cl.dataSafety 2 BFD_FTX_AGENT
               cl.reqServices 0
               cl.optServices 0
               cl.extendSize 0
               cl.s_shelfPri 0
               cl.s_readAhead 0
               cl.acl 0
               cl.rsvd_sec1 0
               cl.rsvd_sec2 0
               cl.rsvd_sec3 0

               RECORD 1 bcnt 160 version 0 type 1 BSR_XTNTS
               type 0 BSXMT_APPEND
               chainVdIndex 0
               chainMCId page 0 cell 0
               tertiaryVdIndex 0
               tertiaryMCId page 0 cell 0
               blksPerPage 16
               segmentSize 0
               delLink.nextMCId page 0 cell 0
               delLink.prevMCId page 0 cell 0
               delRst.mcid page 0 cell 0
               delRst.vdIndex 0
               delRst.xtntIndex 0
               delRst.offset 0
               delRst.blocks 0
               xu.nwf.nwPgCnt 0
               xu.nwf.nwrPage 0
               xu.nwf.notWrit[0] 00000000
               xu.nwf.notWrit[1] 00000002
               xu.x.mcellCnt 0
               xu.x.xCnt 3
```

```
xu.x.bsXA[ 0] bsPage 0 vdblk 0
xu.x.bsXA[ 1] bsPage 2 vdblk 64

CELL 6 nextVdIndex 0 linkSegment 0 tag,bfSetTag: 0, 0
nextMCId page 0 cell 7
CELL 7 nextVdIndex 0 linkSegment 0 tag,bfSetTag: 0, 0
nextMCId page 0 cell 8
CELL 8 nextVdIndex 0 linkSegment 0 tag,bfSetTag: 0, 0
nextMCId page 0 cell 9
CELL 9 nextVdIndex 0 linkSegment 0 tag,bfSetTag: 0, 0
nextMCId page 0 cell 10
CELL 10 nextVdIndex 0 linkSegment 0 tag,bfSetTag: 0, 0
nextMCId page 0 cell 11
CELL 11 nextVdIndex 0 linkSegment 0 tag,bfSetTag: 0, 0
nextMCId page 0 cell 12
CELL 12 nextVdIndex 0 linkSegment 0 tag,bfSetTag: 0, 0
nextMCId page 0 cell 13
CELL 13 nextVdIndex 0 linkSegment 0 tag,bfSetTag: 0, 0
nextMCId page 0 cell 14
CELL 14 nextVdIndex 0 linkSegment 0 tag,bfSetTag: 0, 0
nextMCId page 0 cell 15
CELL 15 nextVdIndex 0 linkSegment 0 tag,bfSetTag: 0, 0
nextMCId page 0 cell 16
CELL 16 nextVdIndex 0 linkSegment 0 tag,bfSetTag: 0, 0
nextMCId page 0 cell 17
CELL 17 nextVdIndex 0 linkSegment 0 tag,bfSetTag: 0, 0
nextMCId page 0 cell 18
CELL 18 nextVdIndex 0 linkSegment 0 tag,bfSetTag: 0, 0
nextMCId page 0 cell 19
CELL 19 nextVdIndex 0 linkSegment 0 tag,bfSetTag: 0, 0
nextMCId page 0 cell 20
CELL 20 nextVdIndex 0 linkSegment 0 tag,bfSetTag: 0, 0
nextMCId page 0 cell 21
CELL 21 nextVdIndex 0 linkSegment 0 tag,bfSetTag: 0, 0
nextMCId page 0 cell 22
CELL 22 nextVdIndex 0 linkSegment 0 tag,bfSetTag: 0, 0
nextMCId page 0 cell 23
CELL 23 nextVdIndex 0 linkSegment 0 tag,bfSetTag: 0, 0
nextMCId page 0 cell 24
CELL 24 nextVdIndex 0 linkSegment 0 tag,bfSetTag: 0, 0
nextMCId page 0 cell 25
CELL 25 nextVdIndex 0 linkSegment 0 tag,bfSetTag: 0, 0
nextMCId page 0 cell 26
CELL 26 nextVdIndex 0 linkSegment 0 tag,bfSetTag: 0, 0
nextMCId page 0 cell 27
CELL 27 nextVdIndex 0 linkSegment 0 tag,bfSetTag: 0, 0
nextMCId page 0 cell 0
```

B.3.3   The *vfragpg(8)* Command

The *vfragpg(8)* command allows you to see the structure of a single
header page in a fragment file. Use showfile -x /usr/.tags/1 to locate the
logical block number of the page.

Syntax:

```
vfragpg special page_lbn
```

TABLE B–8 Flags for the *vfragpg(8)* Command

FLAGS	DESCRIPTION
special	The block special device name
page_lbn	The LBN of the page to be examined

Vfragpg(8) is obsolete and will not work for AdvFS versions greater than 1. Therefore, the command may not be very useful in Tru64 UNIX version 3.0 and greater.

B.3.4 The *vtagpg(8)* Command

The vtagpg(8) utility translates a 16-block part of a volume of a mounted or unmounted file system and formats it as a tag directory. Use this utility with other file utilities to locate file-structure anomalies for debugging.

If the volume is mounted, then use the "showfile -x" command to get the extent map before calling the *vtagpg(8)* command. If the volume is unmounted, then call the *vbmtchain(8)* command to identify the extent information.

Run the *vtagpg(8)* utility to obtain the root tag directory first because it has entries for each fileset in the domain. Then, run the utility again to view the tag directory for the fileset under investigation. This tag information points to the fileset metadata.

The *vtagpg(8)* utility displays tag entries that map file inode number to primary mcell location.

Syntax:

```
vtagpg special [page_lbn]
```

TABLE B–9 Flags for the *vtagpg(8)* Command

FLAG	DESCRIPTION
special	The volume on which the tag directory is located
page_lbn	The LBN of the page to be examined; the default is zero.

Example:

```
# showfile -x /mnt/.tags
Id Vol PgSz Pages XtntType Segs SegSz I/O Perf File
```

```
3.8001 4 16 1 simple ** ** ftx 100% .tags

extentMap: 1
pageOff      pageCnt   vol    volBlock      blockCnt
0            1         4      20112         16
extentCnt: 1

# showfile -x /mnt/.tags/3

Id                 Vol PgSz Pages XtntType Segs SegSz I/O   Perf File
3.8001             4   16   1     simple   **   **    ftx   100% 3

extentMap: 1
pageOff  pageCnt  vol  volBlock  blockCnt
0        1        4    20112     16
extentCnt: 1

# /sbin/advfs/vtagpg /dev/vol/vol02
TAG PAGE LBN 0 nextFreePage 6183 nextFreeMap 28 currPage197824
numAllocTMaps 0 numDeadTMaps 6182 padding 6144
================================================================================
tMapA[  24]  seqNo 32767 nextMap    4 vdIndex65535 bfMCId page 0    cell 4
tMapA[  97]  seqNo 32767 nextMap    4 vdIndex65535 bfMCId page 0    cell 4
tMapA[ 155]  seqNo 31998 nextMap 256 vdIndex 12   bfMCId page 8    cell 0
tMapA[ 156]  seqNo 32766 nextMap    0 vdIndex65535 bfMCId page 0    cell 0
tMapA[ 161]  seqNo 32760 nextMap    0 vdIndex65535 bfMCId page 0    cell 0
tMapA[ 162]  seqNo 32759 nextMap    0 vdIndex65535 bfMCId page 0    cell 0
tMapA[ 224]  seqNo 24834 nextMap   -1 vdIndex 0    bfMCId page 7727 cell 31
tMapA[1022]  seqNo 10884 nextMap    0 vdIndex 1622 bfMCId page 0    cell 0
```

B.3.5   The *vlsnpg(8)* Command

Given the device and the LBN, the *vlsnpg(8)* utility displays the logical sequence number (LSN) of the page of the log. The page takes on the LSN of its first record. This command can be used in a script to loop through LSNs for several pages to find the end of the log.

Syntax:

```
vlsnpg special [page_lbn]
```

TABLE B–10   Flags for the *vlsnpg(8)* Command

FLAG	DESCRIPTION
special	The volume on which the page is located
page_lbn	The LBN of the requested page to be examined; the default is zero.

Example:

```
# /sbin/advfs/vlsnpg /dev/vol/vol02
197824
```

B.3.6 The *shfragbf(8)* Command

Use this command to display summary information on the fragment file.

Syntax:

```
shfragbf [-t frag_list] /<mount_point>/.tags/1
```

TABLE B–11   Flags for the *shfragbf(8)* Command

FLAG	DESCRIPTION
-t frag_list	The name of the fragment list to examine
mount_point	The fileset mount point of the file system to examine

The '-t' flag is undocumented and doesn't provide any useful information for Tru64 UNIX versions greater than 4.0A.

Example:

The following example illustrates how to use *shfragbf(8)* to examine the fragment lists on the /usr file system.

```
# /sbin/advfs/shfragbf /usr/.tags/1
Type  Grps   bad   Frags  free   in-use Bytes  free    in-use
----  ----   ----  ----   ----   ----   ----   ----    ----
0k    1      0     127    127    0      0k     0k      0k
1k    51     0     6477   21     6456   6477k  21k     6456k
2k    72     0     4536   92     4444   9072k  184k    8888k
3k    86     0     3612   11     3601   10836k 33k     10803k
4k    81     0     2511   27     2484   10044k 108k    9936k
5k    65     0     1625   23     1602   8125k  115k    8010k
6k    53     0     1113   5      1108   6678k  30k     6648k
7k    56     0     1008   11     997    7056k  77k     6979k

Percent Free Frags per Group Histogram
Type  Grps   9%  19% 29% 39% 49% 59% 69% 79% 89% 99% 100%
----  ----   --- --- --- --- --- --- --- --- --- --- ---
0k    1      0   0   0   0   0   0   0   0   0   0   1
1k    51     51  0   0   0   0   0   0   0   0   0   0
2k    72     70  0   0   0   0   0   1   1   0   0   0
3k    86     85  1   0   0   0   0   0   0   0   0   0
4k    81     79  0   1   0   0   0   1   0   0   0   0
5k    65     64  0   0   0   0   0   0   0   1   0   0
6k    53     53  0   0   0   0   0   0   0   0   0   0
7k    56     54  0   1   1   0   0   0   0   0   0   0

fragbf occupies 59520k bytes
57720k in-use, 695k free, 465k overhead, 640k wasted
```

B.4   The "New" Metadata Examination Commands

The commands discussed in this section are updated versions of the older AdvFS troubleshooting commands discussed in the previous sections. For Tru64 UNIX version 5.0 and greater, these commands will format the V4 on-disk structure, which includes the reserved BMT (RBMT), as well as the structures that existed in previous versions. Therefore, you can also use these commands to look at the older V3 domains you bring forward from Tru64 UNIX 4.0x. These tools are a dramatic step forward in capability and usability when compared to the commands we have already discussed in this appendix.

With the "new" commands, several special operands can be used. The following is a description:

bmt_id: The BMT file on an AdvFS volume or a BMT file that has been saved by the utility as a dump_file. Use the following format:

```
volume_id | [-F] dump_file
```

You can use the '-F' option to force the utility to interpret the dump_file parameter as a file name if it has the same name as a domain name.

sbm_id: The SBM file on an AdvFS volume or an SBM file that has been saved by the utility as a dump_file. Use the following format:

```
volume_id | [-F] dump_file
```

You can use the '-F' option to force the utility to interpret the dump_file parameter as a file name if it has the same name as a domain name.

frag_id: This argument specifies a fragment file on an AdvFS volume or a fragment file that has been saved by the utility as a dump_file. Use the following format:

```
domain_id fileset_id | [-F] dump_file
```

You can use the '-F' option to force the utility to interpret the dump_file parameter as a file name if it has the same name as a domain name.

log_id: This qualifier specifies a log file in an AdvFS domain or a log file that has been saved by the utility as a dump_file. Use the following format:

```
domain_id | volume_id | [-F] dump_file
```

You can use the '-F' option to force the utility to interpret the dump_file parameter as a file name if it has the same name as a domain name.

domain_id: This option specifies an AdvFS file domain using the following format:

```
[-r] [-D] domain
```

By default, the utility opens all volumes using block device special files; however, you can specify the '-r' flag to operate on one of the raw devices of the domain instead of the block device. If you specify the '-D' flag, the utility interprets the name you supply as a domain name.

volume_id: This specifies an AdvFS volume using the following format:

```
[-V] volume | domain_id volume_index
```

You can specify the '-V' option to force the utility to interpret the name you supply in the volume argument as a volume name. The volume argument also can be a full or partial pathname, for example /dev/disk/dsk12a or dsk12a. If you specify a partial pathname, the tool will always open the character device special file.

Alternatively, specify the volume by using arguments for its domain, domain_id, and its volume index number, volume_index.

fileset_id: This specifies an AdvFS fileset using the following format:

```
[-S] fileset | -T fileset_tag
```

You can specify the '-S' option to force the command to interpret the name you supply as a fileset name. You can also specify the fileset by entering either the name of the fileset, fileset, or the fileset's tag number, '-T fileset_tag'.

file_id: This qualifier specifies a file name in the following format:

```
file | [-t] file_tag
```

You can specify the file by entering either the fileset relative pathname, file, or the file's tag number, '-t file_tag'.

dump_file: This qualifier specifies the name of a file that contains the output from this utility.

page: This qualifier specifies the file page number of a file.

The following is specific to the *nvbmtpg(8)* command:

mcell: Specifies the number of a metadata cell (mcell) in a BMT file.

The following are specific to the *nvlogpg(8)* and *nvfragpg(8)* commands:

page_offset: Specifies the offset relative to the start or the end of the active region in the log file.

record_offset: Specifies a byte offset in a page of the log file.

The following is specific to the *vsbmpg(8)* command:

entry: Specifies the index of the SBM word on the page.

B.4.1   The *nvbmtpg(8)* Command

The *nvbmtpg(8)* utility is a powerful tool that supercedes *vbmtpg(8)* and *vods(8)*. It can be used only on Tru64 UNIX version 5.0 and higher. This tool doesn't require as much knowledge of the internals of AdvFS, which makes it preferable to the older tools.

Syntax:

```
nvbmtpg [-R] [-v] { domain_id | bmt_id } [-f]
nvbmtpg [-R] [-v] bmt_id page [-f]
nvbmtpg [-R] [-v] bmt_id page mcell [-c]
nvbmtpg [-R] [-v] bmt_id [-a]
nvbmtpg [-R] [-v] domain_id fileset_id [file_id] [-c]
nvbmtpg [-R] [-v] { domain_id | volume_id } -l
nvbmtpg [-R] [-v] bmt_id -s b block [-c]
nvbmtpg [-R] [-v] domain_id fileset_id -s f frag [-c]
nvbmtpg [-R] [-v] { bmt_id | domain_id [fileset_id] } -s t
tag [-c]
nvbmtpg [-R] [-v] volume_id -b block [mcell]
nvbmtpg [-R] volume_id -d dump_file
```

TABLE B–12   Flags for the *nvbmtpg(8)* Command

FLAG	DESCRIPTION
-a	Displays all the pages in the BMT.
-b block	Displays the LBN of a disk block on an AdvFS volume.
-c	Displays the entire chain of mcells. Alternatively, continue to search.
-d dump_file	Dumps the contents of the specified BMT file into dump_file.
-f	Displays the number of free mcells.
-l	Displays the deferred delete list of mcells.
-R	Displays information about the RBMT, instead of information about the BMT.
-s b block	Searches for the specified LBN of a disk block on an AdvFS volume.
-s f frag	Searches for the specified number of a file fragment in the frag file for a fileset.
-s t tag	Searches for the file tag number containing one or all of the BMT files for an mcell.
-v	Verbose mode. Displays all the data in a specified mcell.

Example:

Here is an example of the "standard" or "nonverbose" output from the *nvb-mtpg(8)* command when used to examine all of the BMT pages for the first volume of a domain, based on the tag number in the /<mountpoint>/.tags directory. This is similar to the way the older *vbmtpg(8)* and *vods(8)* tools worked.

```
# /sbin/advfs/nvbmtpg M-10 -a
==================================================================
FILE "M-10" BMT page 0
------------------------------------------------------------------
CELL 0 next mcell volume page cell 0 0 0 bfSetTag,tag 0,0

RECORD 0 bCnt 8 BSR_MCELL_FREE_LIST
headPg 0

RECORD 1 bCnt 12 BSR_DEF_DEL_MCELL_LIST
nextMCId page,cell 0,0 prevMCId page,cell 0,0

------------------------------------------------------------------
CELL 1 next mcell volume page cell 1 0 2 bfSetTag,tag -2,1

RECORD 0 bCnt 92 BSR_ATTR
type BSRA_VALID

RECORD 1 bCnt 80 BSR_XTNTS
type BSXMT_APPEND chain mcell volume page cell 0 0 0

firstXtnt mcellCnt 1 xCnt 2
bsXA[ 0] bsPage 0 vdBlk 28320 (0x6ea0)
bsXA[ 1] bsPage 8 vdBlk -1

RECORD 2 bCnt 64 BSR_BFS_QUOTA_ATTR
Blocks hard limit 0, soft limit 0, blkTLimit 0
Files hard limit 0, soft limit 0, fileTLimit 0

------------------------------------------------------------------
CELL 2 next mcell volume page cell 0 0 0 bfSetTag,tag -2,1

RECORD 0 bCnt 220 BSR_BFS_ATTR
setName "test" state BFS_READY bfSetId.dirTag 1

RECORD 1 bCnt 36 BSR_SET_SHELVE_ATTR
flags MSS_NO_SHELVE

------------------------------------------------------------------
CELL 3 next mcell volume page cell 0 0 0 bfSetTag,tag 1,1

RECORD 0 bCnt 92 BSR_ATTR
type BSRA_VALID

RECORD 1 bCnt 80 BSR_XTNTS
type BSXMT_APPEND chain mcell volume page cell 0 0 0
firstXtnt mcellCnt 1 xCnt 1
bsXA[ 0] bsPage 0 vdBlk -1

------------------------------------------------------------------
```

```
CELL 4 next mcell volume page cell 1 0 5 bfSetTag,tag 1,2

RECORD 0 bCnt 92 BSR_ATTR
type BSRA_VALID

RECORD 1 bCnt 80 BSR_XTNTS
type BSXMT_APPEND chain mcell volume page cell 0 0 0
firstXtnt mcellCnt 1 xCnt 2
bsXA[ 0] bsPage 0 vdBlk 28448 (0x6f20)
bsXA[ 1] bsPage 1 vdBlk -1

RECORD 2 bCnt 64 BSR_BF_INHERIT_ATTR
dataSafety BFD_NIL reqServices 1 extendSize 0

RECORD 3 bCnt 8 BMTR_FS_TIME
last sync Tue Oct 12 20:06:02 1999

----------------------------------------------------------------
CELL 5 next mcell volume page cell 0 0 0 bfSetTag,tag 1,2

RECORD 0 bCnt 92 BMTR_FS_STAT
st_mode 40755 (S_IFDIR) st_uid 0 st_gid 0 st_size 8192
st_nlink 3 dir_tag 2 st_mtime Tue Oct 12 20:05:47 1999

----------------------------------------------------------------
CELL 6 next mcell volume page cell 0 0 0 bfSetTag,tag 1,3

RECORD 0 bCnt 92 BSR_ATTR
type BSRA_VALID

RECORD 1 bCnt 80 BSR_XTNTS
type BSXMT_APPEND chain mcell volume page cell 0 0 0
firstXtnt mcellCnt 1 xCnt 2
bsXA[ 0] bsPage 0 vdBlk 28464 (0x6f30)
bsXA[ 1] bsPage 1 vdBlk -1

RECORD 2 bCnt 92 BMTR_FS_STAT
st_mode 40700 (S_IFDIR) st_uid 0 st_gid 0 st_size 8192
st_nlink 2 dir_tag 2 st_mtime Tue Oct 12 20:05:47 1999

----------------------------------------------------------------
CELL 7 next mcell volume page cell 0 0 0 bfSetTag,tag 1,4

RECORD 0 bCnt 92 BSR_ATTR
type BSRA_VALID

RECORD 1 bCnt 80 BSR_XTNTS
type BSXMT_APPEND chain mcell volume page cell 0 0 0
firstXtnt mcellCnt 1 xCnt 2
bsXA[ 0] bsPage 0 vdBlk 28480 (0x6f40)
bsXA[ 1] bsPage 1 vdBlk -1

RECORD 2 bCnt 92 BMTR_FS_STAT
st_mode 100640 (S_IFREG) st_uid 0 st_gid 20 st_size 8192
st_nlink 1 dir_tag 2 st_mtime Tue Oct 12 20:05:47 1999

----------------------------------------------------------------
CELL 8 next mcell volume page cell 0 0 0 bfSetTag,tag 1,5

RECORD 0 bCnt 92 BSR_ATTR
```

```
type BSRA_VALID

RECORD 1 bCnt 80 BSR_XTNTS
type BSXMT_APPEND chain mcell volume page cell 0 0 0
firstXtnt mcellCnt 1 xCnt 2
bsXA[ 0] bsPage 0 vdBlk 28496 (0x6f50)
bsXA[ 1] bsPage 1 vdBlk -1

RECORD 2 bCnt 92 BMTR_FS_STAT
st_mode 100640 (S_IFREG) st_uid 0 st_gid 20 st_size 8192
st_nlink 1 dir_tag 2 st_mtime Tue Oct 12 20:05:47 1999
```

Example:

Here, we show the same BMT file as in the previous example, but this shows the verbose output, which gives a great deal of detail.

```
# /sbin/advfs/nvbmtpg -v M-10 -a
============================================================
FILE "M-10" BMT page 0
----------------------------------------------------------------
--------------
pageId 0 megaVersion 4
freeMcellCnt 19 nextFreePg -1 nextfreeMCId page,cell 0,9
----------------------------------------------------------------
CELL 0 linkSegment 0 bfSetTag 0 (0.0) tag 0 (0.0)
next mcell volume page cell 0 0 0

RECORD 0 bCnt 8 version 0 BSR_MCELL_FREE_LIST (7)
headPg 0

RECORD 1 bCnt 12 version 0 BSR_DEF_DEL_MCELL_LIST (14)
nextMCId page,cell 0,0 prevMCId page,cell 0,0

----------------------------------------------------------------
CELL 1 linkSegment 0 bfSetTag -2 (fffffffe.0) tag 1 (1.8001)
next mcell volume page cell 1 0 2

RECORD 0 bCnt 92 version 0 BSR_ATTR (2)
type BSRA_VALID (3)
bfPgSz 16 transitionId 3
cloneId 0 cloneCnt 0 maxClonePgs 0
deleteWithClone 0 outOfSyncClone 0
cl.dataSafety BFD_FTX_AGENT (2)
cl reqServices 1 optServices 0 extendSize 0 rsvd1 0
rsvd2 0 acl 0 rsvd_sec1 0 rsvd_sec2 0 rsvd_sec3 0

RECORD 1 bCnt 80 version 0 BSR_XTNTS (1)
type BSXMT_APPEND (0)
chain mcell volume page cell 0 0 0
blksPerPage 16 segmentSize 0
delLink next page,cell 0,0 prev page,cell 0,0
delRst volume,page,cell 0,0,0 xtntIndex 0 offset 0 blocks 0
firstXtnt mcellCnt 1 xCnt 2
bsXA[ 0] bsPage 0 vdBlk 28320 (0x6ea0)
bsXA[ 1] bsPage 8 vdBlk -1
```

```
RECORD 2 bCnt 64 version 0 BSR_BFS_QUOTA_ATTR (18)
blkHLimitHi,blkHLimitLo 0,0 (0)
blkSLimitHi,blkSLimitLo 0,0 (0)
fileHLimitHi,fileHLimitLo 0,0 (0)
fileSLimitHi,fileSLimitLo 0,0 (0)
blkTLimit 0, fileTLimit 0, quotaStatus 1420
unused1 0, unused2 0, unused3 0, unused4 0

----------------------------------------------------------------
CELL 2 linkSegment 1 bfSetTag -2 (fffffffe.0) tag 1 (1.8001)
next mcell volume page cell 0 0 0

RECORD 0 bCnt 220 version 0 BSR_BFS_ATTR (8)
bfSetId.domainId 3803dad7.cb9b5 (Tue Oct 12 20:05:27 1999)
bfSetId.dirTag 1 (1.8001)
fragBfTag 1 (1.8001)
nextCloneSetTag 0 (0.0) origSetTag 0 (0.0)
nxtDelPendingBfSet 0 (0.0)
state BFS_READY flags 0x0
cloneId 0 cloneCnt 0 numClones 0
fsDev 0xb559151f freeFragGrps 0 oldQuotaStatus 0
uid 0 gid 1 mode 0744 setName "test"
fsContext[0], fsContext[1] 2.8001 (rootTag)
fsContext[2], fsContext[3] 3.8001 (tagsTag)
fsContext[4], fsContext[5] 4.8001 (userQuotaTag)
fsContext[6], fsContext[7] 5.8001 (groupQuotaTag)
fragGrps[0] firstFreeGrp -1 lastFreeGrp -1
fragGrps[1] firstFreeGrp -1 lastFreeGrp -1
fragGrps[2] firstFreeGrp -1 lastFreeGrp -1
fragGrps[3] firstFreeGrp -1 lastFreeGrp -1
fragGrps[4] firstFreeGrp -1 lastFreeGrp -1
fragGrps[5] firstFreeGrp -1 lastFreeGrp -1
fragGrps[6] firstFreeGrp -1 lastFreeGrp -1
fragGrps[7] firstFreeGrp -1 lastFreeGrp -1

RECORD 1 bCnt 36 version 0 BSR_SET_SHELVE_ATTR (17)
flags MSS_NO_SHELVE (0x4)
smallFile 5
readAhead 0
readAheadIncr 5
readAheadMax 50
autoShelveThresh 100
userId 0
shelf 0

----------------------------------------------------------------
CELL 3 linkSegment 0 bfSetTag 1 (1.8001) tag 1 (1.8001)
next mcell volume page cell 0 0 0

RECORD 0 bCnt 92 version 0 BSR_ATTR (2)
type BSRA_VALID (3)
bfPgSz 16 transitionId 3
cloneId 0 cloneCnt 0 maxClonePgs 0
deleteWithClone 0 outOfSyncClone 0
cl.dataSafety BFD_FTX_AGENT (2)
cl reqServices 1 optServices 0 extendSize 0 rsvd1 0
```

```
rsvd2 0 acl 0 rsvd_sec1 0 rsvd_sec2 0 rsvd_sec3 0

RECORD 1 bCnt 80 version 0 BSR_XTNTS (1)
type BSXMT_APPEND (0)
chain mcell volume page cell 0 0 0
blksPerPage 16 segmentSize 0
delLink next page,cell 0,0 prev page,cell 0,0
delRst volume,page,cell 0,0,0 xtntIndex 0 offset 0 blocks 0
firstXtnt mcellCnt 1 xCnt 1
bsXA[ 0] bsPage 0 vdBlk -1
bsXA[ 1] bsPage 0 vdBlk 0 (0x0)

---------------------------------------------------------------
CELL 4 linkSegment 0 bfSetTag 1 (1.8001) tag 2 (2.8001)
next mcell volume page cell 1 0 5

RECORD 0 bCnt 92 version 0 BSR_ATTR (2)
type BSRA_VALID (3)
bfPgSz 16 transitionId 3
cloneId 0 cloneCnt 0 maxClonePgs 0
deleteWithClone 0 outOfSyncClone 0
cl.dataSafety BFD_FTX_AGENT (2)
cl reqServices 1 optServices 0 extendSize 0 rsvd1 0
rsvd2 0 acl 0 rsvd_sec1 0 rsvd_sec2 0 rsvd_sec3 0

RECORD 1 bCnt 80 version 0 BSR_XTNTS (1)
type BSXMT_APPEND (0)
chain mcell volume page cell 0 0 0
blksPerPage 16 segmentSize 0
delLink next page,cell 0,0 prev page,cell 0,0
delRst volume,page,cell 0,0,0 xtntIndex 0 offset 0 blocks 0
firstXtnt mcellCnt 1 xCnt 2
bsXA[ 0] bsPage 0 vdBlk 28448 (0x6f20)
bsXA[ 1] bsPage 1 vdBlk -1

RECORD 2 bCnt 64 version 0 BSR_BF_INHERIT_ATTR (16)
dataSafety BFD_NIL
reqServices 1
optServices 0
extendSize 0
clientArea 0 0 0 0
rsvd1 0
rsvd2 0
rsvd_sec1 0
rsvd_sec2 0
rsvd_sec3 0

RECORD 3 bCnt 8 version 0 BMTR_FS_TIME (251)
last sync Tue Oct 12 20:06:02 1999

---------------------------------------------------------------
CELL 5 linkSegment 1 bfSetTag 1 (1.8001) tag 2 (2.8001)
next mcell volume page cell 0 0 0

RECORD 0 bCnt 92 version 0 BMTR_FS_STAT (255)
st_ino 2 st_mode 40755 (S_IFDIR) st_nlink 3 st_size 8192
st_uid 0 st_gid 0 st_rdev 0 major 0 minor 0
```

```
st_mtime Tue Oct 12 20:05:47 1999 st_umtime 0
st_atime Tue Oct 12 20:08:09 1999 st_uatime 676399000
st_ctime Tue Oct 12 20:05:47 1999 st_uctime 0
fragId.frag 0 fragId.type 0 BF_FRAG_ANY fragPageOffset 0
dir_tag 2 (2.8001) st_flags 0 st_unused_1 0 st_unused_2 0

-------------------------------------------------------------
CELL 6 linkSegment 0 bfSetTag 1 (1.8001) tag 3 (3.8001)
next mcell volume page cell 0 0 0

RECORD 0 bCnt 92 version 0 BSR_ATTR (2)
type BSRA_VALID (3)
bfPgSz 16 transitionId 3
cloneId 0 cloneCnt 0 maxClonePgs 0
deleteWithClone 0 outOfSyncClone 0
cl.dataSafety BFD_FTX_AGENT (2)
cl reqServices 1 optServices 0 extendSize 0 rsvd1 0
rsvd2 0 acl 0 rsvd_sec1 0 rsvd_sec2 0 rsvd_sec3 0

RECORD 1 bCnt 80 version 0 BSR_XTNTS (1)
type BSXMT_APPEND (0)
chain mcell volume page cell 0 0 0
blksPerPage 16 segmentSize 0
delLink next page,cell 0,0 prev page,cell 0,0
delRst volume,page,cell 0,0,0 xtntIndex 0 offset 0 blocks 0
firstXtnt mcellCnt 1 xCnt 2
bsXA[ 0] bsPage 0 vdBlk 28464 (0x6f30)
bsXA[ 1] bsPage 1 vdBlk -1

RECORD 2 bCnt 92 version 0 BMTR_FS_STAT (255)
st_ino 3 st_mode 40700 (S_IFDIR) st_nlink 2 st_size 8192
st_uid 0 st_gid 0 st_rdev 0 major 0 minor 0
st_mtime Tue Oct 12 20:05:47 1999 st_umtime 0
st_atime Tue Oct 12 20:05:47 1999 st_uatime 0
st_ctime Tue Oct 12 20:05:47 1999 st_uctime 0
fragId.frag 0 fragId.type 0 BF_FRAG_ANY fragPageOffset 0
dir_tag 2 (2.8001) st_flags 0 st_unused_1 0 st_unused_2 0

-------------------------------------------------------------
CELL 7 linkSegment 0 bfSetTag 1 (1.8001) tag 4 (4.8001)
next mcell volume page cell 0 0 0

RECORD 0 bCnt 92 version 0 BSR_ATTR (2)
type BSRA_VALID (3)
bfPgSz 16 transitionId 3
cloneId 0 cloneCnt 0 maxClonePgs 0
deleteWithClone 0 outOfSyncClone 0
cl.dataSafety BFD_FTX_AGENT (2)
cl reqServices 1 optServices 0 extendSize 0 rsvd1 0
rsvd2 0 acl 0 rsvd_sec1 0 rsvd_sec2 0 rsvd_sec3 0

RECORD 1 bCnt 80 version 0 BSR_XTNTS (1)
type BSXMT_APPEND (0)
chain mcell volume page cell 0 0 0
blksPerPage 16 segmentSize 0
delLink next page,cell 0,0 prev page,cell 0,0
```

```
delRst volume,page,cell 0,0,0 xtntIndex 0 offset 0 blocks 0
firstXtnt mcellCnt 1 xCnt 2
bsXA[ 0] bsPage 0 vdBlk 28480 (0x6f40)
bsXA[ 1] bsPage 1 vdBlk -1

RECORD 2 bCnt 92 version 0 BMTR_FS_STAT (255)
st_ino 4 st_mode 100640 (S_IFREG) st_nlink 1 st_size 8192
st_uid 0 st_gid 20 st_rdev 0 major 0 minor 0
st_mtime Tue Oct 12 20:05:47 1999 st_umtime 0
st_atime Tue Oct 12 20:05:47 1999 st_uatime 0
st_ctime Tue Oct 12 20:05:47 1999 st_uctime 0
fragId.frag 0 fragId.type 0 BF_FRAG_ANY fragPageOffset 0
dir_tag 2 (2.8001) st_flags 0 st_unused_1 0 st_unused_2 0

-----------------------------------------------------------
CELL 8 linkSegment 0 bfSetTag 1 (1.8001) tag 5 (5.8001)
next mcell volume page cell 0 0 0

RECORD 0 bCnt 92 version 0 BSR_ATTR (2)
type BSRA_VALID (3)
bfPgSz 16 transitionId 3
cloneId 0 cloneCnt 0 maxClonePgs 0
deleteWithClone 0 outOfSyncClone 0
cl.dataSafety BFD_FTX_AGENT (2)
cl reqServices 1 optServices 0 extendSize 0 rsvd1 0
rsvd2 0 acl 0 rsvd_sec1 0 rsvd_sec2 0 rsvd_sec3 0

RECORD 1 bCnt 80 version 0 BSR_XTNTS (1)
type BSXMT_APPEND (0)
chain mcell volume page cell 0 0 0
blksPerPage 16 segmentSize 0
delLink next page,cell 0,0 prev page,cell 0,0
delRst volume,page,cell 0,0,0 xtntIndex 0 offset 0 blocks 0
firstXtnt mcellCnt 1 xCnt 2
bsXA[ 0] bsPage 0 vdBlk 28496 (0x6f50)
bsXA[ 1] bsPage 1 vdBlk -1

RECORD 2 bCnt 92 version 0 BMTR_FS_STAT (255)
st_ino 5 st_mode 100640 (S_IFREG) st_nlink 1 st_size 8192
st_uid 0 st_gid 20 st_rdev 0 major 0 minor 0
st_mtime Tue Oct 12 20:05:47 1999 st_umtime 0
st_atime Tue Oct 12 20:05:47 1999 st_uatime 0
st_ctime Tue Oct 12 20:05:47 1999 st_uctime 0
fragId.frag 0 fragId.type 0 BF_FRAG_ANY fragPageOffset 0
dir_tag 2 (2.8001) st_flags 0 st_unused_1 0 st_unused_2 0

-----------------------------------------------------------
CELL 9 linkSegment 0 bfSetTag 0 (0.0) tag 0 (0.0)
next mcell volume page cell 0 0 10

-----------------------------------------------------------
CELL 10 linkSegment 0 bfSetTag 0 (0.0) tag 0 (0.0)
next mcell volume page cell 0 0 11

-----------------------------------------------------------
CELL 11 linkSegment 0 bfSetTag 0 (0.0) tag 0 (0.0)
next mcell volume page cell 0 0 12
```

```
------------------------------------------------------------
CELL 12 linkSegment 0 bfSetTag 0 (0.0) tag 0 (0.0)
next mcell volume page cell 0 0 13

------------------------------------------------------------
CELL 13 linkSegment 0 bfSetTag 0 (0.0) tag 0 (0.0)
next mcell volume page cell 0 0 14

------------------------------------------------------------
CELL 14 linkSegment 0 bfSetTag 0 (0.0) tag 0 (0.0)
next mcell volume page cell 0 0 15

------------------------------------------------------------
CELL 15 linkSegment 0 bfSetTag 0 (0.0) tag 0 (0.0)
next mcell volume page cell 0 0 16

------------------------------------------------------------
CELL 16 linkSegment 0 bfSetTag 0 (0.0) tag 0 (0.0)
next mcell volume page cell 0 0 17

------------------------------------------------------------
CELL 17 linkSegment 0 bfSetTag 0 (0.0) tag 0 (0.0)
next mcell volume page cell 0 0 18

------------------------------------------------------------
CELL 18 linkSegment 0 bfSetTag 0 (0.0) tag 0 (0.0)
next mcell volume page cell 0 0 19

------------------------------------------------------------
CELL 19 linkSegment 0 bfSetTag 0 (0.0) tag 0 (0.0)
next mcell volume page cell 0 0 20

------------------------------------------------------------
CELL 20 linkSegment 0 bfSetTag 0 (0.0) tag 0 (0.0)
next mcell volume page cell 0 0 21

------------------------------------------------------------
CELL 21 linkSegment 0 bfSetTag 0 (0.0) tag 0 (0.0)
next mcell volume page cell 0 0 22

------------------------------------------------------------
CELL 22 linkSegment 0 bfSetTag 0 (0.0) tag 0 (0.0)
next mcell volume page cell 0 0 23

------------------------------------------------------------
CELL 23 linkSegment 0 bfSetTag 0 (0.0) tag 0 (0.0)
next mcell volume page cell 0 0 24

------------------------------------------------------------
CELL 24 linkSegment 0 bfSetTag 0 (0.0) tag 0 (0.0)
next mcell volume page cell 0 0 25

------------------------------------------------------------
CELL 25 linkSegment 0 bfSetTag 0 (0.0) tag 0 (0.0)
next mcell volume page cell 0 0 26

------------------------------------------------------------
CELL 26 linkSegment 0 bfSetTag 0 (0.0) tag 0 (0.0)
next mcell volume page cell 0 0 27
```

```
-----------------------------------------------------------------
CELL 27 linkSegment 0 bfSetTag 0 (0.0) tag 0 (0.0)
next mcell volume page cell 0 0 0
```

B.4.2   The *nvfragpg(8)* Command

The *nfragpg(8)* command gives formatted output of the fragment file on a Tru64 UNIX 5.0 AdvFS file system.

Syntax:

```
nvfragpg [-v] [-f] frag_id

nvfragpg [-v] [-f] frag_id page

nvfragpg volume_id -b block

nvfragpg [-v] [-f] domain_id fileset_id -d dump_file
```

TABLE B–13   Flags for the *nvfragpg(8)* Command

FLAG	DESCRIPTION
-b block	The LBN of a disk block on an AdvFS volume
-d dump_file	The name of a file that contains the output of this utility
-f	Displays the frag free list.
-v	Displays all the data in a frag file.

Example:

This example shows how to get the frag file summary information for a mounted AdvFS. You will notice that because the file system is mounted, an error is received unless you use the '-r' flag.

```
# df | grep root2
root2_domain#root 262144 85568 165392 35% /cluster/members
/member2/boot_partition

# /sbin/advfs/nvfragpg root2_domain root
open_vol: open for volume "/dev/disk/dsk5a" failed: Device
busy

# /sbin/advfs/nvfragpg -r root2_domain root
=================================================================
DOMAIN "root2_domain"
-----------------------------------------------------------------
frag    type   free  1K   2K   3K    4K    5K   6K   7K    totals
groups  0      0     0    1    1     0     0    1    3
frags   -      0     0    42   31    0     0    18   91
frags   used   -     0    0    2     9     0    0    2     13
disk    space  0K    0K   0K   128K  128K  0K   0K   128K  384K
space   used   -     0K   0K   6K    36K   0K   0K   14K   56K
space   free   0K    0K   0K   120K  88K   0K   0K   112K  320K
```

```
overhead 0K     0K    0K    1K    1K    0K    0K    1K   3K
wasted – 0K     0K    1K    3K    0K    0K    1K    5K
% used – 0%     0%    4%    28%   0%    0%    9%    14%
```

Example:

This example shows how to look at a single, formatted block from the frag file using the *nvfragpg(8)* command.

```
# /sbin/advfs/nvfragpg -r root2_domain root 32

=====================================================

DOMAIN "root2_domain" VDI 1 (/dev/rdisk/dsk5a) lbn 192496 set
tag 1 FRAG page 32

---------------------------------------------------------------------

self 32 fragType BF_FRAG_4K version 1 freeFrags 22 firstFrag 257
nextFreeGrp -1 nextFreeFrag -1 lastFreeFrag -1
setId 38876d30.100594c.1.8001
free slots:
40 44 48 52 56 60 64 68 72 76 80 84 88 92 96 100
104 108 112 116 120 124
```

B.4.3   The *nvlogpg(8)* Command

The *nvlogpg(8)* command displays formatted output from the transaction log for a domain on a system.

Syntax:

```
nvlogpg log_id
nvlogpg [-v | -B] log_id page [record_offset [-f]]
nvlogpg [-v | -B] log_id { -R | -a }
nvlogpg [-v | -B] log_id { -s | -e } [page_offset]
nvlogpg domain_id | volume_id -d dump_file
nvlogpg [-v | -B] volume_id -b block
```

TABLE B–14   Flags for the *vlogpg(8)* Command

FLAG	DESCRIPTION
-a	All the pages in the log file to be displayed
-B	Brief mode. Only the transaction ID for each log file entry is to be displayed.
-b block	The LBN of a disk block on an AdvFS volume
-d dump_file	The name of a file that will hold the contents of the specified log file
-e	Displays the last active record in the log file

TABLE B–14 Flags for the *vlogpg(8)* Command (Continued)

FLAG	DESCRIPTION
-f	Follows all of the subtransactions of the parent transaction.
-s	Displays the first active record in the log file.
-v	Verbose mode. Displays all of the data in the specified log, page, or record.

Example:

This is an example of how the *nvlogpg(8)* tool can be used to examine basic information about the transaction log for a domain called "root2_domain."

```
# /sbin/advfs/nvlogpg -r root2_domain

==============================================================
DOMAIN "root2_domain" VDI 1 (/dev/rdisk/dsk5a)
--------------------------------------------------------------
The log is 512 pages long.
There is 1 page of active records in the LOG.
The first LOG record is on page 228 at offset 1386.
The last LOG record is on page 228 at offset 1386
```

Example:

Here, we show the more detailed output from *nvlogpg(8)* for a single page in the log. Some of the output has been truncated for readability.

```
# /sbin/advfs/nvlogpg -r root2_domain 228

==============================================================
DOMAIN "root2_domain" VDI 1 (/dev/rdisk/dsk5a) lbn 3776 LOG
page 228
--------------------------------------------------------------
dmnId 38876d30.100594c (Thu Jan 20 15:16:48 2000) pgType
BFM_FTXLOG (3)
pgSafe 1 chkBit 0 curLastRec 1386 prevLastRec 1354 thisPa-
geLSN 45808
firstLogRec page 9 offset 121 lsn 1524

--------------------------------------------------------------
RECORD OFFSET 0 wordCnt 32 clientWordCnt 20 segment 0 lsn
45808
nextRec page 228 offset 32 lsn 45810
prevRec page 227 offset 1984 lsn 45806
prevClientRec page 65535 offset 65535 lsn 0
firstSeg page 228 offset 0 lsn 45808

agentId FTA_BS_BMT_PUT_REC_V1 (5)
type ftxDoneLR, level 0, atomicRPass 2, member 0
ftxId 5c0, bfDmnId 38876d30.100594c
crashRedo page 228 offset 0 lsn 45808
```

```
contOrUndoRBcnt 0, rootDRBcnt 0, opRedoRBcnt 0

----------------------------------------------------------------
RECORD OFFSET 32 wordCnt 32 clientWordCnt 20 segment 0 lsn
45810
nextRec page 228 offset 64 lsn 45812
prevRec page 228 offset 0 lsn 45808
prevClientRec page 65535 offset 65535 lsn 0
firstSeg page 228 offset 32 lsn 45810

agentId FTA_BS_BMT_PUT_REC_V1 (5)
type ftxDoneLR, level 0, atomicRPass 2, member 0
ftxId 5c1, bfDmnId 38876d30.100594c
crashRedo page 228 offset 32 lsn 45810
contOrUndoRBcnt 0, rootDRBcnt 0, opRedoRBcnt 0

----------------------------------------------------------------
RECORD OFFSET 64 wordCnt 32 clientWordCnt 20 segment 0 lsn
45812
nextRec page 228 offset 96 lsn 45814
prevRec page 228 offset 32 lsn 45810
prevClientRec page 65535 offset 65535 lsn 0
firstSeg page 228 offset 64 lsn 45812

agentId FTA_BS_BMT_PUT_REC_V1 (5)
type ftxDoneLR, level 0, atomicRPass 2, member 0
ftxId 5c2, bfDmnId 38876d30.100594c
crashRedo page 228 offset 64 lsn 45812
contOrUndoRBcnt 0, rootDRBcnt 0, opRedoRBcnt 0

----------------------------------------------------------------
RECORD OFFSET 96 wordCnt 32 clientWordCnt 20 segment 0 lsn
45814
nextRec page 228 offset 128 lsn 45816
prevRec page 228 offset 64 lsn 45812
prevClientRec page 65535 offset 65535 lsn 0
firstSeg page 228 offset 96 lsn 45814

agentId FTA_BS_BMT_PUT_REC_V1 (5)
type ftxDoneLR, level 0, atomicRPass 2, member 0
ftxId 5c3, bfDmnId 38876d30.100594c
crashRedo page 228 offset 96 lsn 45814
contOrUndoRBcnt 0, rootDRBcnt 0, opRedoRBcnt 0

----------------------------------------------------------------
RECORD OFFSET 128 wordCnt 32 clientWordCnt 20 segment 0 lsn
45816
nextRec page 228 offset 160 lsn 45818
prevRec page 228 offset 96 lsn 45814
prevClientRec page 65535 offset 65535 lsn 0
firstSeg page 228 offset 128 lsn 45816

agentId FTA_BS_BMT_PUT_REC_V1 (5)
type ftxDoneLR, level 0, atomicRPass 2, member 0
ftxId 5c4, bfDmnId 38876d30.100594c
crashRedo page 228 offset 128 lsn 45816
contOrUndoRBcnt 0, rootDRBcnt 0, opRedoRBcnt 0
```

```
------------------------------------------------------------
RECORD OFFSET 160 wordCnt 32 clientWordCnt 20 segment 0 lsn
45818
nextRec page 228 offset 192 lsn 45820
prevRec page 228 offset 128 lsn 45816
prevClientRec page 65535 offset 65535 lsn 0
firstSeg page 228 offset 160 lsn 45818

agentId FTA_BS_BMT_PUT_REC_V1 (5)
type ftxDoneLR, level 0, atomicRPass 2, member 0
ftxId 5c5, bfDmnId 38876d30.100594c
crashRedo page 228 offset 160 lsn 45818
contOrUndoRBcnt 0, rootDRBcnt 0, opRedoRBcnt 0

[snip]
------------------------------------------------------------
RECORD OFFSET 1386 wordCnt 32 clientWordCnt 20 segment 0 lsn
45892
nextRec page 65535 offset 65535 lsn 0
prevRec page 228 offset 1354 lsn 45890
prevClientRec page 65535 offset 65535 lsn 0
firstSeg page 228 offset 1386 lsn 45892

agentId FTA_BS_BMT_PUT_REC_V1 (5)
type ftxDoneLR, level 0, atomicRPass 2, member 0
ftxId 5ea, bfDmnId 38876d30.100594c
crashRedo page 228 offset 1386 lsn 45892
contOrUndoRBcnt 0, rootDRBcnt 0, opRedoRBcnt 0
------------------------------------------------------------
dmnId 38876d30.100594c (Thu Jan 20 15:16:48 2000) pgType
BFM_FTXLOG (3)
```

B.4.4   The *nvtagpg(8)* Command

You can use the *nvtagpg(8)* to gather formatted output of blocks from a domain's root tag directory.

Syntax:

```
nvtagpg [-v] tag_id

nvtagpg [-v] tag_id { page | -a }

nvtagpg [-v] fileset_id file_id

nvtagpg domain_id fileset_id -d dump_file

nvtagpg domain_id -d dump_file

nvtagpg volume_id -b block
```

TABLE B–15   Flags for the *nvtagpg(8)* Command

FLAG	DESCRIPTION
-a	Displays all of the pages in the file.
-b block	The LBN of a disk block on an AdvFS volume
-d dump_file	The name of a file that will hold the contents of the specified tag file
-v	Verbose mode. Displays all of the data in a specified tag file.

Example:

```
# /sbin/advfs/nvtagpg -r root1_domain -a
================================================================
DOMAIN "root1_domain" VDI 1 (/dev/rdisk/dsk3a) lbn 96 root
TAG page 0
----------------------------------------------------------------
currPage 0
numAllocTMaps 1 numDeadTMaps 0 nextFreePage 0 nextFreeMap 3
tMapA[1] tag 1 seqNo 1 primary mcell (vol,page,cell) 1 0 1
```

B.4.5   The *vsbmpg(8)* Command

The *vsbmpg(8)* tool is another one of the "new" tools that produces formatted output of blocks from the SBM file on a domain. The output will look like a hex dump, which is helpful for troubleshooting situations because a bitmap is what the SBM file is. The usual troubleshooting scenario for the SBM is trying to figure out how a particular bit is set or was cleared improperly. The hex dump output shows if something stomped on the SBM.

Syntax:

```
vsbmpg [-v] sbm_id | domain_id
vsbmpg sbm_id page [entry]
vsbmpg sbm_id -a
vsbmpg sbm_id -i index
vsbmpg sbm_id -B block
vsbmpg volume_id -b block
vsbmpg volume_id -d dump_file
```

TABLE B–16   Flags for the *vsbmpg(8)* Command

FLAG	DESCRIPTION
-a	Displays all of the pages in the SBM file.
-B block	Displays the portion of the SBM that maps the specified block.
-b block	A starting block of a part of an AdvFS volume that you want to format as an SBM page
-d dump_file	The name of a file that will contain the output from this command
-i index	Displays the SBM word specified by the index
-v	Verbose mode. Checks the checksum on each page of the storage bitmap.

Example:

This example illustrates the use of the *vsbmpg(8)* command to display all of the pages in the SBM on a domain called "num_domain."

```
# /sbin/advfs/vsbmpg -r num_domain 1 -a

===========================================================
DOMAIN "num_domain" VDI 1 (/dev/rvol/rootdg/vol_num) lbn 112
SBM page 0
-----------------------------------------------------------
lgSqNm 0 xor 003ffcff
index block mapInt[]
  0 0x000000 ffffffff ffffffff ffffffff ffffffff
  4 0x000800 ffffffff ffffffff ffffffff ffffffff
  8 0x001000 ffffffff ffffffff ffffffff ffffffff
 12 0x001800 ffffffff ffffffff ffffffff ffffffff
 16 0x002000 000000ff 00000000 00000000 00000000
 20 0x002800 00000000 00000000 00000000 00000000
 24 0x003000 00000000 00000000 00000000 00000000
 28 0x003800 00000000 00000000 00000000 00000000
 32 0x004000 00000000 00000000 00000000 00000000
 36 0x004800 00000000 00000000 00000000 00000000
 40 0x005000 00000000 00000000 00000000 00000000
 44 0x005800 00000000 00000000 00000000 00000000
 48 0x006000 00000000 00000000 00000000 00000000
 52 0x006800 00000000 00000000 00000000 003ffc00
 56 0x007000 00000000 00000000 00000000 00000000
 60 0x007800 00000000 00000000 00000000 00000000
 64 0x008000 00000000 00000000 00000000 00000000

[snip]

2028 0x0fd800 00000000 00000000 00000000 00000000
2032 0x0fe000 00000000 00000000 00000000 00000000
2036 0x0fe800 00000000 00000000 00000000 00000000
2040 0x0ff000 00000000 00000000 00000000 00000000
2044 0x0ff800 00000000 00000000
```

B.4.6 The *savemeta(8)* Command

The *savemeta(8)* tool is a korn shell script that saves the metadata for a given domain. It uses the other "new" tools' features for writing out a binary file as its output. It is used primarily for sending diagnostic data to the Customer Support Center for analysis on a damaged domain.

Syntax:

```
savemeta [-LSTtfr] domain savedir
```

TABLE B–17   Flags for the *savemeta(8)* Command

FLAG	DESCRIPTION
domain	The domain for which to gather the information
savedir	The directory to use for saving the metadata information
-L	This flag tells the tool not to write the domain's log. The default if this flag is not specified is to write the log information.
-S	This flag tells the tool not to write the domain's SBM. The default if this flag is not specified is to write the SBM information.
-T	This flag tells the tool not to write the domain's root tag directory. The default if this flag is not specified is to write the domain's root tag directory information.
-t	This flag tells the tool not to write the domain's fileset tag. The default if this flag is not specified is to write the domain's fileset tag information.
-f	This flag tells the tool not to write the domain's frag file. The default if this flag is not specified is to write the domain's frag file information.
-r	This flag allows the tool to be used on mounted but corrupted AdvFS domains. This flag is new in Tru64 UNIX 5.1.

B.5 Undocumented Commands

There was a time when the few tools available to repair and gather in-depth data about AdvFS were hidden in the /usr/field directory and were undocumented. These tools shipped with the operating system prior to the release of Tru64 UNIX 4.0. At that time, some of these tools were moved to the /sbin/advfs directory and some were not. Of those that moved, some were documented and some were removed. This section discusses those that fall into the latter category. Here, we provide some documentation, examples, and tips for running the tools, if you happen to find yourself on an older Tru64 UNIX system and need these commands. For version 4.0 and higher, these commands should not be useful because newer tools have replaced them. In those cases, we give you the name of the newer tool.

B.5.1 The *msfsck(8)* Command

This is the AdvFS bitfile-subsystem metadata structure checker. It verifies low-level metadata structures like the BMT, SBM, and tag directories and displays errors based on what it finds. It will not correct any problems, however.

The file domain must be inactive to run *msfsck(8)*, or the results could be incorrect. You also need at least one mounted fileset (*msfsck(8)* uses the .tags directory in the fileset to access the metadata).

This undocumented tool is available for Tru64 UNIX version 3.x in the /usr/field directory. There is no version of this tool for 4.0 and higher. For 4.0 and higher versions, the *verify(8)* command replaces this tool.

Syntax:

```
msfsck [-t] domain [fileset]
```

TABLE B–18   Flags for the *msfsck(8)* Command

FLAG	DESCRIPTION
domain	The domain to be checked for metadata corruption
fileset	The fileset to be checked. If the fileset is left off, then the fileset of the current working directory is used, if appropriate.
-t	Displays the mcell totals after the command runs.

Example:

This example illustrates use of the *msfsck(8)* command without the '-t' flag and the resulting output.

```
# /usr/field/msfsck usr_domain

Checking disks...
check_disk: checking storage allocated on disk /dev/rz0g
check_rec: bad bitfile state - DELETING
  disk: 1, mcell id (page.cell): 1205.5
  set tag: 1.32769 (0x00000001.0x00008001)
  tag: 14559.32832 (0x000038df.0x00008040)
check_rec: bad bitfile state - DELETING
  disk: 1, mcell id (page.cell): 1253.8
  set tag: 1.32769 (0x00000001.0x00008001)
  tag: 14253.32872 (0x000037ad.0x00008068)

Checking mcell list...
```

```
Checking mcell position field...

Checking tag directories...
check_tagdirs: in-mem tag does not have a matching on-disk tag
  set tag: 1.32769 (0x00000001.0x00008001)
  tag: 14253.32872 (0x000037ad.0x00008068)
check_tagdirs: in-mem tag does not have a matching on-disk tag
  set tag: 1.32769 (0x00000001.0x00008001)
  tag: 14559.32832 (0x000038df.0x00008040)
```

Example:

The following is an example of a successful run of the msfsck tool using the '-t' flag. In this case, the tool reported no errors in the metadata. The DELET-ING messages are benign and do not indicate a problem with the file system.

```
# /usr/field/msfsck -t usr_domain usr

Checking disks...
check_disk: checking storage allocated on disk /dev/rz0g
check_rec: bad bitfile state - DELETING
  disk: 1, mcell id (page.cell): 413.24
  set tag: 1.32770 (0x00000001.0x00008002)
  tag: 20499.32941 (0x00005013.0x000080ad)
check_rec: bad bitfile state - DELETING
  disk: 1, mcell id (page.cell): 1458.14
  set tag: 1.32770 (0x00000001.0x00008002)
  tag: 20336.32777 (0x00004f70.0x00008009)
check_rec: bad bitfile state - DELETING
  disk: 1, mcell id (page.cell): 1461.25
  set tag: 1.32770 (0x00000001.0x00008002)
  tag: 20408.32781 (0x00004fb8.0x0000800d)
display_mcell_totals: mcell count breakdown
Inuse:46410
  Primary:22160
  Secondary:3578
  Extent:20670
  Other:2
  Bad:0
Free:14574
Total:60984

Checking mcell list...

Checking mcell position field...

Checking tag directories...
check_tagdirs: in-mem tag does not have a matching on-disk tag
  set tag: 1.32770 (0x00000001.0x00008002)
  tag: 20499.32941 (0x00005013.0x000080ad)
check_tagdirs: in-mem tag does not have a matching on-disk tag
  set tag: 1.32770 (0x00000001.0x00008002)
  tag: 20336.32777 (0x00004f70.0x00008009)
check_tagdirs: in-mem tag does not have a matching on-disk tag
  set tag: 1.32770 (0x00000001.0x00008002)
  tag: 20408.32781 (0x00004fb8.0x0000800d)
```

Example:

This example was a run of *msfsck(8)* on a large customer domain (176 MB and 10 volumes) that was reporting corruption. In this case, volume 4 (/dev/vol/p1dg/vol40) had a hardware problem, which corrupted the data on the volume.

```
# showfdmn p1_domain

Id                    Date Created              LogPgs     Domain Name
3283a45b.000eb2f0     Fri Nov 8 16:21:31 1996   512        p1_domain

Vol   512-Blks       Free % Used   Cmode   Rblks   Wblks   Vol Name
1L    17672560   16146096     9%      on     128     128    /dev/vol/p1dg/vol32
 2    17672560   16464192     7%      on     128     128    /dev/vol/p1dg/vol33
 3    17672560   16224832     8%      on     128     128    /dev/vol/p1dg/vol34
 4    17672560   17642432     0%      on     128     128    /dev/vol/p1dg/vol40
 5    17672560   16478208     7%      on     128     128    /dev/vol/p1dg/vol41
 6    17672560   16702736     5%      on     128     128    /dev/vol/p1dg/vol48
 7    17672560   16812000     5%      on     128     128    /dev/vol/p1dg/vol57
 8    17672560   16929552     4%      on     128     128    /dev/vol/p1dg/vol42
 9    17672560   16580704     6%      on     128     128    /dev/vol/p1dg/vol49
10    17672560   16529264     6%      on     128     128    /dev/vol/p1dg/vol56
      -------------------- ------
      176725600 166510016     6%

# cd /t2k/recbufCDR.p1

# /usr/field/msfsck -t p1_domain recbufCDR.p1

Checking disks...
check_disk: checking storage allocated on disk /dev/vol/p1dg/vol32
display_mcell_totals: mcell count breakdown
Inuse:1610
  Primary:815
  Secondary:182
  Extent:606
  Other:7
  Bad:0
Free:2030
Total:3640

check_disk: checking storage allocated on disk /dev/vol/p1dg/vol33
display_mcell_totals: mcell count breakdown
Inuse:1580
  Primary:820
  Secondary:185
  Extent:574
  Other:1
  Bad:0
Free:2060
Total:3640

check_disk: checking storage allocated on disk /dev/vol/p1dg/vol34
display_mcell_totals: mcell count breakdown
Inuse:1620
```

```
      Primary:825
      Secondary:190
      Extent:604
      Other:1
      Bad:0
   Free:2020
   Total:3640

check_disk: checking storage allocated on disk /dev/vol/p1dg/vol40
check_mcells: tag is non-nil but set tag is nil
   disk: 4, mcell id (page.cell): 41.5
   next mcell id (page.cell): 0.0
   next disk index: 2
   link segment: 0
   tag: 32769.0 (0x00008001.0x00000000)
   set tag: 0.0 (0x00000000.0x00000000)
check_mcells: tag is non-nil but set tag is nil
   disk: 4, mcell id (page.cell): 41.12
   next mcell id (page.cell): 0.16
   next disk index: 0
   link segment: 0
   tag: 2.32769 (0x00000002.0x00008001)
   set tag: 0.0 (0x00000000.0x00000000)

[snip]

display_mcell_totals: mcell count breakdown
Inuse:800
   Primary:402
   Secondary:334
   Extent:42
   Other:22
   Bad:12
Free:6468
Total:7268

check_disk: checking storage allocated on disk /dev/vol/p1dg/vol41
display_mcell_totals: mcell count breakdown
Inuse:1609
   Primary:824
   Secondary:179
   Extent:605
   Other:1
   Bad:0
Free:2031
Total:3640

check_disk: checking storage allocated on disk /dev/vol/p1dg/vol48
display_mcell_totals: mcell count breakdown
Inuse:1587
   Primary:823
   Secondary:187
   Extent:576
   Other:1
   Bad:0
Free:2053
```

```
Total:3640

check_disk: checking storage allocated on disk /dev/vol/p1dg/vol57
display_mcell_totals: mcell count breakdown
Inuse:1602
  Primary:820
  Secondary:191
  Extent:590
  Other:1
  Bad:0
Free:2038
Total:3640

check_disk: checking storage allocated on disk /dev/vol/p1dg/vol42
display_mcell_totals: mcell count breakdown
Inuse:900
  Primary:480
  Secondary:173
  Extent:246
  Other:1
  Bad:0
Free:2740
Total:3640

check_disk: checking storage allocated on disk /dev/vol/p1dg/vol49
display_mcell_totals: mcell count breakdown
Inuse:907
  Primary:481
  Secondary:175
  Extent:250
  Other:1
  Bad:0
Free:2733
Total:3640

check_disk: checking storage allocated on disk /dev/vol/p1dg/vol56
display_mcell_totals: mcell count breakdown
Inuse:900
  Primary:484
  Secondary:174
  Extent:240
  Other:2
  Bad:0
Free:2740
Total:3640

insert_set_tag: can't get bitfile set params
error: -1093, E_NO_SUCH_BF_SET (-1093)
set tag: 3.16 (0x00000003.0x00000010)
insert_tag: can't insert set tag
set tag: 3.16 (0x00000003.0x00000010)
tag: 32769.131164 (0x00008001.0x0002005c)

[snip]

check_tagdirs: in-mem tag does not have a matching on-disk tag
```

```
set tag: 2.32769 (0x00000002.0x00008001)
tag: 16.0 (0x00000010.0x00000000)

# rmvol /dev/vol/p1dg/vol40 p1_domain
rmvol: Removing volume '/dev/vol/p1dg/vol40' from domain 'p1_domain'
rmvol: Can't find file set hdr - tag 3.16
rmvol: Can't remove volume '/dev/vol/p1dg/vol40' from domain 'p1_domain'
```

B.5.2   The *vchkdir(8)* Command

The *vchkdir(8)* command is the AdvFS directory structure checker and fixer. It verifies that the directory structure is correct, that all directory entries reference a valid file (tag), and that all files (tags) have a directory entry.

The file domain must be inactive to run *vchkdir(8)*. The fileset to be checked and fixed must be mounted. File systems that are massively corrupted so they cannot be mounted are not candidates for this tool.

This undocumented tool is available for 3.x located in the /usr/field directory. There is a version of this tool for 4.0 and higher located on the /sbin/advfs directory. For 4.0 and higher versions, the *verify(8)* command replaces this tool.

Syntax:

```
vchkdir [-d | -f] [-q | -v] <mount-point>
```

TABLE B–19   Flags for the *vchkdir(8)* Command

FLAG	DESCRIPTION
mount_point	The mount point of the fileset that needs to be checked
-f	Creates symbolic links in "<mount-point>/lost+found/" to all files (tags) that do not contain a directory entry; these are called lost files. This flag also removes directory entries that do not point to valid tags.
-d	Deletes lost files and it will delete corrupted directories.
-v	Displays verbose output.
-q	Displays nonverbose, or quiet, output. This is the default.

Note that you may need to run *vchkdir(8)* several times to clean up a fileset.

Example:

The following is an example of a successful run of *vchkdir(8)* on an uncorrupted domain.

```
# /sbin/advfs/vchkdir -v /junk
path : /junk
dev/fset : efs_dmn#efs
type : advfs
advfs id : 0x33f8551d.00064ecb.1

Scanning directories and files ...
ino = 2, size = 8192, mode = 0040755 /junk/
ino = 3, size = 8192, mode = 0040700 /junk/.tags/
ino = 4, size = 8192, mode = 0100640 /junk/quota.user
ino = 5, size = 8192, mode = 0100640 /junk/quota.group
ino = 6, size = 12139184, mode = 0100755 /junk/steves_stuff

Scanning tags ...
ino = 2, size = 8192, mode = 0040755
ino = 3, size = 8192, mode = 0040700
ino = 4, size = 8192, mode = 0100640
ino = 5, size = 8192, mode = 0100640
ino = 6, size = 12140544, mode = 0100755

Searching for lost files ...
ino = 2, dirLinks = 3, tagLinks = 1
ino = 3, dirLinks = 2, tagLinks = 1
ino = 4, dirLinks = 1, tagLinks = 1
ino = 5, dirLinks = 1, tagLinks = 1
ino = 6, dirLinks = 1, tagLinks = 1
```

B.5.3   The *vods(8)* Command

Displays the BMT on-disk structure. It is primarily a low-level debugging tool that is replaced by other tools in Tru64 UNIX 4.0 and greater.

Syntax:

```
vods char_special [page_lbn]
```

TABLE B–20   Flags for the *vods(8)* Command

FLAG	DESCRIPTION
char_special	This is the character special device for an AdvFS volume in the domain you want to examine.
page_lbn	The LBN for the page to examine; the default value is 32.

This undocumented tool is available for Tru64 UNIX 3.x located in the /usr/field directory and 4.0 and higher located in the /sbin/advfs directory.

Example:

This example is a customer run of the *vods(8)* utility on a Tru64 UNIX 3.2D system run to determine why they could not mount a multivolume file system. It was later determined that there was a corruption in the virtual disk

(AdvFS volume) count (vdCnt) field in the metadata was out of sync with the true number of volumes (in this case, four).

```
decfs2:boring# mount -t advfs boring#nh /mnt
boring#nh on /mnt: I/O error

decfs2:boring# showfsets boring
showfsets: can't show set info for domain 'boring'
showfsets: error = E_VOLUME_COUNT_MISMATCH (-1059)

From /var/adm/messages:

Jul 25 14:02:02 decfs2 vmunix: Volume count mismatch for
domain boring. boring expects 65534 volumes,
Jul 25 14:02:02 decfs2 vmunix: /etc/fdmns/boring has 4 links.

decfs1:/# ls /etc/fdmns/boring
vol01 vol02 vol03 vol04

decfs1:tmp# /usr/field/vods /dev/rvol/dg-boring/vol01
PAGE LBN 32 megaVersion 3 nextFreePg 0 freeMcellCnt 21 pageId 0
nextfreeMCId cell 7 page 0
============================================================

CELL 0 nextVdIndex 1 linkSegment 0 tag,bfSetTag: -6, -2
nextMCId cell 4 page 0
============================================================

RECORD 0 bcnt 92 version 0 type 2 BSR_ATTR

[Snip...]

RECORD 2 bcnt 52 version 0 type 15 BSR_DMN_MATTR
seqNum 1
delPendingBfSet 0
uid 0
gid 1
mode 0744
vdCnt 65534
filler_uint16T 0
bfSetDirTag -8
ftxLogTag -9
ftxLogPgs 512
```

B.5.4   The *logread(8)* Command

The *logread(8)* utility is used to give formatted output of the transaction log for an AdvFS file domain. This command has been replaced by the *vlogpg(8)* command in Tru64 UNIX 4.0.

The *logread(8)* command reads a specified number of records from the log. If you specify one or more read-types, then *logread(8)* will read the log accordingly. '-F' reads up to "records" records from the log starting from the tail. '-B' and '-l' read "records" records from the log starting at the head. If you specify one or more data-types, then *logread(8)* will also display the data in the specified data-type(s).

Syntax:

```
logread [-f | -b | -l | -a] [-d | -x] records log_file
```

TABLE B–21   Flags for the *logread(8)* Command

FLAG	DESCRIPTION
records	The number of records in the log to print out
log_file	The full path of the log file in the .tags directory
-f	Reads the log forward. This is the default.
-b	Reads the log backward.
-l	Reads the log backward using client links.
-a	Does all read types.
-d	Displays record contents in hex (one word at a time). This is the default.
-x	Displays record contents according to flyweight transaction formats.

Example:

This example illustrates using *logread(8)* to print out the first two records in a transaction log located on volume 1 of the domain mounted on the /junk mount point.

```
# /usr/field/logread 2 /junk/.tags/M-9

Read Log Forward

0 lsn; 0, 0 (pg, offset); 131 words; bwdLink 0, 65535, 65535
+ + +( 3, 1)Dn; RP 2; 3 ftxId; Crla 2, 0, 0
bs_bitfile_create; Undo Bcnt: 32 RootDn Bcnt: 32 recRedo
lcnt: 104
  bfsTag: -2.0, tag: -8.0, page: 0, numX: 2
  pgBoff: 24, bcnt: 8
  pgBoff:  8, bcnt: 4

  bfsTag: -2.0, tag: -6.0, page: 1, numX: 3
  pgBoff:   0, bcnt:  16
  pgBoff: 316, bcnt:   8
  pgBoff: 308, bcnt: 292

4 lsn; 0, 143 (pg, offset); 44 words; bwdLink 2, 0, 0
+ + + +( 4, 1)Dn; RP 1; 3 ftxId; Crla 2, 0, 0
bs_bmt_alloc_link_mcell; Undo Bcnt: 16 recRedo lcnt: 29
  bfsTag: -2.0, tag: -6.0, page: 1, numX: 4
  pgBoff:   0, bcnt: 16
  pgBoff: 608, bcnt:  8
  pgBoff: 600, bcnt: 28
  pgBoff: 308, bcnt:  6
```

```
# /usr/field/logread 1 /junk/.tags/M-9

Read Log Forward

0 lsn; 0, 0 (pg, offset); 131 words; bwdLink 0, 65535, 65535
+ + +( 3, 1)Dn; RP 2; 3 ftxId; Crla 2, 0, 0
bs_bitfile_create; Undo Bcnt: 32 RootDn Bcnt: 32 recRedo lcnt: 104
   bfsTag: -2.0, tag: -8.0, page: 0, numX: 2
   pgBoff: 24,  bcnt: 8
   pgBoff:  8,  bcnt: 4

   bfsTag: -2.0,   tag: -6.0, page: 1, numX: 3
   pgBoff:   0, bcnt: 16
   pgBoff: 316, bcnt: 8
   pgBoff: 308, bcnt: 292
```

B.6   The *shblk(8)* Command

The *shblk(8)* command produces a hex dump of a specified number of blocks on a character or block special device. This command really has no special relationship to AdvFS except that it ships in the AdvFS base subset. The output is a simple hex dump, with no special AdvFS formatting.

Syntax:

```
shblk [-sb start_block] [-bc block_count] special
```

TABLE B–22   Flags for the *shblk(8)* Command

FLAG	DESCRIPTION
special	A block or character special device file to be examined
-sb start_block	The first block to read
-dc block_count	The number of blocks to read

Example:

In this example, we illustrate how to use *shblk(8)* to look at a hex dump of the first block of the transaction log on the domain steve_domain.

```
# df /steve1
steve_domain#steve1 500000 32 491040 0% /steve1

# showfdmn steve_domain

Id                    Date Created          LogPgs Version  Domain Name
37d5bffa.0004579e Tue Sep 7 20:46:34 1999  512     4        steve_domain

Vol  512-Blks   Free    % Used  Cmode  Rblks   Wblks   VolName
1L   100000     91488   9%      on     16384   16384   /dev/vol/dg1/vol01
2    100000     99888   0%      on     16384   16384   /dev/vol/dg1/vol02
3    100000     99888   0%      on     16384   16384   /dev/vol/dg1/vol03
```

```
4      100000      99888      0%      on      16384      16384      /dev/vol/dg1/vol04
5      100000      99888      0%      on      16384      16384      /dev/vol/dg1/vol05
       ----------  ----------------
       500000      491040     2%
```

```
# cd /steve1/.tags
```

```
# showfile -x M-9
Id               Vol  PgSz  Pages  XtntType  Segs  SegSz   I/O    Perf  File
ffffffff7.0000    1    16    512    simple    **    **    async  100%  M-9
```

```
extentMap: 1
pageOff pageCnt vol volBlock blockCnt
0 512 1 128 8192
extentCnt: 1
```

```
# /sbin/advfs/shblk -sb 128 -bc 1 /dev/rvol/dg1/vol01
```

```
128: 00000002 00000003 37d5bffa 0004579e 00000001 ffff0000 00000000 00000002
128: ffffffff 00000000 ffffffff 00000000 ffffffff 00000000 00000000 00000002
128: 00000017 0000000b 00000002 00000000 00000001 00000200 00000004 37d5bffa
128: 0004579e 00000000 00000002 00000075 00000000 00000000 00000000 00000000
128: 00000000 05bcafe1 00000000 00000000 00000000 00000000 000015db 00000000
128: 00000000 00000000 40151030 00000001 00000000 00000000 00000005 00000000
128: 00000000 05bcafe1 00000000 00000000 00000000 00000000 000015dd 00000000
128: 00000000 00000000 401510d0 00000001 00000000 00000000 00000005 00000000
128: 00000000 05bcafe1 00000000 00000000 00000000 00000000 000015df 00000000
128: 00000000 00000000 40151170 00000001 00000000 00000000 00000005 00000000
128: 40154280 00000001 00000000 00000000 00000007 00000000 00000007 00000000
128: 6e6b6e55 006e776f 00000000 00000000 00000000 00000000 00000005 00000000
128: 00000000 05bcafe1 00000000 00000000 00000000 00000000 000015e1 00000000
128: 00000000 00000000 40151210 00000001 00000000 00000000 00000005 00000000
128: 40154300 00000001 00000000 00000000 00000007 00000000 00000007 00000000
128: 6e6b6e55 006e776f 00000000 00000000 00000000 00000000 00000005 00000000
```

The fsck(8)
Command Operation

This appendix discusses the UFS structure checker, *fsck(8)*, operation in detail. As discussed in Chapter 5, *fsck(8)* performs UFS detection and correction based on the command flags and responses given by the user. Operation of *fsck(8)* is broken down into phases, and each phase is responsible for performing a distinct function for either detecting or correcting a file system inconsistency. The following sections are meant to update the section of the ULTRIX document (Jeltema 1990–1992) for Tru64 UNIX that describes each phase and detail about what the tool is doing. This information can be quite valuable when diagnosing *fsck(8)* as it works on sticky file system corruption.

C.1   Data Structures and Concepts

During Phase 1, *fsck(8)* constructs several internal tables and bitmaps; an understanding of these aids in our discussion of the operation of the tool.

TABLE C–1   Data Structures Used by *fsck(8)*

DATA STRUCTURE	DESCRIPTION
statemap	A table that indicates the current state of each inode. The possible states are USTATE, FSTATE, DSTATE, and CLEAR.
blockmap	A bitmap of allocated frags in the file system, as computed from the inode table
lncntp	A table of inode link counts, initially created by recording the link count field of every allocated inode
duplist	A table of duplicate blocks (DUPs), for example, any frags that are allocated by more than one inode
badlncnt	A table of allocated inodes that have invalid inodes associated with them

The *fsck(8)* command has two basic modes of operation: interactive and preen. In preen mode, *fsck(8)* corrects a limited subset of file system problems automatically. In Tru64 UNIX, this mode is used by *bcheckrc(8)* during the system boot to check UFSs before mounting them. The AdvFSs are ignored by *fsck(8)* in any mode of operation, of course.

System administrators who would like to check and correct file system problems with total control over the results should use *fsck(8)* in interactive mode. In this mode, the tool checks the consistency of a file system and stops when an inconsistency is detected. At this point, it asks the user a yes or no question as to whether to correct the problem and continue or not. Generally, a "yes" response means to correct and continue and a "no" response means do not correct, but continue, if possible. If *fsck(8)* cannot continue, then it will exit.

The following sections describes the various phases *fsck(8)* uses to perform its function.

C.2   Setup Phase: Check Superblock Consistency

Prior to beginning the work of checking and/or correcting the file system, *fsck(8)* must first verify the consistency of the superblock. The size of several internal data areas depends on the file system size and other parameters, which are contained in the superblock.

While the file system is being read in from disk, the following checks are performed:

- the superblock magic number (fs_magic)
- the superblock size field (fs_sbsize)
- the number of cylinder groups (fs_ncg)
- cylinders per group (fs_cpg)
- the total number of cylinders in the file system (fs_ncyl)

Additionally, *fsck(8)* checks the following superblock parameters on this phase:

- The optimization preference is a valid value of either space or time (fs_optim).
- The minfree is a valid number from 0 to 99 (fs_minfree).
- The interleave value is valid from 1 to number of sectors (fs_interleave).
- The fs_npsect is in the valid range.
- If requested, convert the file system to the newer 4.2BSD format.

The tool also checks all the volatile fields in the superblock against those in the alternate superblock in the last cylinder group of the file system. Once the superblock is determined to be valid, the clean field is checked to determine whether further processing is necessary (preen mode only).

Bookkeeping activities performed in the setup phase include obtaining memory for blockmap, statemap, and lncntp (see Table C–1). Bits are set in blockmap corresponding to preallocated file system areas. The superblock cylinder group summary area data are read in this phase for use in Phase 1.

C.3   Phase 1: Check Blocks and Sizes

The primary purpose of Phase 1 is to verify that the fields in the inodes make sense, and that disk block address pointers in inodes are valid. In Phase 1, *fsck(8)* loops through every cylinder group and every inode, checking the following:

- Makes sure that each cylinder group magic number (cg_magic) is correct.

- Ensures that the spare fields (cg_spare) of all inodes are zero.

- Checks that inodes 0 and 1 are unallocated and all fields are zero. These inodes are never used by the file system.

  For each allocated inode, *fsck(8)* does the following:

- Checks that the bit for the inode in the used inode bitmap (cg_iused) is set.

- Takes special action if the inode is of type BADBLK.

- Makes sure the file type is valid.

- Checks if the file size (cg_size) in non-negative.

- Checks if the unused direct disk block pointers (cg_db) in the inode are null.

- For a block or character special file, sees that the file size is zero and (redundantly) that all disk block address pointers but the first are null.

- Checks that the addresses in the direct (cg_db) and indirect (cg_ib) disk block address pointers are within the appropriate range.

- Makes sure the fragments pointed to by the direct and indirect disk block address pointers are not duplicated.

- Checks that the indirect disk block address pointers corresponding to blocks above the top of the file are null.

- Verifies that the number of sectors allocated to the file as determined from the contents of the disk block address pointers matches the value maintained in the inode (di_blocks).

For each allocated inode, the following bookkeeping computations are done:

- Makes sure that the inode link count (di_nlink) is recorded in lncntp.

- Checks if the link count is zero or negative; the inode number is entered in badlncnt.

- Ensures that a counter for the number of allocated inodes is incremented.

- Sets the statemap entry indicating whether this inode is a directory (DSTATE) or a non-directory (FSTATE). When BAD or DUP errors are encountered for this inode, the state is changed to CLEAR.

- Enters the inode numbers with DUP errors in the duplist. The first occurrence of the same DUP block is placed in the unique section of duplist. Additional occurrences of the same DUP block are placed in the non-unique section.

- Checks that bits are set in blockmap for each valid fragment claimed in the inode's disk block address pointers.

- Checks that a counter for all used fragments is adjusted to account for the fragments claimed by this node.

For each unallocated inode, *fsck(8)* checks that:

- The bit for the inode in the used inode bitmap is clear.

- The size, mode, and all disk block address pointers are zero. An unused inode should have null values for all fields.

For each unallocated inode, the following bookkeeping calculations are done:

- Increments an internal free inode counter.

- Sets the statemap entry to USTATE.

When all inodes in a cylinder group have been processed, checks that:

- The number of free inodes found in the cylinder group matches the value contained in the summary area for the cylinder group (cg_cs.cs_nifree).

- The cylinder group summary area (cg_cs) agrees with the superblock cylinder summary area data read in during the setup phase.

C.4   Phase 2: Check Pathnames

The purpose of Phase 2 is to ensure that the values of the entries in each of the directories are appropriate and make sense. The *fsck(8)* tool first validates the integrity of the root inode of the file system (inode 2) by checking the following:

- The root inode is allocated and is a directory type.

- The root inode was not marked to be cleared because of BAD/DUP errors in Phase 1.

Starting at the root, *fsck(8)* then traverses the entire directory tree, examining every directory. Specifically, *fsck(8)* checks the following for each directory:

- length of the full pathname for each directory entry is less than the maximum allowable number of characters.

- The directory size is non-zero.

- The size of the directory is at least large enough to hold entries for '.' and '..'.

- The directory does not contain corrupted entries. Each entry in the directory file is examined, and *fsck(8)* checks that:

  a. The value of the inode field (d_ino) is less than the maximum number of inodes in the file system.

  b. The entry length (d_reclen) is non-zero but falls within the boundary of the directory chunk.

  c. The entry aligns to a four-byte boundary.

  d. The entry length is at least as large as the size of the directory entry as computed by the DIRSIZ macro.

  e. The length of the name field (d_namelen) is less than 256.

  f. The name (d_name) does not contain any embedded null characters.

g. The first directory entry is '.', and the inode field contains the directory inode number.

h. The second directory entry is '..', and the inode field contains the directory inode number of the parent directory.

i. No other directory entries besides the first and second are named '.' and '..'.

j. The inode associated with each directory entry is flagged as allocated in statemap.

k. The inode is not flagged to be cleared in statemap due to either BAD or DUP errors.

Bookkeeping operations done in Phase 2 include:

- Changes a directory inode's state in statemap from DSTATE to FSTATE when *fsck(8)* descends into it. When Phase 2 completes, any entries in statemap which are flagged as DSTATE are not attached to the root file system and will be inserted into lost+found during Phase 3.

- Repairs any corrupted directory entries.

- Reduces the lncntp value for the inode associated with each directory entry by one. If the file system is clean, then all entries in lncntp are zero at the completion of Phase 2.

C.5   Phase 3: Check Connectivity

At this point, statemap entries for all directories attached at the root inode directory hierarchy have the value FSTATE. Any DSTATE entries remaining are directories, which have somehow been disconnected from the directory tree. Phase 3 finds disconnected directory trees and attaches them to lost+found. The actions of Phase 3 are:

- Scans the statemap for a DSTATE entry.

- When one is found, traverses the tree containing the orphan upwards until no '..' directory entry can be found, or the entry for '..' is not DSTATE in statemap.

- Locates the lost+found directory; if an empty space large enough for the entry exists, then an entry is added pointing to the subtree. The name of the entry is the inode number of the root of the tree.

- Runs Phase 2 processing against the newly attached tree. As a result, Phase 2 diagnostics can appear during Phase 3.

C.6   Phase 4: Check Reference Counts

The main purpose of this phase is to determine whether the link counts in the inodes are consistent with the link counts as inferred from the directory structure. Also, inodes flagged CLEAR or DSTATE in statemap are cleared in this phase.

The *fsck(8)* tool examines the statemap entry for every inode in the file system for the following:

- If the entry is USTATE, then there is nothing to do.

- If the entry is CLEAR or DSTATE, removes the inode. DSTATE entries will exist if the file system contained orphan directories and it was not possible to attach them to lost+found.

- If the entry is FSTATE and lncntp is zero for that inode, fsck(8) searches badlncnt for this inode. This situation can occur if a file was deleted, but a process had it open and the system died before the process closed the file.

- If the entry is FSTATE and lncntp is nonzero for that inode, fsck(8) compares the lncntp value with the link count in the inode.

Once all inodes have been processed, the number of free inodes calculated by *fsck(8)* is compared against the value in the superblock summary area (fs_cstotal.cs_nifree).

C.7   Phase 5: Check Cylinder Groups

This phase compares the cylinder group block information with the bitmaps and tables built based on the contents of the inodes and directories. This phase takes no corrective action (with the exception of the block/frag totals in the superblock); problems found in Phase 5 are corrected by Phase 6. Specifically, *fsck(8)* checks the following in Phase 5:

- The cylinder group magic number is correct (cg_magic).

- Blocks marked as free in the cylinder group free-block bitmap (cg_free) do not correspond to preallocated file system areas.

- The free-block bitmap in the cylinder group block agrees with the blockmap as constructed by *fsck(8)*.

- The values of the cylinder group block's fragment summary array (cg_frsum) agree with the values computed from the blockmap.

- The per-cylinder free-block totals in the cylinder group block (cg_btot) agree with the values computed from the blockmap.

- The rotational free-block table in the cylinder group block (cg_b) agrees with the table as computed from the blockmap.

- The total number of free blocks recorded in the superblock (fs_cstotal.cs_nbfree) agrees with the value computed from the blockmap.

- The total number of free fragments recorded in the superblock (fs_cstotal.cs_nffree) agrees with the value computed from the blockmap.

C.8   Phase 6: Salvage Cylinder Groups

In this phase, all of the cylinder group blocks are completely rebuilt based on the information derived from the inode tables; however, the *fsck(8)* tool does not limit itself to rebuilding just those cylinder groups in which errors were found. No error messages are printed in this phase because it only computes the contents of the cylinder group blocks based on inode information that is already considered correct.

Glossary

Access control list—An object that is associated with a file and that contains entries specifying the access that individual users or groups of users have to the file.

ACL—See access control list.

Adapter—A device that converts the protocol and hardware interface of one bus type to that of another without changing the functionality of the bus.

Advanced file system—One of the supported file systems in Tru64 UNIX.

AdvFS—See advanced file system.

AdvFS Volume—See virtual disk.

Alpha microprocessor—A powerful 64-bit microprocessor developed in the early 1990s by Digital Equipment Corp. It is the primary processor family supported by Tru64 UNIX, as well as by Open VMS and Linux.

Bad block replacement—The procedure used to locate a replacement block, mark the bad block as replaced, and move the data from the bad block to the replacement block. Most modern disk drives can perform this function with no assistance from the operating system. The disk may or may not report that it has done so.

BAS—See bitfile access system.

BBR—See bad block replacement.

Bitfile—An AdvFS structure that consists of an array of eight-kilobyte pages, named via a tag. In the BAS layer a bitfile and a file are synonymous.

Bitfile access system—The lowest layer in the AdvFS internal structure. The BAS is concerned primarily with bitfile manipulations, buffer cache management, domain and volume management, transaction and log management, and storage placement and management.

Bitfile metadata cell (mcell)—In AdvFS, these records are stored in the BMT, which are roughly equivalent to inodes in UFS.

Bitfile metadata table—A dynamic AdvFS structure, which contains all of the mcells for a volume in a domain. In Tru64 UNIX version 5.0 and higher, the BMT contains mcells for nonreserved files only.

Block device—A special device file in UNIX, which is really a handle into the device structures of the kernel. It provides a mechanism by which processes on the system can perform operations on devices using standard UNIX system calls.

BMT—See bitfile metadata table.

Boot—The process by which the operating system activates itself on a computer system such that the system can be used to do useful work.

Boot blocks—The area on the beginning of a bootable disk where code is stored that begins the process by which the operating system loads itself into memory.

Buffer—See cache.

Buffer cache (bufcache)—A special cache in Tru64 UNIX that stores UFS metadata. The default size of the buffer cache is 3 percent of the physical memory of the system.

Cache—A specially organized area of memory by which access to slow devices can be made to appear faster by leveling out usage peaks.

Cache flushing—Clearing out "dirty" elements of the dedicated memory by writing the contents out to slow storage device.

CAM—See common access method.

CDFS—See CD-ROM file system.

CD-ROM file system—One of the supported file systems in Tru64 UNIX. This file system type is used to access CD-ROM disks that are laid out in the ISO 9660 and Rock Ridge Extensions format.

CDSL—See context-dependent symbolic link.

Character device—A device special file in UNIX that provides byte-by-byte access to a physical device.

Clone file set—A specialize fileset that makes a copy of the metadata and implements a copy-on-write semantic for the data blocks that allows for consistent backups of one of the filesets of an AdvFS file domain.

Cluster—A group of file system blocks that are read and/or written to the file system at one time.

Cluster device ID—This identifier will have the cluster desired properties that it is unique, universal, and invariant.

Common access method—The SCSI control mechanism employed by Tru64 UNIX.

Concatenated plex—A single copy of a mirrored volume in the LSM. A volume with no mirrors contains only one plex.

Configuration copies—A metadata structure stored in the private region of the LSM disks that describes the disk group.

Context-dependent symbolic link—A special type of symbolic link, introduced in Tru64 UNIX version 5.0, in which the character string "{memb}" is resolved at runtime to the member of the cluster. Therefore, a clusterwide shared boot disk can use this facility to have its own member-specific files.

Cooked device—See block device.

Cylinder—A logical representation of all the tracks located on all the platter sides the same fixed distance from the disk spindle.

Cylinder group—A set of adjacent cylinders in UFS that are used to optimize access to the data located on disk by reducing the need for seeks. The default number of cylinders in a cylinder group in UFS is 16; however, this number can be changed when the file system is created with *newfs(8)*.

DAC—See discretionary access control.

Dead tag—An AdvFS file tag that has used all of its sequence numbers and can no longer be used on the file system.

Defragment—A process by which multiple discontinuous extents are assembled in a contiguous fashion on disk. The *defragment(8)* command is an AdvFS utility that performs the defragment process for user data files.

Device driver—Part of the UNIX kernel that defines how physical devices are accessed using the standard system calls such as *read(2)*, *write(2)*, *select(2)*, and *ioctl(2)*.

Device special file—A special file type in UNIX that, when accessed, initiates activity between a user process and a device driver in the kernel. The device files are usually kept in the /dev directory by convention, but they can be located anywhere.

Differential SCSI bus—A method of communicating between two SCSI devices that decides whether a bit is considered a high or a low bit by measuring the difference in voltage between the two data lines on the bus rather than an absolute voltage.

Directory—An on-disk special file in UNIX that provides the file name to inode translation for the other files in the file system. A directory can also become a mount point by using the *mount(8)* command to attach another file system.

Discretionary access control—Mechanism used to control access by restricting a subject's access to an object. It is generally used to limit a user's access to a file. In this type of access control, the file owner controls other users' accesses to the file.

Disk—A physical device used for random, persistent storage access. A single disk consists of only a single spindle, but any device that presents to the operating system as a single disk is sometimes referred to as a disk in UNIX. Intelligent RAID controllers, such as a Compaq Storageworks HSZ70, present a single unit to the operating system in this way.

Disk block—A fixed-size, contiguous area on disk. It is the smallest addressable data unit transferred between the operating system and a disk. The size of a disk block in Tru64 UNIX is always 512 bytes.

Disk group—An association of disks in LSM used for creating logical volumes. Every LSM configuration has a root disk group (rootdg) and possibly others.

Disk head—A physical device that reads the data on a single side of a platter. All heads are connected to a single actuator arm that moves all the heads together.

Disk label—Information that is physically located at block 0 of any disk device. The disk label contains the partition table and other physical disk attributes defined in the *disklabel(4)* man page.

Division of privileges—A notion that users who do not have root can accomplish certain "privileged" operations on the system. It is also a mechanism that allows nonroot users to accomplish privileged operations by using a special utility.

DNS—See domain name service.

Domain—See file domain.

Domain name service—A hierarchical, distributed mechanism used to uniquely identify host names on the global Internet or an Intranet.

Domain table—An internal table of activated AdvFS file domains consisting of an array of domain structures.

DoP—See division of privileges.

EFS—See extent file system.

Encapsulated volume—See nopriv disk.

Encapsulation—Process for creating an LSM volume by converting an existing file system.

Extended file attributes—A name and value pair that is contained in a variable-size structure called a property list.

Extent—A contiguous set of complete eight-kilobyte file system blocks that contains all or part of a file's data. A file that has more than one extent is considered to be fragmented. A highly fragmented file must have many extents to negatively impact performance.

Extent file system—The file system, based on AdvFS, that was used for the hierarchical storage manager product.

FAS—See file access system.

Fibre channel—A relatively new SCSI hardware standard that uses fiber optic cables rather than copper wires for interconnecting the devices.

FIFO—See first-in first-out.

File—An entity, which is a storing mechanism for information in an operating system.

File access system—The top layer of the AdvFS structure that allows access to the lower BAS layer bitfiles like normal UNIX files.

File domain—A set of AdvFS volumes that contains files. A file uses storage from one or more of the volumes to which the domain is associated.

File-on-file file system (FFS)—One of the supported file systems in Tru64 UNIX.

Fileset—The mountable entity in an AdvFS file domain that contains the files and directory structure of the file system.

File striping—Using the AdvFS stripe command, a large and heavily accessed file's read and write performance can be improved by spreading the file's blocks across the volumes in the file domain.

File system—A storage organization mechanism. It is the hierarchical interface between the I/O subsystem and user-level utilities.

File system block—The smallest size entity that is written and read from a file system in an atomic fashion. In Tru64 UNIX all file system blocks are a fixed size of 8192 bytes.

File system type (fstype)—The underlying mechanism for storing, retrieving, and manipulating files on a storage medium that can be accessed through a UNIX standard interface.

File type—The file systems in UNIX support multiple types of files that are used for different purposes. The most common file types are regular, directory, symbolic link, character and block devices, named pipes, and sockets.

First-in first-out—A queuing mechanism in which the first element to enter is the first one to exit. The elements are taken in order of arrival.

Fragment (frag)—A portion of a file system block, which is used to store a file or portion of a file that is too small and cannot occupy an entire block.

Fragmented—A fragmented file has many small extents of storage. A fragmented volume has a few large extents of free storage.

FWD SCSI—Fast wide differential SCSI. One of the standards defined by the SCSI suite standard.

Generation number—A one-up number stored in an AdvFS tag or UFS inode structure that, along with the tag or inode number, uniquely defines that file on a file system.

Hierarchical storage manager—A defunct Tru64 UNIX product, based on the AdvFS that allowed files to be automatically off-loaded to optical storage based on a high water mark.

Hierarchical storage operating firmware—This is the controlling firmware for the HS series of controllers. Some of the things this firmware allows the user to do are create units, check errors, monitor performance, and manipulate disks.

HSG—An intelligent fibre channel–based RAID controller from Compaq Computer Corporation. There is one controller currently in this series, the HSG80.

HSM—See hierarchical storage manager.

HSOF—See hierarchical storage operating firmware.

HSZ—An intelligent SCSI-based RAID controller from Compaq Computer Corporation. There are several controllers in the series, including the HSZ40, HSZ50, HSZ70, and HSZ80.

IEEE—Institute of Electronic and Electrical Engineers.

Initiator—A device connected to a SCSI bus that can initiate commands to a target.

ISO 9660—An international standard, which describes volume and file structures for information exchange on a CD-ROM volume.

Lazy write—The asynchronous mechanism by which AdvFS updates some of its structures on disk. The updates are not made immediately but are queued and handled at a later time.

Least recently used—A queuing mechanism in which the element chosen has been accessed the farthest in the past. A timestamp scheme must be employed for this to work.

Locality of reference—The concept that blocks should be stored near each other on disk if they are likely to be needed at the same time. In that way all of the needed blocks can be retrieved in the same clustered read operation.

Logical Storage Manager—A product of the Compaq Computer Corporation that is used to create logical volumes that can contain file systems on a Tru64 UNIX system. The LSM is based on the Veritas Volume Manager (VxVM) code by Veritas, Inc.

Logical unit number—A SCSI entity that is used, along with the bus and target numbers, to define a device's nexus.

Logical volume—A term that refers to a pseudo-block device that can be used for raw storage or to contain a file system just like any real block device, but which contains part, all, or multiple block devices.

Logical volume manager—An obsolete subsystem used to create logical volumes in Tru64 UNIX.

LoR—See locality of reference.

LRU—See least recently used.

LSM—See logical storage manager.

LSM volume—See logical volume.

LUN—See logical unit number.

LVM—See logical volume manager.

Mcell—See bitfile metadata cell.

Mcell ID—A number associated with each AdvFS file that is used for access to bitfiles in the BAS layer.

Metadata—Data that are used to describe user file data in a file system. For AdvFS, SBM and BMT are examples of metadata. For UFS, the inode and superblock are examples of metadata.

Migrate—The move of part or all of a file's data blocks in an AdvFS domain from one volume to another. A migration can be initiated explicitly by using the *migrate(8)* command, or implicitly by using *rmvol(8)*, *defragment(8)*, or *balance(8)* utilities.

Minfree—A number given in percent that defines the point over which the system will no longer allow nonroot users on a UFS to create or append files. The default minfree value for UFS on Tru64 UNIX is 10 percent.

Mirror—See plex.

Mirroring—Also known as RAID level 1, mirroring provides redundancy by writing all data to two or more drives simultaneously. It provides redundancy from loss of any single drive, but it tends to be expensive because of the complete replication of drives.

Mount—A mechanism for associating a directory in UNIX with a file system that makes it available for use on the system. There is also a command, *mount(8)*, that performs the mount function in UNIX.

Mount point—Any regular directory in a UNIX file system, which is used as the reference point for the root of any file system.

Mount structure—An internal data structure in UNIX used to keep file system statistics and other mounted file system information.

Mount table—An internal linked list of mount structures that describes all of the currently mounted file systems on a Tru64 UNIX system.

Namei cache—An in-memory structure that stores recently accessed file name to vnode translations.

Network File System—One of the supported file systems in Tru64 UNIX. Originally developed by Sun Microsystems, the NFS facilitates transparent sharing of files on a network of heterogeneous computers.

Network file system daemon (nfsd)—The network file system server daemon.

Network file system I/O daemon (nfsiod)—The network file system client daemon.

Network Information System—Formerly known as the Yellow Pages (YP) service, it is a way to distribute the system databases such as passwd, group, networks, and hosts files among a group of UNIX systems. The systems that share database are said to be in the same NIS domain.

NFS—See Network File System.

NIS—See Network Information System.

Nopriv disk—An LSM entity in which a file system has been encapsulated to add the blocks in. Unlike sliced and simple disks, no private region is associated with it.

ODS—See on-disk structure.

On-disk structure—The method by which a file system's blocks are laid out on a physical disk.

Optimization preference—In UFS, a file system that becomes full will not perform well when fragments are implemented. Thus, the option is available to turn off the use of fragments, thus performing better. This is known as setting an optimization preference of time. When fragments are in use, the optimization preference is for space. Fragments optimize the space utilization on the file system, but they can have a negative impact on performance.

Partition—A logical slice of a physical UNIX disk. There are eight partitions of any Tru64 UNIX disk that are named 'a' through 'h'.

Partition table—A logical table that lists the partitions, sizes, offsets, and file system types. It is found in Tru64 UNIX in the physical disk label on block 0 of any labeled disk.

Plex—A single copy of a mirrored volume. A plex can be either striped, RAID 5, or concatenated.

POSIX—A set of standards defined by the Institute of Electronic and Electrical Engineers (IEEE) that describes different aspects of the UNIX operating system. Tru64 UNIX complies with most of the existing and proposed standards and is active in the committees that define them. See *standards(4)* man page for which standards the operating system currently supports.

Preferred plex—A mirrored LSM volume can have a preferred plex designated that will always be referred to first for access to a needed block.

Property list—A portion of a file's metadata that contains extended file attributes that can be set either by the operating system or by a user-level application.

Protocol—A mechanism by which two entities are able to communicate with one another.

Protocol stack—An implementation of a protocol on a computer system. The most common protocol stack on a Tru64 UNIX system is an implementation of the TCP/IP suite, although others exist.

Pseudo-device—A device driver that does not have any physical hardware associated with it.

Quota—A per-user or per-group restriction imposed on usage of a file system. It can be imposed based on the number of files or the blocks that can be used on a per-file system basis. AdvFS has the additional capability of restricting usage on a per-fileset basis.

RAID—See redundant array of independent disks.

Raw device—See character device.

RBMT—See reserved bitfile metadata table.

Recursion—See recursion.

Redundant Array of Independent Disks—A mechanism by which many disks can be used in concert to present a single logical volume to the system to which it is attached. The is usually done for cost savings, redundancy, or performance reasons.

Reserved bitfile metadata table—An AdvFS structure in Tru64 UNIX version 5.0 and higher that contains all of the mcells for the reserved files in a volume in a domain. The BMT contains mcells for nonreserved files.

Rock ridge extensions—A defined set of extensions to the CD-ROM file system format, which makes the CD appear and behave more like a UFS. It uses these extensions to provide things like permissions, additional file types, POSIX file names, file timestamps, and much more.

Root directory—The top-level directory in any UNIX system. It is the mount point for the root file system and is referenced absolutely by the name '/'.

Rootdg—See root disk group.

Root disk group—The primary disk group in any LSM configuration. Any system must have at least one disk in rootdg to be viable.

Root file system—The file system that is mounted at a system's root directory. This file system has valid boot blocks, a kernel loader, and a kernel in order to start the boot process for the system.

Root privileges—Privileges associated with the root user on a UNIX system. Sometimes also called "rootly powers."

Root user—The ultimate privileged user on a UNIX system, who usually performs all the system administration activities on the system. The root user has a user ID of 0, and its home directory is located at the root of the system.

Round-robin—A real-time scheduling algorithm, in which tasks are assigned to a resource in a cyclical pattern, usually based on a time allotment.

SAN—See storage area network.

SBM—See storage bit map.

SCSI—See small computer system interface.

Sector—See disk block.

Set GID bit—A UNIX permissions bit that, when set on a program, allows the process executing it to assume the group identity of its group owner.

Set UID bit—A UNIX permissions bit that, when set on a program, allows the process executing it to assume the user identity of its user owner.

Shell—A program that provides an interactive environment for a user on a UNIX system by which commands can be executed. It can also be used to interpret commands in a file known as a shell script.

Simple Disk—An LSM concept in which an entire disk is dedicated to LSM. This type of disk has a separate partition for the public and private regions.

Single system image—The desire for all disparate systems in a cluster to appear as a single large system to the user.

Sliced disk—An LSM concept in which only a single partition is dedicated to be used. In this type of disk, both the public and private regions are located in the same partition.

Small computer system interface—A hardware and protocol standard for connecting devices (targets) to a computer system (initiator).

Snapshot—An LSM plex that is used to make an exact duplicate of an existing plex for the purposes of making a consistent backup.

Software RAID—A method for implementing RAID within an operating system. The LSM is an example of a software RAID product.

Sparse file—A file that contains "holes." A sparse file does not have blocks allocated on disk for the entire size of the file as reported in the file size field in the stat structure.

Spindle—Another name for a single spinning disk device. Also, a spindle is another name of the shaft around which the platters on a disk drive spin.

Sticky bit—A permissions bit that, when set on a directory, allows a user creating files to retain control, but which allows many users to have global write access to the directory.

Stripe—The number of disks in a striped plex multiplied by the stripe width.

Striped plex—A plex on which RAID level 0 has been implemented.

Striping—Also known as RAID level 0, data is split across drives, resulting in higher data throughput. Striping provides no redundancy for the volume because loss of a single disk causes loss of the entire logical unit.

Storage area network—A relatively new term used to describe storage that behaves like a network-attached device.

Storage bit map—The AdvFS metadata file that keeps track of free space on the volume. There is one SBM file for each volume in a file domain.

Subdisk—A set of contiguous blocks in a block device that can be used to construct plexes in an LSM environment.

Superblock—The primary data structure that describes a UFS.

SWXCR—A RAID controller made by Compaq for use with its hardware platforms.

Tag—A structure in AdvFS that roughly equates to an inode in UFS. The tag number is actually two hexadecimal numbers separated by a dot, consisting of the tag number and a sequence number. All tags on a file system must be unique; once a tag number is reused it is assigned a new sequence number. When all of the sequence numbers have been used, the tag number is known as a dead tag and is no longer used on that file system again.

.tags directory—A special directory located in the root of every fileset of every AdvFS domain. This directory is used for access into the BAS layer from the FAS layer with the use of special Tru64 UNIX utilities.

Target—A SCSI device that performs an operation requested by an initiator. The target number is determined by the address of the device on a SCSI bus.

Track—A single circumference of a disk platter under a single head located a fixed distance from the disk spindle.

Transaction log—An internal AdvFS structure implemented as a circular buffer on disk. It is used to keep track of changes to metadata so that uncompleted actions can be cleaned up if necessary. There is one transaction log per domain stored on one of its volumes.

UBC—See unified buffer cache.

UFS—See UNIX file system.

Unified buffer cache—A portion of the VM subsystems managed pages that are used to cache file system blocks.

UNIX—A modern multiuser and multitasking operating system originally developed by Ken Thompson and Dennis Ritchie at AT&T Bell Labs in the early 1970s. One of its chief benefits and keys to its longevity has been its portability, which is made possible because most of the system was designed in C.

UNIX file system—One of the supported file systems in Tru64 UNIX. The handle used for file access is the inode.

VFS—See virtual file system.

Virtual disk—An AdvFS entity that consists of a single block device and that is used to construct a file domain. An AdvFS file domain can contain up to 256 virtual disks.

Virtual file system—A set of operations and objects for manipulating files in a file system–independent manner. The handle used for file access is the vnode.

Volume configuration daemon (vold)—The vold is responsible for the interface of the LSM utilities to the kernel. All LSM configuration database changes are centralized through it.

Volume extended I/O daemon (voliod)—The voliod utility starts, stops, or reports on LSM error daemons and volume log I/O daemons.

Vnode—A virtual node used as a file handle into the VFS. The vnode contains file system–independent and dependent parts that refer to an actual file somewhere on a disk.

Winchester drive—See disk.

Write-back cache—A cache update mechanism that allows the controller to report that a write is complete when the cache has been written to, but the disk has not yet been updated. The controller updates the disk with the cached information at a later time.

Write-through cache—A cache update mechanism that retains host write requests in read cache. The data are written to the storage device only when the host makes a write request. The operation is not complete until data to be written have been received by the disk.

Bibliography

Bach, M. J. *The Design of the UNIX Operating System.* Boston, MA: Prentice-Hall, 1986.

Berkeley Software Distribution. *The 4.4BSD System Manager's Manual.* Sebastopol, CA: A USENIX Association Book, O'Reilly & Associates, Inc., 1994.

Brock, J. D. *AdvFS Internals Course Notes.* Institute for Software Advancement, 1997.

Cheek, M. *Digital UNIX System Administrator's Guide.* Boston, MA: Digital Press, 1999.

Compaq Computer Corporation. *Digital UNIX Internal Course Notes,* version 4.0, 1994.

Compaq Computer Corporation. *Digital UNIX System Performance and Tuning Guide,* section 2.2.6, version 4.0D, 1996.

Compaq Computer Corporation. *Digital UNIX System Administration Guide,* version 4.0, 1996.

Compaq Computer Corporation. *Digital UNIX Security Guide,* version 4.0, 1996.

Compaq Computer Corporation. *Tuning Tru64 UNIX for Internet Servers,* version 2.3, Compaq White Paper, 1998.

Goodheart, B., and J. Cox. *The Magic Garden Explained. The Internals of UNIX System V Release 4.* Sydney, Australia: Prentice Hall, 1994.

Institute of Electrical and Electronics Engineers. *Information Technology—Portable Operating System Interface (POSIX) Part 1: System Application Program Interface (API) [C Language],* 1990.

Irlam, G. *UNIX File Size Survey—1993.* http://www.base.com/gordoni/ufs93.html, email: gordoni@home.base.com, 1993.

Jeltema, B. Structure of the ULTRIX File System. A Description of the On-Disk Data Structures, in *ULTRIX 4.4 Supplemental Documentation.* Maynard, MA: Digital Equipment Corporation, 1990a.

Jeltema, B. What fsck is Really Doing, in *ULTRIX 4.4 Supplemental Documentation.* Maynard: MA: Digital Equipment Corporation, 1990b.

Kernighan, B.W., and R. Pike. *The UNIX Programming Environment.* Englewood Cliffs, NJ: Prentice Hall, 1984.

Kleinman, S.R. *Vnodes: An Architecture for Multiple File System Types in Sun UNIX.* Proceedings of the Summer 1986 USENIX Technical Conference, June 1986, pp. 238–247.

McKusick, M.K., W.N. Joy, S.J. Leffler, and R. S. Fabry. A Fast File System for UNIX, ACM Transactions on Computer Systems. *Association for Computing Machinery* 2 (3):181–197, 1984.

McKusick, M.K., and T.J. Kowalski. FSCK: The UNIX File System Check Program, in *4.4BSD System Manager's Manual,* 3:1–21. Sebastopol, CA: O'Reilly & Associates, Inc., 1994.

McKusick, M.K., K. Bostic, M.J. Karels, and J.S. Quarterman. *The Design and Implementation of the 4.4 BSD UNIX Operating System.* Reading, MA: Addison Wesley, 1986.

Millsap, C.V. *Making the Decision to use UNIX Raw Devices.* Oracle Corporation, revision 1.8, 1992.

Nemeth, E., G. Snyder, S. Seebass, and T.R. Hein, *The UNIX System Administration Handbook.* Englewood Cliffs, NJ: Prentice-Hall, 1995.

Neuner, S. *Configuring LSM & AdvFS for Performance.* Presentation slides, Digital UNIX Technical Symposium, 1995.

Neuner, S. *A Tour of LSM.* Presentation slides, Digital UNIX Technical Symposium, 1995.

Peterson, S. *Design Specification for Alleviating AdvFS BMT Exhaustion Problem.* Compaq Internal Document, revision 1.1, 1997.

Ritchie, D.M., and K. Thompson, *The UNIX Time-Sharing System.* Communications of the ACM 17 (7):365–375, 1974.

Saxon, M.S. Using fsck. A Guide to the UNIX File System Check Program. *login* 10 (3): 13–26, 1985.

Stern, H. *Managing NFS and NIS.* Sebastopol, CA: O'Reilly and Associates, 1992.

Stern, H. *Looking for Mr. Good Block.* Sun Microsystems, 1994.

Stern, H. *A File by any Other Name.* Sun Microsystems, 1995.

Stevens, W.R. *Advanced Programming in the UNIX Environment.* Reading, MA: Addison-Wesley, 1992.

Stoppani, P. *The Hitchhiker's Guide to the Advanced File System.* Compaq Internal Document, revision 1.2, 1995.

Sun Microsystems, Inc., *Network File System Protocol Specification.* RFC 1094, DDN Network Information Center, SRI International, 1989.

Sun Microsystems, Inc., *NFS Version 3 Protocol Specification.* RFC 1813, DDN Network Information Center, SRI International, 1995.

Tanenbaum, A.S. *Computer Networks.* Englewood Cliffs, NJ: Prentice Hall, 1989.

Vahalia, U. UNIX Internals. *The New Frontiers.* Englewood Cliffs, NJ: Prentice Hall, 1996.

White, B. *Optimizing Oracle Database/DIGITAL UNIX Systems Environments.* Compaq White Paper, 1998.

Yim, W. *DEC OSF/1 Logical Storage Manager Cookbook.* Compaq Internal Document, revision 1.0, 1994.

Index